HAWAI'I

Where to Stay and Eat
for All Budgets

Must-See Sights
& Local Secrets

Ratings You Can Trust

Fodor's Travel Publications   New York, Toronto, London, Sydney, Auckland
www.fodors.com

FODOR'S HAWAI'I 2005
Editor: Amanda Theunissen

Editorial Production: Jacinta O'Halloran
Editorial Contributors: John Penisten, Cathy Sharpe, Shannon Wianecki, Paul Wood, Maggie Wunsch
Maps: David Lindroth, *cartographer*; Rebecca Baer and Bob Blake, *map editors*
Design: Fabrizio La Rocca, *creative director*; Guido Caroti, *art director*; Melanie Marin, *senior picture editor*
Production/Manufacturing: Angela L. McLean
Cover Photo (Na Pali, Kaua'i): Catherine Karnow

ISBN 1-4000-1397-6

ISSN 0071-6421

SPECIAL SALES
This book is available for special discounts for bulk purchases for sales promotions or premiums. Special editions, including personalized covers, excerpts of existing books, and corporate imprints, can be created in large quantities for special needs. For more information, write to Special Markets/Premium Sales, 1745 Broadway, MD 6-2, New York, New York 10019, or e-mail specialmarkets@randomhouse.com.

AN IMPORTANT TIP & AN INVITATION
Although all prices, opening times, and other details in this book are based on information supplied to us at press time, changes occur all the time in the travel world, and Fodor's cannot accept responsibility for facts that become outdated or for inadvertent errors or omissions. So **always confirm information when it matters,** especially if you're making a detour to visit a specific place. Your experiences—positive and negative—matter to us. If we have missed or misstated something, **please write to us.** We follow up on all suggestions. Contact the Hawai'i editor at editors@fodors.com or c/o Fodor's at 1745 Broadway, New York, NY 10019.

PRINTED IN THE UNITED STATES OF AMERICA

10 9 8 7 6 5 4 3 2 1

DESTINATION HAWAI'I

Just try to describe Hawai'i without saying "paradise." In this place of ineffable beauty, the word is not a cliché, but actually an understatement. O'ahu is the most visited island, yet even here the landscape is so rugged that many developers have just walked away. Maui is dominated by luxury resorts, but also has a dormant volcano and the ultimate scenic drive—Hāna Highway. On the Big Island, ancient ruins and sleepy towns with melodic names punctuate a landscape of tropical forests, pasturelands, and barren lava fields. From Waimea Canyon to the perfect dunes of Polihale Beach, Kaua'i is paradise's prettiest subdivision. Moloka'I is where Hawaiians themselves unwind, drawn to the island's peace and quiet. Tiny Lāna'i is big on natural wonder, including Hulopo'e Beach, where spinner dolphins put on quite a show. Expect to make some tough choices during your trip. Every day you'll have to choose between embarking on high adventure—hiking in a volcano, learning to hang ten—or simply heading for the nearest crescent of palm-shaded sand to do nothing at all. Only in paradise. Aloha!

Tim Jarrell, Publisher

CONTENTS

1 O'ahu   *1*

2 Maui   *97*

3 The Big Island of Hawai'i   *189*

4 Kaua'i   *291*

5 Moloka'i   *363*

ABOUT THIS BOOK

The best source for travel advice is a like-minded friend who's just been where you're headed. But with or without that friend, you'll be in great shape to find your way around your destination once you've learned to find your way around your Fodor's guide.

SELECTION
Our goal is to cover the best properties, sights, and activities in their category, as well as the most interesting communities to visit. We make a point of including local food-lovers' hot spots as well as neighborhood options, and we avoid all that's touristy unless it's really worth your time. You can go on the assumption that everything in this book is recommended wholeheartedly by our writers and editors. Flip to **On the Road with Fodor's** to learn more about who they are. It goes without saying that no property pays to be included.

RATINGS
Orange stars ★ denote sights and properties that our editors and writers consider the very best in the area covered by the entire book. These, the best of the best, are listed in the **Fodor's Choice** section in the front of the book. Black stars ★ highlight the sights and properties we deem **Highly Recommended**, the don't-miss sights within any region. In cities, sights pinpointed with numbered map bullets ❶ in the margins tend to be more important than those without bullets.

SPECIAL SPOTS
Pleasures & Pastimes focuses on experiences that reveal the spirit of the destination. Watch for **Off the Beaten Path** sights. Some are out of the way, some are quirky, and all are worth while. When the munchies hit, look for **Need a Break?** suggestions.

TIME IT RIGHT
Check **On the Calendar** up front and chapters' **Timing** sections for weather and crowd overviews and best days and times to visit.

SEE IT ALL
Use Fodor's exclusive **Great Itineraries** as a model for your trip. Either follow those that begin the book, or mix regional itineraries from several chapters. In cities, **Good Walks** guide you to important sights in each neighborhood; ▶ indicates the starting points of walks and itineraries.

BUDGET WELL
Hotel and restaurant price categories from ¢ to $$$$ are defined in the opening pages of each chapter—expect to find a balanced selection for every budget. For attractions, we always give standard adult admission fees; reductions are usually available for children, students, and senior citizens. Look in **Discounts & Deals** in Smart Travel Tips for information on destination-wide ticket schemes.

BASIC INFO
Smart Travel Tips lists travel essentials for the entire area covered by the book; city- and region-specific basics end each chapter. To find the best way to get around, see the transportation section; see individual modes of travel ("By Car," "By Train") for details.

ON THE MAPS	Maps throughout the book show you what's where and help you find your way around. Black and orange numbered bullets ❶❶ in the text correlate to bullets on maps.
BACKGROUND	We give background information within the chapters in the course of explaining sights as well as in **CloseUp** boxes and in **Understanding Hawai'i** at the end of the book. To get in the mood, review **Books & Movies**. The **Vocabulary** pages can be invaluable.
FIND IT FAST	Within the book, chapters are arranged in a roughly clockwise direction starting with O'ahu. Chapters are divided into small regions, within which towns are covered in logical geographical order; attractive routes and interesting places between towns are flagged as **En Route**. Heads at the top of each page help you find what you need within a chapter.
DON'T FORGET	**Restaurants** are open for lunch and dinner daily unless we state otherwise; we mention dress only when there's a specific requirement and reservations only when they're essential or not accepted—it's always best to book ahead. Unless otherwise noted, **hotels** have private baths, phone, TVs, and air-conditioning and operate on the European Plan (a.k.a. EP, meaning without meals). We always list facilities but not whether you'll be charged extra to use them, so when pricing accommodations, find out what's included.
SYMBOLS	

Many Listings

★ Fodor's Choice
★ Highly recommended
⊠ Physical address
✦ Directions
🏛 Mailing address
☎ Telephone
🖷 Fax
⊕ On the Web
✉ E-mail
🎫 Admission fee
☉ Open/closed times
► Start of walk/itinerary
Ⓜ Metro stations
▭ Credit cards

Outdoors

⛳ Golf
⛺ Camping

Hotels & Restaurants

🏨 Hotel
🛏 Number of rooms
♨ Facilities
🍴 Meal plans
✕ Restaurant
🔖 Reservations
🎩 Dress code
🚬 Smoking
🍷 BYOB
✕🏨 Hotel with restaurant that warrants a visit

Other

☺ Family-friendly
🛈 Contact information
⇨ See also
⊠ Branch address
☞ Take note

ON THE ROAD WITH FODOR'S

A trip takes you out of yourself. Concerns of life at home completely disappear, driven away by more immediate thoughts—about, say, what marvels await the next day, or where you'll have dinner. That's where Fodor's comes in. We make sure that you know all your options, so you don't miss something just around the next bend because you didn't know it was there. Because the best memories of your trip might well have nothing to do with what you came to Hawai'i to see, we guide you to sights large and small all over the region. You might set out to simply splash around in O'ahu's crystal waters, but back at home you find yourself unable to forget spotting humpback whales off Maui's shores or kayaking along Kaua'i's majestic coast. With Fodor's at your side, serendipitous discoveries are never far away.

Our success in showing you every corner of Hawai'i is a credit to our extraordinary writers. Although there's no substitute for travel advice from a good friend who knows your style, our contributors are the next best thing—the kind of people you would poll for travel advice if you knew them.

John Penisten, who updated the Big Island chapter, is a 30-year resident of Hilo. As a freelance travel writer and photographer, he's published in a number of outlets locally, nationally and internationally. His extensive guidebook work includes an adventure guide to Hawaii and guides to Kaua'i and the Big Island for Prima Publishing.

Cathy Sharpe, our Smart Travel Tips updater, was born and reared on O'ahu. For more than 13 years, she worked at a Honolulu public relations agency representing major travel industry clients. Now living in Maryland, she is a public relations and advertising consultant. Cathy returns home at least once a year to visit family and friends, relax at her favorite beaches, and enjoy island cuisine.

Shannon Wianecki, who was raised on Maui, updated the Maui and Lāna'i chapters. With a decade of experience working in the Island's tourism industry, she knows its secrets well. She has contributed to various publications including *Maui Time Magazine.*

Paul Wood, writer, teacher, and freelance journalist, has lived on Maui since 1976. In addition to updating the Moloka'i chapter in this guide, he wrote Fodor's *Escape To The Hawaiian Islands,* and he contributes regularly to magazines interested in Hawaii-based topics. To find out about his humorous story collection *False Confessions,* go to http://pauldevlinwood.com.

Maggie Wunsch, our O'ahu and Kaua'i updater, felt the lure of Hawai'i during her first visit to O'ahu as a child. She returned to the island when she started college and has been there ever since. A freelance journalist, Maggie's travelogues, stories, and writings about Hawai'i's people, places, and events can be found on radio, television, in print, and on the Internet.

1 O'ahu

Third-largest of the Hawaiian Islands, O'ahu is home to 75 percent of the state's population. On the south side of the island in the shadow of Diamond Head, Waikīkī is a 2½-mi hot spot with more than 31,000 hotel rooms and condominiums, and scores of restaurants and shopping. Waikīkī is part of Honolulu, the state's capital. The East O'ahu ring, the area directly east of Honolulu around and beyond the Ko'olau Mountains, has one of the island's famous snorkeling destinations, some interesting ruins, and Sea Life Park, Hawai'i's version of Sea World. The north and west parts of the island are rural, dotted with small plantation towns. Surfers flock to the famed North Shore.

2 Maui

The lush island of Maui, second-largest of the Hawaiian chain, takes its nickname, Valley Isle, from its topographic profile—an arc slung between the peaks of two volcanoes. Hāna, on Maui's eastern shore, is a sleepy little town where you might still be able to get a sense of what Hawai'i was like before T-shirt tourism. The journey here is half the attraction: the Hāna Highway snakes down the eastern coast, and it's easily one of the most spectacular drives in the world. West Maui, "the Golf Coast," has resort after resort. Haleakalā, a 10,023-foot dormant volcano, towers in the distance—you could fit Manhattan inside its great crater. The former whaling town of Lahaina livens up the west coast with shops and restaurants.

3 The Big Island of Hawai'i

If you like your paradises uncrowded, come to the Big Island. It's almost twice the size of all the other Hawaiian Islands combined, and it hangs off the eastern end of the chain like an anchor. It's a formidable piece of land to cover in one vacation, and therefore is generally divided into six sightseeing areas: Hilo on the eastern side; Hāmākua, the northern seacoast; Kohala, the northern mountainous region with the northwest coastline; Kona, the western seaside village of Kailua-Kona together with the Upcountry coffee region; Ka'u and the vast stretches of lava and desert to the south; and Puna, east of Kīlauea volcano. Of course, the volcano itself is always a major attraction—it's still spewing red and orange lava, which is constantly finding new paths, thereby changing the very face of the island. The Big Island is the youngest of the chain, and like the typical younger sibling, it's biding its time, poised to take the spotlight as the most exciting destination in Hawai'i.

4 Kaua'i

Kaua'i's location may be one of the reasons why it stays off many tourists' radar: it's the westernmost of the major islands, with only Ni'ihau, the sparsely populated "Forbidden Isle," close to it. Dismissing Kaua'i as an afterthought would be a mistake, however. The oldest of the Hawaiian Islands, Kaua'i's 550 square mi are rich in natural and cultural history. The banks of Kaua'i's bubbling Wailua River on the eastern shoreline attracted the first Polynesian settlers. Visitors now populate the beaches of its Coconut Coast or head south to the sunny resort of Poʻipū. The cooler, damper north shore is verdant and lush, a startling contrast to Kauaʻi's western side with its Waimea Canyon, called the "Grand Canyon of the Pacific."

⑤ Molokaʻi

Molokaʻi is shaped like a slipper, with the toe pointing toward Maui's west shore. Ten miles wide and 38 mi long, Molokaʻi is made up of two volcanic mountains connected by a plain. Visitors readily embrace the down-to-earth charm of the "Friendly Isle." In the island's highest reaches you can explore Kamakou Preserve, a 2, 774-acre wildlife refuge. There is also plenty of snorkeling, swimming, and sunbathing.

⑥ Lānaʻi

Lānaʻi is the smallest of the populated islands and is below Molokaʻi, right off Maui's west coast. Lānaʻi's only population center is Lānaʻi City, smack in the middle of the island. The town is surrounded by natural wonders: Garden of the Gods, an eerie hilltop strewn with colorful boulders to the northwest; breathtaking Hulopoʻe Beach to the south; and Lānaʻihale, the highest point on the island, to the east. Lānaʻi used to be all about pineapples—until the Great Hawaiian Pineapple Crash of the 1980s—but now the fields are mostly gone and the focus is on the two luxury resorts, the Mānele Bay Hotel on the south shore and the Lodge at Kōʻele near Lānaʻi City.

GREAT ITINERARIES

Many Hawai'i visitors simply loll in a chaise lounge during their stay. If you would prefer to take a peek at several islands, let this 14-day itinerary be your guide.

O'ahu in 3 days

O'ahu is a good place to start your tour, with its frequent air service from the mainland and its scores of restaurants and hotels. On the first morning, rise early to make the steep walk to Diamond Head, for a panorama of the city and beaches. Once you've soaked up the vista, take in a bit of history at the USS *Bowfin*, the USS *Missouri*, and the *Arizona* Memorial. Then spend some time exploring the shops, restaurants, and other attractions of Waikīkī—including the Waikīkī Aquarium and the Bishop Museum, known for its collection of Polynesiana.

On day two, drive around Diamond Head to watch the windsurfers, then follow the coast to Hanauma Bay and the windward town of Kailua. Take side trips to the Nu'uanu Pali Lookout, where the view is spectacular, and the Byodo-In Temple, a replica of the Kyoto original, on your way to the Polynesian Cultural Center. Pick up a souvenir or two in its open-air shopping village. It's a long, dark drive back to Waikīkī, so you might want to stay at a local bed-and-breakfast.

On your third day, continue along the North Shore, stopping at Waimea Valley and Waimea Bay, a popular picnic spot, en route back to Waikīkī. In Honolulu, explore the lei stands and herb shops in the city's Chinatown. Then take a guided tour of America's only royal residence, 'Iolani Palace, and stroll around Mission Houses Museum, the homes of Hawai'i's first

missionaries, and Kawaiaha'o Church, built out of local coral blocks.

Kaua'i in 2 days

On the Garden Isle, begin by making the 90-minute drive from Līhu'e around the south shore of the island and up to spectacular Waimea Canyon. Lookouts en route give you wonderful views of the entire panorama. Kōke'e State Park is at the northern end of the canyon, a true wilderness full of colorful flowers. Return the way you came, stopping en route as time permits to visit the National Tropical Botanical Gardens and

the eclectic shops at Kilohana. Plan your trip to allow time to arrive at Po'ipū Beach and catch the sunset over the Pacific—a sight you won't soon forget.

On your final day, cruise up the Wailua River to the Fern Grotto; take a flight-seeing tour; and stop at Kīlauea Lighthouse, built in 1913 and towering over the Kīlauea Point National Wildlife Refuge, and the Hanalei Valley Overlook, where fields of taro stretch before you almost as far as you can see. Spend your last evening watching the sunset at Hanalei Bay.

Moloka'i in 2 days

This long, small island doesn't take long to explore. The best strategy is to see just a little each day to allow time to kick back and relax. West Moloka'i is mostly given over to the 53,000-acre Moloka'i Ranch, the largest local landholder. In tiny Maunaloa, which anchors the area, start by shopping at the old market and kite shop, on the brief main street. Later head for wide Pāpōhaku Beach, the island's nicest and most private strand and one of the state's most sensational, with its stunning white sand. At dinnertime head for the nearby Lodge at Moloka'i Ranch. Its restaurant, although the most

formal on the island, is casual and comfortable.

The next day—and it will be a full one—reserve ahead to tour Kalaupapa, to which people afflicted with Hansen's disease (leprosy) were once relegated; Father Damien, a Catholic priest, cared for the community's residents until he succumbed to the disease in 1889. Make the tortuous 3-mi trip via the Moloka'i Mule Ride or fly in. Before you catch an evening flight to Maui, take in the stupendous view of the peninsula from Pālā'au State Park.

Maui & Lāna'i in 4 days

Maui, which inspires people to call it the Valley Isle, is the second-largest landfall in the state. Start your Maui sojourn in 'Īao Valley State Park, where a 2,000-foot-high spire known as 'Īao Needle rises from the valley floor and easy hikes lead through forests. Afterward take 'Īao Valley Road into Wailuku, where it becomes Main Street. Many of the old buildings in this drowsy little town are .... ational Register of H......... ......y House, former home of prominent 19th-

century missionaries Edward and Caroline Bailey, displays period furniture and artifacts. Next, follow Route 30 south a couple of miles to the 120-acre Maui Tropical Plantation, a sort of agricultural theme park, to tour former sugarcane fields, get an overview of the growing processes, and

catch lively demonstrations of such activities as lei-making and coconut-husking. Then head over to the Alexander & Baldwin Sugar Museum near Kahului.

The next day, if it's sunny, make the fabulous four-hour drive to Hāna. It's 55 mi of bridges, turns, and vistas showcasing classic Hawaiian scenery. Keep an eye out en route for waterfalls, pools, swimming holes, hiking trails, lookout points, and other stopping places. Overnight in Hāna, a one-time company town devoted to the sugar industry that's now almost entirely focused on tourism.

In the morning visit aviator Charles Lindbergh's grave and 'Ohe'o Gulch, where there are many waterfalls more than 100 feet high with idyllic pools at the bottom. The place is perfect for picnicking and sunbathing and can get very crowded. Backtracking along the Hāna Highway, end the day exploring historic Lahaina. After you've explored Lahaina's antique buildings, go on to Kā'anapali to spend the night. The next morning, get up early for a ferry ride out of Lahaina to Lāna'i. You'll need to arrange a jeep rental in advance; Adventure Lāna'i Eco Centre is your best bet, since they can, schedule permitting, meet you at the dock with your jeep. Once you're on the road, take Route 440 to Lāna'i City. Then take Keōmuku Highway north to Polihua Road through the dryland forest of the Kānepu'u Preserve until you reach Garden of the Gods, a lunar plateau scattered with red boulders of all shapes and sizes. Retrace your steps and end your day with a late afternoon swim at Hulopo'e Beach. Turn in your rental and head back to Lahaina for dinner and a good night's sleep.

If you can handle another early morning, on your last day rise before dawn to see the sun come up over the immense crater of Haleakalā, the volcano whose lava flow created all of East Maui. The crater is now the centerpiece of Haleakalā National Park, which is full of hiking trails. At lovely Hosmer Grove, you can pick up a trail map; the Sliding Sands trail off the top of the crater shows off some amazingly colorful scenery: lush forests keep company with red desertlike terrain.

Big Island in 3 days

After arriving in Hilo, the county seat of the island and the fourth-largest city in the state, drive up Waiānuenue Avenue about a mile (stay to the right) as far as exquisite Rainbow Falls. It's beautiful when the sun is shining, and rainbows form above the mist if the sun is right in the morning. Then travel north of Hilo for 7 mi along Route 19 and turn right onto the 4-mi scenic bypass that skirts Hawai'i Tropical Botanical Garden, before rejoining the highway. Next turn left inland toward the small and unprepossessing town of Honomū and drive 4 mi to 'Akaka Falls State Park, where a 20-minute walk yields the rewarding sight of the park's two cascades—the 400-foot Kahuna Falls and the 442-foot 'Akaka Falls. Spend the afternoon in Hawai'i Volcanoes National Park, exploring its lava tubes, mineral formations, steam vents, and tropical plants—and, if you're lucky, catching the sight of lava flowing from Kīlauea Volcano. Get a feel for the volcanic terrain in just a short time with a visit to Halema'uma'u Crater, a steam-clouded pit inside the Kīlauea Caldera, or with a hike along the blackened Devastation Trail.

Begin day two with a drive up the Hāmākua Coast to Waimea to visit the Kamuela Museum and tour the Parker Ranch Visitor Center and Museum. Take the mountain road to the plantation villages of Hāwī and Kapa'au to visit the statues of King Kamehameha and his Pu'ukoholā Heiau before heading to the sunny Kohala Coast resorts; don't miss the nearby petroglyph carvings, and look for the snowcapped summit of Mauna Keʻa. The next morning head south through Hōlualoa, Kealakekua, and Captain Cook, stopping for a bit at Puʻuhonua o Hōnaunau National Historic Park, about 20 mi south of Kailua-Kona. If you have time, continue on to Ka Lae, the southernmost point in the United States. This windswept and grassy area gives a realistic glimpse of Hawaiʻi's past. When you've seen it all, head back to Kailua-Kona and the Astronaut Ellison S. Onizuka Space Center, a tribute to Hawaiʻi's first astronaut. Spend the rest of the day shopping and relaxing in Kailua-Kona.

Long days of sunshine and fairly mild year-round temperatures make Hawai'i an all-season destination. Most resort areas are at sea level, with average afternoon temperatures of 75°F–80°F during the coldest months of December and January; during the hottest months of August and September the temperature often reaches 90°F. Only at high elevations does the temperature drop into the colder realms, and only at mountain summits does it reach freezing.

Most travelers head to the Islands during winter. From mid-December through mid-April, visitors from the mainland and other areas covered with snow find Hawai'i's sun-splashed beaches and balmy trade winds appealing. This high season means that fewer travel bargains are available; room rates average 10–15 percent higher during this season than the rest of the year.

Rainfall can be high in winter, particularly on the north and east shores of each island. Generally speaking, you are guaranteed sun and warm temperatures on the west and south shores no matter what time of year. Kaua'i's and the Big Island's northern sections get more annual rainfall than the rest of Hawai'i, and so much rain falls on Kaua'i's Mount Wai'ale'ale (approximately 472 inches of rain, or 39 feet), that it's considered the wettest place on earth.

Climate

Moist trade winds drop their precipitation on the north and east sides of the islands, creating tropical climates, while the south and west sides remain hot and dry with desertlike conditions. Higher "Upcountry" elevations typically have cooler, and often misty conditions.

The following are average maximum and minimum temperatures for Honolulu; the temperatures throughout the Hawaiian Islands are similar.

🔊 Forecasts **Weather Channel Connection** ☎ 900/932-8437 95¢ per minute from a Touch-Tone phone ⊕ www.weather.com.

HONOLULU, O'AHU

Jan.	80F	27C	May	85F	29C	Sept.	88F	31C
	65	18		70	21		73	23
Feb.	80F	27C	June	86F	30C	Oct.	87F	31C
	65	18		72	22		72	22
Mar.	81F	27C	July	87F	31C	Nov.	84F	29C
	69	21		73	23		69	21
Apr.	83F	28C	Aug.	88F	31C	Dec.	81F	27C
	69	21		74	23		67	19

ON THE CALENDAR

Hawai'i has so many festivals and special events, that no matter when you go you'll be arriving just in time for the party. You can watch pro surfers and golfers do their thing, sample Island cuisine, learn to hula, or go to a rodeo—just be sure to book way ahead if you're coinciding your trip with any of the major festivals, particularly the Merrie Monarch Festival in April.

WINTER

Dec.

Triple Crown of Surfing (☎ 808/638–7700 O'ahu) : The world's top pro surfers gather on the North Shore for big winter waves and tough competition. **Honolulu Marathon** (☎ 808/734–7200 O'ahu) : Watch or run in one of the country's most popular marathons. **Bodhi Day** (☎ 808/536–7044 all Islands) : The traditional Buddhist Day of Enlightenment is celebrated at temples statewide. **Kaua'i Products Fair** (☎ 808/246–0988 Kaua'i) : Crafts, fruit, plants, clothes, and entertainment are available at this monthlong outdoor market (weekends only). **Festival of Lights** (☎ 808/523–4674 in O'ahu, 808/828–0014 in Kaua'i, 808/667–9175 in Maui) : Islands celebrate the holiday season with electric light parades, decorated city buildings, and events. **Christmas** (all Islands): Hotels outdo each other in such extravagant exhibits and events as Santa arriving by outrigger canoe. **Christmas Lighting of the Banyan Tree** (☎ 808/310–1117 Maui) : Five thousand lights cover the historic banyan tree on Front Street. **Pacific Handcrafters Guild's Annual Christmas Fair** (☎ 808/254–6788 O'ahu) : Craftspeople display their art and fine crafts at this two-day event at Thomas Square Park. **Rainbow Classic** (☎ 808/956–6501 O'ahu) : The UH Warriors and seven top-ranked mainland college basketball teams compete at the University of Hawai'i between Christmas and New Year's Day. **Hawai'i International Film Festival** (☎ 808/528–3456 O'ahu and Neighbor Islands) : The visual feast showcases films from the United States, Asia, and the Pacific and includes seminars with filmmakers and critics. **Passport to International Cultures** (☎ 808/886–8811 Big Island) : A cultural journey of food and fun at the Kings' Shop in Waikoloa, showcases Waikoloa Beach Resort chefs and their cuisine, plus live cultural entertainment and a visit by Santa Claus.

Jan.–Feb.

Chinese New Year Celebrations (☎ 808/533–3181 O'ahu, 808/310–1117 Maui, 808/553–3876 Moloka'i) : The Chinese New Year is welcomed with a Narcissus Festival pageant, coronation ball, cooking demonstrations, street fairs, fireworks, and lion dances. **HulaFest Week** (☎ 808/871–4141) : On February 1, the best college football players square off in the Hula Bowl, concluding this five-day festival on Maui which includes a lū'au, surf classic and Heisman golf tournament. **Sony Open Golf in Hawa'i Tournament** (☎ 808/523–7888 O'ahu) : Top golf pros tee off at the Wai'alae Country Club.

Jan.	**Aloha State Square and Round Dance Festival** (☎ 808/672–3646 O'ahu) : A full week of dancing, workshops, and fun with callers and dancers from around the world. **Cherry Blossom Festival** (☎ 808/ 949–2255 O'ahu) : This popular celebration of all things Japanese includes a run, cultural displays, cooking demonstrations, music, and crafts. It runs through March. **Morey Boogie World Body Board Championships** (☎ 808/396–2326 O'ahu) : The world's best body boarders compete at Banzai Pipeline.
Feb.	**NFL Pro Bowl** (☎ 808/526–4400 O'ahu) : A week after the Super Bowl this annual pro-football all-star game is played at Aloha Stadium. **Pacific Masters & Senior Amateur Golf Tournament** (☎ 800/576–1081 Kaua'i) : This six-day tournament held at Princeville Resort draws golfers from across North America. **Sand-Castle Building Contest** (☎ 808/956–7225 O'ahu) : Students of the University of Hawai'i School of Architecture showcase their skills with some amazing and unusual sand sculpture at Kailua Beach Park. **Whale Week** (☎ 800/942–5311 Maui) : A parade, run, ocean swim, regatta, children's carnival, silent auction, and celebration honoring the humpback whales that visit Maui each winter.
Feb.–Mar.	**Buffalo's Annual Big Board Surfing Classic** (☎ 808/951–7877 O'ahu) : The event features surfing as it used to be, on old-fashioned 12- to 16-foot boards.

SPRING

Mar.	**Opening Day of Polo Season** (☎ 808/947–6511 O'ahu) : Games are held at Mokule'ia and Waimānalo every Sunday at 2 PM through August. **O'ahu Kite Festival** (☎ 808/661–4766 O'ahu) : Kite-flying demonstrations, workshops, and competitions are held at Kapi'olani Park. **Annual Kona Brewers Festival** (☎ 808/334–2739 Big Island) : This gathering of 25 beer brewers and 25 restaurants at the Kona Beach lū'au grounds is the biggest of its kind in the islands. **East Maui Taro Festival** (☎ 808/248–8972 Maui) : Held in Hāna, this three-day festival focuses on all things taro, including poi. **Honolulu Festival** (☎ 808/ 926–2424 O'ahu) : Dozens of events held at various O'ahu locations to promote cultural understanding, economic cooperation, and ethnic harmony between the people of Hawai'i and Asia-Pacific. The festival culminates with a grand parade down Kalakaua Avenue. **Kaua'i Marathon** (☎ 808/826–6244 Kaua'i) : The 26.2-mi course begins in Poipu and treks through Kaua'i Coffee land not normally open to the public. **Prince Kuhio Celebration of the Arts** (☎ 808/742–3770 Kaua'i) : A tribute to a beloved Hawai'i monarch. The day includes commemorative ceremonies at the prince's birthplace in Po'ipū and re-creation of a Hawaiian village at the Hyatt Regency Kaua'i.
Apr.	**Merrie Monarch Festival** (☎ 808/935–9168 Big Island) : A full week of ancient and modern hula competitions begins with a parade the

Saturday morning following Easter Sunday. Tickets must be purchased (and hotel rooms reserved) months in advance; the competition is held at the Edith Kanaka'ole Auditorium in Hilo. **Celebration of the Arts** (☎ 808/669–6200 Maui) : For three days, the Ritz-Carlton, Kapalua pays tribute to Hawai'i's culture with hula, art workshops, a lū'au, and Hawaiian music concerts. Most activities are free. **The 'Ulupalakua Thing!** (☎ 808/875–0457 Maui) : Maui County holds its annual agriculture trade show and sampling with rides, games, and other entertainment at Tedeschi Vineyards, 'Ulupalakua. **Buddha Day** (☎ 808/536–7044 all Islands) : Flower pageants are staged at Buddhist temples to celebrate Buddha's birth. **Crazy Shirts Surf Series** (☎ 800/550–7873 O'ahu) : The Hawai'i Amateur Surfing Association presents this surf competition, including longboarding and bodyboarding. **Earth Day Ho'olaule'a and Lū'au** (☎ 808/826–6404 Kaua'i) : Five days of celebrations honoring the earth and local culture culminate in a huge, all-you-can-eat lū'au. **Hawai'ian Scottish Festival and Games** (☎ 808/988–7872 O'ahu) : Scottish songs, tartans, crafts, food, and traditional Highland athletic competitions make up this festival at Kapi'olani Park.

May	**Lei Day** (☎ 808/547–7393 all Islands) : This annual flower-filled celebration on May 1 includes music, hula, food, and lei-making competitions. **Prince Albert Music Festival** (☎ 808/826–7546 Kaua'i) : Princeville's signature event attracts local musicians and distinguished American composers, plus there are hula performances and art and cultural exhibits. **Ka Hula Piko** (☎ 808/672–3220 Moloka'i) : A community celebration of the birth of hula is marked by performances, storytelling, Hawaiian food, crafts, and lectures at Pāpōhaku Beach Park. **World Ocean Games** (☎ 808/521–4322 O'ahu) : Ten days of events celebrate the sea with lifeguard competitions, boating, and more. **Ka Ulu Lauhala O Kona Festival** (☎ 800/329–5226 Big Island) : A celebration of Hawaiian arts, crafts, and music with Kupuna Elizabeth Lee at the King Kamehameha Kona Beach Hotel. **World Fire Knife Dance Competition** (☎ 800/367–7060 O'ahu) : This international competition of Samoan Fire Knife dancing concludes the Polynesian Cultural Center's weeklong "We Are Samoa" Festival. **In Celebration of Canoes** (☎ 888/310–1117 Maui) : Master canoe carvers from around the Pacific carve canoes from logs throughout the week. A parade of canoes, concerts, and cultural demonstrations also are featured.
May–June	**50th State Fair** (☎ 808/682–5767 O'ahu) : Produce, exhibits, food stands, amusement rides, and live entertainment are at Aloha Stadium over several weekends. **Hawai'ian Airlines World Ocean Games** (☎ 808/521–4322 O'ahu) : This 10-day festival includes international lifeguard and water sports competitions. **Lantern Floating at Keahi Lagoon** (☎ 808/947–2814 O'ahu) : A Buddhist ceremony with 700 floating lanterns pays tribute to peace and departed ancestors at Keahi Lagoon Beach Park. Last Monday in May.

SUMMER	
June	**King Kamehameha Day** (☎ 808/536–0333 all Islands) : Parades and fairs abound, and twin statues of Hawai'i's first king—in Honolulu on O'ahu and in Kapa'au on the Big Island—are draped in giant lei. **Taste of Honolulu** (☎ 808/536–1015 O'ahu) : One of O'ahu's best food events, it includes two days of sampling from the finest restaurants in town and entertainment on the grounds of the Honolulu Civic Center. **Pu'uhonua O Hōnunau Festival** (☎ 808/328–2288 Big Island) : Ancient Hawaiian games, hula, food tasting, lau hala, and coconut-frond weaving demonstrations take place at the historic City of Refuge. **The Maui Film Festival at Wailea** (☎ 888/999–6330 Maui) : Special movie screenings, premieres under-the-stars, contemporary Hawaiian music, and The Taste of Wailea are the highlights of this festival. **Kaua'i Annual Hula Exhibition** (☎ 808/335–6466 Kaua'i) : An evening of Hawaiian and Polynesian chants, music, and hula at the War Memorial Convention Hall.
July	**Kapalua Wine and Food Symposium** (☎ 800/669–0244 Maui) : Wine and food experts and enthusiasts gather for tastings, discussions, and dinners at this four-day event at Kapalua Resort. **Makawao Statewide Rodeo** (☎ 808/572–9565 Maui) : This old-time Upcountry rodeo, held at the Oskie Rice Arena in Makawao on July 4 weekend, includes a parade and three days of festivities. **Parker Ranch Rodeo** (☎ 808/885–7311 Big Island) : In beautiful Waimea, see how the Hawaiian cowboy, the *paniolo,* works the circuit. **Independence Day** (all Islands): The national holiday on July 4 is celebrated with fairs, parades, and fireworks. Special activities include an outrigger canoe regatta with 30 events held on and off Waikīkī Beach. **Prince Lot Hula Festival** (☎ 808/839–5334 O'ahu) : A whole day of hula unfolds beneath the towering trees of O'ahu's Moanalua Gardens. It is believed to be Hawai'i's oldest and largest noncompetitive hula event. **Kīlauea Volcano Wilderness Marathon and Rim Runs** (☎ 808/329–1758 Big Island) : More than 1,000 athletes from Hawai'i, the mainland, and Japan run 26.2 mi across Ka'ū desert, 5 mi around the Kīlauea Caldera rim, and 5.5 mi into Kīlauea Iki Crater. The event takes place in Hawai'i Volcanoes National Park. **Queen Lili'uokalani Keiki Hula Competition** (☎ 808/521–6905 O'ahu) : Tickets for this popular children's hula competition are usually available at the end of June and sell out soon after. **Kōloa Plantation Days** (☎ 808/822–0734 Kaua'i) : A weeklong tribute to Kaua'i's plantation heritage on the island's south shore, featuring a sunset *ho'olaule'a, paniolo* rodeo, plantation tennis tournament, Hawaiian Olympics, golf putting tournament, craft fair, and ethnic cooking demonstrations. The festivities end with a parade and festival in Kōloa Town with entertainment, local food, and crafts.
July–Aug.	**Bon Odori Season** (☎ 808/661–4304 all Islands) : Buddhist temples invite everyone to festivals that honor ancestors and feature Japanese

o-bon dancing. **Hawai'i State Farm Fair** (☎ 808/848–2074 O'ahu) : This 10-day fair with farm products, agricultural exhibits, crafts, a petting zoo, contests, and a country market is held at Aloha Stadium.

Aug.	**BayFest** (☎ 808/254–7653 O'ahu) : This event is the largest military festival of its kind in Hawai'i—with rides, water sports, contests, food, and entertainment—at Kane'ohe Marine Corps Base. **International Festival of the Pacific** (☎ 808/934–0177 Big Island) : Music; dance; a lantern parade; floats; sporting events; and food from Japan, China, Korea, Portugal, Tahiti, New Zealand, and the Philippines round out this event. **Hawaiian International Billfish Tournament** (☎ 808/329–6155 Big Island) : This international marlin fishing tournament, held in Kailua-Kona, includes a parade and a full week of cultural events. The **Maui Onion Festival** (☎ 808/661–4567 Maui) : This lighthearted and food-filled celebration of Maui's most famous crop takes place at Whalers Village, Kā'napali. **Poke Contest** (☎ 808/874–1111 Maui) : Chefs from throughout the Islands convene at the Maui Prince Hotel to compare renditions of this prized local specialty.

FALL

Sept.	**Maui Writers Conference** (☎ 808/879–0061 Maui) : Best-selling authors and powerhouse agents and publishers offer advice—and a few contracts—to aspiring authors and screenwriters at this Labor Day weekend gathering. **Annual Hupuna Beach Prince Hotel Sam Choy Poke Festival** (☎ 808/880–3021 Big Island) : Chefs show off their renditions of this local delicacy. **Taste of Lahaina** (☎ 888/310–1117 Maui) : Maui's best chefs compete for top cooking honors, and samples of their entries are sold at a lively open-air party. **Hawaiian Canoe Festival** (☎ 808/524–1377 O'ahu) : Two weeks of events celebrate the role of the canoe in Polynesian life. **Kaua'i Mokihana Festival** (☎ 808/822–2166 Kaua'i) : This two-day islandwide event combines music, crafts, dancing, and hula competitions. **Hawai'i Garlic Festival and "Home Grown" Products** (☎ 808/528–7388 O'ahu) : A two-day festival of garlic cuisine created by Hawai'i and mainland chefs, children's games and activities, displays, and entertainment.
Sept.–Oct.	**Aloha Festivals** (☎ 808/923–1811 all Islands ⊕ www.gohawaii.com) : This traditional celebration, started in 1946, preserves Hawaiian native culture. Crafts, music, dance, pageantry, street parties, and canoe races are all part of the festival.
Oct.	**Ironman Triathlon World Championships** (☎ 808/329–0063 Big Island ⊕ www.ironmanlive.com) : This popular annual sporting event has competitors swimming, running, and bicycling. **Moloka'i Hoe Canoe Race** (☎ 808/259–7112 Moloka'i and O'ahu) : More than 100 teams from around the world cross the Moloka'i Channel to O'ahu and finish in Waikīkī. **Princess Kaiulani Keiki Hula Festival** (☎ 808/

922–5811 Oʻahu) : Children ages 5–12 perform hulas in honor of Princess Kaiulani. A Hawaiian arts and crafts fair is also held. **Hawaiiana Festival** (☏ 808/742–3770 Kauaʻi) : A three-day series of educational programs designed to teach the customs, crafts, and spirits of Hawaiʻi's native people, plus entertainment and lūʻau take place at the Hyatt Regency Kauaʻi Resort &Spa.

Nov. | **King Kalakaua Kupuna and Keiki Hula Festival** (☏ 808/329–1532 Big Island) : Both children and *kupuna* (adults 55 years and older) compete at this popular hula contest. **Kona Coffee Cultural Festival** (☏ 808/326–7820 Big Island) : A weeklong celebration, including two parades and a family day with ethnic foods and entertainment at Hale Halawai Recreation Pavilion, follows the coffee harvest. **Hawaiʻi's Big Island Festival** (☏ 808/326–7820 Big Island) : This celebration of diversity explores the cultures, cuisines, and healing traditions of islanders. **Waikīkī ArtFest** (☏ 808/696–6717 Oʻahu) : More than 75 of Oʻahu's finest artists and handcrafters demonstrate and sell their products at Kapiolani Park. **A Birthday Celebration for a King** (☏ 808/538–1471 Oʻahu) : ʻIolani Palace commemorates King Kalakaua's birthday with entertainment and decorations of red, white, and blue bunting and Hawaiian flags adorning the palace and grounds. **Hula O Na Keiki** (☏ 800/262–8450 Maui) : Children from Hawaiʻi, California, Las Vegas and Japan compete in this annual contest held at the Kāʻanapali Beach Hotel.

PLEASURES & PASTIMES

Acres of Parkland The Islands have a total of seven national parks, national historic parks, and national memorials, along with more than 75 state parks and historic sites. The two national parks are centered around one of the Islands' most exciting attractions: volcanoes. Kīlauea volcano in the Big Island's Hawai'i Volcanoes National Park has been in a state of constant eruption since 1982, and at times, you can catch a glimpse of molten lava hissing into the ocean. Maui's Haleakalā draws a large number of tourists who make the two-hour drive to the summit to see the sun rise. At any time of day, however, you will find plenty of sights on, in, and around the dormant volcano.

Other national areas run the gamut from royal fishponds to ancient places of worship to Pearl Harbor memorials. State parks range from the 2½-acre wayside stop at O'ahu's Nu'uanu Pali Lookout to the 6,175-acre Nā Pali Coast State Park on Kaua'i.

Golfing Many of the Islands' challenging and beautiful links have been designed by such legends as Arnold Palmer, Ben Crenshaw, and Robert Trent Jones Jr. Maui's greens get the most press due to several nationally televised pro tournaments, especially the EMC Kā'anapali Classic in October, where top Senior PGA players compete. Maui also has a stunning trio of 18-holers clinging to the slopes of Haleakalā volcano.

Not to be outdone, the Big Island has many courses that serve as emerald oases in the midst of black, barren lava fields. On Kaua'i and O'ahu, golf enthusiasts have the enviable task of choosing between fairways that tumble down the sides of mountains, leapfrog across rocky crevices beside the ocean, or serve as nesting areas and playgrounds for black swans. Even Lāna'i has two championship courses.

Lū'au Feasting Just about everyone who comes to Hawai'i goes to at least one lū'au. Traditionally, lū'au last for days, with feasts, sporting events, hula, and song. But at today's scaled-down version you're as likely to find macaroni salad on the buffet as poi, and heaps of fried chicken beside kālua pig.

If you want authenticity, look in the newspaper to see if a church or civic club is holding a lū'au fund-raiser. You'll not only be welcome, you'll experience some downhome Hawaiiana.

Miles of Beaches To many O'ahu's Waikīkī Beach epitomizes Hawai'i's beach culture. This hotel-studded strip is tough to beat for convenience to restaurants and shopping, but the big waves are on the North Shore's Sunset Beach and along Waimea Bay. Kailua Beach Park is the site of international windsurfing competitions; its neighbor, Lanikai Beach is often referred to as the most beautiful beach in the world; and, Makapu'u Beach, near Sea Life Park, has some of the best body surfing in the state.

The sun arcs slowly over Maui's beaches, because, according to legend, the demigod Maui caught the culprit in his lasso and demanded longer daylight hours. You can catch the rays in seclusion on the sands of Mākena, admire windsurfing skills at Ho'okipa, or people-watch at the resort-lined Kā'anapali Beach.

Kaua'i's beaches have found fame as movie sets. And white, black, and green-sand beaches are attractions in their own right on the Big Island. Even Moloka'i and Lāna'i can claim their share of sandy retreats, such as Moloka'i's 3-mi-long Pāpōhaku Beach, the largest white-sand beach in the state; and Lāna'i's Hulopo'e Beach, which has great snorkeling.

Safety deserves a mention here. Ocean waves and currents are often unpredictable, so be careful, even if you are an experienced swimmer. Watch for signs warning of dangerous undertows or invasions of stinging jellyfish, and check to see if your chosen beach has a lifeguard—many do not.

In true aloha spirit, there's no such thing as a private beach in Hawai'i— even those fronting luxury hotels are open to the public.

Scuba Diving
As the Islands emerged millions of years ago, molten lava spilled into the sea and cooled to form cavernous rooms, archways, pinnacles needling skyward, and networks of tunnels called lava tubes. Hawai'i's colorful coral reefs are home to nearly 600 species of tropical fish, including parrot fish, yellow butterfly fish, and the official state fish, the aggressive humuhumunukunukuāpua'a. Other residents include green sea turtles; acrobatic spinner dolphins; graceful manta rays and spotted eagle rays; and cruising white-tip, black-tip, hammerhead, sandbar, and tiger sharks. With all this going on underwater, it's no wonder Hawai'i is among the most popular scuba diving destinations in the world.

Surfing
Surfers from around the world come to ride Hawai'i's formidable waves, including the bone-rattling Banzai Pipeline. Indeed, O'ahu's North Shore is an excellent place to view the veterans, especially during high-surf in December and January. For first-time surfers, Waikīkī Beach on O'ahu and Lahaina on Maui are probably the two best spots to pick up the basics; there are plenty of schools staffed by experienced local surfers who will be happy to show you the ropes.

FODOR'S CHOICE

Fodor's Choice
★

The sights, restaurants, hotels, and other travel experiences on these pages are our editors' top picks—our Fodor's Choices. They're the best of their type in the area covered by the book—not to be missed and always worth your time. In the destination chapters that follow, you will find all the details.

LODGING

$$$$	**Four Seasons Resort Huālalai, Big Island.** A resort that movie moguls dream of, with two-story bungalows by the ocean's edge.
$$$$	**Halekūlani, O'ahu.** This resort is one of the world's most sumptuous retreats.
$$$$	**Kaua'i Marriott Resort and Beach Club, Kaua'i.** Oceanfront lagoons, a spa, beachfront dining, golf, and tennis make this resort a destination unto itself.
$$$$	**Lodge at Kō'ele, Lāna'i.** Fireplaces warm this sprawling mountain retreat in the cool highlands.
$$$$	**The Lodge at Moloka'i Ranch.** City slickers never had it so good; Moloka'i's plushest accommodations are in this Old West-style lodge.
$$$$	**Princeville Resort, Kaua'i.** This cliffside resort is Kaua'i's most romantic getaway.
$$$$	**Ritz-Carlton, Kapalua, Maui.** A magnificent setting, terraced swimming pools, and exemplary service make for an island ideal.
$$$–$$$$	**Turtle Bay Resort, O'ahu.** At the ocean's edge, cottages offer a private, elegant getaway within steps of fine dining, golf, tennis, and hiking.
$$–$$$	**Old Wailuku Inn, Maui.** This beautiful historic property in a quiet Wailuku neighborhood has been lovingly restored.
$$	**Kilauea Lodge, Big Island.** This rustic country inn is nestled in the cool fern forest near Hawai'i Volcanoes National Park.

BUDGET LODGING

$	**Hotel Moloka'i, Moloka'i.** Nothing can beat this simple seaside hotel for unfeigned, down-home aloha spirit.

RESTAURANTS

$$$–$$$$	**Capische, Maui.** This restaurant is doubly charmed—an exquisite menu paired with the island's best sunset view.

$$$–$$$$	**Orchids at the Halekulani, O'ahu.** Enjoy splendid seafood surrounded by a riot of orchids in this oceanside restaurant.
$$$–$$$$	**Pahu i'a at Four Seasons Resort Huālalai, Big Island.** At night, spotlights illuminate the surf—just feet from your table.
$$$	**Formal Dining Room, Lodge at Kō'ele, Lāna'i.** Fresh local ingredients reign in this elegant Upcountry restaurant.
$$–$$$	**Hoku's at the Kāhala Mandarin Oriental, O'ahu.** Endless ocean views, attentive staff, and a menu that travels the world—from Indian nan to Asian stir-fries.
$$–$$$	**Mama's Fish House, Maui.** Mama's mixes the best mai tais on the island, and the fish arrives fresh-off-the-boats every morning.

BUDGET RESTAURANTS

$	**Hamura Saimin, Līhu'e, Kaua'i.** Do as approximately 999 others do each day: come here for a delicious bowl of *saimin*.
¢–$	**Kanemitsu Bakery and Restaurant, Moloka'i.** Don't miss the sweet, round Moloka'i bread baked on the premises.

BEACHES

Anaeho'omalu Beach, Big Island. A beautiful golden-sand crescent complete with ancient fishponds.

Hāpuna Beach, Big Island. In summer this clean, wide white-sand beach is perfect for snorkeling and scuba diving.

Hulopo'e Beach, Lāna'i. The island's only swimming beach is great for snorkeling.

Lanikai Beach, O'ahu. Buttery sand, turquoise waters, and sumptuous sunrises make this a classic postcard beach.

Lydgate Beach Park, Kaua'i. This is a family-friendly beach at its best: snorkeling ponds, a playground, and a beach that begs for a good stroll.

Nāpili Beach, Maui. This sparkling white beach forms a secluded cove that's tailor-made for romantics.

Pāpōhaku Beach, Moloka'i. You can always find a private section of glorious white sand on the island's longest beach.

Polihale Beach Park, Kaua'i. Come for the breathtaking views of rugged cliffs; surf and currents make swimming dangerous.

Wai'ānapanapa State Park, Maui. Travelers on the Road to Hāna are rewarded with black sand contrasting with green Naupaka leaves.

OUTDOOR ACTIVITIES

Hiking Haleakalā Crater, Maui. You can visit six different climate zones here on the cliffs of this dormant volcano.

Ironman Triathlon, Big Island. The mother of all triathlons takes place each October with 1,500 of the world's top athletes.

Kayaking, Kaua'i. For beginners there's the Wailua River; experienced kayakers can take to the open sea by the majestic Na'pali Coast.

Mule rides, Moloka'i. Meander down some of the highest sea cliffs in the world.

QUINTESSENTIAL HAWAI'I

Garden of the Gods, Lāna'i. This surreal landscape is scattered with red and black lava formations, with the blue Pacific in the background.

Hanauma Bay Nature Preserve, O'ahu. A magnificent tropical fishbowl, perfect for sunbathing, swimming, or snorkeling.

Kalaupapa National Historical Park, Moloka'i. This park combines natural grandeur with one of the most poignant and inspiring stories in state history.

Mauna Kea, Big Island. Hawai'i's tallest mountain is a sublime experience at both sunrise and sunset.

Road to Hāna, Maui. Fifty-five miles of curvy road forge a path through Maui's rain forest.

USS *Arizona* Memorial, O'ahu. The gleaming white memorial is a powerful testament.

SMART TRAVEL TIPS

Finding out about your destination before you leave home means you won't squander time organizing everyday minutiae once you've arrived. You'll be more streetwise when you hit the ground as well, better prepared to explore the aspects of Hawai'i that drew you here in the first place. The organizations in this section can provide information to supplement this guide; contact them for up-to-the-minute details, and consult the A to Z sections that end each chapter for facts on the various topics as they relate to the state's many regions. Happy landings!

AIR TRAVEL

Hawai'i is a major destination link for flights traveling to and from the U.S. mainland, Asia, Australia, New Zealand, and the South Pacific. Some of the major airline carriers serving Honolulu fly direct to the islands of Maui, Kaua'i, and the Big Island, allowing you to bypass connecting flights out of Honolulu. For the more spontaneous traveler, island-hopping is easy, with flights departing every 20 to 30 minutes daily until mid-evening. International travelers also have options: O'ahu and the Big Island are gateways to the United States.

BOOKING

When you book, look for nonstop flights and remember that "direct" flights stop at least once. Try to avoid connecting flights, which require a change of plane. Two airlines may operate a connecting flight jointly, so ask whether your airline operates every segment of the trip; you may find that the carrier you prefer flies you only part of the way. To find more booking tips and to check prices and make online flight reservations, log on to www.fodors.com.

CARRIERS

From the U.S. mainland, Delta serves Honolulu and Maui. Continental and Northwest fly into Honolulu. From the West Coast of the United States, American and United fly to Honolulu, Maui, the Big Island, and Kaua'i. United also flies from Denver to Honolulu and the Big Island.

Aloha Airlines flies from California—Burbank, Oakland, and Orange County—to Honolulu, Maui and the Big Island, and from Las Vegas to Honolulu and Maui. Aloha also flies from Vancouver, British Columbia, to Honolulu, and offers connecting services from Phoenix, AZ and Reno, NV. Hawaiian Airlines serves Honolulu and Maui from Las Vegas, Los Angeles, Ontario, Phoenix, Portland, Sacramento, San Diego, San Francisco, and Seattle. In addition to Aloha and Hawaiian, Island Air and Pacific Wings also provide interisland service. Paragon Airlines offers private charter service to all the Islands.

🗗 Major Airlines American ☎ 800/433-7300. Continental ☎ 800/523-3273. Delta ☎ 800/221-1212. Northwest ☎ 800/225-2525. United ☎ 800/241-6522.

🗗 Direct Flights from the U.K. Air New Zealand ☎ 0800/028-4149. American ☎ 0208/572-5555. Continental ☎ 0800/776-464. Delta ☎ 0800/414-767. United ☎ 0845/844-4777. Trailfinders ✉ 1 Threadneedle St., London EC2R 8JX ☎ 0207/628-7628 can arrange bargain flights.

🗗 Interisland Flights Aloha Airlines ☎ 800/367-5250. Hawaiian Airlines ☎ 800/367-5320. Island Air ☎ 800/323-3345. Pacific Wings ☎ 888/575-4546. Paragon Airlines ☎ 800/428-1231.

CHECK-IN & BOARDING

Always **find out your carrier's check-in policy.** Plan to arrive at the airport about two hours before your scheduled departure time for domestic flights and 2½ to 3 hours before international flights. You may need to arrive earlier if you're flying from one of the busier airports or during peak air-traffic times. Plan to **arrive at the airport 45 to 60 minutes before departure for interisland flights.**

Although the Neighbor Island airports are smaller and more casual than Honolulu International, during peak times they can also be quite busy. Allot extra travel time to all airports during morning and afternoon rush-hour traffic periods. Prior to check-in, all luggage being taken out of Hawai'i must pass agricultural inspection. Fruit, plants, and processed foods that have been labeled and packed for export (including pineapples, papaya, coconuts,

flowers, and macadamia nuts) are permitted. Fresh fruit and other agricultural items, including seed lei are not, and will be confiscated.

To avoid delays at airport-security checkpoints, try not to wear any metal. Jewelry, belt and other buckles, steel-toe shoes, barrettes, and underwire bras are among the items that can set off detectors.

Assuming that not everyone with a ticket will show up, airlines routinely overbook planes. When everyone does, airlines ask for volunteers to give up their seats. In return, these volunteers usually get a several-hundred-dollar flight voucher, which can be used toward the purchase of another ticket, and are rebooked on the next flight out. If there are not enough volunteers, the airline must choose who will be denied boarding. The first to get bumped are passengers who checked in late and those flying on discounted tickets, so get to the gate and check in as early as possible, especially during peak periods.

Always **bring a government-issued photo ID** to the airport; even when it's not required, a passport is best.

CUTTING COSTS

The least expensive airfares to Hawai'i are priced for round-trip travel and must usually be purchased in advance. Airlines generally allow you to change your return date for a fee; most low-fare tickets, however, are nonrefundable. It's smart to call a number of airlines and check the Internet; when you are quoted a good price, book it on the spot—the same fare may not be available the next day, or even the next hour. Always check different routings and look into using alternate airports. Also, price off-peak flights, which may be significantly less expensive than others. Travel agents, especially low-fare specialists (⇨ Discounts & Deals), are helpful.

Consolidators are another good source. They buy tickets for scheduled flights at reduced rates from the airlines, then sell them at prices that beat the best fare available directly from the airlines. (Many also offer reduced car-rental and hotel rates.) Sometimes you can even get your money back if you need to return the ticket. Carefully read the fine print detailing penalties for changes and cancellations, purchase the ticket with a credit card, and confirm your consolidator reservation with the airline.

Check local and community newspapers when you're on the Islands for deals and coupons on interisland flights.

In Hawai'i, Aloha Airlines and Hawaiian Airlines offer travelers multi-island air passes that allow unlimited interisland travel during a specific time period at a reduced rate. Aloha Airlines' passes will save you more money than Hawaiian Airlines', but they must be used between the first and last days of the month—Hawaiian Airlines' passes are valid for any 30 consecutive days.

When you fly as a courier, you trade your checked-luggage space for a ticket deeply subsidized by a courier service. There are restrictions on when you can book and how long you can stay. Some courier companies list with membership organizations, such as the Air Courier Association and the International Association of Air Travel Couriers; these require you to become a member before you can book a flight.

Many airlines, singly or in collaboration, offer discount air passes that allow foreigners to travel economically in a particular country or region. These visitor passes usually must be reserved and purchased before you leave home. Information about passes often can be found on most airlines' international Web pages, which tend to be aimed at travelers from outside the carrier's home country. Also, try typing the name of the pass into a search engine, or search for "pass" within the carrier's Web site.

7 Consolidators AirlineConsolidator.com ☎ 888/468-5385 ⊕ www.airlineconsolidator.com; for international tickets. **Best Fares** ☎ 800/880-1234 or 800/576-8255 ⊕ www.bestfares.com; $59.90 annual membership. **Cheap Tickets** ☎ 800/377-1000 or 800/652-4327 ⊕ www.cheaptickets.com. **Expedia** ☎ 800/397-3342 or 404/728-8787 ⊕ www.expedia.com. **Hotwire** ☎ 866/468-9473 or 920/330-9418 ⊕ www.hotwire.com. **Now Voyager Travel** ✉ 45 W. 21st St., Suite 5A New York, NY 10010 ☎ 212/459–

1616 🖷 212/243-2711 ⊕ www.nowvoyagertravel. com. **Onetravel.com** ⊕ www.onetravel.com. **Orbitz** ☎ 888/656-4546 ⊕ www.orbitz.com. **Priceline. com** ⊕ www.priceline.com. **Travelocity** ☎ 888/709-5983, 877/282-2925 in Canada, 0870/876-3876 in the U.K. ⊕ www.travelocity.com.

7 Courier Resources Air Courier Association/ Cheaptrips.com ☎ 800/280-5973 or 800/282-1202 ⊕ www.aircourier.org or www.cheaptrips.com; $34 annual membership. **International Association of Air Travel Couriers** ☎ 308/632-3273 ⊕ www. courier.org; $45 annual membership. **Now Voyager Travel** ✉ 45 W. 21st St., Suite 5A, New York, NY 10010 ☎ 212/459-1616 🖷 212/243-2711 ⊕ www. nowvoyagertravel.com.

7 Discount Passes Aloha Airlines ☎ 800/367-5250. **Hawaiian Airlines** ☎ 800/367-5320.

All Asia Pass, Cathay Pacific, ☎ 800/233-2742, 800/268-6868 in Canada ⊕ www.cathay-usa.com or www.cathay.ca. **Boomerang Pass**, Qantas, ☎ 800/227-4500, 0845/774-7767 in the U.K., 131-313 in Australia, 0800/808-767 in New Zealand (outside Auckland), 03/578-900 in Auckland ⊕ www.qantas.com. **FlightPass**, EuropebyAir, ☎ 888/387-2479 ⊕ www.europebyair.com. **Pacific Explorer Airpass**, Hideaway Holidays, ☎ 02/9743-0253 in Australia 🖷 02/9743-3568 in Australia, 530/325-4069 in the U.S. ⊕ www. hideawayholidays.com.au. **Polypass**, Polynesian Airlines, ☎ 800/264-0823 or 808/842-7659, 020/8846-0519 in the U.K., 1300/653737 in Australia, 0800/800-993 in New Zealand ⊕ www. polynesianairlines.co.nz. **SAS Air Passes**, Scandinavian Airlines, ☎ 800/221-2350, 0870/6072-7727 in the U.K., 1300/727707 in Australia ⊕ www. scandinavian.net.

ENJOYING THE FLIGHT

State your seat preference when purchasing your ticket, and then repeat it when you confirm and when you check in. For more legroom, you can request one of the few emergency-aisle seats at check-in, if you're capable of moving obstacles comparable in weight to an airplane exit door (usually between 35 pounds and 60 pounds)—a Federal Aviation Administration requirement of passengers in these seats. Seats behind a bulkhead also offer more legroom, but they don't have underseat storage. Don't sit in the row in front of the emergency aisle or in front of a bulkhead, where seats may not recline.

Ask the airline whether a snack or meal is served on the flight. If you have dietary concerns, request special meals when booking. These can be vegetarian, low-cholesterol, or kosher, for example. It's a good idea to pack some healthful snacks and a small (plastic) bottle of water in your carry-on bag. On long flights, try to maintain a normal routine, to help fight jet lag. At night, get some sleep. By day, eat light meals, drink water (not alcohol), and **move around the cabin** to stretch your legs. For additional jet-lag tips consult *Fodor's FYI: Travel Fit & Healthy* (available at bookstores everywhere).

Smoking policies vary from carrier to carrier. Many airlines prohibit smoking on all of their flights; others allow smoking only on certain routes or certain departures. Ask your carrier about its policy.

FLYING TIMES

Flying time is about 10 hours from New York, 8 hours from Chicago, 5 hours from Los Angeles, and 15 hours from London, not including layovers.

HOW TO COMPLAIN

If your baggage goes astray or your flight goes awry, complain right away. Most carriers require that you **file a claim immediately.** The Aviation Consumer Protection Division of the Department of Transportation publishes *Fly-Rights,* which discusses airlines and consumer issues and is available online. You can also find articles and information on mytravelrights.com, the Web site of the nonprofit Consumer Travel Rights Center.

Airline Complaints Aviation Consumer Protection Division ✉ U.S. Department of Transportation, Office of Aviation Enforcement and Proceedings, C-75, Room 4107, 400 7th St. SW, Washington, DC 20590 ☎ 202/366-2220 ⊕ airconsumer.ost.dot.gov. **Federal Aviation Administration Consumer Hotline** ✉ for inquiries: FAA, 800 Independence Ave. SW, Washington, DC 20591 ☎ 800/322-7873 ⊕ www.faa.gov.

RECONFIRMING

Check the status of your flight before you leave for the airport. You can do this on your carrier's Web site, by linking to a flight-status checker (many Web booking

services offer these), or by calling your carrier or travel agent.

AIRPORTS

Hawai'i's major airport is Honolulu International, on O'ahu, 20 minutes (9 mi) west of Waikīkī. To travel interisland from Honolulu, you can depart from either the interisland terminal or the commuter-airline terminal, located in two separate structures adjacent to the main overseas terminal building. A free bus service, the Wiki Wiki Shuttle, operates between terminals.

Maui has two major airports: Kahului Airport, which handles major airlines and interisland flights, and Kapalua–West Maui Airport, served by Aloha Airlines and Pacific Wings. If you're staying in West Maui and you're flying in from another island, you can avoid an hour's drive from the Kahului Airport by flying into Kapalua–West Maui Airport. The tiny town of Hāna in East Maui also has an airstrip, served by commuter planes from Honolulu and charter flights from Kahului and Kapalua. Flying here is a great option if you want to avoid the long drive to Hāna from one of the other airports.

Those flying to the Big Island of Hawai'i regularly land at one of two fields. Kona International Airport at Keāhole, on the west side, best serves Kailua-Kona, Keauhou, and the Kohala Coast. Hilo International Airport is more appropriate for those going to the east side. Waimea-Kohala Airport, called Kamuela Airport by residents, is used primarily for commuting among the Islands.

On Kaua'i, visitors fly into Līhu'e Airport, on the east side of the island.

Moloka'i's Ho'olehua Airport is small and centrally located, as is Lāna'i Airport. Both rural airports handle a limited number of flights per day. Visitors coming from the mainland to these islands must first stop in O'ahu and change to an interisland flight.

Airport Information The Big Island: **Kona International Airport at Keāhole** ☎ 808/329-3423; Kaua'i: **Līhu'e Airport** ☎ 808/246-1448. Lāna'i: **Lāna'i Airport** ☎ 808/565-6757. Maui: **Kahului Airport** ☎ 808/872-3893; **Kapalua–West Maui**

Airport ☎ 808/669-0623; Moloka'i: Ho'olehua Airport ☎ 808/567-6361. O'ahu: Honolulu International Airport ☎ 808/836-6413. Hāna Airport ☎ 808/248-8208. Hilo International Airport ☎ 808/934-5838; Waimea-Kohala Airport ☎ 808/887-8126.

BIKE TRAVEL

Hawai'i's natural beauty, breathtaking coastal routes, and year-round fair weather make it attractive to explore by bike. However, on many roads, bicycle lanes are limited or nonexistent, and cyclists must contend with heavy traffic on the more populated islands; biking on O'ahu and Maui may require some skillful maneuvering. Bike routes on the Neighbor Islands include the challenge of riding the Big Island's 225-mi circle-island route, cycling downhill at Maui's Haleakalā crater, exploring the lush routes of tropical Kaua'i, and mastering off-road mountain biking on Lāna'i and Moloka'i. You can rent bikes for some solo cruising, join local cycling clubs for their weekly rides, or hit the road with outfitters for tours that go beyond the well-traveled paths.

71 Bike Maps Division of Forestry and Wildlife, Kaua'i ☎ 808/274-3433. Division of Forestry and Wildlife, Maui ☎ 808/984-8100. Honolulu City and County Bike Coordinator ☎ 808/527-5044.

71 Rentals Bike Hawai'i ☎ 877/683-7433 O'ahu ⊕ www.bikehawaii.com. The Bike Shop ☎ 808/593-8079 O'ahu. B&L Bike & Sports ☎ 808/329-3309 Big Island. Blue Sky Rentals ☎ 808/947-0101 O'ahu. Kaua'i Cycle and Tour ☎ 808/821-2115 Kaua'i. Lāna'i EcoAdventure Centre ☎ 808/565-7737 Lāna'i ⊕ www.adventurelanai.com. Moloka'i Bicycle ☎ 808/553-3931 Moloka'i. Outfitters Kaua'i ☎ 808/742-9667 Kaua'i or 888/742-9887 ⊕ www.outfitterskauai.com. West Maui Cycles ☎ 808/661-9005 Maui.

BIKES IN FLIGHT

Most airlines accommodate bikes as luggage, provided they are dismantled and boxed; check with individual airlines about packing requirements. Some airlines sell bike boxes, which are often free at bike shops, for about $20 (bike bags can be considerably more expensive). International travelers often can substitute a bike for a piece of checked luggage at no charge; otherwise, the cost is about $100. Most U.S. and Canadian airlines charge $40–$80 each way.

BOAT & FERRY TRAVEL

Ferry travel in the Islands is limited to daily service between Lahaina, Maui, and Mānele Bay, Lāna'i. The 9-mi crossing costs $50 round-trip per person and takes about 45 minutes or so, depending on ocean conditions (which can make this trip a rough one). Reservations are essential.

71 Expeditions Lāna'i Ferry ☎ 800/695-2624 ⊕ www.go-lanai.com.

BUSINESS HOURS

Even people in paradise have to work. Generally local business hours are weekdays 8–5. Banks are usually open Monday–Thursday 8:30–3 and until 6 on Friday. Some banks have Saturday-morning hours.

Many self-serve gas stations stay open around-the-clock, with full-service stations usually open from around 7 AM until 9 PM. U.S. post offices are open weekdays 8:30 AM–4:30 PM and Saturday 8:30–noon. On O'ahu, the Ala Moana post office branch is the only branch, other than the main Honolulu International Airport facility, that stays open until 4 PM on Saturday.

MUSEUMS & SIGHTS

Most museums generally open their doors between 9 AM and 10 AM and stay open until 5 PM Tuesday–Saturday. Many museums operate with afternoon hours only on Sunday and close on Monday. Visitor-attraction hours vary throughout the state, but most sights are open daily with the exception of major holidays such as Christmas. **Check local newspapers upon arrival for attraction hours and schedules if visiting over holiday periods.** The local dailies carry a listing of "What's Open/What's Not" for those time periods.

SHOPS

Stores in resort areas sometimes open as early as 8, with shopping-center opening hours varying from 9:30 to 10 on weekdays and Saturday, a bit later on Sunday. Bigger malls stay open until 9 weekdays and Saturday and close at 5 on Sunday. Boutiques in resort areas may stay open as late as 11.

BUS TRAVEL

Getting around by bus is an option on O'ahu, but on Neighbor Islands services are limited and car rental is recommended. O'ahu's transportation system, known just as TheBus, is one of the island's best bargains. Fares per ride are $2, and with more than 68 bus routes you can even do an O'ahu circle-island tour.

The Big Island's Hele-On Bus travels a Kailua-Kona–to–Hilo route once daily except Sunday for $5.25 each way. There are limited routes to other areas. The Ali'i Shuttle runs daily from the Keauhou Resort area to the village of Kailua-Kona every 1–1½ hours from 8:30 AM–7:40 PM. Fares are $2 each way. On Kaua'i, the Kaua'i Bus travels two main routes, one going north to Hanalei from Līhu'e and one going south from Līhu'e to Kekaha. Routes don't come close to many of the island's resorts or best-known attractions but do wind through residential towns. Holo Ka'a Public Transit System has routes in South, West, and Central Maui. Fares depend on the route.

7 Ali'i Shuttle ☏ 808/938-1112 on the Big Island. Hele-On Bus ☏ 808/961-8744 on the Big Island. Holo Ka'a Public Transit System ☏ 808/879-2828 on Maui. Kaua'i Bus ☏ 808/241-6410 on Kaua'i. TheBus ☏ 808/848-5555 on O'ahu ⊕ www.thebus.org.

CAMERAS & PHOTOGRAPHY

Today's underwater "disposable" cameras can provide terrific photos for those once-in-a-lifetime underwater experiences. Film developing is available on all of the Islands. Many hotel/resort sundries stores offer the service, and larger department stores, such as Long's Drugs, have one-hour service for regular film developing and overnight service for panoramic film.

The *Kodak Guide to Shooting Great Travel Pictures* (available at bookstores everywhere) is loaded with tips.

7 Photo Help Kodak Information Center ☏ 800/242-2424 ⊕ www.kodak.com.

EQUIPMENT PRECAUTIONS

Don't pack film or equipment in checked luggage, where it is much more susceptible to damage. X-ray machines used to view checked luggage are extremely powerful and therefore are likely to ruin your film. Try to ask for hand inspection of film, which becomes clouded after repeated exposure to airport X-ray machines, and keep videotapes and computer disks away from metal detectors. Always keep film, tape, and computer disks out of the sun. Carry an extra supply of batteries, and be prepared to turn on your camera, camcorder, or laptop to prove to airport security personnel that the device is real.

CAR RENTAL

You can rent anything from a $26-a-day econobox to a $1,100-a-day Ferrari. It's wise to make reservations in advance, especially if visiting during peak seasons or for major conventions or sporting events.

Rates in Honolulu begin at $38 a day ($164 a week) for an economy car with air-conditioning, automatic transmission, and unlimited mileage. Rates on Maui begin at $32 a day ($144 a week) for the same. This does not include vehicle registration fee and weight tax, insurance, sales tax and a $3-per-day Hawai'i state surcharge.

7 Major Agencies Alamo ☏ 800/327-9633 ⊕ www.alamo.com. Avis ☏ 800/331-1212, 800/879-2847 or 800/272-5871 in Canada, 0870/606-0100 in the U.K., 02/9353-9000 in Australia, 09/526-2847 in New Zealand ⊕ www.avis.com. Budget ☏ 800/527-0700, 0870/156-5656 in the U.K. ⊕ www.budget.com. Dollar ☏ 800/800-4000, 0800/085-4578 in the U.K. ⊕ www.dollar.com. Hertz ☏ 800/654-3131, 800/263-0600 in Canada, 0870/844-8844 in the U.K., 02/9669-2444 in Australia, 09/256-8690 in New Zealand ⊕ www.hertz.com. National Car Rental ☏ 800/227-7368, 0870/600-6666 in the U.K. ⊕ www.nationalcar.com.

CUTTING COSTS

For a good deal, book through a travel agent who will shop around. Also, **price local car-rental companies,** which usually carry pre-owned cars—a popular rental option for the Islands, although the service and maintenance may not be as good as those of a major player. Remember to ask about required deposits, cancellation penalties, and drop-off charges if you're planning to pick up the car in one city and leave it in another. If you're traveling during a holiday period, make sure that a confirmed reservation guarantees you a car.

Many rental companies in Hawai'i offer coupons for discounts at various attractions that could save you money later on in your trip. Consolidators that specialize in air travel can offer good rates on cars as well (⇨ Air Travel). Remember to ask about required deposits, cancellation penalties, and drop-off charges if you're planning to pick up the car in one city and leave it in another. If you're traveling during a holiday period, also make sure that a confirmed reservation guarantees you a car.

🏠 **Local Agencies AA Aloha Cars-R-Us** ☎ 800/655-7989 ⊕ www.hawaiicarrental.com. **JN Car and Truck Rentals** ☎ 800/475-7522, 808/831-2724 on O'ahu ⊕ www.jnautomotive.com. **Ho'okipa Haven** ☎ 808/579-8282 or 800/398-6284 ⊕ www.hookipa.com on Maui. **VIP Car Rentals** ☎ 808/922-4605 on O'ahu.

INSURANCE

When driving a rented car you are generally responsible for any damage to or loss of the vehicle. You also may be liable for any property damage or personal injury that you may cause while driving. Before you rent, see what coverage you already have under the terms of your personal auto-insurance policy and credit cards.

For about $9 to $25 a day, rental companies sell protection, known as a collision- or loss-damage waiver (CDW or LDW), that eliminates your liability for damage to the car; it's always optional and should never be automatically added to your bill. However, **make sure you have enough coverage to pay for the car.** If you do not have auto insurance or an umbrella policy that covers damage to third parties, purchasing liability insurance and a CDW or LDW is highly recommended.

REQUIREMENTS & RESTRICTIONS

In Hawai'i you must be 21 years of age to rent a car and you must have a valid driver's license and a major credit card.

Those under 25 will pay a daily surcharge of $15–$25.

In Hawai'i your unexpired mainland driver's license is valid for rental for up to 90 days.

SURCHARGES

Before you pick up a car in one city and leave it in another, ask about drop-off charges or one-way service fees, which can be substantial. Also inquire about early-return policies; some rental agencies charge extra if you return the car before the time specified in your contract while others give you a refund for the days not used. To avoid a hefty refueling fee, fill the tank just before you turn in the car, but be aware that gas stations near the rental outlet may overcharge. It's almost never a deal to buy the tank of gas that's in the car when you rent it; the understanding is that you'll return it empty, but some fuel usually remains. Surcharges may apply if you're under 25 or if you take the car outside the area approved by the rental agency. You'll pay extra for child seats (about $8 a day), which are compulsory for children under four, and usually for additional drivers (up to $25 a day, depending on location).

CAR TRAVEL

Technically, the Big Island of Hawai'i is the only island you can completely circle by car, but each island offers plenty of sightseeing from its miles of roadways. O'ahu can be circled except for the roadless west-shore area around Ka'ena Point. Elsewhere, major highways follow the shoreline and traverse the island at two points. Rush-hour traffic (6:30 to 8:30 AM and 3:30 to 6 PM) can be frustrating around Honolulu and the outlying areas, as many thoroughfares allow no left turns due to contra-flow lanes. Traffic on Maui can be very bad branching out from Kahului to and from Pā'ia, Kīhei and Lahaina. Drive here during peak hours and you'll know why local residents are calling for restrictions on development. Parking along many streets is curtailed during these times, and towing is strictly practiced. Read curbside parking signs before leaving your vehicle, even at a meter.

GASOLINE

Regardless of today's fluctuating gas prices, you can pretty much count on having to pay more at the pump for gasoline on the Islands than on the U.S. mainland.

ROAD CONDITIONS

It's difficult to get lost in most of Hawai'i. Roads and streets, although they may challenge the visitor's tongue, are well marked. **Keep an eye open for the Hawai'i Visitors and Convention Bureau's red-caped King Kamehameha signs,** which mark major attractions and scenic spots. Ask for a map at the car-rental counter. Free publications containing good-quality road maps can be found on all Islands.

The Big Island and O'ahu have well-maintained roads, which can be easily negotiated and do not require a four-wheel-drive vehicle. Kaua'i has a well-maintained highway running south from Līhu'e to Barking Sands Beach; a spur at Waimea takes you along Waimea Canyon to Kōke'e State Park. A northern route also winds its way from Līhu'e to end at Hā'ena, the beginning of the rugged and roadless Nā Pali Coast. Maui also has its share of impenetrable areas, although four-wheel-drive vehicles rarely run into problems on the island. Although Moloka'i and Lāna'i have fewer roadways, car rental is still worthwhile and will allow plenty of interesting sightseeing. **Opt for a four-wheel-drive vehicle** if dirt-road exploration holds any appeal.

RULES OF THE ROAD

Be sure to **buckle up.** Hawai'i has a strictly enforced seat-belt law for front-seat passengers. Children under four must be in a car seat (available from car-rental agencies). Children 18 and under, riding in the backseat, are also required by state law to use seat belts. The highway speed limit is usually 55 mph. In-town traffic moves from 25 to 40 mph. Jaywalking is very common, so be particularly watchful for pedestrians, especially in congested areas such as Waikīkī. Unauthorized use of a parking space reserved for persons with disabilities can net you a $150 fine.

Asking for directions will almost always produce a helpful explanation from the locals, but you should be prepared for an island term or two. Instead of using compass directions, remember that Hawai'i residents refer to places as being either *mauka* (toward the mountains) or *makai* (toward the ocean) from one another. Other directions depend on your location: in Honolulu, for example, people say to "go Diamond Head," which means toward that famous landmark, or to "go *'ewa,*" meaning in the opposite direction. A shop on the mauka–Diamond Head corner of a street is on the mountain side of the street on the corner closest to Diamond Head. It all makes perfect sense once you get the lay of the land.

CHILDREN IN HAWAI'I

Sunny beaches and many family-oriented cultural sites, activities, and attractions make Hawai'i a very *keiki-* (child-) friendly place. Here kids can swim with a dolphin, surf with a boogie board, check out an active volcano, or ride a sugarcane train. Parents should **use caution on beaches and during water sports.** Even waters that appear calm can harbor powerful rip currents. Be sure to **read any beach-warning guides your hotel may provide. Ask around for kid-friendly beaches** that might have shallow tide pools or are protected by reefs. And remember that the sun's rays are in operation full-force year-round here. Sunblock for children is essential. If you are renting a car, don't forget to arrange for a car seat when you reserve. For general advice about traveling with children, consult *Fodor's FYI: Travel with Your Baby* (available in bookstores everywhere).

Most major resort chains in Hawai'i offer children's activity programs for kids ages 5 to 12. These kid clubs provide opportunities to learn about local culture, make friends with children from around the world, and experience age-appropriate activities while giving moms and dads a "time-out." Upon arrival, check out the daily local newspapers for children's events. The *Honolulu Advertiser's* "TGIF" section each Friday includes a section on keiki activities with a local flavor.

FLYING

If your children are two or older, ask about children's airfares. As a general rule, infants under two not occupying a seat fly at greatly reduced fares or even for free. But if you want to guarantee a seat for an infant, you have to pay full fare. Consider flying during off-peak days and times; most airlines will grant an infant a seat without a ticket if there are available seats.

Experts agree that it's a good idea to use safety seats aloft for children weighing less than 40 pounds. Airlines set their own policies: if you use a safety seat, U.S. carriers usually require that the child be ticketed, even if he or she is young enough to ride free, because the seats must be strapped into regular seats. And even if you pay the full adult fare for the seat, it may be worth it, especially on longer trips. Do **check your airline's policy about using safety seats during takeoff and landing.** Safety seats are not allowed everywhere in the plane, so get your seat assignments as early as possible.

When reserving, request children's meals or a freestanding bassinet (not available at all airlines) if you need them. But note that bulkhead seats, where you must sit to use the bassinet, may lack an overhead bin or storage space on the floor.

LODGING

Families can't go wrong choosing resort locations that are part of larger hotel chains such as Hilton, Sheraton, Outrigger, and Westin. Many of these resorts are on the best beaches on each island, have activities created for children, and are centrally located. Outrigger's "Ohana" brand hotels are off the beachfront but provide great value at good prices. Many condominium resorts now also offer children's activities and amenities during holiday periods. Most hotels in Hawai'i allow children under a certain age to stay in their parents' room at no extra charge, but others charge for them as extra adults; be sure to find out the cutoff age for children's discounts. Also **check for special seasonal programs,** such as "kids eat free" promotions.

🏨 **Best Choices Aston Hotels Resort Quest International** ☎ 800/922-7866 🌐 www.aston-hotels.

com. **Four Seasons Hotels and Resorts** ☎ 800/819-5053 🌐 www.fourseasons.com. **Hilton** ☎ 800/774-1500 🌐 www.hilton.com. **Hyatt Hotels & Resorts** ☎ 888/591-1234 🌐 www.hyatt.com. **Marriott** ☎ 888/236-2427 🌐 www.marriott.com. **Outrigger Hotels** ☎ 800/688-7444 🌐 www.outrigger.com. **Starwood Hotels and Resorts** ☎ 888/625-5144 for Westin and Sheraton, 800/325-3589 for Luxury Collection, 877/946-8357 for W Hotels 🌐 www.starwood.com.

SIGHTS & ATTRACTIONS

Top picks for children run the gamut from natural attractions kids can enjoy for free to some fairly expensive amusements. On O'ahu, favorites include surfing lessons at Waikīkī Beach, hiking Diamond Head, snorkeling Hanauma Bay, learning about marine life at Sea Life Park, splashing about the 29-acre Hawaiian Waters Adventure Park, and touring through South Pacific cultures at the Polynesian Cultural Center. On Maui, kid favorites include the Sugarcane Train that runs between Lahaina and Kā'anapali, snorkeling to Molokini Island, and whale-watching after a visit to the Maui Ocean Center. Visiting Hawai'i Volcanoes National Park, star gazing atop Mauna Kea, touring the Mauna Loa Macadamia Factory near Hilo, swimming with dolphins at the Hilton Waikoloa, and horseback riding at Parker Ranch are fun things to do on the Big Island.

Kaua'i is where kids go to explore film locations such as Peter Pan's Never-Never Land and Jurassic Park. They can learn to water-ski on the Wailua River, visit Kōke'e National Park, or just spend the day swimming Po'ipū's sunny south shores. Lāna'i and Moloka'i are great islands for adventurous youngsters. At Sheraton Moloka'i Lodge and Beach Village, families can sleep in canvas bungalows and enjoy everything from star gazing and spear fishing to horseback riding with a paniolo (Hawaiian cowboy). On Lāna'i, four-wheel-drive off-road adventure tours take families to destinations such as Shipwreck Beach and Mānele Bay, where the dolphins sometimes come to play.

Places that are especially appealing to children are indicated by a rubber-duckie icon (🐤) in the margin.

CONSUMER PROTECTION

Whether you're shopping for gifts or purchasing travel services, **pay with a major credit card** whenever possible, so you can cancel payment or get reimbursed if there's a problem (and you can provide documentation). If you're doing business with a particular company for the first time, contact your local Better Business Bureau and the attorney general's offices in your state and (for U.S. businesses) the company's home state as well. Have any complaints been filed? Finally, if you're buying a package or tour, always consider travel insurance that includes default coverage (⇨ Insurance).

🛈 **BBBs Council of Better Business Bureaus** ✉ 4200 Wilson Blvd., Suite 800, Arlington, VA 22203 ☎ 703/276-0100 🖷 703/525-8277 ⊕ www.bbb.org.

CRUISE TRAVEL

When Pan Am's amphibious *Hawai'i Clipper* touched down on Pearl Harbor's waters in 1936, it marked the beginning of the end of regular passenger-ship travel to the Islands. From that point on, the predominant means of transporting visitors would be by air, not by sea. Today, however, cruising to Hawai'i is making a comeback.

Norwegian Cruise Lines offers four "freestyle" cruises (no set meal times, less formal clothing, more nightlife choices) with Hawai'i itineraries. Norwegian's two new U.S.-flagged ships, *Pride of America* and *Pride of Aloha* sail interisland on three-, four-, and seven-day schedules. To get the best deal on a cruise, **consult a cruise-only travel agency.**

Even if you choose, as most travelers do, to travel by air to the Islands, you can get the flavor of what the luxury-cruise era in Hawai'i was like by checking out Aloha Tower Marketplace's Boat Day Celebrations in Honolulu. Vessels stopping here are met upon arrival by hula dancers and the kind of entertainment and floral festivities that once greeted travelers almost

a century ago. Contact Aloha Tower Marketplace for a boat-day schedule upon arrival.

To learn how to plan, choose, and book a cruise-ship voyage, consult *Fodor's FYI: Plan & Enjoy Your Cruise* (available in bookstores everywhere).

🛈 **Aloha Tower Marketplace** ✉ 1 Aloha Tower Dr., at Piers 8, 9, and 10, Honolulu ☎ 808/528-5700 ⊕ www.alohatower.com. **Carnival** ☎ 888/227-6482 ⊕ www.carnival.com. **Celebrity** ☎ 800/722-5941 ⊕ www.celebritycruises.com. **Crystal Cruises** ☎ 800/804-1500 ⊕ www.crystalcruises.com. **Cunard** ☎ 800/728-6273 ⊕ www.cunard.com. **Holland America** ☎ 877/724-5425 ⊕ www.hollandamerica.com. **Norwegian Cruise Lines** ☎ 800/327-7030 ⊕ www.norwegiancruiselines.com. **Princess** ☎ 800/774-6237 ⊕ www.princess.com. **Royal Caribbean Cruise Line** ☎ 800/398-9819 ⊕ www.royalcaribbean.com. **Seabourn** ☎ 800/929-9391 ⊕ www.seabourn.com.

CUSTOMS & DUTIES

When shopping abroad, keep receipts for all purchases. Upon reentering the country, **be ready to show customs officials what you've bought.** Pack purchases together in an easily accessible place. If you think a duty is incorrect, appeal the assessment. If you object to the way your clearance was handled, note the inspector's badge number. In either case, first ask to see a supervisor. If the problem isn't resolved, write to the appropriate authorities, beginning with the port director at your point of entry.

IN AUSTRALIA

Australian residents who are 18 or older may bring home A$400 worth of souvenirs and gifts (including jewelry), 250 cigarettes or 250 grams of cigars or other tobacco products, and 1,125 ml of alcohol (including wine, beer, and spirits). Residents under 18 may bring back A$200 worth of goods. Members of the same family traveling together may pool their allowances. Prohibited items include meat products. Seeds, plants, and fruits need to be declared upon arrival.

🛈 **Australian Customs Service** ⬡ Regional Director, Box 8, Sydney, NSW 2001 ☎ 02/9213-2000 or 1300/363263, 02/9364-7222 or 1800/020-504 quarantine-inquiry line ☎ 02/9213-4043 ⊕ www. customs.gov.au.

IN CANADA

Canadian residents who have been out of Canada for at least seven days may bring in C$750 worth of goods duty-free. If you've been away fewer than seven days but more than 48 hours, the duty-free allowance drops to C$200. If your trip lasts 24 to 48 hours, the allowance is C$50. You may not pool allowances with family members. Goods claimed under the C$750 exemption may follow you by mail; those claimed under the lesser exemptions must accompany you. Alcohol and tobacco products may be included in the seven-day and 48-hour exemptions but not in the 24-hour exemption. If you meet the age requirements of the province or territory through which you reenter Canada, you may bring in, duty-free, 1.5 liters of wine *or* 1.14 liters (40 imperial ounces) of liquor *or* 24 12-ounce cans or bottles of beer or ale. Also, if you meet the local age requirement for tobacco products, you may bring in, duty-free, 200 cigarettes and 50 cigars. Check ahead of time with the Canada Customs and Revenue Agency or the Department of Agriculture for policies regarding meat products, seeds, plants, and fruits.

You may send an unlimited number of gifts (only one gift per recipient, however) worth up to C$60 each duty-free to Canada. Label the package UNSOLICITED GIFT—VALUE UNDER $60. Alcohol and tobacco are excluded.
🚩 **Canada Customs and Revenue Agency** ⊠ 2265 St. Laurent Blvd., Ottawa, Ontario K1G 4K3 ☎ 800/461-9999 in Canada, 204/983-3500, 506/636-5064 ⊕ www.ccra.gc.ca.

IN HAWAI'I

Plants and plant products are subject to regulation by the Department of Agriculture, both on entering and leaving Hawai'i. Upon leaving the Islands, you'll have to have your bags X-rayed and tagged at one of the airport's agricultural inspection stations before you proceed to check-in. Pineapples and coconuts with the packer's agricultural inspection stamp pass freely; papayas must be treated, inspected, and stamped. All other fruits are banned for export to the U.S. mainland. Flowers pass except for gardenia, rose leaves, jade vine, and mauna loa. Also banned are insects, snails, soil, cotton, cacti, sugarcane, and all berry plants.

You'll have to **leave dogs and other pets at home.** A 120-day quarantine is imposed to keep out rabies, which is nonexistent in Hawai'i. If specific pre- and post-arrival requirements are met, animals may qualify for a 30-day or 5-day-or-less quarantine.
🚩 **U.S. Customs and Border Protection** ⊠ for inquiries and equipment registration, 1300 Pennsylvania Ave. NW, Washington, DC 20229 ⊕ www.cbp. gov ☎ 877/287-8667, 202/354-1000 ⊠ for complaints, Customer Satisfaction Unit, 1300 Pennsylvania Ave. NW, Room 5.2C, Washington, DC 20229.

IN NEW ZEALAND

All homeward-bound residents may bring back NZ$700 worth of souvenirs and gifts; passengers may not pool their allowances, and children can claim only the concession on goods intended for their own use. For those 17 or older, the duty-free allowance also includes 4.5 liters of wine or beer; one 1,125-ml bottle of spirits; and either 200 cigarettes, 250 grams of tobacco, 50 cigars, *or* a combination of the three up to 250 grams. Meat products, seeds, plants, and fruits must be declared upon arrival to the Agricultural Services Department.
🚩 **New Zealand Customs** ⊠ Head office: The Customhouse, 17–21 Whitmore St., Box 2218, Wellington ☎ 09/300-5399 or 0800/428-786 ⊕ www.customs. govt.nz.

IN THE U.K.

From countries outside the European Union, including the United States, you may bring home, duty-free, 200 cigarettes, 50 cigars, 100 cigarillos, or 250 grams of tobacco; 1 liter of spirits or 2 liters of fortified or sparkling wine or liqueurs; 2 liters of still table wine; 60 ml of perfume; 250 ml of toilet water; plus £145 worth of other goods, including gifts and souvenirs. Prohibited items include meat products, seeds, plants, fruits, and dairy products.
🚩 **HM Customs and Excise** ⊠ Portcullis House, 21 Cowbridge Rd. E, Cardiff CF11 9SS ☎ 0845/010–

9000 or 0208/929–0152 advice service, 0208/929–6731 or 0208/910–3602 complaints ⊕ www.hmce.gov.uk.

DISABILITIES & ACCESSIBILITY

The Society for the Advancement of Travel for the Handicapped has named Hawai'i the most accessible vacation spot for people with disabilities. Ramped visitor areas and specially equipped lodgings are relatively common. Travelers with vision impairments who use a guide dog don't have to worry about quarantine restrictions. All you need to do is present documentation that the animal is a trained guide dog and has a current inoculation record for rabies. Access Aloha Travel is the state's only travel planner specializing in the needs of Hawai'i-bound travelers with disabilities. The company can arrange accessible accommodations, sightseeing, dining, activities, medical equipment rentals and personal care attendants. Access Aloha also rents wheelchairs and scooter vans on O'hu and Maui.

7 **Local Resources Disability and Communication Access Board** ⊠ 919 Ala Moana Blvd., Room 101, Honolulu 96814 ☎ 808/586-8121. **Access Aloha Travel** ⊠ 414 Kuwili St., Suite 101, Honolulu 96817 ☎ 800/480-1143 or 008/545-1143 ☎ 808/545-7657 ⊕ www.accessalohatravel.com.

LODGING

Travelers with disabilities and people using wheelchairs find it easy to get around Hawai'i's resorts and hotels, with indoor-outdoor layouts that are easily navigated. If choosing a smaller hotel or a condo or apartment rental, inquire about ground-floor accommodations and **check to see if rooms will accommodate wheelchairs and if bathrooms are accessible.** Many hotels now offer special-needs rooms featuring larger living spaces and bathrooms equipped for guests who require additional assistance.

Despite the Americans with Disabilities Act, the definition of accessibility seems to differ from hotel to hotel. Some properties may be accessible by ADA standards for people with mobility problems but not for people with hearing or vision impairments, for example.

If you have mobility problems, ask for the lowest floor on which accessible services are offered. If you have a hearing impairment, check whether the hotel has devices to alert you visually to the ring of the telephone, a knock at the door, and a fire/emergency alarm. Some hotels provide these devices without charge. Discuss your needs with hotel personnel if this equipment isn't available, so that a staff member can personally alert you in the event of an emergency.

If you're bringing a guide dog, get authorization ahead of time and write down the name of the person with whom you spoke.

RESERVATIONS

When discussing accessibility with an operator or reservations agent, ask hard questions. Are there any stairs, inside *or* out? Are there grab bars next to the toilet *and* in the shower/tub? How wide is the doorway to the room? To the bathroom? For the most extensive facilities meeting the latest legal specifications, opt for newer accommodations. If you reserve through a toll-free number, consider also calling the hotel's local number to confirm the information from the central reservations office. Get confirmation in writing when you can.

SIGHTS & ATTRACTIONS

Many of Hawai'i's sights and attractions are accessible to travelers with disabilities. The state's number-one attraction, Hawai'i Volcanoes National Park, includes a drive-through volcano. The Honolulu Department of Parks and Recreation provides "all-terrain" wheelchairs and beach mats at several beach parks on O'ahu. Accessible Vans of Hawaii rents wheelchairs and scooter vans on O'ahu, Maui, and the Big Island. In addition, the company can arrange accessible accommodations, sightseeing, dining, activities, medical-equipment rentals, and personal care attendants.

7 **Accessible Vans of Hawaii** ☎ 800/303-3750 ⊕ www.accessiblevanshawaii.com. **Honolulu Department of Parks and Recreation** Therapeutic Recreation Unit ☎ 808/692-5461 Therapeutic Recreation Unit ⊕ www.co.honolulu.hi.us/parks/programs/beach.

TRANSPORTATION

Paratransit Services (HandiVan) will take you to a specific destination on Oʻahu—not on sightseeing outings—in vans with lifts and lock-downs. With a HandiVan Pass, one-way trips cost $2. Passes are free and can be obtained from the Department of Transportation Services, which is open weekdays 7:45–4:30; you'll need a doctor's written confirmation of your disability or a Paratransit ID card. Application forms also can be obtained in advance of your visit by calling the Department of Transportation Services or going online. Handi-Cabs of the Pacific also operates ramp-equipped vans with lock-downs in Honolulu. Fares are $10 plus $2.40 per mi for curbside service and $20 plus $2.40 per mile for door-to-door service. Reservations at least 48 hours in advance are required by both companies, so plan ahead.

Those who prefer to do their own driving may rent hand-controlled cars from Alamo, Avis, Budget, Dollar, Hertz and National. You can use the windshield card from your own state to park in spaces reserved for people with disabilities. All require at least 48 hours notice.

⚑ Alamo ☎ 800/651-1223. **Avis** ☎ 800/321-3712. **Budget** ☎ 800/526-6408. **Dollar** ☎ 800/367-5171. **Hertz** ☎ 800/654-3011. **National** ☎ 800/227-7368. **Department of Transportation Services** ✉ 650 S. King St., 2nd floor, Honolulu 96813 ☎ 808/523-4083. **Handi-Cabs of the Pacific** ☎ 808/524-3866. **Paratransit Services (HandiVan)** ☎ 808/456-5555.

⚑ Complaints Aviation Consumer Protection Division (⇨ Air Travel) for airline-related problems. **Departmental Office of Civil Rights** ✉ for general inquiries, U.S. Department of Transportation, S-30, 400 7th St. SW, Room 10215, Washington, DC 20590 ☎ 202/366-4648 🖷 202/366-9371 ⊕ www.dot.gov/ost/docr/index.htm. **Disability Rights Section** ✉ NYAV, U.S. Department of Justice, Civil Rights Division, 950 Pennsylvania Ave. NW, Washington, DC 20530 ☎ ADA information line 202/514-0301, 800/514-0301, 202/514-0383 TTY, 800/514-0383 TTY ⊕ www.ada.gov. **U.S. Department of Transportation Hotline** ☎ for disability-related air-travel problems, 800/778-4838 or 800/455-9880 TTY.

TRAVEL AGENCIES

In the United States, the Americans with Disabilities Act requires that travel firms serve the needs of all travelers. Some agencies specialize in working with people with disabilities.

⚑ Travelers with Mobility Problems Access Adventures/B. Roberts Travel ✉ 206 Chestnut Ridge Rd., Scottsville, NY 14624 ☎ 585/889-9096 ⊕ www.brobertstravel.com ✎ dltravel@prodigy.net, run by a former physical-rehabilitation counselor. **Access Aloha Travel** ✉ 414 Kuwili St., Suite 101, Honolulu, HI 96817 ☎ 800/480-1143 🖷 808/545-7657 ⊕ www.accessalohatravel.com. **Accessible Vans of America** ✉ 9 Spielman Rd., Fairfield, NJ 07004 ☎ 877/282-8267, 888/282-8267, 973/808-9709 reservations 🖷 973/808-9713 ⊕ www.accessiblevans.com. **Accessible Vans of Hawaii** ✉ 355 Hukulike St., Suite 121A, Kahului, HI 96732 ☎ 808/871-7785 or 800/303-3750 🖷 808/871-7536 ⊕ www.accessiblevanshawaii.com. **CareVacations** ✉ No. 5, 5110-50 Ave., Leduc, Alberta, Canada, T9E 6V4 ☎ 780/986-6404 or 877/478-7827 🖷 780/986-8332 ⊕ www.carevacations.com, for group tours and cruise vacations. **Flying Wheels Travel** ✉ 143 W. Bridge St., Box 382, Owatonna, MN 55060 ☎ 507/451-5005 🖷 507/451-1685 ⊕ www.flyingwheelstravel.com.

⚑ Travelers with Developmental Disabilities New Directions ✉ 5276 Hollister Ave., Suite 207, Santa Barbara, CA 93111 ☎ 805/967-2841 or 888/967-2841 🖷 805/964-7344 ⊕ www.newdirectionstravel.com. **Sprout** ✉ 893 Amsterdam Ave., New York, NY 10025 ☎ 212/222-9575 or 888/222-9575 🖷 212/222-9768 ⊕ www.gosprout.org.

DISCOUNTS & DEALS

Be a smart shopper and compare all your options before making decisions. A plane ticket bought with a promotional coupon from travel clubs, coupon books, and direct-mail offers or purchased on the Internet may not be cheaper than the least expensive fare from a discount ticket agency. And always keep in mind that what you get is just as important as what you save.

DISCOUNT RESERVATIONS

To save money, look into discount reservations services with Web sites and toll-free numbers, which use their buying power to get a better price on hotels, airline tickets (⇨ Air Travel), even car rentals. When booking a room, always **call the hotel's local toll-free number** (if one is available) rather than the central reservations number—you'll often get a better price. Always ask about special packages or corporate rates.

F Airline Tickets **Air 4 Less** ☎ 800/AIR4LESS; low-fare specialist.

F Hotel Rooms **Accommodations Express** ☎ 800/444-7666 or 800/277-1064 ⊕ www.acex.net. **Hotels.com** ☎ 800/246-8357 ⊕ www.hotels.com. **Quikbook** ☎ 800/789-9887 ⊕ www.quikbook.com. **Steigenberger Reservation Service** ☎ 800/223-5652 ⊕ www.srs-worldhotels.com. **Turbotrip.com** ☎ 800/473-7829 ⊕ www.turbotrip.com.

PACKAGE DEALS

Don't confuse packages and guided tours. When you buy a package, you travel on your own, just as though you had planned the trip yourself. Fly/drive packages, which combine airfare and car rental, are often a good deal. In cities, ask the local visitor's bureau about hotel and local transportation packages that include tickets to major museum exhibits or other special events.

EATING & DRINKING

Food in Hawai'i is a reflection of the state's diverse cultural makeup and tropical location. Fresh seafood is the hallmark of Hawai'i regional cuisine, and its preparations are drawn from across the Pacific Rim, including Japan, the Philippines, Korea, and Thailand. But Hawaiian food is a cuisine in its own right. Meals in resort areas are costly but often excellent. In general, when you order a regular coffee, you get coffee with milk and sugar.

The restaurants we list are the cream of the crop in each price category.

CATEGORY	COST
$$$$	over $30
$$$	$20–$30
$$	$12–$20
$	$7–$12
¢	under $7

Prices are for one main course at dinner.

MEALTIMES

Unless otherwise noted, the restaurants listed in this guide are open daily for lunch and dinner.

RESERVATIONS & DRESS

Hawai'i is decidedly casual. Aloha shirts and shorts or long pants for men and island-style dresses or casual resort wear for women are standard attire for evenings in most hotel restaurants and local eateries. T-shirts and shorts will do the trick for breakfast and lunch.

Reservations are always a good idea; we mention them only when they're essential or not accepted. Book as far ahead as you can, and reconfirm as soon as you arrive. (Large parties should always call ahead to check the reservations policy.) We mention dress only when men are required to wear a jacket or a jacket and tie.

SPECIALTIES

Fish, fruit, and fresh island-grown produce are the base of Hawai'i regional cuisine. The "plate lunch" is the heart of most Hawaiians' days and usually consists of grilled teriyaki chicken, beef, or fish, served with two scoops of white rice and two side salads. *Poke,* marinated raw tuna, is a local hallmark.

WINE, BEER & SPIRITS

Hawai'i has a new generation of microbreweries, including on site microbreweries at many restaurants. On Maui, check out Tedeschi Vineyards, where you can tour a beautiful island estate and get a taste of sweet pineapple wine. The drinking age in Hawai'i is 21 years of age, and a photo ID must be presented to purchase alcoholic beverages. Bars are open until 2 AM; venues with a cabaret license can stay open until 4 AM. No matter what you might see in the local parks, drinking alcohol in public parks or on the beaches is illegal. It is also illegal to have open containers of alcohol in motor vehicles.

F Tedeschi Vineyards ✉ Kula Hwy., 'Ulupalakua Ranch, Maui ☎ 808/878-6058 ⊕ www.mauiwine.com.

ECOTOURISM

Hawai'i's connection to its environment is spiritual, cultural, and essential to its survival. You'll find a rainbow of natural attractions to explore, from the ribbons of beaches to volcanic peaks, where lava shows after dark are spectacular. There are

13 climatic regions in the world, and Maui and the Big Island offer ecotravelers a glimpse of 11 of them. Much of Kaua'i's natural beauty can be seen only on foot. Its Nā Pali Coast/Waimea Canyon/Kōke'e trail network includes 28 trails totaling some 45 mi rich in endemic species of flora and fauna. Maui offers the exhilaration of a rain-forest hike in Hāna, the cool Upcountry climes of Kula, and the awe-inspiring Haleakalā Crater. Moloka'i and Lāna'i, two of the least-developed islands, hold adventures best experienced on foot and by four-wheel-drive vehicle, or even by mule. Eco-touring in Hawai'i gives you the opportunity to learn from local guides who are familiar with the *aina* (land) and Hawai'i's unique cultural heritage. Many of these tours take clients to locations less traveled, so it helps to be in good physical shape. The views at the ends of these roads are an exceedingly rich reward.

Nature and all its ornaments are sacred to Hawaiians, so before taking pieces of lava rock home for souvenirs, listen to what residents (and some vacationers) will tell you: don't touch! Hapless travelers who take "souvenir" rocks speak of "bad-luck" consequences in the form of stalled cars, travel delays, and bouts of illness. Park rangers spin tales about lava rocks mailed from around the world with attached tales of woe and pleas for the rocks to be put back. If nothing else, with millions of visitors a year, there aren't enough cool rocks to go around.

During the winter months, be sure to watch the beachfronts for endangered sea turtles, or recently laid nests. If you spot one, notify local authorities—they'll be thankful for your help in tracking these elusive creatures.

↗ **Alternative-Hawai'i** ☎ 808/695-5113 ⊕ www. alternative-hawaii.com. **Hawai'i Ecotourism Association** ☎ 877/300-7058 ⊕ www. hawaiiecotourism.org.

ETIQUETTE & BEHAVIOR
Hawai'i was admitted to the Union in 1959, so residents can be pretty sensitive when visitors refer to their own hometowns as "back in the States." Remember, **when in Hawai'i, refer to the contiguous 48 states as "the mainland" and not as the United States.** When you do, you won't appear to be such a *malahini* (newcomer).

GAY & LESBIAN TRAVEL
A few small hotels and some bed-and-breakfasts in Hawai'i are favored by gay and lesbian visitors; Purple Roofs is a listing agent for gay-friendly accommodations in Hawai'i. Pacific Ocean Holidays specializes in prearranging package tours for independent gay travelers. The organization also publishes the *Pocket Guide to Hawai'i,* an online directory of gay and gay-friendly businesses and community resources on O'ahu, Maui, Kaua'i and the Big Island.

For details about the gay and lesbian scene, consult *Fodor's Gay Guide to the USA* (available in bookstores everywhere).

↗ Local Resources **Pacific Ocean Holidays** ⌂ Box 88245, Honolulu 96830 ☎ 808/923-2400 or 800/735-6600 ⊕ www.gayHawaii.com. **Purple Roofs** ⊕ www.purpleroofs.com.

↗ Gay- & Lesbian-Friendly Travel Agencies **Different Roads Travel** ✉ 8383 Wilshire Blvd., Suite 520, Beverly Hills, CA 90211 ☎ 323/651-5557 or 800/429-8747 (Ext. 14 for both) 🖷 323/651-5454 ⌨ lgernert@tzell.com. **Kennedy Travel** ✉ 130 W. 42nd St., Suite 401, New York, NY 10036 ☎ 212/840-8659, 800/237-7433 🖷 212/730-2269 ⊕ www. kennedytravel.com. **Now, Voyager** ✉ 4406 18th St., San Francisco, CA 94114 ☎ 415/626-1169 or 800/255-6951 🖷 415/626-8626 ⊕ www.nowvoyager. com. **Skylink Travel and Tour/Flying Dutchmen Travel** ✉ 1455 N. Dutton Ave., Suite A, Santa Rosa, CA 95401 ☎ 707/546-9888 or 800/225-5759 🖷 707/636-0951; serving lesbian travelers.

HEALTH
Hawai'i is known as the Health State. The life expectancy here is 79 years, the longest in the nation. Balmy weather makes it easy to remain active year-round, and the low-stress aloha attitude certainly contributes to general well-being. When visiting the Islands, however, there are a few health issues to keep in mind.

The Hawai'i State Department of Health recommends that you drink 16 ounces of water per hour to avoid dehydration when hiking or spending time in the sun. **Use** sunblock, **wear UV-reflective sunglasses, and protect your head with a visor or hat for shade.** If you're not acclimated to warm, humid weather you should allow plenty of time for rest stops and refreshments. When visiting freshwater streams, be aware of the tropical disease leptospirosis, which is spread by animal urine and carried into streams and mud. Symptoms include fever, headache, nausea, and red eyes. If left untreated it can cause liver and kidney damage, respiratory failure, internal bleeding, and even death. To avoid this, don't swim or wade in freshwater streams or ponds if you have open sores and **don't drink from any freshwater streams or ponds.**

On the Islands, fog is a rare occurrence, but there can often be "vog," an airborne haze of gases released from volcanic vents on the Big Island. During certain weather conditions such as "Kona Winds," the vog can settle over the Islands and wreak havoc with respiratory and other health conditions, especially asthma or emphysema. If susceptible, stay indoors and get emergency assistance if needed.

DIVERS' ALERT
Do not fly within 24 hours of scuba diving.

PESTS & OTHER HAZARDS
The Islands have their share of bugs and insects that enjoy the tropical climate as much as visitors do. Most are harmless but annoying. When planning to spend time outdoors in hiking areas, **wear long-sleeved clothing and pants** and **use mosquito repellent containing deet.** In very damp places you may encounter the dreaded local centipede. On the Islands they usually come in two colors, brown and blue, and they range from the size of a worm to an 8-inch cigar. Their sting is very painful, and the reaction is similar to bee- and wasp-sting reactions. When camping, **shake out your sleeping bag before climbing in, and check your shoes in the morning,** as the centipedes like cozy places. If planning on hiking or traveling in remote areas, always carry a first-aid kit and appropriate medications for sting reactions.

HOLIDAYS
Major national holidays are New Year's Day; Martin Luther King Jr. Day (3rd Mon. in Jan.); Presidents' Day (3rd Mon. in Feb.); Memorial Day (last Mon. in May); Independence Day (July 4); Labor Day (1st Mon. in Sept.); Columbus Day (2nd Mon. in Oct.); Thanksgiving Day (4th Thurs. in Nov.); Christmas Eve and Christmas Day; and New Year's Eve.

In addition, Hawai'i celebrates Prince Kūhiō Day (Mar. 26), King Kamehameha Day (June 11), and Admission Day (3rd Fri. in Aug.). State, city, and county offices as well as many local companies are closed for business.

INSURANCE
The most useful travel-insurance plan is a comprehensive policy that includes coverage for trip cancellation and interruption, default, trip delay, and medical expenses (with a waiver for preexisting conditions).

Without insurance you'll lose all or most of your money if you cancel your trip, regardless of the reason. Default insurance covers you if your tour operator, airline, or cruise line goes out of business—the chances of which have been increasing. Trip delay covers expenses that arise because of bad weather or mechanical delays. Study the fine print when comparing policies.

U.K. residents can buy a travel-insurance policy valid for most vacations taken during the year in which it's purchased (but check preexisting-condition coverage).

Always **buy travel policies directly from the insurance company;** if you buy them from a cruise line, airline, or tour operator that goes out of business you probably won't be covered for the agency or operator's default, a major risk. Before making any purchase, review your existing health and home-owner's policies to find what they cover away from home.

▶ Travel Insurers In the U.S.: **Access America** ✉ 2805 N. Parham Rd., Richmond, VA 23294 ☎ 800/284-8300 🖷 804/673-1491 or 800/346-9265 ⊕ www.accessamerica.com. **Travel Guard International** ✉ 1145 Clark St., Stevens Point, WI 54481 ☎ 715/345-0505 or 800/826-1300 🖷 800/955-8785 ⊕ www.travelguard.com.

FOR INTERNATIONAL TRAVELERS

For information on customs restrictions, *see* Customs & Duties.

CAR RENTAL

When picking up a rental car, non-U.S. residents need a reservation voucher for any prepaid reservations that were made in the traveler's home country, a passport, a driver's license, and a travel policy that covers each driver.

CAR TRAVEL

Gas costs range from $2 to $2.50 a gallon. Stations are plentiful. Most stay open late (24 hours along large highways and in big cities), except in rural areas, where Sunday hours are limited and where you may drive long stretches without a refueling opportunity. Highways are well paved. Interstate highways—limited-access, multilane highways whose numbers are prefixed by "I–"—are the fastest routes. Interstates with three-digit numbers encircle urban areas, which may have other limited-access expressways, freeways, and parkways as well. Tolls may be levied on limited-access highways. So-called U.S. highways and state highways are not necessarily limited-access but may have several lanes.

Along larger highways, roadside stops with rest rooms, fast-food restaurants, and sundries stores are well spaced. State police and tow trucks patrol major highways and lend assistance. If your car breaks down on an interstate, pull onto the shoulder and wait for help, or have your passengers wait while you walk to an emergency phone (available in most states). If you carry a cell phone, dial *55, noting your location on the small green roadside mileage markers.

Driving in the United States is on the right. Do obey speed limits posted along roads and highways. Watch for lower limits in small towns and on back roads. On weekdays between 6 and 10 AM and again between 4 and 7 PM expect heavy traffic. To encourage carpooling, some freeways have special lanes for so-called high-occupancy vehicles (HOV)—cars carrying more than one passenger.

Bookstores, gas stations, convenience stores, and rest stops sell maps (about $3) and multiregion road atlases (about $10).

CONSULATES & EMBASSIES

7 Australia Australian Consulate ☒ 1000 Bishop St., Honolulu 96813 ☎ 808/524–5050.

7 Canada Canadian Consulate ☒ 1000 Bishop St., Honolulu 96813 ☎ 808/524–5050.

7 New Zealand New Zealand Consulate ☒ 900 Richards St., Room 414, Honolulu 96813 ☎ 808/543–7900.

7 United Kingdom British Consulate ☒ 1000 Bishop St., Honolulu 96813 ☎ 808/524–5050.

CURRENCY

The dollar is the basic unit of U.S. currency. It has 100 cents. Coins are the copper penny (1¢); the silvery nickel (5¢), dime (10¢), quarter (25¢), and half-dollar (50¢); and the golden $1 coin, replacing a now-rare silver dollar. Bills are denominated $1, $5, $10, $20, $50, and $100, all mostly green and identical in size; designs and background tints vary. In addition, you may come across a $2 bill, but the chances are slim. The exchange rate at this writing is US$1.78 per British pound, .74¢ per Canadian dollar, .73¢ per Australian dollar, and .63¢ per New Zealand dollar.

ELECTRICITY

The U.S. standard is AC, 110 volts/60 cycles. Plugs have two flat pins set parallel to each other.

EMERGENCIES

For police, fire, or ambulance, **dial 911** (0 in rural areas).

INSURANCE

Britons and Australians need extra medical coverage when traveling overseas.

7 Insurance Information In the U.K.: **Association of British Insurers** ☒ 51 Gresham St., London EC2V 7HQ ☎ 020/7600–3333 ☐ 020/7696–8999 ⊕ www.abi.org.uk. In Australia: **Insurance Council of Australia** ☒ Insurance Enquiries and Complaints, Level 12, Box 561, Collins St. W, Melbourne, VIC 8007 ☎ 1300/780808 or 03/9629–4109 ☐ 03/9621–2060 ⊕ www.iecltd.com.au. In Canada: **RBC Insurance** ☒ 6880 Financial Dr., Mississauga, Ontario L5N 7Y5 ☎ 800/668–4342 or 905/816–2400 ☐ 905/813–4704 ⊕ www.rbcinsurance.com. In

New Zealand: **Insurance Council of New Zealand** ✉ Level 7, 111-115 Customhouse Quay, Box 474, Wellington ☎ 04/472-5230 🖷 04/473-3011 ⊕ www.icnz.org.nz.

MAIL & SHIPPING

You can buy stamps and aerograms and send letters and parcels in post offices. Stamp-dispensing machines can occasionally be found in airports, bus and train stations, office buildings, drugstores, and the like. You can also deposit mail in the stout, dark blue, steel bins at strategic locations everywhere and in the mail chutes of large buildings; pickup schedules are posted. You can deposit packages at public collection boxes as long as the parcels are affixed with proper postage and weigh less than one pound. Packages weighing one or more pounds must be taken to a post office or handed to a postal carrier.

For mail sent within the United States, you need a 37¢ stamp for first-class letters weighing up to 1 ounce (23¢ for each additional ounce) and 23¢ for postcards. You pay 80¢ for 1-ounce airmail letters and 70¢ for airmail postcards to most other countries; to Canada and Mexico, you need a 60¢ stamp for a 1-ounce letter and 50¢ for a postcard. An aerogram—a single sheet of lightweight blue paper that folds into its own envelope, stamped for overseas airmail—costs 70¢.

To receive mail on the road, have it sent c/o General Delivery at your destination's main post office (use the correct five-digit ZIP code). You must pick up mail in person within 30 days and show a driver's license or passport.

PASSPORTS & VISAS

When traveling internationally, carry your passport even if you don't need one (it's always the best form of ID) and **make two photocopies of the data page** (one for someone at home and another for you, carried separately from your passport). If you lose your passport, promptly call the nearest embassy or consulate and the local police.

Visitor visas aren't necessary for Canadian or European Union citizens, or for citizens of Australia who are staying fewer than 90 days.

🇦🇺 **Australian Citizens Passports Australia** ☎ 131-232 ⊕ www.passports.gov.au. **United States Consulate General** ✉ MLC Centre, Level 59, 19-29 Martin Pl., Sydney, NSW 2000 ☎ 02/9373-9200, 1902/941-641 fee-based visa-inquiry line ⊕ usembassy-australia.state.gov/sydney.

🇨🇦 **Canadian Citizens Passport Office** ✉ to mail in applications: 200 Promenade du Portage, Hull, Québec J8X 4B7 ☎ 819/994-3500, 800/567-6868, 866/255-7655 TTY ⊕ www.ppt.gc.ca.

🇳🇿 **New Zealand Citizens New Zealand Passports Office** ✉ For applications and information, Level 3, Boulcott House, 47 Boulcott St., Wellington ☎ 0800/22-5050 or 04/474-8100 ⊕ www.passports.govt.nz. **Embassy of the United States** ✉ 29 Fitzherbert Terr., Thorndon, Wellington ☎ 04/462-6000 ⊕ usembassy.org.nz. **U.S. Consulate General** ✉ Citibank Bldg., 3rd floor, 23 Customs St. E, Auckland ☎ 09/303-2724 ⊕ usembassy.org.nz.

🇬🇧 **U.K. Citizens U.K. Passport Service** ☎ 0870/521-0410 ⊕ www.passport.gov.uk. **American Consulate General** ✉ Danesfort House, 223 Stranmillis Rd., Belfast, Northern Ireland BT9 5GR ☎ 028/9032-8239 🖷 028/9024-8482 ⊕ usembassy.org.uk. **American Embassy** ✉ for visa and immigration information or to submit a visa application via mail (enclose an SASE), Consular Information Unit, 24 Grosvenor Sq., London W1 1AE ☎ 09055/444-546 for visa information (per-minute charges), 0207/499-9000 main switchboard ⊕ usembassy.org.uk.

TELEPHONES

All U.S. telephone numbers consist of a three-digit area code and a seven-digit local number. Within many local calling areas, you dial only the seven-digit number. Within some area codes, you must dial "1" first for calls outside the local area. To call between area-code regions, dial "1" then all 10 digits; the same goes for calls to numbers prefixed by "800," "888," "866," and "877"—all toll free. For calls to numbers preceded by "900" you must pay—usually dearly.

For international calls, dial "011" followed by the country code and the local number. For help, dial "0" and ask for an overseas operator. The country code is 61 for Australia, 64 for New Zealand, 44 for the United Kingdom. Calling Canada is the same as calling within the United States. Most local phone books list country codes and U.S. area codes. The country code for the United States is 1.

For operator assistance, dial "0." To obtain someone's phone number, call directory assistance at 555–1212 or occasionally 411 (free at many public phones). To have the person you're calling foot the bill, phone collect; dial "0" instead of "1" before the 10-digit number.

At pay phones, instructions often are posted. Usually you insert coins in a slot (usually 25¢–50¢ for local calls) and wait for a steady tone before dialing. When you call long-distance, the operator tells you how much to insert; prepaid phone cards, widely available in various denominations, are easier. Call the number on the back, punch in the card's personal identification number when prompted, then dial your number.

LANGUAGE

English is the primary language on the Islands, so you can get away without knowing much Hawaiian. Making the effort to learn some words of this lyrical language can be rewarding, however. Despite the length of many Hawaiian words, the Hawaiian alphabet is actually one of the world's shortest, with only 12 letters: the five vowels, *a, e, i, o, u,* and seven consonants, *h, k, l, m, n, p, w.* Hawaiian words you are most likely to encounter during your visit to the Islands are *aloha, mahalo* (thank you), *keiki* (child), *haole* (Caucasian or foreigner), *mauka* (toward the mountains), *makai* (toward the ocean), and *pau* (finished, all done). Hawaiian history includes waves of immigrants, each bringing their own language. To communicate with each other, they developed a sort of slang known as "pidgin." If you listen closely, you will know what is being said by the inflections and by the extensive use of body language. For example, when you know what you want to say but don't know how to say it, just say "you know, da kine." For an informative and somewhat-hilarious view of things Hawaiian, check out Jerry Hopkins's series of books titled *Pidgin to the Max* and *Fax to the*

Max, available at most local bookstores in the Hawaiiana sections.

LEI GREETINGS

When you walk off a long flight, perhaps a bit groggy and stiff, nothing quite compares with a Hawaiian lei greeting. The casual ceremony ranks as one of the fastest ways to make the transition from the worries of home to the joys of your vacation. Though the tradition has created an expectation that everyone receives this floral garland when they step off the plane, the state of Hawai'i cannot greet each of its nearly 7 million annual visitors.

Still, it's easy to **arrange for a lei ceremony for yourself or your companions before you arrive.** Contact one of the following companies if you have not signed up with a tour company that provides it. If you really want to be wowed by the experience, request a lei of tuberoses, some of the most divine-smelling blossoms on the planet. Greeters of Hawai'i requires 48 hours' notice and charges $20.95 to $30.95 per person; add $10 for late notification. Kama'āina Leis, Flowers & Greeters requires two days' notice and charges $12.65 for a standard greeting on O'ahu and $15 on the Neighbor Islands.

7 Greeters of Hawai'i ☎ 800/366-8559 🖷 800/926-2644 ⊕ www.greetersofhawaii.com. **Kama'āina Leis, Flowers & Greeters** ☎ 808/836-3246 or 800/367-5183 🖷 808/836-1814.

LODGING

No matter what your budget, there is a place for you in Hawai'i. Large city-size resorts fill the Islands' most scenic shores. Family-style condominiums have many of the amenities of fine hotels, and it's possible to find some at reasonable prices. Vacation rentals and B&Bs are becoming increasingly popular as visitors look for a real slice of Hawai'i away from the crowds. Often tucked into nooks of the Islands you would normally never see, they are competitively priced, highly personalized, and great for relaxing.

The lodgings we list are the cream of the crop in each price category. We always list the facilities that are available, but we don't specify whether they cost extra.

When pricing accommodations, always ask what's included and what costs extra.

Assume that hotels operate on the European Plan (EP, with no meals) unless we specify that they use the Continental Plan (CP, with a Continental breakfast), Breakfast Plan (BP, with a full breakfast), Modified American Plan (MAP, with breakfast and dinner), or the Full American Plan (FAP, with all meals).

CATEGORY	COST
$$$$	over $200
$$$	$150–$200
$$	$100–$150
$	$60–$100
¢	under $60

Prices are for two people in a standard double room in high season, including tax and service.

APARTMENT & HOUSE RENTALS

If you want a home base that's roomy enough for a family and comes with cooking facilities, consider a furnished rental. These can save you money, especially if you're traveling with a group. Home-exchange directories sometimes list rentals as well as exchanges.

◪ International Agents **Hideaways International** ✉ 767 Islington St., Portsmouth, NH 03801 ☎ 603/430–4433 or 800/843–4433 🖷 603/430–4444 ⊕ www.hideaways.com, annual membership $145. **Hometours International** ✉ 1108 Scottie La., Knoxville, TN 37919 ☎ 865/690–8484 or 866/367–4668 ⊕ thor.he.net/~hometour/. **Vacation Home Rentals Worldwide** ✉ 235 Kensington Ave., Norwood, NJ 07648 ☎ 201/767–9393 or 800/633–3284 🖷 201/767–5510 ⊕ www.vhrww.com.

HOME EXCHANGES

If you would like to exchange your home for someone else's, join a home-exchange organization, which will send you its updated listings of available exchanges for a year and will include your own listing in at least one of them. It's up to you to make specific arrangements.

◪ Exchange Clubs **HomeLink International** ✍ Box 47747, Tampa, FL 33647 ☎ 813/975–9825 or 800/638–3841 🖷 813/910–8144 ⊕ www.homelink. org; $110 yearly for a listing, online access, and a catalog; $70 without catalog. **Intervac U.S.** ✉ 30 Corte San Fernando, Tiburon, CA 94920 ☎ 800/756–4663 🖷 415/435–7440 ⊕ www.intervacus.com; $125

yearly for a listing, online access, and a catalog; $65 without catalog.

HOSTELS

No matter what your age, you can save on lodging costs by staying at hostels. Most hostels in Hawai'i cater to a lively international crowd of backpackers, surfers, and windsurfers; those seeking intimacy or privacy should seek out a B&B.

In some 4,500 locations in more than 70 countries around the world, Hostelling International (HI), the umbrella group for a number of national youth-hostel associations, offers single-sex, dorm-style beds and, at many hostels, rooms for couples and family accommodations. Membership in any HI national hostel association, open to travelers of all ages, allows you to stay in HI-affiliated hostels at member rates; one-year membership is about $28 for adults (C$35 for a two-year minimum membership in Canada, £14 in the U.K., A$52 in Australia, and NZ$40 in New Zealand); hostels charge about $10–$30 per night. Members have priority if the hostel is full; they're also eligible for discounts around the world, even on rail and bus travel in some countries.

◪ Organizations **Hostelling International–USA** ✉ 8401 Colesville Rd., Suite 600, Silver Spring, MD 20910 ☎ 301/495–1240 🖷 301/495–6697 ⊕ www. hiusa.org. **Hostelling International–Canada** ✉ 205 Catherine St., Suite 400, Ottawa, Ontario K2P 1C3 ☎ 613/237–7884 or 800/663–5777 🖷 613/237–7868 ⊕ www.hihostels.ca. **YHA England and Wales** ✉ Trevelyan House, Dimple Rd., Matlock, Derbyshire DE4 3YH, U.K. ☎ 0870/870–8808, 0870/770–8868, 0162/959–2600 🖷 0870/770–6127 ⊕ www.yha.org.uk. **YHA Australia** ✉ 422 Kent St., Sydney, NSW 2001 ☎ 02/9261–1111 🖷 02/9261–1969 ⊕ www.yha.com.au. **YHA New Zealand** ✉ Level 1, Moorhouse City, 166 Moorhouse Ave., Box 436, Christchurch ☎ 03/379–9970 or 0800/278–299 🖷 03/365–4476 ⊕ www.yha.org.nz.

HOTELS

All hotels listed have private bath unless otherwise noted.

◪ Toll-Free Numbers **Aston Hotels Resort Quest International** ☎ 800/922–7866 ⊕ www. aston-hotels.com. **Best Western** ☎ 800/528–1234 ⊕ www.bestwestern.com. **Choice** ☎ 800/424–6423

⊕ www.choicehotels.com. **Comfort Inn** ☎ 800/424-6423 ⊕ www.choicehotels.com. **Days Inn** ☎ 800/325-2525 ⊕ www.daysinn.com. **Doubletree Hotels** ☎ 800/222-8733 ⊕ www.doubletree.com. **Embassy Suites** ☎ 800/362-2779 ⊕ www. embassysuites.com. **Fairfield Inn** ☎ 800/228-2800 ⊕ www.marriott.com. **Fairmont Hotels & Resorts Inn** ☎ 800/257-7544 ⊕ www.fairmont.com. **Four Seasons** ☎ 800/332-3442 ⊕ www.fourseasons. com. **Hilton** ☎ 800/445-8667 ⊕ www.hilton. com. **Holiday Inn** ☎ 800/465-4329 ⊕ www. ichotelsgroup.com. **Howard Johnson** ☎ 800/446-4656 ⊕ www.hojo.com. **Hyatt Hotels & Resorts** ☎ 800/233-1234 ⊕ www.hyatt.com. **La Quinta** ☎ 800/531-5900 ⊕ www.lq.com. **Marriott** ☎ 800/228-9290 ⊕ www.marriott.com. **Outrigger Hotels** ☎ 800/688-7444 ⊕ www.outrigger.com. **Quality Inn** ☎ 800/424-6423 ⊕ www.choicehotels.com. **Radisson** ☎ 800/333-3333 ⊕ www.radisson.com. **Ramada** ☎ 800/228-2828, 800/854-7854 international reservations ⊕ www.ramada.com or www. ramadahotels.com. **Red Lion and WestCoast Hotels and Inns** ☎ 800/733-5466 ⊕ www.redlion.com. **Renaissance Hotels & Resorts** ☎ 800/468-3571 ⊕ www.renaissancehotels.com/. **Ritz-Carlton** ☎ 800/241-3333 ⊕ www.ritzcarlton.com. **Sheraton** ☎ 800/325-3535 ⊕ www.starwood.com/sheraton. **Sleep Inn** ☎ 800/424-6423 ⊕ www.choicehotels. com. **Starwood Hotels & Resorts** ☎ 888/325-5144 for Westin and Sheraton, 800/325-3589 for Luxury Collection, 877/946-8357 for W Hotels ⊕ www. starwood.com. **Westin Hotels & Resorts** ☎ 800/228-3000 ⊕ www.starwood.com/westin.

MEDIA

Hawai'i is wired to a variety of media, including network television, cable television, Web-based media, newspapers, magazines, and radio. Many of the resorts and hotels throughout the Islands include an additional visitor-information channel on your in-room television. Consult your in-room directory to get channel and scheduling information and to find out the special activities or events that might be happening during your visit.

NEWSPAPERS & MAGAZINES

Each of the Islands has its own daily newspaper, available through many hotel bell desks; in sundry stores, restaurants, and cafés; and at newsstands. Many hotels will deliver one to your room upon request. The *Honolulu Advertiser* is O'ahu's morn-

ing and Sunday paper; the *Honolulu Star-Bulletin* is O'ahu's evening paper. *West Hawai'i Today* is the Big Island's Kona Coast newspaper, and the *Hawai'i Tribune-Herald* serves the Hilo side of the island. On Maui, it's the *Maui News*. On Kaua'i, it's the *Garden Island* and *Kaua'i Times*. The *Honolulu Weekly* is a great guide for arts and alternative events, and the *Pacific Business News* provides the latest in business news. The monthly *Honolulu Magazine* focuses on O'ahu issues and happenings. Check out local bookstores for Neighbor Island magazines, some of which publish on a quarterly schedule.

RADIO & TELEVISION

Radio airwaves on the Islands are affected by natural terrain, so don't expect to hear one radio station islandwide. For Hawaiian music, tune your FM radio dial to 98.5 KDNN (O'ahu), 100.3 KCCN (O'ahu), 99.5 KHUI (O'ahu), 105.1 KINE (O'ahu), 100.3 KAPA (East Hawai'i), 99.1 KAGB (West Hawai'i), 93.5 KPOA (Maui), and 95.9 KSRF (Kaua'i). News junkies can get their fill of news and talk by tuning to the AM radio dial and the following island stations: 590 KSSK (O'ahu), 650 KHNR (O'ahu), 830 KHVH (O'ahu), 990 KHBZ (O'ahu), 1080 KWAI (O'ahu), 670 KPUA (East Hawai'i), 620 KIPA (West Hawai'i), 1110 KAOI (Maui), 570 KQNG (Kaua'i). National Public Radio enthusiasts can tune to the FM dial for NPR programming on 88.1 KHPR (O'ahu), 89.3 KIPO (O'ahu) and 90.7 KKUA (Maui). On Kaua'i check out the only commercial-free public radio station on the Islands, KKCR, at 90.9 and 91.9 FM. It broadcasts Hawaiian music, jazz, blues, rock, and reggae, as well as talk shows on local issues.

On O'ahu, many residents wake up with Perry & Price on KSSK AM 59 or FM 92. The lively duo provides news, traffic updates, and weather reports between "easy-listening" music and phone calls from listeners from 5 to 10 AM.

Television channels on the Islands are plentiful between network and cable channels. Channel allocation varies by island and location. On O'ahu, you can find the following network programming with its channel and local affiliate call sign: FOX (2) KHON, ABC (4) KITV, UPN/WB (5) KHVE, CBS (9) KGMB, PBS (10) KHET, and NBC (13) KHNL.

MONEY MATTERS

Many of the Islands' best attractions and activities, such as beaches and hiking, can be found in the form of natural beauty and cost nothing to view. You'll pay 50¢ for a daily newspaper, $1.50 to ride the bus anywhere on O'ahu, and from $45 on up to attend a lū'au. Large museums cost between $8 and $15 per entry; smaller ones can cost from $3 to $6. Prices throughout this guide are given for adults. Substantially reduced fees are almost always available for children, students, and senior citizens. For information on taxes, see Taxes.

ATMS

Automatic teller machines for easy access to cash are everywhere on the Islands. ATMs can be found in shopping centers, small convenience and grocery stores, inside hotels and resorts, as well as outside most bank branches. For a directory of locations, call 800/424–7787 for the Master-Card/Cirrus/Maestro network or 800/843–7587 for the Visa/Plus network.

CREDIT CARDS

Most major credit cards are accepted throughout the Islands and are required to rent a car. When making reservations, double-check to ensure that the lodging, restaurant, or attraction you are planning to visit accepts them. In smaller concessions, B&Bs, and fast-food outlets, expect to pay cash.

Throughout this guide, the following abbreviations are used: **AE**, American Express; **D**, Discover; **DC**, Diners Club; **MC**, MasterCard; and **V**, Visa.

🔁 Reporting Lost Cards American Express ☎ 800/992–3404. **Diners Club** ☎ 800/234–6377. **Discover** ☎ 800/347–2683. **MasterCard** ☎ 800/622–7747. **Visa** ☎ 800/ 847–2911.

NATIONAL & STATE PARKS

Hawai'i has seven national parks. On Maui is the summit and crater of the Haleakalā volcano, at Haleakalā National Park. Moloka'i's Kalaupapa National Historical Park was once a leper colony where victims of Hansen's disease were sent into exile in the late 1800s and cared for by Father Damien, a Belgian missionary. On the island of O'ahu, the USS *Arizona* Memorial at Pearl Harbor is overseen by the National Park Service.

The Big Island, Hawai'i's largest island, has four national parks. Hawai'i Volcanoes National Park is the state's number one attraction, where vents have been spewing lava for nearly 20 years. The other three are Pu'uhonua O Hōnaunau National Historical Park, Pu'ukoholā Heiau National Historical Site, and Kaloko-Honokōhau National Historical Park, all of which give a glimpse into Hawai'i's rich cultural history.

Hawai'i's 52 state parks encompass more than 25,000 acres on five islands and include many of its most beautiful beaches and coastal areas. The State Parks Division of the Hawai'i State Department of Land and Natural Resources can provide information on state parks and historic areas.

Look into discount passes to save money on park entrance fees. For $50, the National Parks Pass admits you (and any passengers in your private vehicle) to all national parks, monuments, and recreation areas, as well as other sites run by the National Park Service, for a year. (In parks that charge per person, the pass admits you, your spouse and children, and your parents, when you arrive together.) Camping and parking are extra. The $15 Golden Eagle Pass, a hologram you affix to your National Parks Pass, functions as an upgrade, granting entry to all sites run by the NPS, the U.S. Fish and Wildlife Service, the U.S. Forest Service, and the Bureau of Land Management. The upgrade, which expires with the parks pass, is sold by most national-park, Fish-and-Wildlife, and BLM fee stations. A major percentage of the proceeds from pass sales funds National Parks projects.

Both the Golden Age Passport ($10), for U.S. citizens or permanent residents who are 62 and older, and the Golden Access

Passport (free), for persons with disabilities, entitle holders (and any passengers in their private vehicles) to lifetime free entry to all national parks, plus 50% off fees for the use of many park facilities and services. (The discount doesn't always apply to companions.) To obtain them, you must show proof of age and of U.S. citizenship or permanent residency—such as a U.S. passport, driver's license, or birth certificate—and, if requesting Golden Access, proof of disability. The Golden Age and Golden Access passes are available only at NPS-run sites that charge an entrance fee. The National Parks Pass is also available by mail and via the Internet.

🔢 **National Parks National Park Foundation** ✉ 11 Dupont Circle NW, 6th floor, Washington, DC 20036 ☎ 202/238–4200 ⊕ www.nationalparks.org. **National Park Service** ✉ National Park Service/ Department of Interior, 1849 C St. NW, Washington, DC 20240 ☎ 202/208–6843 ⊕ www.nps.gov. **National Parks Conservation Association** ✉ 1300 19th St. NW, Suite 300, Washington, DC 20036 ☎ 202/223–6722 ⊕ www.npca.org.

🔢 **Passes by Mail & Online National Park Foundation** ⊕ www.nationalparks.org. **National Parks Pass** National Park Foundation ⬤ Box 34108, Washington, DC 20043 ☎ 888/467–2757 ⊕ www. nationalparks.org; include a check or money order payable to the National Park Service, plus $3.95 for shipping and handling (allow 8 to 13 business days from date of receipt for pass delivery), or call for passes.

🔢 **State Parks State Parks Division, Hawai'i State Department of Land and Natural Resources** ✉ 1151 Punchbowl St., Room 310, Honolulu 96813 ☎ 808/587–0300 ⊕ www.hawaii.gov.

PACKING

Hawai'i is casual: sandals, bathing suits, and comfortable, informal clothing are the norm. In summer synthetic slacks and shirts, although easy to care for, can be uncomfortably warm. You'll easily find a bathing suit in Hawai'i, but **bring a bathing cap with you if you wear one.** You can waste hours searching for one.

Probably the most important thing to tuck into your suitcase is sunscreen. This is the tropics, and the ultraviolet rays are powerful. Doctors advise putting on sunscreen when you get up in the morning.

Don't forget to **reapply sunscreen periodically during the day,** since perspiration can wash it away. Consider using sunscreens with a sun protection factor (SPF) of 15 or higher. There are many tanning oils on the market in Hawai'i, including coconut and *kukui* (the nut from a local tree) oils, but they can cause severe burns. Too many Hawaiian vacations have been spoiled by sunburn and even sun poisoning. Hats and sunglasses offer important sun protection, too. Both are easy to find in island shops, but if you already have a favorite packable hat or sun visor, bring it with you, and don't forget to wear it. All major hotels in Hawai'i provide beach towels.

As for clothing in the Hawaiian Islands, there's a saying that when a man wears a suit during the day, he's either going for a loan or he's a lawyer trying a case. Only a few upscale restaurants require a jacket for dinner. The aloha shirt is accepted dress in Hawai'i for business and most social occasions. Shorts are acceptable daytime attire, along with a T-shirt or polo shirt. There's no need to buy expensive sandals on the mainland—here you can get flip-flops for a couple of dollars and off-brand sandals for $20. Golfers should remember that many courses have dress codes requiring a collared shirt; call courses you're interested in for details. If you're not prepared, you can pick up appropriate clothing at resort pro shops. If you're visiting in winter or planning to visit a high-altitude area, **bring a sweater or light- to medium-weight jacket.** A polar fleece pullover is ideal, and makes a great impromptu pillow.

In your carry-on luggage, pack an extra pair of eyeglasses or contact lenses and enough of any medication you take to last a few days longer than the entire trip. You may also ask your doctor to write a spare prescription using the drug's generic name, as brand names may vary from country to country. In luggage to be checked, **never pack prescription drugs, valuables, or undeveloped film.** And don't forget to carry with you the addresses of offices that handle refunds of lost traveler's checks. Check *Fodor's How to Pack* (available at online retailers and bookstores everywhere) for more tips.

To avoid customs and security delays, carry medications in their original packaging. Don't pack any sharp objects in your carry-on luggage, including knives of any size or material, scissors, nail clippers, and corkscrews, or anything else that might arouse suspicion.

To avoid having your checked luggage chosen for hand inspection, don't cram bags full. The U.S. Transportation Security Administration suggests packing shoes on top and placing personal items you don't want touched in clear plastic bags.

CHECKING LUGGAGE

You're allowed to carry aboard one bag and one personal article, such as a purse or a laptop computer. Make sure what you carry on fits under your seat or in the overhead bin. Get to the gate early, so you can board as soon as possible, before the overhead bins fill up.

Baggage allowances vary by carrier, destination, and ticket class. On international flights, you're usually allowed to check two bags weighing up to 70 pounds (32 kilograms) each, although a few airlines allow checked bags of up to 88 pounds (40 kilograms) in first class. Some international carriers don't allow more than 66 pounds (30 kilograms) per bag in business class and 44 pounds (20 kilograms) in economy. On domestic flights, the limit is usually 50 to 70 pounds (23 to 32 kilograms) per bag. In general, carry-on bags shouldn't exceed 40 pounds (18 kilograms). Most airlines won't accept bags that weigh more than 100 pounds (45 kilograms) on domestic or international flights. Expect to pay a fee for baggage that exceeds weight limits. Check baggage restrictions with your carrier before you pack.

Airline liability for baggage is limited to $2,500 per person on flights within the United States. On international flights it amounts to $9.07 per pound or $20 per kilogram for checked baggage (roughly $640 per 70-pound bag), with a maximum of $634.90 per piece, and $400 per passenger for unchecked baggage. You can buy additional coverage at check-in for about $10 per $1,000 of coverage, but it often excludes a rather extensive list of items, shown on your airline ticket.

Before departure, itemize your bags' contents and their worth, and label the bags with your name, address, and phone number. (If you use your home address, cover it so potential thieves can't see it readily.) Include a label inside each bag and **pack a copy of your itinerary.** At check-in, make sure each bag is correctly tagged with the destination airport's three-letter code. Because some checked bags will be opened for hand inspection, the U.S. Transportation Security Administration recommends that you leave luggage unlocked or use the plastic locks offered at check-in. TSA screeners place an inspection notice inside searched bags, which are re-sealed with a special lock.

If your bag has been searched and contents are missing or damaged, file a claim with the TSA Consumer Response Center as soon as possible. If your bags arrive damaged or fail to arrive at all, file a written report with the airline before leaving the airport.

F Complaints U.S. Transportation Security Administration Contact Center ☎ 866/289-9673 ⊕ www.tsa.gov.

SAFETY

Hawai'i is generally a safe tourist destination, but it's still wise to follow the same common sense safety precautions you would normally follow in your own hometown. Hotel and visitor-center staff can provide information should you decide to head out on your own to more remote areas. **Rental cars are magnets for break-ins, so don't leave any valuables in the car, not even in a locked trunk.** Avoid poorly lighted areas, beach parks, and isolated areas after dark as a precaution. When hiking, **stay on marked trails,** no matter how alluring the temptation might be to stray. Weather conditions can cause landscapes to become muddy, slippery, and tenuous, so staying on marked trails will lessen the possibility of a fall or getting lost. Ocean safety is of the utmost importance when visiting an island destination.

Don't swim alone, and follow the international signage posted at beaches that alerts swimmers to strong currents, man-of-war jellyfish, sharp coral, high surf, sharks, and dangerous shore breaks. At coastal lookouts along cliff tops, heed the signs indicating that waves can climb over the ledges. Check with lifeguards at each beach for current conditions, and **if the red flags are up, indicating swimming and surfing are not allowed, don't go in.** Waters that look calm on the surface can harbor strong currents and undertows, and not a few people who were just wading have been dragged out to sea.

LOCAL SCAMS

Be wary of those hawking "too good to be true" prices on everything from car rentals to attractions. Many of these offers are just a lure to get you in the door for time-share presentations. When handed a flyer, read the fine print before you make your decision to participate.

WOMEN IN HAWAI'I

Women traveling alone are generally safe on the Islands, but always follow the safety precautions you would use in any major destination. When booking hotels, **request rooms closest to the elevator,** and always keep your hotel-room door and balcony doors locked. Stay away from isolated areas after dark; camping and hiking solo are not advised. If you stay out late visiting nightclubs and bars, **use caution when exiting night spots** and returning to your lodging.

SENIOR-CITIZEN TRAVEL

Hawai'i is steeped in a tradition that gives great respect to elders, or *kupuna,* and considers them "keepers of the wisdom." Visitors may not be so esteemed, but senior citizens traveling in Hawai'i will find discounts, special senior citizen–oriented activities, and buildings with easy access. Many lodging facilities have discounts for members of the American Association of Retired Persons (AARP).

To qualify for age-related discounts, mention your senior-citizen status up front when booking hotel reservations (not when checking out) and before you're seated in restaurants (not when paying the bill). Be sure to have identification on hand. When renting a car, ask about promotional car-rental discounts, which can be cheaper than senior-citizen rates.

⊞ Educational Programs Elderhostel ✉ 11 Ave. de Lafayette, Boston, MA 02111-1746 ☎ 877/426–8056, 978/323–4141 international callers, 877/426–2167 TTY 🖷 877/426–2166 ⊕ www.elderhostel.org. **Interhostel** ✉ University of New Hampshire, 6 Garrison Ave., Durham, NH 03824 ☎ 603/862–1147 or 800/733–9753 🖷 603/862–1113 ⊕ www.learn.unh.edu.

SHOPPING
KEY DESTINATIONS

On O'ahu, Ala Moana Center is one of the largest shopping spots; it's within easy walking distance of the west end of Waikīkī. The Royal Hawaiian Shopping Center is centrally located in Waikīkī itself. Farther away, you'll find Ward Centers, Aloha Tower Marketplace, and the Kāhala Mall.

The Neighbor Islands offer more in the way of smaller strips of shops. Still, it's possible to find larger stores grouped in areas such as Kaua'i's Kukui Grove Center in Līhu'e, Maui's Ka'ahumanu Shopping Center and Maui Mall in Kahului, the Shops at Wailea and Whaler's Village in Kā'anapali, the Big Island's Prince Kūhiō Shopping Plaza in Hilo, King's Shops in Waikoloa, the Shops at Mauna Lani, and Keauhou Shopping Village and Lanihau Center in Kailua-Kona. Exclusive shops can often be found in the lobbies of luxury hotels.

SMART SOUVENIRS

Aloha shirts and resort wear, Hawaiian-music recordings, shell leis, coral jewelry, traditional quilts, island foods, Kona coffee, and koa-wood products are just a few of the gifts that visitors to Hawai'i treasure. For the more elegant gift items, check out the Hawaiian boutiques in major island shopping centers as well as those tucked away in smaller shopping areas in residential districts. Island crafts fairs and swap meets offer a bargain bazaar of standard items such as T-shirts and tiki statues as well as the original works of local artisans.

WATCH OUT

Souvenirs made from coral or tortoise shell may not have been harvested legally, so in the interest of preserving Hawai'i's environment, it's best to avoid these.

SPORTS & THE OUTDOORS

If you like to swim, hike, fish, bike, scuba dive, kayak, or play golf, Hawai'i is your kind of place. Alternative Hawai'i's Web site provides detailed information on hiking, diving, camping, kayaking, and outfitters on each island. The environment is particularly fragile here, so whatever you do outdoors, don't forget to tread lightly.
F Alternative Hawai'i ☎ 808/695-5113 ⊕ www.alternative-hawaii.com.

BEACHES

Hawai'i's beaches are the stuff of legend, with white sand wedged between palm trees and turquoise water, or even colorful black and green stretches of sand. All beaches are free and open to the public unless otherwise noted—even the most luxurious hotels have to share their beachfronts. Note that riptides and strong undertows can challenge even the strongest swimmers, so if you see a beach where no one is swimming, ask a local about its safety before diving in. **Use care when diving into lagoons** as well, as they often are not as deep as they appear. Alcohol is not permitted on most beaches.

GOLF

Hawai'i is known for its golf, with many high-profile tournaments on TV each year. To experience the glory for yourself, check with your hotel concierge or golf shop to arrange tee times, or call the courses listed in the chapters directly.

HIKING & CAMPING

Hiking is a wonderful way to explore the Islands, but **don't stray off trails,** and be sure to **wear sturdy hiking shoes,** especially if you're doing lava hikes. When camping, **be prepared for radical weather shifts,** especially at high altitudes. Haleakalā National Park, for example, can reach 85°F by day and drop to 35°F by night. Fog, wind, and rain can and do blow in with little or no warning. Ask local outdoor shops which areas are best for you based on your fitness level and camping experience. Note that Hawai'i doesn't have drive-to camping sites; most locations require a hike in or a night on the beach.

KAYAKING

Kayaking is an excellent low-impact way to enjoy the scenery. Kayak rentals are available on each island, and you can arrange guided trips. **Remain close to shore** if you don't want to be whooshed out to sea. Check with the kayak rental shop for weather advisories.

SCUBA DIVING & SNORKELING

Underwater Hawai'i is breathtaking, but diving tends to be pricey. You can arrange trips with countless outfitters, or rent equipment on your own. Whether snorkeling or diving, remember **never to go alone,** and be sure to **ask at the dive shop about rip currents and places to avoid.** Undersea life is extremely fragile, so **don't touch (or take) the coral,** and **watch that your fins don't hit the reefs** behind you.

STUDENTS IN HAWAI'I

Hawai'i is a popular destination for exchange students from around the world, who mainly attend the University of Hawai'i in Honolulu. Contact your hometown university about study and internship possibilities. To check out the student scene on the Islands, stop by any of the University of Hawai'i campuses or community college campuses, and read the *Honolulu Weekly* upon arrival for club and event information. Be sure to ask about discounts for students at all museums and major attractions and be prepared to show ID to qualify.
F IDs & Services **STA Travel** ⊠ 10 Downing St., New York, NY 10014 ☎ 212/627-3111, 800/777-0112 24-hr service center 🖷 212/627-3387 ⊕ www.sta.com. **Travel Cuts** ⊠ 187 College St., Toronto, Ontario M5T 1P7, Canada ☎ 800/592-2887 in the U.S., 416/979-2406 or 866/246-9762 in Canada 🖷 416/979-8167 ⊕ www.travelcuts.com.

TAXES
SALES TAX

There is a 4.16% state sales tax on all purchases, including food. A hotel room tax of 7.25%, combined with the sales tax of 4%, equals an 11.41% rate added onto your hotel bill. A $3-per-day road tax is also assessed on each rental vehicle.

TIME
Hawai'i is on Hawaiian Standard Time, 5 hours behind New York, 2 hours behind Los Angeles, and 10 hours behind London.

When the U.S. mainland is on daylight saving time, Hawai'i is not, so add an extra hour of time difference between the Islands and U.S. mainland destinations. You may also find that things generally move more slowly here. That has nothing to do with your watch—it's just the laid-back way called Hawaiian time.

TIPPING
Tip cab drivers 15% of the fare. Standard tips for restaurants and bar tabs run from 15% to 20% of the bill, depending on the standard of service. Bellhops at hotels usually receive $1 per bag, more if you have bulky items such as bicycles and surfboards. Tip the hotel room maid $1 per night, paid daily. Tip doormen $1 for assistance with taxis; tips for concierge vary depending on the service. For example, tip more for "hard-to-get" event tickets or dining reservations.

TOURS & PACKAGES
Because everything is prearranged on a prepackaged tour or independent vacation, you spend less time planning—and often get it all at a good price.

BOOKING WITH AN AGENT
Travel agents are excellent resources. But it's a good idea to collect brochures from several agencies, as some agents' suggestions may be influenced by relationships with tour and package firms that reward them for volume sales. If you have a special interest, find an agent with expertise in that area; the American Society of Travel Agents (ASTA; ⇨ Travel Agencies) has a database of specialists worldwide. You can log on to the group's Web site to find an ASTA travel agent in your neighborhood.

Make sure your travel agent knows the accommodations and other services of the place being recommended. Ask about the

hotel's location, room size, beds, and whether it has a pool, room service, or programs for children, if you care about these. Has your agent been there in person or sent others whom you can contact?

Do some homework on your own, too: local tourism boards can provide information about lesser-known and small-niche operators, some of which may sell only direct.

BUYER BEWARE
Each year consumers are stranded or lose their money when tour operators—even large ones with excellent reputations—go out of business. So check out the operator. Ask several travel agents about its reputation, and try to **book with a company that has a consumer-protection program.** (Look for information in the company's brochure.) In the United States, members of the United States Tour Operators Association are required to set aside funds ($1 million) to help eligible customers cover payments and travel arrangements in the event that the company defaults. It's also a good idea to choose a company that participates in the American Society of Travel Agents' Tour Operator Program; ASTA will act as mediator in any disputes between you and your tour operator.

Remember that the more your package or tour includes, the better you can predict the ultimate cost of your vacation. Make sure you know exactly what is covered, and beware of hidden costs. Are taxes, tips, and transfers included? Entertainment and excursions? These can add up.

🇿 Tour-Operator Recommendations **American Society of Travel Agents** (⇨ Travel Agencies). **National Tour Association** (NTA) ⊠ 546 E. Main St., Lexington, KY 40508 ☎ 859/226-4444 or 800/682-8886 🖷 859/226-4404 ⊕ www.ntaonline.com. **United States Tour Operators Association** (USTOA) ⊠ 275 Madison Ave., Suite 2014, New York, NY 10016 ☎ 212/599-6599 🖷 212/599-6744 ⊕ www.ustoa.com.

TRANSPORTATION AROUND HAWAI'I
Renting a car is definitely recommended for those who plan to move beyond their hotel lounge chair. With the exception of

O'ahu, public transportation is extremely limited, and even if you are staying in Honolulu or Waikīkī you may want a car if you plan to do any exploring or if you're short on time. **Reserve your vehicle in advance,** particularly during peak travel times and on the smaller islands, where the car-rental fleets are limited. Most major companies have airport counters and complimentary transportation for pickup/drop-off back at the airport upon departure.

Taxis can also be found at island airports, through your hotel doorman, in the more popular resort areas, or by contacting local taxi companies by telephone. Flag-down fees are $2, and each additional mile is $1.70. Most companies will also provide a car and driver for half-day or daylong island tours if you absolutely don't want to rent a car, and a number of companies also offer personal guides. Remember, however, that rates are quite steep for these services, ranging from $100 to $200 or more per day.

TRAVEL AGENCIES

A good travel agent puts your needs first. Look for an agency that has been in business at least five years, emphasizes customer service, and has someone on staff who specializes in your destination. In addition, **make sure the agency belongs to a professional trade organization.** The American Society of Travel Agents (ASTA)—the largest and most influential in the field with more than 20,000 members in some 140 countries—maintains and enforces a strict code of ethics and will step in to help mediate any agent-client disputes involving ASTA members if necessary. ASTA (whose motto is "Without a travel agent, you're on your own") also maintains a Web site that includes a directory of agents. (If a travel agency is also acting as your tour operator, *see* Buyer Beware *in* Tours & Packages.)

⑦ **Local Agent Referrals American Society of Travel Agents (ASTA)** ⊠ 1101 King St., Suite 200, Alexandria, VA 22314 ☎ 703/739-2782 or 800/965-2782 24-hr hot line ᐧ 703/684-8319 ⊕ www.astanet.com. **Association of British Travel Agents**

⊠ 68-71 Newman St., London W1T 3AH ☎ 020/7637-2444 ᐧ 020/7637-0713 ⊕ www.abta.com. **Association of Canadian Travel Agencies** ⊠ 130 Albert St., Suite 1705, Ottawa, Ontario K1P 5G4 ☎ 613/237-3657 ᐧ 613/237-7052 ⊕ www.acta.ca. **Australian Federation of Travel Agents** ⊠ Level 3, 309 Pitt St., Sydney, NSW 2000 ☎ 02/9264-3299 or 1300/363-416 ᐧ 02/9264-1085 ⊕ www.afta.com.au. **Travel Agents' Association of New Zealand** ⊠ Level 5, Tourism and Travel House, 79 Boulcott St., Box 1888, Wellington 6001 ☎ 04/499-0104 ᐧ 04/499-0786 ⊕ www.taanz.org.nz.

VISITOR INFORMATION

Before you go, contact the Hawai'i Visitors & Convention Bureau (HVCB) for general information on each island, free brochures that include an accommodations and car-rental guide, and an entertainment and dining guide containing one-line descriptions of bureau members. Take a virtual visit to Hawai'i on the Web, which can be most helpful in planning many aspects of your vacation. The HVCB site has a calendar section that allows you to see what local events are in place during the time of your stay.

Learn more about foreign destinations by checking government-issued travel advisories and country information. For a broader picture, consider information from more than one country.

⑦ **Tourist Information Hawai'i Visitors & Convention Bureau** ⊠ 2270 Kalakaua Ave., Suite 801, Honolulu 96817 ☎ 808/923-1811, 800/464-2924 for brochures ⊕ www.gohawaii.com. In the U.K. contact the **Hawai'i Visitors & Convention Bureau** ᐧ Box 208, Sunbury, Middlesex TW16 5RJ ☎ 020/8941-4009 ⊕ www.gohawaii.com. Send a £2 check or postal order for an information pack.

⑦ **Government Advisories Consular Affairs Bureau of Canada** ☎ 800/267-6788 or 613/944-6788 ⊕ www.voyage.gc.ca. **U.K. Foreign and Commonwealth Office** ⊠ Travel Advice Unit, Consular Division, Old Admiralty Building, London SW1A 2PA ☎ 0870/606-0290 or 020/7008-1500 ⊕ www.fco.gov.uk/travel. **Australian Department of Foreign Affairs and Trade** ☎ 300/139-281 travel advice, 02/6261-1299 Consular Travel Advice Faxback Service ⊕ www.dfat.gov.au. **New Zealand Ministry of Foreign Affairs and Trade** ☎ 04/439-8000 ⊕ www.mft.govt.nz.

WEB SITES

Do check out the World Wide Web when planning your trip. You'll find everything from weather forecasts to virtual tours of famous cities. Be sure to visit Fodors. com (⊕ www.fodors.com), a complete travel-planning site. You can research prices and book plane tickets, hotel rooms, rental cars, vacation packages, and more. In addition, you can post your pressing questions in the Travel Talk section. Other planning tools include a currency converter and weather reports, and there are loads of links to travel resources.

For more information on Hawai'i, visit ⊕ www.gohawaii.com, the official Web site of the Hawai'i Visitors & Convention Bureau.

Other sites to check out include ⊕ www. bigisland.org (Big Island Visitors Bureau); ⊕ www.visitmaui.com (Maui County Visitors Bureau); ⊕ www.visit-oahu.com (O'ahu Visitors Bureau); ⊕ www. kauaivisitorsbureau.org (Kaua'i Visitors Bureau); and ⊕ www.molokai-hawaii. com (Moloka'i Visitor Information).

The Web site ⊕ www.search-hawaii.com has an engine that can search all linked Hawaiian Web pages by topic or word.

Visit ⊕ www.hshawaii.com for the Hawai'i State vacation planner; ⊕ www.kauai-hawaii.com for Kaua'i visitor information; ⊕ www.honoluluweekly.com for a weekly guide to the arts, entertainment, and dining in Honolulu; and ⊕ www.hawaii.gov, the state's official Web site, for all information on the destination, including camping.

O'AHU
THE GATHERING PLACE

MEET O'AHU'S FRIENDLIEST FISH
at Hanauma Bay Nature Preserve ⇨*p.35*

BE BLOWN AWAY BY 360° VIEWS
on the extinct volcanic peak of
Diamond Head ⇨*p.14*

WIPE OUT! . . . OR TRY NOT TO
at a surfing school in Waikīkī ⇨*p.84*

FORGET YOUR "TO DO" LIST
on a private lānai at the Turtle Bay Resort ⇨*p.63*

PAY TRIBUTE TO THE KING OF SURF
at the Duke Kahanamoku Statue ⇨*p.7*

INDULGE IN 180 FEET OF SEAFOOD
at Todai, in Waikīkī ⇨*p.42*

Updated by
Maggie
Wunsch

O'AHU IS WHERE THE SPIRIT OF ALOHA WAS BORN, and it's still Hawai'i's most exciting, cosmopolitan gathering place, with an eclectic blend of people, customs, and cuisines. Outside of the urbanity of Honolulu, you'll find all the tropical splendor for which the Islands are famous. Part of O'ahu's dramatic appearance lies in its majestic highlands: the western Wai'anae Mountains rise 4,000 feet above sea level, and the verdant Ko'olau Mountains cross the island's midsection at elevations of more than 3,000 feet. Eons of wind and weather erosion have carved these ranges' sculptured, jagged peaks; deep valleys; sheer green cliffs; and dynamic vistas. At the base of these mountains more than 50 beach parks lie draped like a beautiful lei, each known for a different activity, be it snorkeling, surfing, swimming, or sunbathing.

Third-largest of the Hawaiian Islands and covering 608 square mi, O'ahu was formed by two volcanoes that erupted 4 to 6 million years ago. Honolulu, the nation's 12th-largest city, is here, and 80% of Hawai'i's 1.2 million residents call the island home. Somehow, amid all this urban development, you are never more than a glimpse away from a breathtaking ocean or mountain view.

Hawai'i's last kings and queens ruled from 'Iolani Palace in Downtown Honolulu. Today, 'Iolani stands as an elegant tribute to Hawai'i's rich history as a kingdom, republic, territory, and state. Even in the days of royalty, the virtues of Waikīkī as a vacation destination were recognized. Long processions of *ali'i* (nobility) made their way across streams and swamps, past the duck ponds, to the coconut groves and the beach.

By the 1880s guest houses were scattered along the south shore like so many seashells. The first hotel, the Moana (now the Sheraton Moana Surfrider), was built at the turn of the 20th century and christened the First Lady of Waikīkī. The Moana's inaugural room rates of $1.50 per night were the talk of the town. In 1927 the "Pink Palace of the Pacific," the Royal Hawaiian Hotel, was built by the Matson Navigation Company to accommodate travelers arriving on luxury liners. It was opened with a grand ball, and Waikīkī was officially launched as a first-class tourist destination—duck ponds, taro patches, and all.

December 7, 1941, brought that era to a close with the bombing of Pearl Harbor and America's entry into the war in the Pacific. The Royal Hawaiian was turned over to American military forces and became a respite for war-weary soldiers and sailors. But with victory came the postwar boom, and by 1952 Waikīkī had 2,000 hotel rooms. Today, hundreds of thousands of visitors sleep in the more than 33,000 rooms of Waikīkī's nearly 160 hotels and condominiums. Waikīkī continues to serve as home base for countless day trips full of cultural and scenic eco-adventures. Visitors can stroll along Kūhiō Beach and check out the city-sponsored Brunch on the Beach and Sunset on the Beach events each month, as well as meander along the historic Waikīkī walking trail. There are free nightly Hawaiian music and dance performances on the Kūhiō Beach stage.

A massive redesign of the Kālia Road and Beachwalk area as well as a complete renovation of the famous International Marketplace is sched-

1

Numbers in the text correspond to numbers in the margin and on the Waikīkī, Downtown Honolulu, and Oʻahu maps.

If you have 1 day

If you have a short layover on your way to another island or if you can tear yourself away from a convention (or a honeymoon resort) for just one day of sightseeing, the first thing you should do is treat yourself to a dawn hike up **Diamond Head State Monument and Park** ⑱, then have breakfast at one of Waikīkī's beachfront restaurants. Next, take the bus or drive to nearby Ala Moana Shopping Center, which has stores to satisfy all souvenir needs. Buy a carryout lunch from its eclectic, international food court; cross Ala Moana Boulevard; and picnic, sun, and swim at Ala Moana Beach Park. Go on a late-afternoon outrigger canoe ride with one of Waikīkī's beach attendants, followed by mai tais and Hawaiian music at sunset at the **Halekūlani** ❼ or **Royal Hawaiian Hotel** ❽.

If you have 3 days

On your first day, dig in by following the Waikīkī and/or Kapiʻolani Park tours described in this chapter. Start the second day at the **Hawaiʻi Maritime Center** ⑲ in Downtown Honolulu, followed by shopping and lunch at the adjacent **Aloha Tower Marketplace** ⑳. For a view from atop the building that was once the tallest structure in Honolulu, go next door for a short elevator ride to the Aloha Tower's observation deck. Explore historic Downtown Honolulu before heading back to Waikīkī for sunset and dinner. On day three, get an early start so you arrive at **Hanauma Bay Nature Preserve** ㊴ by 7:30, before the crowds. Take a break from the sun with a stop a little farther north along the coast at **Sea Life Park** ㊱, which features some splashy marine shows. From here, follow the East Oʻahu Ring tour in reverse, back to Waikīkī.

If you have 5 days

Devote the first day to Waikīkī, the second to Downtown Honolulu, and the third to East Oʻahu. On the fourth day, get an early start in order to see the **USS *Arizona* Memorial** and **Battleship *Missouri* Memorial** ㊸, since the lines lengthen throughout the morning. Or take the early morning boat tour to Pearl Harbor. From there, drive to the **Bishop Museum** ㊶ and spend some time immersed in Hawaiiana. Keep the rest of the day low-key until evening, when you can take in a cocktail or dinner show followed by dancing. Devote the fifth day to the North Shore. Drive to **Haleʻiwa** ㊻ for breakfast and shopping, then tour **Waimea Valley Audubon Center** ㊼, and finish with a late-afternoon or early-evening visit to the **Polynesian Cultural Center** ㊾.

uled to be underway in 2005 with completion set for 2007. The Kālia/Beachwalk project under the direction of Outrigger Enterprises, plans to turn its older hotels from the 1960s into one modern hotel, retail, and entertainment complex that will feature more outdoor gathering places and a Hawaiian-music preservation hall. In the heart of Waikīkī, the International Marketplace is being redesigned to bring back some of the grandeur of the site that was once owned by Hawaii's Queen Emma.

Walking paths, a stream, and the historic banyans will be at the center of a retail and restaurant complex that will also feature venues for hula and Hawaiian storytelling.

With Waikīkī leading the way, O'ahu maintains its status as an exciting destination, with more things to see, more places to eat, and more things to do than on all the other Hawaiian Islands combined.

Exploring O'ahu

O'ahu is a mixed bag, with enough attractions and adventures to easily fill an entire vacation. Waikīkī is the center of the island's visitor industry and home to its largest concentration of accommodations, stores, restaurants, and nightclubs. Dominated by Diamond Head Crater, Waikīkī's less populated eastern end includes a zoo, an aquarium, and a beautiful park designed for sports from jogging to kite-flying. Take some time to explore the neighborhoods just outside Waikīkī, such as Kaimukī, whose main street, Wai'alae Avenue, boasts a century of different architectural styles alongside boutique shopping and a world of cuisines in the guise of tiny neighborhood eateries. Kāhala has some of the most luxurious real estate on the island. Ala Moana, west of Waikīkī, is brimming with shops that begin with the Ala Moana Center and continue with the five retail complexes of Victoria Ward Centers. Farther west is Downtown Honolulu, the center of Hawai'i's capital city, a bustling blend of history and modern-day commerce. Along its edges, historic Chinatown awaits.

The East O'ahu coast is fringed with white-sand beaches and turquoise seas, and you can drive right over the top of the Ko'olau Mountains. Breeze past modern residential neighborhoods such as Hawai'i Kai to the sleepy slopes of Waimānalo. Finally, a circle-island tour takes you to central, northern, and windward O'ahu, where shoes and cell phones give way to sandy toes and uninterrupted relaxation. Explore the Ewa Plains and O'ahu's "second" resort destination of Ko Olina. Take a time-out to discover the local windward communities of Kailua and Kaneohe, whose beaches are a haven for family fun. On the North Shore, Hale'iwa is a visit back in time, and in winter, it is the place to catch a glimpse of ocean waves that reach heights of 20 feet and more.

To stay oriented on the island, keep in mind that directions on O'ahu are often given as *mauka* (toward the mountains) or *makai* (toward the ocean). In Honolulu and Waikīkī, you may also hear people referring to "Diamond Head" (toward that landmark) and *'ewa*—away from Diamond Head.

About the Restaurants

O'ahu's cuisines are as diverse as its population, with Asian, European, and Pacific flavors most prevalent. Here, the Asian influence can even be found at the corner McDonald's where the menu is posted in both English and kanji. While you're exploring O'ahu's banquet of choices, be sure to sample Hawai'i regional cuisine, also known variously as Euro-Asian or Pacific Rim.

Scenic Drives

A drive around O'ahu brings you face-to-face with its sheer natural beauty. Roll past the wave-dashed eastern shore, with its photogenic beaches and cliffs. Drive through the central plains past acres of red soil, once rich in pineapple and now supporting diversified crops, such as coffee. Head to the North Shore, a reflection of old O'ahu with its rickety storefronts and trees hanging heavy with bananas and papaya. Forget the air-conditioning, roll down the windows, and smell the salt air along the windward coast, where the view is dominated by mountains chiseled by centuries of winds, rains, and waterfalls.

Water Sports

Whether you soar above them, sail on them, or dive into them, the waters surrounding O'ahu are an ocean-lover's dream. The seas off Waikīkī call to novices looking for a surfing lesson or outrigger canoe ride, while the North Shore beckons accomplished wave riders. Snorkeling and scuba diving at Hanauma Bay, on the island's eastern tip, bring you face-to-face with a rainbow of sea creatures. Honolulu's Kewalo Basin is the starting point for most fishing charters, and the Honolulu harborfront piers serve as home port for many luxury cruise excursions. Windsurfers and ocean kayakers head to the beaches of the windward side, Lanikai in particular.

About the Hotels

O'ahu's lodgings range from sprawling resorts to intimate, low-rise hideaways. First-time visitors who wish to be in the heart of the island's activity can find it all in Waikīkī. Guests do well by this south-shore tourist mecca since shops, restaurants, nightlife, and the beach are nearby. Business travelers prefer to stay on the eastern edge of Waikīkī, near the Hawai'i Convention Center, or in Downtown Honolulu's sole hotel. Windward, leeward, and north-shore digs are casual and shorter on amenities but have charms all their own.

WHAT IT COSTS				
$$$$	**$$$**	**$$**	**$**	**¢**
RESTAURANTS over $30	$20–$30	$12–$20	$7–$12	under $7
HOTELS over $200	$150–$200	$100–$150	$60–$100	under $60

Restaurant prices are for one main course at dinner. Hotel prices are for two people in a standard double room in high season, including tax and service.

Timing

The ideal seasons to visit O'ahu are spring and fall, when fewer tourists are around and the weather is warm, but not too warm. Fall is additionally fun thanks to the Aloha Festivals, a monthlong program of free Hawaiian-style celebrations and special events. Festival highlights on O'ahu include a floral parade and evening block parties downtown and in Waikīkī. Come December, Downtown Honolulu is a veritable wonderland during its holiday Festival of City Lights.

WAIKĪKĪ

If Hawai'i is America's most exotic, most unique state, then Waikīkī is its generator, keeping everything humming. On the dry, sunny side of O'ahu, it takes all the natural splendors of the Islands and mixes them with elegance and daring to create an international playground in the middle of the Pacific.

A tropical retreat since the days of Hawai'i's kings and queens, Waikīkī sparkles along 2½ mi of spangled sea from the famous Diamond Head Crater to the east to the Ala Wai Yacht Harbor to the west. Separated on its northern boundary from the sprawling city of Honolulu by the broad Ala Wai Canal, Waikīkī is 3½ mi from Downtown Honolulu and worlds apart from any other city in the world. You may find yourself saying such things as *aloha* and *mahalo* (thank you), and don't be surprised if you start planning your next trip while you're still lazing on Waikīkī's sunny, hypnotic shores.

a good walk

A good place to start a Waikīkī walking tour is the **Ala Wai Yacht Harbor ❶ ▶**, home to an armada of pleasure boats and two members-only yacht clubs. It's just makai of the Renaissance 'Ilikai Waikīkī at 1777 Ala Moana Boulevard. From here head toward the main intersection of Ala Moana Boulevard and Kālia Road, turn right at the large sculpture of hula dancers signaling the entry to **Hilton Hawaiian Village Beach Resort and Spa ❷**, and wander through this 22-acre resort complex past gardens and waterfalls.

Continue makai on Kālia Road to Fort DeRussy, home of the **U.S. Army Museum ❸**. Across the street, on Saratoga Road, nestled snugly amid the commerce of Waikīkī, is an oasis of tranquility: the teahouse at the **Urasenke Foundation ❹**, where the art of Hawaiian hospitality bows to the art of the centuries-old Japanese tea ceremony.

With a little taste of Asia and some Zen for the road, head mauka on Saratoga Road until you reach Kalākaua Avenue. Then turn right toward Diamond Head. At the intersection with Lewers Street, stop and peer into the lobby of the **First Hawaiian Bank ❺** for a quick view of the island's history in six massive wall murals. Diagonally across Kalākaua Avenue is one of Waikīkī's architectural landmarks, the **Gump Building ❻**.

Walk down Lewers Street toward the ocean. It dead-ends at the impressive **Halekūlani ❼**, one of Waikīkī's most prestigious hotels, famed for its elegant hospitality. From the Halekūlani stroll toward Diamond Head along the paved oceanside walkway. It leads past the Sheraton Waikīkī to the gracious, historic, and very pink **Royal Hawaiian Hotel ❽**. Return to Kalākaua Avenue and continue walking toward Diamond Head.

On the makai side of Kalākaua Avenue you'll see the oldest hotel in Waikīkī, the venerable **Sheraton Moana Surfrider ❾**. Wander through the breezy lobby to the wide back porch, called the Banyan Veranda, or take a quick tour through tourism history in the Moana's second-floor historical room. From here, walk down the beach and head toward Diamond Head. Next to Kalākaua Avenue, just to the right of the Duke

Kahanamoku Statue on the makai side, you'll find the four **Kahuna (Wizard) Stones of Waikīkī** ⑩. Legend has it that these stones hold magical powers. Sadly, however, the stones are often overlooked and, more often than not, irreverently draped with wet towels. The **Duke Kahanamoku Statue** ⑪ pays tribute to the memory of one of Hawai'i's most beloved surfers and swimmers. Every weekend evening at sunset, the torches along the beach are lit from this statue to the stage one block 'ewa, where free hula entertainment kicks off Waikīkī after-dark celebrations.

Continue your walk four blocks farther down Kalākaua Avenue toward Diamond Head; then turn mauka onto 'Ōhua Avenue and you'll find the only church in Waikīkī with its own building, the Roman Catholic St. Augustine's. Saturday evening services include hymns sung by a Tongan choir. As you exit the front entrance of the Church, turn left on Kalākaua Avenue to the intersection of Kalākaua and Kapahulu avenues. On the makai side, you will see a six-foot-tall bronze surfboard, which indicates the beginning of the **Waikīkī Historic Trail** ⑫. This 2-mi walk passes 20 bronze surfboard markers that feature photos and text highlighting Waikīkī's rich, historic past.

TIMING   Allow yourself at least one full day for this walk, and time it so that you'll wind up on Waikīkī Beach at sunset. Many shops and attractions are open every day of the year from sunup to way past sundown to cater to the body clocks of tourists from around the world. Note, however, that the Urasenke Foundation tea ceremonies take place only on Wednesday and Friday mornings. Hawai'i's location near the equator can make the midday sun quite warm. Since sunburns and dehydration can be vacation spoilers, you might want to take a time-out for a leisurely lunch at one of Waikīkī's beachfront restaurants, or slip inside one of Waikīkī's chic air-conditioned boutiques for some cool island wear.

What to See

▶ ❶ **Ala Wai Yacht Harbor.** Every other summer the Trans-Pacific yacht race from Los Angeles makes its colorful finish here, complete with flags and onboard parties. The next Trans-Pac is estimated to arrive in July 2005. No matter when you visit Hawai'i, if you want a taste of what life on the water could be like, stroll around the docks and check out the variety of craft, from houseboats to luxury cruisers. Home to both the Waikīkī and Hawai'i Yacht Clubs, the waiting list for permanent boat slips here is at least a decade. ✉ *1599 Ala Moana Blvd., oceanside across from Waikīkī Prince Hotel, Waikīkī.*

❶ **Duke Kahanamoku Statue.** This bronze statue was erected in honor of Hawai'i's celebrated surfer and swimmer. Known as the "father of modern surfing," Duke won his first gold medal for the 100-meter freestyle at the 1912 Olympics. When the statue was first placed here, it caused a wave of controversy because the Duke is standing with his back to the ocean, something no safety-conscious surfer would ever do. ✉ *Two blocks Diamond Head of the Sheraton Moana Surfrider on Kalākaua Ave., Waikīkī* ✑ *Free.*

❺ **First Hawaiian Bank.** Get a glimpse of Hawaiian history kept safe in this Waikīkī bank, where half a dozen murals depict the evolution of Hawai-

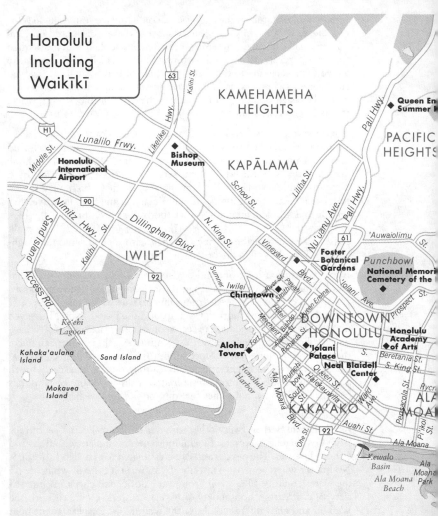

Honolulu Including Waikīkī

KAMEHAMEHA HEIGHTS

Queen En
Summer

PACIFIC
HEIGHTS

Lunalilo Frwy.

Honolulu International Airport

Bishop Museum

KAPĀLAMA

'Auwaiolimu St.

Nimitz Hwy.

Dillingham Blvd.

IWILEI

Foster Botanical Gardens

Punchbowl

National Memori Cemetery of the

Iwilei
Chinatown

DOWNTOWN HONOLULU

Honolulu Academy of Arts

Aloha Tower

Honolulu Harbor

'Iolani Palace

Neal Blaidell Center

S. King St.

Beretania St.

KAKA'AKO

Ala Moana Blvd.

Auahi St.

Ala Moana

ALA
MOA

Ke'ehi Lagoon

Kahaka'aulana Island

Sand Island

Mokauea Island

Kewalo Basin
Ala Moana Beach

Ala Moana Park

Māmala Bay

0 ————————— 2 miles
0 ————————— 3 km

Honolulu Watershed Forest Reserve

MĀNOA

PĀLOLO

MAKIKI
HEIGHTS

Round Top Dr.

Nehoa St.

Manoa Rd.

Wilder
Ave.

ST. LOUIS
HEIGHTS

WILHELMINA
RISE

Punahou

Lunalilo Fwy.

University Ave.

O'ahu

St. Louis

Pālolo Ave.

10th Ave.

Wilhelmina

16th Ave.

Beretania St.

King St.

H1

MŌ'ILI'ILI

Kapi'olani Blvd.

Wai'alae Ave.

KAPAHULU

8th Ave.

10th Ave.

12th Ave.

Lunalilo Fwy.

a Moana
opping
nter

Hawai'i
Convention
Center

Ala Wai Canal

Date St.

Ala Wai
Golf Course

Pāhoa

KAIMUKĪ

16th Ave.

Makapu'u

KĀHALA

Ala Wai
Yacht
Harbor

Fort
DeRussy

Kalākaua Ave.

Ala Wai Blvd.

Kapahulu

Alohea Ave.

Kīlauea Ave.

WAIKĪKĪ

Kāhala
Ave.

Waikīkī
Beach

**Honolulu
Zoo**

Monsarrat Ave.

Diamond Head Rd.

◆

Kapi'olani
Park

**Waikīkī
Aquarium**

◆

Diamond
Head

▲

Diamond Head Rd.

Diamond
Head Beach

Waikīkī

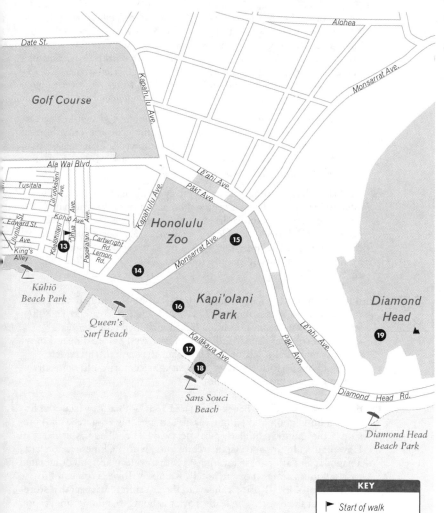

Date St.

Alohea

Golf Course

Monsarrat Ave.

Kapahulu Ave.

Ala Wai Blvd.

Lē'ahi Ave.

Tusitala

Pākī Ave.

Lili'uokalani Ave.

Kūhiō Ave.

Edward St.

Ka'iulani Ave.

'Ohua Ave.

Honolulu
Zoo

15

St. Edward St.

Ka'iolani

Cartwright
Rd.

Papa'kalani
Rd.

Lemon
Rd.

Kūhiō
Ave.

13

King's
Alley

Kūhiō
Beach Park

14

Monsarrat Ave.

Queen's
Surf Beach

16

Kapi'olani
Park

Lē'ahi Ave.

Pākī Ave.

Diamond
Head

19

17

Kalākaua Ave.

18

Sans Souci
Beach

Diamond Head Rd.

Diamond Head
Beach Park

KEY
► *Start of walk*

ian culture. The impressive panels were painted between 1951 and 1952 by Jean Charlot (1898–1979), whose work is represented in Florence at the Uffizi Gallery and in New York at both the Metropolitan Museum and the Museum of Modern Art. The murals are beautifully lighted at night, with some panels visible from the street. ✉ *2181 Kalākaua Ave., Waikīkī* ☎ *808/943–4670* 🖃 *Free* 🕐 *Mon.–Thurs. 8:30–4, Fri. 8:30–6.*

6 Gump Building. Built in 1929 in Hawaiian-colonial style, with Asian architectural motifs and a blue-tile roof, this structure once housed Hawai'i's premier store, Gump's, which was known for high-quality Asian and Hawaiian objects. It's now home to a Louis Vuitton boutique. ✉ *2200 Kalākaua Ave., Waikīkī.*

7 Halekūlani. Maintaining an air of mystery within its tranquil setting, the modern Halekūlani hotel is centered on a portion of its original (1917) beachfront estate, immortalized as the setting for the 1925 Charlie Chan detective novel, *The House Without a Key.* For a view of an orchid blossom unlike any other, take a peek at the swimming pool with its huge orchid mosaic on the bottom. ✉ *2199 Kālia Rd., Waikīkī* ☎ *808/923–2311.*

If it's lunchtime or close to sunset, linger at the Halekūlani and get a table at **House Without a Key** (✉ 2199 Kālia Rd., Waikīkī ☎ 808/ 923–2311). The restaurant has a light lunch menu and serves wonderful tropical drinks and *pūpū* (appetizers) before dinner. Enjoy the view and the sounds of the Hawaiian steel guitar, and watch graceful hula performed nightly beneath the centuries-old *kiawe* tree (kiawe is a mesquite-type wood).

2 Hilton Hawaiian Village Beach Resort and Spa. With a little island in Kahanamoku Lagoon and palm trees all around, this 20-acre Waikīkī resort is the quintessential tropical getaway. The village is a blend of Hawaiian sculpture and Asian architecture, with a Chinese moon gate, a pagoda, and a Japanese farmhouse with a waterwheel, all dominated by a tall mosaic mural of the hotel's Rainbow Tower. You can browse for souvenirs in all price ranges at the 90 different specialty stores throughout the resort. The Kālia Tower is home to a miniature version of the Bishop Museum, designed to give visitors an interactive glimpse of the history of Polynesia. ✉ *2005 Kālia Rd., Waikīkī* ☎ *808/949–4321.*

10 Kahuna (Wizard) Stones of Waikīkī. According to legend, these boulders preserve the magnetic legacy of four Tahitian sorcerers—Kapaemahu, Kinohi, Kapuni, and Kahaloa. The stones are said to have healing powers for all who come here to honor these legendary figures. ✉ *Waikīkī Beach, just 'ewa of the Duke Kahanamoku Statue Waikīkī.*

8 Royal Hawaiian Hotel. Affectionately nicknamed the Pink Palace of the Pacific, this legendary hotel sticks out amid the high-rises on Waikīkī Beach like a pink confection. The Royal Hawaiian opened in 1927, and the lobby is reminiscent of an era when visitors to the Islands arrived on luxury liners. A stroll through the Royal's coconut grove garden is like a walk back to a time when Waikīkī was still a sleepy, tropical paradise. ⊠ *2259 Kalākaua Ave., Waikīkī* ☏ *808/923–7311.*

★ **❾** **Sheraton Moana Surfrider.** Listed on the National Register of Historic Places, this intricate beaux arts–style hotel was christened the First Lady of Waikīkī when she opened her doors at the turn of the 20th century. With period furnishings and historical exhibits, this landmark holds plenty of Hawai'i nostalgia. Visit the **Historical Room** in the rotunda above the main entrance to see the collection of old photographs and memorabilia dating from the opening of the hotel. ⊠ *2365 Kalākaua Ave., Waikīkī* ☏ *808/922–3111.*

need a break? Since 1901, travelers to Waikīkī have sought respite in the shade of the **Moana's Banyan Veranda** (⊠ 2365 Kalakaua Ave., Waikīkī ☏ 808/922–3111), where afternoon high tea has become tradition. Steps away from the ocean, you can close your eyes and linger over teas fragrant with the essence of tropical fruit like mango and papaya. Tea time sandwiches and desserts are sweet additions and a reward for those who brave the rigors of surfing and swimming here in the waters of Waikīkī, once called the "playground of the kings."

❹ **The Urasenke Foundation.** The teahouse here, built in 1951, was the first of its kind to be built outside Japan. If you are looking for a slice of serenity in Waikīkī, this is a good place to find it. The meditative ceremony reflects the influences of centuries of Zen Buddhism. Each ceremony lasts approximately 30 minutes; you can participate or just watch. Wear something comfortable enough for sitting on the floor (but no shorts, please). ⊠ *245 Saratoga Rd., Waihīhi* ☏ *808/923–3059* 🖅 *Minimum donation $3* ☺ *Wed. and Fri. 10–noon.*

❸ **U.S. Army Museum.** This museum at Fort DeRussy has an intimidating collection of war memorabilia. The major focus is on World War II, but exhibits range from ancient Hawaiian weaponry to displays relating to the Vietnam War. It's within Battery Randolf (Building 32), a bunker built in 1911 as a key to the defense of Pearl Harbor and Honolulu. Some of its walls are 22 feet thick. Guided group tours can be arranged; self-guided audio tours are also available. ⊠ *Fort DeRussy, Bldg. 32, Kālia Rd., Waikīkī* ☏ *808/438–2822, 808/422–0561 for recorded information* 🖅 *Free* ☺ *Tues.–Sun. 10–4:15.*

⓬ **Waikīkī Historic Trail.** Take a walk back in time to the Waikīkī of yesteryear along this scenic 2-mi route. Twenty "bronze surfboard" markers provide not only a written description of the sights along the way, but also include photography taken at those very same spots over the last 100 years. You'll get an intimate glance into Waikīkī's history as the playground of royalty, celebrities, and generations of tourists.

Begin your tour of the trail at the standing bronze surfboard next to the Duke Kahanamoku statue. Free 90-minute guided walking tours begin at the statue at 9 AM weekdays and 4:30 PM Saturday. ⊠ *Waikīkī Beach, Diamond Head side of Sheraton Moana Surfrider, Waikīkī* ☏ *808/841–6442* ⊕ *www.waikikihistorictrail.com.*

Kapiʻolani Park & Diamond Head

Kapiʻolani Park, established during the late 1800s by King Kalākaua and named after his queen, is a 500-acre expanse where you can play all sorts of sports, enjoy a picnic, see wild animals, or hear live music. It lies in the shadow of Diamond Head Crater, perhaps Hawaiʻi's most famous natural landmark. Diamond Head got its name from sailors who thought they had found precious gems on its slopes. The diamonds proved to be volcanic refuse.

a good walk

The ʻewa end of Kapiʻolani Park is occupied by the **Honolulu Zoo ⑬** ☞, on the corner of Kalākaua and Kapahulu avenues. On weekends look for the Zoo Fence Art Mart, on Monsarrat Avenue outside the zoo, on the Diamond Head side, for affordable artwork by contemporary artists.

Across Monsarrat Avenue, between Kalākaua Avenue and Pākī Avenue in Kapiʻolani Park, is the **Waikīkī Shell ⑭**, Honolulu's outdoor concert venue. Cut across the park toward the ocean to the **Kapiʻolani Bandstand ⑮**, where you'll hear more free island tunes on days when community events are taking place.

Cross Kalākaua Avenue toward the ocean to the **Waikīkī Aquarium ⑯** and its neighbor, the **Waikīkī War Memorial Natatorium ⑰**, an open-air swimming stadium built in 1927 to commemorate lives lost in World War I.

As it leaves Kapiʻolani Park, Kalākaua Avenue forks into Diamond Head Road, a scenic 2-mi stretch popular with walkers and joggers, and winds around the base of Diamond Head alongside the ocean, passing handsome Diamond Head Lighthouse (not open to the public). Lookout areas offer views of the surfers and windsurfers below. The hike to the summit of **Diamond Head State Monument and Park ⑱** requires strenuous walking. To save time and energy, drive, don't walk, along Diamond Head Road, turn left at Monsarrat Avenue, head a mile up the hill, and look for a sign on the right to the entrance to the crater. Drive through the tunnel to the inside of the crater. The trail begins at the parking lot.

TIMING   Budget a full day to see Kapiʻolani Park and Diamond Head. If you want to hike up to the crater's summit, do it before breakfast. That way you beat not only the heat but the crowds. Hiking Diamond Head takes an hour round-trip, but factor in some extra time to enjoy the views from the top. Keep an eye on your watch if you're there at day's end, because the gates close promptly at 6. If you want to see the Honolulu Zoo, it's best to get there right when it opens, since the animals are livelier in the cool of the morning. Give the aquarium an hour, including 10 minutes in its Sea Visions Theater. For the best seats at the 10 AM Pleasant Hawaiian Hula Show, get to Kapiʻolani Park by 8 or so.

What to See

★ ⑱   **Diamond Head State Monument and Park.** Panoramas from this 760-foot extinct volcanic peak, once used as a military fortification, extend from Waikīkī and Honolulu in one direction and out to Koko Head in the other, with surfers and windsurfers scattered like confetti on the cresting waves below. This 360-degree perspective is a great orientation for first-time visitors of both this island, its neighbors, and this pyroclastic volcano. On a clear day you can even see the islands of Maui and Molokaʻi if you look to your left. The ¾-mi trail starts at the crater floor, and although most guidebooks say there are 99 steps to the top, that's only true of the first flight—there are four flights altogether! New lighting inside the summit tunnel and spiral staircase eases the way to the top. Take bottled water with you on this hike to ensure that you stay hydrated under the tropical sun. ⊠ *Diamond Head Rd. at 18th Ave., Waikīkī* ☏ *808/587–0285* ⊕ *www.state.hi.us/dlnr/dsp/oahu.html* ⊑ *$1 per person, $5 per vehicle.* ☉ *Daily 6–6.*

🖑 🏴 ⓭ **Honolulu Zoo.** There are bigger and better zoos, but this one is lovely, and on Wednesday evenings in summer, the zoo puts on "The Wildest Show in Town," a free concert series. The best part of the zoo is its 7½-acre African savanna, where animals roam freely on the other side of hidden rails and moats. To get a glimpse of the Hawaiʻi state bird, check out the Kipuka Nene Sanctuary. If you're visiting during a full moon, ask about the "Twilight" tours of the Zoo's nocturnal animals who are active only after dusk. At the petting zoo, kids can pet a llama and meet Abbey, the zoo's resident monitor lizard. If your visit is timed right, you might also consider a family sleepover inside the zoo during its "Snooze in the Zoo" events, which take place on a Friday or Saturday night at the end of each month. ⊠ *151 Kapahulu Ave., Waikīkī* ☏ *808/971–7171* ⊕ *www.honoluluzoo.org* ⊑ *$6* ☉ *Daily 9–4:30.*

ⓕ **Kapiʻolani Bandstand.** A replica of the Victorian Kapiʻolani Bandstand, which was originally built in the late 1890s, is Kapiʻolani Park's centerpiece for community entertainment and concerts. Check out the "Bandstand Jams," held at 5:30 every Friday, with concert performances ranging from contemporary Hawaiian to jazz to reggae. The nation's only city-sponsored band, the Royal Hawaiian Band, performs free concerts on Sunday afternoons. Local newspapers list entertainment information. ⊠ *ʻEwa end of Kapiʻolani Park, mauka side of Kalākaua Ave., Waikīkī.*

★ 🖑 ⓰ **Waikīkī Aquarium.** This amazing little attraction harbors more than 2,500 organisms and 420 species of Hawaiian and South Pacific marine life, endangered Hawaiian monk seals, sharks, and the only chambered nautilus living in captivity. The Edge of the Reef exhibit showcases five different types of reef environments found along Hawaiʻi's shorelines. Check out the Sea Visions Theater, the biodiversity exhibit, and the self-guided audio tour, which is included with admission. Programs include "Exploring the Reef at Night," "Shark Nites," "Stingray Tracking," and "Aquarium After Dark" activities. ⊠ *2777 Kalākaua Ave., Waikīkī* ☏ *808/923–9741* ⊕ *www.waquarium.org* ⊑ *$7* ☉ *Daily 9–4:30.*

⓮ **Waikīkī Shell.** Local people bring a picnic and grab one of the 6,000 "grass seats" (lawn seating) for music under the stars. Here's a chance to enjoy some of Hawaiʻi's best musicians as well as visiting guest artists. Concerts are held May 1 to Labor Day, with a few winter dates, weather permitting. Check the newspapers to see who is performing. ⊠ *2805 Monsarrat Ave., Waikīkī* ☏ *808/924–8934* ⊕ *www.blaisdellcenter.com.*

⑰ Waikīkī War Memorial Natatorium. This 1927 World War I monument, dedicated to the 102 Hawaiian servicemen who lost their lives in battle, stands proudly—its 20-foot archway, which was completely restored in 2002, is floodlighted at night. The 100-meter saltwater swimming pool is closed to the public; it was the training spot for Olympians Johnny Weissmuller and Buster Crabbe and the U.S. Army during World War II. ⊠ *2777 Kalākaua Ave., Waikīkī.*

You can enjoy breakfast, lunch, or dinner outdoors beneath the shade of a *hau* tree at the New Otani Kaimana Beach Hotel, next to the Waikīkī War Memorial Natatorium. Dubbed the **Hau Tree Lānai** (⊠ 2863 Kalākaua Ave. ☎ 808/921–7066), it's a little jewel if you want open-air oceanfront refreshment.

Downtown Honolulu

Honolulu's past and present play a delightful counterpoint throughout the downtown sector. Modern skyscrapers stand directly across from the Aloha Tower, which was built in 1926 and was, until the early 1960s, the tallest structure in Honolulu. Buildings here tell the story of Hawai'i's history in architecture, from the Chinatown buildings of the late 1800s to the 21st-century design of the First Hawaiian Building. Washington Place, built in 1846, was the home of Queen Lili'uokalani until her death in 1917, and until 2003 it served as the residence for Hawai'i's governors. A new governor's residence has been built alongside Washington Place, and plans are under way to open Washington Place to the public as a historical museum.

To reach Downtown Honolulu from Waikīkī by car, take Ala Moana Boulevard to Alakea Street. There are public parking lots (50¢ per half hour for the first two hours) in buildings along Alakea Street and Bethel Street, two blocks 'ewa. Keep in mind that parking in most downtown lots is expensive ($3.50 per half hour).

a good walk

Begin at the **Hawai'i Maritime Center ⑲ ▶** at the harborfront, across Ala Moana Boulevard from Alakea Street in Downtown Honolulu. This museum traces the history of Hawai'i's love affair with the sea. Just 'ewa of the Hawai'i Maritime Center is **Aloha Tower Marketplace ⑳**, a complex of harborside shops and restaurants where you can also view the luxury cruise liners in port and the traditional Hawaiian Boat Days celebrations that greet each arrival.

Cross Ala Moana Boulevard, walk a block 'ewa, and turn mauka on Ft. Street Mall, a pedestrian walkway, until you reach King Street. Turn left, and after a few blocks you'll reach **Chinatown ㉑**, the old section of Downtown Honolulu. Here you can find a Buddhist temple, a Japanese shrine, shops, art galleries, restaurants, and a big open market.

Walk back toward Diamond Head along King Street until it intersects with Bishop Street. On the mauka side is lovely **Tamarind Park ㉒**, a popular lunchtime picnic spot for Honolulu's workforce, which gathers under its shady plumeria, *kukui,,* monkeypod—and one tamarind—trees.

Downtown Honolulu

Foster Botanical Gardens

Kuan Yin Temple

'A'ala St.

River St.

61

'Iolani Ave.

Lunalilo Frwy.

Maunakea

Nu'uanu

Kukui St.

Vineyard Blvd.

N. Beretania

River St.

Queen Emma

Ketaulike

21

Maunakea

N. Hotel St.

Pauahi

Nu'uanu

Fort St.

S. Bishop St.

Miller St.

Punchbowl St.

Smith

King St.

Bethel St.

S. Hotel St.

Alakea

Richards St.

Merchant St.

22

23

26

S. Beretania St.

31

24

Queen St.

27

28

Fort St.

Mililani

25

29

S. King St.

20

30

19

Ala Moana Blvd.

Honolulu Harbor

Punchbowl St.

South St.

Kapi'olani Blvd.

Pohukaina

Keauhou

Queen St.

Cooke

Kawaiaha'o

Waimanu

Haniwai

Auahi St.

Keawe

Coral

Cooke

'Ohe

Halekauwila

Kamani

Ward Ave.

Auahi St.

92

'Ahui

Kewalo Basin

KEY

▶ *Start of walk*

0   550 yards

0   500 meters

Continue down King Street and hang a left onto Richards Street. At the corner of Richards and Hotel streets is the No. 1 Capitol District Building, which houses Hawaiʻi's newest museum (opened in late 2002), the **Hawaiʻi State Art Museum** ㉓. Walk back along Richards Street toward King Street until you reach **ʻIolani Palace** ㉔, on the left-hand side. This graceful Victorian structure was built by King David Kalākaua in 1882. Also on the palace grounds is the Kalākaua Coronation Bandstand, where the Royal Hawaiian Band performs at noon most Fridays.

Across King Street from ʻIolani Palace is Aliʻiōlani Hale, the judiciary building that once served as the parliament hall during the kingship era. In front of it is the gilded **Kamehameha I Statue** ㉕, which honors Hawaiʻi's greatest monarch. Walk one block mauka up Richards Street to tour the **Hawaiʻi State Capitol** ㉖. Almost across the street from the state capitol is Washington Place, the home of Hawaiʻi's governor.

Return to King Street via Punchbowl Street, stay on the mauka side, and proceed in a Diamond Head direction. Walk past the palace again until you come to the massive stone **Hawaiʻi State Library** ㉗, a showcase of architectural restoration. At Punchbowl Street is **Honolulu Hale** ㉘, or City Hall. Across the street is the **Kawaiahaʻo Church** ㉙, perhaps Hawaiʻi's most famous religious structure. On the Diamond Head side of the Kawaiahaʻo Church is the **Mission Houses Museum** ㉚, where the first American missionaries in Hawaiʻi lived. From here it's three long blocks toward Diamond Head to Ward Avenue and one block mauka to Beretania Street, but the **Honolulu Academy of Arts** ㉛ is worth the extra mileage (you might choose to drive there instead). It houses a world-class collection of Western and Asian art.

TIMING Downtown Honolulu merits a full day of your time. Be sure to stop by the palace Tuesday–Saturday, the only days tours are offered. Remember that the Mission Houses Museum is closed Sunday and Monday and the Honolulu Academy of Arts is closed Monday. Saturday morning is the best time to walk through Chinatown; that's when the open-air markets do their biggest business with local families. A walk through Chinatown can take at least an hour, as can tours of the Mission Houses and ʻIolani Palace. Wrap up your day at sunset with refreshments or dinner back at the Aloha Tower Marketplace, which stays open late into the evening, with live entertainment on the harborfront.

What to See

 ㉛ ㉚ **Aloha Tower Marketplace.** Two stories of shops and kiosks feature island-inspired clothing, jewelry, art, and home furnishings. The Marketplace, located on the Honolulu Harborfront, also has indoor and outdoor restaurants, as well as live entertainment. For a bird's-eye view of this working harbor, take a free ride up to the observation deck of Aloha Tower, which anchors the market. The Marketplace's location makes it an ideal spot for watching the arrival of cruise ships. On Hawaiian Boat Days, the waterfront comes alive with entertainment and hula dancers who greet and send off the arriving and departing ships. ✉ *1 Aloha Tower Dr., at Piers 8, 9, and 10, Downtown Honolulu* ☎ *808/528–5700 or 808/566–2337 for entertainment info* ⊕ *www.alohatower.com* ☉ *Daily 9–9, restaurants 9 AM–2 AM.*

HONOLULU'S 15-BLOCK MELTING POT

HONOLULU'S CHINATOWN *was established in the late 1800s by laborers looking for a new life after their contracts with the* sugar plantations ended. The neighborhood—bordered by North Beretania Street and North King Street to the north and south and Bethel Street and River Street to the east and west—has a tumultuous and fascinating history. It was twice destroyed by fire, first in 1886 and again in 1900 (the later fire was deliberately set to clear the area of the bubonic plague), but was lovingly rebuilt both times, and by the 1930s it was a real center of influence, namely because of its prime location just minutes from Honolulu Harbor. In the 1940s, however, the neighborhood became notorious as the seedy stomping ground of military personnel, who found their way here to sample the exotic food, as well as the bars, pool halls, tattoo parlors, and prostitution houses. For years after, Chinatown was crime-ridden and many of its historic buildings fell into disrepair. It wasn't until 1973, when the federal government declared the neighborhood a historic area, that Chinatown's slow upswing began. Since then new residential buildings and commercial space have been added and many cultural gems have been restored.

Today, visiting a revitalized Chinatown is like taking a two-hour tour throughout Asia. At its heart is the **O'ahu Marketplace** (⊠ N. King and Kekaulike Sts.), where everything a Chinese chef could desire is on display. The neighborhood still retains much of its original architecture—notable are the Chinatown Police Station and the Hawai'i Theatre Center. Even amid the flurry of modern retail outlets, including the Maunakea Marketplace, Mahalo Antique Mall, and the more

contemporary Chinese Cultural Plaza, are places of calm in the Taoist Lum Sai Ho Tong Society Temple, the Shinto Izumo Taisha Mission Cultural Hall, and the Kuan Yin Buddhist Temple. The wild orchid gardens at the **Foster Botanical Garden** (⊠ N. Vineyard Blvd. at Nu'uanu Ave. ☎ 808/522–7060), open daily 9–4, are perfect for quiet contemplation.

The contemporary side of Chinatown is just as exciting. Though there's plenty of yesteryear to be found in the herb and antique shops, Chinatown is also a great place to shop for chic modern-day accoutrements. Additionally, Nu'uanu Avenue, north of Hotel Street known as "NOHO" is packed with art galleries and trendy clubs.

Of course, one of the main reasons to visit this lively neighborhood is the food. Don't miss the udon noodles at the **Yat Hung Chow Noodle Factory** (⊠ 150 N. King St. ☎ 808/531–7982). Equally delicious are the pastries at **Shung Chong Yuein** (⊠ 1027 Maunakea St. ☎ 808/ 531–1983).

㉑ Chinatown. Noodle factories and herb shops, lei stands and acupuncture studios, art galleries and Chinese and Thai restaurants make up this historic neighborhood. A major highlight is the colorful O'ahu Market, an open-air emporium with hanging pigs' heads, display cases of fresh fish, row after row of exotic fruits and vegetables, and vendors of all ethnic backgrounds. Check out the Chinese Cultural Plaza's Moongate stage for cultural events, especially around the Chinese New Year. A walking map of the area can be downloaded from the Web site listed below. ⊠ *King St. between Smith and River Sts., Chinatown* ⊕ *www. chinatownhi.com.*

need a break? There are Chinese, Thai, Japanese, Korean, and Italian food stalls at **Maunakea Marketplace** (⊠ 1120 Maunakea St., Chinatown ☎ 808/524–3409), one block mauka of King Street. The food is flavorful and reasonably priced. A courtyard has some seating.

㉙ Hawai'i Maritime Center. The story of the Islands begins on the seas. The **Kalākaua Boat House** has interactive exhibits where you can learn about Hawai'i's whaling days, the history of Honolulu Harbor, the Clipper seaplane, and surfing and windsurfing in Hawai'i. Moored next to the Boat House is the *Falls of Clyde.* Built in 1778, this four-masted, square-rigged ship once brought tea from China to the U.S. west coast and is now used as a museum. Self-guided audio tours are available in English, Japanese, and Korean. ⊠ *Ala Moana Blvd. at Pier 7, Downtown Honolulu* ☎ 808/536–6373 ⊕ *www.holoholo.org/maritime* 🎟 *$7.50* ۞ *Daily 8:30–5.*

㉓ Hawai'i State Art Museum. The second floor of the State Capitol District Building has 12,000 feet of gallery space dedicated to the art of Hawai'i in all its ethnic diversity. The Diamond Head Gallery features new acquisitions and thematic shows from the State Art Collection and the State Foundation on Culture and the Arts. The 'Ewa Gallery houses more than 150 works documenting Hawai'i's visual-arts history since becoming a state in 1959. Also included are a sculpture gallery as well as a café, a gift shop, and educational meeting rooms. ⊠ *250 South Hotel St., 2nd fl., Downtown Honolulu* ☎ 808/586–0307 ⊕ *www.state.hi.us/sfca* 🎟 *Free* ۞ *Tues.–Sat. 10–4.*

㉖ Hawai'i State Capitol. The capitol's architecture is richly symbolic: the columns look like palm trees, the legislative chambers are shaped like volcanic cinder cones, and the central court is open to the sky, representing Hawai'i's open society. Replicas of the Hawai'i state seal, each weighing 7,500 pounds, hang above both its entrances. The building, which in 1969 replaced 'Iolani Palace as the seat of government, is surrounded by reflecting pools, just as the Islands are embraced by water. ⊠ *215 S. Beretania St., Downtown Honolulu* ☎ 808/586–0146 🎟 *Free* ۞ *Guided tours upon request weekday afternoons.*

㉗ Hawai'i State Library. This beautifully renovated main library, originally built in 1913, is wonderful to explore. Its Samuel M. Kamakani Room, on the first floor in the mauka courtyard, houses an extensive Hawai'i and Pacific book collection and pays tribute to Kamakani, one of

Hawai'i's noted historians. ⊠ *478 King St., Downtown Honolulu* ☏ *808/586–3500* ☐ *Free* ⊙ *Mon. and Fri.–Sat. 9–5, Tues. and Thurs. 9–8, Wed. 10–5.*

㉛ Honolulu Academy of Arts. The academy dates to 1927 and has an impressive permanent collection that includes Hiroshige's ukiyo-e Japanese prints, donated by James Michener; Italian Renaissance paintings; and American and European art. Six open-air courtyards provide a casual counterpart to the more formal galleries. The Luce Pavilion complex has a traveling-exhibit gallery, a Hawaiian gallery, a café, and a gift shop. The Academy Theatre screens art films. There are select Islamic-art tours offered by the academy's art center which take you to the Doris Duke Foundation for Islamic Art, located within Duke's former Diamond Head estate, Shangri-La. Tours of this estate require reservations in advance. Guided tours of the academy are available Tuesday–Saturday at 11 AM and Sunday at 1:15 PM. Call about special exhibits, concerts, and films. ⊠ *900 S. Beretania St., Downtown Honolulu* ☏ *808/532–8700* ⊕ *www.honoluluacademy.org* ☐ *$7 Academy, $25 Shangri-La Islamic Art Tours* ⊙ *Tues.–Sat. 10–4:30, Sun. 1–5.*

㉘ Honolulu Hale. This Mediterranean Renaissance–style building was constructed in 1929 and serves as the center of city government. Stroll through the cool, open-ceiling lobby with exhibits of local artists, and time your visit to coincide with one of the free concerts sometimes offered in the evening, when the building stays open late. During the winter holiday season, the Hale becomes the focal point for the annual Honolulu City Lights Festival program. ⊠ *530 S. King St., Downtown Honolulu* ☏ *808/523–4654* ☐ *Free* ⊙ *Weekdays 8–4:30.*

㉔ 'Iolani Palace. Built in 1882 on the site of an earlier palace and beautifully restored since, this is America's only royal residence. (Bucking the stereotype of the primitive islander, the palace had electricity and telephone lines installed even before the White House did.) It contains the thrones of King Kalākaua and his successor (and sister) Queen Lili'uokalani. Downstairs galleries showcase the royal jewelry, and kitchen and offices of the monarchy. The palace is open for guided tours only, and reservations are essential. Take a look at the gift shop, formerly the 'Iolani Barracks, built to house the Royal Guard. ⊠ *King and Richards Sts., Downtown Honolulu* ☏ *808/522–0832* ⊕ *www.iolanipalace.org* ☐ *Grand Tour $20, downstairs galleries only $10* ⊙ *Tues.–Sat. 8:30–2, with tours beginning on the half hour.*

need a break? For an exotic lunch stop by **Duk's Bistro** (⊠ 1188 Maunakea St., Chinatown ☏ 808/531–6325), a tiny three-room eatery facing Chinatown's busiest street and featuring a French-Vietnamese menu. Spring for the shrimp, mushroom, and taro spring rolls or have a "Meal in a Bowl," brimming with rice noodles and fresh island vegetables.

㉕ Kamehameha I Statue. This downtown landmark pays tribute to the Big Island chieftain who united all the warring Hawaiian Islands into one kingdom at the turn of the 18th century. The statue, which stands with one arm outstretched in welcome, is one of three originally cast in Paris, France, by American sculptor T. R. Gould; the original version is in Kapa'au, on the Big Island, near the king's birthplace. Each year on the king's birthday, June 11, the statue is draped in fresh lei that reach lengths of 18 feet and longer. ⊠ *417 S. King St., outside Ali'iōlani Hale, Downtown Honolulu.*

㉙ **Kawaiaha'o Church.** Fancifully called Hawai'i's Westminster Abbey, this 14,000-coral-block house of worship witnessed the coronations, weddings, and funerals of generations of Hawaiian royalty. Each of the building's coral blocks was quarried from reefs offshore at depths of more than 20 feet and transported to this site. Interior woodwork was created from the forests of the Ko'olau Mountains. The upper gallery has an exhibit of paintings of the royal families. The graves of missionaries and of King Lunalilo are in the yard. Services in English and Hawaiian are held each Sunday. Although there are no guided tours, you can look around the church at no cost. ⊠ *957 Punchbowl St., at King St., Downtown Honolulu* ☎ *808/522–1333* ☞ *Free* ☉ *English service Sun. at 8* AM *and Wed. at 6* PM, *Hawaiian service Sun. at 10:30* AM.

㉚ **Mission Houses Museum.** The determined Hawai'i missionaries arrived in 1820, gaining royal favor and influencing every aspect of island life. Their descendants became leaders in government and business. You can walk through their original dwellings, including a white-frame house that was prefabricated in New England and shipped around the Horn— it is Hawai'i's oldest wooden structure. The museum hosts living history programs, candlelight museum tours, and crafts fairs. Certain areas of the museum may be seen only on a one-hour guided tour. The museum also offers historic-downtown walking tours on Thursday at 10 AM; reservations are required 24 hours in advance. ⊠ *553 S. King St., Downtown Honolulu* ☎ *808/531–0481* ⊕ *www.lava.net/~mhm* ☞ *$10, walking tour $15* ☉ *Tues.–Sat. 9–4; guided tours at 9:45, 11:15, 1, and 2:30.*

㉒ **Tamarind Park.** From jazz and Hawaiian tunes to the strains of the U.S. Marine Band, music fills this pretty park most Fridays at noon. Do as the locals do: pick up lunch at one of the many carryout restaurants and find a bench or patch of grass. ⊠ *Corner of Bishop and S. King Sts., Downtown Honolulu* ☞ *Free.*

The East O'ahu Ring

At once historic and contemporary, serene and active, the east end of O'ahu holds within its relatively small area remarkable variety and picture-perfect scenery of windswept cliffs and wave-dashed shores.

a good drive

From Waikīkī there are two routes to Lunalilo Freeway (H-1). On the Diamond Head end, go mauka on Kapahulu Avenue and follow the signs to the freeway. On the 'ewa end, take Ala Wai Boulevard and turn mauka at Kalākaua Avenue, staying on it until it ends at Beretania Street, which is one-way going left. Turn right off Beretania Street at Pi'ikoi Street, and the signs will direct you onto the freeway heading west.

Take the freeway exit marked Pali Highway (Route 61), one of three roads that cut through the Ko'olau Mountains. On the right is the **Queen Emma Summer Palace** 32 ▶. The colonial-style white mansion, which once served as the summer retreat of King Kamehameha IV and his wife, Queen Emma, is now a museum.

As you drive toward the summit of the highway, the road is lined with sweet ginger in summer and red poinsettias in winter. If it has been raining, waterfalls will be tumbling down the chiseled cliffs of the Ko'olau. If it is very windy, those waterfalls can look as if they are traveling up the cliffs, not down, making them a sight to behold.

Watch for the turn to the **Nu'uanu Pali Lookout** 33. There is a small parking lot and a lookout wall from which you can see all the way up and down the windward coast—a view that Mark Twain called the most beautiful in the world.

As you follow the highway down the other side of the mountain, continue straight along what becomes Kailua Road. If you're interested in Hawaiian history, look for the YMCA at the Castle Hospital junction of Kalaniana'ole Highway and Kailua Road. Behind it is **Ulupō Heiau** 34, an ancient outdoor shrine. Ready for a detour? Head straight on Kailua Road to Kailua Beach Park, which many people consider the best on the island. The road twists and turns, so watch the signs.

Retracing your route back to Castle Junction, turn left at the intersection onto Kalaniana'ole Highway. Soon you will come to the small town of **Waimānalo** 35. Waimānalo's two beaches are Bellows Beach, great for swimming and bodysurfing, and Waimānalo Beach Park, also safe for swimming.

Another mile along the highway, on the right, is **Sea Life Park** 36, home to the world's only "wholphin," the offspring of a whale and a dolphin. Across the highway from Sea Life Park is Makapu'u Beach, a beautiful cove that is great for seasoned bodysurfers but treacherous for weak swimmers. The road winds up a hill, at the top of which is a turnoff on the makai side to **Makapu'u Point** 37.

Next you'll see the inviting Sandy Beach. Tempting as this beach looks, it is not advisable to swim here because the waves are powerful and the rip currents more than tricky. From here the road twists and turns next to steep cliffs along the Koko Head shoreline. Offshore, the islands of Moloka'i and Lāna'i call like distant sirens, and every once in a while Maui is visible in blue silhouette. For the best photos, pull into the parking lot at **Hālona Blowhole** 38. At the top of the hill on the makai side of the road is the entrance to **Hanauma Bay Nature Preserve** 39, one of O'ahu's most famous snorkeling destinations.

From here back to Waikīkī the highway passes several residential communities called Hawai'i Kai, Niu Valley, and 'Āina Haina, each of which has a small shopping center where you can pick up a soda or a snack. Right before you turn off from Kalaniana'ole Highway there's a long stretch of green on the makai side. This is the private Wai'alae Country Club, scene of the televised annual Sony Open golf tournament.

Take the Kīlauea Avenue exit. Turn left at the stoplight onto Kīlauea Avenue. Here you'll see Kāhala Mall, an upscale shopping complex with yuppie eateries, high-fashion stores, and eight movie theaters. A few blocks past the mall, take a left on Hunakai Street and follow it until it dead-ends at Kāhala Avenue. Turn right and drive through **Kāhala** ⓐ, O'ahu's wealthiest neighborhood. Kāhala Avenue becomes Diamond Head Road. Follow it straight to Kapi'olani Park. Stay on the right side of the park until you hit Kapahulu Avenue. Take a left, and you're back in Waikīkī.

TIMING   If Hanauma Bay is your main focus, don't try to do the tour on Tuesday, when the park is closed. Also note that the bay is best in the early hours before the waters are churned up. You could reverse the above directions and get there first thing in the morning, before the crowds. Allow two hours for Hanauma Bay, two hours for Sea Life Park, and one for Queen Emma Summer Palace. Another tip: look up to the top of the mountains and, if it's clear, head directly to the Nu'uanu Pali Lookout. It's a shame to get there only to find the view obscured by clouds or fog. Temperatures at the summit are several degrees cooler than in warm Waikīkī, so bring a jacket along.

What to See

ⓧ **Hālona Blowhole.** Below a scenic turnout along the Koko Head shoreline, this oft-photographed lava tube that sucks the ocean in and spits it out in lofty plumes may or may not perform, depending on the currents. Look to your right to see the tiny beach below that was used to film the wave-washed love scene in *From Here to Eternity*. In winter, it's a good spot to watch whales at play. Take your valuables with you and lock your car, because this scenic location is a hot spot for petty thieves. ✉ *Kalaniana'ole Hwy., 1 mi east of Hanauma Bay.*

ⓧ **Hanauma Bay Nature Preserve.** This bay was created when the exterior
Fodor'sChoice wall of a volcanic crater collapsed, opening it to the sea and thereby giv-
★ ing birth to O'ahu's most famous snorkeling destination. Even from the overlook, the horseshoe-shape bay is a beauty, and you can easily see the reefs through the clear aqua waters. The wide beach is a great place for sunbathing and picnics. This is a marine conservation district, and regulations prohibit feeding the fish. Visitors are required to go through the Bay's Education Center before trekking down to the Bay. The Center provides a cultural history of the area and exhibits about the importance of protecting its marine life. Check out the "Today at the Bay" exhibit for up-to-date information on daily tides, ocean safety warnings and event activities. Food concessions and equipment rentals are also on-site. Come early to get parking, as the number of visitors allowed per day is limited. Call for current conditions. Weather permitting, Hanauma Bay by Starlight events are held on Saturday, extending the opening hours to 10 PM. ✉ *7455 Kalaniana'ole Hwy.* ☎ *808/396–4229* ✉ *Donation $5; parking $1; mask, snorkel, and fins rental $8; tram from parking lot down to beach $1.50* ☉ *Wed.–Mon. 6–6.*

ⓧ **Kāhala.** O'ahu's wealthiest neighborhood has streets lined with multi-million-dollar homes and the classy Kāhala Mandarin Oriental Hawai'i hotel, which attracts a prestigious clientele. At intervals along tree-lined

Kāhala Avenue are narrow lanes that provide public access to Kāhala's magnificent coastal beaches. Kāhala is home to the private Wai'alae Golf Course, site of the annual Sony Open PGA golf tournament each January. ⊠ *East of Diamond Head.*

㊲ Makapu'u Point. This spot has breathtaking views of the ocean, mountains, and the windward islands. The peninsula jutting out in the distance is **Mōkapu,** site of a U.S. Marine base. The spired mountain peak is **Mt. Olomana.** In front of you on the long pier is part of the **Makai Undersea Test Range,** a research facility that is closed to the public. Offshore is **Rabbit Island,** a picturesque cay so named because some think it looks like a swimming bunny.

Nestled in the cliff face is the **Makapu'u Lighthouse,** which became operational in 1909 and has the largest lighthouse lens in America. The lighthouse is closed to the public, but near the Makapu'u Point turnout you'll find the start of a mile-long paved road (closed to traffic). Hike up to the top of the 647-foot bluff for a closer view of the lighthouse and, in winter, a great whale-watching vantage point. ⊠ *Kalaniana'ole Hwy., turnout above Makapu'u Beach.*

㉝ Nu'uanu Pali Lookout. This panoramic perch looks out to windward O'ahu. It was in this region that King Kamehameha I drove defending forces over the edges of the 1,000-foot-high cliffs, thus winning the decisive battle for control of O'ahu. From here, you can see views that stretch from Kaneohe Bay to Chinaman's Hat, a small island off the coast, and beyond. It's a windy spot, so hang on to your hat. Lock your car if you get out, because break-ins have occurred here. ⊠ *Top of Pali Hwy.* ☉ *Daily 9–4.*

▶ **㉜ Queen Emma Summer Palace.** Queen Emma and her family used this stately white home, built in 1848, as a retreat from the rigors of court life in hot and dusty Honolulu during the mid-1800s. It has an eclectic mix of European, Victorian, and Hawaiian furnishings and has excellent examples of Hawaiian quilts and koa-wood furniture as well as the queen's wedding dress and other memorabilia. ⊠ *2913 Pali Hwy.* ☎ *808/595–6291* ⊕ *www.daughtersofhawaii.org* ⊠ *$5* ☉ *Guided tours daily 9–4.*

㉖ Sea Life Park. Dolphins leap and spin, penguins frolic, and a killer whale performs impressive tricks at this marine-life attraction 15 mi from Waikīkī at scenic Makapu'u Point. In addition to a 300,000-gallon Hawaiian reef aquarium, you'll find the Pacific Whaling Museum, the Hawaiian Monk Seal Care Center, and a breeding sanctuary for Hawai'i's endangered *Honu* sea turtle. There are several interactive activities such as a stingray encounter, an underwater photo safari, and a "Splash University" dolphin-training session. Inquire about the park's behind-the-scenes tour for a glimpse of dolphin-training areas and the seabird rehabilitation center. ⊠ *41-202 Kalaniana'ole Hwy., Waimānalo* ☎ *808/259–7933 or 886/365–7446* ⊕ *www.sealifepark.com* ⊠ *$24* ☉ *Daily 9:30–5.*

㉞ Ulupō Heiau. Though they may look like piles of rocks to the uninitiated, *heiau* are sacred stone platforms for the worship of the gods and date from ancient times. *Ulupō* means "night inspiration," referring to the legendary *menehune,* a mythical race of diminutive people who supposedly built the heiau under the cloak of darkness. ⊠ *Behind YMCA at Kalaniana'ole Hwy. and Kailua Rd.*

need a break? Generations of children have purchased their beach snacks and sodas at **Kalapawai Market** (⊠ 306 S. Kalāheo Ave.), near Kailua Beach. A windward landmark since 1932, the green-and-white market has distinctive charm. It's a good source for your carryout lunch, since there's no concession stand at the beach.

③⑤ **Waimānalo.** This modest little seaside town flanked by chiseled cliffs is worth a visit. Its biggest draw is its beautiful beach, offering glorious views to the windward side. Down the side roads, as you head mauka, are little farms that grow a variety of fruits and flowers. Toward the back of the valley are small ranches with grazing horses. If you see any trucks selling corn and you're staying at a place where you can cook it, be sure to get some in Waimānalo. It may be the sweetest you'll ever eat, and the price is the lowest on O'ahu. ⊠ *Kalaniana'ole Hwy.*

Around the Island

After visiting three historic attractions in populated West Honolulu, you'll find that the O'ahu landscape turns increasingly rural as you head north. Once carpeted in pineapple and sugarcane plantations, the central plains and the North Shore are now home to ranches, banana farms, and fields of exotic flowers and coffee grown for export. Some plantation towns have become cute with boutiques and little art galleries. Others are just themselves—old, wooden, and picturesque—with small homes surrounded by flowers and tropical-fruit trees.

a good drive Follow H-1 Freeway heading west. Take the exit for Likelike Highway. Stay in the right lane and look for signs to the **Bishop Museum** ④① ⏵. Return to the freeway and head west; the road will merge into the Moanalua Freeway (Route 78). Stay on this past the Pu'uloa Road–Tripler Hospital exit for **Moanalua Gardens** ④②, a lovely park with huge monkeypod trees.

Continuing on the freeway, up over what is known as Red Hill, you'll pass Aloha Stadium, a 50,000-seat arena that hosts the annual NFL Pro Bowl, local football and baseball games, and big-name rock concerts. The Aloha Flea Market is also held here. As you approach the stadium on the freeway, bear right at the sign to 'Aiea, and then merge left onto Kamehameha Highway (Route 99), going south to Pearl Harbor. Turn right at the Hālawa Gate for a tour of the **USS *Arizona* Memorial**, the **Battleship *Missouri* Memorial** ④③, and the USS *Bowfin* Memorial.

Follow H-1 west to Waipahu (Exit 8B) and onto Farrington Highway. Turn right at Waipahu Depot Road and left onto Waipahu Street to reach **Hawai'i's Plantation Village** ④④, a collection of restored original and replicated homes from a 19th-century plantation town.

Take H-1 to H-2 to Route 80 (Kamehameha Highway), heading to Wahiawā, home of the U.S. Army base at Schofield Barracks. Head north until Route 80 meets Route 99, where you'll see a scrubby patch called the Del Monte Pineapple Variety Garden. Unpromising as it looks, it's actually quite interesting, with varieties of the ubiquitous fruit ranging from thumb-size pink ones to big golden ones.

Merge left on Kamehameha Highway and you'll see the **Dole Pineapple Pavilion** ㊺. From here, Kamehameha Highway cuts through pineapple and sugarcane fields. Close to the bottom of the hill, a traffic-light intersection invites you to take the Haleʻiwa bypass road to save time. Don't. Turn left instead and drive to the traffic circle. Go around the circle and continue 7 mi to Mokulēʻia on Route 930. Soon you'll come to Dillingham Airfield, where you can fly in a glider.

Back at the traffic circle, follow the signs to **Haleʻiwa** ㊻, a sleepy plantation town with fashion boutiques, surf shops, restaurants, and the best grilled mahimahi sandwich on the North Shore at Kua ʻAina Sandwich. Leaving Haleʻiwa and continuing along Kamehameha Highway (Route 83), you'll pass the famous North Shore beaches, where the winter surf comes in size extra large. The first of these is the famous big surf spot Waimea Bay. Across the street, on the mauka side of the road, is **Waimea Valley Audubon Center** ㊼. If you're interested in seeing a fine example of an ancient Hawaiian heiau, turn mauka at the Foodland store and take Pūpūkea Road up the steep climb, not quite a mile, to the dirt road on the right, leading to the **Puʻuomahuka Heiau** ㊽.

Continue along the coastal road past more famous surfing beaches, including ʻEhukai and Sunset. If it's wintertime, keep clear of those waves, which sometimes rise as high as 30 feet. Leave the sea to the daring (some say crazy) surfers who ride the towering waves with astounding grace. The only hotel of any consequence in these parts is your next landmark: the Turtle Bay Resort.

As you approach the town of Lāʻie, there is a long stretch of pine trees on the makai side. Look for the entrance to Mālaekahana State Park; on the mauka side is the sprawling **Polynesian Cultural Center** ㊾.

As you continue driving along the shoreline, notice the picturesque little island of Mokoliʻi ("little lizard"), a 206-foot-high sea stack. According to Hawaiian legend, the goddess Hiʻiaka, sister of Pele, slew the dragon Mokoliʻi and flung its tail into the sea, forming the distinct islet. Other dragon body parts—in the form of rocks, of course—were scattered along the base of nearby Kualoa Ridge.

Continue straight on Kahekili Highway (Route 83) and look on your right for **Senator Fong's Plantation and Gardens** ㊿. Two miles farther on the right is the Valley of the Temples and its lovely **Byodo-In Temple** ㊉, a replica of a 900-year-old temple outside Uji, Japan.

Follow Kahekili Highway to Likelike Highway (Route 63), where you turn mauka and head back toward Honolulu through the Wilson Tunnel. The highway leads to Lunalilo Freeway going east. Exit at Pali Highway and go south through Downtown Honolulu on Bishop Street. Then turn left on Ala Moana Boulevard, which leads to Kalākaua Avenue in Waikīkī.

TIMING   Unless you don't plan on stopping at any of the sights, allot nothing less than a day to circle the island. Try to factor in two or three different excursions and time-outs along this scenic North Shore. Don't rush through the Polynesian Cultural Center; instead, devote an afternoon and evening to the center, perhaps stopping first for a morning at Waimea Valley. Note that the center is closed Sunday.

On another day, allow a full afternoon for the Bishop Museum. Inquire also about the "Behind the Scenes" museum tour. Afternoons, you may have to wait as long as two hours to see the USS *Arizona* Memorial. The best bet is to head out there early in the day. Security measures at all military sites are now very strict. If you are planning to visit the USS *Arizona* Memorial, the Battleship *Missouri* Memorial, or the USS *Bowfin* Memorial, be prepared to bring only your "self." No purses, backpacks, diaper bags, waist packs, camera bags, or other "items of concealment" are allowed, and locking those items in your vehicle leaves you vulnerable to local petty thieves on the lookout for rental-car targets. A baggage storage facility will hold items for $2 each while you are on tour of the Harbor. Hale'iwa deserves two hours: factor in some extra North Shore time for hiking, relaxing on a beach, kayaking, taking a glider ride, and having a snack. Wear flip-flops but bring a pair of walking shoes as well.

The weather is mercurial on the North Shore. It can be sunny and clear in Waikīkī and cloudy in the country. Bring along a light jacket, a hat, and sunscreen. Then you'll be ready for anything.

What to See

43 Battleship *Missouri* Memorial. The USS *Missouri* saw action from World War II to the Persian Gulf War, and on these decks the agreement for Japanese surrender to end World War II was signed. The famed battleship, now moored about 1,000 feet from the *Arizona*, serves as a museum and interactive educational center. Tours start at the visitor center located between the USS *Arizona* Memorial and the U.S.S. *Bowfin* Memorial. A trolley transports you to the navy's Ford Island, where you can board the "Mighty Mo," take a tour, and see how 2,400 sailors lived and worked together in the shadow of its 16-inch guns. Tours range from a deluxe "Captain's Tour" to a behind-the-scenes "Explorer Tour" that explores the battleship's fire and machinery rooms. Come dressed in attire suitable for climbing up and down the ship's ladders. ⊠ *Pearl Harbor* ☎ *808/423–2263 or 888/877–6477* ⊕ *www.ussmissouri.com* ⊠ *$16 general admission, guided tours $22–$49* ⊙ *Daily 9–5.*

▶ **41 Bishop Museum.** Founded in 1889 by Charles R. Bishop as a memorial to his wife, Princess Bernice Pauahi, the museum began as a repository for the royal possessions of this last direct descendant of King Kamehameha the Great. Today it is the Hawai'i State Museum of Natural and Cultural History and houses more than 24.7 million items that tell the history of the Hawaiian Islands and their Pacific neighbors. The Hawaiian Hall houses world-famous displays of Polynesian artifacts: lustrous feather capes, the skeleton of a giant sperm whale, photography and crafts displays, and an authentic, well-preserved grass house inside a two-story 19th-century Victorian style gallery. Also check out the planetarium, daily hula and Hawaiian crafts demonstrations, special exhibits, and the Shop Pacifica. The building alone, with its huge Victorian turrets and immense stone walls, is worth seeing. ⊠ *1525 Bernice St.* ☎ *808/847–3511* ⊕ *www.bishopmuseum.org* ⊠ *$14.95* ⊙ *Daily 9–5.*

51 **Byodo-In Temple.** Tucked away in the back of the Valley of the Temples cemetery is a replica of the 11th-century Temple at Uji in Japan. A 2-ton carved wooden statue of the Buddha presides inside the main temple building. Next to the temple building are a meditation house and gardens set dramatically against the sheer, green cliffs of the Koʻolau Mountains. You can ring the 5-foot, 3-ton brass bell for good luck and feed some 10,000 carp that inhabit the garden's 2-acre pond. ⊠ *47-200 Kahekili Hwy., Kāneʻohe* ☎ *808/239–8811* ⊠ *$2* ⊙ *Daily 8:30–4:30.*

45 **Dole Pineapple Pavilion.** Celebrate Hawaiʻi's famous golden fruit at this promotional, tourist-oriented center with exhibits, a huge gift shop, a snack concession, educational displays, and the world's largest maze. Although much more sophisticated than its original 1950 fruit stand, the Pavilion is filled with souvenir options galore, and kids love the 1.7-mi Pineapple Garden Maze, which is made up of 11,400 tropical plants and trees. Take a self-guided Garden Tour or hop aboard the Pineapple Express for a 20-minute train tour to learn a bit about life on a pineapple plantation. ⊠ *64-1550 Kamehameha Hwy.* ☎ *808/621–8408* ⊕ *www.dole-plantation. com* ⊠ *Pavilion free, maze $5, train $3.50* ⊙ *Daily 9–5.*

46 **Haleʻiwa.** During the 1920s this seaside hamlet was a trendy retreat at the end of a railroad line. During the 1960s hippies gathered here, followed by surfers. Today Haleʻiwa is a fun mix, with old general stores and contemporary boutiques, galleries, and eateries. Be sure to stop in at **Liliʻuokalani Protestant Church,** founded by missionaries in the 1830s. It's fronted by a large, stone archway built in 1910 and covered with night-blooming cereus. ⊠ *Follow H-1 west from Honolulu to H-2 north, exit at Wahiawā, follow Kamehameha Hwy. 6 mi, turn left at signaled intersection, then right into Haleʻiwa* ⊕ *www. haleiwamainstreet.com.*

need a break? For a real slice of Haleʻiwa life, stop at **Matsumoto's** (⊠ 66-087 Kamehameha Hwy. ⊕ www.matsumotoshaveice.com), a family-run business in a building dating from 1910, for shave ice in every flavor imaginable. For something different, order a shave ice with adzuki beans—the red beans are boiled until soft, mixed with sugar, and then placed in the cone with the ice on top.

44 **Hawaiʻi's Plantation Village.** Starting in the 1800s, immigrants came to these islands like so many waves against the shore. Tour authentically furnished buildings, both original and replicated, that re-create and pay tribute to Hawaiʻi's sugar plantation era. See a Chinese social hall; a Japanese shrine, sumo ring, and saimin stand; a dental office; and historic homes at this "living museum" 30 minutes from Downtown Honolulu. ⊠ *Waipahu Cultural Gardens Park, 94-695 Waipahu St., Waipahu* ☎ *808/677–0110* ⊕ *www.hawaiiplantationvillage.org* 🖾 *$10* ⊙ *Weekdays 9–3, Sat. 10–3, with guided tours on the hour.*

㊷ Moanalua Gardens. This lovely park is the site of the internationally acclaimed Prince Lot Hula Festival on the third weekend in July. Throughout the year, the Moanalua Gardens Foundation sponsors 3-mi guided walks into Kamananui Valley, usually on Sundays; call for specific times. Self-guided tour booklets ($5) are also available from the Moanalua Gardens Foundation office. ⊠ *1352 Pineapple Pl., Honolulu* ☎ *808/839–5334* ⊕ *www.mgf-hawaii.com* 🖾 *Free, guided hikes $5* ⊙ *Weekdays 8–4:30.*

⟳ ㊾ Polynesian Cultural Center. Re-created, individual villages showcase the lifestyles and traditions of Hawai'i, Tahiti, Samoa, Fiji, the Marquesas Islands, New Zealand, and Tonga. This 45-acre center, 35 mi from Waikīkī, was founded in 1963 by the Church of Jesus Christ of Latter-day Saints. It houses restaurants, hosts lū'aus, and demonstrates cultural traditions such as tribal tattooing, fire dancing, and ancient customs and ceremonies. The expansive open-air shopping village carries Polynesian handicrafts. If you're staying in Honolulu, see the center as part of a van tour so you won't have to drive home late at night after the two-hour evening show. Various packages are available, from basic admission to an all-inclusive deal. ⊠ *55-370 Kamehameha Hwy., Lā'ie* ☎ *808/ 293–3333 or 800/367–7060* ⊕ *www.polynesia.com* 🖾 *$49–$189* ⊙ *Mon.–Sat. 12:30–9:30.*

㊽ Pu'uomahuka Heiau. Worth a stop for its spectacular views from a bluff high above the ocean overlooking Waimea Bay, this sacred spot was once the site of human sacrifices. It's now on the National Register of Historic Places. ⊠ *½ mi north of Waimea Bay on Rte. 83, turn right on Pūpūkea Rd. and drive 1 mi uphill.*

㊿ Senator Fong's Plantation and Gardens. Hiram Fong, the first Asian-American to be elected to Congress, shares his love of Hawaiian flora and fauna by allowing tours of his 700-acre plantation estate. A 45-minute guided tram tour takes you through the estate's five lush valleys, each named for a U.S. president that Fong served under during his 17-year tenure in the Senate. The visitor center has a snack bar and gift shop. ⊠ *47-285 Pūlama Rd., off Kahekili Hwy., 2 mi north of Byodo-In Temple, Kahalu'u* ☎ *808/239–6775* ⊕ *www.fonggarden.net* 🖾 *$10* ⊙ *Tram tours daily 10–4.*

㊸ USS *Arizona* Memorial. A simple, gleaming white structure shields the hulk of the USS *Arizona*, which sank with 1,102 men aboard when the Japanese attacked Pearl Harbor on December 7, 1941. The tour includes a 23-minute documentary with actual news footage from the day of the attack and a shuttle-boat ride to the memorial. Appropriate dress is required (no bathing suits, slippers, or bare feet). ⊠ *National Park Service, Pearl Harbor* ☎ *808/422–0561 or 808/423–2263* ⊕ *www.nps.gov/ usar* 🖾 *Free* ☞ *Tour tickets distributed on a first-come, first-served basis, with 1- to 3-hr waits common; arrive early, tickets are sometimes gone by noon.* ⊙ *Daily 8–3.*

○ ㊼ **Waimea Valley Audubon Center.** You can see the remnants of an early Hawaiian civilization in this valley which is being restored to its natural habitat. This 1,800-acre center is home to 6,000 species of tropical flora and fauna. There are plenty of birds for watching, paths for strolling, and trails for hiking. Picnic in the vicinity of the 45-foot Waihe'e Falls, take a peek at the remains of the Hale O Lono Temple along with other ancient archeological sites and botanical gardens. ✉ *59-864 Kamehameha Hwy., Hale'iwa* ☎ *808/638–9199* 🖉 *$8* ⊙ *Daily 9:30–5.*

┌─────────┐
│ off the │
│ beaten │
│ path   │
└─────────┘

USS *Bowfin* Memorial – Moored near the USS *Arizona* Memorial visitor center, the *Bowfin* is one of only 15 World War II subs still in existence. Dubbed the "Pearl Harbor Avenger," the sub saw nine successful war patrols and is credited with sinking 44 enemy ships while in service. Go aboard and see what life was like for its 80-member crew. Children under four are not admitted. ✉ *11 Arizona Memorial Dr., at Pearl Harbor* ☎ *808/423–1342* ⊕ *www.bowfin. org* 🖉 *$8* ⊙ *Daily 8–4:30.*

BEACHES

For South Seas sun, fun, and surf, O'ahu is a dream destination, but first some words of caution: when approaching any Hawaiian beach, heed signs indicating current surf conditions. If they warn of dangerous surf or currents, pay attention. Most beaches have lifeguards, although two exceptions are Kahana and Mālaekahana. Waikīkī is only 21 degrees north of the equator, so the sun here is very strong. No alcoholic beverages are allowed, and no matter which beach you choose, lock your car and never, ever leave your valuables unattended.

Waikīkī Beaches

The 2½-mi strand called Waikīkī Beach actually extends from Hilton Hawaiian Village on one end to Kapi'olani Park and Diamond Head on the other. Areas along this sandy strip have separate names but subtle differences. Beach areas are listed here from west to east.

Kahanamoku Beach. Named for Hawai'i's famous Olympic swimming champion, Duke Kahanamoku, this beach has decent snorkeling and swimming and a gentle surf. Its sandy bottom slopes gradually. The area has a snack concession, showers, a beach-gear and surfboard rental shop, catamaran cruises, and a sand volleyball court. ✉ *In front of Hilton Hawaiian Village Beach Resort and Spa.*

★ **Ft. DeRussy Beach.** Sunbathers, swimmers, and windsurfers enjoy this beach, one of the widest in Waikīkī, fronting the military hotel, the Hale Koa, and the U.S. Army Museum. It trails off to a coral ocean bottom with fairly good snorkeling. There are volleyball courts, food stands, picnic tables, dressing rooms, and showers. ✉ *In front of Fort DeRussy and Hale Koa Hotel.*

Gray's Beach. Named for a little lodging house called Gray's-by-the-Sea, which stood here in the 1920s, this beach is known for two good surf-

CloseUp
TIE THE KNOT WITH AN ISLAND TWIST

S **O MANY COUPLES** *have gotten married in Hawai`i that an island wedding is starting to become a cliché. However, there's no shortage of reasons to get married in paradise—just think of all the money you'll save if you get hitched in swimsuits—and no matter what your budget or style, you can say your "I dos" on any one of Hawai`i's islands.*

First off, you'll need to take care of the legalities. Hawai`i state law is fairly forgiving: there are no state-residence or U.S.-citizenship requirements, nor is blood work required. However, both parties must be at least 18 years of age to apply for a marriage license, and proof of age is required—18-year-olds must present a certified copy of a birth certificate; those 19 and older may present a valid ID or driver's license. The State does not issue licenses for same-sex couples.

The prospective bride and groom must appear together before a marriage license agent to apply. The license is issued at the time of application, granted you've been approved and have forked over the $60 fee (bring cash). The license is good within the state of Hawai`i for up to 30 days.

You can apply for a marriage license through the State Department of Health (O`ahu: ⊠ Room 101, 1250 Punchbowl St., Honolulu ☎ 808/586–4544 ⊠ Big Island: ⊠ State Office Building, 75 Aupuni St., Hilo ☎ 808/974–6008 ⊠ Kaua`i: ⊠ 3040 Umi St., Lihue ☎ 808/241–3498 ⊠ Maui: ⊠ State Building, 54 High St., Wailuku ☎ 808/984–8210 for Maui, 808/565–6411 for Lana`i, 808/553–3663 for Moloka`i). The Honolulu office is open weekdays 8–4.

The actual planning of your big day can be just as involved and unromantic as it is on the mainland, and Hawai`i has no shortage of professional wedding planners. The Hawai`i Visitors & Convention Bureau has a wedding and honeymoon registry that will assist with information on everything from finding a location to hiring the caterer and photographer. To register, go to the HVCB Web site at www.gohawaii.com and click on Weddings and Honeymoons. At your request, they can put you in touch with reliable freelance planners. Keep in mind that though there are high-priced planners at all the ritzy resorts, a simple yet memorable outdoor ceremony can be arranged for a few hundred dollars. Don't forget leis for the bride and groom, and be sure to ask the person presiding over the ceremony to give a special blessing in Hawaiian.

Believe it or not, the Hawaiian language has no word for "romance." Instead, islanders live in the spirit of it. Hawai`i is a destination where you can recite your vows at sunset or sunrise, on beaches, on lava rock, on a golf course, or even underwater. Can you imagine a better beginning for the rest of your life?

ing spots called Paradise and Number Threes just beyond its reef. High tides often cover the narrow beach. ⊠ *In front of Halekūlani.*

★ **Kahaloa and Ulukou Beaches.** Possibly the best swimming and lots of activities are available along this little stretch of Waikīkī Beach. Take a catamaran or outrigger canoe ride out into the bay, unless you're ready to try your skill at surfing. ⊠ *In front of Royal Hawaiian Hotel and Sheraton Moana Surfrider.*

Kūhiō Beach Park. This beach is a hot spot for shoreline and beach ac-
Fodor'sChoice   tivities. Check out the Kūhiō Beach stage nightly at 6:30 for free hula
★   and Hawaiian-music performances; weekends there's a torch-lighting ceremony at sunset as well. Surf lessons for beginners are available from the beach center here every half hour. ⊠ *Past the Sheraton Moana Surfrider Hotel to Kapahulu Ave. pier.*

Queen's Surf. A great place for a sunset picnic, this beach is beyond the seawall, toward Diamond Head, at what's known as the "other end of Waikīkī." It was once the site of Queen Lili'uokalani's beach house. A mix of families and gay couples gathers here, and it seems as if someone is always playing a steel drum. There are good shade trees, picnic tables, and a changing house with showers. ⊠ *Across from entrance to Honolulu Zoo.*

Sans Souci. Nicknamed Dig-Me Beach because of its outlandish display of skimpy bathing suits, this small rectangle of sand is nonetheless a good sunning spot for all ages. Children enjoy its shallow, safe waters, and the shore draws many ocean kayakers and outrigger canoeists. Serious swimmers and triathletes also swim in the channel here, beyond the reef. There's no food concession, but near one end is the Hau Tree Lānai restaurant. ⊠ *Makai side of Kapi'olani Park, between New Otani Kaimana Beach Hotel and Waikīkī War Memorial Natatorium.*

Diamond Head Beach. This narrow strip of beach is not good for swimmers due to the reef just offshore, but it's still a great spot for watching windsurfers and wave boarders strut their skills across the water. Parking is located on Diamond Head Road, just past the Diamond Head Lighthouse. From the parking area, look for an opening in the makai wall where an unpaved trail leads down to the beach.

Beaches Around O'ahu

Hanauma Bay Nature Preserve. The main attraction here is snorkeling.
Fodor'sChoice   The coral reefs are clearly visible through the turquoise waters of this
★   sunken volcanic crater half open to the ocean. It is a designated marine preserve and features a marine-life education center for visitors. Visitors must watch a 9-minute video about the preserve before being allowed down to the bay. Although the fish are the tamest you'll view while snorkeling, feeding them is not allowed. The bay is best early in the morning (around 7), before the crowds arrive. It can be difficult to park later in the day. There are changing rooms, showers, and a busy food and snorkel-equipment concession. No smoking is allowed, and the beach is closed on Tuesday. **Hanauma Bay Dive Tours** runs snorkeling, SNUBA, and scuba tours to Hanauma Bay with transportation from Waikīkī hotels. (☎ 808/256–8956) ⊠ *7455 Kalaniana'ole Hwy.* ☎ *808/396–4229* ⌨ *Donation $5; parking $1; mask,*

snorkel, and fins rental $8; tram from parking lot down to beach $1.50 ⊙ *Wed.–Mon. 6–7.*

Sandy Beach. Strong, steady winds make "Sandy's" a kite-flyer's paradise. There's a changing house with indoor and outdoor showers but no food concessions. Unless you are an expert at navigating rip currents and very shallow shore breaks, this beach is dangerous for the casual swimmer—more neck and spine injuries occur here than anywhere else on the island. ⊠ *Makai of Kalaniana'ole Hwy., 2 mi east of Hanauma Bay.*

Makapu'u Beach. Swimming at Makapu'u should be attempted only by strong swimmers and bodysurfers because the swells can be overwhelmingly big and powerful. Instead, consider this tiny crescent cove—popular with locals—as a prime sunbathing spot. Finding parking in the small lot can be tricky. In a pinch, try parking on the narrow shoulder and walking down to the beach. There is a changing house with indoor and outdoor showers. ⊠ *Makai of Kalaniana'ole Hwy., across from Sea Life Park, 2 mi south of Waimānalo.*

★ **Waimānalo Beach Park.** This is a "local" beach busy with picnicking families and active sports fields. Sometimes folks are not very friendly to tourists here, and there have been some incidents of car theft, but the beach itself is one of the island's most beautiful. Expect a wide stretch of sand; turquoise, emerald, and deep-blue seas; and waves full of boogie boarders. ⊠ *Windward side; look for signs makai of Kalaniana'ole Hwy., south of Waimānalo town.*

Bellows Beach. The waves here are great for bodysurfing. Locals come for the fine swimming on weekends and holidays, when the Air Force opens the beach to civilians. There are showers, abundant parking, and plenty of spots for picnicking underneath shady ironwood trees. There is no food concession, but McDonald's and other take-out fare is available right outside the entrance gate. ⊠ *Entrance on Kalaniana'ole Hwy. near Waimānalo town center; signs on makai side of road.*

Kailua Beach Park. Steady breezes attract windsurfers by the dozens to this long, palm-fringed beach with gently sloping sands. You can rent equipment in Kailua and try it yourself. This is a local favorite, so if you want the beach to yourself, head here on a weekday. There are showers, changing rooms, picnic areas, and a concession stand. Buy your picnic provisions at the Kalapawai Market nearby. ⊠ *Windward side, makai of Kailua town; turn right on Kailua Rd. at market, cross bridge, then turn left into beach parking lot.*

Fodor'sChoice **Lanikai Beach Park.** A mile of buttery sand ideal for a stroll, this beach ★ fronts some of the most expensive real estate on the windward side. When the trade winds are active, look for windsurfers. Early birds can watch some spectacular sunrises. ⊠ *Windward side, past Kailua Beach Park; street parking on Mokulua Dr. for various public access points to beach.*

Kahana Bay Beach Park. Local parents often bring their children to wade in safety at this pretty beach cove with very shallow, protected waters. A grove of tall ironwood and pandanus trees keeps the area cool, shady, and ideal for a picnic. An ancient Hawaiian fishpond, which was in use until the '20s, is visible nearby. There are changing houses, showers, and picnic tables. ⊠ *Windward side of island, makai of Kamehameha Hwy., north of Kualoa Park.*

Kualoa Regional Park. This is one of the island's most beautiful picnic, camping, and beach areas. Grassy expanses border a long, narrow stretch of beach with spectacular views of Kāneʻohe Bay and the Koʻolau Mountains. Dominating the view is an islet called Mokoliʻi, which rises 206 feet above the water. You can swim in the shallow areas year-round. The one drawback is that it's usually windy. Refreshments are not sold here so bring a cooler. There are places to shower, change, and picnic in the shade of palm trees. ☒ *Windward side, makai of Kamehameha Hwy., north of Waiāhole.*

Mālaekahana Beach Park. The big attraction here is tiny Goat Island, a bird sanctuary just offshore. At low tide the water is shallow enough—never more than waist high—so that you can wade out to it. Wear sneakers so you don't cut yourself on the coral. Families love to camp in the groves of ironwood trees at Mālaekahana State Park. The beach itself is fairly narrow but long enough for a 20-minute stroll, one-way. The waves are never too big, and sometimes they're just right for the beginning bodysurfer. There are changing houses, showers, and picnic tables. Note that the entrance gates are easy to miss because you can't see the beach from the road. ☒ *Windward side; entrance gates are makai of Kamehameha Hwy., ½ mi north of Lāʻie.*

Sunset Beach. This is one link in the chain of North Shore beaches that extends for miles. It's popular for its gentle summer waves and crashing winter surf. The beach is broad, and the sand is soft. Lining the adjacent highway there are usually carryout truck stands selling shaved ice, plate lunches, and sodas. ☒ *North Shore, 1 mi north of ʻEhukai Beach Park on makai side of Kamehameha Hwy.*

ʻEhukai Beach Park. ʻEhukai is part of a series of beaches running for many miles along the North Shore. What sets it apart is the view of the famous Banzai Pipeline, where the waves curl into magnificent tubes, making it an experienced wave-rider's dream. In spring and summer, the waves are more accommodating to the average swimmer. The long, wide, and generally uncrowded beach has a changing house with toilets and an outdoor shower. Bring along drinks; the nearest store is a mile away. ☒ *North Shore, 1 mi north of Foodland store at Pūpūkea, turn makai off Kamehameha Hwy. directly into the small parking lot bordering highway.*

★ **Waimea Bay.** Made popular in that old Beach Boys song "Surfin' U.S.A.," Waimea Bay is a slice of hang-ten heaven and home to the king-size 25- to 30-foot winter waves. Summer is the time to swim and snorkel in the calm waters. The beach is a broad crescent of soft sand backed by a shady area with tables, a changing house, and showers. Parking is almost impossible in the lot on weekends, so folks just park along the road and walk down. ☒ *North Shore across from Waimea Valley, 3 mi north of Haleʻiwa on makai side of Kamehameha Hwy.*

Haleʻiwa Aliʻi Beach Park. The winter waves are impressive here, but in summer the ocean is like a lake, ideal for family swimming. The beach itself is big and often full of locals. Its broad lawns off the highway invite volleyball and Frisbee games and groups of barbecuers. There is a changing house with showers but no food concessions. Haleʻiwa has everything you need for provisions. ☒ *North Shore, makai side of Kamehameha Hwy., north of Haleʻiwa town center and past harbor.*

Yokohama Bay. You'll be one of the few outsiders at this Wai'anae Coast beach at the very end of the road. It feels and looks remote and untouched, which may explain the lack of crowds. Locals come here to fish and swim in waters that are calm enough for children in summer. The beach is narrow and rocky in places. Bring provisions, because the nearest town is a 15-minute drive away. There are showers and a changing house, plus a small parking lot, but most folks just pull over and park on the side of the bumpy road. ⊠ *Wai'anae Coast, northern end of Farrington Hwy. about 7 mi north of Mākaha.*

Mākaha Beach Park. This beach provides a slice of local life most visitors don't see. Families string up tarps for the day, fire up hibachis, set up lawn chairs, get out the fishing gear, and strum 'ukuleles while they "talk story" (chat). The swimming is generally decent in the summer, but avoid the big winter waves. This was home to the island's first professional surf meet, in 1952. The ¼-mi beach has a changing house and showers and is the site of a yearly big-board surf meet. ⊠ *Wai'anae Coast, 1½ hrs west of Honolulu on H-1 Fwy. and Farrington Hwy., makai side of hwy.*

🐾 ★ **Ala Moana Beach Park.** Ala Moana has a protective reef, which keeps the waters calm and perfect for swimming. After Waikīkī, this is the most popular beach among visitors. To the Waikīkī side is a peninsula called Magic Island, with picnic tables, shady trees, and paved sidewalks ideal for jogging. Ala Moana also has playing fields, changing houses, indoor and outdoor showers, lifeguards, concession stands, and tennis courts. This beach is for everyone, but only in the daytime. It's a high-crime area after dark. ⊠ *Honolulu, makai side of Ala Moana Shopping Center and Ala Moana Blvd.; from Waikīkī take Bus 8 to shopping center and cross Ala Moana Blvd.*

WHERE TO EAT

If you're looking for a meal with a view, explore the restaurants at the upscale hotels and resorts that line O'ahu's shores. Settings can be as casual as a "barefoot bar" or as elegant as a romantic dinner for two under the stars. Beyond Waikīkī are culinary jewels tucked away in shopping centers and residential neighborhoods that specialize in ethnic cuisines. You'll almost never go wrong if you sample the offerings at any establishment whose name ends in the words "Drive Inn." Here you will find the local grinds, which are the staples of the Hawaiian diet: seafood plate lunches and noodle saimin. For snacks and fast food around the island, look for the lunch wagons, usually parked roadside near the beaches.

Waikīkī

Chinese

$$–$$$$ ✕ **Golden Dragon.** You can't beat the view at this restaurant set by a lagoon. On the menu are nearly 65 à la carte dishes and four six-course dinner menus of fine Cantonese, Szechuan, and nouvelle-Chinese dishes prepared by chef Steve Chiang. Two of the house specialties—the Imperial Peking duck and Imperial beggar's chicken (whole chicken wrapped in lotus leaves and baked in a clay pot)—must be ordered 24 hours in advance. To begin your meal, try the fresh scallop soup; end with a dessert of litchi or green-tea ice cream. ⊠ *Hilton Hawaiian Village, 2005 Kālia Rd., Waikīkī* ☎ *808/946–5336* ⌂ *Reservations essential* ▭ *AE, D, DC, MC, V* ⊙ *No lunch.*

Contemporary

$$$–$$$$ ✕ **Hau Tree Lānai.** At breakfast, lunch, or dinner you can eat under graceful *hau* trees, so close to Kaimana Beach you can hear the whisper of the waves. Breakfast offerings include a huge helping of eggs Benedict, poi pancakes, and a delicious salmon omelet. For dinner, try the moonfish, snapper, seafood mixed grill with a Thai chili sauce, or the popular sesame-crusted hoisin rack of lamb. Every first and third Sunday, the restaurant offers an "East Meets West" brunch buffet in partnership with the hotel's Miyako restaurant. ⊠ *New Otani Kaimana Beach Hotel, 2863 Kalākaua Ave., Waikīkī* ☎ *808/921–7066* ⊕ *www.kaimana. com* ⌂ *Reservations essential* ▭ *AE, D, DC, MC, V.*

★ **$$–$$$$** ✕ **Bali by the Sea.** In the Hilton Hawaiian Village, this restaurant is breeze-swept, with an oceanside setting offering glorious views of Waikīkī Beach. The menu is a blend of French and Asian influences, with starters like Kula onion–and–ginger soup. Signature dishes include scallion crusted 'ahi tempura and poached Kona lobster. Another favorite is the roasted-beet salad with caramelized macadamia nuts and goat cheese. Toast the view with a dessert of fresh strawberry champagne soup flavored with mint and macadamia nut ice cream. ⊠ *Hilton Hawaiian Village, 2005 Kālia Rd., Waikīkī* ☎ *808/941–2254* ⌂ *Reservations essential* ▭ *AE, D, DC, MC, V* ⊙ *No dinner Sun.*

$$–$$$ ✕ **Ocean House Restaurant.** Guests are greeted on the front porch at this re-creation of a 1900s plantation home. Tables and booths are spaced for views and covered in rich tropical fabrics. The menu puts forth the bounty of the Pacific with such dishes as coconut lobster skewers, seared peppered scallops, and macadamia nut–crusted sea bass. For beef lovers, there is the slow-roasted prime rib. ⊠ *Outrigger Reef on the Beach hotel, 2169 Kālia Rd., Waikīkī* ☎ *808/923–2277* ▭ *AE, D, DC, MC, V.*

$–$$$ ✕ **Tiki's Grill and Bar.** If you are looking for Hawaiian kitsch, look no further than Tiki's Grill and Bar—you won't find a more fitting tribute to the tiki bars of the '50s and '60s in the rest of Waikīkī. Dishes include salmon glazed with *togarashi*-spiced cane sugar (togarashi is a small, hot, red Japanese chili), Asian vegetable linguine, and Tiki's cheeseburgers topped with fresh Hauula tomatoes. Leave a little room for some tropical libations at the Volcano Bar. Outdoor seating gives requisite views of Waikīkī Beach. ⊠ *Aston Waikīkī Beach Hotel, 2570 Kalākaua Ave., Waikīkī* ☎ *808/923–8454* ▭ *AE, D, DC, MC, V.*

★ **$$** ✕ **Duke's Canoe Club.** This casual beachfront eatery, named after Hawai'i's famous surfer Duke Kahanamoku, is usually crowded (reserve ahead or you'll probably have to wait for a table). Lunchtime is lively, and on the weekend the restaurant hosts sunset concerts on the beach on its outdoor terrace. Fish can be served up Duke's style: baked in a garlic, lemon, and sweet basil glaze to keep it tender and moist. Other Duke's specialties include macadamia-and-crab wontons, seafood coconut curry, mango barbecue ribs, and the decadent Hula Pie. ⊠ *Outrigger Waikīkī on the*

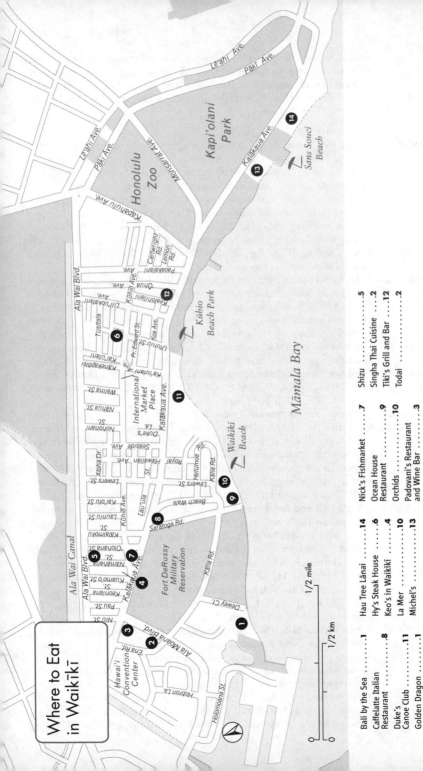

Where to Eat in Waikīkī

Bali by the Sea 1
Caffelatte Italian
Restaurant 8
Duke's
Canoe Club 11
Golden Dragon 1

Hau Tree Lānai 14
Hy's Steak House 6
Keo's in Waikīkī 4
La Mer 10
Michel's 13

Nick's Fishmarket 7
Ocean House
Restaurant 9
Orchids 10
Padovani's Restaurant
and Wine Bar 3

Shizu 5
Singha Thai Cuisine 2
Tiki's Grill and Bar 12
Todai 2

Beach, 2335 Kalākaua Ave., Waikīkī ☎ 808/922–2268 ⊕ www.hulapie. com 🖃 AE, D, DC, MC, V.

French

★ $$$$ ✕ **Padovani's Restaurant and Wine Bar.** Philippe Padovani first gained fame at three top Hawai'i hotels (the Halekūlani, Ritz-Carlton, and Mānele Bay) before opening this hideaway inside the Doubletree Alana Waikīkī. Chef's specialties include the salmon confit in extra-virgin olive oil and lemongrass broth, and a roasted quail stuffed with mushrooms and sausage. Dessert lovers will savor the ginger crème brûlée and the coconut tapioca pudding tropical fruit with raspberry coulis. The dining room has rich gold accents against polished wood. An upstairs wine bar offers 550 different wines and 64 varietals by the glass, single-malt Scotch, a lighter menu, entertainment on weekend evenings, and an enclosed cigar room. ⊠ Doubletree Alana Waikīkī, 1956 Ala Moana Blvd., Waikīkī ☎ 808/946–3456 ⟨ Reservations essential 🖃 AE, D, DC, MC, V.

★ $$$–$$$$ ✕ **La Mer.** In the exotic, oceanfront atmosphere of a Mandalay mansion, you'll be served neoclassic French cuisine that many consider to be the finest in Hawai'i. Here, on the grounds of the Halekūlani hotel, is a room—open to the ocean, and with sweeping views of Diamond Head—as luscious as its menu. French-born chef Yves Garner presides over a menu that includes Hamachi medallions covered with pistachio nuts, roasted Scottish salmon and salmon tartare, and bouillabaisse La Mer–style in a puff pastry. The perfect ending is a symphony of La Mer desserts. ⊠ Halekūlani, 2199 Kālia Rd., Waikīkī ☎ 808/923–2311 ⟨ Reservations essential 🏛 Jacket required 🖃 AE, MC, V ☺ No lunch.

★ $$$ $$$$ ✕ **Michel's.** Back in the splendor of the sweeping oceanfront view in this dining room that is as romantic as it is elegant. Michel's has its roots in traditional French cuisine and at its heart a fusion of island influences. On the menu is Kona lobster steamed in sake, steak tartare, and sautéed abalone with spaghetti squash. Michel's Sunday brunches are sumptuous, with grilled salmon steaks, Maine lobster and bay shrimp salad, along with the classic eggs Benedict. ⊠ 2895 Kalākaua Ave. ☎ 808/923–6552 ⟨ Reservations essential 🖃 AE, D, DC, MC, V.

Italian

$$$$ ✕ **Caffelatte Italian Restaurant.** Every dish at this tiny trattoria run by a Milanese family is worth ordering, from the gnocchi in a thick, rich sauce of Gorgonzola to spinach ravioli served with butter and basil. The tiramisu is the best in town and the sugared orange slices in Russian vodka are a perfect ending to a meal. There's limited seating inside and a few tables outside on the narrow lānai. Be aware that each person must order three courses (appetizer, main course, and dessert). The chef will prepare a special mystery dinner for two for $60. There's no parking, so walk here if you can. ⊠ 339 Saratoga Rd., 2nd level, Waikīkī ☎ 808/924–1414 🖃 AE, DC, MC, V ☺ Closed Tues.

Japanese

$$–$$$$ ✕ **Shizu.** Sample the Japanese cooking styles of teishoku (traditional preparation of fish, rice, soup, and more, served in lacquer bowls) and tableside teppanyaki in a contemporary setting overlooking a Zen-style rock gar-

den. The two teppanyaki rooms have vibrant stained-glass windows with vibrant irises. Here, diners sit around a massive iron grill on which a dexterous chef slices and cooks sizzling meats and vegetables. At dinner, there is an "all you can eat" shabu shabu and sukiyaki special. Try green-tea cheesecake for dessert. ⊠ *Royal Garden at Waikīkī, 440 ʻOlohana St., 4th fl., Waikīkī* ☎ *808/943–0202* ▤ *AE, D, DC, MC, V.*

Seafood

★ **$$$–$$$$** ✕ **Nick's Fishmarket.** The decor is a little dark and retro, with black booths, candlelight, and formal table settings. But here you can indulge in Beluga caviar, Norwegian salmon marinated in sake and honey, and a sumptuous sourdough lobster bisque. In addition, this is one of the few places with abalone on the menu; it's sautéed and served with lobster risotto. Leave room for Vanbana Pie, a decadent combination of bananas, vanilla Swiss-almond ice cream, and hot caramel sauce. ⊠ *Waikīkī Gateway Hotel, 2070 Kalākaua Ave., Waikīkī* ☎ *808/955–6333* ⌖ *Reservations essential* ▤ *AE, D, DC, MC, V.*

$$$–$$$$ ✕ **Orchids.** It seems only fitting that you can hear the waves from this
Fodor'sChoice orchid-filled dining room that lays out the best seafood bar in town, in-
★ cluding sashimi, *poke* (marinated raw fish), and Pacific-crab salad with fresh mango. Try the Madras seafood curry or the miso–marinated sea bass. Poultry dishes include a Peking spiced Muscovy duck breast and tandoori-roasted island chicken. Outdoor and indoor seating is available, with the best views from the lānai. ⊠ *Halekūlani, 2199 Kālia Rd., Waikīkī* ☎ *808/923–2311* ⌖ *Reservations essential* ▤ *AE, MC, V.*

★ **$$$** ✕ **Todai.** Long on seafood and short on decor, this restaurant is a hit with both local residents and tourists alike. Todai has a 180-foot seafood buffet with 40 different kinds of sushi that include salmon skin, sea urchin, eel, and spicy tuna. You'll also find lobster, shrimp tempura, Alaskan snow crab, salad, barbecued ribs, and much more on the buffet. Save room for a Tokyo crepe stuffed with fresh fruit and chocolate filling and topped with whipped cream, or the green-tea cheesecake. ⊠ *1910 Ala Moana Blvd., Waikīkī* ☎ *808/947–1000* ⌖ *Reservations essential* ▤ *AE, D, DC, MC, V.*

Steak

$$$–$$$$ ✕ **Hy's Steak House.** Like most other upscale steak houses, this place has a classic private-club ambience—it's snug and library-like, and the service is outstanding. You can watch the chef perform behind glass. Hy's is famous for its kiawe-broiled New York strip steak, beef Wellington, cold-water lobster tail, and rack of lamb. The Caesar salad is excellent, as are the panfried potatoes. For a final flair, try the flambéed bananas Foster. ⊠ *Waikīkī Park Heights Hotel, 2440 Kūhiō Ave., Waikīkī* ☎ *808/922–5555* ⌖ *Reservations essential* ▤ *AE, DC, MC, V* ✆ *No lunch.*

Thai

★ **$$–$$$** ✕ **Singha Thai Cuisine.** Dishes here are prepared in traditional Thai fashion, with just a sprinkling of Hawaiʻi regional flavorings and traditional French cooking techniques. The macadamia nut–crusted black tiger prawns, vegetarian curry dishes, and Thai chili are wonderful. Singha's beautiful Royal Thai dancers dressed in traditional costume add to the occasion, performing nightly. ⊠ *1910 Ala Moana Blvd., Waikīkī* ☎ *808/941–2898* ⌕ *Reservations essential* ▤ *AE, D, DC, MC, V* ☽ *No lunch.*

★ **$–$$** ✕ **Keo's in Waikīkī.** This twinkling little nook, with tables set amid lighted trees, big paper umbrellas, and sprays of orchids, is a favorite of visiting Hollywood celebrities. Most of the herbs, vegetables, fruits, and flowers found here are grown on owner Keo Sananikone's North Shore farm. Favorites include the Evil Jungle Prince (shrimp, vegetables, or chicken in a sauce flavored with Thai basil, coconut milk, and red chili) and the Panang shrimp and scallop. The Golden Triangle (tiger prawns wrapped in pastry) and the vegetarian crispy fried noodles are two popular appetizers. For dessert, the apple bananas in coconut milk are wonderful. ⊠ *2028 Kūhiō Ave., Waikīkī* ☎ *808/951–9355* ⌕ *Reservations essential* ▤ *AE, D, DC, MC, V* ☽ *No lunch.*

Honolulu

American/Casual

$–$$ ✕ **California Pizza Kitchen.** This duet of dining and watering hole for young fast-trackers is worth the wait for a table. The pizzas have unusual toppings, such as Thai chicken, Peking duck, and Caribbean shrimp. The pastas, like Kung Pao spaghetti, are made fresh daily. The salads come in both half and whole portions. At the Kāhala site, a glass atrium with tiled and mirrored walls and one side open to the shopping mall creates a sidewalk-café effect. The location on the top level of the Ala Moana Center offers a great respite for the weary shopper. ⊠ *Kāhala Mall, 4211 Wai'alae Ave., Kāhala* ☎ *808/737–9446* ⊠ *Ala Moana Shopping Center, 1450 Ala Moana Blvd., Ala Moana* ☎ *808/941–7715* ⌕ *Reservations not accepted* ▤ *AE, D, DC, MC, V.*

$–$$ ✕ **Hard Rock Cafe.** The Honolulu branch of this international chain has its trademark rock-and-roll memorabilia on display along with Hawaiian surfboards and aloha shirts for local flavor. Here, charbroiled burgers hold their own alongside island favorites like 'ahi-steak (yellowfin tuna–steak) sandwiches and watermelon baby-back ribs. Count on loud music, high energy, and busy weekend evenings. ⊠ *1837 Kapi'olani Blvd., Ala Moana* ☎ *808/955–7383* ⌕ *Reservations not accepted* ▤ *AE, MC, V.*

$ ✕ **Cafe Laufer.** Ten minutes from Waikīkī, this eatery is a local favorite not only for its selection of soups, sandwiches, and salads, but also for its desserts. If you have a sweet tooth, consider the linzer torte, Black Forest cake, or chocolate macadamia-nut pastries. The cafe is open until 10 most evenings for those who crave a sweet nightcap to the day. ⊠ *3565 Wai'alae Ave. Kaimuki* ☎ *808/735–7717* ⌕ *Reservations not accepted.* ▤ *AE, MC, V* ☽ *Closed Tues.*

¢–$ ✕ **L&L Drive Inn.** On Monsarrat Avenue in Waikīkī and at more than 60 neighborhood locations throughout the island, the Drive Inn serves up an impressive mix of Asian-American and Hawaiian-style plate lunches. Chicken *katsu* (cutlet), shrimp curry, and seafood mix plates include two scoops of rice and macaroni salad. There are also "mini" versions of the large-portion plates that include just one scoop of starch. It's a quick take-out place to pick up lunch before heading to the nearest beach or park. ⊠ *3045 Monsarrat Ave., Diamond Head* ☎ *808/735–1388* ⚭ *Reservations not accepted* ▭ *No credit cards.*

Barbecue

$–$$ ✕ **Dixie Grill.** This Southern-inspired eatery emphasizes just how much fun food can be. There's even an outdoor sandbox for the kids! Dixie Grill specializes in all things fried, including okra, catfish, and chicken. Also on the menu are baby-back ribs, whole Dungeness crab, and campfire steak prepared with either wet or dry-rub herb sauces. Save room for the sweet-potato pecan pie. ⊠ *404 Ward Ave., Kaka'ako* ☎ *808/ 596–8359* ▭ *AE, D, DC, MC, V.*

Chinese

¢–$ ✕ **Legends Seafood Restaurant.** When touring Chinatown, take time out to try some dim sum at Legends, where you'll hear Chinese spoken as often as English. Try the prawn dumplings and fresh vegetables, or the calamari rings with northern-Chinese spices. To top off your meal, choose the mango gelatin in the shape of a colorful carp. ⊠ *Chinese Cultural Plaza, 100 N. Beretania St., Downtown Honolulu* ☎ *808/532– 1868* ▭ *AE, D, DC, MC, V.*

Contemporary

★ $$$$ ✕ **Chef Mavro.** You can expect nothing less than the most creative of meals from chef-owner George Mavrothalassitis, a James Beard Award-winning chef, who changes the menu every six weeks. Savor Keahole lobster pot-au-feu flavored with sweet basil and braised upcountry root vegetables. For dessert, Mavro's signature *lilikoi malasadas* (passion fruit–flavored Portuguese doughnuts) are served with guava coulis and pineapple-coconut ice cream. Three prix-fixe menus of three, four, or six courses, start at $56, and include recommendations for the perfect pairing of food and wine. ⊠ *1969 S. King St., Mō'ili'ili* ☎ *808/944– 4714* ⊕ *www.chefmavro.com* ⚭ *Reservations essential* ▭ *AE, DC, MC, V* ☺ *No lunch.*

★ $$$–$$$$ ✕ **Alan Wong's.** Chef-owner Alan Wong turns local grinds into beautifully presented epicurean treats. For starters, try the Poki-Pines, crispy wonton 'ahi poke balls on avocado with wasabi sauce. Linger over Kalbi grilled *opah* with shrimp kimchee fried rice. Do dessert right, with Wong Way tiramisu: chocolate espresso *pot de crème* (custard) topped with chiffon cake layers and mascarpone cheese with Kona-coffee *granité* (sugared ice). ⊠ *McCully Court, 1857 S. King St., 3rd fl., Mō'ili'ili* ☎ *808/949–2526* ⊕ *www.alanwongs.com* ▭ *AE, MC, V* ☺ *No lunch.*

$$–$$$$
Fodor'sChoice
★
✕ **Hoku's at the Kāhala Mandarin Oriental.** With a second-story view of magnificent Kāhala Beach, this restaurant has a warmth that comes as much from its attentive staff as it does from the sun filtering in. Order from a world of choices including 'ahi sashimi on seaweed, Indian naan bread baked in a tandoori oven, and a wok-seared Maine lobster. For the vegetarian, Hoku's Rainbow of Vegetables entrée features a colorful platter of veggies that are steamed, grilled, and cooked to perfection. With 24 hours' notice, Hoku's will create a Seafood Tower of shellfish that is both an architectural and epicurean marvel. ⊠ *Kāhala Mandarin Oriental, 5000 Kāhala Ave., Kāhala* ☎ *808/739–8780* ▭ *AE, D, MC, V.*

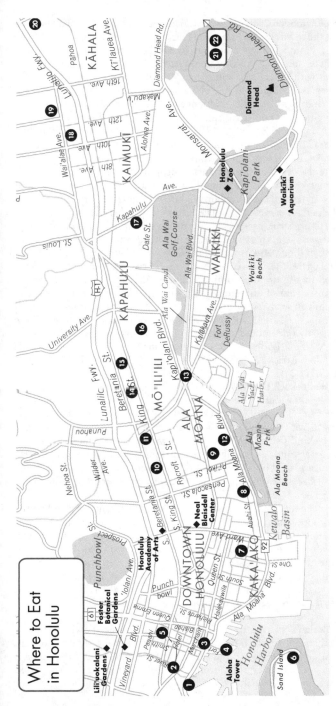

Where to Eat in Honolulu

Alan Wong's **14**
Café Laufer **18**
Cafe Sistina **10**
California
Pizza Kitchen **12, 21**
Chef Mavro **15**

Compadres
Mexican Bar and Grill . . **8**
Dixie Grill **7**
Gordon Biersch
Brewery Restaurant . . . **4**
Hard Rock Cafe **13**

Hoku's at the Kahala
Mandarin Oriental . . . **22**
Indigo
Euroasian Cuisine **2**
Kaka'ako Kitchen **8**
La Mariara **6**

L & L Drive Inn **20**
Legends Seafood
Restaurant **5**
L'Uraku **9**
'Ono Hawaiian Foods . **17**
Palomino **3**

Patisserie **21**
Sam Choy's Breakfast,
Lunch and Crab &
Big Aloha Brewery **1**
Sushi Sasabune **11**
3660 On The Rise . . . **19**
The Willows **16**

★ **$$–$$$** ✕ **Indigo Euroasian Cuisine.** Owner Glenn Chu sets the mood for an evening out on the town: the walls are red brick, the ceilings are high, and from the restaurant's lounge next door comes the sultry sound of late-night jazz. Take a bite of a crispy wonton stuffed with goat cheese or turn up the heat with the roasted tomato-garlic crab soup. For dessert, indulge in the legendary Madame Pele's chocolate volcano. After dinner, saunter over to Indigo's Green Room lounge or Opium Den & Champagne Bar for a nightcap. If you're touring downtown at lunchtime, check out Indigo's Cool Island Buffet. ✉ *1121 Nu'uanu Ave., Downtown Honolulu* ☎ *808/521–2900* ⊕ *www.indigo-hawaii.com* ▭ *AE, D, DC, MC, V.*

$$–$$$ ✕ **L'Uraku.** If you like a little whimsy with your wasabi, then you'll appreciate the decor of this Japanese-European fusion restaurant, which stays sunny with its collection of Kiyoshi hand-painted umbrellas that hang from the ceiling. Chef Hiroshi Fukui's contemporary food stylings are the perfect complement. The menu includes his signature 10 ounce garlic rib-eye steak as well as his crunchy shrimp with wasabi ketchup. Check out L'Uraku's three-course weekender lunch menu. ✉ *1341 Kapi'olani Blvd., Ala Moana* ☎ *808/955–0552* ▭ *AE, D, MC, V.*

★ **$–$$$** ✕ **3660 on the Rise.** This casually stylish eatery is a 10-minute drive from Waikīkī in the up-and-coming culinary mecca of Kaimukī. Sample Chef Russell Siu's Furikake popcorn-shrimp salad, pan-seared Chinese-style Chilean sea bass, or his signature *'ahi katsu* (tuna cutlet) wrapped in nori and deep-fried with a wasabi-ginger sauce. After an evening here you'll easily understand why 3360 continues its rise on the Honolulu culinary scene. Looking for a sweet ending? The banana spring rolls should do the trick. ✉ *3660 Wai'alae Ave., Kaimukī* ☎ *808/737–1177* ▭ *AE, DC, MC, V.*

★ **$–$$$** ✕ **Gordon Biersch Brewery Restaurant.** Snuggling up to Honolulu Harbor, this indoor-outdoor eatery, part of a West Coast–based chain of microbreweries, is Aloha Tower Marketplace's busiest. The menu is American with an island twist, with everything from sweet and spicy vegetable and fish stir-fries to garlic herb-crusted mahimahi with vegetable strings and sweet ginger rice. Ask for tastes of the brewery's dark, medium, and light brews before choosing your favorite. ✉ *Aloha Tower Marketplace, 1 Aloha Tower Dr., Downtown Honolulu* ☎ *808/599–4877* ▭ *AE, D, DC, MC, V.*

$–$$ ✕ **Kaka'ako Kitchen.** If you want the culinary excellence of 3660 on the Rise without the price tag, come to this casual restaurant. Here, the owners of 3660 unleash their skills on the island-style plate lunch. You can order your "two scoops of rice" either white or brown. For vegetarians, the grilled Portobello-mushroom burger served with blue cheese, roasted peppers, lettuce, and tomato on a taro bun is a superb choice. Friday nights, live music adds an additional "local flavor" to the mix. ✉ *Ward Centre, 1200 Ala Moana Blvd., Kaka'ako* ☎ *808/596–7488* ⚑ *Reservations not accepted* ▭ *No credit cards.*

★ **$–$$** ✕ **La Mariana.** Just past Downtown Honolulu, tucked away in the industrial area of Sand Island, is this friendly South Seas–style restaurant. La Mariana has been around for nearly five decades, and the decor is a hodgepodge of everything from glass floats in fish nets to koa-wood tables. Sample the shrimp *lumpia* (Phillipine version of the eggroll) or the seafood-stuffed eggplant au gratin. The Cajun 'ahi is good as either a main entrée or appetizer. The weekend sing-alongs at the piano bar give the place a nostalgic island charm. ⊠ *50 Sand Island Rd., Iwilei* ☎ *808/848–2800* ⊟ *AE, D, DC, MC, V.*

★ **$–$$$** ✗ **Palomino.** A Downtown Honolulu favorite, this art deco Euro-bistro, with handblown glass chandeliers, a grand staircase, and a 50-foot marble-and-mahogany bar, features a menu that fuses French, Spanish, and Italian cuisines. Entrées include Roma style pizzas, spit roasted poultry, strombolis, and seafood that includes roasted garlic- or crab-stuffed prawns. Try the grilled ravioli for a change of pace. ⊠ *Harbor Court, 66 Queen St., 3rd fl., Downtown Honolulu* ☎ *808/528–2400* ⊟ *AE, D, DC, MC, V.*

German

$–$$ ✗ **Patisserie.** By day, this bakery in the Kāhala Mall serves deli food, but five nights a week it turns into a 24-seat restaurant with great German food, a rarity in Hawai'i. The menu is small—only 10 entrées—but any choice is a good one. The Wiener schnitzel is juicy within its crispy crust, and veal ribs are garnished with a sprig of rosemary. Try the potato pancakes, crisp outside and soft inside, joined by a healthy spoonful of applesauce. ⊠ *Kāhala Mall, 4211 Wai'alae Ave., Kāhala* ☎ *808/735–4402* ⚑ *Reservations not accepted* ⊟ *MC, V* ☉ *Closed Sun.–Mon.*

Hawaiian

$$–$$$ ✗ **The Willows.** The exterior of this garden restaurant gives little clue as to the wonderful ambience that awaits within. Man-made ponds are sprinkled among the thatched dining pavilions, and you'll also find a tiny wedding chapel and a gallery gift shop. The food, served buffet-style, includes the trademark Willows curry along with roasted Portobello mushrooms, *laulau* (a steamed bundle of ti leaves containing pork, butterfish, and taro tops), and pineapple-mango barbecued ribs. ⊠ *901 Hausten St., Mō'ili'ili* ☎ *808/952–9200* ⚑ *Reservations essential* ⊟ *AE, D, MC, V.*

¢–$ ✗ **'Ono Hawaiian Foods.** The adventurous in search of a real "local food" experience should head to this no-frills hangout. You know it has to be good if residents are waiting in line to get in. Here you can sample poi, *lomi lomi* salmon (salmon massaged until tender and served with minced onions and tomatoes), laulau, kālua pork (roasted in an underground oven), and *haupia* (a light, gelatin-like dessert made from coconut). Appropriately enough, the Hawaiian word '*ono* means delicious. ⊠ *726 Kapahulu Ave., Kapahulu* ☎ *808/737–2275* ⚑ *Reservations not accepted* ⊟ *No credit cards* ☉ *Closed Sun.*

Italian

$–$$ ✗ **Cafe Sistina.** Sergio Mitrotti has gained quite a following with his inventive Italian-Mediterranean cuisine, which is as artistic as his drawings on the café's walls. The menu combines three generations of family recipes—his grandmother's, his mother's, and his own, which includes a snapper with walnut mint sauce. If you love ravioli, try the asparagus ravioli with a sweet-vermouth cream sauce. On Saturday there's a late-evening menu to feed the lively salsa dance crowd. ⊠ *1314 S. King St., Makīkī* ☎ *808/596–0061* ⊟ *AE, MC, V.*

Japanese

$–$$ ✕ **Sushi Sasabune.** This tiny sushi bar is the home of the island's most famous "trust me" sushi chef, Seiji Kumagawa. Sit back and let him concoct a great meal for you—and don't expect a California roll. The sushi is authentically Japanese but created from such regional delicacies as Nova Scotia salmon and Louisianna blue crab. Sasabune's sushi specials come with miso soup, seaweed salad, and adzuki-bean ice cream. ✉ *1419 S. King St., Mōʻiliʻili* ☎ *808/947–3800* ⚄ *Reservations essential* ▭ *AE, D, DC, MC, V.*

Mexican

$–$$ ✕ **Compadres Mexican Bar and Grill.** The after-work crowd gathers here for potent margaritas and yummy pūpū. An outdoor terrace is best for cocktails only. Inside, the wooden floors, colorful photographs, and lively paintings create a festive setting for imaginative Mexican specialties. Fajitas, baby-back ribs, pork *carnitas* (small bits or shreds of meat), and grilled shrimp are just a few of the many offerings. There's a late-night appetizer menu available until midnight. ✉ *Ward Centre, 1200 Ala Moana Blvd., Ala Moana* ☎ *808/591–8307* ▭ *D, MC, V.*

Seafood

★ $$$ ✕ **Sam Choy's Breakfast, Lunch and Crab & Big Aloha Brewery.** In this casual setting, great for families, diners can get crackin' with crab, chow down on chowders, and fill up with an abundance of both seafood and landlubber fare. This eatery's warehouse size sets the tone for its large portions. An on-site microbrewery brews five varieties of Big Aloha beer. Sam Choy's is in Iwilei past Downtown Honolulu on the highway heading toward Honolulu International Airport. ✉ *580 Nimitz Hwy., Iwilei* ☎ *808/545–7979* ⊕ *www.samchoy.com* ▭ *AE, D, DC, MC, V.*

Around the Island

Haleʻiwa

AMERICAN/ CASUAL

$$ ✕ **Haleiwa Joe's.** A day of surfing or just watching the big-wave riders can work up an appetite. Haleiwa Joe's, located just past the Anahulu Stream Bridge, serves up steaks, prime rib, and seafood such as crunchy coconut shrimp and grilled salmon with Asian pesto sauce. Come in time to watch the sun set over Haleʻiwa Harbor. The bar serves various "small plate" menu items including black and blue ʻahi with a wasabi-ranch dressing. ✉ *66-0011 Kamehameha Hwy., Haleiwa* ☎ *808/637– 8005* ⚄ *Reservations not accepted* ▭ *AE, DC, MC, V.*

★ ¢ ✕ **Kua ʻAina Sandwich.** A must-stop spot during a drive around the island, this North Shore eatery specializes in burgers heaped with bacon, cheese, salsa, and pineapple. It moved to its current location next to Wyland Galleries after it outgrew its tiny spot down the road. The grilled mahimahi sandwich comes with a homemade tartar sauce. The crispy shoestring fries alone are worth the trip. You can also check out Kua ʻAina's south-shore location across from the Ward Centre in Honolulu. ✉ *66-160 Kamehameha Hwy., Haleiwa* ☎ *808/637–6067* ✉ *1116 Auahi St., Ala Moana, Honolulu* ☎ *808/591–9133* ⚄ *Reservations not accepted* ▭ *No credit cards.*

Hawai'i Kai

AUSTRIAN
$$–$$$
✕ **Chef's Table.** This tiny eatery is good for a lunch break while touring East O'ahu or as a getaway dinner spot. Chef Andreas Knapp, formerly of the Kahala Hilton and the Westin Century Plaza, creates dishes that are true to his Austrian heritage. Daily specials, including luscious homemade soups, salads, sauerbratens, and schnitzels, combined with an atmosphere that is friendly, fun, and casual, make the Chef's Table a neighborhood favorite. A European-style brunch is offered Sunday. ⊠ *Hawai'i Kai Towne Center, 333 Keahole St., Hawai'i Kai* ☎ *808/ 394–2433* ▤ *AE, D, DC, MC, V.*

CONTEMPORARY
$$–$$$$
✕ **Roy's.** Two walls of windows offer views of Maunalua Bay and Diamond Head in the distance, and a glassed-in kitchen affords views of what's cooking at this noisy two-story restaurant with a devoted following. The menu matches Hawaiian flavors with Euro-Asian accents. Dishes with a modern flair—crispy calamari and Asian glass noodle salad—share the menu with comfort-food favorites, such as meat loaf with mushroom gravy. ⊠ *Hawai'i Kai Corporate Plaza, 6600 Kalaniana'ole Hwy., Hawai'i Kai* ☎ *808/396–7697* ▤ *AE, D, DC, MC, V.*

Windward O'ahu

AMERICAN
$$–$$$

✗ **Buzz's Original Steakhouse.** This family-owned restaurant is just across the road from Kailua Beach Park and epitomizes the kind of laid-back style you'd expect to find in Hawai'i. Burgers, salads, and fresh-fish sandwiches are the lunch staples; sirloin steak, rack of lamb, and teriyaki chicken top the dinner choices. Lānai seating allows you to catch an ocean breeze while you dine. ⊠ *413 Kawailoa Rd., Kailua* ☎ *808/261–4661* 🖃 *No credit cards.*

$$–$$$

✗ **Lucy's Grill and Bar.** This windward eatery offers outdoor seating and an open-air bar that shakes up a mean martini to go with its eclectic and innovative menu. Begin with the deep-fried kalua pig pastry triangles with a mandarin orange-plum dipping sauce. Seafood offerings include grilled mahimahi, and lemongrass-crusted scallops with a yellow Thai curry. For meat lovers, there are baby-back ribs in sweet hoisin barbecue sauce. Desserts, such as the coconut-chocolate bar with vanilla gelato, are sinfully rich. ⊠ *33 Aulike St., Kailua* ☎ *808/230–8188* 🖃 *MC, V.*

MEXICAN
¢–$

✗ **Bueno Nalo.** The owners of this family-run eatery are dedicated to healthful Mexican cuisine, and the food is reliably good. *Topopo* salad is a heap of greens, tomatoes, onions, tuna, olives, cheese, and beans on top of a tortilla. Combination plates with tacos, enchiladas, and tamales are bargains. Families appreciate the *keiki* (child's) menu for diners 10 and under. Velvet paintings and piñatas add a fun, funky flavor to the setting. ⊠ *20 Kainehe St., Kailua* ☎ *808/263–1999* 🖃 *AE, MC, V.*

WHERE TO STAY

If your dream vacation entails getting away from the usual hustle and bustle, look at the listings in the Around the Island category. If you prefer to be close to the action, go for a hotel or condominium in or near Waikīkī, where most of the island's lodgings are. Except for the peak months of January and February, you'll have little trouble getting a room if you call in advance. Don't be intimidated by published rates. Most hotels offer a variety of package options and special deals, such as sports, honeymoon, room and car, and kids stay/eat free promotions. These extras can make vacations even more affordable, so ask about them when you book.

Below is a selective list of lodging choices in each price category. For a complete list of every hotel and condominium on the island, write or call the Hawai'i Visitors & Convention Bureau for a free *Accommodation Guide.*

Waikīkī

$$$$

🏨 **Aston Waikīkī Beach Tower.** On Kalākaua Avenue, but set back from the street on the mauka side, this 39-story luxury condominium resort has the atmosphere of an intimate vest-pocket hotel. The property has the usual amenities plus views of Waikīkī that you'd expect from a larger beachfront resort. Spacious (1,100–1,400 square feet) one- and two-bedroom suites are appointed with style and feature kitchens that would please a gourmet, twice-daily maid service, washer-dryers, and a private lānai. There's a heated swimming pool. ✉ *2470 Kalākaua Ave., Waikīkī, Honolulu 96815* ☎ *808/926–6400 or 877/997-6667* 🖨 *808/926–7380* ⊕ *www.aston-hotels.com* ⇥ *140 suites* ⟁ *Room service, kitchens, minibars, cable TV, tennis court, pool, sauna, laundry facilities, concierge* ▭ *AE, D, DC, MC, V.*

$$$$
Fodor'sChoice
★
🏨 **Halekūlani.** The sleek oceanside Halekūlani exemplifies the translation of its name—the "house befitting heaven." The service is impeccable, and the mood is tranquil amid the frenetic activity of Waikīkī. Guest rooms, which are spacious and artfully appointed in marble and wood, have ocean views and dozens of little touches such as fruit baskets, 27-inch flat-screen televisions, DVD and CD players, cordless phones, and complimentary wireless Internet service. The hotel has three fine restaurants—House Without a Key, La Mer, and Orchids—a spa, and an oceanside pool with a mesmerizing orchid mosaic. ✉ *2199 Kālia Rd., Waikīkī, Honolulu 96815* ☎ *808/923–2311 or 800/367–2343* 🖨 *808/926–8004* ⊕ *www.halekulani. com* ⇥ *412 rooms, 44 suites* ⟁ *3 restaurants, room service, in-room data ports, in-room safes, minibars, cable TV, pool, spa, hair salon, massage, beach, 3 bars, shops, dry cleaning, concierge, Internet, business services, meeting room* ▭ *AE, DC, MC, V.*

$$$$
🏨 **Hawai'i Prince Hotel Waikīkī.** The Prince is a slim high-rise with the kind of sophisticated interior design generally reserved for a big-city hotel. You know you're in Waikīkī, however, when you look out your window at the Ala Wai Yacht Harbor—all guest rooms have floor-to-ceiling windows with ocean views. The Prince Court offers a subtle blend of Asian, European, and Hawaiian cuisine, while Hakone focuses on the cuisine of Japan. The hotel is within walking distance of the Ala Moana Shopping Center and has its own 27-hole Arnold Palmer–designed golf course in 'Ewa Beach, about a 45-minute hotel-shuttle ride from Waikīkī. ✉ *100 Holomoana St., Waikīkī, Honolulu 96815* ☎ *808/956–1111 or 800/321–6248* 🖨 *808/946–0811* ⊕ *www.hawaiiprincehotel.com* ⇥ *467 rooms, 57 suites* ⟁ *3 restaurants, room service, in-room data ports, in-room safes, minibars, cable TV, 27-hole golf course, pool, gym, hair salon, hot tub, lobby lounge, shops, babysitting, concierge, business services, meeting room* ▭ *AE, DC, MC, V.*

$$$$
🏨 **Hyatt Regency Waikīkī Resort and Spa.** An open-air atrium with a two-story waterfall, shops, live music, and daily entertainment make this one of the liveliest lobbies anywhere, though you may get lost in it. Guest rooms have private lānai and sitting areas. The Na Ho'ola Spa will pamper you with a poolside massage. The Ciao Mein restaurant mixes it up with a menu of both Italian and Chinese food. The hotel is across from Kūhiō Beach and a short walk from Kapi'olani Park. ✉ *2424 Kalākaua Ave., Waikīkī, Honolulu 96815* ☎ *808/923–1234 or 800/633–7313* 🖨 *808/923–7839* ⊕ *www.hyattwaikiki.com* ⇥ *1,212 rooms, 18 suites* ⟁ *5 restaurants, room service, in-room data ports, in-room safes, minibars, cable TV, pool, spa, bar, lobby lounge, shops, children's programs (ages 5–12), concierge, business services, meeting rooms* ▭ *AE, D, DC, MC, V.*

$$$$
🏨 **Outrigger Reef on the Beach.** You can learn to surf or paddle an outrigger canoe at the Reef, which is right on the beach near Ft. DeRussy

Where to Stay in Waikīkī

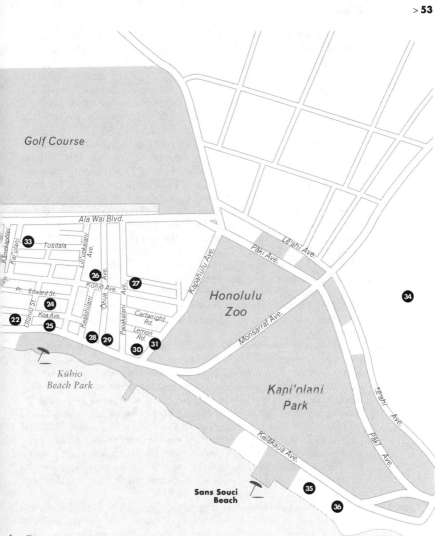

Park. Ask for an ocean view; the other rooms have decidedly less delightful overlooks. For fun, cook your own meal at the lively Shore Bird Oceanside Bar and Grill or pamper yourself at the oceanside Serenity Spa. ⊠ *2169 Kālia Rd., Waikīkī, Honolulu 96815* ☎ *808/923–3111 or 800/688–7444* 🖷 *808/924–4957* ⊕ *www.outrigger.com* ⚓ *846 rooms, 39 suites ⚫ 2 restaurants, room service, refrigerators, cable TV, pool, gym, beach, 4 bars, nightclub, children's programs (ages 5–12), meeting room, no-smoking rooms ☰ AE, D, DC, MC, V.*

★ **$$$$** 🏨 **Outrigger Waikīkī on the Beach.** Outrigger Hotels & Resorts' star property on Kalākaua Avenue stands on some of the nicest sands in Waikīkī. Rooms have a rich plantation feeling with dark wood furnishings and bold colors such as yellow and green. Each room has a lānai. For more than 25 years, the main ballroom has been home to the sizzling Society of Seven entertainers. The beachfront Duke's Canoe Club is a dining hot spot. In late May, this hotel is the headquarters for the World Ocean Games competitions that take place on Waikīkī Beach. ⊠ *2335 Kalākaua Ave., Waikīkī, Honolulu 96815* ☎ *808/923–0711 or 800/688–7444* 🖷 *808/921–9749 or 800/688–7444* ⊕ *www.outrigger.com* ⚓ *500 rooms, 30 suites ⚫ 3 restaurants, room service, in-room data ports, in-room safes, kitchenettes, minibars, cable TV, pool, gym, hot tub, 5 bars, lobby lounge, shops, children's programs (ages 5–13), dry cleaning, laundry facilities, concierge, business services, meeting rooms ☰ AE, D, DC, MC, V.*

$$$$ 🏨 **Renaissance 'Ilikai Waikīkī.** Spacious 600-square-foot guest rooms in two towers overlook Ala Wai Harbor and the ocean. The open-air lobby has cascading waterfalls; torches light the walkways for romantic evening strolls. Some guest rooms have kitchenettes and offer wireless Internet access. For sky-high dining, there's Sarento's Top of the "I" Italian restaurant. ⊠ *1777 Ala Moana Blvd., Waikīkī, Honolulu 96815* ☎ *808/949–3811 or 800/245–4524* 🖷 *808/947–0892* ⊕ *www.ilikaihotel. com* ⚓ *728 rooms, 51 suites ⚫ 3 restaurants, room service, some kitchens, minibars, cable TV, tennis court, 2 pools, health club, outdoor hot tub, massage, 2 lobby lounges, video game room, shops, laundry facilities, Internet, business services, meeting room, car rental ☰ AE, D, DC, MC, V.*

★ **$$$$** 🏨 **Royal Hawaiian Hotel.** Nicknamed the Pink Palace of the Pacific due to its candy-pink exterior, the Royal was built in 1927 by Matson Navigation Company to accommodate its luxury-cruise passengers. It still exudes old-world charm, especially in its rooms in the Historic Wing, which have canopy beds, Queen Anne–style desks, and pink telephones. You can dine by the water's edge at the Surf Room or sip a mai tai at the bar that made that drink famous. In 2004, the hotel's Abhasa Waikiki Spa expanded its garden area by 3,000 square feet, adding four new outdoor treatment cabanas, a lounge, and a dining area. The hotel's Tower Wing received its own face-lift in the same year with new room furnishings and decor, upgraded bathrooms, and updated common areas. ⊠ *2259 Kalākaua Ave., Waikīkī, Honolulu 96815* ☎ *888/488–3535 or 808/923–7311 or 866/500–8313* 🖷 *808/924–7098* ⊕ *www. royal-hawaiian.com* ⚓ *472 rooms, 53 suites ⚫ 2 restaurants, room service, minibars, cable TV, pool, hair salon, spa, beach, bar, children's pro-*

grams (ages 5–12), concierge, business services, meeting room ⊟ *AE, DC, MC, V.*

$$$$ ⊞ **Sheraton Moana Surfrider.** "The First Lady of Waikīkī" opened its doors in 1901 and became the first resort to make famous a little beach called Waikīkī. It has since merged with the newer Surfrider next door, but you can appreciate its history by requesting a room in the Moana Banyan Wing, where each floor has been restored to its original style (each floor is done in a single kind of wood: mahogany, maple, oak, cherry, or koa). These rooms are small by today's standards, but they're well appointed and charming. The Diamond Head Tower rooms offer full views of Waikīkī Beach. Enjoy high tea and Hawaiian music on the Moana's breeze-swept veranda. A recent refreshening of the guest rooms and public areas is in keeping with the style that has earned this Lady her place in Hawaiian history as Waikīkī's most gracious hostess. ⊠ *2365 Kalākaua Ave., Waikīkī, Honolulu 96815* ☎ *888/488–3535 or 808/922–3111 or 866/500–8313* 🖷 *808/923–0308* ⊕ *www.moana-surfrider.com* ➔ *793 rooms, 46 suites* ⊜ *2 restaurants, snack bar, room service, in-room data ports, in-room safes, cable TV, pool, beach, bar, 2 lounges, shops, children's programs (ages 5–12), concierge, meeting room* ⊟ *AE, DC, MC, V.*

$$$$ ⊞ **Sheraton Waikīkī.** Towering over its neighbors, the Sheraton takes center stage on Waikīkī Beach. Guest rooms are spacious, and many have grand views of Diamond Head. Be sure to take the glass-walled elevator up to the Hanohano Room, an elegant dining room with breathtaking panoramas of the ocean and Waikīkī. The Hoʻokipa Center features a hospitality lounge, fitness center, and the center of operations for the hotel's Keiki Aloha children's activity program. ⊠ *2255 Kalākaua Ave., Waikīkī, Honolulu 96815* ☎ *888/488–3535 or 808/922–4422 or 866/500–8313* 🖷 *808/923–8785* ⊕ *www.sheratonwaikiki.com* ➔ *1,709 rooms, 130 suites* ⊜ *3 restaurants, room service, minibars, cable TV, 2 pools, health club, beach, lobby lounge, dance club, shops, children's programs (ages 5–12), concierge, business services, meeting rooms* ⊟ *AE, DC, MC, V.*

$$$$ ⊞ **W Honolulu—Diamond Head.** The W is on the quiet edge of Waikīkī across from Kapiʻolani Park. Guest rooms feature spectacular ocean views, private lānai, 27-inch TVs with Broadband Internet access, CD players, and VCRs/DVDS with a video/DVD library. The luxurious trademark W beds wrap you in 250-thread-count sheets, and rooms are elegantly appointed with teak furnishings in a Balinese motif. The hotel's Wonder Lounge is perfect for an after-work libation. ⊠ *2885 Kalākaua Ave., Waikīkī, Honolulu 96815* ☎ *808/922–1700 or 888/488–3535* 🖷 *808/923–2249* ⊕ *www.starwood.com* ➔ *44 rooms, 4 suites* ⊜ *Restaurant, room service, in-room data ports, minibars, cable TV, in-room VCRs, in-room DVDs, beach, bar, lounge, dry cleaning, laundry service, concierge, business services* ⊟ *AE, D, DC, MC, V.*

★ **$$$$** ⊞ **Waikīkī Beachcomber Hotel.** With an excellent location right across the street from Waikīkī Beach, the Beachcomber is also a short walk from the Royal Hawaiian Shopping Center and the DFS Galleria. Rooms have tropical motifs and private lānai. Three evening shows are presented here: the venerable "Don Ho," "Blue Hawaiʻi," and "The Magic of Polyne-

sia." ✉ *2300 Kalākaua Ave., Waikīkī, Honolulu 96815* ☎ 808/922–
4646 or 800/622–4646 🖷 808/923–4889 ⊕ *www.waikikibeachcomber.
com* 🛏 *500 rooms, 7 suites* ♻ *Restaurant, snack bar, room service, minibars, cable TV, refrigerators, pool, outdoor hot tub, lobby lounge, children's programs (ages 5–12), laundry facilities, meeting rooms,
no-smoking rooms* ▤ *AE, DC, MC, V.*

★ **$$$$** 🏨 **Waikīkī Parc.** This jewel of a boutique hotel is owned by the same
group that manages the Halekūlani across the street, where guests
have signing privileges. Waikīkī Parc offers the same attention to detail in service and architectural design as the larger hotel but lacks a
beachfront location. The lobby is light and airy, and guest rooms are
done in Island pastels with seafoam green accents and plantation-style
shutters that open out to the lānai. Rooms have sitting areas and writing desks. The hotel's Japanese restaurant, Kacho, serves Kyoto cuisine, and the lovely Parc Café is known for its bountiful island-style
buffets. ✉ *2233 Helumoa Rd., Waikīkī, Honolulu 96815* ☎ 808/921–
7272 or 800/422–0450 🖷 808/931–6638 ⊕ *www.waikikiparc.com*
🛏 *298 rooms* ♻ *2 restaurants, room service, in-room data ports, in-
room safes, minibars, cable TV, pool, gym, concierge, business services*
▤ *AE, D, DC, MC, V.*

$$$–$$$$ 🏨 **Aston Waikīkī Beach Hotel.** This Aston hotel is hip to Hawaiiana, pay-
ing tribute to the best of paradise: rooms are done in colors ranging from
pineapple yellow to hot-lava red and feature teak furnishings and retro
hand-painted bamboo curtains. Included with your room is a "breakfast
on the beach" option. This allows you to grab prepackaged à la carte break-
fast items from the poolside food court that can be easily stashed in your
complimentary insulated cooler bag for a day at the beach. Tiki's Bar and
Grill and Wolfgang Puck Express are dining options here. ✉ *2570
Kalākaua Ave., Waikīkī, Honolulu 96815* ☎ 808/922–2511 or 877/997–
6667 🖷 808/922–8785 ⊕ *www.aston-hotels.com* 🛏 *645 rooms, 12
suites* ♻ *Restaurant, in-room data ports, in-room safes, cable TV, pool,
shops, laundry facilities, meeting rooms* ▤ *AE, D, DC, MC, V.*

$$$–$$$$ 🏨 **Aston Waikīkī Sunset.** Families enjoy this high-rise condominium re-
sort near Diamond Head, one block from Waikīkī Beach and two blocks
from the Honolulu Zoo. One- and two-bedroom suites have complete
kitchens, daily maid service, and private lānai. There's also an outdoor
barbecue area, a tennis court, a sauna, and a children's playground. ✉ *229
Paoakalani Ave., Waikīkī, Honolulu 96815* ☎ 808/922–0511 or 800/
922–7866 🖷 808/922–8580 ⊕ *www.aston-hotels.com* 🛏 *307 suites*
♻ *Snack bar, BBQ, in-room data ports, cable TV, kitchens, tennis court,
pool, sauna, shop, playground* ▤ *AE, D, DC, MC, V.*

★ **$$$–$$$$** 🏨 **Hilton Hawaiian Village Beach Resort and Spa.** Sprawling over 22 acres
on Waikīkī's widest stretch of beach, this resort is a destination unto it-
self. Choose from accommodations in five hotel towers surrounded by
lavish gardens, a lagoon, cascading waterfalls, and 60 species of exotic
birds, fish, and fauna. Accommodations range from standard hotel
guest rooms to one- or two-bedroom condo-style units. Check out the
sublime Mandara Spa and Holistic Wellness Center or immerse your-
self in Hawaiian culture at the Bishop Museum at the Kālia Hawaiian
Cultural Activities Center. There are 20 restaurants and lounges to cater

to every taste and 90 boutiques where you can get everything from Hawaiian musical instruments to designer clothing. ⊠ *2005 Kālia Rd., Waikīkī, Honolulu 96815* ☎ *808/949–4321 or 800/221–2424* 🖷 *808/947–7898* ⊕ *www.hiltonhawaiianvillage.com* ⤳ *3,432 rooms, 365 suites, 264 condominiums* ♢ *18 restaurants, room service, in-room data ports, in-room safes, minibars, cable TV, 5 pools, gym, spa, beach, snorkeling, 8 bars, shops, babysitting, children's programs (ages 5–12), dry cleaning, laundry service, concierge, Internet, business services, meeting room, car rental, no-smoking rooms* ▭ *AE, D, DC, MC, V.*

★ **$$$–$$$$** 🏨 **New Otani Kaimana Beach Hotel.** Polished to a shine, this hotel is open to the trade winds and furnished with big, comfortable chairs. The ambience is cheerful and charming, and the lobby has a happy, unpretentious feel. Best of all, it's right on the beach at the quiet end of Waikīkī, practically at the foot of Diamond Head. Rooms are smallish but very nicely appointed with soothing pastels, off-white furnishings, and private lānai. Enjoy your meals beachside at the Hau Tree Lanai. ⊠ *2863 Kalākaua Ave., Waikīkī, Honolulu 96815* ☎ *808/923–1555 or 800/356–8264* 🖷 *808/922–9404* ⊕ *www.kaimana.com* ⤳ *119 rooms, 6 suites* ♢ *2 restaurants, room service, in-room data ports, in-room safes, minibars, cable TV, refrigerators, gym, hair salon, lobby lounge, babysitting, concierge, meeting rooms* ▭ *AE, D, DC, MC, V.*

$$$–$$$$ 🏨 **Sheraton Princess Kaiulani.** Just across from Waikīkī Beach on the land that was once the Ainahau Estate home of Princess Victoria Kaiulani, this hotel keeps alive the traditions of old Hawai'i, with furnishings that include Hawaiian quilts and artwork. Arts-and-crafts demonstrations and a historical-hotel tour take place during the day, and at night there's poolside hula on the Lava Stage. The hotel has two restaurants: the Pikake Terrace, for casual outdoor dining, and Momoyama Japanese Restaurant. ⊠ *120 Kaiulani Ave., Waikīkī, Honolulu 96815* ☎ *888/488–3535 or 808/922–5811 or 866/500–8313* 🖷 *808/931–4577* ⊕ *www.princesskaiulani.com* ⤳ *1,150 rooms, 10 suites* ♢ *2 restaurants, room service, in-room data ports, cable TV, pool, gym, lobby lounge, children's programs (ages 5–12), business services* ▭ *AE, D, DC, MC, V.*

$$$–$$$$ 🏨 **Waikīkī Beach Marriott Resort.** On the eastern edge of Waikīkī, this hotel is across from Kūhiō Beach and close to Kapi'olani Park, the zoo, and the aquarium. Deep Hawaiian woods and bold tropical colors fill the hotel's two towers, which have ample courtyards and public areas open to ocean breezes and sunlight. The Kealohilani Tower's spacious guest rooms are some of the largest in Waikīkī, and the Paokalani Tower's Diamond Head side rooms offer breathtaking views of Diamond Head crater and Kapi'olani Park. Dine at the Kuhio Beach Grill, listen to the legendary Genoa Keawe perform on the Moana Terrace on Thursday evenings or reserve your table for the "One" variety dinner show. ⊠ *2552 Kalākaua Ave., Waikīkī, Honolulu 96815* ☎ *808/922–6611 or 800/367–5370* 🖷 *808/921–5222* ⊕ *www.marriottwaikiki.com* ⤳ *1,337 rooms, 9 suites* ♢ *3 restaurants, room service, in-room safes, minibars, cable TV, refrigerators, tennis court, 2 pools, gym, 2 lounges, concierge, business services, meeting rooms* ▭ *AE, D, MC, V.*

$$$ 🏨 **Doubletree Alana Waikīkī.** The lobby of this 19-story high-rise is modern and attractive, with rotating exhibits of local artists' work. Guest rooms have private lānai with panoramic views of Waikīkī, the ocean, or the mountains. The staff of this boutique property has a reputation for absolute attention to detail. Those doing business globally like the 24-hour business center. Also open round-the-clock is the fitness center. The signature restaurant here is Padovani's Restaurant and Wine Bar. ⊠ *1956 Ala Moana Blvd., Waikīkī, Honolulu 96815* ☎ *808/941–7275 or 800/222–8733* ⊜ *808/949–0996* ⊕ *www.alana-doubletree. com* ⤐ *268 rooms, 45 suites* ⚐ *Restaurant, room service, in-room data ports, in-room safes, minibars, cable TV, refrigerators, pool, gym, lobby lounge, concierge, business services, no-smoking rooms* ⊟ *AE, D, MC, V.*

$$$ 🏨 **Ohana East.** Formerly the Outrigger East, this hotel is the flagship property for Ohana Hotels in Waikīkī. It's just two blocks from the beach and a quarter mile from Kapi'olani Park, with easy access to Waikīkī activities and trolley and bus routes. You can stay in standard hotel rooms or suites with kitchenettes. All rooms have Nintendo systems for restless kids. ⊠ *150 Kaiulani Ave., Waikīkī, Honolulu 96815* ☎ *808/922–5353 or 800/462–6262* ⊜ *808/926–4334* ⊕ *www. ohanahotels.com* ⤐ *423 rooms, 22 suites* ⚐ *4 restaurants, room service, in-room data ports, in-room safes, some kitchenettes, refrigerators, room TVs with video games, pool, gym, hair salon, bar, laundry facilities* ⊟ *AE, D, DC, MC, V.*

$$–$$$$ 🏨 **Ilima Hotel.** This 17-story condominium-style hotel has large studios with two double beds and full kitchens; you can also opt for a suite with a spacious lānai. Located on a side street near the Ala Wai Canal, the Ilima is a short walk away from Waikīkī Beach and the Royal Hawaiian Shopping Center. ⊠ *445 Nohonani St., Waikīkī, Honolulu 96815* ☎ *808/923–1877 or 888/864–5462* ⊜ *808/924–2617* ⊕ *www.ilima. com* ⤐ *99 units* ⚐ *In-room data ports, in-room safes, kitchens, cable TV, pool, gym, sauna, laundry facilities* ⊟ *AE, DC, MC, V.*

$$–$$$$ 🏨 **Radisson Waikīkī Prince Kūhiō.** Two blocks from Kūhiō Beach, this 37-story high-rise is on the Diamond Head end of Waikīkī. Hawaiian-print bedspreads and artwork in sepia, cream, and earth tones decorate the rooms. Cupid's, the lobby lounge, plays Hawaiian music, and Trellises, the hotel restaurant, hosts a sumptuous seafood buffet on Friday and Saturday evenings. ⊠ *2500 Kūhiō Ave., Waikīkī, Honolulu 96815* ☎ *808/922–8811 or 800/557–4422* ⊜ *808/923–0330* ⊕ *www.radisson. com/waikikihi* ⤐ *620 rooms* ⚐ *Restaurant, room service, in-room data ports, cable TV, pool, gym, hot tub, lobby lounge, Internet, business services* ⊟ *AE, D, DC, MC, V.*

$$–$$$$ 🏨 **Royal Garden at Waikīkī.** From the outside, this 25-story boutique hotel looks like a residential Waikīkī high-rise. But step inside and it whispers elegance, from the marble and etched glass in the lobby to the genuine graciousness of the staff. Guest rooms have sitting areas, private lānai, and marble and brass baths. The hotel's Chez Michel by Cascada restaurant serves French-inspired island cuisine. There's a free shuttle service to and from Kapi'olani Park, Ala Moana Shopping Center, Royal Hawaiian Shopping Center, and duty-free shops. ⊠ *440 'Olohana St., Waikīkī, Honolulu 96815* ☎ *808/943–0202 or 800/367–5666* ⊜ *808/ 946–8777* ⊕ *www.royalgardens.com* ⤐ *202 rooms, 18 suites* ⚐ *2* restaurants, room service, in-room safes, cable TV, refrigerators, 2 pools, gym, lobby lounge, Internet, business services, meeting room ☰ AE, D, DC, MC, V.

$$–$$$$ 🏨 **Queen Kapi'olani Hotel.** A half block from the shore, this 19-story hotel appeals to those in search of clean, basic accommodations within walking distance of the beach and Waikīkī's main attractions. Some rooms have kitchenettes, and the third floor has a large pool and sundeck. ✉ *150 Kapahulu Ave., Waikīkī, Honolulu 96815* ☎ *808/922–1941 or 800/367–2317* 🖨 *808/924–1982* ⊕ *www.queenkapiolani.com* 🛏 *307 rooms, 7 suites* ౿ *2 restaurants, room service, in-room data ports, kitchenettes, refrigerators, cable TV, pool, bar, laundry facilities, meeting rooms* ☰ *AE, D, DC, MC, V.*

$$–$$$$ 🏨 **Waikīkī Joy.** This boutique hotel is a lesser-known gem. The location is great, tucked away on a quiet side street next to the DFS Galleria. One tower has all suites, and another has standard hotel rooms. Units have either ocean or partial ocean views. Each has a lānai, an in-room Jacuzzi, a deluxe stereo system, and a control panel by the bed. The hotel's private karaoke rooms are great places for entertaining friends. Complimentary Continental breakfast is served daily. ✉ *320 Lewers St., Waikīkī, Honolulu 96815* ☎ *808/923–2300 or 877/997–6667* 🖨 *808/ 922–8785* ⊕ *www.aston-hotels.com* 🛏 *50 rooms, 44 suites* ౿ *Restaurant, in-room data ports, in-room safes, kitchenettes, minibars, cable TV, pool, sauna, lobby lounge* ☰ *AE, D, DC, MC, V* ⊙⊙ *CP.*

$$–$$$ 🏨 **Aston Coconut Plaza Hotel.** With its small size and intimate service, Coconut Plaza is a true boutique hotel. Tropical plantation decor features rattan furnishings and floral bedspreads. Guest rooms have private lānai, and all except standard-view rooms come with kitchenettes. Free Continental breakfast is served daily on the lobby veranda. The hotel is only three blocks from the beach on the Ala Wai Canal. ✉ *450 Lewers St., Waikīkī, Honolulu 96815* ☎ *808/923–8828 or 877/997–6667* 🖨 *808/922–8785* ⊕ *www.aston-hotels.com* 🛏 *70 rooms, 11 suites* ౿ *In-room data ports, in-room safes, some kitchenettes, pool, hair salon, laundry facilities, meeting rooms* ☰ *AE, D, DC, MC, V* ⊙⊙ *CP.*

$$–$$$ 🏨 **Waikīkī Sand Villa.** The Villa's rooms are definitely on the small side, but they're clean and fairly comfortable. All rooms are equipped with T1 Internet access, and there's even a Webcam set up at the hotel's sand bar so you can chat with friends and family back home. Complimentary breakfast is served daily in the hotel's breakfast room or at tables outside by the swimming pool. Studio accommodations are also available. The hotel is three blocks from the beach across from the Ala Wai Canal. ✉ *2375 Ala Wai Blvd., Waikīkī, Honolulu 96815* ☎ *808/ 922–4744 or 800/247–1903* 🖨 *808/923–2541* ⊕ *www.sandvillahotel. com* 🛏 *212 rooms* ౿ *Restaurant, in-room data ports, in-room safes, refrigerators, pool, hot tub, bar, shop; no a/c in some rooms.* ☰ *AE, D, DC, MC, V* ⊙⊙ *CP.*

$$ 🏨 **Diamond Head Bed and Breakfast.** The two guest rooms at this bed-and-breakfast on the southeastern edge of Kapi'olani Park are big, have private baths, and open to a lānai and large backyard that makes the hustle and bustle of Waikīkī seem miles away. This traditional Hawaiian-style home is filled with Hawaiian heirlooms including an extra large koa hand-carved bed once belonging to a member of Hawaiian royalty. A minimum two-night stay is required. Reservations should be made three to four months in advance. ⊠ *3240 Noela Dr., Waikīkī, Honolulu 96815* 🕾 *808/985–7488* 🖷 *808/967–8610* ⊠ *Reservations: Hawai'i's Best Bed and Breakfasts, Box 758, Volcano, 96765* 🕾 *808/885–4550 or 800/262–9912* ⊕ *www.bestbnb.com* ⤳ *2 rooms* ☼ *No a/c, no room phones* ▭ *No credit cards* ⊙⊙ *BP.*

$–$$$ ⊡ **The Breakers.** The Breakers' six two-story buildings surround the pool and overlook gardens filled with tropical flowers. A throwback to the early 1960s, guest rooms have Japanese-style shoji doors. Rooms come with kitchenettes, bathrooms with shower only, and lānai. Guests return here year after year to soak up the laid-back old Hawai'i atmosphere. It's a half block from the beach and from Waikīkī restaurants. ⊠ *250 Beach Walk, Waikīkī, Honolulu 96815* 🕾 *808/923–3181 or 800/ 426–0494* 🖷 *808/923–7174* ⊕ *www.breakers-hawaii.com* ⤳ *64 units* ☼ *Restaurant, kitchenettes, pool, bar* ▭ *AE, DC, MC, V.*

$–$$$ ⊡ **Patrick Winston's Waikīkī Condos.** This 24-unit condominium complex has budget, standard, and deluxe two-bedroom units. Each has its own individual decor, but all have full kitchens, ceiling fans, sofa beds, and lānai. For nostalgia buffs, ask about the "Blue Hawaii" or "Hawaii 5-0" themed suites. Owner Patrick Winston can provide everything from exercise equipment to rice cookers to tips on the best places to dine on the island. ⊠ *417 Nohonani St., Waikīkī, Honolulu 96815* 🕾 *808/ 922–3894 or 800/545–1948* 🖷 *808/924–3332* ⊕ *www. winstonswaikikicondos.com* ⤳ *24 units* ☼ *Fans, in-room data ports, kitchens, pool, laundry facilities; no a/c.* ▭ *AE, DC, MC, V.*

$–$$ ⊡ **Aloha Punawai.** This family-operated apartment hotel is across the street from Ft. DeRussy Beach and within walking distance of shops and restaurants. The studios have bathrooms with showers only, but each unit comes with a full kitchen, cable television, and a lānai. Furnishings are simple and spartan. You can opt for telephone service or forgo the distraction. ⊠ *305 Saratoga Rd., Waikīkī, Honolulu 96815* 🕾 *808/923– 5211 or 866/713–9694* 🖷 *808/923–5211* ⊕ *www.alternative-hawaii. com/alohapunawai* ⤳ *19 units* ☼ *Kitchens, cable TV, laundry facilities; no phones in some rooms* ▭ *AE, DC, MC, V.*

$–$$ ⊡ **Holiday Inn–Waikīkī.** This Holiday Inn is conveniently located just two blocks from the beach and a 10-minute walk from both the Hawai'i Convention Center and Ala Moana Shopping Center. It offers the standard, reliable chain amenities with tropical-motif rooms. ⊠ *1830 Ala Moana Blvd., Waikīkī, Honolulu 96815* 🕾 *808/955–1111 or 888/992– 4545* 🖷 *808/947–1799* ⊕ *www.holiday-inn-waikiki.com* ⤳ *199 rooms, 6 suites* ☼ *Restaurant, in-room data ports, in-room safes, kitchenettes, cable TV, pool, gym, laundry facilities, shop, business services.* ▭ *AE, DC, MC, V.*

$–$$ ⊡ **Marc Hawai'i Polo Inn and Tower.** This boutique hotel fronts Ala Moana Boulevard, just one block from Ala Moana Shopping Center and Ala Moana Beach Park, on the 'ewa end of Waikīkī. Rooms are small, with tropic-style furnishings. Tower rooms have kitchenettes. The Inn's decor pays tribute to the Hawai'i polo enthusiasts who play in season on both

O'ahu's windward and north shores. ☒ *1696 Ala Moana Blvd., 96815* ☎ *808/949–0061 or 800/535–0085* ⊕ *www.marcresorts.com* ⤴ *106* ⚭ *Restaurant, in-room safes, some kitchenettes, cable TV, pool, laundry facilities* ☰ *AE, DC, MC, V.*

$–$$ ⌨ **Waikīkī Hāna.** Smack-dab in the middle of Waikīkī and a block away from the beach, this eight-story hotel is convenient for exploring just about every shop, restaurant, and activity in O'ahu's tourist hub. Accommodations are clean and plain. Many rooms have their own lānai. Pay a little extra per day and you can rent a refrigerator. The Super Chef restaurant on the ground floor offers casual, convenient dining for breakfast, lunch, and dinner. ☒ *2424 Koa Ave., Waikīkī, Honolulu 96815* ☎ *808/926–8841 or 800/367–5004* ☐ *808/924–3770* ⊕ *www.castleresorts.com* ⤴ *70 rooms, 2 suites* ⚭ *Restaurant, in-room safes, kitchenettes, cable TV, hair salon, lobby lounge, laundry facilities* ☰ *AE, DC, MC, V.*

¢–$ ⌨ **Royal Grove Hotel.** This flamingo-pink family-oriented hotel is reminiscent of Miami. With just six floors, it is one of Waikīkī's smaller hotels. The lobby is comfortable; the rooms, though agreeably furnished, have neither themes nor views. Go for the higher-end rooms if possible—economy rooms have no air-conditioning and more street noise. The hotel is about two blocks from the beach, and the pool area is bright with tropical flowers. Don't be surprised if members of the Fong family, who own and run the place, cook up a potluck dinner with some 'ukulele entertainment, just so guests can meet each other. Weekly and monthly rates are available. ☒ *151 Uluniu Ave., Waikīkī, Honolulu 96815* ☎ *808/923–7691* ⊕ *www.royalgrovehotel.com* ☐ *808/922–7508* ⤴ *78 rooms, 7 suites* ⚭ *Kitchenettes, pool; no a/c in some rooms* ☰ *AE, D, DC, MC, V.*

Honolulu

★ $$$$ ⌨ **Kāhala Mandarin Oriental Hawai'i.** Minutes away from Waikīkī, on the quiet side of Diamond Head, this elegant oceanfront hotel is hidden in the wealthy neighborhood of Kāhala. Rooms combine touches of Asia and old Hawai'i, with mahogany furniture, teak parquet floors, hand-loomed area rugs, local art, and grass-cloth wall coverings. If you're adventurous, you may want to reserve ahead to interact with dolphins in the hotel's impressive 26,000-square-foot lagoon. For the ultimate in pampering, book a spa suite at the Kahala Spa. Dine at the eclectic Hoku's, or beachfront in your own cabana at Cabana's Seaside Grill. ☒ *5000 Kāhala Ave., Kāhala, Honolulu 96816* ☎ *808/739–8888 or 800/367–2525* ☐ *808/739–8800* ⊕ *www.mandarinoriental.com/kahala* ⤴ *341 rooms, 29 suites* ⚭ *5 restaurants, room service, in-room data ports, in-room safes, minibars, cable TV, pool, gym, spa, beach, dive shop, lobby lounge, concierge, business services, meeting room* ☰ *AE, D, DC, MC, V.*

$$$–$$$$ ⌨ **Aston at the Executive Centre Hotel.** Here's a great option for the corporate traveler who wants to avoid Waikīkī. Downtown Honolulu's only hotel is an all-suite high-rise in the center of the business district, within walking distance of the Aloha Tower Marketplace and 10 minutes from

Honolulu International Airport. Suites are on the top 10 floors of a 40-story glass-walled tower, providing views of downtown and Honolulu Harbor. Each unit has a separate living area and kitchenette stocked with cold beverages. Some units have washer-dryers. The hotel offers a round-the-clock business center and health spa. Guests receive free Continental breakfast and a newspaper daily. ✉ *1088 Bishop St., Downtown Honolulu 96813* ☎ *808/539–3000 or 877/997–6667* ☒ *808/523–1088* ⊕ *www.aston-hotels.com* ⬦ *116 suites* ⚖ *Restaurant, in-room data ports, in-room safes, kitchenettes, cable TV, pool, gym, spa, business services, meeting rooms* ▭ *AE, DC, MC, V* ⍾⊙⍾ *CP.*

$$–$$$$ ⊞ **Ala Moana Hotel.** This hotel is at the entrance to Waikīkī near the popular Ala Moana Shopping Center (they're connected by a pedestrian ramp), Victoria Ward Centers, the Hawai'i Convention Center, and Ala Moana Beach Park. Most rooms in this 36-story high-rise have a lānai with a view of Ala Moana Beach, the ocean, or the mountains. Rooms on the 29th to 35th floors have the added luxury of in-room whirlpool baths and free use of the conference room. If you want a panoramic view of Ala Moana Beach, we recommend the one-bedroom junior suites for a wall-to-wall Pacific Ocean view. The hotel's nightclub, Rumours, is popular with the after-work crowd, and the Plantation Cafe is known for its elaborate Sunday brunches and weekend seafood buffets. The swimming pool features a chair lift for those guests who have special needs. ✉ *410 Atkinson Dr., Ala Moana, Honolulu 96814* ☎ *808/955–4811 or 888/367–4811* ☒ *808/944–6839* ⊕ *www.alamoanahotel.com* ⬦ *1,150 rooms, 67 suites* ⚖ *4 restaurants, room service, in-room safes, minibars, cable TV, pool, gym, bar, 2 lobby lounges, dance club, nightclub, meeting room* ▭ *AE, DC, MC, V.*

$$–$$$ ⊞ **Mānoa Valley Inn.** An intimate surprise is tucked away in Mānoa Valley, just 2 mi from Waikīkī. Built in 1919, this stately home is on the National Register of Historic Places. Linger over the complimentary Continental breakfast on the shady backyard lānai each morning and enjoy tropical fruit and cheese in the afternoon. Rooms are furnished in country-inn style, with antique four-poster beds, marble-top dressers, patterned wallpaper, and period antiques. There's a reading room with a TV and VCR. The separate carriage house sleeps four. ✉ *2001 Vancouver Dr., Mānoa, Honolulu 96822* ☎ *808/947–6019 or 800/634–5115* ☒ *808/946–6168* ⊕ *www.manoavalleyinn.com* ⬦ *7 suites, 4 with bath; 1 house* ▭ *AE, DC, MC, V* ⍾⊙⍾ *CP.*

$$–$$$ ⊞ **Pagoda Hotel.** The location, minutes away from Ala Moana Shopping Center and Ala Moana Beach Park, and moderate rates make this a good choice if you're simply looking for a place to sleep and catch a couple of meals. Studios feature kitchenettes with full-size refrigerators, stoves, microwaves, and cooking and dining ware. There are no memorable views because the hotel is surrounded by high-rises. The restaurant is notable for its Japanese gardens and carp-filled waterways. ✉ *1525 Rycroft St., Ala Moana, Honolulu 96814* ☎ *808/941–6611 or 800/367–6060* ☒ *808/955–5067* ⊕ *www.hthcorp.com* ⬦ *362 rooms* ⚖ *1 restaurant, room service, in-room data ports, some kitchenettes, refrigerators, 2 pools, hair salon, shop, laundry facilities, no-smoking rooms* ▭ *AE, D, DC, MC, V.*

Around the Island

★ **$$$$**   J. W. Marriott 'Ihilani Resort & Spa. Forty-five minutes and a world away from the bustle of Waikīkī, the 'Ihilani is in a sleek 17-story building illuminated by a glass-dome atrium. Rooms are 650 square feet and have marble bathrooms with deep soaking tubs, private lānai, teak furnishings, in-room CD players with a selection of CDs, and a high-tech control system (lights, temperature controls, and more). Most rooms have ocean views. Azul is the resort's signature dining room and features contemporary Mediterranean cuisine. The 35,000-square-foot, two-story 'Ihilani Spa has everything from green-tea wraps to authentic Thalasso therapies. There's a Ted Robinson–designed 18-hole championship golf facility. ⊠ *92-1001 'Ōlani St., Kapolei 96707* ☎ *808/679–0079 or 800/626–4446* ☐ *808/679–0080* ⊕ *www.ihilani.com* ⇨ *387 rooms, 63 suites* ♨ *4 restaurants, room service, minibars, cable TV, 18-hole golf course, 6 tennis courts, 2 pools, health club, spa, shops, babysitting, children's programs (ages 5–12), concierge, business services, meeting rooms* ☰ *AE, DC, MC, V.*

$$$$
Fodor'sChoice
★
Turtle Bay Resort. A $35 million renovation has finally restored this resort to a grandeur worthy of its location on O'ahu's scenic North Shore. All rooms now feature lānai to showcase stunning peninsula views. The rooms are stylish, in colors that represent all the shades of the sea and sand. The beach cottages are sumptuous oceanfront retreats complete with Brazilian walnut floors, teak rockers on the lānai, and large marble bathrooms with deep soaking tubs. The resort's signature restaurant is 21 Degrees North. Turtle Bay also has a spa, 12 mi of nature trails, a Hans Heidemann Surf School, and the only 36-hole golf facility on O'ahu. ⊠ *57-091 Kamehameha Hwy. (Box 187), Kahuku 96731* ☎ *808/293–8811 or 800/203–3650* ☐ *808/293–9147* ⊕ *www.turtlebayresort.com* ⇨ *373 rooms, 10 suites, 42 beach cottages* ♨ *4 restaurants, room service, refrigerators, cable TV, 2 18-hole golf courses, 10 tennis courts, 2 pools, gym, spa, beach, horseback riding, lobby lounge, shops, children's programs (ages 5–12), meeting room* ☰ *AE, D, DC, MC, V.*

$–$$$$ Schrader's Windward Country Inn. Though billed as "cottages by the sea," the setting is actually more roadside motel than resort. But Schrader's provides a moderately priced lodging alternative with amenities you won't find in Waikīkī, including complimentary biweekly ocean-reef tours that include snorkeling and kayaking the scenic windward coastline. One- to four-bedroom accommodations are available. Units feature microwaves and refrigerators, and some have full kitchens. Ask for the rooms that open onto Kāne'ohe Bay if you relish the possibility of fishing right off your lānai. ⊠ *47-039 Lihikai Dr., Kāne'ohe 96744* ☎ *808/239–5711 or 800/735–5711* ☐ *808/239–6658* ⊕ *www. hawaiiscene.com/schrader* ⇨ *57 rooms* ♨ *BBQs, kitchenettes, pool* ☰ *AE, D, DC, MC, V.*

¢–$$$$ Backpackers Vacation Inn and Plantation Village. Spartan in furnishings and definitely very casual in spirit, Backpackers is a surfer's kind of place to catch some sleep between wave sets. It's near Waimea Bay on the North Shore at Three Tables Beach and offers double rooms (some with a double bed, others with two single beds), hostel accommodations, and cot-

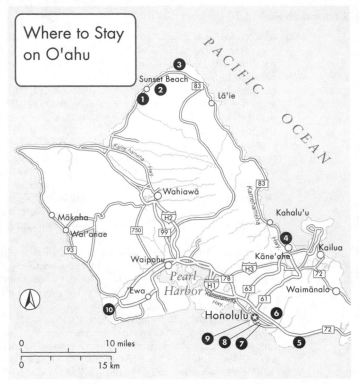

Where to Stay
on Oʻahu

tages. Some accommodations have kitchenettes. It's a three-minute walk to the supermarket. ⊠ 59-788 Kamehameha Hwy., Haleʻiwa 96712 ☎ 808/638–7838 ⊕ www.backpackers-hawaii.com 🖷 808/638–7515 ↩ 25 rooms ☾ Some kitchenettes; no a/c, no phones in some rooms, no TV in some rooms ⊟ MC, V.

¢–$ 🖭 **Breck's on the Beach Hostel.** Just north of Sunset Beach Park, Breck's offers convenient digs along the North Shore, with rooms ranging from basic dormitory to ocean-view balcony apartments that sleep eight people. Guests, usually surfer types from many continents, have access to free body boards and snorkeling equipment. Bicycles and surfboards are also available. Studio apartments have refrigerators and private baths, and the larger balcony apartments include kitchens. Airport pickup is available. A three-night minimum stay is required. ⊠ 59-043 Huelo St., Sunset Beach 96712 ☎ 808/638–7873 ↩ 21 units ☾ Some kitchens, airport shuttle; no a/c in some rooms ⊟ No credit cards.

NIGHTLIFE & THE ARTS

Nightlife on Oʻahu can be as simple as a barefoot stroll in the sand or as elaborate as a dinner show with all the glitter of a Las Vegas production. You can view the vibrant hues of a Honolulu sunset during a cocktail cruise or hear the melodies of ancient chants at a lū'au on a remote west-shore beach.

Waikīkī's Kalākaua and Kūhiō avenues come to life when the sun goes down. Outside Honolulu, offerings are slimmer but equally diverse. Wafting through the night air of O'ahu is the sound of music of every kind—from classical to contemporary. Music has been the language of Hawai'i from the beginning, and O'ahu has the best selection. There is hula everywhere, whether dancers wear sequin skirts in Waikīkī or authentic ti-leaf skirts at Paradise Cove.

The arts thrive alongside the tourist industry. O'ahu has an established symphony, a thriving opera company, chamber music groups, and community theaters. Major Broadway shows, dance companies, and rock stars also make their way to Honolulu. Check the local newspapers—the *Honolulu Advertiser,* the *Honolulu Star-Bulletin,* or the *Honolulu Weekly*—for the latest events.

Bars, Cabarets & Clubs

The drinking age is 21 on O'ahu and throughout Hawai'i. Many bars will admit younger people but will not serve them alcohol. By law, all establishments that serve alcoholic beverages must close by 2 AM. The only exceptions are those with a cabaret license, which have a 4 AM curfew. Most places have a cover charge of $5 to $10.

Honolulu

★ **Aaron's Atop the Ala Moana.** A splendid view, good contemporary dance music, and a sophisticated, well-dressed crowd come together at this Honolulu nightclub, which offers candlelight, a late-night dining menu, and an incomparable 36th-floor view of Honolulu's city lights. ⊠ *Ala Moana Hotel, 410 Atkinson Dr., Ala Moana* ☎ *808/955–4466.*

Anna Bannana's. Generations of Hawai'i college students have spent more than an evening or two at this legendary two-story, smoky dive. A living-room atmosphere makes it a comfortable place to hang out. Here, the music is fresh, loud, and sometimes experimental. Local favorites deliver ultracreative dance music, and the likes of blues singer Taj Mahal have been known to perform. Live music happens Thursday–Saturday, starting at 9 PM. ⊠ *2440 S. Beretania St., Mō'ili'ili* ☎ *808/946–5190.*

Banana Patch Lounge. This hotel lounge is definitely active—the entertainment includes guests strutting their stuff at karaoke. ⊠ *Miramar at Waikīkī Hotel, 2345 Kūhiō Ave., Waikīkī* ☎ *808/922–2077.*

★ **Banyan Veranda.** The Banyan Veranda is steeped in history. From this location the radio program *Hawaii Calls* first broadcast the sounds of Hawaiian music and the rolling surf to a U.S. mainland audience in 1935. Today, a variety of Hawaiian entertainment, with an emphasis on the sounds of the steel guitar, continues to provide the perfect accompaniment to the sounds of the surf. ⊠ *Sheraton Moana Surfrider, 2365 Kalākaua Ave., Waikīkī* ☎ *808/922–3111.*

Blue Tropix. This nightclub features DJs mixing hip-hop and house for the 18-plus crowd. Check out the Big Teeze on Tuesday and XXX Saturday promotions with DJ Kool-E and the Nocturnal Sound Krew. ⊠ *1700 Kapi'olani Blvd., Ala Moana* ☏ *808/944–0001.*

Café Sistina After Hours. This little Italian restaurant goes "Noche Tropical" after hours on Saturday, when some of the island's most enthusiastic salsa dancers kick up their heels to a DJ spinning Tito Puente, Celia Cruz, and Grupo Niche. ⊠ *Café Sistina, 1314 S. King St., Ala Moana* ☏ *808/596–0061.*

The Cellar Nightclub. Head downstairs to the Cellar to get your groove on with an 18-and-over crowd and music mixed by DJs Big John and Sho. Monday is dedicated to hip-hop. ⊠ *205 Lewers St., Waikīkī* ☏ *808/923–9952.*

Chai's Island Bistro. Chai's welcomes some of Hawai'i's top entertainers, such as the Brothers Cazimero (on Wednesday evening), Hapa, and Jake Shimabukuro. There's also a Pacific Rim–cuisine menu with a twist of Thai. ⊠ *Aloha Tower Marketplace, 1 Aloha Tower Dr., Downtown Honolulu* ☏ *808/585–0011.*

Cobalt Lounge. Take the glass elevator up 30 stories to this lounge, in the center of the Hanohano Room, that is definitely "blue" Hawaii. Leather sofas and cobalt blue lighting set the mood. Enjoy the sunset with floor to ceiling windows that offer breathtaking views of Diamond Head and the Waikīkī shoreline. You'll find soft lights, starlight, and dancing nightly. ⊠ *Sheraton Waikīkī, 2255 Kalākaua Ave., Waikīkī* ☏ *808/922–4422.*

☕ **Dave and Buster's.** Located in the Victoria Ward Centers, this restaurant features a stocked bar and lots of amusements ranging from classic billiards to shuffleboard and the latest in video arcade games. DJ Taco spins the tunes nightly after 9 at the Sunset Bar. ⊠ *Ward Entertainment Center, 1030 Auahi St., Ala Moana* ☏ *808/589–5007.*

Don Ho's Grill. This popular waterfront restaurant in the Aloha Tower Marketplace houses the Tiny Bubbles Bar, famous for its "suck 'em up" mai tai, a Don Ho classic. There are karaoke contests on Wednesday evenings and Hawaiian music Wednesday–Sunday at dinnertime with performers like Jerry Santos, Jake Shimabukuro, and Robert Cazimero. On the weekend, dance music plays from 10 PM to 2 AM. ⊠ *Aloha Tower Marketplace, 1 Aloha Tower Dr., Downtown Honolulu* ☏ *808/528–0807.*

Duke's Canoe Club. With its oceanfront spot on Waikīkī Beach, this restaurant presents "Concerts on the Beach" every Friday and Saturday with contemporary Hawaiian musicians like Henry Kapono. National musicians like Jimmy Buffett have also performed here. At Duke's Barefoot Bar, solo Hawaiian musicians take the stage nightly. ⊠ *Outrigger Waikīkī, 2335 Kalākaua Ave., Waikīkī* ☏ *808/922–2268.*

Esprit. Waikīkī's only oceanfront nightclub affords a 180-degree view of the beach. Tito and the Rhythm Klub provide the contemporary tunes that keeps this club's crowd in sync and dancing the night away. ⊠ *Sheraton Waikīkī, 2255 Kalākaua Ave., Waikīkī* ☏ *808/922–4422.*

Fusion Waikīkī. This club features a Paper Doll Revue Drag Show and a Men of Fusion Male Revue, with a fun crowd that spans all genders and persuasions. ⊠ *2260 Kūhiō Ave., 3rd fl., Waikīkī* ☏ *808/924–2422.*

Gordon Biersch Brewery Restaurant. Live duos and trios serenade patrons of the outside bar that flanks Honolulu Harbor. Although there's no dancing, this is the place in Honolulu to see and be seen. ⊠ *Aloha Tower Marketplace, 1 Aloha Tower Dr., Downtown Honolulu* ☎ *808/599–4877.*

Honu Bar and Terrace. Sophisticated and swank, this lobby lounge presents light jazz and island ensembles during the cocktail and sunset hours. ⊠ *Kāhala Mandarin Oriental Hawai'i, 5000 Kāhala Ave., Kāhala* ☎ *808/739–8888.*

Hula's Bar and Lei Stand. Hawai'i's oldest and best-known gay-friendly nightspot offers calming panoramic outdoor views of Diamond Head and the Pacific Ocean by day and a high-energy club scene by night. Check out the soundproof, glassed-in dance floor and the hand-carved koa canoe that hangs above the bar. ⊠ *Waikīkī Grand Hotel, 134 Kapahulu Ave., 2nd fl., Waikīkī* ☎ *808/923–0669.*

Mai Tai Bar at the Royal Hawaiian. Everything is pink, including the beer, at this outdoor bar which offers front-row seating for Waikīkī sunsets and an unobstructed view of Diamond Head. Contemporary Hawaiian music holds center stage here. ⊠ *Royal Hawaiian Hotel, 2259 Kalākaua Ave., Waikīkī* ☎ *808/923–7311.*

Moana Terrace. Three floors up from Waikīkī Beach, this open-air terrace is the home of Aunty Genoa Keawe, the "First Lady of Hawaiian Music." Her falsetto sessions include jams with the finest of Hawai'i's musicians. The Terrace also features a Tahitian hula show at sunset on Monday evenings. ⊠ *Waikīkī Beach Marriott Resort, 2552 Kalākaua Ave., Waikīkī* ☎ *808/922–6611.*

Moose McGillycuddy's Pub and Cafe. Loud bands play for the beach-and-beer gang in a blue-jeans-and-T-shirt setting. Bikini contests are Sunday nights and there is an all male revue Wednesday evenings. ⊠ *310 Lewers St., Waikīkī* ☎ *808/923–0751.*

Nashville Waikīkī. Country music in the tropics? You bet! Put on your *paniolo* (Hawaiian cowboy) duds and mosey on out to the giant dance floor. There are pool tables, dartboards, line dancing, and free dance lessons (Monday, Tuesday, Friday at 7 PM) to boot. ⊠ *Ohana Waikīkī West Hotel, 2330 Kūhiō Ave., Waikīkī* ☎ *808/926–7911.*

Opium Den & Champagne Bar at Indigo's. This bar at the edge of Chinatown resembles a joint right out of a film noir. Jazz plays early in the evening; late-night DJs spin trance, Top 40, funk, disco, and rock. In addition to champagne, happy hour features sake martinis and a sampler menu. ⊠ *Indigo Euroasian Cuisine, 1121 Nu'uanu Ave., Downtown Honolulu* ☎ *808/521–2900.*

Paradise Lounge. Several contemporary Hawaiian acts, including the longtime band Olomana, perform in this pretty outdoor club. ⊠ *Hilton Hawaiian Village, 2005 Kālia Rd., Waikīkī* ☎ *808/949–4321.*

Pier Bar. Here's one of the few places in Honolulu where you can hear live music outdoors and dance underneath the stars. It attracts a grab bag of groups; call ahead to find out who's playing. ⊠ *Aloha Tower Marketplace, 1 Aloha Tower Dr., Downtown Honolulu* ☎ *808/536–2166.*

Pipeline Cafe and Sports Bar. This is two stories of fun with pool, darts, and more. The upstairs sports bar has TVs galore and a skybox view of the dancing below. Music includes both live acts and seasoned DJs. Theme nights add to the excitement. ⊠ *805 Pohukaina St., Kaka'ako* ☎ *808/589–1999.*

Royal Garden at Waikīkī. Some of O'ahu's top jazz stylists perform in the elegant, intimate lobby lounge of this sophisticated hotel. ⊠ *Royal Garden at Waikīkī, 444 'Olohana St., Waikīkī* ☎ *808/943–0202.*

Rumours. The after-work crowd loves this spot, which has dance videos, disco, and throbbing lights. On Saturday "Little Chill" nights, the club plays oldies from the '70s, '80s, and '90s and serves free pūpū. There is "salsa after dark" dancing Thursday evening with free salsa lessons from 6:30 to 7:30. ⊠ *Ala Moana Hotel, 410 Atkinson St., Ala Moana* ☎ *808/955–4811.*

Scruples Beach Club. After the sun goes down, the beach party moves from the sand to this discotheque right off Waikīkī's strip. Dance to the latest alternative, house, and Top 40 music with a clientele that is as diverse as all Hawai'i. Casual attire is welcome. ⊠ *2310 Kuhio Ave. at Nahua St., Waikīkī* ☎ *808/923–9530.*

Shore Bird Oceanside Bar and Grill. This Waikīkī beachfront bar spills right out onto the sand. It has a large dance floor and a 10-foot video screen. Karaoke sing-alongs are held nightly. ⊠ *Outrigger Reef on the Beach hotel, 2169 Kālia Rd., Waikīkī* ☎ *808/922–2887.*

Venus Nightclub. This high-energy social bar, with leather couches ideal for a night of people-watching, features hip-hop, trance, and reggae with guest DJs five nights a week. Attention, ladies: there's a male dance revue Saturday evenings. ⊠ *1349 Kapi'olani Blvd., Ala Moana* ☎ *808/951–8671.*

Virus Entertainment. Here DJs make the music come alive with their mix of house, trance, drum, and bass. On the last Saturday of the month, prepare to get wet at the after-hours foam party. ⊠ *1687 Kapi'olani Blvd., Ala Moana* ☎ *808/951–9881.*

Wave Waikīkī. This venue has stood the test of time, anchoring the Waikīkī entertainment scene for more than two decades. Dance to live rock and roll until 1:30 AM and recorded music after that. It can be a rough scene (the place has seen more than its fair share of drunken fisticuffs), but the bands are tops. Late nights, the music here definitely goes "underground." ⊠ *1877 Kalākaua Ave., Waikīkī* ☎ *808/941–0424.*

Wonder Lounge at the W Diamond Head. A variety of theme dance nights make Friday evenings a wonder to behold here in the lobby of the W Diamond Head. The crowd is full of hip, young professionals who enjoy mai tai martinis and the chance to do some not-so-serious networking. ⊠ *W Honolulu—Diamond Head, 2885 Kalākaua Ave., Waikīkī* ☎ *808/922–1700.*

World Cafe. Honolulu's only upscale billiards nightclub also has a sports bar and dancing to Top-40 tunes. ⊠ *500 Ala Moana Blvd., Ala Moana* ☎ *808/599–4450.*

Zanzabar. DJs spin top hits, from hip-hop to soul and techno to trance, at this elegant and high-energy nightspot in the Waikīkī Trade Center. ⊠ *2255 Kūhiō Ave., Waikīkī* ☎ *808/924–3939.*

Around the Island

The Bay Club. A beautiful place to watch the sun set over the North Shore, this lounge inside the Turtle Bay Resort hosts a variety of local bands that play contemporary Hawaiian tunes. On weekend nights, dance music keeps things rocking on the North Shore. ⊠ *Turtle Bay Resort, 57-091 Kamehameha Hwy., Kahuku* ☎ *808/293–8811.*

Cocktail & Dinner Cruises

Dinner cruises depart either from the piers adjacent to the Aloha Tower Marketplace in Downtown Honolulu or from Kewalo Basin, just 'ewa of Ala Moana Beach Park, and head along the coast toward Diamond Head. There's usually dinner, dancing, drinks, and a sensational sunset. Except as noted, dinner cruises cost approximately $30–$95, cocktail cruises $25–$40. Most major credit cards are accepted.

Ali`i Kai Catamaran. Patterned after an ancient Polynesian vessel, this huge catamaran casts off from Aloha Tower with 1,000 passengers. The deluxe dinner cruise has two open bars, a huge dinner, and an authentic Polynesian show with colorful hula music. The food is good, the after-dinner show loud and fun, and everyone dances on the way back to shore. ⊠ *Pier 5, street level, Honolulu* ☎ *808/539–9400 ext. 5.*

Dream Cruises. The 100-foot motor yacht *American Dream* handles up to 225 guests for evening cruises off the shores of Waikīkī. Decks have plenty of outdoor space for views of the twinkling city lights. The Island Grill dinner cruise includes one mai tai, grilled-steak and -chicken brochette with grilled vegetables, cold *somen* (thin white Japanese noodles made from wheat flour) salad, *haupia* (coconut pudding) chocolate cake, and soft drinks. You pay for extra drinks. Vegetarian meals may be ordered in advance. After a hula demonstration, a DJ spins tunes from the '50s through the '70s. ⊠ *306 Kamani St., Honolulu* ☎ *808/ 592–5200 or 800/400–7300* ⊕ *www.dream-cruises.com.*

Navatek Cruises. The sleek *Navatek* is a revolutionary craft designed to sail smoothly in rough waters, which allows it to power farther along Waikīkī's coastline than its competitors. Choose from sunset dinner buffet or moonlight cruises, or breakfast and lunch whale-watch cruises December–mid-April. Tours leave from Pier 6, next to Aloha Tower Marketplace. ⊠ *Honolulu Harbor* ☎ *808/973–1311* ⊕ *www. atlantisadventures.com.*

Paradise Cruises. Prices vary depending on which deck you choose on the 1,600-passenger, four-deck *Star of Honolulu*. For instance, a seven-course French-style dinner and live jazz on the top deck costs $199. A steak and crab feast on level two costs $105. This ship also features daily Hawaiiana Lunch cruises that offer lei-making and 'ukulele and hula lessons for $42. Evening excursions also take place on the 340-passenger *Starlet I* and 230-passenger *Starlet II*, which offer three-course dinners beginning at $42. ⊠ *1540 S. King St., Honolulu* ☎ *808/983–7827* ⊕ *www.paradisecruises.com.*

Cocktail & Dinner Shows

Some O'ahu entertainers have been around for years, and others have just arrived on the scene. Either way, the dinner-show food is usually buffet-style with a definite local accent. Dinner shows are all in the $55 to $99 range. Cocktail shows run $30 to $43. The prices usually include one cocktail, tax, and gratuity. In all cases, reservations are essential. Be sure to call in advance. You never know when an artist may have switched venues.

Blue Hawai'i: The Show. Jonathan Von Brana sings Elvis Presley tunes that showcase the King's love of the Islands. ⊠ *Waikīkī Beachcomber Hotel, 2300 Kalākaua Ave., Waikīkī* ☎ *808/923–1245* ☉ *Shows Wed.–Mon. at 6:15.*

Creation: A Polynesian Odyssey. This show traces Hawai'i's culture and history, from its origins to statehood. The highlight is a daring Samoan fire-knife dancer. ⊠ *'Āinahau Showroom, Sheraton Princess Ka'iulani Hotel, 120 Ka'iulani Ave., Waikīkī* ☎ *808/931–4660* ☉ *Dinner shows Tues., Thurs., Sat. at 6.*

Don Ho. Don Ho is the singer who put Waikīkī entertainment on the map four decades ago. His song "Tiny Bubbles" became his trademark. His show, a Polynesian revue (with a cast of young and attractive Hawaiian performers), has found the perfect home in this intimate club inside the Waikīkī Beachcomber Hotel. ⊠ *Waikīkī Beachcomber Hotel, 2300 Kalākaua Ave., Waikīkī* ☎ *808/923–3981* ☉ *Shows Sun.–Thurs. at 7, with cocktail and dinner seatings.*

Magic of Polynesia. Hawai'i's top illusionist, John Hirokawa, displays mystifying sleight of hand in this highly entertaining show, which incorporates contemporary hula and island music into its acts. ⊠ *Waikīkī Beachcomber Hotel, 2300 Kalākaua Ave., Waikīkī* ☎ *808/971–4321* ☉ *Nightly at 8.*

ONE. The latest addition to the Waikīkī show scene, this variety show at the Marriott features juggling, illusions, and a high-energy Polynesian revue. ⊠ *Waikīkī Beach Marriott Resort 2552 Kalākaua Ave., Waikīkī* ☎ *808/921–5000* ☉ *Shows Mon., Wed., Fri. at 7.*

★ ☉ **Polynesian Cultural Center.** Easily one of the best on the Islands, this show has soaring moments and an "erupting volcano." The performers are students from Brigham Young University's Hawai'i campus. ⊠ *55-370 Kamehameha Hwy., Lā'ie* ☎ *808/293–3333 or 800/367–7060* ⊕ *www.polynesia.com* ☉ *Mon.–Sat. 12:30–9:30.*

Society of Seven. This lively, popular septet has great staying power and, after more than 25 years, continues to put on one of the best shows in Waikīkī. They sing, dance, do impersonations, play instruments, and, above all, entertain with their contemporary sound. ⊠ *Outrigger Waikīkī on the Beach, 2335 Kalākaua Ave., Waikīkī* ☎ *808/922–6408* ☉ *Tues.–Sat. at 8:30.*

Dance

Every year at least one of mainland America's finer ballet troupes makes the trip to Honolulu for a series of dance performances at the

BEYOND "TINY BUBBLES"

ASK MOST VISITORS *about Hawaiian music and they'll likely break into a lighthearted rendition of "Little Grass Shack." When they're finished, lead them directly to a stereo.*

First, play them a recording of singer Kekuhi Kanahele, whose compositions combine ancient Hawaiian chants with modern melodies. Then ask them to listen to a CD by guitarist Keola Beamer, who loosens his strings and plays slack-key tunes dating to the 1830s. Amaze them with the `ukulele stylings of young Jake Shimabukuro. Share a recording by falsetto virtuoso Amy Hanaiali`i Gilliom, or play the late Israel Kamakawiwo`ole's version of "What a Wonderful World," which has appeared on scores of feature films and national television-series. "Brother Iz," who died in 1997, was a native Hawaiian with a voice so pure, most of his songs were recorded simply with voice and `ukulele. His last album, Alone In Iz World, was released posthumously.

These artists, like many others, are proving just how multifaceted Hawaiian music has become. They're unearthing their island roots in the form of revered songs and chants, and they're reinterpreting them for today's audiences.

Granted, "Little Grass Shack" does have its place in the history books. After Hawai`i became a U.S. territory in 1900, the world discovered its music thanks to touring ensembles who turned heads with swaying hips, steel guitars, and pseudo-Hawaiian lyrics. Once radio and movies got into the act, dreams of Hawai`i came with a saccharine Hollywood sound track.

But Hawaiian music is far more complex. It harks back to the ancient islanders who beat rough-hewn drums, blew haunting calls on conch shells, and intoned chants for their gods. It recalls the voices of 19th-century Christian missionaries who taught islanders to sing in four-part harmony, a style that's still popular today.

The music takes on international overtones thanks to gifts from foreign immigrants: the `ukulele from Portuguese laborers, for instance, and the guitar from Mexican traders. And it's enlivened by a million renderings of "Tiny Bubbles," as entertainers such as Don Ho croon Hawaiian-pop hits for Waikīkī tourists.

Island music came full circle in the late 1960s and '70s, when a few dedicated artists began giving voice to a resurgence of interest in Hawaiian culture, history, and traditions.

Today's artistic trailblazers are digging deep to explore their heritage, and their music reflects that thoughtful search. They go one step further by incorporating such time-honored instruments as nose flutes and gourds, helping them keep pace with the past.

If you want to experience the true essence of Hawaiian music, you must come to Hawai`i. Check ads and listings in local papers for information on concerts, which take place in indoor and outdoor theaters, hotel ballrooms, and cozy nightclubs. When you hear the sound, you'll know it's Hawaiian because it'll make you feel right at home.

Neal Blaisdell Center Concert Hall (⊠ Ward Ave. at King St., Downtown Honolulu, Honolulu ☎ 808/591–2211). A local company, **Ballet Hawai'i** (☎ 808/988–7578), is active during the holiday season with its annual production of *The Nutcracker,* which is usually held at the **Mamiya Theater** (⊠ St. Louis School, 3142 Wai'alae Ave., Kaimukī, Honolulu).

Film

Art, international, classic, and silent films are screened at the little theater at the **Honolulu Academy of Arts** (⊠ 900 S. Beretania St., Downtown Honolulu, Honolulu ☎ 808/532–8768). **Kāhala Mall** (⊠ 4211 Wai'alae Ave., Kāhala, Honolulu ☎ 808/733–6233) has eight movie theaters showing a diverse range of films. It's a 10-minute drive from Waikīkī. **Ward 16 Entertainment Complex** (⊠ 1044 Auahi St., Ala Moana, Honolulu ☎ 808/593–3000) is a 16-screen entertainment complex that also has restaurants like Dave and Buster's and retail outlets like Roxy Sportswear.

The **Hawai'i International Film Festival** (☎ 808/528–3456) may not be Cannes, but it is unique and exciting. During the weeklong festival, held from the end of November to early December, top films from the United States, Asia, and the Pacific are screened day and night at several theaters on O'ahu.

★ ☻ The city-sponsored **Sunset on the Beach** (☎ 808/523–2489) events are held twice a month at various beaches. This is truly a local night out on the town. Find your spot on the beach and enjoy entertainment, food from top local restaurants, and a first-run movie feature on a big screen, all underneath the stars.

Lū'au

Most lū'au emphasize fun over strict adherence to tradition. They generally cost $60–$100. Reservations are essential.

Germaine's Lū'au. This lū'au is billed as being "100 years away from Waikīkī." Expect a lively crowd as you are bused to a private beach 35 minutes from Waikīkī. The bus ride is actually a lot of fun, and the beach and sunset are pleasant. The service is brisk in order to feed everyone on time, and the food is the usual multicourse, all-you-can-eat buffet, but the show is warm and friendly. ☎ *808/949–6626 or 800/367–5665* ☻ *Tues.–Sat. at 6.*

Paradise Cove Lū'au. There are palms and a glorious sunset, and the pageantry is fun, even informative. The food—well, you didn't come for the food, did you? This is another mass-produced event for 1,000 or so. A bus takes you from one of six Waikīkī hotel pickup points to a remote beachfront estate beside a picturesque cove on the western side of the island, 27 mi from Waikīkī. ☎ *808/842–5911* ⊕ *www. paradisecovehawaii.com* ☻ *Daily at 5:30, doors open at 5.*

Polynesian Cultural Center Ali'i Lū'au. An hour's drive from Honolulu, this North Shore O'ahu lū'au is set amid seven re-created Polynesian villages. Dinner is all-you-can-eat traditional lū'au food such as kālua pig and lomi lomi salmon, followed by a world-class revue. ☎ *808/293–3333 or 800/367–7060* ⊕ *www.polynesia.com* ☻ *Mon.–Sat. at 5:30.*

Royal Hawaiian Lū'au. Waikīkī's only oceanfront lū'au offers an exotic, upscale menu and entertainment. With the setting sun, Diamond Head, the Pacific Ocean, and the legendary Pink Palace as a backdrop, this contemporary lū'au might even make you learn to love poi. ☎ *808/923–7311 ☉ Mon. at 6.*

Music

Chamber Music Hawai'i (☎ 808/947–1975) gives 25 concerts a year at the **Honolulu Lutheran Church** (✉ 1730 Punahou St., Makiki Heights, Honolulu), **Honolulu Academy of Arts** (✉ 900 S. Beretania St., Downtown Honolulu, Honolulu), and other locations around the island.

Hawai'i Opera Theater (✉ Neal Blaisdell Center Concert Hall, Ward Ave. and King St., Downtown Honolulu, Honolulu ☎ 808/596–7372 ⊕ www. hawaiiopera.org) has a season which spans January–March and includes such works as *The Barber of Seville, Tristan and Isolde,* and *Madame Butterfly,* performed by renowned international opera stars and guest conductors. All operas are sung in their original language with projected English translation. Tickets range from $27 to $95.

The **Honolulu Symphony Orchestra** (✉ Dole Cannery, 650 Iwilei Rd., Suite 202, Iwilei, Honolulu ☎ 808/792–2000 ⊕ www.honolulusymphony. com ✍ $17–$59) performs at the Neil Blaisdell Concert Hall and is led by the young, dynamic Samuel Wong. The Honolulu Pops series, with some performances underneath the stars summer nights at the Waikīkī Shell, features top local and national artists under the direction of talented conductor-composer Matt Catingub.

Rock concerts are usually performed at the domed **Neal Blaisdell Center Arena** (☎ 808/591–2211). Internationally famous performers pack them in at **Aloha Stadium** (☎ 808/486–9300).

Theater

Because many of today's touring shows and music artists depend on major theatrical sets, lighting, and sound, Hawai'i, already pricey, can be an expensive gig. As a result, not many touring companies manage to stop here—those who do sell out fast. There is strong community support for local performing arts companies. O'ahu has developed several excellent local theater troupes, which present first-rate entertainment on an amateur and semiprofessional level all year long.

Army Community Theatre. This is a favorite for its revivals of musical theater classics, presented in an 800-seat house. The casts are talented, and the fare is great for families. ✉ *Richardson Theater, Fort Shafter, Downtown Honolulu, Honolulu ☎ 808/438–4480 ✍ $14–$20.*

Diamond Head Theater. The repertoire includes a little of everything: musicals, dramas, experimental productions, and classics. This company is in residence five minutes from Waikīkī, right next to Diamond Head. ✉ *520 Makapu'u Ave., Kapahulu, Honolulu ☎ 808/733–0274 ⊕ www. diamondheadtheater.com ✍ $10–$40.*

Hawai'i Theatre Center. Beautifully restored, this Downtown Honolulu theater, built in the 1920s in a neoclassic beaux arts style, hosts a wide variety of performing arts events, including international theatrical productions, international touring acts, festivals, films, and meetings. Historic tours of the theater are offered Tuesday at 11 for $5. Admission for performances varies. ⊠ *1130 Bethel St., Downtown Honolulu, Honolulu* ☎ *808/528–0506* ⊕ *www.hawaiitheatre.com.*

Honolulu Theater for Youth. This group stages delightful productions for children around the Islands from September through May. Call for a schedule. ⊠ *2846 Ualena St., Downtown Honolulu, Honolulu* ☎ *808/ 839–9885* ⊠ *$10.*

John F. Kennedy Theater. Eclectic dramatic offerings—everything from musical theater to Kabuki, Nō, and Chinese opera—are performed at this space at the University of Hawai'i's Mānoa campus. ⊠ *1770 East–West Rd., Mānoa, Honolulu* ☎ *808/956–7655* ⊠ *$9–$12.*

Kumu Kahua. This is the only troupe presenting shows and plays written by local playwrights about the Islands. It stages five or six productions a year. ⊠ *46 Merchant St., Downtown Honolulu, Honolulu* ☎ *808/536–4441* ⊠ *$12–$15.*

Mānoa Valley Theater. Wonderful nonprofessional performances are put on in this intimate theater in Mānoa Valley from September through July. ⊠*2833 E. Mānoa Rd., Mānoa, Honolulu* ☎*808/988–6131* ⊠*$17–$20.*

SPORTS & THE OUTDOORS

Aerial Tours

An aerial tour of the Islands opens up a world of perspective. Looking down from the sky at the outline of the U.S.S. Arizona as it lays in its final resting place in the waters of Pearl Harbor or getting a glimpse of how Mother Nature carves a vast expanse of volcanic crater are the kind of views only seen through an "eye in the sky." If you go, don't forget your camera.

The Original Glider Rides (⊠ Dillingham Airfield, Mokulē'ia ☎ 808/ 677–3404) has been offering piloted glider (sailplane) rides over the northwest end of Oahu's North Shore, since 1970. These are piloted scenic rides for one or two passengers in sleek, bubble-topped, motor-less aircraft. You'll get aerial views of mountains, shoreline, coral pools, windsurfing sails, and in winter, humpback whales. Reservations are recommended; 20- and 30-minute flights leave every 20 minutes daily 10–5. The charge for one passenger is $70; two people fly for $120 (ask about promotional pricing). Check-in with "Mr. Bill" for more information and reservations.

Island Seaplane Service (⊠ 85 Lagoon Drive, Honolulu ☎ 808/836–6273) takes off from Keahi Lagoon and sets you soaring on an aerial tour that is either a half-hour south and eastern O'ahu shoreline tour or an hour Circle Island tour. Get the feel of what Hawai'i air transportation was like during the Pan Am Clipper days for $89 to $139.

Makani Kai Helicopters (✉ 110 Kapalulu Pl., Honolulu ☎ 808/834–5813 ⊕ www.makanikai.com) depart from Honolulu International Airport for helicopter tours of O'ahu by daylight or at sunset. A Waikīkī by Night excursion sends you soaring by the breathtaking Honolulu city lights. Tours range from $99 to $185, with customized charters available from $550 per hour.

Biking

Coastal roads are flat and well paved. On the downside, they're also awash in vehicular traffic. Frankly, biking is no fun in either Waikīkī or Honolulu, but things are a bit better outside the city. Be sure to take along a nylon jacket for the frequent showers on the windward side and remember that Hawai'i is "paradise after the fall": lock up your bike.

Mountain bikes and mopeds are available for rent at **Blue Sky Rentals & Sports Center** (✉ 1920 Ala Moana Blvd., across from the Hilton Hawaiian Village, Waikīkī, Honolulu ☎ 808/947–0101). Rates are $18 per day (from 8 to 6), $26 for 24 hours, and $75 per week—a $100 deposit is required for weekly rentals. Prices include a bike, a helmet, a lock, and a water bottle.

If you want to find some biking buddies, write ahead to the **Hawai'i Bicycling League** (✉ Box 4403, Honolulu 96813 ☎ 808/735–5756 ⊕ www.bikehawaii.com), which can tell you about upcoming races and club rides (frequent on all the Islands).

For biking information and maps, contact the **Honolulu City and County Bike Coordinator** (☎ 808/527–5044).

Camping & Hiking

For a free O'ahu recreation map that outlines the island's 33 major trails, including the visitor-friendly Mānoa Falls Trail, Makapu'u Lighthouse Trail, Wa'ahila Ridge Trail, and Leeward's O'ahu's Kaena Point, contact the **Hawai'i State Department of Land and Natural Resources** (✉ 1151 Punchbowl St., Room 130, Downtown Honolulu, Honolulu 96813 ☎ 808/587–0300 ⊕ www.hawaii.gov).

For a complimentary hiking-safety guide, contact the City and County of Honolulu's **Trails and Access Manager** (☎ 808/973–9782). Ask for a copy of "Hiking on O'ahu: The Official Guide."

For families, the **Hawai'i Nature Center** (✉ 2131 Makiki Heights Dr., Makiki Heights, Honolulu 96822 ☎ 808/955–0100) in upper Makiki Valley conducts a number of programs for both adults and children. The center arranges guided hikes into tropical settings that reveal hidden waterfalls and protected forest reserves.

O'ahu Nature Tours (☎ 808/924–2473 ⊕ www.oahunaturetours.com) offers glorious sunrise, hidden waterfall, mountain forest, rain forest, and volcanic walking tours with an escort who will explain the wealth of native flora and fauna that is your companion along the way.

When on the North Shore, check out the **Trails at Turtle Bay Resort** (✉ Turtle Bay Resort, 57-091 Kamehameha Hwy. ☎ 808/293–8811 ⊕ www.turtlebayresort.com)—more than 12 mi of trails and oceanside pathways on this 880-acre resort. You can pick up a trail and ocean guide for a self-guided tour of the 5 mi of coastline and its exotic plants and trees.

Camping on O'ahu is available at four state parks, 12 county beach parks, and within the grounds of one county botanic garden. Stays are restricted to five nights per month in all beach and state recreation areas, and parks are closed to campers on Wednesday and Thursday evenings. To obtain a free camping permit for state parks, write to the **Department of Land and Natural Resources, State Parks Division** (⌂ Box 621, Honolulu 96809 ☎ 808/587–0300). For county and beach parks, contact the **Honolulu Department of Parks and Recreation** (✉ 650 S. King St., Honolulu 96813 ☎ 808/523–4525). A word of caution: although some O'ahu recreation areas have caretakers and gates that close in the evening for your safety, many others can be quite isolated at night.

Mālaekahana State Park on the North Shore is a local favorite and offers a beachfront setting with two areas that include rest rooms, showers, picnic tables, and drinking water. It's on Kamehameha Highway between Lā'ie and Kahuku. On the windward coast, **Ho'omaluhia Botanic Gardens** (✉ 45-680 Luluku Rd., Kaneohe ☎ 808/523–4525) provides a safe, scenic camping setting at the base of the majestic Ko'olau Mountains. Five grassy camping areas with rest rooms, showers, and drinking water are available on Friday, Saturday, and Sunday evenings only. Permits are free and are issued at the garden daily between 9 and 4.

You can rent everything from tents to backpacks at the **Bike Shop** (✉ 1149 S. King St., Mō'ili'ili, Honolulu ☎ 808/595–0588 ⊕ www.bikeshophawaii.com).

Fitness Centers & Spas

HONOLULU **Abhasa Spa.** Natural organic skin and body treatments are the signature at this spa tucked away in the Royal Hawaiian Hotel's coconut grove. Thalasso therapy with seaweed, vegetarian lifestyle–spa therapies, color-light therapy, Ayurveda body treatments, acupuncture, and body cocooning are all available. ✉ *Royal Hawaiian Hotel, 2259 Kalākaua Ave., Waikīkī* ☎ *808/922–8200* ⊕ *www.royalhawaiian.com.*

Ampy's European Facials and Body Spa. Indulge in this day spa's famous custom aromatherapy facials; massages; and spa packages, including a Gentlemen's Retreat. It's in the Ala Moana Building, adjacent to the Ala Moana Shopping Center. ✉ *1441 Kapi'olani Blvd., Suite 377, Ala Moana* ☎ *808/946–3838.*

Hawaiian Rainforest Salon and Spa. Vichy showers, aromatherapy whirlpool baths, a Korean-style Akasuri body polish, massage treatments, body wraps and facials, as well as complete hair, nail, and makeup services are available here. ✉ *Pacific Beach Hotel, 5th fl., 2490 Kalākaua Ave., Waikīkī* ☎ *808/441–4890* ⊕ *www.pacificbeachhotel.com.*

Mandara Spa at the Hilton Hawaiian Village. Twenty-five treatment rooms, spa suites, an elegant Hawaiian floral tile infinity pool, a full-service hair and nail salon, and a café are included in this spa environment. Treatments combine the healing techniques of Hawai'i, Asia, and Europe. Indulge in the signature "Mandara" massage, which features two massage therapists working in unison. ⊠ *Hilton Hawaiian Village Beach Resort and Spa 2005 Kālia Road, Waikīkī* ☎ *808/949–4321* ⊕ *www. hiltonhawaiianvillage.com.*

Na Ho'ola at the Hyatt Waikīkī. Come here for an authentic Hawaiian spa experience with poolside Lomi Lomi (Hawaiian massage), Reiki treatments, ti-leaf and Polynesian aloe body wraps, and La Stone (Swedish massage combined with the use of hot and cold stones) therapies. The spa also features a fitness center with cardiovascular equipment and an ocean view. ⊠ *2424 Kalākaua Ave., Waikīkī* ☎ *808/921–6097.*

Paul Brown Salon and Day Spa. This is one of the few salons where the principal owner still works the floor. The spa's location makes it an ideal spot to take a break from shopping at the Victoria Ward Centers. Get a tropical-fruit facial or mineral body wrap and follow it up with the Magic Island massage—a combination of Thai, shiatsu, *lomi lomi,* and reflexology. The spa also has a full-service hair and nail salon. ⊠ *Ward Centre, 1200 Ala Moana Blvd., Ala Moana* ☎ *808/591–1881* ⊕ *www. paulbrownhawaii.com.*

Serenity Spa Hawai'i. Aromatherapy treatments, massages, and facials are provided in an atmosphere of serene calm at this day spa, only steps off the beach. If you want to optimize your tanning time, consider this starter: the Golden Touch tanning massage, which combines a massage with tan accelerators, sunscreen and scented oils. ⊠ *Outrigger Reef on the Beach, 2169 Kālia Rd., Waikīkī* ☎ *808/926–2882* ⊕ *www. serenityspahawaii.com.*

SpaHalekulani. SpaHalekulani adds another touch of heaven to the elegance of the Halekūlani Hotel oasis. This spa has no common area, just individualized suites for personalized pampering. SpaHalekulani's signature treatments specialize in exploring the healing traditions found in many of the South Pacific Islands, including Hawaii. For an invigorating massage, we suggest the Japanese Ton Ton Amma (pounders). For your hair, try the restorative Tahitian coconut hair therapy treatment. ⊠ *Halekūlani Hotel 2199 Kālia Road, Waikīkī* ☎ *808/ 931–5322.*

★ **Spa Olakino at the Waikīkī Beach Marriott.** Paul Brown has created a spa facing Waikīkī Beach where you can linger with a cup of tea between treatments, gaze through 75-foot windows at all the activity outside, then be enveloped in a retreat of serenity just steps away. The decor is lush with Hawaiian foliage and sleek Balinese teak furnishings. Treatments include body wraps with green tea and aloe, Thai massage, papaya pineapple facials, and a variety of spa packages for men, women, and couples. ⊠ *Waikīkī Beach Marriott 2552 Kalākaua Ave., Waikīkī* ☎ *808/922– 6611* ⊕ *www.marriottwaikiki.com.*

★ **Spa Suites at the Kāhala Mandarin Oriental.** The Kāhala Mandarin Oriental has created spa suites so sumptuous you may never want to leave. Each suite features a Jacuzzi, a private vanity area, and a private garden in which to relax between treatments. Treatments are custom-designed and merge Hawaiian, Asian, and traditional therapies. If interested in indigenous treatments, ask about the spa's "Envelopment" therapies. After a day on the links, the Golfer's Tonic massage is a hole-in-one for relaxation. ⊠ *Kāhala Mandarin Oriental, 5000 Kāhala Ave., Kāhala* ☎ *808/739–8938.*

24-Hour Fitness. Waikīkī's most accessible fitness center has weight-training machines, cardiovascular equipment, free weights, and a pro shop. Admission is $10 per day for guests of many Waikīkī hotels (call for a list) and $20 for all others. ⊠ *Pacific Beach Hotel, 2nd fl., 2490 Kalākaua Ave., Waikīkī* ☎ *808/971–4653.*

AROUND THE **J. W. Marriott 'Ihilani Resort & Spa.** About 25 minutes from the airport
ISLAND is O'ahu's largest health and fitness center. There are 35,000 square feet of space for classes, weight training, Roman pools, Vichy showers, detoxifying wraps, and exotic revitalizing beauty treatments. Pamper yourself with a deluxe Thalasso therapy with color and aqua essences. Call to get prices and to arrange nonguest privileges. ⊠ *J. W. Marriott 'Ihilani Resort & Spa, 92-1001 'Ōlani St., Kapolei* ☎ *808/679–0079* ⊕ *www.ihilani.com.*

The Spa Luana at Turtle Bay Resort. Luxuriate at the ocean's edge at this serene spa, which offers custom massage treatments and beauty rituals, and includes a full-service hair and nail salon. The Kaomi massage provides deep-tissue relaxation, while the seaweed wrap is a soothing way to detoxify. In addition to in-spa treatments, there are private spa suites, a fitness center and outdoor exercise studio, and a lounge area and juice bar. ⊠ *Turtle Bay Resort, 57-091 Kamehameha Hwy., North Shore* ☎ *808/447–6868* ⊕ *www.turtlebayresort.com.*

Football

Seen nationwide on ESPN on Christmas Day is the collegiate **Hula Bowl** (☎ 808/486–9300) which takes place at Aloha Stadium in Honolulu. The nationally televised **NFL Pro Bowl** (☎ 808/486–9300) is held in early February at Aloha Stadium in Honolulu. The **University of Hawai'i Warriors** (☎ 808/956–6508) take to the field at Aloha Stadium in season, with a big local following. There are often express buses to games from Kapi'olani Park.

Golf

O'ahu has more than three dozen public and private golf courses. Hotel concierges can assist with tee times and transportation. To get a preview before you arrive, check out ⊕ www.808golf.com, which offers a comprehensive online guide to Hawai'i golf, including course descriptions and tee-time reservations. For last-minute tee times, consult Standby Golf at 888/645–2665. Standby Golf has access to 39 courses on Oʻahu; it is possible to book some courses a day ahead of time at reasonable rates.

Ala Wai Golf Course. One of the most popular municipal 18-hole courses is on Waikīkī's mauka end, across the Ala Wai Canal. It's par 70 on 5,867 yards and has a pro shop and a restaurant. There's always a waiting list for tee times, so if you plan to play, call the minute you land. ⊠ *404 Kapahulu Ave., Waikīkī, Honolulu* ☎ *808/733–7387* ✎ *Greens fee $42; cart $16.*

Coral Creek Golf Course. Located on the ʻEwa Beach plains, about 40 minutes from Waikīkī, this 18-hole, 6,808-yard, par-72 course offers wind challenges, ravines, and six lakes lined with coral rock formations. Club rental is available. ⊠ *91-1111 Geiger Rd., ʻEwa Beach* ☎ *808/441–4653* ✎ *Greens fee $125, cart included.*

Hawaiʻi Kai Championship Course. Advance reservations are recommended at this 18-hole, 6,222-yard course and the neighboring 18-hole, 2,386-yard Hawaiʻi Kai Executive Course, both of which overlook East Oʻahu's magnificent coastline. ⊠ *8902 Kalanianaʻole Hwy., Hawaiʻi Kai, Honolulu* ☎ *808/395–2358* ⊕ *www.hawaiikaigolf.com* ✎ *Greens fee weekdays $105 for Championship Course and $37 for Executive Course, weekends $110, cart included.*

Hawaiʻi Prince Golf Club. This 27-hole Arnold Palmer– and Bill Seay–designed course features white sand bunkers, 10 lakes, and a layout that rises and falls in sync with the Waiʻanae Mountain range on the horizon. Visiting players are welcome. ⊠ *91-1200 Ft. Weaver Rd., ʻEwa Beach* ☎ *808/944–4567* ⊕ *www.princeresortshawaii.com* ✎ *Greens fee $90 guests, $135 nonguests, cart included.*

Kahuku Golf Course. This 9-hole walking-only course is played more by locals than by visitors but serves up some stunning North Shore natural beauty. ⊠ *56-501 Kamehameha Hwy., Kahuku* ☎ *808/293–5842* ✎ *Greens fee $20 nonresidents; hand-cart rental $4.*

Ko Olina Golf Club. This Ted Robinson–designed course on Oʻahu's west side is affiliated with the ʻIhilani Resort. Its 18 holes are beautifully landscaped with waterfalls and ponds where black and white swans serve as your gallery. ⊠ *Ko Olina Resort, 92-1220 Aliʻinui Dr., Kapolei* ☎ *808/676–5300* ⊕ *www.koolina.com* ✎ *Greens fee $150, cart included.*

Koʻolau Golf Club. This 18-hole, par-72 course on Oʻahu's windward side in Kaneohe is officially rated by the United States Golf Association as the most difficult golf course in the country. Up for the challenge? ⊠ *45-550 Kionaole Rd., Kaneohe* ☎ *808/236–4653* ⊕ *www. koolaugolfclub.com* ✎ *Greens fee $115, cart included.*

Luana Hills Country Club. The front 9 of this Peter and Perry Dye–designed 18-hole, par-72 course is carved into the slopes of Mt. Olomana and features some of the trademark Dye features like forced carries, bunkers bordered by railroad ties, and ravines carved right into Maunawili Valley. ⊠ *770 Auloa Rd., Kailua* ☎ *808/262–2139* ✎ *Greens fee $100, cart included.*

Mākaha Valley Country Golf Club. Two exceptional 18-hole courses here offer a beautiful valley setting on what was formerly ranch and farm lands. ⊠ 84-627 Mākaha Valley Rd., Wai'anae ☎ 808/695–9578 🖾 Greens fee $125 until noon, $95 noon–2:30, $80 2:30–closing, cart included.

Mililani Golf Club. The tree-lined greens at this par-72, 6,455-yard course afford magnificent views of the surrounding Ko'olau and Wai'anae mountain ranges. Created from former pineapple fields, the original irrigation system was transformed into part of the course's water hazards. ⊠ 95-176 Kuahelani Ave., Mililani ☎ 808/623–2222 ⊕ www.mililanigolf. com 🖾 Greens fee $85, cart included.

Olomana Golf Links. This par-72, 6,326-yard course features hills and some interesting water hazards, not to mention a backdrop of the sheer cliffs of the Ko'olau Mountains. ⊠ 41-1801 Kalanianaole Hwy., Waimānalo ☎ 808/259–7626 🖾 Greens fee $67, cart included.

Turtle Bay Resort Golf Club. Both of Turtle Bay's golf courses are landscaped using the salt-tolerant seashore paspalum grass. The championship par-72 Palmer course measures 6,225 yards and offers a combination of Scottish links–type play along with a tropical back 9. The Fazio course is the only course in the state designed by George Fazio; it's difficult 18th hole features a 160-yard carry over a wetlands bird sanctuary. ⊠ Turtle Bay Resort, 57-091 Kamehameha Hwy., Kahuku ☎ 808/293–8574 🖾 Greens fee $90 guests, $135 nonguests, cart included.

ON THE SIDELINES   The giants of the greens return to Hawai'i every January or February (depending on TV scheduling) to compete in the **Sony Open Golf Tournament** (☎ 808/734–2151), a PGA Tour regular with a $1 million purse. It's held at the exclusive Wai'alae Country Club in Kāhala, and it's always a crowd-pleaser.

Horseback Riding

☘ **Kualoa Ranch.** This ranch across from Kualoa Beach Park leads trail rides in Ka'a'awa, one of the most beautiful valleys in all Hawai'i. Trail rides cost between $57 and $91. Kualoa has other activities as well, such as windsurfing, jet skiing, all-terrain-vehicle trail rides, and children's activities, which may be combined for half- or full-day package rates. ⊠ 49-560 Kamehameha Hwy., Ka'a'awa ☎ 808/237–8515 ⊕ www.kualoa.com.

Happy Trails Hawai'i. Take a guided horseback ride through the verdant Waimea Valley on trails that offer panoramic views from Kaena Point to the famous North Shore surfing spots. Rates vary depending on length of ride and skill level. ⊠ 1 mile mauka up Pupakea Road on the right., Pupakea ☎ 808/638–7433.

Jogging

In Honolulu, the most popular places to jog are the two parks, **Kapi'olani** and **Ala Moana,** at either end of Waikīkī. In both cases, the loop around the park is just under 2 mi. You can run a 4½-mi ring around **Diamond Head crater,** past scenic views, luxurious homes, and herds of other joggers. If you're looking for jogging companions, show up for the free **Honolulu Marathon Clinic,** which starts at the Kapiʻolani Bandstand from March through November, Sunday at 7:30 AM.

Once you leave Honolulu, it gets trickier to find places to jog that are scenic as well as safe. It's best to stick to the well-traveled routes, or ask the experienced folks at the **Running Room** (⊠ 819 Kapahulu Ave., Kapahulu, Honolulu ☎ 808/737–2422) for advice.

The "Honolulu Walking Map" and "The Fitness Fun Map" are free from the **Hawaiʻi State Department of Health Community Resources Section** (⊠ 1250 Punchbowl St., Room 217, Downtown Honolulu, Honolulu ☎ 808/586–4661). These list more than two dozen routes and suggested itineraries for seeing Oʻahu on foot.

ON THE SIDELINES   The **Honolulu Marathon** is a thrilling event to watch as well as to participate in. Join the throngs who cheer at the finish line at Kapiʻolani Park as internationally famous and local runners tackle the 26.2-mi challenge. It's held on the second Sunday in December and is sponsored by the **Honolulu Marathon Association** (☎ 808/734–7200 ⊕ www.honolulumarathon.org).

Tennis

Oʻahu has 181 public tennis courts that are free and open for play on a first-come, first-served basis; you're limited to 45 minutes of court time if others are waiting to play. A complete listing is available free of charge from the **Department of Parks and Recreation** (⊠ Tennis Unit, 650 S. King St., Honolulu 96813 ☎ 808/971–7150 ⊕ www.co.honolulu.hi.us).

Kapiʻolani Park, on the Diamond Head end of Waikīkī, has two tennis locations. The **Diamond Head Tennis Center** (⊠ 3908 Pākī Ave. ☎ 808/971–7150), on the mauka side of Kapiʻolani Park, has nine courts open to the public. There are more than a dozen courts for play at **Kapiʻolani Tennis Courts** (⊠ 2748 Kalākaua Ave. ☎ 808/971–2510). The closest public courts to the ʻewa end of Waikīkī are in **Ala Moana Park** (⊠ Makai side of Ala Moana Blvd. ☎ 808/592–7031).

The **Pacific Beach Hotel** (⊠ 2490 Kalākaua Ave., Waikīkī ☎ 808/922–1233) has rooftop tennis courts that are open to nonguests for a fee.

Forty-five minutes from Waikīkī, on Oʻahu's ʻEwa Plain, are two championship tennis courts at the **Hawaiʻi Prince Golf Club** (⊠ 91-1200 Ft. Weaver Rd., ʻEwa Beach ☎ 808/944–4567); shuttle service is available from the Hawaiʻi Prince Hotel Waikīkī for hotel guests.

Triathlon

Swim-bike-run events are gaining in popularity and number in Hawaiʻi. Most fun to watch (or compete in) is the **Tinman Triathlon** (☎ 808/732–7311), held in mid-July in Waikīkī.

Volleyball

Volleyball is extremely popular on the Islands, and no wonder. Both the men's and women's teams of the **University of Hawai'i** have blasted to a number-one ranking in years past. Crowded, noisy, and very exciting home games are played from September through December (women's) and from January through April (men's) in the university's 10,000-seat Stan Sheriff Arena. ✉ *Lower Campus Rd., Honolulu* ☎ *808/956–4481* 🎟 *$8.*

Water Park

🐚 **Hawaiian Waters Adventure Park.** Get wet and wild at this 29-acre water-theme park with 20 rides including a seven-story speed slide, a football field–size wave pool, inner-tube cruising, and SHAKA, the world's wildest half pipe. A children's water world of delight has a kiddie pool, waterfalls, minislides, and animal floaties. It's in Kapolei, mauka of the H-1 Freeway on Farrington Highway, 15 minutes from the Honolulu International Airport. ✉ *91-400 Farrington Hwy., Kapolei* ☎ *808/ 674–9283* ⊕ *www.hawaiianwaters.com* 🎟 *$34.*

Water Sports

The seemingly endless ocean options can be arranged through any hotel travel desk or beach concession. Try the **Waikīkī Beach Center,** next to the Sheraton Moana Surfrider, or the **C & K Beach Service,** by the Hilton Hawaiian Village (no telephones).

DEEP-SEA FISHING **Inter-Island Sportfishing** (☎ 808/591–8888 ⊕ www.fish-hawaii.com) operates three vessels available for exclusive or shared deep-sea fishing charters. Rates range from $150 to $835 per day, depending on whether you choose an exclusive charter or share one with five other anglers. If the "big one" doesn't get away, Inter-Island will arrange to have your trophy fish mounted and sent to you. Departures for charters are from Kewalo Basin. **Magic Sportfishing** (☎ 808/596–2998 ⊕ www. magicsportfishing.com) offers shared and private charters; rates range from $150 to $850 per day.

OCEAN KAYAKING This dynamic sport is catching on fast on the Islands. On the North Shore, clear kayaks (so you can see the ocean below you as you paddle) for calm water kayaking, and ocean kayaks are available for rental at **Surf 'N Sea** (✉ 62-595 Kamehameha Hwy. ☎ 808/637–9887). You can kayak the "surfing waters of the kings" off Waikīkī with assistance from **Prime Time Sports** (✉ Ft. DeRussy Beach ☎ 808/949–8952). Bob Twogood, a name that is synonymous with O'ahu kayaking, runs a shop called **Twogood Kayaks Hawai'i** (✉ 345 Hahani St., Kailua ☎ 808/262–5656 ⊕ www.aloha.com/~twogood), which makes, rents, and sells the fiberglass crafts. Rates for renting solo and tandem kayaks range from $25 to $50. Twogood also offers guided kayak tours and adventure packages which range from $59 to $89. Kayak rental rates include kayak delivery and pickup across from Kailua Beach.

SAILING **Honolulu Sailing Company** (☎ 808/239–3900 ⊕ www.honsail.com) offers a variety of sailing options as well as sailing instruction. Departures are from Pier 2, Honolulu Harbor.

SCUBA & **Captain Bruce's Hawaii** (☎ 808/373–3590 or 800/535–2487 ⊕ www.
SNORKELING captainbruce.com) offers dives with treks to both East and West Oʻahu dive sites. Two-tank boat dives range from $106 to $122. Certification courses are also available; call for rates. **Reeftrekkers** (☎ 808/943–0588) gives divers an opportunity via the Internet to customize their dive excursions before arrival on the Islands. Two-tank dives range in price from $95 to $105. **South Seas Aquatics** (☎ 808/922–0852 ⊕ www.ssahawaii. com) offers two-tank boat dives at various sites; rates range from $85 to $101. Several certification courses are available; call for rates. On the North Shore, **Surf-N-Sea** (☎ 808/637–3337 ⊕ www.surfnsea.com) conducts a variety of dive excursions, including night dives. A two-tank excursion starts at $65. Night dives begin at $80.

The most famous snorkeling spot in Hawaiʻi is Hanauma Bay. You can get masks, fins, and snorkels at the **rental stand** (☎ 808/395–4725) right at the park. **Hanauma Bay Snorkeling Excursions** (☎ 808/373–5060) provides transport from Waikīkī and costs $30 round-trip, including park admission, snorkeling gear, and lessons. You can pick up snorkeling equipment and site advice from **Snorkel Bob's** (✉ 700 Kapahulu Ave. ☎ 808/735–7944), conveniently located on the way to Hanauma Bay.

Area dive sites include the following:

Hanauma Bay. East of Koko Head, this bay is an underwater state park and a popular dive site. The shallow inner reef gradually drops from 10 to 70 feet at the outer reef. Expect to see butterfly fish, goatfish, parrot fish, surgeon fish, and sea turtles.

Mahi Waiʻanae. This 165-foot minesweeper was sunk in 1982 in the waters just south of Waiʻanae on Oʻahu's leeward coast to create an artificial reef. It's intact and penetrable. Goatfish, tame lemon butterfly fish, blue-striped snapper, and 6-foot moray eels can be seen hanging out here. Depths are from 50 to 90 feet.

Maunalua Bay. East of Diamond Head, Maunalua Bay has several sites, including Turtle Canyon, with lava flow ridges and sandy canyons teeming with green sea turtles of all sizes; *Kāhala Barge,* a penetrable, 200-foot sunken vessel; Big Eel Reef, with many varieties of moray eels; and Fantasy Reef, a series of lava ledges and archways populated with barracuda and eels.

Shark's Cove. You can dive from this North Shore site during summer months only and you should be an experienced diver. Sunlight from above creates a stained-glass effect in the large, roomy caverns. Easily accessible from shore, the cove has depths ranging from 15 to 45 feet. This is the most popular cavern dive on the island.

Three Tables. Named for the trio of flat rocks that break the surface near the beach, this North Shore site has easy access from the shore. Beneath the waves are large rock formations, caverns, and ledges. You can only dive here in the summer months.

SURFING To rent a board in Waikīkī, visit **C&K Beach Service** (☎ no phone), on
★ the beach fronting the Hilton Hawaiian Village. Rentals cost $10 to $15
per hour, depending on the size of the board, and $18 for two hours.
Small group lessons are $50 per hour with board, and they promise to
have you riding the waves by lesson's end.

Surfing and bodysurfing instruction from the staff of Hans Hedemann—
who spent 17 years on the professional surfer World Tour circuit—is
available for $50 per hour for group lessons and $90 for private lessons
at the Waikīkī **Hans Hedemann Surf Hawaii** (☎ 808/923–7779).

Novice surfers can meet with guaranteed success with lessons from
some of Hawai'i's most knowledgeable water-safety experts—off-duty
Honolulu firefighters—who man the boards at one of Hawai'i's hottest
★ ☾ new surfing schools, **Hawaiian Fire, Inc.** (☎ 808/384–8855). Lessons
($97 for group lesson, $139 for private lesson) include equipment,
safety and surfing instruction, and two hours of surfing time (with
lunch break) at a secluded beach near Barbers Point. Transportation is
available from Waikīkī.

North Shore Eco-Surf Tours (☎ 808/638–9503) will set you up with a surf
tour that is not only exhilarating but educational, too. On the North
Shore, rent a short board for $5 an hour or a long board for $7 from a
shop called **Surf-N-Sea** (☎ 808/637–9887). Lessons cost $65 for two hours.

In winter head out to the North Shore to watch the best surfers in the
world hang ten during the **Van's Triple Crown Hawaiian Pro Surfing Championships.** This two-day event, scheduled according to wave conditions,
is generally held at the Banzai Pipeline and Sunset Beach during November and December.

WATER-SKIING **Hawai'i Sports Wakeboard and Water Ski Center** (✉ Koko Marina Shopping Center, 7192 Kalaniana'ole Hwy., Hawai'i Kai ☎ 808/395–3773)
offers instruction and equipment rentals for water-skiing and wake-
boarding, as well as activity packages that combine water sports with
parasailing off East O'ahu's Hawai'i Kai Marina. There are also rides
in inflatable banana boats and bumper tubes for children of all ages.

WINDSURFING This sport was born in Hawai'i, and O'ahu's Kailua Beach is its cradle.
Kailua Sailboard and Kayaks Company (✉ 130 Kailua Rd., Kailua ☎ 808/
262–2555) offers small group lessons, rents equipment, and transports
everything to the waterfront. World champion Robby Naish and his family build and sell boards, rent equipment, provide accommodations referrals, and offer windsurfing and kiteboarding instruction out of **Naish
Hawai'i** (✉ 155A Hamakua Dr., Kailua ☎ 808/261–6067 ⊕ www.
naish.com). A four-hour package, including 90 minutes of instruction,
costs $55. **North Shore Windsurfing School** (✉ 59-452 Makana Rd.,
Hale'iwa ☎ 808/638–8198) offers expert instruction, but you have to
bring your own board. **Surf-N-Sea** (✉ 7192 Kalaniana'ole Hwy., Hale'iwa
☎ 808/637–9887) rents windsurfing gear for $12 per hour; a two-hour
windsurfing lesson costs $65.

Watch the pros jump and spin on the waves during July's **Pan Am Hawaiian Windsurfing World Cup** (☎ 808/734–6999) off Kailua Beach. For

windsurfing competitions off Diamond Head point, check out August's **Wahine Classic** (☎ 808/521–4322), featuring the world's best female boardsailors.

SHOPPING

Honolulu is the number-one shopping spot on the Islands and an international crossroads of the shopping scene. It has sprawling shopping malls, unique boutiques, hotel arcades, neighborhood businesses, and a variety of other enterprises. Major shopping malls are generally open daily 10–9; smaller neighborhood boutiques are usually 9-to-5 operations.

Shopping Centers

In Honolulu

★ **Ala Moana Shopping Center** (⊠ 1450 Ala Moana Blvd., Ala Moana ☎ 808/955–9517 special events and shuttle service) is one of the nation's largest open-air malls and is just five minutes from Waikīkī by bus. More than 240 stores and 60 restaurants make up this 50-acre complex. All of Hawai'i's major department stores are here, including Neiman Marcus, Sears, and Macy's. Palm Boulevard features upscale designer fashions, such as Gucci, Louis Vuitton, Gianni Versace, and Emporio Armani.

Aloha Tower Marketplace (⊠ 1 Aloha Tower Dr., at Piers 8, 9, and 10, Downtown Honolulu ☎ 808/566–2337 ⊕ www.alohatower.com/atm) cozies up to Honolulu Harbor and bills itself as a festival marketplace. Along with restaurants and entertainment venues, it has 80 shops and kiosks selling mostly visitor-oriented merchandise, from expensive sunglasses to souvenir refrigerator magnets.

DFS Galleria Waikīkī (⊠ corner of Kalākaua and Royal Hawaiian Aves., Waikīkī ☎ 808/931–2655) has boutiques of world-class designers—such as Hermès, Cartier, and Calvin Klein—as well as Hawai'i's largest beauty and cosmetic store. An old Hawai'i atmosphere is created by a three-story replica of a 1920s luxury cruise liner; daily live entertainment; and the Waikīkī Walk, with authentic fashions, arts and crafts, and gifts of the Hawaiian Islands. There is also an exclusive boutique floor available to duty-free shoppers only. The Kālia Grill and Starbucks offer a respite for weary shoppers.

Kāhala Mall (⊠ 4211 Wai'alae Ave., Kāhala ☎ 808/732–7736) has 90 retail outlets including Macy's, Gap, Reyn's Aloha Wear, and Barnes & Noble. Restaurants range from quick-bite venues to leisurely meal places. Kāhala Mall's Main Stage spotlights entertaining arts performances ranging from local ballet to contemporary Hawaiian music concerts. Along with an assortment of gift shops, Kāhala Mall also has eight **movie theaters** (☎ 808/733–6233) for post-shopping entertainment. The mall is 10 minutes by car from Waikīkī in the chic residential neighborhood of Kāhala, near the slopes of Diamond Head.

The fashionable **King Kalākaua Plaza** (✉ 2080 Kalākaua Ave., Waikīkī ☎ 808/955–2878), one of Waikīkī's newer shopping destinations, offers flagship stores Banana Republic and Nike Town as well as the All Sports Hawaii Cafe.

The **Royal Hawaiian Shopping Center** (✉ 2201 Kalākaua Ave., Waikīkī ☎ 808/922–0588 ⊕ www.shopwaikiki.com), fronting the Royal Hawaiian and Sheraton Waikīkī hotels, is three blocks long and contains more than 100 stores on four levels. Browse through the Hawaiian Heirloom Jewelry Collection by Philip Rickard, which also has a museum with Victorian jewelry pieces. Bike buffs can check out the Harley-Davidson Motor Clothes and Collectibles Boutique. The center has 15 restaurants, including the Paradiso Seafood Grill, the Cheesecake Factory, and Villa Paradiso, and even has a post office.

2100 Kalākaua (✉ 2100 Kalākaua Ave., Waikīkī ☎ 808/550–4449 ⊕ www.2100kalakaua.com) is the newest addition to the island retail scene. Many of the world's top designers have boutiques in this unique three-story town-house-style center. Its tenants include Chanel, Coach, Tiffany & Co., Yves Saint Laurent, Gucci, and Tod and Bocheron. The bronze statue fronting the center was created by Japanese artist Shige Yamada.

Heading west from Waikīkī toward Downtown Honolulu, you'll run into a section of town with five distinct shopping-complex areas known as ★ the **Victoria Ward Centers** (✉ 1050–1200 Ala Moana Blvd., Ala Moana); there are more than 120 specialty shops and 20 restaurants here. The Ward 16 Entertainment Complex features 16 movie theaters. A "shopping concierge" can assist you in navigating your way through the center's five complexes, which span four city blocks. Two of the largest and most popular complexes are the **Ward Warehouse** and the **Ward Centre**.

Waikīkī Shopping Plaza (✉ 2270 Kalākaua Ave., Waikīkī ☎ 808/923–1111) is across the street from the Royal Hawaiian Shopping Center. Its landmark is a 75-foot water-sculpture gizmo, which looks great when it's working. Walden Books, Guess, Clio Blue jewelers, and Tanaka of Tokyo Restaurant are some of the 50 shops and restaurants on six floors.

Waikīkī has three theme park–style shopping centers. **King's Village** (✉ 131 Ka'iulani Ave., Waikīkī ☎ 808/944–6855) looks like a Hollywood stage set of monarchy-era Honolulu, complete with a changing-of-the-guard ceremony every evening at 6:15; shops include Hawaiian Island Creations Jewelry, Swim City USA Swimwear, and Island Motor Sports. **Waikīkī Town Center** (✉ 2301 Kūhiō Ave., Waikīkī ☎ 808/922–2724) is an open-air complex with a variety of shops ranging from fashions to jewelry. There are free hula shows here Monday, Wednesday, Friday, and Saturday at 7 PM.

Around the Island

★ **Aloha Stadium Swap Meet** (✉ 99-500 Salt Lake Blvd., 'Aiea ☎ 808/486–6704) is a thrice-weekly outdoor bazaar that attracts hundreds of vendors and even more bargain hunters. Every Hawaiian souvenir imaginable can be found here, from coral shell necklaces to bikinis, as well as a variety of ethnic wares, from Chinese brocade dresses to Japanese pottery. There are also ethnic foods, silk flowers, and luggage in aloha floral prints. Wear comfortable shoes, use sunscreen, and bring bottled water to make this outing even more enjoyable. The flea market takes place in the Aloha Stadium parking lot Wednesday and weekends from 6 to 3; the $6 admission fee includes round-trip shuttle service from Waikīkī.

While playing on the North Shore, check out the **North Shore Marketplace** (⊠ 66-250 Kamehameha Hwy., Haleiwa ☎ 808/637–7000) for boutiques like the Silver Moon Emporium for vintage clothing, Patagonia for adventure wear, and North Shore Custom and Design Swimwear for mix-and-match bikinis off the rack.

The **Waikele Premium Outlets** (⊠ H-1 Fwy., Waikele, 30 minutes west of Downtown Honolulu, Waikele ☎ 808/676–5656) reflects Hawai'i's latest craze: manufacturer-direct shopping at discount prices. Among its tenants are the Anne Klein Factory, Donna Karan Company Store, Kenneth Cole, and Saks Fifth Avenue Outlet.

Specialty Stores

Clothing

HIGH FASHION Tucked away on the windward side in Kailua, **Adasa** (⊠ 25 Maluniu Ave., Kailua ☎ 808/263–8500) offers up some of the world's hippest clothing and accessories from designers like Flavio Olivera and Marc ★ Jacobs. **Anne Namba Designs** (⊠ 324 Kamani St., Downtown Honolulu ☎ 808/589 1135) takes the beauty of classic kimonos and creates the most contemporary of fashions. In addition to women's apparel, she also features a men's line and a stunningly beautiful wedding couture line.

Top-of-the-line international fashions for men and women are available at **Mandalay Imports** (⊠ Halekūlani, 2199 Kālia Rd., Waikīkī ☎ 808/922–7766), home of Star of Siam silks and cottons, Anne Namba couture, and designs by Choisy, who works out of Bangkok. **Neiman Marcus** (⊠ Ala Moana Shopping Center, 1450 Ala Moana Blvd., Ala Moana ☎ 808/951–8887) is the trendy end of the high-fashion scene. For the latest in footwear, **Nordstrom Shoes** (⊠ Ward Centre, Ala Moana Blvd., Ala Moana ☎ 808/973–4620) displays an elegant array of pricey styles. **Pzazz** (⊠ 1419 Kalākaua Ave., Waikīkī ☎ 808/955–5800), nicknamed the Ann Taylor of consignment shops, sells high fashion at low prices.

Shanghai Tang (⊠ Ala Moana Shopping Center, Ala Moana ☎ 808/942–9800) first opened as a tailoring shop in Hong Kong, and this store is its 11th branch. The emphasis is on workmanship and the luxury of fine fabrics in the tradition of old-Shanghai tailoring. Shanghai Tang offers custom tailoring for men, women, and children.

ISLAND WEAR For vintage aloha shirts, try **Bailey's Antique Clothing and Thrift Shop** (⊠ 517 ★ Kapahulu Ave., Waikīkī, Honolulu ☎ 808/734–7628). If you're looking for aloha wear that ranges from the bright-and-bold to the cool-and-classy, try **Hilo Hattie** (⊠ 700 N. Nimitz Hwy., Iwilei ☎ 808/535–6500), the world's largest manufacturer of Hawaiian and tropical fashions; it's also a good source for island souvenirs. Free shuttle service is available from Waikīkī. If you plan on surfing or just want to look like a surfer, check out **Local Motion** (⊠ 1958 Kalākaua Ave., Waikīkī, Honolulu ☎ 808/979–7873). This outfitter's flagship store has everything from surfboards to surf wear. For contemporary rayon aloha shirts made in the vintage-style patterns, **Locals Only** (⊠ Ala Moana Shopping Center, Ala Moana, Honolulu ☎ 808/942–1555) offers an exclusive line by Pineapple Juice and Locals Only sportswear. For stylish Hawaiian wear, the kind worn by local men and women, look in one of the branches of **Macy's** (⊠ Ala Moana Shopping Center ⊠ Kāhala Mall ⊠ 1450 Ala Moana Blvd., Ala Moana ☎ 808/941–2345 for all stores) **Native Books and Beautiful Things** (⊠ Ward Warehouse, 1050 Ala Moana Blvd., Ala Moana, Honolulu ☎ 808/596–8885) sells hand-painted, one-of-a-kind clothing created by local artisans.

Ohelo Road (⊠ Kāhala Mall, 4211 Wai'alae Ave., Kāhala, Honolulu ☎ 808/735–5525) carries island-print dresses in materials that make living in the tropics cool year-round. For menswear and select women's and children's aloha wear, try **Reyn's** (⊠ Ala Moana Shopping Center, 1450 Ala Moana Blvd., Ala Moana, Honolulu ☎ 808/949–5929 ⊠ Kāhala Mall, 4211 Wai'alae Ave., Kāhala, Honolulu ☎ 808/737–8313 ⊠ Sheraton Waikīkī, 2255 Kalākaua Ave., Waikīkī, Honolulu ☎ 808/923–0331). For contemporary island wear in fabrics made for a tropical climate, try **Tapestries by Hauoli** (⊠ Ala Moana Shopping Center, Ala Moana, Honolulu ☎ 808/973–0566), which sells machine-washable dresses, pants, tops, and accessories.

Food

Bring home fresh pineapple, papaya, or coconut to savor or share with friends and family. Jam comes in flavors such as pohā, passion fruit, and guava. Kona- and O'ahu-grown Waialua coffee beans have an international following. There are dried-food products such as saimin, haupia, and teriyaki barbecue sauce. All kinds of cookies are available, as well as exotic teas, drink mixes, and pancake syrups. And don't forget the macadamia nuts, from plain to chocolate-covered and brittled. By law, all fresh-fruit products must be inspected by the Department of Agriculture before export. To really impress those back home, pick up a box of gourmet chocolates from the **Honolulu Chocolate Company** (⊠ Ward Centre, 1200 Ala Moana Blvd., Ala Moana ☎ 808/591–2997). Bring home the flavors of Hawai'i, from Kona coffee to macadamia nuts, dipped in the finest of chocolates. For cheap prices on local delicacies, try one of the many **Longs Drugs** (⊠ Ala Moana Shopping Center, 1450 Ala Moana Blvd., 2nd level, Ala Moana ☎ 808/941–4433 ⊠ Kāhala Mall, 4211 Wai'alae Ave., Kāhala ☎ 808/732–0784). **Tropical Fruits Distributors of Hawai'i** (⊠ 651 Ilalo St., Honolulu ☎ 808/847–3224 or 800/697–9100 ⊕ www.dolefruithawaii.com) specializes in packing inspected pineapple and papaya; it will deliver to your hotel and to the airport check-in counter or ship to the mainland United States and Canada.

Gifts

To send home tropical flowers, contact **Hawaiian Greenhouse** (☎ 888/965–8351 ⊕ www.hawaiiangreenhouse.com). To ship exotic orchids, contact the **Kawamoto Nursery** (☎ 808/732–5805 ⊕ www.kawamotoorchids.com).

Pacific-American Gallery (⊠ 100 Holomana St., Waikīkī ☎ 808/942–3767), in the Hawai'i Prince Hotel, presents works in all mediums by emerging native Hawaiian and Pacific Island artists, including pottery, sculpture, paintings and drawings, and photography.

Robyn Buntin Galleries (⊠ 820 S. Beretania St., Downtown Honolulu, Honolulu ☎ 808/545–5572) presents Chinese nephrite-jade carvings, Japanese lacquer and screens, Buddhist sculptures, and other international pieces.

Takenoya Arts (⊠ Halekūlani, 2199 Kālia Rd., Waikīkī ☎ 808/926–1939) specializes in intricately carved netsuke (toggles used to fasten containers to kimonos), both antique and contemporary, and one-of-a-kind necklaces.

Hawaiian Arts & Crafts

Items handcrafted from native Hawaiian wood make lovely gifts. Koa and milo have a beautiful color and grain. The great koa forests are disappearing because of environmental factors, so the wood is becoming valuable; most koa products you'll encounter are produced from wood grown on commercial farms.

You can purchase traditional island comforters, wall hangings, pillows, and other Hawaiian print quilt items at **Hawaiian Quilt Collection** (⊠ Ala Moana Center, 1450 Ala Moana Blvd., Ala Moana ☎ 808/946–2233). For hula costumes and instruments, try **Hula Supply Center** (⊠ 2346 S. King St., Mō'ili'ili ☎ 808/941–5379).

Bring home some aloha you can sink your bare feet into with the exclusive Hawaiian rug collection from **Indich Collection** (⊠ Gentry Pacific Design Center, 560 N. Nimitz Hwy., Downtown Honolulu ☎ 808/524–7769), which features designs that include Hawaiian petroglyphs, banana leafs, and heliconia.

Local residents come to **Island Treasures** (⊠ Koko Marina Center, 7192 Kalaniana'ole Hwy. ☎ 808/396–8827) to shop for gifts that are both unique and within reach of almost every budget. From koa accessories to original artwork, jewelry, beauty products, and home accessories, the quality is outstanding and the creativity of the work makes this a trove for island gifts.

A wonderful selection of Hawaiian arts, crafts, and children's toys can be found at **My Little Secret** (⊠ Ward Warehouse, 1050 Ala Moana Blvd., Ala Moana ☎ 808/596–2990).

Jewelry

Bernard Hurtig's (⊠ Hilton Hawaiian Village Ali'i Tower, 2005 Kālia Rd., Waikīkī ☎ 808/947–9399) sells fine jewelry with an emphasis on 18-karat gold and antique jade. **Haimoff & Haimoff Creations in Gold**

(✉ Halekūlani, 2199 Kālia Rd., Waikīkī ☎ 808/923–8777) sells the work of jewelry designer Harry Haimoff.

If you notice the wrists of local women, you are apt to see Hawaiian heirloom bracelets fashioned in either gold or silver in a number of island-inspired designs. Jewelry, such as these bracelets, that captures the heart of the Hawaiian lifestyle in all its elegant diversity can be found at **Na Hoku** (✉ Ala Moana Center, 1450 Ala Moana, Ala Moana, Honolulu ☎ 808/946–2100).

Coral and pearl jewelry is popular, stunning, and fairly affordable. To see where it comes from and how jewelry is designed using these treasures from the sea, take a tour of the **Maui Divers Jewelry Design Center** (✉ 1520 Liona St., Mō'ili'ili, Honolulu ☎ 808/946–7979).

Philip Rickard (✉ Royal Hawaiian Shopping Center, 2201 Kalākaua Ave., Waikīkī ☎ 808/924–7972) features custom Hawaiian wedding jewelry among this famed jeweler's heirloom design collection.

O'AHU A TO Z

To research prices, get advice from other travelers, and book travel arrangements, visit www.fodors.com.

AIR TRAVEL

Most flights to Honolulu International originate in Los Angeles or San Francisco, which means they are nonstop. Flying time from the West Coast is 4½ to 5 hours. Honolulu also has a number of carriers routing to the islands from the United Kingdom.

CARRIERS   Carriers flying into Honolulu from the mainland United States include Aloha, American, Continental, Delta, Hawaiian, Northwest, and United. Carriers flying from the United Kingdom to Honolulu include Air New Zealand, American, Continental, Delta, and United.

Charter flights are the least expensive and the least reliable—with chronically late departures and occasional cancellations. They also tend to depart less frequently (usually once a week) than do regularly scheduled flights. The savings may be worth the potential annoyance, however. Charter flights serving Honolulu International Airport are available from American Trans Air and Hawaiian Airlines.

🛪 **Air New Zealand** ☎ 800/262-1234 ⊕ www.airnewzealand.com. **Aloha Airlines** ☎ 808/484-1111 ⊕ www.alohaairlines.com. **American** ☎ 808/833-7600 or 800/433-7300 ⊕ www.aa.com. **American Trans Air** ☎ 800/435-9282 ⊕ www.ata.com. **Continental** ☎ 800/523-3273 ⊕ www.continental.com. **Delta** ☎ 800/221-1212 ⊕ www.delta.com. **Hawaiian Airlines** ☎ 808/838-1555 or 800/367-5320 ⊕ www.hawaiianair.com. **Northwest/KLM** ☎ 800/225-2525 ⊕ www.nwa.com. **United** ☎ 800/864-8331 ⊕ www.ual.com.

AIRPORT

More direct flights, by more domestic and international air carriers, arrive at and depart from Honolulu International than at any other airport in Hawai'i. If you find yourself waiting at the airport with extra time on your hands, be sure to visit the Pacific Aerospace Museum, open daily, in the main terminal. It includes a 1,700-square-foot, three-dimensional, multimedia theater presenting the history of flight in Hawai'i, and a full-scale space-shuttle flight deck. Hands-on exhibits include a mission-control computer program tracing flights in the Pacific.

🛈 **Honolulu International Airport** ☎ 808/836-6411 ⊕ www.ehawaiigov.org.

AIRPORT TRANSFERS There are taxis right at the airport baggage-claim exit. At $1.50 start-up plus $2.50 for each mile, the fare to Waikīkī will run approximately $23, plus tip. Drivers are also allowed to charge 30¢ per suitcase. Trans Hawaiian Services runs an airport shuttle service to Waikīkī. The fare is $8 one-way, $15 round-trip. The municipal bus (TheBus) will take you into Waikīkī for only $1.50, but you are allowed only one bag, which must fit on your lap. Some hotels have their own pickup service. Check when you book.

🛈 **TheBus** ☎ 808/848-5555 ⊕ www.thebus.org. **Trans-Hawaiian Services** ☎ 808/566-7300.

BOAT & FERRY TRAVEL

Boat Day used to be the biggest day of the week. Jet travel once obscured that custom, but arriving in Hawai'i by ship is making a comeback. If you have the time, it is one sure way to unwind. Many cruises are planned a year or more in advance and fill up fast. Most cruise-ship companies offer a fare that includes round-trip air travel to the point of embarkation.

Norwegian Cruise Lines' 2,200-passenger *Norwegian Star* vessel offers seven-day cruises to the Hawaiian Islands. Ports of call include O'ahu, Maui, Kaua'i, the Big Island, and Fanning Island in Kiribati.

🛈 **Norwegian Cruise Line (NCL)** ⊠ 7665 Corporate Dr., Miami, FL 33126 ☎ 800/327-7030 ⊕ www.ncl.com.

BIKE & MOPED TRAVEL

Blue Sky Rentals & Sports Center rents mopeds for $35 a day (8–6) and $40 for 24 hours. Mountain bikes from Blue Sky Rentals cost $20 a day, $25 for 24 hours, and $100 for the week, plus a $100 deposit. Big Kahuna rents a variety of motorcycles for $100–$175 a day.

🛈 **Big Kahuna Motorcycle Tours and Rentals** ⊠ 404 Seaside Ave., Waikīkī ☎ 808/924-2736. **Blue Sky Rentals & Sports Center** ⊠ 1920 Ala Moana Blvd., across from Hilton Hawaiian Village, Waikīkī ☎ 808/947-0101.

BUS TRAVEL

You can go all around the island or just down Kalākaua Avenue for $2 on Honolulu's municipal transportation system, affectionately known as TheBus. You're entitled to one free transfer per fare if you ask for it when boarding. Exact change is required, and dollar bills are accepted. A four-day pass for visitors costs $20 and is sold at the more than 30 ABC stores (Hawaiian chain stores that sell sundries and are geared to tourists) in Waikīkī. Monthly passes cost $40.

There are no official bus-route maps, but you can find privately published booklets at most drugstores and other convenience outlets. The important route numbers for Waikīkī are 2, 4, 8, 19, 20, and 58. If you venture afield, you can always get back on one of these.

There are also a number of brightly painted private buses, many free, that will take you to such commercial attractions as dinner cruises, garment factories, and the like.

🚍 **TheBus** ☎ 808/848-5555 ⊕ www.thebus.org.

CAR RENTAL

If you plan to go beyond Waikīkī to tour Oʻahu, renting a car is essential. During peak seasons—summer, Christmas vacations, and February—reservations are necessary. Rental agencies abound in and around the Honolulu International Airport and in Waikīkī. Local agencies rent everything from used cars to classics and pickup trucks.

Cloud Nine Limousine Service provides red-carpet treatment in its chauffeur-driven super-stretch limousines. Rates begin at $50 an hour, plus tax and tip, with a two-hour minimum. Another reliable company is Duke's Limousine Service, which offers a choice of luxury super-stretches, sedans, or SUV limousines, with rates that begin at $50 per hour, with a two-hour minimum.

🚍 **Major Agencies: Avis** ☎ 808/834-5536 or 800/831-2847 ⊕ www.avis.com. **Budget** ☎ 800/527-0700 ⊕ www.budget.com. **Dollar** ☎ 808/831-2330 or 800/800-4000 ⊕ www.dollarcar.com. **Enterprise** ☎ 808/836-2213 or 800/736-8222 ⊕ www.enterprise. com. **Hertz** ☎ 808/831-3500 or 800/654-3011 ⊕ www.hertz.com. **National** ☎ 808/ 831-3800 or 888/868-6207 ⊕ www.nationalcar.com. **Thrifty** ☎ 808/831-2277 or 800/ 847-4389.

🚍 **Local Agencies: JN Car and Truck Rentals** ☎ 808/831-2724 ⊕ www.jnag.com. **Paradise Rent A Car** ☎ 808/946-7777 or 888/882-2277 ⊕ www.paradiserentacar.com. **VIP** ☎ 808/922-4605.

🚍 **Limousine Rentals: Cloud Nine Limousine Service** ☎ 808/524-7999 or 800/524-7999 ⊕ www.cloudninelimos. **Duke's Limousine, Inc.** ☎ 808/738-1878 ⊕ www. dukeslimo.com.

CAR TRAVEL

Oʻahu's drivers are generally courteous, and you rarely hear a horn. People will slow down and let you into traffic with a wave of the hand. A friendly wave back is customary. If a driver sticks a hand out the window in a fist with the thumb and pinky sticking straight out, this is a good thing: it's the *shaka,* the Hawaiian symbol for "hang loose," and is often used to say "thanks," as well.

Hawaiʻi has a seat-belt law for front-seat passengers and those under the age of 18 in the back seats. Children under 40 pounds must be in a car seat, available from your car-rental agency.

It's hard to get lost on Oʻahu. Roads and streets, although perhaps unpronounceable to visitors, are at least well marked. Major attractions and scenic spots are marked by the distinctive HVCB sign with its red-caped warrior. Although it's hard to get lost, driving in Honolulu can be frustrating, as many streets are one-way.

Driving in rush-hour traffic (6:30–8:30 AM and 3:30–5:30 PM) can be exasperating, because left turns are prohibited at many intersections and many roads turn into contra-flow lanes. Parking along many streets is curtailed during these hours, and towing is strictly enforced. Read the curbside parking signs before leaving your vehicle, even at a meter. Remember not to leave valuables in your car. Rental cars are often targets for thieves.

EMERGENCIES

To reach the police, fire department, or an ambulance in an emergency, dial **911**.

A doctor, laboratory-radiology technician, and nurses are always on duty at Doctors on Call. Appointments are recommended but not necessary. Dozens of kinds of medical insurance are accepted, including Medicare, Medicaid, and most kinds of travel insurance.

Kūhiō Pharmacy is Waikīkī's only pharmacy and handles prescription requests only until 4:30 PM. Longs Drugs is open evenings at its Ala Moana location and 24 hours at its South King Street location (15 minutes from Waikīkī by car). Pillbox Pharmacy, located in Kaimukī, will deliver prescription medications for a small fee.

🚩 **Doctors & Dentists: Doctors on Call** ⊠ Sheraton Princess Kaiulani Hotel, 120 Kaiulani Ave., Waikīkī ☎ 808/971-6000.

🚩 **Emergency Services: Coast Guard Rescue Center** ☎ 808/541-2450.

🚩 **Hospitals: Castle Medical Center** ⊠ 640 Ulukahiki, Kailua ☎ 808/263-5500. **Kapiolani Medical Center for Women and Children** ⊠ 1319 Punahou St., Makiki Heights, Honolulu ☎ 808/983-6000. **Queen's Medical Center** ⊠ 1301 Punchbowl St., Downtown Honolulu, Honolulu ▥ 808/538-9011. **Saint Francis Medical Center-West** ⊠ 91-2141 Ft. Weaver Rd., 'Ewa Beach ☎ 808/678-7000. **Straub Clinic** ⊠ 888 S. King St., Downtown Honolulu, Honolulu ☎ 808/522-4000.

🚩 **Pharmacies: Kūhiō Pharmacy** ⊠ Outrigger West Hotel, 2330 Kūhiō Ave., Waikīkī ☎ 808/923-4466. **Longs Drugs** ⊠ Ala Moana Shopping Center, 1450 Ala Moana Blvd., 2nd level, Ala Moana ☎ 808/949-4010 ⊠ 2220 S. King St., Mō'ili'ili ☎ 808/947-2651. **Pillbox Pharmacy** ⊠ 1133 11th Ave., Kaimukī ☎ 808/737-1777.

SIGHTSEEING TOURS

BOAT TOURS O'ahu Wild Side Specialty Tours takes small group charters to O'ahu's Wai'anae Coast for dolphin and turtle encounters, and, during winter months, whale-watching. Boats depart daily from the Wai'anae Harbor. Learn lei-making, coconut frond–weaving or take a 'ukulele or hula lesson while cruising the waters off O'ahu on the morning Hawai'i Cultural Cruise offered by Paradise Cruises. Learn about Hawaiian history and culture through activities, videos, and artifact displays onboard the boat.

Sashimi Fun Fishing offers the perfect Sunset Cruise option for those who want to do more than sip a beverage and watch the scenery go by. Come aboard either a 47- or 60-foot Delta and go sunset bottom fishing. The cruise includes a local barbecue dinner and you can also cook what you catch. Hotel transportation to the boat is included in the package.

Tradewind Charters is a good bet for half-day private charter tours for sailing, snorkeling, and whale-watching. Traveling on these luxury yachts not only gets you away from the crowds but also gives you the opportunity to "take the helm" if you wish. The cruise includes snorkeling at an exclusive anchorage as well as hands-on snorkeling and sailing instruction. Charter prices are approximately $495 for up to six passengers.

🄵 **Paradise Cruises** ✉ Pier 5, Honolulu Harbor, Honolulu ☎ 808/983-7700. **Sashimi Fun Fishing** ☎ 808/955-3474. **Tradewind Charters** ✉ 796 Kalanipuu St., Honolulu ☎ 800/829-4899. **Wild Side Specialty Tours** ✉ Wai'anae Boat Harbor, Slip A11, Wai'anae Boat Harbor ☎ 808/306-7273.

BUS & VAN TOURS There are many ground-tour companies in O'ahu that handle daylong sightseeing excursions. Depending on the size of the tour, travel may be by air-conditioned bus or smaller vans. Vans are recommended because less time is spent picking up passengers, and you get to know your fellow passengers and your tour guide. Ask exactly what the tour includes in the way of actual "get-off-the-bus" stops and "window sights." Most of the tour guides have taken special Hawaiiana classes to learn their history and lore, and many are certified by the state of Hawai'i. Tipping ($10 per person at least) is customary.

E Noa Tours uses minibuses and trolleys and likes to get you into the great outdoors. Polynesian Adventure Tours has motorcoaches, vans, and minicoaches. Polynesian Hospitality provides narrated tours. Roberts Hawai'i has equipment ranging from vans to presidential limousines. Trans Hawaiian Services offers multilingual tours.

Most tour companies offer some version of the standard O'ahu tours listed below.

There are several variations on the Circle Island Tour theme. Some of these all-day tours, ranging from $45 to $65, include lunch. Little Circle tours cover East O'ahu. This is a half-day tour and costs between $25 and $40.

The comprehensive Pearl Harbor and City tour includes the boat tour to Pearl Harbor run by the National Park Service. These tours cost between $35 and $40.

One of the advantages of the Polynesian Cultural Center tour is that you don't have to drive yourself back to Waikīkī after dark if you take in the evening show. The tour is $70–$80 per person.

🄵 **E Noa Tours** ☎ 808/591-9923 🌐 www.enoa.com. **Polynesian Adventure Tours** ☎ 808/833-3000 🌐 www.polyad.com. **Polynesian Cultural Center** ☎ 808/293-3333 or 808/923-1861 🌐 www.polynesia.com. **Polynesian Hospitality** ☎ 808/526-3565. **Roberts Hawai'i** ☎ 808/539-9400 🌐 www.robertshawaii.com. **Trans Hawaiian Services** ☎ 808/566-7300.

THEME TOURS E Noa Tours has certified tour guides who conduct not only Circle Island and Pearl Harbor tours but also shopping tours to the Waikele Premium Outlets.

Hawaiian Island Eco-Tours, Ltd.'s experienced guides take nature lovers and hikers on limited-access trails for tours ranging from hidden waterfalls to bird-watching.

Home of the Brave and Top Gun Tours offers military-history buffs a narrated tour of military bases plus a drive through the National Memorial Cemetery of the Pacific.

Mauka Makai Excursions takes visitors to some of the ancient Hawaiian archaeological, legendary, and nature sites that islanders hold sacred. **⚡ E Noa Tours** ☎ 808/591-9923 ⊕ www.enoa.com. **Hawaiian Island Eco-tours, Ltd** ☎ 808/236-7766 ⊕ www.hikeoahu.com. **Home of the Brave and Top Gun Tours** ☎ 808/396-8112. **Mauka Makai Excursions** ☎ 808/593-3525 ⊕ www.hau-ecotours.com.

UNDERWATER TOURS *Atlantis* Submarines operates two air-conditioned vessels off Waikīkī, which dive up to 100 feet for viewing of a sunken navy-yard oiler, coral gardens, and an artificial reef teeming with tropical fish. Dive cruises are two hours in length and are a popular family activity. Children must be at least 3 feet tall to board. Note: flash photography will not work; use film speed ASA 200 or above without flash. Tours cost $90 and begin from the Hilton Hawaiian Village Resort Pier.
⚡ Atlantis Submarines ⊠ Hilton Hawaiian Village Beach Resort and Spa, 2005 Kālia Rd., Waikīkī, Honolulu 96815 ☎ 808/973-1296.

WALKING TOURS Meet at the Chinese Chamber of Commerce for a fascinating peek into herbal shops, an acupuncturist's office, open-air markets, and specialty stores. The 2½-hour tour sponsored by the Chamber costs $5 and is available every Tuesday at 9:30. Reservations are required.

The Mission Houses Museum offers a two-hour walk through historic Honolulu that begins with an hour-long tour of the Mission Houses before the downtown stroll. Reservations are required. Tours are $8 and operate Thursday and Friday mornings.

The American Institute of Architects (AIA) offers a tour of Downtown Honolulu from an architectural perspective. Tours cost $15 per person and run Tuesday and Saturday mornings at 9:30 AM.

The Hawaii Geographic Society arranges a unique Downtown Honolulu historic-temple and archaeology walking tour (Sunday only upon request) for $10 per person.

History springs to life for young and old alike during Honolulu Time Walks, which come with appropriately costumed narrators and cost $7 to $45. Tours and seminar programs explore the "mysteries" of Honolulu—its haunts, historic neighborhoods, and the different but not always talked about eras in its colorful history.
⚡ AIA Downtown Walking Tour ⊠ American Institute of Architects, 1128 Nu'uanu Ave., Downtown Honolulu, Honolulu ☎ 808/545-4242. **Chinatown Walking Tour** ⊠ Chinese Chamber of Commerce, 42 N. King St., Downtown Honolulu, Honolulu ☎ 808/533-3181. **Hawaii Geographic Society** ☎ 808/538-3952. **Historic Downtown Walking Tour** ⊠ 553 S. King St., Downtown Honolulu, Honolulu ☎ 808/531-0481. **Honolulu Time Walks** ⊠ 2634 S. King St., Suite 3, Downtown Honolulu, Honolulu ☎ 808/943-0371.

TAXIS

You can usually get a taxi right outside your hotel. Most restaurants will call a taxi for you. Rates are $1.50 at the drop of the flag, plus $2.50 per mile. Flat fees can also be negotiated for many destinations—just ask your driver. Drivers are generally courteous, and the cars are in good condition, many of them air-conditioned. For transportation throughout the island, try Charley's Taxi & Tours. SIDA of Hawai'i Taxis, Inc., offers 24-hour island-wide transportation service and multilingual drivers.

🚖 Charley's Taxi & Tours ☎ 808/531-1333. SIDA of Hawai'i Taxis, Inc. ☎ 808/836-0011.

TRANSPORTATION AROUND O'AHU

Waikīkī is only 2½ mi long and ½ mi wide, which means you can usually walk to where you are going. However, if you plan to venture outside of Waikīkī, it's best to rent a car.

TROLLEY TRAVEL

The Waikīkī Trolley has three lines and 40 stops that allow you to design your own itinerary. The Red Line cruises around Waikīkī, Ala Moana, and Downtown Honolulu. The Yellow Line hits major shopping centers and restaurant locations. The Blue Line provides a tour of O'ahu's southeastern coastline, including Hanauma Bay and Sea Life Park. The trolleys depart from the Royal Hawaiian Shopping Center in Waikīkī every 15 minutes daily from 8 to 4:30. Fares range from $18–$25. At press time, there were reports that trolley service may be discontinued; please call ahead to see if trolleys are running.

🚖 Waikīkī Trolley ☎ 808/591-2561 or 800/824-8804 ⊕ www.waikikitrolley.com.

VISITOR INFORMATION

🚖 Activities & Attractions Association of Hawai'i ☎ 808/871-7947 or 800/398-9698 ⊕ www.HawaiiFun.org. Hawai'i Visitors & Convention Bureau ⊠ Waikīkī Business Plaza, 2270 Kalākaua Ave., Suite 801, Honolulu 96815 ☎ 808/923-1811 or 800/464-2924 ⊕ www.gohawaii.com. O'ahu Visitor Bureau ☎ 877/525-6248 ⊕ www.visit-oahu.com. Surf Report ☎ 808/973-4383. Weather ☎ 808/973-4381.

MAUI
THE VALLEY ISLE

2

Updated by
Shannon
Wianecki

"MAUI NŌ KA ʻOI" IS WHAT LOCALS SAY—it's the best, the most, the top of the heap. To those who know Maui well, there's good reason for the superlatives. The second-largest island in the Hawaiian chain, Maui has made an international name for itself with its tropical allure, its arts and cultural activities, and miles of perfect-tan beaches. Maui weaves a spell over the more than 2 million people who visit its shores each year, and many decide to return for good.

Maui residents have quite a bit to do with their island's successful tourism story. In the mid-1970s, savvy marketers on Maui saw a way to increase their sleepy island's economy by positioning it as an island apart. Community leaders started promoting their Valley Isle separately from the rest of the state. They nicknamed West Maui the Golf Coast, luring in heavyweight tournaments that, in turn, would bring more visitors. They attracted some of the finest resorts and hotels in the world, and they became the state's condominium experts, emphasizing the luxurious privacy these accommodations can provide. Maui's visitor count swelled, putting it far ahead of that of the other Neighbor Islands.

Quick growth has led to its share of problems. During the busy seasons—from Christmas to Easter and then again during the summer—West Maui can be overly crowded. Although Maui has widened the road that connects Lahaina and Kāʻanapali, the occasional traffic congestion here might not be what you bargained for. And South Maui's Kīhei still has trouble keeping traffic in motion along its one seaside main drive.

But then consider Maui's natural resources. The island is made up of two volcanoes, one now extinct and the other dormant, that both erupted long ago and joined into one island. The resulting depression between the two is what gives Maui its nickname, the Valley Isle. West Maui's 5,788-foot Puʻu Kukui was the first volcano to form, a distinction that gives that area's mountainous topography a more weathered look. Rainbows seem to grow wild over this terrain as gentle mists fill the deeply eroded canyons.

The Valley Isle's second volcano is the 10,023-foot Haleakalā, a mammoth mountain. If you hike its slopes or peer into its enormous crater, you'll witness an impressive variety of nature, with desertlike terrain butted up against tropical forests.

The island's volcanic history gives Maui much of its beauty. The roads around the island are lined with rich red soil, the fertile foothold for sugarcane. Sugar has disappeared from West Maui, as it has nearly everywhere in the state. But Central Maui is still carpeted with grassy green, thanks to HC&S with its last working mill at Puʻunēnē.

Farmers also appreciate the Valley Isle. On the slopes of Haleakalā, the volcanic richness of the soil has yielded lush results. Sweetly scented flowers bloom large and healthy. Grapes cultivated on Haleakalā's slopes are squeezed for wine and champagne. Horses graze languidly on rolling meadows of the best Upcountry grasses, while jacaranda trees dot the hillsides with spurts of luscious lavender. As the big brute of a volcano slides east and becomes the town of Hāna, lavish rains turn the landscape to jungle, and waterfalls cascade down the crags.

Numbers in the text correspond to numbers in the margins and on the Maui, Lahaina, Kahului-Wailuku, and Road to Hāna maps.

If you have
1 day

This is a tough choice. But how can you miss the opportunity to see **Haleakalā National Park** ③⑦ and the volcano's enormous, otherworldly crater? Sunrise at the summit has become the thing to do. You'll need an hour and a half from the bottom of **Haleakalā Highway** ③⑥ (Route 37) to the summit. Add to that the time of travel to the highway—at least 45 minutes from Lahaina or Kīhei. *The Maui News* posts the hour of sunrise every day. The best experience of the crater takes all day. Start at the summit, hike down Sliding Sands trail, cross the crater floor, and come back up the Halemau'u switchbacks. (This works out best if you leave your car at the Halemau'u trailhead parking lot and get a lift for the last 20-minute drive to the mountaintop.) If you don't hike, leave the mountain early enough to go explore **'Īao Valley State Park** ②⑧, above Wailuku.

If you have
3 days

Give yourself the Haleakalā volcano experience one day, and then rest up a little with a beach-snorkel-exploring jaunt on either West Maui or the South Shore. The South Shore trip will have to include the **Maui Ocean Center** ③① at Mā'alaea. Then drive east, sampling the little beaches in **Wailea** ③③ and getting a good dose of big, golden **Mākena Beach State Park** ③④. Be sure to drive on past Mākena into the rough lava fields, the site of Maui's last lava flows, which formed rugged **La Pérouse Bay** ③⑤. The 'Āhihi-Kīna'u Marine Preserve has no beach, but it's a rich spot for snorkeling.

Or take the West Maui trip through Olowalu, **Lahaina** ④–⑯, and **Kā'anapali** ③, and dodge off the highway to find small beaches in Nāpili, Kahana, **Kapalua** ①, and beyond. The road gets narrow and sensational around **Kahakuloa** ②.

On your third day, explore **Hāna** ⑥①. Drive up to **Pā'ia** ④④ for a meal, pause at **Ho'okipa Beach** ④⑤ for the surf action, and on your way back to Hāna savor the sight of the taro fields of **Ke'anae Arboretum** ⑤③ and **Wailua Overlook** ⑤⑤. Nearly everyone keeps going past Hāna town to **'Ohe'o Gulch** ⑥④.

If you have
5 days

After you've completed the three-day itinerary above, explore Upcountry. Get to the town of **Makawao** ④② and use it as your pivot point. Head north at the town's crossroads and drive around **Ha'ikū** ④⑥ by turning left at the first street (Kokomo Road), right at Ha'ikū Road, then coming back uphill on any of those leafy, twisting gulch-country roads. After you've explored Makawao town, drive out to Kula on the Kula Highway. Stop in little Kēōkea for coffee, and keep driving on Kula Highway to the 'Ulupalakua Ranch History Room at the **Tedeschi Vineyards and Winery** ④①. Add some time in Central Maui to really get to the heart of things, especially **Wailuku** ②③–②⑥, with its old buildings and curious shops. From here you can loop out to **Pā'ia** ④④ and spend some time enjoying beaches in the Spreckelsville area.

Exploring Maui

The island can be split up into five exploring areas—West Maui, Central Maui, the South Shore, Upcountry (including Haleakalā), and the Road to Hāna (East Maui). You can spend a half day to a full day or more in each area, depending on how long you have to visit. The best way to see the whole island is by car, but there are a few good walking tours.

To get yourself oriented, first look at a map of the island. You will notice two distinct circular landmasses. The smaller landmass, on the western part of the island, consists of 5,788-foot Puʻu Kukui and the West Maui Mountains. The interior of these mountains is one of the earth's wettest spots. Annual rainfall of 400 inches has sliced the land into impassable gorges and razor-sharp ridges. Oddly enough, the area's leeward shore—what most people mean when they say "West Maui"—is sunny and warm year-round.

The large landmass on the eastern portion of Maui was created by Haleakalā, the cloud-wreathed volcanic peak at its center. One of the best-known mountains in the world, Haleakalā is popular with hikers and sightseers. This larger region of the island is East Maui. Its dry, leeward South Shore is flanked with resorts, condominiums, beaches, and the busy town of Kīhei. Its windward shore, largely one great rain forest, is traversed by the Road to Hāna.

Between the two mountain areas is Central Maui, the location of the county seat of Wailuku, from which the islands of Maui, Lānaʻi, Molokaʻi, and Kahoʻolawe are governed. It's also the base for much of the island's commerce and industry.

On the Islands, the directions *mauka* (toward the mountains) and *makai* (toward the ocean) are often used.

About the Restaurants

You can eat a great meal every night for a month on Maui without ever dining twice in the same place. The resorts set very high standards, and restaurants elsewhere have risen to the challenge. Maui continues to attract fine chefs, several of whom are known for their trendsetting Hawaiʻi regional cuisine. This growing movement uses fruits and vegetables unique to Hawaiʻi in classic European or Asian ways—spawning such dishes as *ʻahi* (yellowfin tuna) carpaccio, breadfruit soufflé, and papaya cheesecake. Of course, you can find plain old local-style cooking here—particularly if you wander into the less-touristy areas of Wailuku or Kahului, for example. A good "plate lunch" will fulfill your daily requirement of carbohydrates: macaroni salad, two scoops of rice, and an entrée of, say, curry stew, teriyaki beef, or *kālua* (roasted in an underground oven) pig and cabbage.

About the Hotels

The resorts here re-create whatever is beautiful about Maui on the premises, doing their best to improve on nature. And their best is pretty amazing—opulent gardens and fantasy swimming pools with slide-

2

Beaches

Maui's beaches win awards for being the best in the world. (Yes, there are awards for beaches.) Those of Wailea and Kapalua lead the pack. Residents particularly revere Mākena Beach, beyond Wailea—so much so that they launched a successful grassroots campaign to have it preserved as a state park. But don't expect to find the island ringed with sand. In fact, most of the coastline is dramatically craggy; beaches tend to be pockets. Each one has a personality of its own and can be completely explored in a half day. The thin, clean strand of Kā'anapali, though, goes on for 3 mi, past resort after resort. Offshore here, yachts, catamarans, and parasail riders drift across brilliant porcelain-blue water. Many of Maui's beaches are a little difficult to spot from the road, especially where homes and hotels have taken up shoreline property. Just remember that you can go to any beach you want. Access to the sea is a sacred trust in Hawai'i, preserved from ancient times.

Scenic Drives

Maui has bad roads in beautiful places. Lots of visitors take a break from the beach and just go driving, usually taking day trips from their lodgings around Lahaina or Kīhei. Maui's landscape is extraordinarily diverse for such a small island. Your sense of place (and the weather) will seem to change every few miles. If you drive to the top of Haleakalā, you rise from palm-lined beaches to the rare world inhabited by airplanes in only an hour and a half. The Road to Hāna takes you into the tropical rain forest, testing your reflexes behind the wheel on the rain-gouged windward side. Upcountry—around Makawao and Ha'ikū—you can drive into and out of the rain, with rainbows that seem to land on the hood of your car.

Water Sports

The West Maui vacation coast (from Lahaina to Kapalua) centers on Lahaina Harbor, where you can find boats for snorkeling, scuba diving, deep-sea fishing, whale-watching, parasailing, and sunset cocktail–partying. At the harbor, you can learn to surf, catch a ferry to Lāna'i, or grab a seat on a fast inflatable. The South Maui vacation coast has Mā'alaea Harbor and the great snorkeling beaches of Kīhei and Wailea. If you want to walk through the ocean without getting wet, visit the top-notch aquarium in Mā'alaea. If you're a thrill-seeker, drive to Ho'okipa, near Pā'ia, where surfers, kite boarders, and windsurfers catch big waves and big air.

Whale-Watching

One of the best signs of the high intelligence of humpback whales is that they return to Maui every year. Having fattened themselves in subarctic waters all summer, they migrate south in the winter to breed, and thousands of them cruise the Lahaina Roadstead (that is, the leeward Maui sea channel) in particular. From December 15 to May 1 the Pacific Whale Foundation has naturalists stationed in two places—on the rooftop of their headquarters and at the scenic viewpoint on the *pali,* or cliff-side stretch, of the highway into Lahaina. The foundation also runs whale-watch boats that depart every hour of the day. In fact, every boat on the island will go out of its way to watch humpbacks when the opportunity arises—which it does often, as the whales themselves seem to have a penchant for people-watching.

down waterfalls and hidden grottoes (sometimes with swim-up bars in them). In addition, spas, cultural events, championship golf courses, priceless art collections, and tennis clubs make it hard to work up the willpower to leave the resort and go see the real thing. Kā'anapali, the grande dame, sits next to Lahaina's action. Kapalua, farther north, is more private and serene—and catches a bit more wind and rain. Sprawling Wailea on the South Shore has excellent beaches and designer golf courses, each with a distinct personality. Resort prices are not for everyone. Many people compromise on the luxury and find condominium apartments in Nāpili and Kahana (for West Maui) or in Kīhei (South Shore). With a few exceptions, you'll find that accommodations are all clustered along these leeward shores. If you want to stay elsewhere on the island—say, Upcountry or in Hāna (without using the Hotel Hāna-Maui)—seek out a bed-and-breakfast or a rental property.

WHAT IT COSTS				
$$$$	**$$$**	**$$**	**$**	**¢**
RESTAURANTS over $30	$20–$30	$12–$20	$7–$12	under $7
HOTELS over $200	$150–$200	$100–$150	$60–$100	under $60

Restaurant prices are for one main course at dinner. Hotel prices are for two people in a standard double room in high season, including tax and service.

Timing

Although Maui has the usual temperate-zone shift of seasons—a bit rainier in the winter, hotter and drier in the summer—these seasonal changes are negligible on the leeward coasts, where most visitors stay. The only season worth mentioning is tourist season, when the roads around Lahaina and Kīhei get crowded. Peak activity occurs from December through March and picks up again in summer. If traffic is bothering you, get out of town and explore the countryside. During high season, the Road to Hāna tends to clog—well, not clog exactly, but develop little choo-choo trains of cars, with everyone in a line of six or a dozen driving as slowly as the first car. The solution: leave early (dawn) and return late (dusk). And if you find yourself playing the role of locomotive, pull over and let the other drivers pass.

WEST MAUI

West Maui, anchored by the amusing old whaling town of Lahaina, was the focus of development when Maui set out to become a premier tourist destination. The condo-filled beach towns of Nāpili, Kahana, and Honokōwai are arrayed between the stunning resorts of Kapalua and Kā'anapali, north of Lahaina.

Lahaina itself has a notorious past. There are stories of lusty whalers who met head-on with missionaries bent on saving souls. Both groups journeyed to Lahaina from New England in the early 1800s. At first, Lahaina might look touristy, but there's a lot that's genuine here as well. The town has renovated most of its old buildings, which date from the time when it was Hawai'i's capital. Much of the town has been designated a National Historic Landmark, and any new buildings must conform in style to those built before 1920.

Begin this tour in **Kapalua ❶** ⌐. Even if you're not staying there, you'll want to have a look around the renowned Kapalua Bay Hotel and enjoy a meal or snack before you begin exploring. From Kapalua drive north on the Honoapi'ilani Highway (Route 30). This road is paved, but storms now and then make it partly impassable, especially on the winding 8-mi stretch that is only one lane wide, with no shoulder and a sheer drop-off into the ocean. However, you'll discover some gorgeous photo opportunities along the road, and if you go far enough, you'll come to **Kahakuloa ❷**, a sleepy fishing village tucked into a cleft in the mountain. The road pushes on to Wailuku, but you may be tired of the narrow and precipitously winding course you have to take.

From Kahakuloa turn around and go back in the direction from which you came—south toward Kā'anapali and Lahaina, past the beach towns of Nāpili, Kahana, and Honokōwai. If you wish to explore these towns, get off the Upper Honoapi'ilani Highway and drive closer to the water. If you're not staying there, you may want to visit the planned resort community of **Kā'anapali ❸**, especially the Hyatt Regency Maui and the Westin Maui. To reach them, turn right onto Kā'anapali Parkway. Next, head for Lahaina. Before you start your Lahaina trek, take a short detour by turning left from Honoapi'ilani Highway onto Lahainaluna Road, and stop at the **Hale Pa'i ❹**, the printing shop built by Protestant missionaries in 1837. Return down Lahainaluna Road until you reach Front Street and turn left.

Since Lahaina is best explored on foot, use the drive along Front Street to get oriented and then park at or near **505 Front Street ❺**, at the south end of the town's historic and colorful commercial area. Heading back into town, turn right onto Prison Street and you'll come to **Hale Pa'ahao ❻**, which was built from coral blocks. Return to Front Street, where it's a short stroll north to the **Banyan Tree ❼**, one of the town's best-known landmarks and, behind it, the old **Court House ❽**. Next door, also in Banyan Park, stand the reconstructed remains of the waterfront **Fort ❾**. About a half block northwest, you'll find the site of Kamehameha's **Brick Palace ❿**. If you walk to the corner of Front and Dickenson streets, you'll find the **Baldwin Home ⓫**, restored to reflect an early-19th-century house. Next door is the **Master's Reading Room ⓬**, Maui's oldest building.

Wander north or south on Front Street to explore Lahaina's commercial side. At the Wharf Cinema Center, you can see the **Spring House ⓭**, built over a freshwater spring. If you head north on Front Street, you'll come to the **Wo Hing Museum ⓮** on the right. Walk another two blocks north and you'll find the **Seamen's Hospital ⓯**. If it's before dusk and you still have a hankering for just one more stop, try the **Waiola Church and Cemetery ⓰**. Walk south down Front Street, make a left onto Dickenson Street, and then make a right onto Waine'e Street and walk another few blocks to reach the church.

Maui

TO MOLOKA'I

Pailolo Channel

Slaughterhouse Beach

D.T. Fleming Beach

Honokōhau

Kapalua 1
Nāpili
Honolua

Nāpili Beach

Kahakuloa 2

Kahana

30

West Maui Forest Reserve

340

WEST MAUI MTS.

Kahekili Hwy.

Honokōwai

Honoapi'ilani Hwy.

Kā'anapali 3
Kā'anapali Beach

Kahului-Wailuku 17 - 26 see detail map

Ho'okipa Beach 45

Baldwin Beach

44 **Pā'ia**
Hāna Hwy.
Baldwin

Lahaina 4 - 16 see detail map

Kepaniwai Park & Heritage Gardens

'Īao Stream

Kanahā Beach

Kahului

32

Wailuku

Haleakalā Hwy.

37

TO LĀNA'I

'Īao Valley State Park 28 *'Īao* 27

30

Puʻunēnē Ave.

350

Haleakalā Highway 36

Pūlehu Rd.

30

Maui Tropical Plantation 29

Honoapi'ilani Hwy.

380

Mokulele Hwy.

311

Au'au Channel

Honoapi'ilani Hwy.

Maui Ocean Center 31

N. Kīhei Rd.

30

Mā'alaea Small Boat Harbor

Mā'alaea Bay

Kīhei 32

Pi'ilani Hwy.

S. Kīhei Rd.

Haleakalā

Kama'ole Beach Parks

31

Ulua Beach

Waiohuli
Kēōkea 40

Wailea 33

Wailea Beach

Kula Hwy.

Tedeschi Vineyards and Winery 41

37

Ulupalakua Ranch

31

Mākena Beach State Park 34

TO KAHO'OLAWE

Mākena Hwy.

Kanaio

La Pérouse Bay 35

'Alalākeiki Channel

N

0 ————————— 10 miles

0 ————————— 15 km

PACIFIC OCEAN

kū

Ulumalu

365 Rd.

Twin
Falls

47   48

Huelo

Kailua

Waikamoi
Nature Trail

49   Kaumahina State
360   51 Wayside Park

Puahokamoa
Stream   50

52   53   Ke'anae Arboretum

Honomanū Bay   Wailua

54   55   Wailua Overlook

Ke'anae
Overlook

56   57   Nāhiku

Waikāne
Falls

360   Hāna Hwy

Hāna
Airport

Ka'eleku Caverns 58   59

60   Wai'ānapanapa
State Park

Pi'ilanihale
Heiau

Hotel Hāna-Maui   62

61

Hāna

43   Kokomo

Hui No'eau
Visual Arts
Center

kawao

kalani

377

Haleakalā
Crater Rd.

Kōolau
Forest
Reserve

Pi'ina'au Stream

Haleakalā
National Park
Headquarters/
Visitor Center

378   37

Leleiwi
Overlook

Halemau'u

38   Kula Botanical
Gardens

9

Nanea a'o
Kula

Kalahaku
Overlook

Haleakalā

Haleakalā Visitor
Center

Pu'u 'Ula'ula
Overlook

Kahikinui
Forest
Reserve

Haleakalā
National Park

Hāna Forest Reserve

Kōkī Beach

63   Hāmoa
Beach

Mū'olea

64   'Ohe'o Gulch

Kīpahulu

65   Grave of
Charles Lindbergh

Kaupō

31

Pi'ilani Hwy

31

'Alenuihāhā Channel

TO THE BIG ISLAND OF HAWAI'I

KEY
▶ Start of itinerary

TIMING You can walk the length of Lahaina's Front Street in less than 30 minutes if you don't stop along the way. Just *try* not to be intrigued by the town's colorful shops and historic sites. Realistically, you'll need at least a half day—and can easily spend a full day—to check out the area's coastal beaches, towns, and resorts. The Banyan Tree in Lahaina is a terrific spot to be when the sun sets—mynah birds settle in here for a screeching symphony, which can be an event in itself. If you arrange to spend a Friday afternoon exploring Front Street, you can dine in town and hang around for Art Night, when the galleries stay open into the evening and entertainment fills the streets.

What to See

★ ⓫ **Baldwin Home.** In 1835 an early missionary to Lahaina, Ephraim Spaulding, built this attractive thick-walled house of coral and stone. In 1836 Dr. Dwight Baldwin—also a missionary—moved in with his family. The home has been restored and furnished to reflect the period. You can view the living room, with the family's grand piano; the dining room; and Dr. Baldwin's dispensary. The Lahaina Restoration Foundation occupies the building, and its knowledgeable staff is here to answer almost any question about historic sites in town. Ask for its walking-tour brochure. ⊠ *696 Front St., Lahaina* ☎ *808/661–3262* ⊕ *www.hawaiimuseums.org* ⊠ *$3* ⊙ *Daily 10–4.*

❼ **Banyan Tree.** This massive tree, a popular and hard-to-miss meeting place if your party splits up for independent exploring, was planted in 1873. It's the largest of its kind in the state and provides a welcome retreat for the weary who come to sit under its awesome branches. ⊠ *Front St., between Hotel and Canal Sts., Lahaina.*

❿ **Brick Palace.** All that's left of the palace built by King Kamehameha I to welcome the captains of visiting ships are the excavated cornerstones and foundation in front of the Pioneer Inn. Hawai'i's first king lived only one year in the palace because his favorite wife, Ka'ahumanu, refused to stay here. It was then used as a warehouse, storeroom, and meeting house for 70 years, until it collapsed. ⊠ *Makai end of Market St., Lahaina.*

❽ **Court House.** This old civic building was erected in 1859, rebuilt in 1925, and restored to its 1925 condition in 1999. At one time or another it served as a customhouse, post office, vault and collector's office, governor's office, police court, and courtroom. Now it houses museum displays, the Lahaina Arts Society, a visitor center, and, perhaps best of all, a water cooler. ⊠ *649 Wharf St., Lahaina* ☎ *808/661–0111* ⊠ *Free* ⊙ *Daily 9–5.*

❺ **505 Front Street.** The quaint, New England–style mall on this quiet stretch of Front Street has many treasures—notably a resident endangered sea turtle. In 2002 Turtle No. 5690 awed researchers and tourists alike by laying a record eight nests in the sand just steps from the mall. Catching sight of a nestling is rare, but 505's superb restaurants, galleries, bookstore, day spa, and local designer's shop are much more accessible. ⊠ *South end of Front St. near Shaw St., Lahaina.*

Lahaina

❾ **Fort.** Used mostly as a prison, this fortress was positioned so that it could police the whaling ships that crowded the harbor. It was built from 1831 to 1832 after sailors, angered by a law forbidding local women from swimming out to ships, lobbed cannonballs at the town. Cannons raised from the wreck of a warship in Honolulu Harbor were brought to Lahaina and placed in front of the fort, where they still sit today. The building itself is an eloquent ruin. ⊠ *Canal and Wharf Sts., Lahaina.*

❻ **Hale Pa'ahao (Old Prison).** This jailhouse dates to rowdy whaling days. Its name literally means "stuck-in-irons house," referring to the wall shackles and ball-and-chain restraints. The compound was built in the 1850s by convict laborers out of blocks of coral that had been salvaged from the demolished waterfront Fort. Most prisoners were sent here for desertion, drunkenness, or reckless horse riding. Today, a wax figure representing an imprisoned old sailor tells his recorded tale of woe. ⊠ *Waine'e and Prison Sts., Lahaina* 🎟 *Free* ☉ *Daily 8–5.*

❹ **Hale Pa'i.** Protestant missionaries established Lahainaluna Seminary as a center of learning and enlightenment in 1831. Six years later, they built this printing shop. Here at the press, they and their young Hawaiian scholars created a written Hawaiian language and used it to produce a Bible, history texts, and a newspaper. An exhibit displays a replica of the original Rampage press and facsimiles of early printing. The oldest U.S. educational institution west of the Rockies, the seminary now serves as Lahaina's public high school. ⊠ *980 Lahainaluna Rd., Lahaina* 🖀 *808/661–3262* 🖃 *Donations accepted* ☉ *Weekdays 10–3.*

❸ **Kāʻanapali.** The theatrical look of Hawaiʻi tourism—planned resort communities where luxury homes mix with high-rise hotels, fantasy swimming pools, and a theme-park landscape—all began right here in the 1960s. Three miles of uninterrupted white beach and placid water form the front yard for this artificial utopia, with its 40 tennis courts and two championship golf courses. The six major hotels here are all worth visiting just for a look around, especially the Hyatt Regency Maui, which has a multimillion-dollar art collection. At the Whalers Village shopping complex, a small **Whaling Museum** (⊠ Kāʻanapali Pkwy., Suite H16 🖀 808/661–5992 🖃 donations accepted) tells the story of the 19th-century *Moby-Dick* era; it's open daily from 9 AM to 10 PM. ⊠ *2435 Kāʻanapali Pkwy.*

❷ **Kahakuloa.** Untouched by progress, this tiny village is a relic of pre–jet travel Maui. Many remote villages similar to Kahakuloa used to be tucked away in the valleys of this area. This is the wild side of West Maui. True adventurers will find terrific snorkeling and swimming along this coast, as well as some good hiking trails. ⊠ *North end of Honoapiʻilani Hwy.*

▶❶ **Kapalua.** Set in a beautiful secluded spot surrounded by pineapple fields, this resort got its first big boost in 1978, when the Maui Land & Pineapple Company built the luxurious Kapalua Bay Hotel. The hotels host dedicated golfers, celebrities who want to be left alone, and some of the world's richest folks. Kapalua's shops and restaurants are among Maui's finest, but expect to pay high prices. By contrast, the old **Honolua Store** serves informal plate lunches, popular with locals. ⊠ *Bay Dr., Kapalua.*

🄲 **Lahaina–Kāʻanapali & Pacific Railroad.** Affectionately called the Sugarcane Train, this is Maui's only passenger train. It's an 1890s-vintage railway that once shuttled sugar but now moves sightseers between Kāʻanapali and Lahaina. This quaint little attraction with its singing conductor is a big deal for Hawaiʻi but probably not much of a thrill for those more accustomed to trains (though children like it no matter where they grew up). A barbecue dinner with entertainment is offered on Thursday at 5 PM. ⊠ *1½ blocks north of the Lahainaluna Rd. stoplight (at Hinau St.) on Honoapiʻilani Hwy., Lahaina* 🖀 *808/661–0080* 🖃 *Round-trip $15.75, one-way $11.50, dinner train $65* ☉ *Daily 10:15–4.*

⓬ **Master's Reading Room.** This could be Maui's oldest residential building, constructed in 1834. In those days the ground floor was a mission's storeroom, and the reading room upstairs was for sailors. ⊠ *Front and Dickenson Sts., Lahaina* 🖀 *808/661–3262.*

⓯ **Seamen's Hospital.** Built in the 1830s to house King Kamehameha III's royal court, this property was later turned over to the U.S. government, which used it as a hospital for whalers. Next door is a typical **sugar plantation camp residence**, circa 1900. ⊠ *1024 Front St., Lahaina* 🖀 *808/ 661–3262.*

⑬ **Spring House.** Built by missionaries to shelter a freshwater spring, this historic structure now holds a huge Fresnel lens, once used in a local lighthouse that guided ships to Lahaina. ✉ *Wharf Cinema Center, 658 Front St., Lahaina.*

need a break? The sandwiches have real Gruyère and Emmentaler cheese at **Maui Swiss Cafe** (✉ 640 Front St., Lahaina ☎ 808/661–6776)—expensive ingredients with affordable results. The friendly owner scoops the best and cheapest locally made ice cream in Lahaina. Daily lunch specials are less than $6.

⑯ **Waiola Church and Cemetery.** The Waiola Cemetery is actually older than the neighboring church; it dates from the time when Kamehameha's sacred wife, Queen Keōpūolani, died and was buried here in 1823. The first church here was erected in 1832 by Hawaiian chiefs and was originally named Ebenezer by the queen's second husband and widower, Governor Hoapili. Aptly immortalized in James Michener's *Hawai'i* as the church that wouldn't stand, it was burned down twice and demolished in two windstorms. The present structure was put up in 1953 and named Waiola (water of life). ✉ *535 Waine'e St., Lahaina* ☎ *808/ 661–4349.*

⑭ **Wo Hing Museum.** Built by the Wo Hing Society in 1912 as a fraternal society for Chinese residents, this eye-catching building now contains Chinese artifacts and a historic theater that shows Thomas Edison's films of Hawai'i, circa 1898. Upstairs is the only public Taoist altar on Maui. ✉ *858 Front St., Lahaina* ☎ *808/661–5553* ▣ *Donations accepted* ☉ *Daily 10–4.*

CENTRAL MAUI

Kahului, an industrial and commercial town in the center of the island, is home to many of Maui's permanent residents, who find their jobs close by. The area was developed in the early '50s to meet the housing needs of workers for the large sugarcane interests here, specifically those of Alexander & Baldwin. The company was tired of playing landlord to its many plantation workers and sold land to a developer who promised to create affordable housing. The scheme worked, and Kahului became the first planned city in Hawai'i. Ka'ahumanu Avenue (Route 32), Kahului's main street, runs from the harbor to the hills. It's the logical place to begin your exploration of Central Maui.

West of Kahului, Wailuku, the county seat since 1950, is certainly the most charming town in Central Maui. Its name means "Water of Destruction," after a battle that pitted King Kamehameha I against Maui warriors in the 'Īao Valley. Wailuku was a politically important town until the sugar industry began to decline in the 1960s and tourism took hold. Businesses left the cradle of the West Maui Mountains and followed the new market to the shore, where tourists arrived by the boatload. Wailuku still houses the County government, but has the feel of a town that fell asleep for several decades. The charming boutiques and salons now inhabiting Main Street's plantation-style buildings serve as reminders of a bygone era.

a good tour

Begin at the **Alexander & Baldwin Sugar Museum** ⑰ ▶ in Puʻunēnē, directly across from the HC&S sugar mill.

From here, explore Kahului, which looks nothing like the lush, tropical paradise most people envision as Hawaiʻi. Head northwest on Puʻunēnē Avenue all the way to its end at Kaʻahumanu Avenue and turn left. Three blocks ahead you'll see the Sputniklike canvas domes of Kaʻahumanu Center, Maui's largest shopping center. If you turn right at the signal just before that, you'll follow the curve of Kahului Beach Road and see many ships in port at **Kahului Harbor** ⑱. On your left are the cream-and-brown buildings of the **Maui Arts & Cultural Center** ⑲. Continue past the harbor, turn right at Waiehu Beach Road, and about a mile later as you cross the ʻĪao Stream you'll see **Halekiʻi-Pihana Heiau State Monument** ⑳ on the hilltop to your left. Return along the harbor road and make a right turn at Kanaloa Avenue. Return to Kaʻahumanu Avenue on this road, passing **Keōpūolani Park** ㉑ and the War Memorial Stadium, site of the annual Hula Bowl game. Turn right to reach Wailuku (Kaʻahumanu Avenue eventually becomes Wailuku's Main Street). To get a closer look at **Wailuku's Historic District** ㉒, turn right from Main Street onto Market Street, where you can park for free within view of the landmark ʻĪao Theater ㉓. The theater is a good place to begin your walking tour. Many amusing shops line **Market Street** ㉔ between Vineyard and Main streets. From here, it's a short walk along Main Street to **Kaʻahumanu Church** ㉕ on High Street, just around the corner from Main and across the way from the County Court House. Retrieve your car and turn right onto Main Street. After a few blocks, you'll see **Bailey House** ㉖, on your left.

Continue driving uphill, into the mountains. Main Street turns into ʻĪao Valley Road, the air cools, and the hilly terrain gets more lush. Soon you'll come to **Kepaniwai Park & Heritage Gardens** ㉗. ʻĪao Valley Road ends at ʻ**Īao Valley State Park** ㉘, home of the erosion-formed gray and moss-green rock called ʻĪao Needle. This is a great place to picnic, wade in the stream, and explore the paths. Then return to Wailuku and, at the traffic light, turn right onto Route 30. Drive south a couple of miles to the **Maui Tropical Plantation & Country Store** ㉙.

TIMING   The complete itinerary will take a full day. But you can explore Central Maui comfortably in little more than a half day if you whiz through the Maui Tropical Plantation, or save it for another day. If you want to combine sightseeing with shopping, you'll need more time. Hikers may want to expand their outing to a full day to explore ʻĪao Valley State Park.

What to See

★ ▶ ⑰ **Alexander & Baldwin Sugar Museum.** "A&B," Maui's largest landowner, was one of the "Big Five" companies that spearheaded the planting, harvesting, and processing of sugarcane. Although Hawaiian cane sugar is now being supplanted by cheaper foreign versions—as well as by sugar derived from inexpensive sugar beets—the crop was for many years the mainstay of the Hawaiian economy. You'll find the museum in a small,

Kahului Bay

Kahului Harbor

Kamahā Pond

Wai'ale Reservoirs

KEY

▶ Start of itinerary

Kahului-Wailuku

restored plantation manager's house next to the post office and the still-operating sugar refinery (black smoke billows up when cane is burning). Historic photos, artifacts, and documents explain the introduction of sugarcane to Hawai'i and how plantation managers brought in laborers from other countries, thereby changing the Islands' ethnic mix. Exhibits also describe the sugar-making process. ⊠ *3957 Hansen Rd., Pu'unēnē* ☎ *808/871–8058* ⬧ *$5* ⊘ *Mon.–Sat. 9:30–4:30 (last admission at 4).*

★ ㉖ **Bailey House.** This was the home of Edward and Caroline Bailey, two prominent missionaries who came to Wailuku to run the first Hawaiian girls' school on the island, the Wailuku Female Seminary. The school's main function was to train the girls in the "feminine arts." It once stood next door to the Baileys' home, which they called Halehō'ike'ike (House of Display), but locals always called it the Bailey House, and the sign painters eventually gave in. Construction of the house, between 1833 and 1850, was supervised by Edward Bailey himself. The Maui Historical Society runs a museum in the plastered stone house, with a small collection of artifacts from before and after the missionaries' arrival and with Mr. Bailey's paintings of Wailuku. Some rooms have missionary-period furniture. The Hawaiian Room has exhibits on the making of tapa cloth, as well as samples of pre–Captain Cook weaponry. ⊠ *2375A Main St., Wailuku* ☎ *808/244–3326* ⊕ *www. mauimuseum.org* ⊡ *$5* ⊘ *Mon.–Sat. 10–4.*

⑳ Haleki`i-Pihana Heiau State Monument. Stand here at either of the two *heiau*(ancient Hawaiian stone platforms once used as places of worship) and imagine the king of Maui surveying his domain. That's what Kahekili, Maui's last fierce king, did, and so did Kamehameha the Great after he defeated Kahekili's soldiers. Today the view is most instructive. Below, the once-powerful `Iao Stream has been sucked dry and boxed in by concrete. Before you is the urban heart of the island. The suburban community behind you is all Hawaiian Homelands—property owned solely by native Hawaiians. ⊠ *End of Hea Pl., off Kuhio Pl. from Waiehu Beach Rd. (Rte. 340), Kahului* ⊡ *Free* ⊘ *Daily 7–7.*

㉓ `Iao Theater. One of Wailuku's most-photographed landmarks, this charming movie house went up in 1927 and served as a community gathering spot. When restoration work was completed, the Maui Community Theatre resumed its longtime residence here in its historic Wailuku headquarters. The art-deco building is now the showpiece of Wailuku's Main Street. ⊠ *68 N. Market St., Wailuku* ☎ *808/242–6969.*

need a break? **Maui Bake Shop** (⊠ 2092 Vineyard St., Wailuku ☎ 808/242–0064) serves salads, sandwiches, and a variety of light entrées, but what you're really going to crave are the pastries—a feast for the eyes as well as the palate. The pastel-frosted frogs, chicks, rabbits, and mice, made of orange butter-cream cookie dough, are irresistible.

**★ ㉘ `Iao Valley State Park.** When Mark Twain saw this park, he dubbed it the Yosemite of the Pacific. Yosemite it's not, but it is a lovely deep valley with the curious `Iao Needle, a spire that rises more than 2,000 feet from the valley floor. You can take one of several easy hikes from the parking lot across `Iao Stream and explore the jungle-like area. This park has a beautiful network of well-maintained walks, where you can stop and meditate by the edge of a stream or marvel at the native plants and flowers. Mist occasionally rises if there has been a rain, which makes being here even more magical. ⊠ *Western end of Rte. 32* ⊡ *Free* ⊘ *Daily 7–7.*

**㉕ Ka`ahumanu Church.** It's said that Queen Ka`ahumanu attended services on this site in 1832 and requested that a permanent structure be erected. Builders first tried adobe, which dissolved in the rain, then stone. The present wooden structure, built in 1876, is classic New England style, with white exterior walls and striking green trim. You won't be able to see the interior, however, unless you attend Sunday services. There's a service entirely in the Hawaiian language each Sunday morning at 9:30 (there are services in English as well—call for information). ⊠ *Main and High Sts., Wailuku* ☎ *808/244–5189.*

⑱ Kahului Harbor. The island's only deep-draft harbor, Kahului Harbor is Maui's chief port. Cruise ships resembling floating cities stop here once a week, as do cargo ships and smaller vessels, including the occasional yacht. Surfers sometimes use this spot to catch some waves, but it's not a good swimming beach. ⊠ *Kahului Beach Rd., Kahului.*

🖐 ㉑ **Keōpūolani Park.** Maui's "Central Park" covers 101 acres, and—reflecting Maui residents' traditional love of sports—it has seven playing fields. Named for the great Maui queen who was born near here and is buried in Lahaina's Waiola Church cemetery, the park is planted with native species that are still growing to reach their potential. The park also includes Maui Nui, a native-plant botanical garden, and a 3-mi walking path. ⊠ *Kanaloa Ave. next to the YMCA.*

🖐 ㉗ **Kepaniwai Park & Heritage Gardens.** This county park is a memorial to Maui's cultural roots, with picnic facilities and ethnic displays dotting the landscape. Among the displays are an early Hawaiian shack, a New England–style saltbox, a Portuguese-style villa with gardens, and dwellings from such other cultures as China and the Philippines. Next door the Hawai'i Nature Center has an interactive exhibit and hikes good for children.

The peacefulness here belies the history of the area. During his quest for domination, King Kamehameha I brought his troops from the Big Island of Hawai'i to the Valley Isle in 1790 and engaged in a successful and particularly bloody battle against the son of Maui's chief, Kahekili, near Kepaniwai Park. An earlier battle at the site had pitted Kahekili himself against an older Big Island chief, Kalani'ōpu'u. Kahekili prevailed, but the carnage was so great that the nearby stream became known as Wailuku (water of destruction) and the place where fallen warriors choked the stream's flow was called Kepaniwai (the water dam). ⊠ *'Iao Valley Rd., Wailuku* 🎫 *Free* 🕐 *Daily 7–7.*

need a break? For lunch try local favorite **Ba Le** (⊠ 270 Dairy Rd., Kahului 🕿 808/877–2400), in the Kau Kau Corner food court at the Maui Marketplace. The Vietnamese sandwiches—crisp French rolls piled with fresh herbs, vegetables, and your choice of meat—are cheap and delicious. The food court also offers diner fare and plate lunches.

㉔ **Market Street.** An idiosyncratic assortment of shops makes Wailuku's Market Street a delightful place for a stroll. Shops such as the Good Fortune Trading Company and Brown-Kobayashi carry affordable antiques and furnishings, while Gallerie Ha and the White Orchid gift shop are more sophisticated. Cafe Marc Aurel brews excellent espresso which you can sip while sampling the selection of used CDs at the corner music shop. ⊠ *Wailuku.*

★ ⑲ **Maui Arts & Cultural Center.** An epic fund drive by the citizens of Maui led to the creation of this $32 million facility. The top-of-the-line Castle Theater seats 1,200 people on orchestra, mezzanine, and balcony levels; rock stars play the A&B Amphitheater. The MACC (as it's called) also includes a small black box theater, an art gallery with interesting exhibits, and classrooms. The building itself is worth a visit: it incorporates work by Maui artists, and its signature lava-rock wall pays tribute to the skills of the Hawaiians. ⊠ *Above the harbor on Kahului Beach Rd.* 🕿 *808/242–2787, 808/242–7469 box office* 🕐 *Weekdays 9–5.*

🐦 ㉙ **Maui Tropical Plantation & Country Store.** When Maui's once-paramount crop declined in importance, a group of visionaries decided to open an agricultural theme park on the site of this former sugarcane field. The 60-acre preserve, on Route 30 just outside Wailuku, offers a 30-minute tram ride through its fields with an informative narration covering growing processes and plant types. Children will probably enjoy the historical-characters exhibit as well as fruit-testing, coconut-husking, and lei-making demonstrations, not to mention some entertaining spider monkeys. There's a restaurant on the property and a "country store" specializing in Made in Maui products. ✉ *Honoapiʻilani Hwy. (Rte. 30), Waikapu* ☎ *808/244–7643* 🆓 *Free; tram ride with narrated tour $9.50* ⊙ *Daily 9–5.*

㉒ **Wailuku's Historic District.** The National Register of Historic Places lists many of the old buildings here. Old Wailuku town, Maui's county seat, is sleepy but undergoing a small renaissance. Some interesting stores, coffee shops, and galleries dot its nostalgic side streets. You can pick up a free brochure that describes a self-guided walking tour at **Wailuku Main Street Association** (✉ 2062 Main St. ☎ 808/244–3888). ✉ *High, Vineyard, and Market Sts., Wailuku.*

THE SOUTH SHORE

Twenty-five years ago a scant few adventurers lived in Kīhei. Now about one-third of the Maui population lives here in what was one of the fastest-growing towns in America. Traffic lights and mini-malls may not fit your notion of paradise, but Kīhei does offer sun, heat, and excellent beaches. Besides that, the town's relatively inexpensive condos and small hotels make this a home base for many Maui visitors. Great restaurants are easy to find in any price range. At one end of this populous strip, you have Māʻalaea Small Boat Harbor and the Maui Ocean Center, a world-class seawater aquarium. At the other end, lovely Wailea—a resort community to rival those on West Maui—gives way to truly unspoiled coastline.

a good drive

Start with a look at **Māʻalaea Small Boat Harbor** ㉚ ▶, the departure point for many whale-watching trips, snorkel excursions (often out to the tiny crescent island Molokini), and sunset dinner cruises. Then tour the **Maui Ocean Center** ㉛, an aquarium dedicated to the sea life of the North Pacific. When you leave the aquarium, turn right onto Route 30 and then turn right again at the first traffic signal onto North Kīhei Road (Route 31). You're headed toward the town of **Kīhei** ㉜ on a straight road following the long, sandy coastline of Māʻalaea Bay. On your left is marshy Keālia Pond, a state-managed wildlife sanctuary. On your right, ecologically fragile dunes run between the road and the sea. A turnout provides some parking stalls, information about the dunes, and a boardwalk so you can cross the dunes and use the beach. When you get to the long, thin town of Kīhei, you have a choice. You can turn right at the fork in the road and experience the colorful stop-and-go beach route of South Kīhei Road. Or you can turn left and bypass the town on the Piʻilani Highway, hastening to the resort community of **Wailea** ㉝.

THE BOY WHO RAISED AN ISLAND

ACCORDING TO LEGEND, *the island of Maui was named after a demigod whose father, Akalana, kept the heavens aloft and whose* mother, Hina, guarded the path to the netherworld. Of their children, Maui was the only one who possessed magic powers, though he wasn't a good fisherman and was teased mercilessly by his brothers for it. Eventually, the cunning young Maui devised a way to catch his own fish: he distracted his brothers and pulled his line across theirs, switching the hooks and stealing the fish they had caught.

When Maui's brothers caught on to his deception, they refused to take him fishing. To console Maui, his father gave him a magic hook, the Manaiakalani. Akalana said that the hook was fastened to the heavens and when it caught land a new continent would be born. Maui was able to convince his brothers to take him

out one more time. As they paddled deep into the ocean, he chanted a powerful spell, commanding the hook to catch "the Great Fish." The hook caught more than a fish—as they paddled along, mountain peaks were lifted out of the water's depths.

As the mountains began to rise, Maui told his brothers to paddle quickly without looking back. They did so for two days, at which point their curiosity proved too much. One of the brothers looked back, and as he stopped paddling, Maui's magic line snapped, and the hook was lost forever beneath the sea. Maui had intended to raise an entire continent, but because of his brother's weakness, he had only an island to show for his efforts.

If you're looking for the best beach, you might as well flip a coin. There are great beaches all along this coast. At Wailea, you'll drive past grand resorts interspersed with stretches of golf courses and access roads leading down to small but excellent beaches. As you head south on Wailea Alanui Drive, the manicured look of Wailea gives way to wildness and, after a couple of miles, to **Mākena Beach State Park** ❹. Mākena is such a big beach that it has two paved parking areas. Beyond this point the landscape gets wilder and the road gradually fades away in black fields of cracked lava. This is **La Pérouse Bay** ❺.

TIMING   Because it includes so many fine beach choices, this is definitely an all-day excursion—especially if you include a visit to the aquarium. A good way to do this trip is to get active in the morning with exploring and snorkeling, then shower in a beach park, dress up a little, and enjoy the cool luxury of the Wailea resorts. At sunset, settle in for dinner at one of the area's many fine restaurants.

What to See

❸❷ **Kīhei.** This is a community that's still discovering itself. A greenway for bikers and pedestrians is under construction, as is an unchecked surplus of new homes and properties. Moderately priced hotels, condos, and restaurants make the town convenient for visitors. The beaches and the reliably sunny weather are added attractions. The county beach parks such as Kama'ole I, II, and III have lawns, showers, and picnic tables. Remember: beach park or no beach park, the public has a right to the entire coastal strand, and this one in Kīhei has many off-road delights.

㉟ La Pérouse Bay. Beyond Mākena Beach, the road fades away into a vast territory of black lava flows, the result of Haleakalā's last eruption some 200 years ago. This is where Maui received its first official visit by a European explorer—the French admiral Jean-François de Galaup, Comte de La Pérouse, in 1786. Before it ends, the road passes through 'Āhihi-Kīna'u Marine Preserve, an excellent place for morning snorkel adventures.

▶ **㉚ Mā'alaea Small Boat Harbor.** With only 89 slips and so many good reasons to take people out on the water, this active little harbor needs to be expanded. The Army Corps of Engineers has a plan to do so, but harbor users are fighting it—particularly the surfers, who say the plan would destroy their surf breaks. In fact, the surf here is world renowned, especially the break to the left of the harbor called "freight train," said to be the fastest anywhere. ⊠ *Off Honoapi'ilani Hwy. (Rte. 30).*

★ **㉞ Mākena Beach State Park.** "Big Beach" they call it—a huge stretch of coarse golden sand without a house or hotel for miles. A decade ago, Maui citizens campaigned successfully to preserve this beloved beach from development. At the right-hand end of the beach rises the beautiful hill called Pu'u Ōla'i, a perfect cinder cone. A climb over the rocks at this end leads to "Little Beach," where the (technically illegal) clothing-optional attitude prevails.

★ **㉛ Maui Ocean Center.** You'll feel as though you're walking from the seashore down to the bottom of the reef, and then through an acrylic tunnel in the middle of the sea at this aquarium, which focuses on Hawai'i and the Pacific. Special tanks get you close up with turtles, rays, and the unusual creatures of the tide pools. The center is part of a growing complex of retail shops and restaurants overlooking the harbor. ⊠ *Enter from Honoapi'ilani Hwy. (Rte. 30) as it curves past Mā'alaea Harbor; Mā'alaea* 📞 *808/270–7000* ⊕ *www.mauioceancenter.com* 💲*$19* ⊙ *July and Aug., daily 9–6; Sept.–June, daily 9–5.*

★ **㉝ Wailea.** Wailea, the South Shore's resort community, is slightly quieter and drier than its West Side sister, Kā'anapali. Most visitors cannot pick a favorite and stay at both. The luxury of the resorts (edging on overindulgence) and the simple grandeur of the Shops at Wailea make the otherwise stark coast a worthy destination. A handful of perfect little beaches all have public access, and a paved beach walk allows you to stroll among all the properties, restaurants, and sandy coves. A great place to watch whales in the winter, the makai, or ocean, side of the beach walk is landscaped with exceptionally rare native plants.

HALEAKALĀ & UPCOUNTRY

The west-facing upper slopes of Haleakalā are locally called "Upcountry." This region is responsible for much of Hawai'i's produce—lettuce, tomatoes, and sweet Maui onions—but the area is also a big flower producer. As you drive along you'll notice cactus thickets mingled with purple jacaranda, wild hibiscus, and towering eucalyptus trees. Upcountry is also fertile ranch land, with such spreads as the historic 20,000-acre 'Ulupalakua Ranch and 32,000-acre Haleakalā Ranch. In Makawao each July 4, the Maui Roping Club throws its annual rodeo and parade.

a good drive

Take the **Haleakalā Highway** ㊱ ► (Route 37) to **Haleakalā National Park** ㊲ and the mountain's breathtaking summit. Make sure you have a full tank of gas. No service stations exist beyond Kula. Follow Haleakalā Highway up the mountain to the unlikely intersection of Haleakalā Highway and Haleakalā Highway. If you continue straight the road's name changes to Kula Highway (still Route 37). Instead, turn left onto Haleakalā Highway–this is now Route 377. After about 6 mi, make a left onto Crater Road (Route 378). The switchbacks begin here. Near the top of the mountain is the Park Headquarters/Visitor Center, a good spot to stretch your legs and learn a little bit about the park.

Continuing up the mountain, you'll come to several overlooks, including Leleiwi Overlook and Kalahaku Overlook, both with views into the crater. Not far from Kalahaku Overlook you'll find the Haleakalā Visitor Center. Eventually you'll reach the highest point on Maui, the Pu'u 'Ula'ula Overlook.

On the return trip, turn left at the bottom of Crater Road. Drive about 2 mi, and you'll come to **Kula Botanical Gardens** ㊳ on your left. Stop here to admire the abundant tropical flora. Continue south. If you have reservations for tea, turn left up Waipoli Road. Follow the road to the cattle guard, and you'll see the driveway of **Nāneu u'o Kula** ㊴ on the right, where you can munch on lavender scones and survey the scented view. If tea isn't your thing, continue south and you'll join Kula Highway (Route 37) again. Turn left and soak in the slow pace of life when you stumble upon little **Kēōkea** ㊵. Follow the road coastward and you'll reach 'Ulupalakua Ranch headquarters and **Tedeschi Vineyards and Winery** ㊶, where Maui's only island wines can be sampled.

Return toward Kahului on Route 37, the Kula Highway. If you're pressed for time head downhill back to Kahului. Otherwise, turn north on Makawao Avenue (Route 365) toward **Makawao** ㊷, a classic old Hawaiian town. The **Hui No'eau Visual Arts Center** ㊸ is about a mile from Makawao down Baldwin Avenue. From here it's a 7-mi drive down toward the ocean to the Hāna Highway at the town of Pā'ia. Make a left on the Hāna Highway to return to Kahului.

TIMING This can be an all-day outing even without the detours to Tedeschi Vineyards and Makawao. If you start early enough to catch the sunrise from Haleakalā's summit, you'll have plenty of time to explore the mountain, have lunch in Kula or at 'Ulupalakua Ranch, and end your day with dinner in Makawao or Ha'ikū.

What to See

► ㊱ **Haleakalā Highway.** On this road you'll travel from sea level to an elevation of 10,023 feet in only 38 mi—a feat you won't be able to repeat on any other car route in the world. It's not a quick drive, however. It'll take you about two hours—longer if you can't resist the temptation to stop and enjoy the spectacular views. ⊠ *Rte. 37.*

③⑦ **Haleakalā National Park.** Haleakalā Crater is the centerpiece of this
Fodor'sChoice 27,284-acre national park, established in 1916. The crater is actually
★ an erosional valley, flushed out by water pouring from the summit through two enormous gaps. The small hills within the crater are volcanic cinder cones (called *pu'u* in Hawaiian), each with a small crater at its top, and each the site of a former eruption. The mountain has terrific camping and hiking, including a trail that loops through the crater.

Before you head up Haleakalā, call for the latest **park weather conditions** (☎ 808/877–5111). Extreme gusty winds, heavy rain, and even snow in winter are not uncommon. Because of the high altitude, the mountaintop temperature is often as much as 30 degrees cooler than that at sea level. Be sure to bring a jacket.

You can learn something of the volcano's origins and eruption history at the **Park Headquarters/Visitor Center,** at a 7,000-foot elevation on Haleakalā Highway. Maps, posters, and other memorabilia are available at the gift shop here.

Leleiwi Overlook, at about an 8,800-foot elevation on Haleakalā, is one of several lookout areas in the park. If you're here in the late afternoon, it's possible you'll experience a phenomenon called the Brocken Specter. Named after a similar occurrence in East Germany's Harz Mountains, the "specter" allows you to see yourself reflected on the clouds and encircled by a rainbow. Don't wait all day for this, because it's not a daily occurrence.

The famous silversword plant grows amid the desertlike surroundings at **Kalahaku Overlook,** at the 9,000-foot level on Haleakalā. This endangered flowering plant grows only here in the crater at the summit of this mountain. The silversword looks like a member of the yucca family and produces a 3- to 8-foot-tall stalk with several hundred purple sunflowers. At this lookout the silversword is kept in an enclosure to protect it from souvenir hunters and nibbling wildlife.

The **Haleakalā Visitor Center,** at an elevation of 9,740 feet, has exhibits inside, and a trail from here leads to White Hill—a short, easy walk that will give you an even better view of the valley. Hosmer Grove, just off the highway before you get to the visitor center, has campsites and interpretive trails. Park rangers maintain a changing schedule of talks and hikes both here and at the top of the mountain. Call the park for current schedules.

Just before the summit, the **Crater Observatory** offers warmth and shelter, informative displays, and an eye-popping view of the cinder-cone-studded, 7-mi-by-3-mi crater. The highest point on Maui is the **Pu'u 'Ula'ula Overlook,** at the 10,023-foot summit. Here you'll find a glass-enclosed lookout with a 360-degree view. The building is open 24 hours a day, and this is where visitors gather for the best sunrise view. Dawn begins between 5:45 and 7, depending on the time of year. On a clear day you can see the islands of Moloka'i, Lāna'i, Kaho'olawe, and Hawai'i (the Big Island). On a *really* clear day you can even spot O'ahu glimmering in the distance.

On a small hill nearby, you'll see **Science City**, an off-limits research and communications center straight out of an espionage thriller. The University of Hawai'i maintains an observatory here, and the Department of Defense tracks satellites. ⊠ *Haleakalā Crater Rd. (Rte. 378), Makawao* ☎ *808/572–4400* ⊕ *www.nps.gov/hale* ⊠ *$10 per car* ☉ *Park Headquarters/Visitor Center daily 8–4, Haleakalā Visitor Center daily sunrise–3.*

need a break? **Kula Lodge** (⊠ Haleakalā Hwy., Kula ☎ 808/878–2517) serves hearty breakfasts from 6:30 to 11:15, a favorite with hikers coming down from a sunrise visit to Haleakalā's summit, as well as those on their way up for a late-morning tramp in the crater. Spectacular ocean views fill the windows of this mountainside lodge.

㊸ Hui No'eau Visual Arts Center. The main house of this nonprofit cultural center on the old Baldwin estate, just outside the town of Makawao, is an elegant two-story Mediterranean-style villa designed in the 1920s by the defining Hawai'i architect C. W. Dickey. "The Hui" is the grande dame of Maui's well-known arts scene. The exhibits are always satisfying, and the grounds might as well be a botanical garden. The Hui also offers classes and maintains working artists' studios. ⊠ *2841 Baldwin Ave., Makawao* ☎ *808/572–6560* ⊠ *Free* ☉ *Daily 10–4.*

㊵ Keōkea. More of a friendly gesture than a town, this is the last outpost for Maui's cowboys on their way to work at 'Ulupalakua or Kaupō ranch. A coffee tree pushes through the sunny deck at Grandma's Coffee Shop, and tiny Keōkea Gallery sells some of the most original artwork on the island. The only rest room for miles is across the street at the public park, and the view makes stretching your legs worth it.

㊳ Kula Botanical Gardens. This well-kept garden has assimilated itself naturally into its craggy 6-acre habitat. There are beautiful trees here, including native koa (prized by woodworkers) and *kukui* (the state tree, a symbol of enlightenment). There's also a good selection of proteas, the flowering shrubs that have become a signature flower crop of Upcountry Maui. A natural stream feeds into a koi pond, which is also home to a pair of African cranes. ⊠ *638 Kekaulike Hwy. Kula* ☎ *808/878–1715* ⊠ *$5* ☉ *Daily 9–4.*

㊷ Makawao. This once-tiny town has managed to hang on to its country charm (and eccentricity) as it has grown in popularity. The district was originally settled by Portuguese and Japanese immigrants who came to Maui to work the sugar plantations and then moved "Upcountry" to establish small farms, ranches, and stores. Descendants now work the neighboring Haleakalā and 'Ulupalakua ranches. Every July 4 the *paniolo* (Hawaiian cowboy) set comes out in force for the Makawao Rodeo. The crossroads of town—lined with chic shops and down-home eateries—reflects a growing population of people who came here just because they liked it. ⊠ *Intersection of Baldwin and Makawao Aves.*

★ ❸❾ **Nanea a'o Kula.** Reserve a spot for tea or lunch at this lavender farm with a falcon's view. It's *the* relaxing remedy for those suffering from too much sun, shopping, or golf. Owners Ali'i and Lani lead tours through winding paths of therapeutic lavender varieties, proteas, succulents, and rare Maui wormwood. Their logo, a larger-than-life dragonfly, darts above chefs who are cooking up lavender-infused shrimp appetizers out on the lanai. The gift shop abounds with the farm's own innovative lavender products. ✉ *1100 Waipoli Rd. Kula* ☎ *808/878–3004* ⊕ *www.mauikulalavender. com* 🍴 *$25* 🌿 *Reservations essential* ⊙ *Daily 11 AM.*

need a break? One of Makawao's most famous landmarks is **Komoda Store & Bakery** (✉ 3674 Baldwin Ave. ☎ 808/572–7261)—a classic mom-and-pop store that has changed little in three-quarters of a century—where you can get a delicious cream puff if you arrive early enough. They make hundreds but sell out each day.

★ ❹❶ **Tedeschi Vineyards and Winery.** You can tour the winery and its historic grounds, the former Rose Ranch, and sample the island's only wines: a pleasant Maui Blush, Maui Champagne, and Tedeschi's annual Maui Nouveau. The top-seller, naturally, is the pineapple wine. The tasting room is a cottage built in the late 1800s for the frequent visits of King Kalākaua. The cottage also contains the '**Ulupalakua Ranch History Room,** which tells colorful stories of the ranch's owners, the paniolo tradition that developed here, and Maui's polo teams. The old General Store may look like a museum, but in fact it's an excellent pit stop. ✉ *Kula Hwy., 'Ulupalakua Ranch* ☎ *808/878–6058* ⊕ *www.mauiwine.com* 🍴 *Free* ⊙ *Daily 9–5, tours at 10:30 and 1:30.*

THE ROAD TO HĀNA

Fodor'sChoice ★ Don't let anyone tell you **Hāna Highway** is impassable, frightening, or otherwise unadvisable. Because of all the hype, you're bound to be a little nervous approaching it for the first time; but once you try it, you'll wonder if maybe there's somebody out there making it sound tough just to keep out the hordes. The 55-mi road begins in Kahului, where it is a well-paved highway. The eastern half of the road, riddled with turns and bridges, is challenging, and you'll want to stop often so the driver can enjoy the view, too. But it's not a grueling all-day drive. The challenging part of the road takes only an hour and a half. Don't expect a booming city when you get to Hāna. It's the road, which meanders past lush scenery and waterfalls, that's the draw.

a good drive Hāna Highway is the main street in the little town of **Pā'ia** ❹❹ ▶. You'll want to begin with a full tank of gas. There are no gas stations along Hāna Highway, and the stations in Hāna close by 6 PM. You can also pick up a picnic lunch here. Lunch and snack choices along the way are limited to rustic fruit stands. Once the road gets twisty, remember that many residents make this trip frequently. You'll recognize them because they're the ones who'll be zipping around every curve. They've seen this so many times before that they don't care to linger. Pull over to let them pass.

Two miles east of Pā'ia you'll see **Ho'okipa Beach** ㊺, arguably the wind-surfing capital of the world. Two miles later the bottom of Ha'ikū Road offers a right-turn side trip to **Ha'ikū** ㊻, Maui's verdant gulch country. About 6 mi later, at the bottom of Kaupakalua Road, the roadside mile-posts begin measuring the 36 mi to Hāna town. The road's trademark noodling starts about 3 mi after that. All along this stretch of road, wa-terfalls are abundant. Open the windows to enjoy the sounds and smells. There are plenty of places to pull off and park. You'll want to plan on doing this a few times, since the road's curves make driving without a break difficult. When it's raining (which is often), the drive is particu-larly beautiful.

At the fruit stand just after mile marker 2, you can treat yourself to some fresh sugarcane juice. If you're feeling adventurous, follow the path be-yond the stand to the paradisaical waterfalls known as **Twin Falls** ㊼. Swim at your own risk. Dry off and drive on past the sleepy country villages of **Huelo** and **Kailua** ㊽. Between mile markers 9 and 10, the **Waikamoi Nature Trail** ㊾ sign beckons you to explore. About a mile farther you can stop at the bridge over **Puahokamoa Stream** ㊿, where there are more pools and waterfalls. If you'd rather stretch your legs and use a flush toilet, continue another mile to the **Kaumahina State Wayside Park** �51. Near mile marker 14 you'll find yourself driving along a cliff side down into deep, lush **Honomanū Bay** �52. Another 4 mi brings you to the **Ke'anae Ar-boretum** �53, where you can add to your botanical education or enjoy a challenging hike into a forest. Nearby you'll find the **Ke'anae Over-look** �54. Coming up is the halfway mark to Hāna. If you've had enough scenery, this is as good a time as any to turn around and head back to civilization.

Continue from mile marker 20 for about ¾ mi to **Wailua Overlook** �55. After another ½ mi you'll hit the best falls on the entire drive to Hāna, **Waikāne Falls** �56. At about mile marker 25 you'll see a road that heads down toward the ocean and the village of **Nāhiku** �57, once a populous ancient settlement. Just after mile marker 31, turn left onto 'Ula'ino Road. Follow the signs to **Ka'eleku Caverns** �58. You'll need to call ahead to book an underground tour. The road doubles back for a mile, loses its pave-ment, and even crosses a stream just before Kahanu Garden and **Pi'ilani-hale Heiau** �59, the largest in the state. Back on the road and less than ½ mi farther is the turnoff for Hāna Airport. Just beyond mile marker 32 you'll pass **Wai'ānapanapa State Park** �60. Stop at the black-sand beach for a swim. **Hāna** �61 is just minutes away from here. By now the relaxed pace of life which Hāna residents enjoy should have you in its grasp, so you won't be discouraged to learn that 'town' is little more than a gas station, a post office, and a ramshackle grocery. **Hotel Hāna-Maui** �62, with its surrounding ranch, is the mainstay of Hāna's economy.

Just outside Hāna, take a left on Haneo'o Loop to explore lovely **Hāmoa Beach** �63. You can watch the swells roll in or take a dip yourself. You'll then want to drive 10 mi past town to the pools at **'Ohe'o Gulch** �64. Many people travel the mile past 'Ohe'o Gulch to see the **Grave of Charles Lind-bergh** �65. You'll see a ruined sugar mill with a big chimney on the right side of the road and then, on the left, a rutted track leading to Palapala

PACIFIC OCEAN

Huelo
48
Kailua
49 Waikamoi
Nature Trail
51 Kaumahina State
Wayside Park
Puahokamoa 50
Stream
52 Honomanū Bay
Ke'anae Arboretum 53 ○ Wailue
55 Wailua Overlook
54
56 57 Nāhiku
Ke'anae Overlook
Waikāna
Falls
Koolau
Forest
Reserve
Ka'elekut 58 Hāna
Caverns Airport Wai'ānapanapa
59 State Park
Pi'ilanihale 360 60
Heiau
Hotel Hāna-Maui 62
61 Ilūna
Hāna
Forest Kōki
Reserve Beach
Haleakalā National Park
63 Hāmoa
Beach
31
Kahikinui Forest Reserve
Wailua
Kipahulu
Forest
Reserve
64 'Ohe'o Gulch
Kipahulu
65
31 Grave of
Pi'ilani Highway Charles Lindbergh
Kaupō

Alenuihaha Channel

0   4 mi
0   4 km

KEY
---- Dry riverbed
Start of itinerary

Ho'omau Congregational Church. The simple one-room church sits on a bluff over the sea, with the small graveyard on the ocean side. From here, you'll want to return the way you came. The road ahead is quite rough and not recommended for rental cars.

TIMING   With stops, the drive from Pā'ia to Hāna should take you between two and three hours. Lunching in Hāna, hiking, and swimming can easily turn the round-trip into a full-day outing. Since there's so much scenery to take in, try to plan your Road to Hāna drive for a day that promises fair, sunny weather, though the drive can be beautiful when it's raining. For an even more relaxing trip, plan to stay overnight at the Hāna hotel.

What to See

65   **Grave of Charles Lindbergh.** The world-renowned aviator chose to be buried here because he and his wife, writer Anne Morrow Lindbergh, spent a lot of time living in the area in a home they'd built. He was buried here in 1974, next to Palapala Ho'omau Congregational Church. Since this is a churchyard, be considerate and leave everything exactly as you found it. Next to the churchyard on the ocean side is a small county park, a good place for a peaceful picnic. ⊠ *Palapala Ho'omau Congregational Church, Pi'ilani Hwy., Kīpahulu.*

46   **Ha'ikū.** At one time this town vibrated around a couple of enormous pineapple canneries. Now the place is reawakening and becoming a self-reliant community. At the town center, the old cannery has been turned into a rustic mall. Nearby warehouses are following suit. Continue 2 mi up Kokomo Road to see a large pu'u capped with a grove of columnar pines, and the 4th Marine Division Memorial Park. During World War II American GIs trained here for battles on Iwo Jima and Saipan. Locals have nicknamed the cinder cone Giggle Hill, because it was a popular hangout for Maui women and their favorite servicemen. You might want to return to Hāna Highway by following Ha'ikū Road east. This is one of Maui's prettiest drives, and it passes West Kuiaha Road, where a left turn will bring you to a second renovated cannery. ⊠ *Intersection of Ha'ikū and Kokomo Rds.*

63   **Hāmoa Beach.** Indulge in swimming or bodysurfing at this beautiful salt-and-pepper beach. Picnic tables, rest rooms, and showers beneath the idyllic shade of coconut trees offer a more than comfortable rest stop. The road leading to Hāmoa also takes you to **Koki Beach,** where you can watch the Hāna surfers mastering the swells and strong currents, and the seabirds darting over **'Ālau,** the palm-fringed islet off the coast. The swimming is safer at Hāmoa. ⊠ *Haneo'o Loop Rd., 2 mi east of Hāna town.*

61   **Hāna.** The town centers on its lovely circular bay, dominated on the right-hand shore by a pu'u called Ka'uiki. A short trail here leads to a cave, the birthplace of Queen Kā'ahumanu. Two miles beyond town another pu'u presides over a loop road that passes Hāna's two best beaches—Koki and Hāmoa. The hill is called Ka Iwi O Pele (Pele's Bone). This area is rich in Hawaiian history and legend. Offshore here, at tiny 'Ālau Island, the demigod Maui supposedly fished up the Hawaiian islands.

Although sugar was once the mainstay of Hāna's economy, the last plantation shut down in the '40s. In 1946 rancher Paul Fagan built the **Hotel Hāna-Maui** and stocked the surrounding pastureland with cattle. Suddenly, it was the ranch and its hotel that were putting food on most tables. The cross you'll see on the hill above the hotel was put there in memory of Fagan.

For many years, the Hotel Hāna-Maui was the only attraction for diners and shoppers determined to spend some time and money in Hāna after their long drive. Now, the **Hāna Cultural Center Museum** (⊠ Ukea St. ☎ 808/248–8622) also helps to meet that need. Besides operating a well-stocked gift shop, it displays artifacts, quilts, a replica of an authentic *kauhale* (an ancient Hawaiian living complex, with thatch huts and food gardens), and other Hawaiiana. The knowledgeable staff can explain it all to you. ⊠ *Hāna Hwy., mile marker 35.*

Hāna Airport. Think of Amelia Earhart. Think of Waldo Pepper. If these picket-fence runways don't turn your thoughts to the derring-do of barnstorming pilots, you haven't seen enough old movies. Only the smallest planes can land and depart here, and when none of them happen to be around, the lonely wind sock is the only evidence that this is a working airfield. ⊠ *Hāna Hwy. past mile marker 30* ☎ 808/248–8208.

㊾ Honomanū Bay. At mile marker 14 the Hāna Highway drops into and out of this enormous valley, with its rocky black-sand beach. The Honomanū Valley was carved by erosion during Haleakalā's first dormant period. At the canyon's head there are 3,000-foot cliffs and a 1,000-foot waterfall, but don't try to reach them. There's not much of a trail, and what does exist is practically impassable. ⊠ *Hāna Hwy. before Keʻanae.*

★ ㊺ Hoʻokipa Beach. There is no better place on this or any other island to watch the world's best windsurfers in action. The surfers know five different surf breaks here by name. Unless it's a rare day without wind or waves, you're sure to get a show. It's not safe to park on the shoulder. Use the ample parking lot at the county park entrance. ⊠ *2 mi past Pāʻia on Rte. 36.*

㊽ Hotel Hāna-Maui. It's pleasant to stroll around the lobby of this low-key but beautiful property, perhaps on the way to dinner at the restaurant, drinks at the bar, or shopping in the gift stores. The newer Sea Ranch cottages across the road, built to look like authentic plantation housing from the outside, are also part of the hotel. ⊠ *Hāna Hwy., Hāna* ☎ 808/248–8211.

㊽ Huelo and Kailua. This little farm town of Huelo has two quaint churches and several lovely B&Bs. It's a good place to stay if you value privacy, but it also provides an opportunity to meet local residents and learn about a rural lifestyle you might not have expected to find on the Islands. The same can be said for nearby Kailua (mile marker 6), home to Alexander & Baldwin's irrigation employees. ⊠ *Hāna Hwy. near mile marker 5.*

58 Ka'eleku Caverns. Guided tours with Maui Cave Adventures lead amateur spelunkers into a system of gigantic lava tubes, accentuated by colorful underworld formations. Choose your level of exploration—a one-hour walking tour or a two-hour adventure tour. Gear (gloves, flashlight, and hard hat) is provided, and visitors must be at least eight years of age. ⊠ *1¼ mi down 'Ula'ino Rd., off Hāna Hwy.* ☎ *808/248-7308* ⊕ *www.mauicave.com* ⊠ *$29–$59* ⊙ *Tours depart Mon.–Sat. at 11 and 1.*

51 Kaumahina State Wayside Park. The park has a picnic area, rest rooms, and a lovely overlook to the Ke'anae Peninsula. Hardier souls can camp here, with a permit. ⊠ *Hāna Hwy., mile marker 12, Kailua* ☎ *808/984-8109* ⊠ *Free* ⊙ *Weekdays 8–4.*

off the beaten path

KAUPŌ ROAD – The road to Hāna continues all the way around Haleakalā's "back side" through 'Ulupalakua Ranch and into Kula. The desertlike area, with its grand vistas, is unlike anything else on the island, but the road itself is bad, sometimes impassable in winter. The car-rental agencies are smart to call it off-limits to their passenger cars. Most of the residents along the road in these wild reaches also prefer that you stick to the windward side of the mountain. The danger and dust from increasing numbers of speeding jeep drivers are making life tough for the residents, especially in Kaupō, with its 4 mi of unpaved road. The small communities around East Maui cling tenuously to the old ways. Please keep them in mind if you do pass this way.

53 Ke'anae Arboretum. Here's a place to learn the names of the many plants and trees now considered native to Hawai'i. The meandering Pi'ina'au Stream adds a graceful touch to the arboretum and provides a swimming pond besides. You can take a fairly rigorous hike from the arboretum if you can find the trail at one side of the large taro patch. Be careful not to lose the trail once you're on it. A lovely forest waits at the end of the 25-minute hike. ⊠ *Hāna Hwy., mile marker 17, Ke'anae* ⊠ *Free* ⊙ *Daily 24 hrs.*

54 Ke'anae Overlook. From this observation point, you can take in the patchwork-quilt effect the taro farms create below. The people of Ke'anae are working hard to revive this Hawaiian agricultural art and the traditional cultural values that the crop represents. The ocean provides a dramatic backdrop for the farms. In the other direction there are awesome views of Haleakalā through the foliage. This is a great spot for photos. ⊠ *Hāna Hwy. near mile marker 17, Ke'anae.*

57 Nāhiku. In ancient times this was a busy settlement with hundreds of residents. Now only about 80 people live in Nāhiku, mostly native Hawaiians and some back-to-the-land types. A rubber grower planted trees here in the early 1900s. The experiment didn't work out, so Nāhiku was essentially abandoned. The road ends at the sea in a pretty landing. This is the rainiest, densest part of the East Maui rain forest. ⊠ *Makai side of Hāna Hwy., mile marker 25.*

★ **⑥₄** ⌂ **'Ohe'o Gulch.** One branch of Haleakalā National Park runs down the mountain from the crater and reaches the sea here, where a basalt-lined stream cascades from one pool to the next. Some tour guides still call this area "Seven Sacred Pools," but in truth there are more than seven, and they've never been considered sacred. You can park here and walk to the lowest pools for a cool swim. The place gets crowded, though, since most people who drive the Hāna Highway make this their last stop. If you enjoy hiking, go up the stream on the 2-mi hike to **Waimoku Falls.** The trail crosses a spectacular gorge, then turns into a boardwalk that takes you through an amazing bamboo forest. You can pitch a tent in the grassy campground down by the sea. ⌂ *Pi'ilani Hwy., 10 mi south of Hāna.*

need a break? The drive to Hāna wouldn't be as enchanting without a stop or two at one of the countless fruit stands alongside the highway. Every half mile or so a thatched hut tempts passersby with apple bananas, lilikoi, avocados, or starfruit just plucked from the tree. Leave 50¢ or $1 in the can for the folks who live off the land. Definitely take the time to stop just past mile marker 2 on the Hāna Highway, where you can sample fresh sugarcane juice and have a young coconut shucked for you.

About 10 minutes before Hāna town, you can stop for—of all things—espresso. The tiny, colorful **Nahiku Ti Gallery and Coffee Shop** (⌂ between mile markers 27 and 28, Hāna Hwy. ☎ 808/248–8800) sells local coffee, dried fruits and candies, and delicious (if pricey) banana bread. Sometimes the barbecue is fired up and you can try fish skewers or baked breadfruit (an island favorite impossible to find elsewhere). The Ti Gallery sells Hawaiian crafts.

★ ▶ **④₄** **Pā'ia.** This little town on Maui's north shore was once a sugarcane enclave, with a mill and plantation camps. Astute immigrants quickly opened shops to serve the workers, who probably found it easier to buy supplies near home. The town boomed during World War II when the marines set up camp in nearby Ha'ikū. The old HC&S sugar mill finally closed and no sign of the military remains, but the entrepreneurs—in one form or another—are here to stay. In the '70s Pā'ia became a hippie town as dropouts headed for Maui to open boutiques, galleries, and unusual eateries. In the '80s windsurfers discovered nearby Ho'okipa Beach and brought an international flavor to Pā'ia (to the benefit of the unusual eateries). Budget inns have cropped up to accommodate eclectic travelers, and whether you're looking for yoga pants or pumpkin soup, Pā'ia is sure to deliver. ⌂ *Intersection of Baldwin Ave. and Hāna Hwy.*

need a break? Pā'ia is a great place to find food. A French-Caribbean bistro with a sushi bar in back, a French-Indian creperie, a neo-Mexican gourmet restaurant, and a fish market all compete for your patronage near the intersection of Baldwin Avenue and Hāna Highway. This abundance is helpful because Pā'ia is the last place to snack before the pilgrimage to Hāna and the first stop for the famished on the return trip.

Anthony's Coffee Company (✉ 90 Hāna Hwy. ☏ 808/579–8340) roasts its own beans, sells ice cream and picnic lunches, and is a great place to eavesdrop on the local windsurfing crowd. **Charley's Restaurant** (✉ 142 Hāna Hwy. ☏ 808/579–9453) is an easygoing saloon-type hangout with pool tables. **Mana Foods** (✉ 49 Baldwin Ave. ☏ 808/579–8078), the North Shore's natural-foods store, has an inspired deli with wholesome hot and cold items. The long line at **Pā'ia Fishmarket Restaurant** (✉ 2A Baldwin Ave. ☏ 808/579–8030) attests to the popularity of their tasty mahi sandwiches. Fresh fish can also be bought by the pound. Pā'ia has an excellent wine store, the **Wine Corner** (✉ 113 Hāna Hwy. ☏ 808/579–8904), which can be helpful since two good eateries nearby are BYOB.

★ **⑤⑨** **Pi'ilanihale Heiau.** The largest prehistoric monument in Hawai'i, this temple platform was built for a great 16th-century Maui king named Pi'ilani and his heirs. This king also supervised the construction of a 10-foot-wide road that completely encircled the island. (That's why his name is part of most of Maui's highway titles.) Hawaiian families continue to maintain and protect this sacred site as they have for centuries, and they have not been eager to turn it into a tourist attraction. However, they now offer a brochure so you can tour the property yourself. Parties of four or more can reserve a guided tour by calling 48 hours in advance. Tours include the 122-acre **Kahanu Garden,** a federally funded research center focusing on the ethnobotany of the Pacific. ✉ *Left on 'Ula'ino Rd. at mile marker 31 of Hāna Hwy.; the road turns to gravel; continue 1½ mi* ☏ *808/248–8912* 🎟 *Self-guided tours $5, guided tours $10* ☉ *Weekdays 10–2.*

⑤⓪ **Puahokamoa Stream.** The bridge over Puahokamoa Stream is one of many you'll cross en route from Pā'ia to Hāna. It spans pools and waterfalls. Picnic tables are available, so many people favor this as a stopping point, but there are no rest rooms. ✉ *Hāna Hwy. near mile marker 11.*

④⑦ **Twin Falls.** Once a rough trail plastered with "no trespassing" signs, this treasured spot is now easily accessible. You'll know you've found it by the mass of cars surrounding the substantial fruit stand at the trail head. Several deep, emerald pools sparkle beneath waterfalls and offer excellent swimming and photo opportunities. While it's still private property, the "no trespassing" signs have been replaced by colorfully painted arrows pointing away from residences and toward the falls. Swim at your own risk and beware: flash floods here and in all East Maui stream areas can be sudden and deadly. Check the weather before you go. ✉ *Hāna Hwy., past mile marker 2.*

⑥⓪ **Wai'ānapanapa State Park.** The park is right on the ocean, and it's a lovely spot to picnic, hike, or swim. An ancient burial site is nearby, as well as a heiau. Wai'ānapanapa also has one of Maui's only black-sand beaches and some freshwater caves for adventurous swimmers to explore. The water in the tide pools here turns red several times a year. Scientists say it's explained by the arrival of small shrimp, but locals claim the color represents the blood of Popoalaea, who legend says was murdered in one of the caves by her husband, Chief Kaakea. In either case,

Fodor'sChoice
★

the dramatic contrast between the rain-forest green of the cliffs and the black volcanic rock is not to be missed. With a permit you can stay in state-run cabins here for less than $30 a night—the price varies depending on the number of people—but reserve early. They often book up a year in advance. ⊠ *Hāna Hwy. near mile marker 32, Hāna* ☎ *808/984–8109* ☞ *Free.*

56 **Waikāne Falls.** Though not necessarily bigger or taller than the other falls, these are the most dramatic—some say the best—falls you'll find on the road to Hāna. That's partly because the water is not diverted for sugar irrigation. The taro farmers in Wailua need all the runoff. This is a particularly good spot for photos. ⊠ *Hāna Hwy. past mile marker 21, Wailua.*

49 **Waikamoi Nature Trail.** Stretch your car-weary limbs here. A short (if muddy) trail leads through tall eucalyptus trees to a coastal vantage point with a picnic table and barbecue. Signage reminds visitors QUIET, TREES AT WORK and BAMBOO PICKING PERMIT REQUIRED. Awapuhi, or Hawaiian shampoo ginger, sends up fragrant shoots along the trail. ⊠ *Hāna Hwy., between mile markers 9 and 10.*

55 **Wailua Overlook.** From the parking lot you can see Wailua Canyon, but you'll have to walk up steps to get a view of Wailua Village. The landmark in Wailua Village is a church made of coral, built in 1860. Once called St. Gabriel's Catholic Church, the current Our Lady of Fatima Shrine has an interesting legend surrounding it. As the story goes, a storm washed just enough coral up onto the shore to build the church but then took any extra coral back to sea. ⊠ *Hāna Hwy. near mile marker 21, Wailua.*

BEACHES

All of Hawai'i's beaches are free and open to the public—even those that grace the front yards of fancy hotels—so you can make yourself at home on any one of them. Blue beach-access signs indicate rights-of-way through condominium and resort properties.

Although they don't appear often, be sure to pay attention to any signs or warning flags on the beaches. Warnings of high surf or rough currents should be taken seriously. Before you seek shade under a coconut palm, be aware that the trade winds are strong enough to knock fruit off the trees and onto your head. Drinking alcoholic beverages on beaches in Hawai'i is prohibited.

West Maui

"Slaughterhouse" (Mokuleia) Beach. The island's northernmost beach is part of the Honolua-Mokuleia Marine Life Conservation District. "Slaughterhouse" is the surfers' nickname for what is officially Mokuleia. When the weather permits, this is a great place for bodysurfing and sunbathing. Concrete steps and a green railing help you get down the sheer cliff to the sand. The next bay over, Honolua, has no beach but offers one of the best surf breaks in Hawai'i. Often you'll see competitions happening there, with cars pulled off the road and parked in the pineapple field. There are no facilities in this wild area. ⊠ *Mile marker 32 on road past Kapalua.*

CloseUp

FROM MONGOOSE TO MOUNTAIN APPLE

Hawai'i's Flora and Fauna

Hawai'i has the dubious distinction of claiming more extinct and endangered animal species than all of the North American continent. The Hawaiian crow, or 'alalā, for example, has been reduced to a population of only about 15 birds, and most of these have been raised in captivity on the Big Island. The 'alalā is now facing a serious threat from another endangered bird—the 'io, or Hawaiian hawk. Still "protected" although making a comeback from its former endangered status, the nēnē goose, Hawai'i's state bird, roams freely in parts of Maui, Kaua'i, and the Big Island, where mating pairs are often spotted ambling across roads in Hawai'i Volcanoes National Park.

The mongoose is not endangered, although some residents wish it were. Alert drivers can catch a glimpse of the ferretlike animal darting across country roads. The mongoose was brought to Hawai'i in 1883 in an attempt to control the rat population, but the plan had only limited success, because the hunter and hunted rarely met: mongooses are active during the day, rats at night.

At the Kīlauea Point National Wildlife Refuge on Kauai'i, hundreds of Laysan albatross, wedge-tail shearwaters, red-footed boobies, and other marine birds glide and soar within photo-op distance of visitors to Kīlauea Lighthouse. Boobie chicks hatch in the fall and emerge from nests burrowed into cliff-side dirt banks and even under stairs—any launching pad from which the fledgling flyer can catch the nearest air current.

Hawai'i has only two native mammals. Threatened with extinction, the rare Hawaiian bat hangs out primarily at Kealakekua Bay on the Big Island. Also on

the endangered species list, doe-eyed Hawaiian monk seals breed in the northwestern Islands. With only 1,500 left in the wild, you won't catch many lounging on the beaches of Hawai'i's populated islands, but you can see rescued pups and adults along with "threatened" Hawaiian green sea turtles at Sea Life Park and the Waikīkī Aquarium on O'ahu.

Tropical flowers such as plumeria, orchids, hibiscus, red ginger, heliconia, and anthuriums grow wild on all the Islands. Pīkake blossoms make the most fragrant leis, and fragile orange 'ilima (once reserved only for royalty) the most elegant leis. The lovely wood rose is actually the dried seedpod of a species of morning glory. Mountain apple, Hawaiian raspberry, thimbleberry, and strawberry guava provide refreshing snacks for hikers; and giant banyan trees, hundreds of years old, spread their canopies over families picnicking in parks, inviting youngsters to swing from their hanging vines.

Sprouting ruby pom-pom-like lehua blossoms—thought to be the favorite flower of Pele, the volcano goddess— 'ōhi'a trees bury their roots in fields of once-molten lava. Growing on the Big Island as well as the outer slopes of Maui's Haleakalā, exotic protea flourish only at an elevation of 4,000 feet. Within Haleakalā's moonscape crater, the rare and otherworldly silversword—a 7-foot stalk with a single white spike and pale yellow flower found nowhere else on earth—blooms once and then dies.

D. T. Fleming Beach. Because the current can be quite strong, this charming, mile-long sandy cove is better for sunbathing than for swimming. Still it's one of the island's most popular beaches, and there are rest rooms, showers, picnic tables, grills, and paved parking. Part of the beach runs along the front of the Ritz-Carlton, Kapalua. ⊠ *Rte. 30, 1 mi north of Kapalua Resort.*

Kapalua Beach. On the northern side of Nāpili Bay is small, pristine Kapalua Beach. You may have to share sand space with a number of other beachgoers, however, because the area is quite popular for lazing, swimming, and snorkeling. There are showers, rest rooms, and a paved parking lot. ⊠ *Past Bay Club restaurant off Lower Honoapi'ilani Hwy., before Kapalua Bay Hotel.*

Fodor'sChoice **Nāpili Beach.** A sparkling white crescent makes a perfect cove for strolling
★ and sunbathing. It's right outside the Nāpili Kai Beach Club, a popular little resort for honeymooners. But despite this and other condominiums and development around the bay, the facilities here are minimal. There are showers at the far right end of the beach and a tap by the beach-access entrance, where you can wash the sand off your feet, and you're only a few miles south of Kapalua. ⊠ *5900 Lower Honoapi'ilani Hwy.; from upper highway follow cutoff road closest to Kapalua Resort and look for Nāpili Pl. or Hui Dr.*

★ **Kā'anapali Beach.** If you're looking for peace and quiet, this is not the beach for you. But if you want lots of action, lay out your towel here. The beach fronts the big hotels at Kā'anapali and is one of Maui's best people-watching spots: cruises, windsurfers, and parasailers head out from here while the beautiful people take in the scenery. The area around Black Rock has prime snorkeling, and the bravest of the brave dive off the imposing rock into the calm water below. Although no facilities are available, the nearby hotels have rest rooms and some, like the Marriott, have outdoor showers. You're also close to plenty of shops and concession stands. ⊠ *Follow any of 3 Kā'anapali exits from Honoapi'ilani Hwy. and park at any of the hotels.*

The South Shore

Kīhei has excellent beaches right in town, including three beach parks called **Kama'ole I, II,** and **III,** which have showers, rest rooms, picnic tables, and barbecues. Good snorkeling can be done along the rocky borders of the parks. If Kīhei is excellent, though, Wailea is even better. Look for a little road and parking lot between the first two big resorts—the Renaissance and the Marriott. This gets you to **Mōkapu** and **Ulua beaches.** This is a good area for families as the beaches are protected from major swells and several reef formations provide ample tide pools for kids to explore. Note that there have been a lot of break-ins in the parking lot.

★ A road just after the Grand Wailea takes you to **Wailea Beach,** a wide, sandy stretch, with good snorkeling and swimming. There are showers at the north end, though the south end is more accessible and, therefore, more popular with locals. Near the Kea Lani resort, you'll find **Polo Beach,** which is small and uncrowded. You can swim and snorkel here and it's a good place to whale-watch.

★ **Mākena.** Just south of Wailea is the state park at Mākena, with one of the state's most breathtaking beaches. "Big Beach" is a 3,000-foot-long and 100-foot-wide stretch of deep sand abutting aquamarine sea. It's never crowded, no matter how many cars are crammed into the lots. The water is fine for swimming, but the shore drop-off is steep and swells can get big, so use caution. There are portable toilets at each of the three paved entrances. If you climb the cinder cone near the first entrance, you'll discover "Little Beach"—clothing-optional by popular practice. (Officially, nude sunbathing is illegal in Hawai'i.) On Sunday, free spirits of all kinds crowd Little Beach's tiny shoreline for a drumming circle and bonfire. ✉ *Off Wailea Alanui Dr.*

The North Shore

Kanahā Beach. Local folk and windsurfers like this long, golden strip of sand bordered by a wide grassy area. This is a popular Kahului spot for joggers and picnicking families. Kanahā Beach has toilets, showers, picnic tables, and grills. ✉ *Drive through airport and back out to car-rental road (Koeheke), turn right, and keep going.*

★ **Baldwin Beach.** Another local favorite, just west of Pā'ia town, this beach is a big body of comfortable sand. There's not much wave action for bodysurfing, but this is a good place to stretch out, swim, or jog. The county park at the right side of the beach has picnic areas, rest rooms, showers, and sometimes even a lifeguard. ✉ *Hāna Hwy., 1 mi west of Baldwin Ave.*

★ **Ho'okipa Beach.** If you want to see some of the world's finest windsurfers, stop at this beach along Hāna Highway. The sport has become an art—and a career, to some—and its popularity was largely developed right at Ho'okipa. It's also one of Maui's hottest surfing spots, with waves as high as 15 feet. This is not a good swimming beach, nor the place to learn windsurfing, but plenty of picnic tables and barbecue grills are available for hanging out. ✉ *2 mi past Pā'ia on Rte. 36.*

Hāna

Hāmoa Beach. This is the beach that James Michener made famous by deeming it the only North Pacific beach he'd ever seen that truly conjures the South Pacific. Indeed, it is idyllic with its perfect half-moon shape shaded by palm trees. And it's rarely crowded, despite the picnic area that the Hotel Hāna-Maui has set up here for its guests. It's also one of the few Hāna beaches with bathroom facilities. It's better for bodysurfing than swimming. ✉ *2 mi past Hāna off Rte. 36.*

Kōkī Beach. This beach in Hāna offers unusually good bodysurfing because the sandy bottom stays shallow for a long way out. On the down side, there are no facilities here. But this is a wild place rich in Hawaiian lore. Watch conditions, because the riptides here can be mean. ✉ *Haneo'o Loop Rd. 2 mi east of Hāna town.*

Fodor's Choice **Wai'ānapanapa State Park.** The startling contrasts created by white foam,
★ black sand, and green *naupaka* (one of the most common beach plants in Hawai'i) branches bestow a quick fix of paradise on tired travelers. Swimming here is both relaxing and invigorating. The park has rest rooms, picnic tables, and several cultural sites. A dramatic coastal path continues all the way to Hāna. ✉ *Hāna Hwy. near mile marker 32.*

WHERE TO EAT

A history of innovative Pacific Rim cuisine has supplied the island with many good restaurants. Fresh fish, island-grown produce, and simple, stylized presentations characterize the very best. Many of the key players have opened restaurants on both resort shores. Roy's, Sansei, Longhi's, and Marco's have all opened second locations in Kīhei and Wailea, making it even easier for visitors to find outstanding meals. Expect to eat well in any price category.

Except as noted, reservations are not required, but it's never a bad idea to phone ahead to book a table. Restaurants are open daily unless otherwise specified. An aloha shirt and pants for men and a simple dress or pants for women are acceptable in all establishments.

West Maui

American

★ $–$$ ✕ **Lahaina Coolers.** This breezy little café with a surfboard hanging from its ceiling serves such tantalizing fare as Evil Jungle Pasta (pasta with grilled chicken in spicy Thai peanut sauce) and linguine with prawns, basil, garlic, and cream. It also has pizzas, steaks, burgers, and desserts such as a chocolate taco filled with tropical fruit and berry salsa. Pastas are made fresh in-house. Don't be surprised to see a local fisherman walk through or a harbor captain reeling in a hearty breakfast. ⊠ *180 Dickenson St., Lahaina* ☎ *808/661–7082* ▤ *AE, MC, V.*

¢–$ ✕ **The Gazebo Restaurant.** Even locals will stand in line upward of a half hour for a table overlooking the beach at this restaurant, an actual open-air gazebo. The food is standard diner fare, but it's thoughtfully prepared. Breakfast choices include macadamia-nut pancakes and Portuguese-sausage omelets. There are satisfying burgers and salads at lunch. The friendly hotel staff puts out coffee for those waiting in line. ⊠ *Nāpili Shores Resort, 5315 Lower Honoapiʻilani Hwy., Nāpili* ☎ *808/669–5621* ▤ No credit cards ⊘ No dinner.

Continental

$$$$ ✕ **Bay Club.** Dinner by candlelight at this spot on a rocky promontory overlooking the ocean is a romantic way to cap off a day in the sun, especially if you've been swimming at Kapalua Beach just a few yards from the door. You won't want to walk through the richly paneled, elegant interior with sandy feet, however. Island seafood is emphasized, starting with ʻahi tartare for an appetizer and building to the Hawaiian seafood pan roast of prawns, lobster, and scallops cooked in sweet-basil broth. ⊠ *Kapalua Bay Hotel, 1 Bay Dr., Kapalua* ☎ *808/669–5656* ▤ *AE, D, DC, MC, V.*

$$$–$$$$ ✕ **Swan Court.** A grand staircase leads down into a cathedral-ceiling ballroom, and black and white swans glide across a waterfall-fed lagoon at this elegant eatery. Try the crispy scallop dim sum in plum sauce; creamy lobster-coconut bisque brimming with chunks of fish, lobster, shrimp, and button mushrooms; or charbroiled lamb chops in macadamia satay sauce. Arrive early and ask for a table on the left side, where the swans

linger in the evening. The restaurant also serves a breakfast buffet and hosts the off-Broadway hit *Tony and Tina's Wedding.* ⊠ *Hyatt Regency Maui, Kāʻanapali Beach Resort, 200 Nohea Kai Dr., Lahaina* ☎ *808/ 661–1234* ▤ *AE, D, DC, MC, V.*

French

$$$–$$$$ ✕ **Chez Paul.** Since 1975 this tiny roadside restaurant between Lahaina and Māʻalaea in Olowalu has been serving excellent French cuisine to a packed house of repeat customers. Such dishes as fresh local fish poached in white wine with shallots, cream, and capers typify the classical menu. The restaurant's nondescript exterior belies the fine art, linen-draped tables, and wine cellar. Don't blink or you'll miss this small group of buildings huddled in the middle of nowhere. ⊠ *Honoapiʻilani Hwy., 4 mi south of Lahaina, Olowalu* ☎ *808/661–3843* ⌕ *Reservations essential* ▤ *AE, D, MC, V* ⊘ *No lunch.*

★ $$$–$$$$ ✕ **Gerard's.** Owner and celebrated chef Gerard Reversade started cooking at the age of 10, and at 12 he was baking croissants. He honors the French tradition with such exquisitely prepared dishes as rack of lamb in mint crust with thyme jus, and venison cutlets in a port sauce with confit of chestnuts, walnuts, fennel, and pearl onions. The menu changes once a year, but many favorites—such as the sinfully good crème brûlée—remain. A first-class wine list, a lovely room, and celebrity-spotting round out the experience. ⊠ *Plantation Inn, 174 Lahainaluna Rd., Lahaina* ☎ *808/661–8939* ▤ *AE, D, DC, MC, V* ⊘ *No lunch.*

Hawaiian/Pacific Rim

★ $$$–$$$$ ✕ **The Banyan Tree.** Chef Robert Ciborowski crafts the menu at the Ritz-Carlton's current main restaurant, a beautiful space overlooking the Kapalua coast. The coconut, sweet corn, and lemongrass soup garnished with Dungeness crab is legendary; ʻahi carpaccio with green papaya, and Asian-spiced rock shrimp with chive-mustard dipping sauce highlight the list of appetizers. Main courses include roasted mahimahi with chardonnay butter sauce and macadamia nut–crusted lamb chops. Save room for the vanilla-bean crème brûlée, served in half a baby pineapple. ⊠ *Ritz-Carlton, Kapalua, 1 Ritz-Carlton Dr., Kapalua* ☎ *808/ 669–6200* ▤ *AE, D, DC, MC, V.*

★ $$$–$$$$ ✕ **David Paul's Lahaina Grill.** Though the restaurant's namesake is only a consultant now, David Paul's is still a favorite of both locals and tourists alike. Beautifully designed, it's adjacent to the elegant Lahaina Inn in a historic, creaky building on Lahainaluna Road. The celebrated menu is revised seasonally, but you can count on finding the signature tequila shrimp and firecracker rice along with such scrumptious desserts as triple-berry pie. The restaurant has an extensive wine cellar, an in-house bakery, and a baby grand in the lounge. ⊠ *127 Lahainaluna Rd., Lahaina* ☎ *808/667–5117* ▤ *AE, DC, MC, V.*

$$–$$$ ✕ **Hula Grill.** Genial chef-restaurateur Peter Merriman's bustling, family-oriented restaurant is in a re-created 1930s Hawaiian beach house, and every table has an ocean view. You can also dine on the beach, toes in the sand, at the Barefoot Bar, where Hawaiian entertainment is presented every evening. South Pacific snapper is baked with tomato, chili, and cumin aioli and served with a black bean, Maui onion, and avocado

relish. Spareribs are steamed in banana leaves, then grilled with mango barbecue sauce over mesquitelike *kiawe* wood. ✉ *Whalers Village, 2435 Kāʻanapali Pkwy., Kāʻanapali* ☎ *808/667–6636* ▭ *AE, DC, MC, V.*

★ **$$–$$$** ✕ **Iʻo.** From its opening, this restaurant established itself as cutting edge in Lahaina, both for its theatrical interior designed by the artist Dado and for its contemporary Pacific Rim menu. A prized appetizer is the Silken Purse—steamed wontons stuffed with roasted peppers, mushrooms, macadamia nuts, and tofu. Favorite dinners include lemongrass-coconut fish and nori-wrapped rare tuna, served with green-papaya salad. Desserts to savor are the Hawaiian Vintage Chocolate Mousse and the chocolate pâté with Kula strawberries. ✉ *505 Front St., Lahaina* ☎ *808/661–8422* ▭ *AE, D, DC, MC, V* ☉ *No lunch.*

$$–$$$ ✕ **Plantation House Restaurant.** It's hard to decide which is better here, the food or the view. Hills, grassy volcanic ridges lined with pine trees, and fairways that appear to drop off into the ocean provide an idyllic setting. The specialty is fresh island fish prepared according to different "tastes"—Upcountry Maui, Asian-Pacific, Provence, and others. The breeze through the large shuttered windows can be cool, so you may want to bring a sweater or sit by the fireplace. ✉ *Plantation Course Clubhouse, 2000 Plantation Club Dr., past Kapalua* ☎ *808/669–6299* ▭ *AE, MC, V.*

★ **$$–$$$** ✕ **Roy's Kahana Bar & Grill.** Roy Yamaguchi's own sake brand "Y" and Hawaiian fusion specialties such as shrimp with sweet-and-spicy chili sauce keep regulars returning for more. Locals know to order the incomparable chocolate soufflé immediately after being seated. Next door, Roy's somewhat quieter restaurant Nicolina caters to a spice-loving crowd with grilled Southwestern chicken with chili hash, and smoked-and-peppered duck with gingered sweet potatoes. All three restaurants, two in Kahana and one in Kīhei, are in supermarket parking lots—it's not the view that excites, it's the food. ✉ *Kahana Gateway Shopping Center, 4405 Honoapiʻilani Hwy., Kahana* ☎ *808/669–6999 for Roy's, 808/669–5000 for Nicolina* ✉ *Safeway Shopping Center, 303 Piikea Ave., Kīhei* ☎ *808/891–1120* ▭ *AE, D, DC, MC, V.*

¢–$ ✕ **Honokowai Okazuya.** Don't expect to sit down at this miniature restaurant sandwiched between a dive shop and a salon—this is strictly a take-out joint. You can order local plate lunches, Chinese, vegetarian, or sandwiches. The spicy eggplant is delicious, and the fresh chow fun noodles are bought up quickly. ✉ *3600-D Lower Honoapiʻilani Hwy., Lahaina* ☎ *808/665–0512* ▭ *No credit cards* ☉ *Closed Sun. and daily 2:30–4:30.*

Italian

$$–$$$ ✕ **Longhi's.** A Lahaina establishment, Longhi's has been around since 1976, serving great Italian pasta as well as sandwiches, seafood, beef, and chicken dishes. The pasta is homemade, and the in-house bakery turns out breakfast pastries, desserts, and fresh bread. Even on a warm day, you won't need air-conditioning with two spacious, breezy, open-air levels to choose from. The black-and-white tile floors are a nice touch. Now there's a branch on the South Shore, at the Shops at Wailea. ✉ *888 Front St., Lahaina* ☎ *808/667–2288* ✉ *The Shops at Wailea, 3750 Wailea Alanui Dr., Wailea* ☎ *808/891–8883* ▭ *AE, D, DC, MC, V.*

Where to Eat on Maui

★ **$–$$** ✕ **Penne Pasta.** Heaping plates of flavorful pasta and low-key, unintrusive service make this restaurant the perfect alternative to an expensive night out in Lahaina. The osso buco (Thursday's special) is sumptuous, and the traditional salad niçoise overflows with generous portions of olives, peppers, garlic 'ahi, and potatoes. It's wise for two people to split a salad and entrée, as portions are large. ✉ *180 Dickenson St., Lahaina* ☎ *808/661–6633* ▭ *AE, D, DC, MC, V* ⊘ *No lunch weekends.*

Japanese

★ **$$–$$$$** ✕ **Kai.** Master sushi chef Norio Yamamoto sits at the helm of this intimate sushi bar, hidden behind the bar at the Ritz-Carlton, Kapalua. There's a small menu, but your best bet is to let Chef Norio design the meal. He might have yellowtail cheeks, fresh sea urchin, and raw lobster. He also makes lobster-head soup, a Japanese comfort food. ✉ *Ritz-Carlton, Kapalua, 1 Ritz-Carlton Dr., Kapalua* ☎ *808/669–6200* ▭ *AE, D, DC, MC, V.*

★ **$$–$$$** ✕ **Sansei.** One of the best-loved restaurants on the island, Sansei is Japanese with a Hawaiian twist. Inspired dishes include *panko*-crusted 'ahi (panko are Japanese bread crumbs), spicy fried calamari, mango-and-crab-salad roll, and a decadent foie gras *nigiri* (served on rice without seaweed) sushi. Desserts often use local fruit; the Kula-persimmon crème brûlée is stunning. The new location in Kīhei is a popular karaoke hangout, serving late-night sushi at half price. ✉ *Kapalua Shops, 115 Bay Dr., Kapalua* ☎ *808/666–6286* ✉ *Kīhei Town Center, 1881 S. Kīhei Rd., Kīhei* ☎ *808/879–0004* ▭ *AE, D, MC, V* ⊘ *No lunch.*

Seafood

★ **$$$–$$$$** ✕ **Pacific'O.** You can sit outdoors at umbrella-shaded tables near the water's edge, or find a spot in the breezy, marble-floor interior. The exciting menu features fresh 'ahi-and-ono tempura, in which the two kinds of fish are wrapped around *tobiko* (flying-fish roe), then wrapped in nori, and wok-fried. There's a great lamb dish, too—a whole rack of sweet New Zealand lamb, sesame-crusted and served with roasted macadamia sauce and Hawaiian chutney. Live jazz is played Thursday through Saturday from 9 to midnight. ✉ *505 Front St., Lahaina* ☎ *808/667–4341* ▭ *AE, D, DC, MC, V.*

$–$$ ✕ **Kimo's.** On a warm Lahaina day, it's a treat to relax at an umbrella-shaded table on the lānai, sip a mai tai, and watch sailboats glide into and out of the harbor. Outstanding seafood is just one of the options here; also good are Hawaiian-style chicken and pork dishes, and burgers. Try the signature dessert, Hula Pie: vanilla–macadamia nut ice cream topped with chocolate fudge and whipped cream in an Oreo-cookie crust. ✉ *845 Front St., Lahaina* ☎ *808/661–4811* ▭ *AE, DC, MC, V.*

Central Maui

American

¢–$ ✕ **Iao Cafe.** This casual café serves inventive and healthful weekday lunches. The seared 'ahi sandwich with wasabi mayonnaise is always on the menu, and every Friday brings crab cakes with sweet chili aioli. There are daily specials, too, such as curried chicken salad and blackened mahimahi. ⊠ *2051 Main St., Wailuku* ☎ *808/244–6816* ▤ *No credit cards* ⊗ *Closed weekends.*

¢ ✕**Maui Bake Shop.** Wonderful breads baked in brick ovens from 1935, hearty lunch fare, and irresistible desserts make this a popular spot in Central Maui. Baker José Krall was trained in France, and his wife, Claire, is a Maui native whose friendly face you'll often see when you walk in. Standouts include the focaccia and homemade soups. ⊠ *2092 Vineyard St., Wailuku* ☎ *808/242–0064* ▤ *AE, D, MC, V* ⊗ *Closed Sun. No dinner.*

Chinese

$ ✕**Dragon Dragon.** Whether you're a party of 10 or 2, this is the place to share seafood-tofu soup or spareribs with garlic sauce. Tasteful, simple decor complements the solid menu. Fresh Dungeness crab is offered with four sauce selections. The restaurant shares parking with the Maui Megaplex and makes a great pre- or postmovie stop. ⊠ *In Maui Mall, 70 E. Kaahumanu Ave., Kahului* ☎ *808/893–1628* ▤ *AE, D, MC, V.*

Hawaiian

¢–$ ✕**A.K.'s Café.** Nearly hidden between auto-body shops and karaoke bars is this wonderful, bright cafe. Affordable, tasty entrées such as grilled tenderloin with wild mushrooms or garlic-crusted ono with ginger relish come with a choice of two sides. The flavorful dishes are healthy, too—Chef Elaine Rothermal previously instructed island nutritionists on how to prepare health-conscious versions of local favorites. Try the Hawaiian french-fried sweet potatoes, the steamed *ulu* (breadfruit), or the poi. ⊠ *1237 Lower Main, Wailuku* ☎ *808/244–8774* ▤ *D, MC, V* ⊗ *Closed Sun.*

Italian

$–$$ ✕**Marco's Grill & Deli.** This convenient eatery outside Kahului Airport (look for the green awning) serves reliable Italian food that's slightly overpriced. Homemade pastas appear on the extensive menu, along with an unforgettably good Reuben sandwich and the best tiramisu on the island. The local business crowd fills the place for breakfast, lunch, and dinner. The Kīhei branch is in a gorgeous new building with a grand piano. ⊠ *444 Hāna Hwy., Kahului* ☎ *808/877–4446* ⊠ *1445 S. Kīhei Rd., Kīhei* ☎ *808/874–4041* ▤ *AE, D, DC, MC, V.*

Japanese

$ ✕**Restaurant Matsu.** Sit at a common table and eat authentic Japanese fare along with the locals—*katsu* (cutlet) dishes and curries served with white rice, or bowls of saimin or *udon* noodles with tempura. ⊠ *161 Ala Maha St., Kahului* ☎ *808/871–0822* ▤ *No credit cards.*

Latin

★ $$–$$$ ✕**Mañana Garage.** Parked in downtown Kahului is this restaurant, which makes the most of its automobile theme—it's probably the only place you'll have your wine served out of buckets with crankshaft stems. Chef Tom Lelli's cuisine ranges from Cuban to Brazilian to Mexican, with a few Hawaiian touches thrown in for good measure. The best dishes include ceviche marinated in coconut milk and lime, 'ahi sashimi, and quesadillas made with homemade corn tortillas. For dessert, the pound-cake ice-cream sandwich with sweet potato and praline is a must.

There's lively music on the weekends. ⊠ *33 Lono Ave., Kahului* ☎ *808/873–0220* ⊟ *AE, D, MC, V* ⊙ *No lunch weekends.*

Thai

$–$$ ✕ **Saeng's Thai Cuisine.** Choosing a dish from the six-page menu here requires determination, but the food is worth the effort, and most dishes can be tailored to your taste buds: hot, medium, or mild. Begin with spring rolls and a dipping sauce, move on to such entrées as Evil Prince Chicken (cooked in coconut sauce with Thai herbs), or red-curry shrimp, and finish up with tea and tapioca pudding. Asian artifacts, flowers, and a waterfall decorate the dining room, and tables on a veranda satisfy lovers of the outdoors. ⊠ *2119 Vineyard St., Wailuku* ☎ *808/244–1567* ⊟ *AE, MC, V.*

Vietnamese

★ $$–$$$ ✕ **A Saigon Café.** The only storefront sign announcing this small, delightful hideaway is one reading OPEN. Once you find it, treat yourself to *banh hoi chao tom,* more commonly known as "shrimp pops burritos" (ground marinated shrimp, steamed and grilled on a stick of sugarcane). Vegetarian fare is also well represented here—try the green-papaya salad. Fresh island fish is always available. The white interior serves as a backdrop for Vietnamese carvings in this otherwise unadorned space. Background music includes one-hit wonders from the early '70s. ⊠ *1792 Main St., Wailuku* ☎ *808/243–9560* ⊟ *D, MC, V.*

★ ¢   ✕ **Ba Le.** Tucked into the mall's food court is the best, cheapest fast food on the island. The famous soups, or *pho,* come laden with seafood or rare beef, fresh basil, bean sprouts, and lime. Tasty sandwiches are served on crisp French rolls—lemongrass chicken is a favorite. The word is out, so the place gets busy at lunchtime, though the wait is never long. ⊠ *Kau Kau Corner food court, Maui Marketplace, 270 Dairy Rd., Kahului* ☎ *808/877–2400* ⊟ *AE, D, DC, MC, V.*

The South Shore

American

$$–$$$ ✕ **Joe's Bar & Grill.** With friendly service, a great view of Lāna'i, and such dishes as New York strip steak with caramelized onions, wild mushrooms, and Gorgonzola cheese crumble, there are lots of reasons to stop in at this spacious, breezy spot. Owners Joe and Bev Gannon, who run the immensely popular Hāli'imaile General Store, have brought their flair for food home to roost in this comfortable treetop-level restaurant at the Wailea Tennis Club, where you can dine while watching court action from a balcony seat. ⊠ *131 Wailea Ike Pl., Wailea* ☎ *808/875–7767* ⊟ *AE, MC, V.*

★ $–$$ ✕ **Maui Onion.** Forget the overrated Cheeseburger in Paradise in Lahaina—Maui Onion has the best burgers on the island, hands down, and phenomenal onion rings as well. They coat the onions in pancake batter, then dip them in panko, then fry them 'til they're golden brown. ⊠ *Renaissance Wailea, 3550 Wailea Alanui Dr., Wailea* ☎ *808/879–4900* ⊟ *AE, D, DC, MC, V.*

Hawaiian/Pacific Rim

$$$–$$$$ ✕ **Humuhumunukunukuāpua'a.** Wrestle with the restaurant's formidable name—the name of the state fish—or simply watch the fish swim by in the 2,100-gallon tank at the bar. The thatch-roofed building actually floats on a lagoon, creating an atmosphere which tends to outshine the food. Sweet-corn and lobster soup with poached rock shrimp and basil puree is a standout, as is the sesame-crusted mahimahi with coconut rice, baby bok choy, and black bean miso sauce. You can fetch your own spiny lobster (which is best simply grilled) from a cage below the water's surface. You may have to fetch your own drinks as well; the service is notoriously slow. ⊠ *Grand Wailea Resort, 3850 Wailea Alanui Dr., Wailea* ☎ *808/875–1234* ▭ *AE, D, DC, MC, V.*

★ **$$$–$$$$** ✕ **Spago.** Celebrity chef and owner Wolfgang Puck wisely brought his fame to this gorgeous locale. Giant sea-anemone prints, modern-art-inspired lamps, and views of the shoreline give diners something to look at while waiting. The solid menu delivers with dishes like seared scallops with asparagus and *pohole* (fiddlehead fern) shoots, and "chinois" lamb chops with Hunan eggplant. The beef dish, with braised celery, Armagnac, and horseradish potatoes, may be the island's priciest—but devotees swear it's worth every cent. ⊠ *Four Seasons Resort, 3900 Wailea Alanui Dr., Wailea* ☎ *808/879–2999* ▭ *AE, D, DC, MC, V* ⊗ *No lunch.*

$$–$$$ ✕ **Hula Moons.** This delightful oceanside spot is full of memorabilia chronicling the life of Don Blanding, an artist and poet who became Hawai'i's unofficial ambassador of aloha in the 1930s. The vegetarian appetizer of fresh pohole ferns, Hāna tomatoes, and Kula onions is fabulous. Try the bamboo-steamed whole *moi,* a fish once reserved for Hawaiian royalty, or the tangy braised short ribs. Sunday brunch is one of the most lavish on the island, and the wine list is extensive. You can dine inside, poolside, or on the terrace. ⊠ *Marriott Wailea Resort, 3700 Wailea Alanui Dr., Wailea* ☎ *808/879–1922* ▭ *AE, D, DC, MC, V.*

Irish

$–$$ ✕ **Mulligan's on the Blue.** If you're hankering for bangers and mash or shepherd's pie, stop in here. You'll be greeted by a nearly all-Irish staff, and before you know it, you'll be sipping a heady pint of Guinness. Breakfast is a good value for the area, and the view is one of the best. Live music makes evenings fun. ⊠ *100 Kaukahi St., Wailea* ☎ *808/874–1131* ▭ *AE, D, DC, MC, V.*

Italian

$$$–$$$$
Fodor's Choice
★ ✕ **Capische.** Hidden up at the quiet Blue Diamond Resort, this restaurant is one local patrons would like kept secret. A circular stone atrium gives way to a small piano lounge, where you'll find the best sunset view on the island. You can count on the freshness of the ingredients in superb dishes like the quail saltimbocca, and the saffron *vongole*—a colorful affair of squid-ink pasta and spicy saffron broth. Intimate and well conceived, Capische, with its seductive flavors and ambience, makes for a romantic night out. ⊠ *Blue Diamond Resort, 555 Kaukahi St., Wailea* ☎ *808/879–2224* ▭ *AE, D, DC, MC, V* ⊗ *No lunch.*

$$$–$$$$ ✕ **Sarento's on the Beach.** Chef George Gomes, formerly of A Pacific Café, heads the kitchen at South Maui's newest Italian restaurant. The beachfront setting is irresistible, and the menu features both traditional Italian dishes—like penne Calabrese and seafood *fra diavolo*—as well as inventions such as swordfish saltimbocca, a strangely successful entrée with a prosciutto, Bel Paese, radicchio, and porcini-mushroom sauce. The wine list includes some affordable finds. ⊠ *2980 S. Kīhei Rd., Kīhei* ☎ *808/875–7555* ⊟ *AE, D, DC, MC, V* ⊘ *No lunch.*

$–$$ ✕ **Caffe Ciao.** Chef Dino Bugica brings Italy to the Fairmont Kea Lani. Authentic, fresh gnocchi and lobster risotto taste especially delicious in the open-air café, which overlooks the swimming pool. For casual European fare, try a poached-tuna salad, grilled panini, or pizza from the wood-burning oven. Additionally, locals have long known Caffe Ciao's sister deli as the sole source for discerning palates: delectable pastries, tapenades, mustards, and even $50 bottles of truffle oil. ⊠ *Fairmont Kea Lani, 4100 Wailea Alanui Dr., Wailea* ☎ *808/875–4100* ⊟ *AE, D, DC, MC, V.*

Japanese

$$$–$$$$ ✕ **Hakone.** Well-regarded Japanese food is served at this restaurant in the Maui Prince hotel. A full six-course *kaiseki* meal—with small dishes of raw, cooked, hot, cold, sweet, and savory items—is $58, a good value for the quality of food presented. Impeccably fresh sushi, traditional cooked dishes, and an impressive sake list round out the menu. The Sunday-night sushi buffet is popular. ⊠ *Maui Prince, 5400 Mākena Alanui Rd., Mākena* ☎ *808/874–1111* ⊟ *AE, MC, V* ⊘ *No lunch.*

★ ¢–$$ ✕ **Hirohachi.** A stone's throw from the flashier Sansei, Hirohachi has been serving authentic Japanese fare for years. Owner Hiro has discerning taste—he buys only the best from local fishermen and imports many ingredients from Japan. Order with confidence—even if you can't read the Japanese specials posted on the wall—everything on the menu is high quality. ⊠ *1881 S. Kīhei Rd., Kīhei* ☎ *808/875–7474* ⊟ *AE, MC, V* ⊘ *Closed Mon.*

Seafood

★ $$$–$$$$ ✕ **Nick's Fishmarket Maui.** This romantic spot serves fresh seafood in the simplest preparations: mahimahi with Kula-corn relish, 'ahi pepper fillet, and *opakapaka* with rock shrimp in a lemon-butter-caper sauce. Everyone seems to love the Greek Maui Wowie salad made with local onions, tomatoes, avocado, feta cheese, and bay shrimp. Service is somewhat formal, but it befits the beautiful food presentations and extensive wine list. ⊠ *Fairmont Kea Lani, 4100 Wailea Alanui Dr., Wailea* ☎ *808/879–7224* ⊟ *AE, D, DC, MC, V* ⊘ *No lunch.*

$$–$$$ ✕ **Māʻalaea Waterfront Restaurant.** At this harborside establishment, fresh fish is prepared in a host of sumptuous ways: baked in buttered parchment paper; imprisoned in ribbons of angel-hair potato; or topped with tomato salsa, smoked chili pepper, and avocado. The varied menu also lists an outstanding rack of lamb and veal scallopini. Tourists come early to dine at sunset on the outdoor patio. Enter Māʻalaea at the Maui Ocean Center and then follow the blue WATERFRONT RESTAURANT signs to the third condominium. ⊠ *50 Hauʻoli St., Māʻalaea* ☎ *808/244–9028* ⊟ *AE, D, DC, MC, V* ⊘ *No lunch.*

$–$$ ✕ **Blue Marlin Harborfront Grill & Bar.** This is a casual, less expensive alternative to the Māʻlaea Waterfront Restaurant. It's as much a bar as it is a grill, but the kitchen nonetheless sends out well-prepared, substantial servings of fresh fish, burgers, and salads. The sidewalk tables have a lovely view of the harbor. ⊠ *Māʻalaea Harbor Village, corner of Old Māʻalaea Rd. and Honoapiʻilani Hwy., next to the Maui Ocean Center; Māʻalaea* ☎ *808/244–8844* ▭ *AE, MC, V.*

Thai

★ **$–$$** ✕ **Thai Cuisine.** Fragrant tea and coconut-ginger chicken soup begin a satisfying meal at this excellent Thai restaurant. The care that goes into the decor here (reflected in the glittering Buddhist shrines, fancy napkin folds, and matching blue china) also applies to the cuisine. The lean and moist meat of the red-curry duck rivals similar dishes at resort restaurants, and the fried bananas with ice cream are wonderful. ⊠ *In Kukui Mall, 1819 S. Kīhei Rd., Kīhei* ☎ *808/875–0839* ▭ *AE, D, DC, MC, V.*

East Maui

American

¢–$ ✕ **Café Oʻlei.** Your best bet for a casual lunch in Makawao, this restaurant paved the way for three other popular locations island-wide. Especially recommended are the quinoa salad and the snow-crab-and-avocado sandwich on focaccia. Seating is outdoors only. ⊠ *Paniolo Courtyard, 3673 Baldwin Ave., Makawao* ☎ *808/573–9065* ▭ *No credit cards* ☾ *Closed Sun. No dinner.*

★ ¢–$ ✕ **Pauwela Café.** Ultracasual and ultrafriendly, this spot just off Hāna Highway is worth the detour. Order a kālua-pork sandwich and a piece of coffee cake and pass the afternoon. The large breakfast burritos and homemade soups are also good. ⊠ *375 W. Kuiaha Rd., off Hāna Hwy, past Haʻikū Rd., Haʻikū* ☎ *808/575–9242* ▭ *No credit cards* ☾ *No dinner.*

Eclectic

$–$$ ✕ **Jacque's.** Jacque, an amiable French chef, won the hearts of the windsurfing crowd when he opened this hip, ramshackle bar and restaurant. French-Caribbean dishes like Jacque's Crispy Little Poulet reveal the owner's expertise. The outdoor seating can be a little chilly at times; coveted spots at the sushi bar inside are snatched up quickly. ⊠ *120 Hāna Hwy., Pāʻia* ☎ *808/579–8844* ▭ *AE, D, MC, V.*

¢–$ ✕ **Cafe Des Amis.** Papier-mâché wrestlers pop out from the walls at this small creperie. French crepes with Gruyère and Indian wraps with lentil curry are among the choices, all served with wild greens and sour cream or chutney on the side. For dessert, of course, are more crepes—filled with chocolate, Nutella, cane sugar, or banana. ⊠ *42 Baldwin Ave., Pāʻia* ☎ *808/579–6373* ▭ *AE, D, MC, V.*

Hawaiian/Pacific Rim

★ **$$–$$$** ✕ **Hāliʻimaile General Store.** What do you do with a lofty wooden building that was a tiny town's camp store in the 1920s and is surrounded by sugarcane and pineapple fields? If you're Bev and Joe Gannon, you invent a legendary restaurant. The Szechuan barbecued salmon and rack of lamb Hunan-style are classics, as is the sashimi napoleon appetizer: a tower of crispy wontons layered with ʻahi and salmon. Pastry chef Teresa Gannon makes an unbelievable pineapple upside-down cake. The restaurant even has its own cookbook. ⊠ *900 Hāliʻimaile Rd., left at exit off Rte. 37, 5 mi from Hāna Hwy., Hāliʻimaile* ☎ *808/572–2666* ⊟ *MC, V.*

Italian

$$–$$$ ✗ **Casanova Italian Restaurant & Deli.** The pizzas, baked in a brick wood-burning oven imported from Italy, are the best on the island. This is a good Italian dinner house in an out-of-the-way location. Casanova is also known for its daytime deli and, at night, for its extra-large dance floor and entertainment by well-known island and mainland musicians. ⊠ *1188 Makawao Ave., Makawao* ☎ *808/572–0220* ⊟ *D, DC, MC, V.*

Mexican

$–$$ ✗ **Milagro's.** Delicious fish tacos are found at this corner hangout, along with a selection of fine tequilas. Latin fusion recipes ignite fresh fish and vegetables. The people-watching can be fun here, under the awning shade at the junction of Baldwin Avenue and Hāna Highway. Lunch and happy hour (3–5) are the best values; the prices jump at dinnertime. ⊠ *3 Baldwin Ave., Pāʻia* ☎ *808/579–8755* ⊟ *AE, D, DC, MC, V.*

$–$$ ✗ **Polli's.** This Mexican restaurant in the paniolo town of Makawao not only offers standards such as enchiladas, chimichangas, and fajitas but will also prepare any item on the menu with seasoned tofu or vegetarian taco mix—and the meatless dishes are just as good. A special treat are the *bunuelos*—light pastries topped with cinnamon, maple syrup, and ice cream. The intimate interior is plastered with colorful sombreros and other cantina knickknacks. ⊠ *1202 Makawao Ave., Makawao* ☎ *808/572–7808* ⊟ *AE, D, DC, MC, V.*

★ ¢ ✗ **Maui's Best Tamales.** The owner of this tiny tamale haven can sometimes be seen surrounded by towers of fresh Kula corn. From these she makes indisputably "Maui's best tamales." Her daily specials—chipotle pork or chicken mole—are divine. The small shopping center offers scant seating, so take your tamales to go, and find somewhere nearby to admire the awesome view. ⊠ *In Pukalani Sq., 81 Makawao Ave., Pukalani* ☎ *808/573–2998* ⊟ *No credit cards* ☉ *Closed after 6 PM.*

Seafood

$$$–$$$$ ✗ **Mama's Fish House.** A stone- and shell-engraved path leads you up to
Fodor'sChoice what would be, in an ideal world, a good friend's house. The Hawaiian nautical theme inside is hospitable and fun, but the real treat here is the fish—baked in a creamy caper sauce or steamed in traditional lūʻau leaves. The menu even lists which boat reeled in your fish. The chicken, steak, and kālua pig dishes are worth trying, too, and the beachside restaurant serves the best mai tais on the island, bar none. About 1½ mi east of Paʻia on Hāna Highway, Mama's is marked by a tiny fishing boat perched above the entrance. ⊠ *799 Poho Pl., Kūʻau* ☎ *808/579–8488* ⌂ *Reservations essential* ⊟ *AE, D, DC, MC, V.*

Steak

$$–$$$ ✗ **Makawao Steak House.** A restored 1927 house on the slopes of Haleakalā is the setting for this paniolo restaurant, which serves consistently good prime rib, rack of lamb, and fresh fish. Three fireplaces, friendly service, and an intimate lounge create a cozy, welcoming atmosphere. ⊠ *3612 Baldwin Ave., Makawao* ☎ *808/572–8711* 🚬 *D, DC, MC, V* ⊗ *No lunch.*

WHERE TO STAY

Updated by
Shannon
Wianecki

Maui has the highest percentage of upscale hotel rooms and the highest average accommodation cost of any Hawaiian island. The quality level—and the opulence quotient—is way up there, making this one of the best places in the world to indulge in a first-class resort vacation. But Maui also has the state's highest concentration of condominium units; many are oceanfront and offer the amenities of a hotel suite without the cost.

The county officially sanctions relatively few B&Bs, not wanting to siphon business from the hotels. However, many alternative accommodations offer seclusion and a countryside experience, especially Upcountry and in Hāna. Most of these are better described as guest cottages—or guesthouses—that skip the breakfast part of B&B and offer provisions and privacy instead. Rates for most B&Bs range from $40 to as much as $150 per night.

West Maui

$$$$ 🏨 **Hyatt Regency Maui.** This resort underwent a $19 million room renovation in 2002, which has resulted in a softer color scheme and colonial-style furniture, rounded out by Hawaiian-quilt wall hangings. There is also a museum-quality art collection; a seemingly endless swimming pool, with swim-through grottoes and a 130-foot water slide; fantasy landscaping (the builders used 10,000 tons of rock to fabricate the environment) with splashing waterfalls; and the Spa Moana, an oceanfront, full-service facility. ⊠ *Kā'anapali Beach Resort, 200 Nohea Kai Dr., Lahaina 96761* ☎ *808/661–1234 or 800/233–1234* 🖶 *808/667–4499* ⊕ *www.mauihyatt.com* ⬫ *815 rooms ♨ 4 restaurants, in-room safes, cable TV with movies and video games, 2 18-hole golf courses, 6 tennis courts, pool, health club, spa, beach, 6 bars, library, children's programs (ages 3–12), Internet, no-smoking floors* 🚬 *AE, D, DC, MC, V.*

$$$$ 🏨 **Kā'anapali Ali'i.** Yes, this is a condominium, but you'd never know it: the four 11-story buildings are put together so well you still have the feeling of seclusion. Instead of tiny rooms you can choose between one- and two-bedroom apartments. Each has lovely amenities: a chaise in an alcove, a bidet, a sunken living room, a whirlpool, oak kitchen cabinets, and a separate dining room. The Kā'anapali Ali'i is maintained like a hotel, with daily maid service, an activities desk, and a 24-hour front desk. ⊠ *50 Nohea Kai Dr., Lahaina 96761* ☎ *808/667–1400 or 800/642–6284* 🖶 *808/661–1025* ⊕ *www.classicresorts.com* ⬫ *264 units ♨ Kitchens, in-room safes, 18-hole golf course, 6 tennis courts, 2 pools, sauna, beach, laundry facilities* 🚬 *AE, D, DC, MC, V.*

$$$$ 🏨 **Kapalua Bay Hotel.** Fronting what was once voted America's best beach, at lovely Kapalua Bay, this hotel has a real Maui feel to it. The exterior is understated white and natural wood, and the open lobby, filled with

Where to Stay on Maui

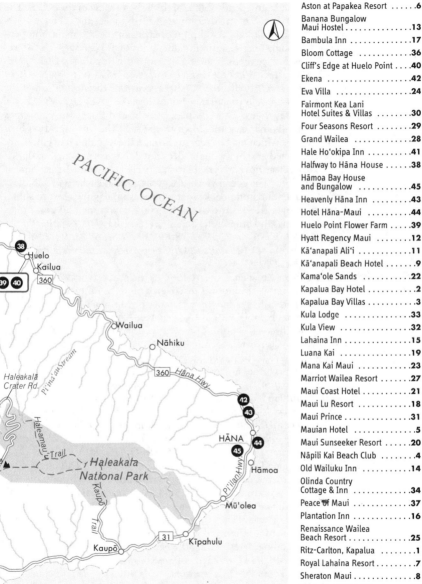

PACIFIC OCEAN

flowering vanda and dendrobium orchids, has a view of the ocean. The plantation-style rooms are decorated in earth tones, and all have views of Lānaʻi and Molokaʻi. A shopping plaza outside the main hotel entrance has some fine restaurants and boutiques. Guests receive preferred rates and tee times at three golf courses in Kapalua. ⊠ *1 Bay Dr., Kapalua 96761* ☎ *808/669–5656 or 888/488–3535* 🖷 *808/669–4694* ⊕ *www.starwood.com/hawaii* 🖘 *209 rooms* ♨ *3 restaurants, cable TV, golf privileges, 6 tennis courts, 2 pools, beach* ⊟ *AE, DC, MC, V.*

$$$$ 🏨 **Kapalua Bay Villas.** This complex of two- and three-story buildings is built on hills that cascade down to the sea. The one- and two-bedroom condos, which may be rented through the Kapalua Bay Hotel, are privately owned and individually decorated. Each is assigned to one of five luxury categories and is regularly inspected to ensure that standards are maintained. The ocean views are great, with the island of Molokaʻi in the distance and humpback whales (in season) passing close to shore. Renters enjoy a free shuttle to the Kapalua Bay Hotel and guest rates for golf, tennis, and other hotel amenities. ⊠ *1 Bay Dr., Kapalua 96761* ☎ *808/669–5656 or 800/367–8000* 🖷 *808/669–4694* ⊕ *www. kapaluabay.com* 🖘 *125 units* ♨ *Golf privileges, laundry facilities, concierge* ⊟ *AE, D, DC, MC, V.*

$$$$ 🏨 **Ritz-Carlton, Kapalua.** Construction of the property was halted when
Fodor'sChoice a Hawaiian burial ground was discovered, and the hotel was moved up
★ the hill, where it has commanding views of Molokaʻi. Rooms are spacious and comfortable with oversize marble bathrooms and lānai overlooking the three-level pool. There's a wonderful democracy of service here: everyone is treated equally like a VIP. A full-time cultural adviser, Clifford Naeʻole, educates employees and guests alike in Hawaiian tradition. Golf privileges are available at three 18-hole courses in Kapalua. ⊠ *1 Ritz-Carlton Dr., Kapalua 96761* ☎ *808/669–6200 or 800/262–8440* 🖷 *808/665–0026* ⊕ *www.ritzcarlton.com* 🖘 *548 rooms* ♨ *3 restaurants, cable TV with movies, in-room safes, 18-hole golf course, golf privileges, 10 tennis courts, pool, health club, hair salon, massage, beach, lobby lounge, shops, children's programs (ages 5–12), laundry service, Internet, business services* ⊟ *AE, D, DC, MC, V.*

$$$$ 🏨 **Royal Lahaina Resort.** What distinguishes the Royal Lahaina are the two-story cottages, each divided into four units. The bedrooms open to the trade winds on two sides. The upstairs units each have a private lānai, and downstairs units share one—all lānai have stunning ocean or golf-course views. The walkway to the courtyard wedding gazebo is lined with stepping-stones engraved with the names of past brides and grooms and their wedding dates. ⊠ *2780 Kekaʻa Dr., Lahaina 96761* ☎ *808/ 661–3611 or 800/447–6925* 🖷 *808/661–3538* ⊕ *www.hawaiihotels. com* 🖘 *592 rooms* ♨ *3 restaurants, cable TV, 18-hole golf course, 11 tennis courts, 3 pools, beach* ⊟ *AE, D, DC, MC, V.*

$$$$ 🏨 **Sheraton Maui.** The six buildings that make up this understated resort are set among dense gardens on Kāʻanapali's best stretch of beach. Rooms come with ocean, mountain, or garden views. The swimming pool looks like a natural lagoon, with rock waterways and wooden bridges. Best of all, the hotel sits next to the 80-foot-high "Black Rock," from which divers leap in a nightly torch-lighting ritual. ⊠ *2605 Kāʻana-*

pali Pkwy., Lahaina 97671 ☎ *808/661–0031 or 888/488–3535* 🖷 *808/661–0458* ⊕ *www.starwood.com/hawaii* ➳ *510 rooms* ♨ *2 restaurants, in-room safes, refrigerators, 3 tennis courts, pool, health club, hair salon, hot tub, spa, beach, lobby lounge, children's programs (ages 5–12), laundry facilities, business services* ▤ *AE, D, DC, MC, V.*

$$$$ ▥ **The Westin Maui Resort & Spa.** The cascading waterfall in the lobby of this hotel gives way to an "aquatic playground" with five heated swimming pools, abundant waterfalls (15 at last count), lagoons, and a premier beach. The water features combined with an indoor/outdoor yoga studio, spa and fitness center, and privileges at two 18-hole golf courses make this an active resort. Relaxation is by no means forgotten. Elegant dark wood furnishings in the rooms accentuate the crisp linens of "Heavenly Beds." The brand-new, 13,000-square-foot Heavenly Spa features 11 treatment rooms and a yoga studio. ✉ *2365 Kā'anapali Pkwy., Lahaina 96761* ☎ *808/667–2525 or 888/488–3535* 🖷 *808/661–5831* ⊕ *www.starwood.com/hawaii* ➳ *761 rooms* ♨ *3 restaurants, cable TV with movies, golf privileges, 5 pools, spa, health club, hair salon, 3 hot tubs, beach, lobby lounge, babysitting, children's programs (ages 12 and under), Internet, meeting rooms* ▤ *AE, D, DC, MC, V.*

$$$–$$$$ ▥ **Aston at Papakea Resort.** Although this oceanfront condominium has no beach, there are several very close by. And with classes on swimming, snorkeling, pineapple cutting, and more, you'll have plenty to keep you busy. Papakea has built-in privacy because its units are spread out among 11 low-rise buildings on some 13 acres of land; bamboo-lined walkways between buildings and fish-stocked ponds add to the serenity. Note that there's a two-night minimum stay. ✉ *3543 Honoapi'ilani Hwy., Lahaina 96761* ☎ *808/669–4848 or 800/922–7866* 🖷 *808/922–8785* ⊕ *www.aston-hotels.com* ➳ *36 studios, 224 1-bedroom units, 104 2-bedroom units* ♨ *Kitchens, putting green, 4 tennis courts, 2 pools, hot tub, sauna, children's programs (ages 5–12), laundry facilities* ▤ *AE, MC, V.*

★ $$$ ▥ **Kā'anapali Beach Hotel.** This attractive, old-fashioned hotel is full of aloha. Locals say that it's the only resort on the island where visitors can get a true Hawaiian experience. The vintage-style Mixed Plate restaurant, known locally for its native cuisine program, has displays honoring the many cultural traditions represented by the staff: the employees themselves contributed the artifacts. The spacious rooms are simply decorated in wicker and rattan and face the beach beyond the courtyard. There are complimentary classes in authentic hula dancing, lei-making, and 'ukulele playing. ✉ *2525 Kā'anapali Pkwy., Lahaina 96761* ☎ *808/661–0011 or 800/262–8450* 🖷 *808/667–5978* ⊕ *www.kaanapalibeachhotel.com* ➳ *430 rooms* ♨ *3 restaurants, cable TV with movies, in-room safes, golf privileges, pool, beach, lobby lounge* ▤ *AE, D, DC, MC, V.*

$$$ ▥ **Mauian Hotel.** If you're looking for a quiet place to stay, this sedate hotel way out in Nāpili may be for you. The rooms have neither televisions nor telephones—such noisy devices are relegated to the 'Ohana Room, where a Continental breakfast is served daily. The simple two-story buildings date from 1959, but have been renovated with bright, modern furnishings, including conveniently equipped kitchens. Best of all, the 2-acre property opens out onto lovely Nāpīli Bay. ✉ *5441 Lower Honoapiʻilani Hwy., Napīli 96761* 🕾 *808/669–6205 or 800/367–5034* 🖷 *808/669–0129* 🌐 *www.mauian.com* 🖙 *44 rooms* ⚲ *Pool, hair salon, shuffleboard, laundry facilities; no room phones, no room TVs* ▭ *AE, D, MC, V* ❍ *CP.*

$$$ 🏨 **Nāpili Kai Beach Club.** Located on 10 beautiful beachfront acres—the beach here is one of the best on the West Side for swimming and snorkeling—the Nāpili Kai draws a loyal following. Hawaiian-style rooms are done in sea-foam green, mauve, and rattan; shoji doors open onto your lānai, with the beach and ocean right outside. The rooms closest to the beach have no air-conditioning, but ceiling fans usually suffice. This is a family-friendly place, with children's programs and free classes in hula and lei-making. Packages that include a car, breakfast, and other extras are available if you stay five nights or longer. ✉ *5900 Lower Honoapiʻilani Hwy., Nāpili Bay 96761* 🕾 *808/669–6271 or 800/367–5030* 🖷 *808/669–5740* 🌐 *www.napilikai.com* 🖙 *162 rooms* ⚲ *Fans, kitchenettes, cable TV, 2 putting greens, 4 pools, exercise equipment, hot tub, beach, shuffleboard, children's programs (ages 6–12), dry cleaning, concierge, Internet; no a/c in some rooms* ▭ *AE, MC, V.*

★ $$–$$$$ 🏨 **Plantation Inn.** Charm and luxury set apart this inn, which is on a quiet street in the heart of Lahaina. Filled with Victorian and Asian furnishings, it's reminiscent of a southern plantation home. Secluded lānai draped with hanging plants face a central courtyard, pool, and a garden pavilion perfect for morning coffee. Each guest room or suite is decorated differently, with hardwood floors, French doors, antiques, four-poster beds, and ceiling fans. Suites have kitchenettes and whirlpool baths. A generous breakfast is included in the room rate, and one of Hawaiʻi's best French restaurants, Gerard's, is on-site. ✉ *174 Lahainaluna Rd., Lahaina 96761* 🕾 *808/667–9225 or 800/433–6815* 🖷 *808/667–9293* 🌐 *www.theplantationinn.com* 🖙 *18 rooms* ⚲ *Restaurant, fans, refrigerators, cable TV, pool, hot tub, free parking, Internet,* ❍ *BP* ▭ *AE, MC, V.*

★ $$–$$$ 🏨 **Lahaina Inn.** This antique jewel right in the heart of town is classic Lahaina—a two-story wooden building that will transport you back to the turn of the 20th century. The nine small rooms and three suites shine with authentic period restoration and furnishings, including quilted bedcovers, antique lamps, and Oriental carpets. You can while away the hours in a wicker chair on your balcony. An excellent Continental breakfast is served in the parlor. ✉ *127 Lahainaluna Rd., Lahaina 96761* 🕾 *808/661–0577 or 800/669–3444* 🖷 *808/667–9480* 🌐 *www. lahainainn.com* 🖙 *9 rooms, 3 suites* ⚲ *No room TVs, no smoking* ▭ *AE, D, MC, V* ❍ *CP.*

The South Shore

★ $$$$ 🏨 **Fairmont Kea Lani Hotel Suites & Villas.** This dramatic resort with a gleaming white exterior is a replica of Las Hadas in Manzanilla, Mexico, and it's the best value in upscale Wailea. Spacious one-bedroom suites in the main hotel have dining lānai and marble bathrooms. Two- and three-bedroom villas on the beach offer more seclusion; each has a private plunge pool and a full kitchen. Service here is as good as what you'd find at hotels with double the price tag, and such special touches as guava juice and cool towels at check-in set this hotel apart. Another plus: one of Maui's best restaurants, Nick's Fishmarket, is on the premises. ⊠ *4100 Wailea Alanui Dr., Wailea 96753* ☎ *808/875–4100 or 800/882–4100* 🖶 *808/875–1200* ⊕ *www.kealani.com* 🖙 *413 suites, 37 villas* ⚂ *3 restaurants, snack bar, microwaves, refrigerators, in-room VCRs, golf privileges, 3 pools, health club, hair salon, 2 hot tubs, beach, lobby lounge, shops, children's programs (ages 5–12), Internet* ☰ *AE, D, DC, MC, V.*

★ **$$$$** ▦ **Four Seasons Resort.** Thoughtful luxuries—like Evian spritzers poolside and room-service staff who toast your bread in-room—earned this Maui favorite its impeccable reputation. The property itself has tremendous appeal, with spectacular floral arrangements, courtyards, waterfalls, fountains, and private cabanas adjoining Wailea Beach. Most rooms have an ocean view and you'll find terry robes and whole-bean coffee grinders in each. Choose between three good restaurants, including Wolfgang Puck's Spago. A recently renovated spa promises further pampering. Access to three 18-hole golf courses and "Wimbledon West," with 11 championship tennis courts, is included. ⊠ *3900 Wailea Alanui Dr., Wailea 96753* ☎ *808/874–8000 or 800/334–6284* 🖶 *808/874–6449* ⊕ *www.fshr.com* 🖙 *380 rooms* ⚂ *3 restaurants, in-room safes, cable TV with movies and video games, refrigerators, golf privileges, 2 tennis courts, pool, health club, massage, spa, beach, bicycles, badminton, croquet, volleyball, 2 bars, recreation room, babysitting, Internet,* ☰ *AE, D, DC, MC, V.*

$$$$ ▦ **Grand Wailea.** Sunny opulence is everywhere at this 40-acre resort. Elaborate water features include a 2,000-foot multilevel "canyon riverpool" with slides and grottos. The Spa Grande offers guests everything from aerobics classes to hydrotherapy massage. Spacious ocean-view rooms are outfitted with overstuffed chaises, comfortable writing desks, and oversize tubs. Access to three 18-hole golf courses and tennis privileges are available. The resort also has one of Maui's most legendary—and least pronounceable—restaurants, Humuhumunukunukuāpua'a. ⊠ *3850 Wailea Alanui Dr., Wailea 96753* ☎ *808/875–1234 or 800/888–6100* 🖶 *808/874–2442* ⊕ *www.grandwailea.com* 🖙 *779 rooms* ⚂ *5 restaurants, in-room safes, cable TV with movies, golf privileges, 3 pools, health club, spa, beach, windsurfing, 6 bars, recreation room, shops, children's programs (ages 5–12), Internet* ☰ *AE, D, DC, MC, V.*

$$$$ ▦ **Kama'ole Sands.** Eleven four-story buildings wrap around 15 acres of grassy slopes with swimming pools, a small waterfall, and barbecues. It's a good choice for the active traveler; there are tennis and volleyball courts to keep you in shape. Condos are well appointed with modern conveniences, but there's a relaxed, almost retro feel to the place. All units have kitchens, laundries, and private lānai. The property has a 24-hour front desk and an activities desk, and it is across the road from Kama'ole Beach Park III. ⊠ *2695 S. Kīhei Rd., Kīhei 96753* ☎ *808/874–8700 or 800/367–5004* 🖶 *808/879–3273* ⊕ *www.castle-group.com* 🖙 *11 studios; 211 1-bedroom, 83 2-bedroom, and 4 3-bedroom units* ⚂ *Restaurant, 4 tennis courts, pool, wading pool, volleyball; no a/c in some rooms* ☰ *AE, D, DC, MC, V.*

$$$$ 🏨 **Marriott Wailea Resort.** The Marriott (formerly the Outrigger) was built before current construction laws were put in place, so rooms sit much closer to the crashing surf than at most resorts—Wailea Beach is just a few steps away. The tropical lobby and interior spaces showcase a remarkable collection of Hawaiian and Pacific Rim artifacts. All of the spacious rooms have private lānai and are styled with a tropical theme. The grounds are accented with palm, banana, and torch ginger varieties. There are golf privileges at three nearby courses, as well as tennis privileges at the Wailea Tennis Club. The Mandara Spa provides beauty and relaxation treatments as well as massage. ⊠ *3700 Wailea Alanui Dr., Wailea 96753* ☎ *808/879–1922 or 800/922–7866* 🖷 *808/874–8331* ⊕ *www.outriggerwailea.com* 🛏 *516 rooms* ⌂ *3 restaurants, in-room safes, cable TV with video games, golf privileges, 3 pools, hair salon, 2 hot tubs, massage, spa, beach, children's programs (ages 5–12), dry cleaning, laundry service, Internet, business services* ▤ *AE, D, DC, MC, V.*

$$$$ 🏨 **Maui Prince.** The attention given to service, style, and presentation at this hotel is apparent from the minute you walk into the delightful open-air lobby. Rooms on five levels surround the courtyard, which has a Japanese garden with a bubbling stream. Room decoration is understated, in tones of mauve and beige. ⊠ *5400 Mākena Alanui Rd., Mākena 96753* ☎ *808/874–1111 or 800/321–6284* 🖷 *808/879–8763* ⊕ *www.princeresortshawaii.com* 🛏 *310 rooms* ⌂ *4 restaurants, in-room safes, some in-room VCRs, 2 18-hole golf courses, 6 tennis courts, 2 pools, exercise equipment, hot tub, beach, badminton, croquet, shuffleboard, children's programs (ages 5–12), business services, meeting rooms* ▤ *AE, DC, MC, V.*

$$$–$$$$ 🏨 **Maui Coast Hotel.** You might never notice this elegant hotel because it's set back off the street. The standard rooms are fine—very clean and modern—but the best deal is to pay a little more for one of the suites. In these you'll get an enjoyable amount of space and jet nozzles in the bathtub. You can sample nightly entertainment by the large, heated pool or utilize the new fitness center until 10 PM. Six-mile-long Kama'ole Beach is across the street. ⊠ *2259 S. Kīhei Rd., Kīhei 96753* ☎ *808/874–6284, 800/895–6284, or 800/426–0670* 🖷 *808/875–4731* ⊕ *www.westcoasthotels.com* 🛏 *265 rooms, 114 suites* ⌂ *2 restaurants, in-room safes, refrigerators, cable TV with movies, 2 tennis courts, fitness center, pool, 2 hot tubs, dry cleaning, laundry service* ▤ *AE, D, DC, MC, V.*

$$$–$$$$ 🏨 **Renaissance Wailea Beach Resort.** Most of the rooms here are positioned on fantastic Mōkapu Beach. A giant ceremonial canoe enhances the lobby area. Outside, you'll find exotic gardens, waterfalls, and reflecting ponds. A decent value package offers discounts at the restaurants and the hotel's own lū'au, performed on site three nights a week. The VIP Mōkapu Beach Club building has 26 luxury accommodations and its own concierge, pool, and beach cabanas. Mōkapu Beach Club guests have access to the nearby golf and tennis facilities. ⊠ *3550 Wailea Alanui Dr., Wailea 96753* ☎ *808/879–4900 or 800/992–4532* 🖷 *808/874–6128* ⊕ *www.renaissancehotels.com* 🛏 *345 rooms* ⌂ *3 restaurants, cable TV with movies and video games, Internet, refrigerators, 2 pools, health club, hot tub, beach, basketball,*

Ping-Pong, shuffleboard, lobby lounge, children's programs (ages 5–12) ▤ *AE, D, DC, MC, V.*

$$$–$$$$ ⌂ **Wailea Villas.** The Wailea Resort started out with three fine condominiums, named, appropriately, Wailea 'Ekahi, Wailea 'Elua, and Wailea 'Ekolu (Wailea One, Two, and Three). Since then, Wailea has added the Grand Champions Villas, and the adjoining Mākena Resort has built Mākena Surf and Polo Beach Club. All have large units with exceptional views and access to five of the island's best beaches. The Wailea 'Elua Village, Polo Beach Club, and Mākena Surf are the more luxurious properties, with rates to match. ⊠ *3750 Wailea Alanui Dr., Wailea 96753* ☎ *808/879–1595 or 800/367–5246* 🖷 *808/874–3554* ⊕ *www.drhmaui. com* ⇨ *9 studios, 94 1-bedroom, 157 2-bedroom, and 10 3-bedroom apartments* ♨ *6 pools; no a/c in some rooms,* ▤ *AE, MC, V.*

★ **$$** ⌂ **Mana Kai Maui.** This unsung hero of South Maui hotels may be older, but that only means it's closer to the beach—beautiful Keawakapu. Hotel rooms with air-conditioning are remarkably affordable for the location. Two-room condos with private lānais benefit from the hotel amenities, such as daily maid service and discounts at the oceanfront restaurant downstairs. Shoji screens and bamboo furniture complement the marvelous ocean views, which in winter are punctuated by the visiting humpback whales. ⊠ *2960 S. Kīhei Rd., Kīhei 96753* ☎ *808/879– 2778 or 800/367–5242* 🖷 *808/879–7825* ⊕ *www.crhmaui.com* ⇨ *98 rooms* ♨ *Restaurant, cable TV, in-room safes, refrigerators, pool, hot tub, beach, salon, meeting rooms* ▤ *AE, D, DC, MC, V.*

$$ ⌂ **Maui Lu Resort.** This was the first hotel in Kīhei; the main lobby was the summer home of the original owner, a Canadian logger. Over the years the Maui Lu has added numerous wooden buildings and cottages to its 28 acres. It's a little reminiscent of a rustic lodge and shows some wear, but the rooms are comfortable and some have their own private coves. Of the 120 rooms, 50 are on the beach. The rest are across South Kīhei Road on the main property. ⊠ *575 S. Kīhei Rd., Kīhei 96753* ☎ *808/ 879–5881 or 800/922–7866* 🖷 *808/879–4627* ⊕ *www.aston-hotels.com* ⇨ *120 rooms* ♨ *Restaurant, in-room safes, refrigerators, 2 tennis courts, pool, beach, lounge* ▤ *AE, D, DC, MC, V.*

$–$$ ⌂ **Luana Kai.** Here's a prime example of a condominium-by-the-sea, perfect for setting up house for at least four days (the required minimum). There are three different room plans, suited for couples, families, or friends traveling together. Each one comes with everything you need to make yourself at home—a fully equipped kitchen, dishwasher, laundry, television, VCR, and stereo equipment. The pool's a social place, with five gas grills, a full outdoor kitchen, and saunas. The beach is down the road a ways—but the place adjoins a grassy county park with tennis courts. ⊠ *940 S. Kīhei Rd., Kīhei 96753* ☎ *808/879–1268 or 800/669– 1127* 🖷 *808/879–1455* ⊕ *www.luanakai.com* ⇨ *113 units* ♨ *Ceiling fans, putting green, 4 tennis courts, pool, sauna, shuffleboard; no a/c* ▤ *AE, DC, MC, V.*

$ ⌂ **Maui Sunseeker Resort.** This hotel is a great value for the area, private and relaxed. You can opt for a studio, a one-bedroom, or the two-bedroom penthouse; all have kitchenettes and full baths, as well as barbecue facilities and easy access to the 4-mi stretch of beach outside.

✉ *551 S. Kīhei Rd., Kīhei 96753* ☎ *808/879–1261 or 800/532–6284*
🖷 *808/874–3877* ⊕ *www.mauisunseeker.com* ⇨ *3 units* ⚲ *Kitchenettes, cable TV, laundry facilities* ⊟ *MC, V.*

East Maui

★ **$$$$** ⌸ **Hotel Hāna-Maui.** Small, secluded, and quietly luxurious, the Hotel Hāna is a departure from the usual resort accommodations. Tranquility envelops the ranch setting, with its unobstructed views of the Pacific. Spacious rooms (680 to 830 square feet) have bleached-wood floors, authentic kapa-print fabric furnishings, and sumptuously stocked mini-bars at no extra cost. Nine treatment rooms, spa suites, and a heated *watsu* pool complement the state-of-the-art fitness center. The once-maligned restaurant has had a makeover. Chef Larry Quirit, an island native who has worked in California and Italy, introduced organic produce and locally caught fish to the Pacific Rim menu. The Sea Ranch Cottages, with individual hot tubs, are the best value. A shuttle takes you to beautiful Hāmoa Beach. ✉ *Hāna Hwy.* ⌂ *Box 9, Hāna 96713* ☎ *808/248–8211 or 800/321–4262* 🖷 *808/248–7264* ⊕ *www. hotelhanamaui.com* ⇨ *19 rooms, 47 cottages, 1 house* ⚲ *2 restaurants, 2 tennis courts, 2 pools, hot tub, gym, spa, beach, horseback riding, bar, Internet, library; no room TVs* ⊟ *AE, D, DC, MC, V.*

$$$–$$$$ ⌸ **Heavenly Hāna Inn.** An impressive Japanese gate marks the entrance to this small upscale inn. Lush gardens surround the three suites, all under one roof, but each with a separate entrance. Rooms are lovingly spare, with Japanese overtones, and the furniture was built with exotic woods by Hāna residents. There is also a traditional Japanese tearoom. ✉ *Hāna Hwy. near mile marker 32* ⌂ *Box 790, Hāna 96713* ☎ *808/248–8442* ⊕ *www.heavenlyhanainn.com* ⇨ *3 suites* ⚲ *Fans; no a/c, no room phones, no kids under 15, no smoking* ⊟ *AE, D, MC, V.*

$$ ⌸ **Kula Lodge.** This hotel isn't typically Hawaiian: the lodge inexplicably resembles a chalet in the Swiss Alps, and two units even have gas fireplaces. Charming and cozy in spite of the nontropical ambience, it's a good spot for a romantic stay. Units are in two wooden cabins; four have lofts in addition to the ample bed space downstairs. On 3 acres, the lodge has startling views of Haleakalā and two coasts, enhanced by the surrounding tropical gardens. The property has an art gallery and a protea store that will pack flowers for you to take home. ✉ *Haleakalā Hwy. (Rte. 377)* ⌂ *R.R. 1, Box 475, Kula 96790* ☎ *808/ 878–2517 or 800/233–1535* 🖷 *808/878–2518* ⊕ *www.kulalodge.com* ⇨ *5 units* ⚲ *Restaurant, shop; no a/c, no room phones, no room TVs* ⊟ *AE, MC, V.*

Guesthouses & Bed & Breakfasts

Despite the name, many of these small-scale accommodations (both rooms and cottages) choose not to interrupt your privacy with breakfast. Instead they'll provide you with Upcountry or tropical surroundings that will enchant you, and a kitchen that will let you do your own thing.

$$$–$$$$ ⌸ **Ekena.** "Ekena" means Garden of Eden, and the grounds here are full of tropical fruit trees and exotic flowers; a hillside location makes for commanding views of the ocean. There are two houses, each with a fully equipped kitchen. Jasmine, the smaller of the two, is suited to parties of two. The main house, Sea Breeze, is huge (2,600 square feet), with two large suites, but occupancy is restricted to a maximum of four people. There's a minimum stay of three days. ⊠ *Off Hāna Hwy.* ☐ *Box 728, Hāna 96713* ☎ *808/248–7047* ⊕ *www.maui.net/~ekena* ⇆ *2 houses* ☐ *Fans, cable TV, in-room VCRs, laundry facilities; no a/c, no kids under 14* ▭ *No credit cards.*

★ **$$$–$$$$** ▢ **Hāmoa Bay House & Bungalow.** This Balinese-inspired property is sensuous and secluded—a private sanctuary in a fragrant jungle. There are two buildings: the main house is 1,300 square feet and contains two bedrooms, one of them a suite set apart by a breezeway; there's a screened veranda with an ocean view and an outdoor lava-rock shower accessible to all guests. The 600-square-foot bungalow is a treetop perch with a giant bamboo bed and a hot tub on the veranda. Hāmoa Beach is a short walk away. A three-day minimum stay applies. ⊠ *Hāna Hwy.* ☐ *Box 773, Hāna 96713* ☎ *808/248–7884* 🖷 *808/248–7047* ⊕ *www. hamoabay.com* ⇆ *1 house, 1 bungalow* ☐ *Kitchen, in-room VCRs, laundry facilities; no kids under 14, no smoking* ▭ *No credit cards.*

$$$–$$$$ ▢ **Huelo Point Flower Farm.** Set on a 300-foot cliff overlooking Waipio Bay, this 2-acre estate has verdant foliage and views. The Gazebo Cottage is small with a half bath, kitchenette, and an outdoor shower. The Carriage House has cathedral ceilings, a loft bedroom with a queen-size bed, a den with a double bed, and two spacious decks. The two-bedroom, one-bath guesthouse has floor-to-ceiling glass windows, a spacious patio, and a private hot tub facing the ocean. The Main House, with 22-foot cathedral ceilings, a sunken tub in the master bath, and a large patio with a private hot tub, can accommodate up to eight. The orchard and ozonated pool are special treats. Don't try to find this secluded inn at night. ⊠ *Door of Faith Rd., off Hāna Hwy.* ☐ *Box 1195, Pa'ia 96779* ☎ *808/572–1850* ⊕ *www.maui.net/~huelopt* ⇆ *4 units* ☐ *In-room VCRs, pool, hot tub; no a/c* ▭ *No credit cards.*

$$–$$$$ ▢ **Olinda Country Cottage & Inn.** The restored Tudor home and adjacent cottage are so far up Olinda Road above Makawao you'll keep thinking you must have passed it. The inn, which sits amid an 8½-acre protea farm surrounded by forest and some wonderful hiking trails, has five accommodations: two upstairs bedrooms with private baths; the downstairs Pineapple Sweet; a romantic cottage, which looks like a dollhouse from the outside; and best of all, Hidden Cottage, which has a private hot tub. Bring warm clothes—the mountain air can be chilly. ⊠ *2660 Olinda Rd., Olinda 96768* ☎ *808/572–1453* ☎ *800/932–3435* ⊕ *www.mauibnbcottages.com* ⇆ *3 rooms, 2 cottages* ☐ *No smoking, no a/c* ▭ *No credit cards.*

★ **$$–$$$** ▢ **Cliff's Edge at Huelo Point.** Breathtakingly situated 300 feet above an emerald bay (frequented by turtles and dolphins) this off-the-beaten-path retreat is well worth the drive. Skylights let the stars in above the king-size bed in the penthouse room of the main house. All rooms have lavishly tiled baths, Balinese and Tommy Bahamas furnishings, and spacious kitchenettes. Thoughtful, hotel-type amenities—locally made soaps and jams—complete an already perfect setting for relaxation. The private, two-bedroom guesthouse is 100% equipped, with its own hot tub, full kitchen, and satellite TV. A studio with an infinity pool is planned. ✉ *Door of Faith Rd., off Hāna Hwy.* 🕾 *Box 1095, Haiku 96708* 🕾 *808/572–4530* 🌐 *www.cliffsedge.com* 🛏 *3 rooms, 1 house* ☙ *TV in some rooms, kitchen, kitchenettes, pool, 2 hot tubs; no a/c* ⭤ *CP* ⊟ *No credit cards.*

$$–$$$ 🏨 **Old Wailuku Inn.** This historic home, built in 1924, may be the ulti-
Fodor's Choice mate Hawaiian B&B. Each room is decorated with the theme of a
★ Hawaiian flower, and the flower motif is worked into the heirloom Hawaiian quilt on each bed. Other features include 10-foot ceilings, floors of native hardwoods, and (depending on the room) some delightful bathtubs. The first-floor rooms have private gardens. A hearty breakfast is included. ✉ *2199 Kahoʻokele St., Wailuku 96793* 🕾 *808/244–5897 or 800/305–4899* 🌐 *www.mauiinn.com* 🛏 *7 rooms* ☙ *In-room VCRs, library, Internet* ⊟ *AE, D, DC, MC, V* ⭤ *BP.*

$$ 🏨 **Bambula Inn.** This casual sprawling house in a quiet Lahaina residential area has two studio apartments, one attached to the house and one free-standing. No breakfast is served; this is a move-in-and-hang-out beach house. Just across the street is a small beach, and moored just offshore is a sailboat hand-built by the owner. He likes to take his guests out for whale-watching and sunset sails, no charge. He also provides snorkel equipment. This is a friendly, easygoing way to visit Lahaina. ✉ *518 Ilikahi St., Lahaina 96761* 🕾 *808/667–6753 or 800/544–5524* 🕾 *808/667–0979* 🌐 *www.bambula.com* 🛏 *2 studios* ☙ *Fans, kitchens, kitchenettes, cable TV; no a/c in some rooms* ⊟ *D, MC, V.*

$$ 🏨 **Bloom Cottage.** The name comes from the abundance of roses and other flowers that surround this well-run, classic B&B. This is life in the slow lane, with quiet, privacy, and a fireplace for when the evenings are nippy. The furnishings are very Ralph Lauren, with a cowhide flourish suited to this ranch-country locale. The 1906 house has three rooms and is good for four to six people willing to share a single bathroom. The cottage is ideal for a couple. ✉ *229 Kula Hwy., Kula 96790* 🕾 *808/579–8282* 🕾 *661/393–5015* 🌐 *www.hookipa.com/bloom_cottage.html* 🛏 *3 rooms, 1 cottage* ☙ *No a/c, no smoking* ⊟ *AE, D, MC, V.*

$$ 🏨 **Eva Villa.** The waterfall and lilies at this elegant B&B's entrance instantly remind you that you're on vacation. Located in the neighborhood above Wailea, Eva Villa is both quiet and welcoming. Three modern, 600-square-foot suites come furnished with queen-size beds and sleeper sofas, kitchens stocked with Continental breakfasts, and access to the pool and Jacuzzi. Rick and Dale Pounds, the congenial owners who live on-property, even provide guests with a farewell CD of island photos and music. The real treasure, however, is the 360° ocean and mountain view from the rooftop patio, accompanied by a telescope. ✉ *815 Kumulani Dr., Wailea 96753* 🕾 *808/874–6407* 🌐 *www.maui.bnb.com* 🛏 *3 suites* ☙ *BBQ, fans, cable TV, kitchens, pool, hot tub, laundry, Internet* ⭤ *CP.*

$–$$ 🏨 **Silver Cloud Guest Ranch.** Silver Cloud is in cowboy country, on the high mountainside beyond Kula and just 5 mi before ʻUlupalakua Ranch. The noble Plantation House, with six rooms, surveys pasturelands and a spellbinding panorama of islands and sea. Silence is a chief attraction in this offbeat but magnificent part of Maui. In addition to the main house, the ranch has the separate Lānai Cottage and five studios with kitchenettes (good for families) arranged like a bunkhouse in a horseshoe shape. A complete breakfast with fresh fruit and juice is served out of the Plantation House kitchen every morning. ✉ *1373 Thompson Rd.* ☎ *R.R. 2, Box 201, Kula 96790* ☎ *808/878–6101 or 800/532–1111* 📠 *808/878–2132* ⊕ *www.maui.net/~slvrcld* ⤴ *11 rooms, 1 cottage* ⚘ *Some kitchenettes, horseback riding* ▭ *AE, D, DC, MC, V* ⍁⏐ *BP.*

$ ⌨ **Hale Hoʻokipa Inn.** This handsome 1924 Craftsman-style house in the heart of Makawao town is a good base for excursions to the crater or to Hāna. The owner has lovingly furnished it with antiques and fine art. (She's also a certified tour guide who likes to take guests on hikes.) She has divided the house into three single rooms, each prettier than the next, and the South Wing, which sleeps four and includes the kitchen. All rooms have private claw-foot baths and Continental breakfast is served. This inn matches most people's notion of Grandma and Grandpa's house. ✉ *32 Pakani Pl., Makawao 96768* ☎ *808/572–6698* 📠 *808/572–2580* ⊕ *www.maui.net/~mauibnb* ⤴ *3 rooms, 1 2-bedroom suite, 1 cottage* ⚘ *Cable TV, library; no a/c* ▭ *No credit cards* ⍁⏐ *CP.*

$ ⌨ **Halfway to Hāna House.** A private studio on Maui's lush rural north coast, this serene retreat includes a two-person hammock, surrounding organic gardens, and great ocean views. It's a short walk from here to natural pools, waterfalls, and hiking areas. The room comes with optional Continental breakfast and a well-supplied kitchenette—all the equipment you need to do your own thing. A three-night minimum stay is required. ✉ *Hāna Hwy.* ☎ *Box 675, Haʻikū 96708* ☎ *808/572–1176* 📠 *808/572–3609* ⊕ *www.halfwaytohana.com/paradise.html* ⤴ *1 room* ⚘ *Kitchenette; no a/c* ▭ *No credit cards*

$ ⌨ **Kula View.** This affordable home-away-from-home sits in peaceful, rural Kula. At an elevation of 2,000 feet, the climate is pleasantly temperate. Guests stay in the entire upper floor of a tastefully decorated house with a private entrance, deck, and gardens. A commanding view of Haleakalā stretches beyond the French doors. The hostess provides an "amenity basket," a very popular Continental breakfast, advice on touring, and even beach towels or warm clothes for your crater trip. ✉ *600 Holopuni Rd., Kula 96790* ☎ *808/878–6736* ⊕ *www.kulaview.com* ⤴ *1 room* ⚘ *Kitchenette; no a/c* ▭ *No credit cards* ⍁⏐ *CP.*

¢–$ ⌨ **Peace of Maui.** The small Upcountry community of Haliʻimaile, 2 mi closer to the coast than Makawao and near both Baldwin Avenue and Haleakalā Highway, is well situated for accessing the rest of the island. This small inn is a good choice for budget-minded travelers who want to be out and active all day. Six rooms in a "lodge" have pantries and mini-refrigerators. The kitchen and bathroom are shared. There's also a separate cottage with its own kitchen and facilities. You'll have sweeping views of the north shore and the mountains here. ✉ *1290 Haliʻimaile Rd., Haliʻimaile 96768* ☎ *808/572–5045 or 888/475–5045* ⊕ *www. peaceofmaui.com* ⤴ *6 rooms, 1 cottage* ⚘ *Cable TV, car rental; no a/c,* ▭ *No credit cards.*

¢   ⌨ **Banana Bungalow Maui Hostel.** A typical lively and cosmopolitan hostel, Banana Bungalow offers the cheapest accommodations on the island. Private rooms have one queen or two single beds; clean bathrooms are down the hall. Dorm rooms are available for $17.50 per night. Free daily tours to waterfalls, beaches, and Haleakalā Crater make this a stellar deal. (Yes, the tours are *free.*) The property's amenities include free high-speed Internet access in the common room, kitchen privileges, a Jacuzzi, and banana trees ripe for the picking. Tucked in an out-of-the-way corner of Wailuku, the old building has splendid mountain views. ⊠ *310 N. Market St., Wailuku 96793* ☎ *808/244–5090 or 800/846–7835* ⊕ *www.mauihostel.com* ⥻ *38 rooms* ⚘ *BBQ, kitchen, laundry facilities, Internet; no a/c* ▭ *MC, V.*

NIGHTLIFE & THE ARTS

Nightlife on Maui might be better labeled "evening life." The quiet island has little of Waikīkī's after-hours decadence. But before 10 PM there's a lot on offer, from lū'au shows and dinner cruises to concerts. Lahaina still tries to uphold its reputation as a party town and succeeds wildly every Halloween when thousands converge on Front Street.

The **Maui Arts & Cultural Center** (⊠ Above the harbor on Kahului Beach Rd. ☎ 808/242–2787) is the backbone of Maui's arts and entertainment. The complex includes the 1,200-seat Castle Theater, which hosts international performances and weekly film showings; a 4,000-seat amphitheater for large outdoor concerts; and the 350-seat McCoy Theater for plays and recitals. For information on current programs, check the **Events Box Office** (☎ 808/242–7469) or the *Maui News.*

For nightlife of a different sort, children and astronomy buffs should try stargazing at **Tour of the Stars,** a one-hour program held nightly on the roof of the Hyatt Regency Maui in Kā'anapali. You can look through giant binoculars and a deep-space telescope. The program is run by an astronomer. A romantic program for couples, with roses and chocolate, is held on Friday and Saturday nights at 11. Check in at the hotel lobby 15 minutes prior to starting time. ⊠ *Lahaina Tower, Hyatt Regency Maui, 200 Nohea Kai Dr., Lahaina* ☎ *808/661–1234 Ext. 4727* ▭ *$25* ☉ *Nightly at 8, 9, and 10; Fri. and Sat. romantic program at 11.*

Bars & Clubs

With a little homework, good music and high times can be had on Maui. *Maui Times Magazine,* a free publication found at most stores and restaurants, will help you find out who's playing where. The *Maui News* also publishes an entertainment schedule in its Thursday edition of "Maui Scene."

Contemporary Music

Kahale's Beach Club. A friendly, informal hangout, Kahale's offers live music (usually Hawaiian), drinks, and burgers every day from 10 AM 'til 2 in the morning. ⊠ *36 Keala Pl., Kīhei* ☎ *808/875–7711.*

Lobby Lounge. In the comfort of the Four Seasons lobby, you can listen to contemporary and Hawaiian music played by some of the island's best musicians. At sunset, a hula dancer joins the performance. In addition, the menu is far superior to regular lounge fare—it offers selections from all of the resort's restaurants. ⊠ *Four Seasons Resort, 3900 Wailea Alanui Dr., Wailea* ☎ *808/874–8000.*

Jazz

Moana Bakery and Cafe. While its name doesn't lend itself to visions of late nights on the town, this popular North Shore restaurant is an intimate venue for jazz and blues duos, and the occasional flamenco guitarist. The menu is good, too. ⊠ *71 Baldwin Ave. Pa'ia* ☎ *808/579–9999.*
Pacific'O. This highly recommended restaurant is also a reliable place to hear live jazz on the beach. It's a mellow, Pacific sort of jazz—naturally—and it plays from 9 until midnight Thursday through Saturday. Guest musicians—George Benson, for example—often sit in. ⊠ *505 Front St., Lahaina* ☎ *808/667–4341.*

Rock

Casanova Italian Restaurant & Deli. Popular Casanova claims to be the best place on the island for singles. When a DJ isn't spinning, contemporary musicians play blues, country and western, rock and roll, and reggae. Past favorites have included Kool and the Gang, Los Lobos, and Taj Mahal. Expect a cover charge on nights featuring live entertainment. ⊠ *1188 Makawao Ave., Makawao* ☎ *808/572–0220.*
Cheeseburger in Paradise. This Front Street hangout is known for—what else?—big beefy cheeseburgers (not to mention a great spinach-nut burger). Locals also know it as a great place to tune in to live bands playing rock and roll, Top 40, and oldies from 4:30 PM to closing. There's no dance floor, but the second-floor balcony is a good place to watch Lahaina's Front Street action. ⊠ *811 Front St., Lahaina* ☎ *808/661–4855.*
Hapa's Brewhaus & Restaurant. Well-loved local performer Willi K. owns Monday nights at this club, which has a large stage, a roomy dance floor, state-of-the-art light and sound systems, and tier seating. Crowds pile in on this and other nights for live music, televised sports, and fine brews. ⊠ *Lipoa Center, 41 E. Lipoa St., Kīhei* ☎ *808/879–9001.*
Hard Rock Cafe. Maui's version of the Hard Rock is popular with young locals as well as visitors who like their music *loud.* ⊠ *Lahaina Center, 900 Front St., Lahaina* ☎ *808/667–7400.*
Moose McGillycuddy's. The Moose offers no-cover live music on Tuesday and Thursday and draws a young crowd that comes to enjoy the burgers and beer, dancing and mingling. ⊠ *844 Front St., Lahaina* ☎ *808/667–7758.*
Mulligan's on the Blue. Perfect pints of Guinness and late-night fish-and-chips—who could ask for more? Add to that live entertainment (including Sunday-evening Irish jams), gorgeous sunset views, an optimal resort location, and a dance floor, and you've got one of Maui's busiest nighttime hangouts. ⊠ *Blue Golf Course, 100 Kaukahi St., Wailea* ☎ *808/874–1131.*
The Sly Mongoose. Off the beaten tourist path, the Sly Mongoose is the seediest dive bar in town, and one of the friendliest. The bartender will know your name and half your life history inside of 10 minutes, and she makes the strongest mai tai on the island. ⊠ *1036 Limahana Pl., Lahaina* ☎ *808/661–8097.*

Tsunami's. You can dance to hip-hop, house, techno, reggae, and Top 40 hits in this sophisticated, high-tech disco, where laser beams zigzag high above a futuristic dance floor. The music plays from 9 to 1 on Friday and Saturday nights. Expect a dress code—no jeans or T-shirts—and a $10 cover charge. ⊠ *Grand Wailea, 3850 Wailea Alanui Dr., Wailea* ☎ *808/875–1234.*

Dinner & Sunset Cruises

***America II* Sunset Sail.** The star of this two-hour cruise is the craft itself—a 1987 America's Cup 12-m class contender that is exceptionally smooth and steady. ⊠ *Lahaina Harbor, Lahaina* ☎ *808/667–2195* ☒ *$39.*

***Kaulana* Cocktail Cruise.** This two-hour sunset cruise (with a bit of whale-watching in season) has a *pūpū* (appetizers) menu, open bar, and live music. ⊠ *Lahaina Harbor, Lahaina* ☎ *808/871–1144* ☒ *$39.*

Pride Charters. A 65-foot catamaran built specifically for Maui's waters, the *Pride of Maui* has a large cabin, a large upper sundeck for unobstructed viewing, and a stable, comfortable ride. Evening cruises include cocktails and *pūpūs* such as wontons and chicken teriyaki sticks. Daytime sailing and snorkeling trips are also available. ⊠ *Mā'alaea Harbor, Mā'alaea* ☎ *808/242–0955* ☒ *$47.*

Scotch Mist Charters. A two-hour champagne sunset sail is offered on the 25-passenger Santa Cruz 50 sloop *Scotch Mist II.* ⊠ *Lahaina Harbor, Lahaina* ☎ *808/661–0386* ☒ *$45.*

Film

There are megaplexes showing first-run movies in Kukui Mall, Lahaina Center, Maui Mall, and Ka'ahumanu Shopping Center. Check local papers for showtimes.

Maui Film Festival. In this ongoing celebration, quality films that may not show up at the local megaplex are screened Wednesday evenings. Screenings in Maui's most luxurious movie house—Castle Theater at Maui Arts & Cultural Center—are accompanied by live music and poetry readings in the Candlelight Cafe. In summer, the festival attracts big-name celebrities to Wailea for cinema under the stars. The annual "Celestial Cinema" includes music, hula, and Hawaiian storytelling. ☎ *808/572–3456 for recorded program information* ⊕ *www.mauifilmfestival.com.*

Lū'au & Revues

★ **The Feast at Lele.** "Lele" is an older, more traditional name for Lahaina. This "feast" is redefining the lū'au by crossing it with island-style fine dining in an intimate beach setting. Both the show and the five-course meal express the spirit of a specific island culture—Hawaiian, Samoan, Tongan, or Tahitian. The wine list and liquor selections are excellent. ⊠ *505 Front St., Lahaina* ☎ *808/667–5353* ⚶ *Reservations essential* ☒ *$95* ☉ *Mon.–Sat. at 5:30 in winter and 6:30 in summer.*

"'Ulalena" at Maui Theater. One of Maui's hottest tickets, "'Ulalena" is a 75-minute musical extravaganza that is well received by audiences and Hawaiian-culture experts alike. Cirque de Soleil-inspired, the ensemble cast (20 singer-dancers and a five-musician orchestra) mixes native rhythms and stories with acrobatic performance. High-tech stage wizardry gives an inspiring introduction to island culture. It has auditorium seating, and beer and wine are for sale at the concession stand. There are dinner-theater packages in conjunction with top Lahaina restaurants. ✉ *878 Front St., Lahaina* ☎ *808/661–9913 or 877/688–4800* ⚑ *Reservations essential* 🎟 *$48–$68* ⊙ *Tues.–Sat. at 6 PM.*

Nāpili Kai Beach Club Keiki Hula Show. Expect to be charmed as well as entertained when 30 children ages 6 to 17 take you on a dance tour of Hawai'i, New Zealand, Tahiti, Samoa, and other Polynesian islands. The talented youngsters make their own ti-leaf skirts and fresh-flower leis. They give the leis to the audience at the end of the show. This is a non-professional but delightfully engaging review, and the 80-seat oceanfront room is usually sold out. ✉ *Nāpili Kai Beach Club, 5900 Lower Honoapi'ilani Hwy., Nāpili* ☎ *808/669–6271* 🎟 *$50* ⊙ *Dinner Fri. at 6, show at 7:30.*

Old Lahaina Lū'au. This is the best lū'au you'll find on Maui. It's small, personal, and authentic and is performed in an outdoor theater designed specifically for traditional Hawaiian entertainment. The setting feels like an old seaside village. In addition to fresh fish and grilled steak and chicken, you'll get all-you-can-eat traditional lū'au fare: kālua pig, chicken long rice, *lomi lomi* salmon (massaged until tender and served with minced onions and tomatoes), *haupia* (coconut pudding), and other treats. You'll also get all you can drink. Guests sit either on tatami mats or at tables. Then there's the entertainment: a musical journey from old Hawai'i to the present with hula dancing, chanting, and singing. ✉ *1251 Front St., makai of the Lahaina Cannery Mall, Lahaina* ☎ *808/667–1998* 🎟 *$79* ⊙ *Nightly at 5:45.*

Warren & Annabelle's. Magician Warren Gibson entices his guests into a swank nightclub with red carpets and a gleaming mahogany bar and plies them with appetizers (coconut shrimp, crab cakes), desserts (rum cake, crème brûlée), and "smoking cocktails." Then he performs tableside magic while his ghostly assistant, Annabelle, tickles the ivories. The show is fun, and all the better for not being too slick. Note that this is a nightclub, so no one under 21 is allowed. ✉ *Lahaina Center, 900 Front St.* ☎ *808/667–6244* ⚑ *Reservations essential* 🎟 *$39.95* ⊙ *Mon.–Sat. at 5.*

Theater

Baldwin Theatre Guild. Dramas, comedies, and musicals are presented by this group about eight times a year. The guild has staged such favorites as *The Glass Menagerie, Brigadoon,* and *The Miser.* Musicals are held in the 1,200-seat Community Auditorium. All other plays are presented in the Baldwin High School Mini Theatre. ✉ *1650 Ka'ahumanu Ave., Kahului* ☎ *808/984–5673* 🎟 *$8.*

Maui Academy of Performing Arts. For a quarter-century this group has offered fine performances as well as dance and drama classes for children and adults. It has presented such plays as *Peter Pan, Jesus Christ Superstar,* and *The Nutcracker.* Call ahead for performance venue. ✉ *81 N. Church St., Wailuku* ☎ *808/244–8760* 💲 *$10–$12.*

Maui Community Theatre. The oldest dramatic group on the island—it was started in the early 1900s—is now staging about six plays a year. Each July the group also holds a fund-raising variety show, which can be a hoot. ✉ *'Iao Theatre, 68 N. Market St., Wailuku* ☎ 808/242–6969 💲 *Musicals $10–$15, nonmusicals $8–$13.*

Seabury Hall Performance Studio. This college-preparatory school above Makawao town offers a season of often supercharged shows in its satisfying small theater and two dance studios. The school's formula is to mix talented kids with seasoned adults and innovative, even offbeat, concepts. Dance concerts are always a hit. ✉ *480 Olinda Rd., 1 mi north of Makawao crossroads* ☎ *808/573–1257* 💲 *$7–$12.*

Tony and Tina's Wedding. The longest-running off-Broadway hit ever, this show couldn't have found a more apt backdrop than the Hyatt's Swan Court. If you didn't come to Maui with a wedding party, or you need relief from the party you did come with, immerse yourself in the hilarity of a faux Italian wedding. Typical reception fare is served—lasagna, fish, Caesar salad, and wedding cake. Heckling is allowed; the more you participate, the more fun you have. ✉ *Hyatt Regency Maui, Kā'anapali Resort, 200 Nohea Kai Dr., Lahaina* ☎ *808/661–1234* 💲 *$76.50* ⊙ *Mon.–Sat. at 6:30.*

SPORTS & THE OUTDOORS

Biking

Maui County has designated hundreds of miles of bike paths on Maui's roads, making biking safer and more convenient than in the past. Painted bike lanes make it possible for a rider to travel all the way from Mākena to Kapalua, and you'll see dozens of hardy souls pedaling under the hot Maui sun. Some people rent a bike just to ride around the resort where they're staying. Bikes rent for $10 to $20 a day. Several companies offer downhill bike tours from the top of Haleakalā all the way to the coast.

Island Biker (✉ 415 Dairy Rd., Kahului ☎ 808/877–7744) rents standard front-shock bikes and road bikes for $29 a day or $95 per week; helmets are included. **West Maui Cycles** (✉ 1087 Limahana St., Lahaina ☎ 808/661–9005) offers an assortment of cycles, including front-suspension bikes for $40 per day, full-suspension bikes for $50 per day, and standard hybrid bikes for $20 per day.

Camping & Hiking

Fodor'sChoice Let's start with the best—hiking **Haleakalā Crater** (✉ Haleakalā Crater
★ Rd., Makawao ☎ 808/572–4400) at Haleakalā National Park. The recommended way to explore the crater is to go in two cars and ferry your-

selves back and forth between the head of Halemau'u Trail and the summit. This way, you can hike from the summit down Sliding Sands Trail, cross the crater floor, investigate the Bottomless Pit and Pele's Paint Pot, then climb out on the switchback trail (Halemau'u). When you emerge, the shelter of your waiting car will be very welcome. Give yourself eight hours for the hike; take a backpack with lunch, water, and a reliable jacket for the beginning and end of the hike. This is a demanding trip, but you will never regret or forget it.

If you want to stay longer than a day, plan on overnighting in one of the national park's three cabins or two campgrounds. The cabins are equipped with bunk beds, wood-burning stoves, fake logs, and kitchen gear. To reserve a cabin you have to plan at least three months in advance and hope the lottery system is kind to you. Contact the **National Park Service** (🖃 Box 369, Makawao 96768 ☎ 808/572–9306). The tent campsites are easy to reserve on a first-come, first-served basis. Just make sure to stop at park headquarters to register on your way in.

Just as you enter Haleakalā National Park, **Hosmer Grove** offers an hour-long loop trail into the cloud forest that will give you insight into Hawai'i's fragile ecology. You can pick up a map at the trailhead. Park rangers conduct guided hikes on a changing schedule. There are six campsites (no permit needed), pit toilets, drinking water, and cooking shelters.

Another good hiking spot—and something totally unexpected on a tropical island—is **Polipoli Forest.** During the Great Depression the government began a program to reforest the mountain, and soon cedar, pine, cypress, and even redwood took hold. It's cold and foggy here, and often wet or at least misty. To reach the forest, take Route 37 all the way out to the far end of Kula. Then turn left at Route 377. After about a half mile, turn right at Waipoli Road. First you'll encounter switchbacks; after that it's just plain bad—but passable. There are wonderful trails, a small campground, and a cabin that you can rent from the Division of State Parks. Write far in advance for the **cabin** (🖃 Box 1049, Wailuku 96793 ☎ 808/244–4354); for the campground, you can wait until you arrive in Wailuku and visit the **Division of State Parks** (🖃 54 High St. ☎ 808/984–8109).

'Ohe'o Gulch is a branch of Haleakalā National Park, located past Hāna on the Pi'ilani Highway. This is the starting point of one of the best hikes on Maui—the 2-mi trek upstream to the 400-foot **Waimoku Falls.** Along the way you can take side trips and swim in the stream's basalt-lined pools. Then the trail bridges a sensational gorge and passes onto a boardwalk through a mystifying forest of giant bamboo. Down at the grassy sea cliffs, you can camp, no permit required, although you can stay only three nights. Toilets, grills, and tables are available here, but there's no water and open fires aren't allowed.

A great avenue into the island's untrammeled wilderness is Maui's chapter of the **Sierra Club** (🖃 71 Baldwin Ave., Pā'ia ☎ 808/579–9802 ⊕ www.hi.sierraclub.org/maui). Rather than venturing out on your own, you may want to join one of the club's hikes into pristine forests and valley isle watersheds, or along ancient coastal paths. Several hikes a month are led by informative naturalists who carry first aid kits and arrange waivers to access private land. Some outings include volunteer service, but most are just for fun. Bring your own food and water, sturdy shoes, and a suggested donation of $5—a true bargain.

For excursions into remote areas, contact **Maui Eco Adventures** (⊠ 180 Dickenson St., Suite 101, Lahaina ☎ 808/661–7720 or 877/661–7720). The ecologically minded company leads hikes into private or otherwise inaccessible areas. Hikes, which can be combined with kayaking, mountain biking, or sailing trips, explore botanically rich valleys in Kahakuloa and East Maui.

Fitness & Spa Centers

Most spas and fitness centers on Maui are in hotels. Generally, spa services are available to both guests and nonguests, whereas fitness centers are for guests only. If your hotel does not have a facility, ask whether privileges are available at another hotel. Those listed provide the most comprehensive services.

The Spa at Four Seasons Resort. This fully renovated, comprehensive spa offers massage, facials, wraps, and signature services such as the Mango Salt Glow (an exfoliating body scrub using mango sorbet) in a relaxing new treatment facility. Oceanside and couples massage are available. ⊠ 3900 Wailea Alanui Dr., Wailea ☎ 808/874–8000 or 800/334–6284.

★ **Spa Grande, Grand Wailea.** At 50,000 square feet, this is the largest spa on the island. The "Termé Circuit," with five different therapeutic baths and a loofah scrub, is available separately for $80, or free with a treatment. Spa services—massages, facials, wraps, and the like—go up in price from there. The gym, which has state-of-the- art cardio equipment, is a separate facility, and access is complimentary for hotel guests. ⊠ 3850 Wailea Alanui Dr., Wailea ☎ 808/875–1234 or 800/888–6100.

★ **Spa Kea Lani, Fairmont Kea Lani Hotel Suites & Villas.** One of the island's smallest spas may well be its nicest. There are only nine treatment rooms, but each is state-of-the-art. Massage tables are hydraulic, so your therapist can move you into the perfect position for your specific needs. The signature Iliili Stone Massage is practiced by experts who harvest their own stones nearby. Use of the gym, open 24 hours a day, is free to hotel guests. ⊠ 4100 Wailea Alanui Dr., Wailea ☎ 808/875–4100 or 800/659–4100.

Spa Luna. If hotel spa prices are a little intimidating, try this day spa, which is also an aesthetician's school. Located in the former Hā'iku Cannery, it offers services ranging from facials to massage to microdermabrasion. You can opt for professional services or take advantage of the student clinics. The students are subject to rigorous training, and their services are offered at a fraction of the regular cost. ⊠ Hā'iku Cannery, 810 Hā'iku Rd., Hā'iku ☎ 808/575–2440.

Spa Moana, Hyatt Regency Maui. Spa Moana has oceanfront views from the gym, which is free to hotel guests. Treatment areas are serene. The

THE HUMPBACK'S WINTER HOME

THE HUMPBACK WHALES' *attraction to Maui is legendary. More than half the North Pacific's humpback population winters in Hawai`i. At one time there were thousands of the huge mammals, but a history of overhunting and marine pollution dwindled the world population to about 1,500. In 1966, humpbacks were put on the endangered species list, which restricts boats and airplanes from getting too close.*

Experts believe the humpbacks keep returning to Hawaiian waters because of the warmth. Winter is calving time, and the young whales, born with little blubber, probably couldn't survive in the frigid Alaskan waters. No one has ever seen a whale give birth here, but experts know that calving is their main winter activity, since the 1- and 2-ton youngsters suddenly appear while the whales are in residence.

Between November and April boats leave the wharves at Lahaina and Mā`alaea in search of the massive creatures, merely to observe and enjoy their awe-inspiring size in closer proximity. As it's almost impossible not to see whales during winter on Maui, you'll want to prioritize: is adventure or comfort your aim? If close encounters with the giants of the deep are your desire, pick a smaller boat that guarantees sightings. Afternoon trips are generally rougher as the wind picks up, but some say this is when the most surface action occurs. If an impromptu marine-biology lesson sounds fun, go with the Pacific Whale Foundation. For those wanting to sip mai tais as whales cruise calmly by, stick with a sunset cruise on a boat with a full bar and buffet.

Every captain aims to please during whale season, getting as close as legally possible. Crew members know when a whale is about to dive (after several waves of its heart-shape tail) but rarely can

predict breaches (when the whale hurls itself up and almost entirely out of the water). Don't forget to bring sunscreen, light long sleeves, and a hat you can secure. Weather can be extreme at sea, especially as the wind picks up. Arrive early to find parking—this can be a particular challenge at Mā`alaea Harbor.

Pacific Whale Foundation *(⊠ Kealia Beach Plaza, 101 N. Kīhei Rd., Kīhei ☎ 808/ 879–8811) pioneered whale-watching back in 1979 and now runs four boats. During humpback season PWF has a marine naturalist stationed at McGregor Point Lookout (on the cliffs heading into Lahaina).*

*Whale-watching trips can be booked by the **Ocean Activities Center** (⊠ 1847 S. Kīhei Rd., Suite 205, Kīhei ☎ 808/879– 4485). **Island Marine** (⊠ 658 Front St., Lahaina ☎ 808/661–8397) takes passengers out on the West Side. **Pride Charters** (⊠ 208 Kenolio Rd., Kīhei ☎ 808/874–8835) offers two-hour cruises narrated by a naturalist.*

spa offers traditional treatments such as Thai massage and shiatsu, as well as its own signature services, such as the Káanapali Coffee Scrub (treatment times come in Tall, Grande, and Vente). ⊠ *200 Nohea Kai Dr., Lahaina* ☎ *808/661–1234 or 800/233–1234.*

Waihua, Ritz-Carlton, Kapalua. The gym here is the island's most elegant, right down to the chilled washcloths waiting for you after your workout. Unique services include butler-drawn baths in your room, complete with theme music and champagne, mai tais, or fresh juice. All the traditional spa services are offered, too, including massages from Swedish to lomi lomi. ⊠ *1 Ritz-Carlton Dr., Kapalua* ☎ *808/669–6200 or 800/262–8440.*

Outside the resorts, the most convenient and best-equipped fitness center is **24-Hour Fitness** (⊠ 150 Hāna Hwy., Kahului ☎ 808/877–7474); day passes are $20. The **Maui Family YMCA** (⊠ 250 Kanaloa Ave., Kahului ☎ 808/242–9007) offers $10 day passes.

Golf

How do you keep your mind on the game in a place like Maui? The views make it very hard. Nonetheless Maui has become one of the world's premier golf-vacation destinations. The island's major resorts all have golf courses, each of them stunning. They're all open to the public, and most lower their greens fees after 2 PM on weekday afternoons.

Elleair Golf Course. Bill Newis designed this privately owned course, which is independent of the resorts, to take advantage of its lofty location above Kīhei town. You'll get panoramic views not only out to sea but also across Haleakalā. ⊠ *1345 Pi'ilani Hwy., Kīhei* ☎ *808/874–0777* ⚑ *Greens fee $90, cart included.*

Kā'anapali Golf Courses. Two of Maui's most famous courses are here: the North Course, designed by Robert Trent Jones Sr., and the South Course, laid out by Arthur Jack Snyder. ⊠ *Kā'anapali Beach Resort, Kā'anapali* ☎ *808/661–3691* ⚑ *Greens fee $130 guests, $150 nonguests; cart included.*

Kapalua Golf Club. The club has three 18-holers—the Village Course and the Bay Course, both designed by Arnold Palmer, and the Plantation Course, designed by Ben Crenshaw. Kapalua is well known to television-sports watchers. ⊠ *300 Kapalua Dr., Kapalua* ☎ *808/669–8044* ⚑ *Greens fee $135 guests, $220 nonguests, $85 twilight special after 1:30; cart included; club rental $45.*

Mākena Golf Course. There are two lovely 18-hole courses here, North and South, designed by Robert Trent Jones Jr. Of all the resort courses, this one is the most remote. At one point, golfers must cross a main road, but there are so few cars that this poses no problem. ⊠ *5415 Mākena Alanui Rd., Kīhei* ☎ *808/879–3344* ⚑ *Greens fee $90 guests, $120 nonguests; cart included.*

Sandalwood Golf Course. Sandalwood has a unique location on the slopes of the West Maui Mountains just south of Wailuku, with elevated views of Haleakalā. ⊠ *2500 Honoapi'ilani Hwy., Wailuku* ☎ *808/242–4653* ⚑ *Greens fee $80, $50 after noon and all day Tues. and Thurs.; cart included.*

Wailea Golf Club. The club has three courses: the Gold and the Blue, which were designed by Arthur Jack Snyder, and the newer Emerald, designed by Robert Trent Jones Jr. In his design, Snyder incorporated ancient lava-rock walls to create an unusual golfing experience. ⊠ *100 Wailea Golf Club Dr., Wailea* ☎ *808/875–5111* ⬧ *Greens fee $120 guests, $160 nonguests, $95 twilight price (Blue course only); cart included.*

Maui has municipal courses, where the fees are lower. Be forewarned, however, that the weather can be cool and wet, and the locations may not be convenient. The **Waiehu Municipal Golf Course** is on the northeast coast of Maui a few miles past Wailuku. ⊠ *Off Rte. 340, West Maui* ☎ *808/244–5934 or 808/270–7400* ⬧ *Greens fee $26 weekdays, $30 weekends; cart $8.30 per person.*

ON THE SIDELINES

Maui has a number of golf tournaments, most of which are of professional caliber and worth watching. Many are also televised nationally. One attention-getter is the **Mercedes Championships** (☎ 808/669–2440) held in January. This is the first official PGA tour event, held on Kapalua's Plantation Course. The Aloha Section of the Professional Golfers Association of America hosts the **Verizon Hall of Fame** (☎ 808/669–8877) championship at the Plantation Course in May. A clambake feast on the beach tops off the **Kapalua Clambake Pro-Am** (☎ 808/669–8812) in July.

Over in Wailea, in June, on the longest day of the year, self-proclaimed "lunatic" golfers start out at first light to play 100 holes of golf in the annual **Ka Lima O Maui** (☎ 808/875–5111), a fund-raiser for local charities. The nationally televised **Senior Skins** (☎ 808/875–5111) in January pits four of the most respected Senior PGA players against one another.

Hang Gliding

Armin Engert of **Hang Gliding Maui** (☎ 808/572–6557 ⊕ www.hanggglidingmaui.com) will take you on an instructional powered hang-gliding trip out of Hāna Airport. A 25- to 30-minute flight lesson costs $95, and a 50- to 60-minute lesson is $165. Snapshots of your flight from a wing-mounted camera cost an additional $25.

Helicopter Tours

Helicopter flight-seeing excursions can take you over the West Maui Mountains, Hāna, and Haleakalā. This is a beautiful, exciting way to see the island, and the *only* way to see some of its most dramatic areas. Tour prices usually include a videotape of your trip so you can relive the experience at home. Prices run from about $125 for a half-hour rainforest tour to $340 for a two-hour mega-experience that includes a champagne toast on landing.

It takes about 90 minutes to travel inside the volcano, then down to the village of Hāna. Some companies stop in secluded areas for refreshments. Helicopter-tour operators throughout the state come under sharp scrutiny for passenger safety and equipment maintenance. Don't be afraid to ask about a company's safety record, flight paths, age of equipment, and level of operator experience. Noise levels are a concern as well; residents have become pretty vocal about regulating this kind of pollution.

The highly recommended **Blue Hawaiian Helicopters** (✉ Kahului Heliport, Hangar 105, Kahului 96732 ☎ 808/871–8844 ⊕ www.bluehawaiian. com), has provided aerial adventures in Hawai'i since 1985, and it has the best service and safety record. Its ASTAR helicopters are air-conditioned and have noise-blocking headsets for all passengers.

Sunshine Helicopters (✉ Kahului Heliport, Hangar 107, Kahului 96732 ☎ 808/871–0722 or 800/544–2520 ⊕ www.sunshinehelicopters.com) offers tours of Maui and Moloka'i in its *Black Beauty* aircraft.

Outrigger-Canoe Races

Polynesians first traveled to Hawai'i by outrigger canoe, and racing the traditional craft has always been a favorite pastime on the Islands. Canoes were revered in old Hawai'i, and no voyage could begin without a blessing, ceremonial chanting, and a hula performance to ensure a safe journey. At Whalers Village in May, the two-day launch festivities for the **Ho'omana'o Challenge Outrigger Sailing Canoe World Championship** (☎ 808/661–3271) include a torch-lighting ceremony, arts-and-crafts demonstrations, and a chance to observe how the vessels are rigged— as well as the start of the race.

Parasailing

Parasailing is an easy and fun way to earn your wings: just strap on a harness attached to a parachute, and a powerboat pulls you up and over the ocean from a launching dock or from a boat's platform. Note that to reduce interference with whales, no "thrill craft"—including parasails—are allowed in Maui waters from December 15 to April 15.

West Maui Para-Sail (☎ 808/661–4060) offers both 400- and 800-foot flights, ranging from $48 to $55—early-bird flights are cheapest. For safety reasons, passengers must weigh more than 100 pounds, or two must be strapped together in tandem. The group will be glad to let you experience a "toe dip" or "freefall" if you request it.

Polo

Polo is popular on Maui. From April through June Haleakalā Ranch hosts "indoor" contests on a field flanked by side boards. The field is on Route 377, 1 mi from Route 37. During the "outdoor" polo season, mid-August to the end of October, matches are held at Olinda Field, 1 mi above Makawao on Olinda Road. There is a $5 admission charge for most games, which start at 1:30 PM on Sunday. The sport has two special events. The **Oskie Rice Memorial Tournament** occurs on Memorial Day. The **High Goal Benefit,** held on the last Sunday in October, draws challengers from Argentina, England, South Africa, New Zealand, and Australia. For information, contact ☎ 808/877–7744.

Rodeos

With dozens of working cattle ranches throughout the Islands, many youngsters learn to ride a horse before they can drive a car. Mauians love their rodeos and put on several for students at local high schools throughout the year. Paniolos get in on the action, too, at three major annual events: the Oskie Rice Memorial Rodeo, usually staged the weekend after Labor Day; the Cancer Benefit Rodeo in April, held at an arena 3 mi east of Pā'ia; and Maui's biggest event, drawing competitors from all the Islands as well as the U.S. mainland, the 4th of July Rodeo, which comes with a full parade and other festivities that last for days. Spectator admission fees to the competitions vary from free to $7. Cowboys are a tough bunch to tie down to a phone, but you can try calling the **Maui Roping Club** (☎ 808/572–2076) for information.

Sporting Clays

Skillfully designed to fit inside the crater of a large cinder cone, **Papaka Sporting Clays** (☒ 1679 Kahakai St., Kīhei ☎ 808/879–4441) is an outdoor arcade dedicated to the art of shooting. The 5-stand course includes "Springing Teal," "High Pheasant," and "Busting Bunnies" (no real bunnies involved; the targets are clay disks). Certified instructors outfit you with a vest, earplugs, eye protection, a shotgun, and instruction. They can pick you up in the Kīhei-Wailea area or at 'Ulupalakua Ranch by appointment any morning or afternoon. The cost is $99 for 75 targets. Spectators can come along for free.

Tennis

Most courts charge by the hour but will let players continue after their initial hour for free, provided no one is waiting. In addition to the facilities listed below, many hotels and condos have courts open to nonguests for a fee. The best free courts are the five at the **Lahaina Civic Center** (☒ 1840 Honoapi'ilani Hwy., Lahaina ☎ 808/661–4685), near Wahikuli State Park. They're available on a first-come, first-served basis.

Kapalua Tennis Garden. This complex, home to the Kapalua Tennis Club, serves the Kapalua Resort with 10 courts, four lit for night play, and a pro shop. You'll pay $10 an hour if you're a guest, $12 if you're not. ☒ *100 Kapalua Dr., Kapalua* ☎ *808/669–5677.*

Wailea Tennis Club. The club has 11 Plexipave courts (its famed grass courts are, sadly, a thing of the past), lessons, rentals, and ball machines. On weekday mornings clinics are given to help you improve your ground strokes, serve, volley, or doubles strategy. Rates are $27 per hour per court. ☒ *131 Wailea Ike Pl., Kīhei* ☎ *808/879–1958 or 800/332–1614.*

ON THE SIDELINES At the Kapalua Jr. Vet/Sr. Tennis Championships in May, where the minimum age is 30, players have been competing in singles and doubles events since 1979. On Labor Day, the Wilson Kapalua Open Tennis Tournament, Maui's grand prix of tennis, calls Hawai'i's hottest hitters to volley for a $12,000 purse at Kapalua's Tennis Garden and Village Tennis Center. Also at the Tennis Center, Women's International Tennis Association professionals rally with avid amateurs in a week of pro-am and pro-doubles competition during the Kapalua Betsy Nagelsen Tennis Invitational in December. All events are put on by the **Kapalua Tennis Club** (☎ 808/669–5677).

The Wailea Open Tennis Championship is held in spring or summer on the Plexipave courts at the **Wailea Tennis Club** (☎ 808/879–1958).

Water Sports

DEEP-SEA FISHING
If fishing is your sport, Maui is the place for it. You'll be able to throw in hook and bait for fish such as 'ahi, *aku* (skipjack tuna), barracuda, bonefish, *kawakawa* (bonito), mahimahi, Pacific blue marlin, ono, and *ulua* (jack crevalle). On Maui you can fish throughout the year, and you don't need a license.

Plenty of fishing boats run out of Lahaina and Mā'alaea harbors. If you charter a boat privately, expect to spend in the neighborhood of $600 a day. But you can share the boat for much cheaper. As a rule, the captain keeps the catch and will fillet a nice piece for you to grill up at your home or hotel.

Finest Kind Inc. (✉ Lahaina Harbor, Slip 7 ⌂ Box 10481, Lahaina 96767 ☎ 808/661–0338) has four boats: *Finest Kind,* a 37-foot Merritt; *Reel Hooker,* and *Ikaika Kai,* both 35-foot Bertrams; and *Exact,* a 31-foot Bertram. The company specializes in live bait. **Hinatea Sportfishing** (✉ Lahaina Harbor, Slip 27, Lahaina 96761 ☎ 808/667–7548) has a 41-foot Hatteras, and offers full-day, shared-boat tours beginning at $160 per person. **Luckey Strike Charters** (✉ Lahaina Harbor, Slip 50, Lahaina 96767 ☎ 808/661–4606 ⊕ www.luckeystrike.com) has two boats, the *Luckey Strike II,* a 50-foot Delta sportfishing vessel, and the *Kanoa,* a 31-foot Uniflite Sport Fisher. It offers four-, six-, and eight-hour shared-boat trips starting at $115 per person. **Ocean Activities Center** (✉ 1847 S. Kīhei Rd., Suite 205, Kīhei 96753 ☎ 808/879–4485 or 800/798–0652) books trips out of Mā'alaea Harbor, offering full-day tours for $135 per person on a 37-foot Tolleycraft. Or you can join the crew on 3-hour high-speed trolling adventures aboard the *Maka Kai,* or the *Wailea Kai,* two 65-foot Power Cats. For $89 you'll get a pole, and a steak-and-chicken barbecue lunch. Spectators ride along for $40. Finally, you can keep your catch on their popular bottom fishing tour, running from 4 to 8 PM for $110 a pole.

KAYAKING
The sport has been gaining popularity on the island, and kayaking off the coast of Maui can be a leisurely paddle or a challenge, depending on your location, your inclination, and the weather. The company to contact is **Maui Sea Kayaking** (☎ 808/572–6299 ⊕ www.maui.net/~kayaking). It takes small parties to secret spots and takes great care in customizing its outings. For example, the guides accommodate kayakers with disabilities as well as senior kayakers, and they also offer kid-size gear. Among their more unusual programs are kayak surfing and wedding-vow renewal.

KITE BOARDING
Catapulting up to 100 feet in the air above the breaking surf, the pioneers of kite boarding hardly seem of this world. Silken kites hold the athletes aloft for precious seconds—long enough for the execution of mind-boggling tricks—then deposit them back in the sea. This new sport is not for the weak-kneed. Injury is so likely, in fact, companies are not allowed to rent equipment. Beginners must take lessons, then

purchase their own gear. Devotees swear after your first few lessons, committing to buy your kite is easy.

Contact **Kite Surfing Maui** (✉ 22 Hāna Hwy., Kahului ☎ 808/873–0015 ⊕ www.ksmaui.com) for "flight lessons." Pro kite boarders will induct you at "Kite Beach," providing instruction, equipment, snacks, and FAA guidelines (seriously, there are rules about avoiding airplanes at nearby Kahului Airport). If you're not inclined to take to the air yourself, live vicariously at **Red Bull's King of the Air** (✉ Ho'okipa Beach Park ☎ 808/573–3322 ⊕ www.redbullkingoftheair) showcase contest each fall. Contenders travel from as far as Poland and Norway for the chance to be crowned king or queen of the air.

RAFTING These high-speed, inflatable craft are nothing like the raft that Huck Finn used to drift down the Mississippi. While passengers grip straps, these rafts fly, skimming and bouncing, across the sea. Because they're so maneuverable, they go where the big boats can't—secret coves, sea caves, and unvisited beaches. **Ocean Riders** (✉ Lahaina 96767 ☎ 808/661–3586 ⊕ www.mauioceanriders.com) takes people all the way around the island of Lāna'i. For snorkeling or gawking, the "back side" of Lāna'i is one of Hawai'i's unsung marvels.

SAILING Because of its proximity to the smaller islands of Moloka'i, Lāna'i, Kaho'olawe, and Molokini, Maui can provide some of Hawai'i's best sailing experiences. Most sailing operations like to combine their tours with a meal, some throw in snorkeling or whale-watching, and others offer a sunset cruise.

The best and longest-running operation is the Coon family's **Trilogy Excursions** (✉ Lahaina ☎ 808/661–4743 or 800/874–2666). They have six beautiful multihulled sailing craft, and the crews treat passengers with genuine warmth and affection. A full-day catamaran cruise to Lāna'i includes a guided van tour of the island, a barbecue lunch, beach volleyball, and a "Snorkeling 101" class, in which you can test your skills in the waters of Hulopo'e Marine Preserve. (Trilogy has exclusive commercial access.) Snorkeling gear is supplied. The company also offers a Molokini snorkel cruise.

The Hyatt Regency Maui's **Kiele V** (☎ 808/661–1234), a 55-foot luxury catamaran, does daily (except Wednesday) snorkel sails; afternoon cocktail sails; and, in season, whale-watching sails. **Mahana Na'ia** (✉ Mā'alaea Harbor ☎ 808/871–8636) provides good service and food on its comfortable catamaran cruise. This boat specializes in snorkel trips to Molokini.

Maui–Moloka'i Sea Cruises (☎ 808/242–8777) features the 92-foot *Prince Kuhio,* one of the largest air-conditioned cruise vessels in Maui waters. Programs include snorkeling and whale-watching cruises. **Scotch Mist Charters** (☎ 877/464–6284 or 808/661–0386) takes a maximum of 25 on snorkeling, sunset, or whale-watching trips aboard a 50-foot Santa Cruz sailing yacht.

SCUBA DIVING Maui is just as scenic underwater as it is on dry land. In fact, some of the finest diving spots in Hawai'i lie along the Valley Isle's western and southwestern shores. If you're a certified diver, you can rent gear at any Maui dive shop simply by showing your PADI or NAUI card. Unless you're familiar with the area, however, it's probably best to hook up with a dive shop for an underwater tour.

Dive shops island-wide sell and rent equipment and give lessons and certification. Before signing on with any of these outfitters, however, it's a good idea to ask a few pointed questions about your guide's experience, the weather outlook, and the condition of the equipment. Shops provide equipment with proof of certification, as well as introductory dives ($100–$160) for those who aren't certified.

Ed Robinson's Diving Adventures (⊠ 50 Koki St. Kīhei ☎ 808/879–3584 or 800/635–1273) offers diving instruction, charters, and underwater photo trips. **Happy Divers** (⊠ 888 Puiki St., Lahaina ☎ 808/669–0123) specializes in small group trips; beginners can wet their feet with single dives or take a three-day PADI certification course. **Lahaina Divers** (⊠ 143 Dickenson St., Lahaina ☎ 808/667–7496 ⊕ www.lahainadivers.com) offers tours of Maui, Molokini, and Lānaʻi; boats are accessible for passengers with disabilities. **Maui Dive Shop** (⊠ 1455 S. Kīhei Rd., Kīhei ☎ 808/873–3388) offers scuba charters, diving instruction, and equipment rental from six locations island-wide, with its main office in Kīhei.

Area dive sites are accessible either by beach or boat and include the following:

Honolua Bay has beach entry. This West Maui marine preserve is alive with many varieties of coral and tame tropical fish, including large ulua, *kāhala*, barracuda, and manta rays. With depths of 20 to 50 feet, this is a popular summer dive spot. Generally high surf prohibits winter dives.

Exploring the back side of **Molokini Crater** at ʻAlalākeiki Channel makes for an exciting boat dive. The crescent-shape islet, formed by the eroding top of a volcano, is a marine preserve ranging 10 to 80 feet in depth. The numerous tame fish and brilliant coral dwelling within the crater make it a popular introductory dive site.

SNORKELING The same boats which offer whale-watching, sailing, and diving trips also do snorkeling. Trips include lunch, gear, instruction, possible whale-watching, and usually visits to more than one site. Molokini Crater, that little bowl of land off the coast of Wailea, is a popular snorkeling spot only accessible by boat. For about $65, you can spend a half day at Molokini, with meals provided.

For a personal introduction to Maui's undersea universe, the indisputable authority is **Ann Fielding's Snorkel Maui** (⌂ Box 1107, Makawao 96768 ☎ 808/572–8437). A marine biologist, Fielding—formerly with the University of Hawaiʻi, Waikīkī Aquarium, and the Bishop Museum and the author of several guides to island sea life—is the Carl Sagan of Hawaiʻi's reef cosmos. She'll not only show you fish, but she'll also introduce you to *individual* fish. This is a good first experience for dry-behind-the-ears types. Snorkel trips, which cost $75, include lunch.

You can find some good snorkeling spots on your own. Secluded **Windmill Beach** (⊠ take Rte. 30 3½ mi north of Kapalua, then turn onto the dirt road to the left) has a superb reef for snorkeling. A little more than 2 mi south of Windmill Beach, a dirt road leads to **Honolua Bay.** The coral formations on the right side of the bay are particularly dramatic. You'll find **Nāpili Bay,** one beach south of the Kapalua Resort, quite good for snorkeling.

Almost the entire coastline from Kā'anapali south to Olowalu offers fine snorkeling. Favorite sites include the area just out from the cemetery north of Wahikuli State Park, near the lava cone called **Black Rock,** on which Kā'anapali's Sheraton Maui Hotel is built; and the shallow coral reef south of Olowalu General Store.

The coastline from Wailea to Mākena is also good. The best snorkeling is found near the rocky fringes of Wailea's **Mōkapu, Ulua, Wailea,** and **Polo** beaches.

Between Polo Beach and Mākena Beach (turn right on Mākena Road just past Mākena Surf Condo) lies **Five Caves,** where you'll find a maze of underwater grottoes below offshore rocks. This spot is recommended for experienced snorkelers only, since the tides can get rough. At Mākena, the waters around the **Pu'u Ōla'i** cinder cone provide great snorkeling.

If you need gear, **Snorkel Bob's** (⊠ Nāpili Village Hotel, 5425 Lower Honoapi'ilani Hwy., Nāpili ☎ 808/669–9603 ⊠ 2411 S. Kīhei Rd., Kīhei ☎ 808/879–7449 ⊠ 1217 Front St., Lahaina ☎ 808/661–4421) will rent you a mask, fins, and a snorkel and throw in a carrying bag, map, and snorkel tips for as little as $5 per day.

SURFING   Maui's diverse coastline has surf for every level of waterman or woman. Beginners can hang ten at Kīhei's **Cove Park** (⊠ S. Kīhei Rd. Kīhei), a sometimes crowded but reliable 1-to 2-foot break. Long- or short-boarders can paddle out anywhere alongside Lahaina's coastline, such as at **Launiupoko State Wayside** (⊠ Honoapi'ilani Hwy., near mile marker 18). South Shore waves tend to break in gentle sets all summer long. The North Shore is another story. Winter waves pound the northern coast, attracting water champions from every corner of the world. Adrenaline addicts are towed in by jet ski to a legendary, deep-sea break called *Jaws.* Waves here periodically tower upwards of 40 feet, dwarfing the helicopters seeking to capture unbelievable photos.

Whatever your skill, there's a board, a break, and even a surf guru to accommodate you. The right-footed gurus at **Goofy Foot** (⊠ 505 Front St., Lahaina ☎ 808/244–9283 ⊕ www.goofyfootsurfschool.com) will encourage you to stand up and surf. Their safari shop is just steps away from "Breakwall," a great beginner's spot. Two-hour classes with five or fewer students are $55, and six-hour classes with lunch and an ocean-safety course are $250. **Hawai'i Ultimate Adventures** (⊠ 4242 Lower Honoapi'ilani Hwy. ☎ 808/669–3720 ⊕ www.hawaiiultimate.net) offers specialized instruction for kids and watchful instruction for all ages. The owners also provide gear and act as guides on waterfall hikes and kayak trips. The **Nancy Emerson School of Surfing** (⊠ 358 Papa Pl.,

Suite F, Kahului ☎ 808/244–7873 ⊕ www.surfclinics.com) will get even the most shaky novice riding with its pioneering "Learn to Surf in One Lesson" program. A private lesson with Nancy herself—a pro surfer and occasional stunt double—costs $200 for one hour or $305 for two hours; lessons with her equally qualified instructors are $95 for one hour and $150 for two hours. Group lessons are $75 for two hours.

Take lessons or go solo at **Big Kahuna** (⊠ Island Surf Bldg. 1993 S. Kīhei Rd. #2, Kīhei ☎ 808/875–6395). Surfboard rentals are a deal at $15 for two hours, or $20 for the day. (The boards are soft boards, it's $5 more for fiberglass). The shop also rents kayaks and snorkel gear, and is located conveniently across from Cove Park. **Hāna Highway Surf** (⊠ 69 Hāna Hwy., Pā'ia ☎ 808/579–8999) rents good boards for $20 per day. **Second Wind** (⊠ 111 Hāna Hwy., Kahului ☎ 808/877–7467) rents surfboards for a mere $18 per day or $90 per week. Check out www.mauisurf.com for additional information on surf schools and surf rules on Maui.

ON THE SIDELINES Even if you aren't a surfer, watching can be exhilarating. **Ho'okipa Beach Park** (⊠ 2 mi past Pā'ia on Hana Hwy.) is where modern-day surfing, windsurfing, and kite boarding began on Maui. This is an easy place to view the action, with paved parking areas and picnic pavilions in the park. Glassy, near-perfect waves can be seen at **Honolua Bay,** on the northern tip of West Maui. To get there, continue 2 mi north of D. T. Fleming Park on Honuapilani Hwy. (Rte 30) and take a left onto the dirt road next to a pineapple field; a path leads down the cliff to the beach. In January, the **Maui Rusty Pro** invites professionals to compete for a $40,000 purse at Honolua Bay. The **Local Motion Surfing** competition follows in May.

WINDSURFING When Ho'okipa Bay was discovered by windsurfers three decades ago, this windy beach 10 mi east of Kahului gained an international reputation. The spot is blessed with optimal wave-sailing wind and sea conditions and, for experienced windsurfers, can offer the ultimate experience. Other locations around Maui are good for windsurfing as well—Kanahā, for example—but Ho'okipa is unrivaled.

Windsurfing aficionados can rent equipment—or get lessons—from the experts islandwide. Lessons range from 2-hour introductory classes to 5-day advanced "flight school" and cost upwards of $40. A great launching site, **Kanahā Beach Park** (⊠ behind Kahului Airport) is dedicated to beginners in the morning hours, before the waves and wind really get roaring. The professionals at **Action Sports Maui** (⊠ 6 E.Waipulani Rd. Kīhei ☎ 808/871–5857 ⊕ www.actionsportsmaui.com) will meet you at Kanahā, outfit you with a "quiver" of sails, and guide you through your first "jibe" or turn. **Maui Windsurf Company** (⊠ 22 Hāna Hwy., Kahului ☎ 808/877–4816) has a drive-through service and a no-hassle equipment pickup and drop-off system. **Maui Windsurfari** (⊠ 360 Papa Pl. #205, Kahului ☎ 808/871–7766 or 800/736–6284 ⊕ www.windsurfari.com) specializes in windsurfing vacation packages, offering a full range of services including accommodation bookings and high-tech-gear rental. **Second Wind** (⊠ 11 Hāna Hwy., Kahului ☎ 808/

877–7467) rents boards with two sails for $43 per day. Boards with three sails go for $48 per day.

ON THE
SIDELINES Few places lay claim to as many windsurfing tournaments as Maui. The Valley Isle is generally thought to be the world's preeminent wind-surfing location. Board-sailing experts travel from around the globe to compete on its waves. In March the **Hawaiian Pro Am Windsurfing** competition gets under way. In April the **Da Kine Hawaiian Pro Am** lures top windsurfers, and the **Aloha Classic World Wave Sailing Championships** takes place in October. All are held at Ho'okipa Bay, right outside the town of Pā'ia. For competitions featuring amateurs as well as professionals, check out the **Maui Race Series** (☎ 808/877–2111), six events held at Kanahā Beach in Kahului in summer, when winds are the strongest and a lack of big waves makes conditions excellent for the slalom (speed-racing) course. Competitors maneuver their boards close to shore, and the huge beach provides plenty of seating and viewing space.

SHOPPING

Shopping is, of course, abundant in the resort areas. Whether you're searching for a dashboard hula dancer or something a little more up-market, you can probably buy it on Front Street in Lahaina or South Kīhei Road in Kīhei. But don't miss the great boutiques lining the streets of small towns like Pā'ia and Makawao. You can purchase upscale fashions and art while strolling through these charming, quieter communities.

Local artisans turn out gorgeous work in a range of prices. Special souvenirs include rare hardwood bowls and boxes, prints of sea life, Hawaiian quilts, and specialty food products like Kona coffee. A group that calls itself Made on Maui exists solely to promote the products of its members—items ranging from pottery and paintings to Hawaiian teas and macadamia caramel corn. You can identify the group by its distinctive Haleakalā logo.

Business hours for individual shops on the island are usually 9 to 5, seven days a week. Shopping centers tend to stay open later (until 9 or 10 at least one night of the week).

Shopping Centers
Azeka Place Shopping Center. Kīhei offers this large and bustling place. Azeka I is the older half, on the makai side of the street. Azeka II, on the mauka side, has a Longs Drugs and several good lunch stops. ⊠ *1280 S. Kīhei Rd., Kīhei.*
Ka'ahumanu Center. This is Maui's largest mall with more than 75 stores, movie theaters, an active stage, and a food court. The mall's impressive rooftop, composed of a series of manta ray–like umbrella shades, is easily spotted. Stop at Camellia Seed Shop for what the locals call "crack seed," a delicacy made from dried fruits, nuts, and sugar. Other interesting stops here include Maui Hands—purveyor of prints, paintings, woodwork, and jewelry by some of the island's finest artists—and such

mall standards as Macy's, Gap, and Waldenbooks. ✉ *275 Ka'ahumanu Ave., Kahului* ☎ *808/877–3369.*

Kama'ole Shopping Center. Residents of Kīhei favor the locally owned shops at this small shopping center. ✉ *2463 S. Kīhei Rd., Kīhei.*

Lahaina Cannery Mall. Set in a building reminiscent of an old pineapple cannery are 50 shops and an active stage. The mall hosts fabulous free events year-round (like the International Jazz Festival). Recommended stops include Na Hoku, purveyor of striking Hawaiian heirloom jewelry and pearls; Totally Hawaiian Gift Gallery; and Kite Fantasy, one of the best kite shops on Maui. An events schedule is available on the Web site. ✉ *1221 Honoapi'ilani Hwy., Lahaina* ☎ *808/661–5304* ⊕ *www.lahainacannery.com.*

Lahaina Center. Island department store Hilo Hattie Fashion Center anchors the complex and puts on a free hula show at 2 PM every Wednesday and Friday. In addition to Hard Rock Cafe, Banana Republic, and a four-screen cinema, you will find a replica of an ancient Hawaiian village complete with three full-size thatch huts built with 10,000 feet of Big Island 'ōhi'a wood, 20 tons of *pili* grass, and more than 4 mi of handwoven coconut *senit* (twine). There's all that *and* validated parking. ✉ *900 Front St., Lahaina* ☎ *808/667–9216.*

Maui Mall. The anchor stores here are Longs Drugs and Star Market, and there's a good Chinese restaurant, Dragon Dragon. The Tasaka Guri Guri Shop is an oddity. It's been around for nearly a hundred years, selling an ice cream–like confection called "guri guri." The mall also has a whimsically designed 12-screen megaplex. ✉ *70 Ka'ahumanu Ave., Kahului* ☎ *808/877–7559.*

Maui Marketplace. On the busy stretch of Dairy Road, just outside the Kahului Airport, this behemoth marketplace couldn't be more conveniently located. The 20-acre complex houses several outlet stores and big retailers, such as Pier One Imports, Sports Authority, and Borders Books & Music. Sample local food at the Kau Kau Corner food court. ✉ *270 Dairy Rd., Kahului* ☎ *808/873–0400.*

Rainbow Mall. This mall is one-stop shopping for condo guests—it offers video rentals, Hawaiian gifts, pizza, and a liquor store. ✉ *2439 S. Kīhei Rd., Kīhei.*

The Shops at Wailea. Stylish, upscale, and close to most of the resorts, this mall brings high fashion to Wailea. Luxury boutiques such as Gucci, Fendi, Cos Bar, and Tiffany & Co. have shops, as do less expensive chains like Gap, Guess, and Tommy Bahama's. Several good restaurants face the ocean, and regular Wednesday-night events include live entertainment, art exhibits, and fashion shows. ✉ *3750 Wailea Alanui Dr., Wailea* ☎ *808/891–6770.*

Whalers Village. Chic Whalers Village has a whaling museum and more than 50 restaurants and shops. Upscale haunts include Louis Vuitton, Ferragamo, Versace, and Chanel Boutique. The complex also offers some interesting diversions: Hawaiian artisans display their crafts daily; hula dancers perform on an outdoor stage weeknights from 7 to 8; and three films spotlighting whales and marine history are shown daily for free at the Whale Center of the Pacific. ✉ *2435 Kā'anapali Pkwy., Kā'anapali* ☎ *808/661–4567.*

Grocery Stores

Foodland. In Kīhei town center, this is the most convenient supermarket for those staying in Wailea. It's open round-the-clock. ⊠ *1881 S. Kīhei Rd., Kīhei* ☏ *808/879–9350.*

Mana Foods. You'll find the best selection of organic produce on the island, as well as a great hot and cold deli at this health food store. ⊠ *49 Baldwin Ave., Pā'ia* ☏ *808/579–8078.*

Lahaina Square Shopping Center Foodland. This Foodland serves West Maui and is open daily from 6 AM to midnight. ⊠ *840 Waine'e St., Lahaina* ☏ *808/661–0975.*

Safeway. Safeway has three stores on the island open 24 hours daily. ⊠ *Lahaina Cannery Mall, 1221 Honoapi'ilani Hwy., Lahaina* ☏ *808/667–4392* ⊠ *170 E. Kamehameha Ave., Kahului* ☏ *808/877–3377* ⊠ *277 Piikea Ave., Kīhei* ☏ *808/891–9120.*

Specialty Stores

Art

Maui has more art per square mile than any other Hawaiian island—maybe more than any other U.S. county. There are artists' guilds and co-ops and galleries galore all over the island. Art shows are held throughout the year at the Maui Arts & Cultural Center. The Lahaina Arts Society presents **Art in the Park** under the town's historic banyan tree every Friday and Saturday from 9 to 5. Moreover, the town of Lahaina hosts **Art Night** every Friday from 7 to 10. Galleries open their doors (some serve refreshments) and musicians stroll the streets. Similar festivities occur at **WOW!** on Wednesday, from 6:30 to 9:30 PM at the Shops at Wailea.

Avalene Gallery. Avalene Gallery shows the work of Jan Kasprzycki, Steve Smeltzer, and Lisa Kasprzycki. Jan Kasprzycki, one of Hawai'i's best-known colorists, is currently working on "NightScapes," a series of large portraits of cities and towns worldwide. Smeltzer's sculpture is whimsical and colorful. Kasprzycki's daughter, Lisa, is a wonderful painter in her own right, working mostly in oil on canvas and wood. ⊠ *1156 Makawao Ave., Makawao* ☏ *808/572–8500.*

Hot Island Glassblowing Studio & Gallery. With the glass-melting furnaces glowing bright orange and the shop loaded with mesmerizing sculptures and functional pieces, this is an exciting place to visit. The working studio, set back from Makawao's main street in "The Courtyard," is owned by a family of glassblowers. ⊠ *3620 Baldwin Ave., Makawao* ☏ *808/572–4527.*

★ **Hui No'eau Visual Arts Center.** Not only are the grounds a pleasure to visit, but the Hui's gift shop sells unique pieces from local artists, as does the pottery studio in back. ⊠ *2841 Baldwin Ave., Makawao* ☏ *808/572–6560.*

Lahaina Galleries. Works of both national and international artists are displayed at the gallery's two locations in West Maui. ⊠ *728 Front St., Lahaina* ☏ *808/667–2152* ⊠ *Kapalua Resort, Bay Dr., Kapalua* ☏ *808/669–0202.*

Martin Lawrence Galleries. Martin Lawrence displays the works of noted mainland artists, including Andy Warhol and Keith Haring, in a bright and friendly gallery. ⊠ *Lahaina Market Place, Front St. and Lahainaluna Rd., Lahaina* ☎ *808/661–1788.*

★ **Maui Crafts Guild.** This is one of the most interesting galleries on Maui. Set in a two-story wooden building alongside the highway, the Guild is crammed with treasures. Resident artists craft everything in the store— from Norfolk-pine bowls to *raku* (Japanese lead-glazed) pottery to original sculpture. The prices are surprisingly low. Upstairs, gorgeous pieces of handcrafted hardwood furniture are on display. ⊠ *43 Hāna Hwy., Pā'ia* ☎ *808/579–9697.*

★ **Maui Hands.** This gallery shows work by dozens of local artists, including paniolo-theme lithographs by Sharon Shigekawa, who knows whereof she paints: she rides each year in the Kaupō Roundup. ⊠ *3620 Baldwin Ave., Makawao* ☎ *808/572–5194* ⊠ *Ka'ahumanu Center, 275 Ka'ahumanu Ave., Kahului* ☎ *808/877–0368.*

Viewpoints Gallery. Viewpoints calls itself Maui's only fine-arts collective; it is a cooperative venture of about two dozen Maui painters and sculptors. ⊠ *3620 Baldwin Ave., Makawao* ☎ *808/572–5979.*

Village Gallery. This gallery, with two locations on the island, showcases the works of such popular local artists as Betty Hay Freeland, Wailehua Gray, Margaret Bedell, George Allen, Joyce Clark, Pamela Andelin, Stephen Burr, and Macario Pascual. ⊠ *120 Dickenson St., Lahaina* ☎ *808/661–4402* ⊠ *Ritz-Carlton, 1 Ritz-Carlton Dr., Kapalua* ☎ *808/ 669–1800.*

Clothing

ISLAND WEAR **Hilo Hattie Fashion Center.** Hawai'i's largest manufacturer of aloha shirts and mu'umu'u also carries brightly colored blouses, skirts, and children's clothing. ⊠ *Lahaina Center, 900 Front St., Lahaina* ☎ *808/661–8457.*

Tommy Bahama's. It's hard to find a man on Maui who *isn't* wearing a TB-logo aloha shirt. For better or worse, here's where you can get yours. On the way out, be sure to grab a Barbados Brownie at the restaurant, which is attached to the shop. ⊠ *The Shops at Wailea, 3750 Wailea Alanui Dr., Wailea* ☎ *808/875–9983.*

RESORT WEAR If you're not in the mood for a matching aloha shirt and mu'umu'u ensemble, check out the malls and franchise stores like **Honolua Surf Company** (⊠ 845 Front St., Lahaina ☎ 808/661–8848). This chain is popular with young men and women for surf trunks, casual clothing, and accessories.

Some of the smaller boutiques around the island offer a great selection of upscale resort wear and casual sportswear. Head to Baldwin Avenue in Makawao, and Hāna Highway in Pā'ia for a string of several good shops. Listed below are some you might otherwise miss.

Maggie Coulombe. Maggie Coulombe's cutting-edge fashions have the style of SoHo and the heat of the Islands. The designs here are unique and definitely worth a look, even if you don't buy. ⊠ *505 Front St., Lahaina* ☎ *808/662–0696.*

Maui Girl. This is *the* place for swimwear, cover-ups, beach hats, and sandals. Maui Girl designs its own suits and imports teenier versions from

Brazil as well. Whatever your size, tops and bottoms can be purchased separately. ⊠ *13 Baldwin Ave., Pā'ia* ☎ *808/579–9266.*

Nell. The Fairmont Kea Lani's boutique carries stylish resort wear for women. ⊠ *Fairmont Kea Lani, 4100 Wailea Alanui Dr., Wailea* ☎ *808/875–4100.*

Sisters & Company. Opened by four sisters, this little shop has a lot to offer—current brand-name clothing such as Tamara Katz and ener-chi, locally made jewelry, beach sandals, and gifts. Sister No. 3, Rhonda, runs a tiny, ultrahip hair salon in back. ⊠ *1913 S. Kīhei Rd., Kīhei* ☎ *808/875–9888.*

Flea Market

Maui Swap Meet. This Saturday flea market is the biggest bargain on Maui, with crafts, gifts, souvenirs, fruit, flowers, jewelry, antiques, art, shells, and lots more. ⊠ *Rte. 350, off S. Pu'unēnē Ave., Kahului* 🖃 *50¢* ⊙ *Sat. 5:30 AM–noon.*

Food

Local produce—pineapples, papayas, coconuts, or Maui onions—and Made in Maui jams and jellies make great souvenirs. Cook Kwee's Maui Cookies have gained quite a following, as have Maui Potato Chips. Both are available in most Valley Isle grocery stores. Coffee sellers now have Maui-grown and -roasted beans alongside the better-known Kona varieties.

Remember that fresh fruit must be inspected by the U.S. Department of Agriculture before it can leave the state, so it's safest to buy a box that has already passed muster.

Airport Flower & Fruit Co. Ready-to-ship pineapples, Maui onions, papayas, and fresh coconuts are available by phone. ☎ *808/243–9367 or 800/922–9352.*

Maui Coffee Roasters. This café and roasting house near Kahului Airport is the best stop for Kona and Island coffees. The salespeople give good advice and will ship items. You even get a free cup of joe in a signature to-go cup when you buy a pound of coffee. ⊠ *444 Hāna Hwy., Unit #B, Kahului* ☎ *808/877–2877* ⊕ *www.hawaiiancoffee.com.*

Take Home Maui. These folks will supply, pack, and deliver produce to the airport or your hotel. ⊠ *121 Dickenson St., Lahaina* ☎ *808/661–8067 or 800/545–6284.*

Gifts

Lahaina Printsellers Ltd. Hawai'i's largest selection of original antique maps and prints pertaining to Hawai'i and the Pacific is available here. It also sells museum-quality reproductions and original oil paintings from the Pacific Artists Guild. A second, smaller shop is open at 505 Front Street. ⊠ *Whalers Village, 2435 Kā'anapali Pkwy., Kā'anapali* ☎ *808/667–7617.*

Lei Spa. In addition to being a day spa, this is a wonderful place to buy soaps, lotions, and shampoos, almost all of which are made on Maui. ⊠ *505 Front St., Lahaina* ☎ *808/661–1178.*

White Orchid. Maui's wedding-business boom prompted White Orchid Wedding to expand its business by opening a gift shop. It offers tasteful gifts including colorful home furnishings, photo albums, Maui-made products, and art objects. ⊠ *1961 Vineyard St., Wailuku* ☎ *808/ 242–8697.*

Hawaiian Crafts

The arts and crafts native to Hawai'i are first on the list for many visiting shoppers. Such woods as koa and milo grow only in certain parts of the world, and because of their increasing scarcity, prices are rising. Artisans turn the woods into bowls, trays, and jewelry boxes that will last for years. Look for them in galleries and museum shops.

★ **Hāna Coast Gallery.** One of the best places to shop on the island, this 3,000-square-foot gallery has fine art and jewelry on consignment from local artists. ⊠ *Hotel Hāna-Maui, Hāna Hwy., Hāna* ☎ *808/248–8636 or 800/637–0188.*

Hāna Cultural Center. The center sells distinctive island quilts and other Hawaiian crafts. ⊠ *Ukea St., Hāna* ☎ *808/248–8622.*

Kīhei Kalama Village Marketplace. This is a fun place to investigate. Shaded outdoor stalls sell everything from printed and hand-painted T-shirts and sundresses to jewelry, pottery, wood carvings, fruit, and gaudily painted coconut husks—all made by local craftspeople. ⊠ *1941 S. Kīhei Rd., Kīhei* ☎ *808/879–6610.*

Jewelry

Haimoff & Haimoff Creations in Gold. This shop carries the original work of several jewelry designers, including the renowned Harry Haimoff. ⊠ *Kapalua Resort* ☎ *808/669–5213.*

Jessica's Gems. Jessica's has a good selection of Hawaiian heirloom jewelry, and its Lahaina store specializes in black pearls. ⊠ *Whalers Village, 2435 Kā'anapali Pkwy., Kā'anapali* ☎ *808/661–4223* ⊠ *858 Front St., Lahaina* ☎ *808/661–9200.*

Lahaina Scrimshaw. Here you can buy brooches, rings, pendants, cuff links, tie tacks, and collector's items adorned with intricately carved sailors' art. ⊠ *845A Front St., Lahaina* ☎ *808/661–8820* ⊠ *Whalers Village, 2435 Kā'anapali Pkwy., Kā'anapali* ☎ *808/661–4034.*

Master Touch Gallery. The exterior of this shop is as rustic as all the old buildings of Makawao, so there's no way to prepare yourself for the elegance of the handcrafted jewelry displayed within. Owner David Sacco truly has the "master touch." The extravagant new shop in Wailea is perhaps more befitting of the designs. ⊠ *3655 Baldwin Ave., Makawao* ☎ *808/572–6000* ⊠ *The Shops at Wailea, 3750 Wailea Alanui Dr., Wailea* ☎ *808/875–5555.*

Maui Divers. This company has been crafting gold and coral into jewelry for more than 20 years. ⊠ *640 Front St., Lahaina* ☎ *808/661–0988.*

MAUI A TO Z

To research prices, get advice from other travelers, and book travel arrangements, visit www.fodors.com.

AIR TRAVEL

You can fly to Maui from the mainland United States or from Honolulu. Flight time from the West Coast to Maui is about 5 hours; from the Midwest, expect about an 8-hour flight; and coming from the East Coast will take about 10 hours, not including layovers. Maui is the most visited of the Neighbor Islands and therefore the easiest to connect to on an interisland flight. Honolulu–Kahului is one of the most heavily traveled air routes in the nation.

CARRIERS   United flies nonstop to Kahului from Los Angeles and San Francisco. American also flies into Kahului, with one stop in Honolulu, from Dallas and Chicago, and nonstop from Los Angeles. Delta has through service to Maui daily from Salt Lake City, Atlanta, and Los Angeles and one nonstop flight daily from Los Angeles. Hawaiian Airlines has direct flights to Kahului from the U.S. West Coast.

Continental, Hawaiian, and Northwest fly from the mainland to Honolulu, where Maui-bound passengers can connect with a 40-minute interisland flight. Flights generally run about $75 one-way between Honolulu and Maui and are available from Hawaiian Airlines, Aloha Airlines, and Island Air.

🔲 **Aloha Airlines** ☎ 808/244-9071, 800/367-5250 from U.S. mainland ⊕ www.alohaairlines.com. **American** ☎ 800/433-7300 ⊕ www.aa.com. **Continental** ☎ 800/523-3273 ⊕ www.continental.com. **Delta** ☎ 800/221-1212 ⊕ www.delta.com. **Hawaiian Airlines** ☎ 800/882-8811 ⊕ www.hawaiianair.com. **Island Air** ☎ 800/652-6541 ⊕ www.islandair.com. **Northwest** ☎ 800/225-2525 ⊕ www.nwa.com. **United** ☎ 800/241-6522 ⊕ www.ual.com.

AIRPORTS

Kahului Airport is efficient and remarkably easy to navigate. Its main disadvantage is its distance from the major resort destinations in West Maui. Kahului is the only airport on Maui that has direct service from the mainland.

If you're staying in West Maui, you might be better off flying into the Kapalua–West Maui Airport. The only way to get to the Kapalua–West Maui Airport is on an interisland flight from Honolulu because the short runway accommodates only small planes. Set in the midst of a pineapple field with a terrific view of the ocean far below, the little airport provides one of the most pleasant ways to arrive on the Valley Isle.

Hāna Airport isn't much more than a landing strip. Only commuter Aloha Island Air flies here, landing twice a day from Honolulu (via Moloka'i and Kahului) and departing 10 minutes later. The morning flight originates in Princeville, Kaua'i. When there is no flight, the tiny terminal usually stands eerily empty, with no gate agents, ticket takers, or other people in sight.

🔲 **Hāna Airport** ☎ 808/248-8208. **Kahului Airport** ☎ 808/872-3800 or 808/872-3830. **Kapalua–West Maui Airport** ☎ 808/669-0623.

AIRPORT   The best way to get from the airport to your destination—and to see
TRANSFERS   the island itself—is in your own rental car. Most major car-rental companies have desks or courtesy phones at each airport. They also can provide a map and directions to your hotel from the airport.

It will take you about an hour, with traffic in your favor, to get from Kahului Airport to a hotel in Kapalua or Kāʻanapali and 30 to 40 minutes to go to Kīhei or Wailea.

Shuttles also run between the airport and the Kāʻanapali and Kapalua resorts during daylight hours at regular intervals.

If you are flying into Hāna Airport and staying at the Hotel Hāna-Maui, your flight will be met. If you have reserved a rental car, the agent will usually know your arrival time and meet you. Otherwise you can call Dollar Rent A Car to pick you up.

Maui has more than two dozen taxi companies, and they make frequent passes through the Kahului and Kapalua–West Maui airports. If you don't see a cab, you can call La Bella Taxi for island-wide service from the airport. Call Kīhei Taxi if you're staying in the Kīhei, Wailea, or Mākena area. Charges from Kahului Airport to Kāʻanapali run about $57; to Wailea, about $36; and to Lahaina, about $50.
🚹 **Kīhei Taxi** ☎ 808/879-3000. **La Bella Taxi** ☎ 808/242-8011.

BOAT & FERRY TRAVEL
Approaching the Valley Isle on the deck of a ship is an unforgettable experience. Watching the land loom ever larger conjures up the same kinds of feelings the early Polynesians probably had on their first voyage—except they didn't get the kind of lavish treatment those on board a luxury cruise ship routinely receive. You can book passage through American Hawaiʻi Cruises, which offers seven-day interisland cruises departing from Honolulu on the S.S. *Constitution* and the S.S. *Independence*. Or ask about the company's seven-day cruise-resort combination packages.

The quieter islands of Lānaʻi and Molokaʻi can be visited by ferries from Lahaina. The *Maui Princess,* a 118-foot luxury yacht will bear you to the "friendly isle" of Molokaʻi for $40 one-way, leaving early and returning late once daily. Ferries to Mānele Bay Harbor on Lānaʻi cross the channel five times daily. Trips take 45 minutes and cost $25 each way.
🚹 **American Hawaiʻi Cruises** ✉ 2 North Riverside Plaza, Chicago, IL 60606 ☎ 312/466-6000 or 800/765-7000. **Expeditions** ☎ 808/661-3756 or 800/695-2624 ⊕ www.golanai.com. **Molokaʻi Ferry** ☎ 808/662-3355 ⊕ www.molokaiferry.com

BUS TRAVEL
Maui has a limited bus system, run by a private company, Akina Tours. Air-conditioned buses transport visitors around the West Maui and South Maui areas only. Inexpensive one-way, round-trip, and all-day passes are available. The Holo Kaʻa Public Transit System has routes in South, West, and Central Maui.
🚹 **Akina Bus Service/Holo Kaʻa Public Transit System** ☎ 808/879-2828 ⊕ www.akinatours.com

CAR RENTAL
During peak seasons—summer, and Christmas through Easter—be sure to reserve your car well ahead of time if you haven't booked a room-car package with your hotel. Expect to pay about $35 a day—before

taxes, insurance, and extras—for a compact car from one of the major companies. You can get a less-expensive deal from one of the locally owned budget companies. There is a $2 daily road tax on all rental cars in Hawai'i.

Budget, Dollar, and National have courtesy phones at the Kapalua–West Maui Airport; Hertz and Alamo are nearby. All of the above, plus Avis, have desks at or near Maui's major airport in Kahului. Roberts Tours offers car rentals through package tours. Quite a few locally owned companies rent cars on Maui, including Aloha Rent-A-Car, which will pick you up at Kahului Airport or leave a vehicle for you if your flight comes in after-hours.

Major Agencies: Alamo ☎ 800/327–9633 ⊕ www.alamo.com. **Avis** ☎ 800/331–1212, 800/879–2847 in Canada ⊕ www.avis.com. **Budget** ☎ 800/527–7000, 800/268–8900 in Canada ⊕ www.budget.com. **Dollar** ☎ 808/248–8237 or 800/800–4000 ⊕ www.dollar.com. **Hertz** ☎ 800/654–3011, 800/263–0600 in Canada ⊕ www.hertz.com. **National** ☎ 800/227–7368 ⊕ www.nationalcar.com.

Local Agencies: Aloha Rent-A-Car ☎ 808/877–4477 or 877/452–5642. **Rent-A-Jeep** ☎ 808/877–6626. **Roberts Tours** ☎ 808/523–9323.

CAR TRAVEL

Maui has some 120 mi of coastline and less than one-quarter of its land mass is inhabited. To see the island, your best bet is a car. Roads generally have two lanes, sometimes four, and sometimes only one—ancient highways which bridge staggering valleys in testimony to their bygone engineers. The two difficult roads on Maui are Hāna Highway (Rte. 36) and an 8-mi scenic stretch of one-lane highway between Kapalua and Wailuku on the north side of the West Maui Mountains. If you're going to attempt the partially paved, patched, and bumpy road between Hāna and 'Ulupalakua, take a four-wheel-drive vehicle. Be forewarned: rental-car companies prohibit travel on roads they've determined might damage the car. If you break down, you're on your own for repairs. And, if you need to ask for directions, try your best to pronounce the multi-vowel road names. Locals don't use (or know) highway route numbers and will respond to them with looks as lost as yours.

EMERGENCIES

In an emergency, dial **911** to reach an ambulance, the police, or the fire department.

For emergency road service, there is a Honolulu-based AAA. A dispatcher will send a tow truck, but you will need to tell the driver where to take your car. Don't forget to carry your membership card with you.

For medical assistance in West Maui, call Doctors on Call. Or try a walk-in clinic at Whalers Village, West Maui Health Care Center, which was created by two doctors in 1980 to treat visitors to West Maui. It is open daily from 8 AM to 10 PM. Kīhei Clinic Medical Services is in the central part of the Valley Isle and is geared toward working with visitors in Kīhei and Wailea.

Doctors: Doctors on Call ✉ Hyatt Regency Maui, Nāpili Tower, Suite 100, 200 Nohea Kai Dr., Lahaina ☎ 808/667–7676. **Kīhei Clinic Medical Services** ✉ 2349 S. Kīhei Rd.,

Suite D, Kīhei ☎ 808/879-1440. **West Maui Health Care Center** ✉ 2435 Kā'anapali Pkwy., Suite H-7, Kā'anapali ☎ 808/667-9721.

🔳 **Emergency Services: AAA** ☎ 800/222-4357. **Coast Guard Rescue Center** ☎ 800/552-6458.

🔳 **Hospitals: Hāna Medical Center** ✉ Hāna Hwy., Hāna ☎ 808/248-8294. **Kula Hospital** ✉ 204 Kula Hwy., Kula ☎ 808/878-1221. **Maui Memorial Hospital** ✉ 221 Mahalani St., Wailuku ☎ 808/244-9056.

🔳 **Pharmacies: Kīhei Professional Pharmacy** ✉ 41 E. Lipoa Kīhei ☎ 808/879-8499. **Kmart Stores** ✉ 424 Dairy Rd. Kahului ☎ 808/871-5677. **Valley Isle Pharmacy** ✉ 130 Prison St. Lahaina ☎ 808/661-4747.

LODGING

APARTMENT RENTALS

Besides the condos listed in the Where to Stay section, which operate like hotels and offer hotel-like amenities, Maui has condos you can rent through central booking agents. Most agents represent more than one condo complex (some handle single-family homes as well), so be specific about what kind of price, space, facilities, and amenities you want. The following are multiproperty agents.

🔳 **Aston Hotels & Resorts** ✉ 2255 Kūhiō Ave., 18th fl., Honolulu 96815 ☎ 800/342-1551 ⊕ www.aston-hotels.com. **Captain Cook Resorts** ✉ 1024 Kapahulu Ave., Honolulu 96816 ☎ 808/738-5507 or 800/854-8843. **Destination Resorts** ✉ 3750 Wailea Alanui Dr., Wailea 96753 ☎ 800/367-5246 ⊕ www.drhmaui.com. **Hawai'i Condo Exchange** ✉ 1817 El Cerrito Pl., Los Angeles, CA 90068 ☎ 800/442-0404. **Kīhei Maui Vacations** ✉ Box 1055, Kīhei 96753 ☎ 800/542-6284 ⊕ www.kmvmaui.com. **Marc Resorts Hawai'i** ✉ 2155 Kalakaua Ave., Suite 706, Honolulu 96815 ☎ 800/535-0085 ⊕ www.marcresorts.com. **Maui Windsurfari** ✉ 425 Koloa St., Kahului 96732 ☎ 808/871-7766 or 800/736-6284 ⊕ www.windsurfari.com.

BED-AND-BREAKFASTS

The Maui Visitors Bureau refers callers to Bed & Breakfast Hawai'i. Bed and Breakfast Honolulu has statewide listings, with about 50 B&Bs on Maui. Bed & Breakfast Maui-Style has listings for about 50 B&Bs on Maui. Island Bed & Breakfast, headquartered on Kaua'i, has listings throughout the state and handles about 35 B&Bs on Maui. A directory is available for $12.95.

🔳 **Bed & Breakfast Hawai'i** ☎ 808/733-1632 ⊕ www.bandb-hawaii.com. **Bed and Breakfast Honolulu** ☎ 808/595-7533 or 800/288-4666 ⊕ www.hawaiibnb.com. **Bed & Breakfast Maui-Style** ☎ 808/879-7865. **Island Bed & Breakfast** ☎ 808/822-7771 or 800/733-1632.

MOPED TRAVEL

You can rent mopeds on the West Side at Wheels R Us for $26 a day. On the South Shore, try Wheels USA at Rainbow Mall. Rates are $16.95 a day. Expect to pay a hefty deposit, up to $300, if you don't use a credit card. Be especially careful navigating roads where there are no designated bicycle lanes. Note that helmets are optional on Maui, but eye protection is not.

🔳 **Wheels R Us** ✉ 741 Waine'e St., Lahaina ☎ 808/667-7751. **Wheels USA** ✉ 2439 S. Kīhei Rd., Kīhei ☎ 808/875-1221.

SHUTTLE TRAVEL

If you're staying in the right hotel or condo, there are a few shuttles that can get you around the area. Akina Tours double-decker West Maui Shopping Express ferries passengers to and from Kā'anapali, Kapalua, Honokōwai, and Lahaina from 8 AM to 10 PM. The fare is $1 per person each way, and schedules are available at most hotels.

The free Kā'anapali Trolley Shuttle runs within the resort between 9 AM and 11 PM and stops automatically at all hotels and at condos when requested. All Kā'anapali hotels have copies of schedules, or you can call the Kā'anapali Operation Association.

The Wailea Shuttle and the Kapalua Shuttle run within their respective resorts and are free. Schedules are available throughout each resort. ⓘ **Akina Bus Service** ☏ 808/870-2828 ⊕ www.akinatours.com. **Kā'anapali Operation Association** ☏ 808/661-7370.

SIGHTSEEING TOURS

BUS & VAN TOURS This is a big island to see in one day, so tour companies combine various sections—either Haleakalā, 'Īao Needle, and West Maui, or Hāna and its environs. Contact companies for their current offerings. Often hotels have tour desks to facilitate arrangements.

A tour of Haleakalā and Upcountry is usually a half-day excursion and is offered in several versions by different companies for about $50 and up. The trip often includes stops at a protea farm and at Tedeschi Vineyards and Winery, the only place in Maui where wine is made. A Haleakalā sunrise tour starts before dawn so that you can get to the top of the dormant volcano before the sun peeks over the horizon. Some companies throw in champagne to greet the sunrise.

A tour of Hāna is almost always done in a van, since the winding road to Hāna just doesn't provide a comfortable ride in bigger buses. Of late, Hāna has so many of these one-day tours that it seems as if there are more vans than cars on the road. Still, to many it's a more relaxing way to do the drive than behind the wheel of a car. Guides decide where you stop for photos. Tours run from $70 to $120.

Ground tour companies are usually statewide and have a whole fleet of vehicles. Some use air-conditioned buses, whereas others prefer smaller vans. Then you've got your minivans, your microbuses, and your minicoaches. The key is how many passengers each will hold. Be sure to ask how many stops you'll get on your tour, or you may be disappointed to find that all your sightseeing is done through a window.

Most of the tour guides have been in the business for years. Some were born on the Islands and have taken special classes to learn more about their culture and lore. They expect a tip ($1 per person at least), but they're just as cordial without one.

Polynesian Adventure Tours uses large buses with floor-to-ceiling windows. The drivers are fun and really know the island. Roberts Hawai'i Tours is one of the state's largest tour companies, and its staff can arrange tours with bilingual guides if asked ahead of time.

Temptation Tours' president, Dave Campbell, has targeted members of the affluent older crowd (though almost anyone would enjoy these tours) who don't want to be herded onto a crowded bus. He provides exclusive tours in his plush six-passenger limovan and specializes in full-day tours to Haleakalā and Hāna, ranging from $110 to $249. Dave's "Ultimate" Hāna tour includes lunch at Hotel Hāna-Maui.

🔒 **Polynesian Adventure Tours** ✉ 400 Hāna Hwy., Kahului 96732 ☎ 808/877-4242 or 800/622-3011 ⊕ www.polyad.com. **Roberts Hawai'i Tours** 🏠 Box 247, Kahului 96732 ☎ 808/871-6226 or 800/767-7551 ⊕ www.roberts-hawaii.com. **Temptation Tours** ✉ 211 'Āhinahina Pl., Kula 96790 ☎ 808/877-8888.

<table>
<tr><td>HIKING &
WALKING TOURS</td><td>Hike Maui is the oldest hiking company on the Islands, and its rain-forest, mountain-ridge, crater, coastline, and archaeological-snorkel hikes are led by such knowledgeable folk as ethnobotanists and marine biologists. Prices range from $59 to $135 for hikes of 5 to 10 hours, including lunch. Hike Maui supplies waterproof day packs, rain ponchos, first-aid gear, water bottles, and transportation to the site.</td></tr>
</table>

Paths in Paradise is a small company offering specialized hikes into wetlands, rain-forest areas, and the crater. The owner, Renate Gassman-Duvall, is an expert birder and biologist. She helps hikers spot native honeycreepers feeding on lehua blossoms and supplies them with bird and plant check cards. Half-day hikes run $110, and full-day hikes are $135, with lunch and gear provided.

In 'Īao Valley, the Hawai'i Nature Center leads interpretive hikes for children and their families.

🔒 **Hawai'i Nature Center** ✉ 875 'Īao Valley Rd., Wailuku 96793 ☎ 808/244-6500. **Hike Maui** 🏠 Box 330969, Kahului 96733 ☎ 808/879-5270 ⊕ www.hikemaui.com. **Paths in Paradise** 🏠 Box 667, Makawao ☎ 808/579-9294 ⊕ www.mauibirdhikes.com.

<table>
<tr><td>HORSEBACK
TOURS</td><td>Several companies on Maui offer horseback riding that's far more appealing than the typical hour-long trudge over a dull trail with 50 other horses.</td></tr>
</table>

Adventures on Horseback conducts five-hour outings into secluded parts of Maui. The $185 tours traverse ocean cliffs on Maui's north shore, follow the slopes of Haleakalā, and pass along streams, through rain forests, and near waterfalls, where riders can stop for a dip in a fresh-water pool. Tours include breakfast, lunch, and refreshments.

Charley's Trail Rides & Pack Trips require a stout physical nature—but not a stout physique: riders must weigh less than 200 pounds. Overnight trips go from Kaupō—a *tiny* village nearly 20 mi past Hāna—up the slopes of Haleakalā, where you spend the night in the crater. Charley is a bona fide paniolo, and tours with him include meals, park fees, and camping supplies for $250 per person. Book several weeks in advance if you'd prefer a cabin instead of a tent.

Pony Express Tours will take you on horseback into Haleakalā Crater. The half-day ride goes down to the crater floor for a picnic lunch. The full-day excursion covers 12 mi of terrain and visits some of the crater's unusual formations. You don't need to be an experienced rider, but the longer ride can be tough if you're unathletic. The company also offers one- and two-hour rides on Haleakalā Ranch for $55 to $155.

🔒 **Adventures on Horseback** 🏠 Box 1419, Makawao 96768 ☎ 808/242-7445 ⊕ www.mauihorses.com/aoh. **Charley's Trail Rides & Pack Trips** 🏠 c/o Kaupō Kaupō Ranch,

Kaupō 96713 ☎ 808/248-8209. **Pony Express Tours** ⌖ Box 535, Kulā 96790 ☎ 808/
667-2200 or 808/878-6698 ⊕ ponyexpresstours.com.

THEME TOURS   Once you have your bearings, you may want a tour that's a bit more
specialized. For example, you might want to bike down a volcano, ride
an ATV, or immerse yourself in art.

Art lovers will admire the spectacular resort collections. A free tour of
the Hyatt Regency Maui's art collection and gardens starts at 11 on
Monday, Wednesday, and Friday and winds through the multimillion-
dollar collection of Asian and Pacific art. Among the treasures are Chinese cloisonné, Japanese dragon pots, Thai elephant bells, Hawaiian
quilts, and contemporary work. If you're not fond of group tours, just
pick up a copy of the hotel's "Art Guide" for a fascinating do-it-yourself experience.

The diverse art collection at the Grand Wailea rivals that of an international art museum. Sculptures, artifacts, stained-glass windows, a
200,000-piece ceramic-tile mosaic, paintings, and assorted works by Léger,
Warhol, Picasso, Botero, and noted Hawaiian artists decorate the
grounds. Tours leave from the resort's Napua Gallery at 10 on Tuesday
and Friday. Nonguests pay $6.

If biking down the side of Haleakalā Crater sounds like fun, several companies are ready to assist you. Maui Downhill vans will shuttle you to
the mountaintop, help you onto a bike, and follow you as you coast down
through clouds and gorgeous scenery. Lunch or breakfast is included,
depending on your trip's start time; treks cost $150. Maui Mountain
Cruisers bike trips are $125 including lunch; nonbikers can ride down
Haleakalā in a van for $55.

Haleakalā ATV Tours explore the mountainside in their own unique
way: propelled through the forest on 350 cc, four-wheel-drive Honda
Rancher all-terrain vehicles. The adventures begin at Haleakala Ranch
and rev right up to the pristine Waikamoi rain-forest preserve. Kids
under 15 ride alongside in the exciting Argo Conquest, an eight-
wheeled amphibious vehicle. Two-hour trips go for $90, and 3½-hour
trips are $139.

The Maui Pineapple Plantation Tour takes you right into the fields in a
company van. The 2½-hour, $26 trip gives you first-hand experience of
the operation and its history, some incredible views of the island, and
the chance to pick a fresh pineapple for yourself. Tours depart weekday mornings and afternoons from the Kapalua Logo Shop.
🏃 **Grand Wailea** ⊠ 3850 Wailea Alanui Dr., Wailea 96753 ☎ 808/875-1234.
Haleakalā ATV Tours ⌖ Box 703, Kula 96790 ☎ 808/661-0288 ⊕ www.atvmaui.
com. **Hyatt Regency Maui** ⊠ Kā'anapali Beach Resort, 200 Nokea Kai Dr., Lahaina
96761 ☎ 808/661-1234. **Maui Downhill** ⊠ 199 Dairy Rd., Kahului 96732 ☎ 808/871-
2155 or 800/535-2453 ⊕ www.mauidownhill.net. **Maui Mountain Cruisers** ⌖ Box
1356, Makawao 96768 ☎ 808/871-6014 ⊕ www.mauicruisers.com. **Maui Pineapple
Plantation Tour** ⊠ Kapalua Resort Activity Desk, 500 Office Rd., Kapalua 96761
☎ 808/669-8088.

TAXIS

For short hops between hotels and restaurants, taxis can be a convenient way to go, but you'll have to call ahead. Even busy West Maui doesn't have curbside taxi service. Long distances between towns spike the prices; you'd be smart to use taxis just for the areas in which they're located. Ali'i Cab covers West Maui, and Kīhei Taxi serves Central Maui.

To really arrive in style, you might consider Classy Taxi. The company offers limos, convertibles, and a 1929 Model A Ford Phaeton for a regular cab's fare.

Arthur's Limousine Service offers a chauffeured super-stretch Lincoln complete with bar and two TVs for $88 per hour. Arthur's fleet also includes less grandiose Lincoln Town Cars for $65 per hour with a two-hour minimum. If you want to stretch out with a company on the South Shore, call Wailea Limousine Service. Despite the name, this company also provides limousines to the Lahaina area.

🚖 **Ali'i Cab** ☎ 808/661-3688. **Arthur's Limousine Service** ☎ 808/871-5555 or 800/345-4667. **Classy Taxi** ☎ 808/665-0003. **Kīhei Taxi** ☎ 808/879-3000. **Wailea Limousine Service** ☎ 808/875-4114, 808/661-4114 in Lahaina.

VISITOR INFORMATION

The Maui Visitors Bureau can provide you with brochures and information. Visitor Channel 7 televises visitor information 24 hours a day, including video tours, restaurant previews, and activities information.

National Weather Service/Maui Forecast covers the islands of Maui, Moloka'i, and Lāna'i.

🚖 **Maui Visitors Bureau** ✉ 1727 Wili Pā Loop, Wailuku 96793 ☎ 800/525-6284 🖨 808/244-1337 ⊕ www.visitmaui.com. **National Weather Service/Maui Forecast** ☎ 808/877-5111.

THE BIG ISLAND OF HAWAI'I
THE VOLCANO ISLE

3

Updated by
John Penisten

NEARLY TWICE AS LARGE AS ALL THE OTHER Hawaiian Islands combined, Hawai'i (known as the Big Island to avoid confusion with the state name) is used to setting records. Perhaps most dramatically, it has the world's most active volcano: the east rift zone below Halema'uma'u on Kīlauea has been spewing lava intermittently since January 3, 1983. The island's southern tip is the southernmost point in the United States, although to the southeast, far beneath the ocean's surface, Lōihi, a sea mount bubbling lava, is slowly building another Hawaiian island, due to emerge in about 100,000 years. If you measure Mauna Kea from its origins 32,000 feet beneath the ocean's surface to its 13,796-foot peak, it is the tallest mountain in the world. The Keck Observatory on its summit, with one of the world's most powerful telescopes, searches the universe from the clearest place on earth for peering into the heavens.

With its diverse climate and terrain, the Big Island offers skiing (but only for experts) in winter and year-round sunshine on its southern and western shores, where the temperature averages 69°F to 84°F in July and 53°F to 75°F in January. So much rain falls near Hilo, the island's major city, that a botanical garden at Onomea Bay provides umbrellas to enter its tropical jungle. By contrast, land along the Kona-Kohala Coast feels desertlike, with uninhabited stretches of lava.

In earlier times, Hawai'i's kings and queens lived and played along the Kona-Kohala Coast. King Kamehameha I was born close to its northern shores, near Mo'okini Heiau, built around the end of the 5th century (a *heiau* is a stone platform that was used as a site of worship). All along the water's edge are reminders of earlier inhabitants. At Kawaihae, two heiau—Pu'ukoholā and Mailekini—mark the site of Kamehameha's final victory in 1810 in his battle to unite the Hawaiian Islands.

Developers are becoming increasingly aware of the cultural significance and rich history of the '*āina* (land). Attempts are being made to preserve and restore the bits and pieces of Hawai'i's past that come to light when a bulldozer rakes the land. You'll find historic markers scattered along trails and roadways, at hotel grounds, and in parks. Resorts, such as the Waikoloa Beach Marriott, the Fairmont Orchid Hawai'i, Kona Village, and Ohana Keauhou Beach Resort, conduct tours of petroglyph fields and historic sites. The Waikoloa Beach Marriott, the Four Seasons Resort Hualālai, and the Mauna Lani Bay Hotel and Bungalows have restored the fishponds that once supplied the tables of Hawaiian royalty.

The drive along the Hāmākua Coast from Hilo, the island's county seat and the fourth-largest city in the state, to Waimea, a fast-growing wealthy cowboy town, shows recent developments on the island. Sugarcane stalks no longer wave in the breeze. They have been replaced by orchards of macadamia-nut trees, eucalyptus, and specialty crops (from lettuce to strawberries) raised for chefs who prepare regional cuisine. Macadamia nuts are big business on the Big Island, supplying 90% of the state's yield. Diversification—coffee; anthuriums and orchids; ginger; tomatoes; sweet corn; papayas; bananas; kava (used in the

Numbers in the text correspond to numbers on the maps in this chapter.

If you have 1 day

Fly directly to Hilo and rent a car or take a prearranged tour to see **Hawai'i Volcanoes National Park** ㉙–㉞. Ask about area hikes to explore Halema'uma'u Crater, Thurston Lava Tube, fern forests, and Devastation Trail.

If you have 3 days

Start in **Kailua-Kona** ㊽–㊿, learning about Big Island history. Then spend the afternoon at a beach. On the second day, head for **Hawai'i Volcanoes National Park** ㉙–㉞ early so you'll have time to sightsee along the way. Take Queen Ka'ahumanu Highway, turning inland to **Waimea** ㉖–㉙. If you have time take a side trip to the **Waipi'o Valley Overlook** ㉚. On your third day, consider a morning snorkel cruise to Kealakekua Bay. As an alternative, drive down to **Ka Lae** ㉝, through **South Kona and Ka'u** ㊱–㊲, to get an impression of what Hawai'i was like before developers. Stretch your legs hiking to Green Sand Beach. If you prefer to sightsee, head north and explore the **Kohala District** ㊱–㉙. As you wind your way up the coast, stop at the **Pu'ukoholā Heiau National Historic Site** ㊱. There are several restaurants in Kawaihae, and the sugar-plantation towns of **Hāwī and Kapa'au** ㉒ have several little galleries and eateries. Pause in Kapa'au to see the **King Kamehameha Statue** ㉓ and then continue to the **Pololū Valley** ㉔ overlook.

If you have 8 days

Split your stay between three hotels. Stay the first night in **Hilo** ❶–⓲, where you can do a little sightseeing and visit the farmers' market. Rise early the second day to move to new accommodations closer to the volcano. Explore the town of **Pāhoa** ⓳ and its surroundings on your way to **Hawai'i Volcanoes National Park** ㉙–㉞, where you'll want to spend most of the third day.

On the fourth day, move on to the southwestern shore. Drive back through Hilo to enjoy sightseeing along the **Hāmākua Coast** ㉚–㉚. If time permits, take a guided tour into Waipi'o Valley. Check into a hotel, condo or B&B along the fabulous Kohala Coast or in the Kailua-Kona resort town area. Make day five primarily a beach day, adding a snorkel cruise or a run into **Kailua-Kona** ㊽–㊿ for lunch and some souvenir shopping. Save the morning of the sixth day to discover North Kohala. After hiking, biking, or horseback riding in the area, check out the little towns of **Hāwī and Kapa'au** ㉒. On the return drive, history comes alive at **Mo'okini Heiau** ㉑, **Lapakahi State Historical Park** ㉚, and the **Pu'ukoholā Heiau National Historic Site** ㊱.

On the seventh day, take the high road through Kona coffee country and head south from Kailua-Kona via the artists' colony of Hōlualoa to **Kainaliu** ㊶. Visit the **Greenwell Site** ㊷; then drive down to **Kealakekua Bay** ㊸ and check out **Hikiau Heiau** ㊹ and the **Captain Cook Monument** ㊿. Be sure to explore **Pu'uhonua O Hōnaunau** ㊱. Finally take a spin through Ka'u past lava fields and coffee orchards to **Ka Lae** ㊽, the United States's most southern point.

The last day of your trip should be one of rest and relaxation—a leisurely breakfast and a brief trip to the beach or golf course. Or, do some last-minute shopping before departing.

pharmaceutical industry); and even goat cheese, vanilla, and cacao—is adding a new chapter to the agricultural history of the state.

Although Kīlauea Volcano remains the greatest attraction to visitors, business owners in all sections of the economy have combined efforts to make the island exciting, welcoming, and fun. Ongoing airport expansions in the Kona area reflect their success. In Hilo, despite the rain, the farmers' market remains the most inspiring in the state, displaying colorful produce reflecting the island's full range of climates and ethnic traditions. In North Kohala, the statue of King Kamehameha I has been spruced up in the red and yellow colors of royalty, and the area draws an increasing number of visitors to its plantation past. Gated communities are sprouting up along the entire coast, and even remote South Point has become well worth the long drive as visitors seek out the more remote and adventurous sites of the Big Island.

Exploring the Big Island

The first secret to enjoying the Big Island: rent a car. The second: stay more than three days, or return again and again until you have seen all the facets of this fascinating place. With 266 mi of coastline made up of white-coral, black-lava, and a dusting of green-olivine beaches, and with its cliffs of lava and emerald gorges slashing into jutting mountains, the Big Island can be overwhelming. Depending on the number of days you have available, it would be best to divide your time between the Hilo and Kona sides of the island in order to take in the attractions of each side.

If your schedule allows a week or 10 days on the island, you might want to spend a couple of nights in the historic town of Hilo, followed by two nights at a bed-and-breakfast near Hawai'i Volcanoes National Park and another night in Waimea before finishing up your vacation at a resort on the sunny west side of the island. It's best to follow this in east coast–to–west coast order for accommodations, although the itinerary could be easily reversed. If you're short of time, head straight for Hawai'i Volcanoes National Park on your first day, and briefly visit Hilo before traveling the Hāmākua Coast route and making your new base in Kailua-Kona that night.

Directions on the island are often referred to as *mauka* (toward the mountains) and *makai* (toward the ocean).

A word of caution: the Big Island is truly big; some areas are largely undeveloped and without amenities for miles on end. Each year, unmarked trails and dangerous currents claim the lives of unprepared adventurers. Swim and hike only in areas that are established and designated as safe. Take plenty of drinking water when hiking, along with proper footwear and clothing for the area. And always let someone know where you are going.

About the Restaurants

In resort restaurants along the Kohala Coast, upscale eateries in Waimea, and elsewhere, cutting-edge chefs cook with the freshest local produce,

3

Flora & Fauna

On the Big Island, 11 distinct climatic zones across 4,038 square mi are home to hundreds of indigenous plants and birds that are among the most endangered species on Earth. Even the warm waters are unlike oceans elsewhere. More than 30% of marine mammals, such as the Hawaiian monk seal and Hawaiian spinner dolphins, are endemic. Humpback whales, which can be seen from late December to early April, and green sea turtles, visible year-round, are Big Island attractions.

Hitting the Links

Many of the Big Island's courses are emerald oases in the midst of black, barren lava fields. They were designed by world-renowned architects, and on several of the courses—which range from mountainsides to green seaside havens—the challenges are as extraordinary as the views. Towering over them is snowcapped, 13,796-foot Mauna Kea, home of Poli'ahu, the Hawaiian snow goddess.

Hiking

The ancient Hawaiians blazed many trails across their archipelago, and many of these paths can still be hiked today. Part of the King's Trail at 'Anaeho'omalu winds through a field of lava rocks covered with prehistoric carvings meant to communicate stories of births, deaths, marriages, and other family events. In Hawai'i Volcanoes National Park, trails crisscross the volcanic landscape. You can explore a lava tube or cave, or circle a *kīpuka* (verdant island surrounded by lava). In addition, the serenity of remote beaches, such as the black-sand beach at Pololū, is accessible only to hikers.

Horseback Riding

With its *paniolo* (cowboy) heritage, the Big Island is a great place for equestrians. Riders can gallop through green Upcountry pastures, ride to Kealakekua Bay to see the Captain Cook Monument, saunter into Waipi'o Valley for a taste of old Hawai'i, or venture around the rim of Pololū Valley on mules.

Scuba Diving

Kealakekua Bay State Historical and Underwater Park Marine Preserve has depths from 15 feet to more than 110 feet and is popular with experienced divers. Pine Trees, in North Kona, is an area that includes such sites as Carpenter's House, Golden Arches, and Pyramid Pinnacles—two underwater lava towers with tubes, arches, false Moorish idols, and large schools of butterfly fish. Plane Wreck Point, off Keāhole Point, is for expert divers only. Damselfish, fantail, and filefish hover around in the shadows. Red Hill, south of Kona, encompasses large caverns and lava tubes.

Shopping

Galleries abound in Kailua-Kona, North Kohala, Waimea, Holualoa, Volcano, Hilo, and even in such out-of-the-way burgs as Kukuihaele and Honomū. Coffee drinkers will want to bring back some Kona coffee, grown on the western slopes of the Big Island. Look for the "100% Pure Kona Coffee" label. Locally grown macadamia nuts also make great gifts. You'll find them everywhere and processed in every way—from chocolate-covered to garlic-dusted.

fish, and herbs, creating intriguing blends of flavors that reflect the island's varied ethnic background. Events such as the Great Waikoloa Food, Wine and Music Fest at the Hilton Waikoloa Village, and Cuisines of the Sun at Mauna Lani Bay Hotel draw hundreds of guests to starlit open-air dinners celebrating the bounty of the isle's land and waters.

About the Hotels

Accommodations vary tremendously: from sunny "destination" resorts to condominiums on cool mountaintops to family-style B&Bs in green little towns geared more toward fishing and farming than vacationing. This is the beauty of a trip to this island: you can sample that elusive thing called "the real Hawai'i" and also have time to experience the ultimate luxury vacation. But be aware that you'll need a car or a taxi if you choose to stay outside the resort areas. Also, quality and prices vary enormously away from the resorts.

WHAT IT COSTS				
$$$$	**$$$**	**$$**	**$**	**¢**
RESTAURANTS over $30	$20–$30	$12–$20	$7–$12	under $7
HOTELS over $200	$150–$200	$100–$150	$60–$100	under $60

Restaurant prices are for a main course. Hotel prices are for two people in a standard double room, including tax and service.

Timing

Touring the Big Island is appealing at any time of year. Although traffic can be heavy in town areas at times, the country roads are somewhat less busy. The weather remains basically stable year-round. It's a rare day when Kailua-Kona and the Kohala Coast are not sunny and warm, though deluges can occur in January and February. It's difficult to predict weather in Hilo. The tropical climate here produces 130 inches of rain annually which is equally distributed throughout the year; so there is no real distinct wet or dry season although winter showers tend to be heavier and more frequent. If you are traveling in winter, you are apt to get wet on the Hāmākua and East Hawai'i side. The volcano area is always cooler because of the higher elevation, so bring a sweater or light jacket.

HILO

Hilo is a town of both modern and rustic buildings stretching from the banks of the Wailuku River to Hilo Bay, where a few hotels rim stately Banyan Drive. Nearby, the 30-acre Lili'uokalani Gardens, a formal Japanese garden with arched bridges and waterways, was created in the early 1900s to honor the area's Japanese sugar plantation laborers. It also became a safety zone after a devastating tidal wave swept away businesses and homes on May 22, 1960, killing 60 people.

Though the center of government and commerce for the island, Hilo is primarily a residential town. Mansions with perfectly kept yards of lush tropical foliage surround older wooden houses with rusty corrugated roofs. It's a friendly community, populated primarily by descendants of the contract laborers—Japanese, Chinese, Filipino, Puerto Rican, and Portuguese—brought in to work the sugarcane fields during the 1800s. Bring your umbrella: the rainfall averages 130 inches per year!

When the sun shines and the snow glistens on Mauna Kea, 25 mi in the distance, Hilo sparkles. In the rain the town takes on the look of an impressionist painting—greenery muted alongside weather-worn brown, red, and blue buildings. Several of these buildings have been spruced up to revitalize the downtown area. Often the rain blows away by noon and a colorful arch appears in the sky. One of Hilo's nicknames is the City of Rainbows.

The whole town has fewer than 1,000 hotel rooms, most of them strung along Banyan Drive. By contrast, the eight Kohala Coast resorts alone have more than 3,704 rooms combined. Nonetheless, Hilo, with a population of almost 50,000 in the entire district, is the fourth-largest city in the state and home to the University of Hawai'i at Hilo.

a good tour

Historic downtown Hilo is best explored on foot. Start your excursion in front of the public library, on Waiānuenue Avenue, four blocks from Kamehameha Avenue. Here, you'll find the ponderous **Naha and Pinao stones ❶** ▶, which legend says King Kamehameha I was able to lift as a teenager, thus foretelling that someday he would be a powerful king. Cross the road to walk southeast along Kapi'olani Street, and turn right on Haili Street to visit the historic **Lyman Mission House and Museum ❷**. Back on Haili Street, follow this busy road toward the ocean; on your right you'll pass **Haili Church ❸**.

Soon you'll reach **Keawe Street ❹** with its plantation-style architecture. Stop at the **Big Island Visitors Bureau ❺** on the right-hand corner for maps and brochures before taking a left. You'll bump into Kalākaua Street; for a quick respite turn left and rest on the benches in **Kalākaua Park ❻**.

Continue makai on Kalākaua Street to visit the **Pacific Tsunami Museum ❼** on the corner of Kalākaua and Kamehameha Avenue. After heading three blocks east, you'll come across the **S. Hata Building ❽**, which has interesting shops and restaurants and the **Mokupapapa: Discovery Center for Hawaii's Remote Coral Reefs Museum**. Just next door, on either side of Mamo Street, is the **Hilo Farmers' Market ❾**.

Once you've fully explored Hilo, take a drive to some of the area's outlying sights. Begin this excursion driving southwest from the cluster of hotels along **Banyan Drive ❿**. **Lili'uokalani Gardens ⓫**, on the right, has Japanese gardens and an arched footbridge to **Coconut Island ⓬**. When you reach the intersection of Banyan Drive and Kamehameha Avenue at the bridge over the Waiakea Fish Pond/Wailoa River, turn right on Kamehameha and head toward downtown, then turn left at the traffic signal onto Pauahi Street, then left again into Wailoa State Park. Close to the Waiakea Fish Pond is the **Wailoa Center ⓭**.

From Wailoa State Park and Wailoa Center, go back to Pauahi Street, turn right back to Kamehameha Avenue and the bayfront, and take a left to downtown on Kamehameha Avenue. Follow Kamehameha Av-

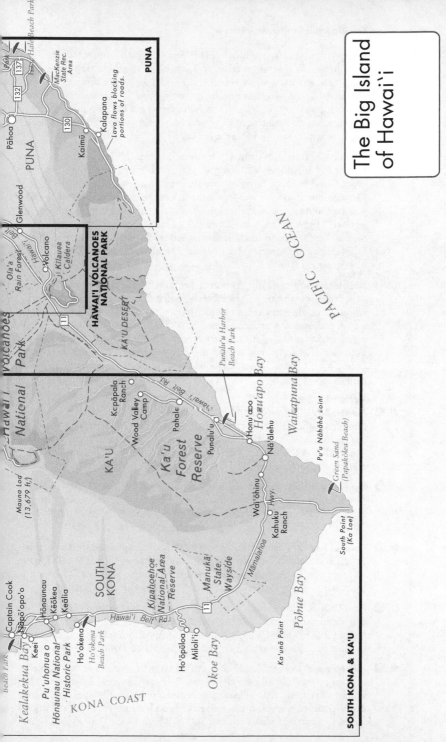

The Big Island of Hawai'i

enue as it passes along a block inland from the bayfront and winds into downtown. At the intersection of Kamehameha and Waiānuenue Avenue, turn left for a short ride to two popular sights a couple of miles outside town. When the road forks, after about a mile in a southwest direction, stay to the right to reach **Rainbow Falls** ⑭. Two miles farther up the road, also on the right, you'll come across the photogenic Boiling Pots at the base of **Pe'epe'e Falls** ⑮.

Drive back to the Bayfront Highway and take a right. It intersects with Highway 11, Kanoelehua Avenue, which takes you directly to the volcano. Close to Hilo, however, are three more attractions. On the right, just past mile marker 4, you'll pass the sign for **Pana'ewa Rain Forest Zoo** ⑯. Just five minutes up Stainback Highway, it's a great stop for children. Back on Highway 11, 5 to 6 mi south of Hilo, turn left when you reach the marker for **Mauna Loa Macadamia Factory** ⑰. On your return to Hilo, find serenity and tropical beauty at the **Nani Mau Gardens** ⑱ on Makalika Street off Route 11.

TIMING   Rain is inevitable in Hilo. Expect to get rained on here, as the 130 inches of annual precipitation are equally distributed throughout the year. Allow a full day to explore Hilo if you want to take in all the sights, less if you skip the museums and have little interest in shopping. Remember that morning hours are generally cooler for walking the streets than late afternoon, when the humidity can soar. It's definitely worth timing a visit for a Wednesday or Saturday, when the farmers' market is in full swing.

What to See

★ ⑩   **Banyan Drive.** The more than 50 leafy banyan trees with aerial roots dangling from their limbs were planted some 60 to 70 years ago by visiting celebrities. You'll find such names as Amelia Earhart and Franklin Delano Roosevelt on plaques on the trees. ⊠ *Begin at Hawai'i Naniloa Resort; 93 Banyan Dr.*

⑤   **Big Island Visitors Bureau.** Marked by a red-and-white Hawaiian-warrior sign, the bureau is worth a visit for brochures, maps, and up-to-date, friendly insider advice. ⊠ *250 Keawe St. (corner of Haili St.)* ☎ *808/961–5797* ⊕ *www.bigisland.org* ⊙ *Weekdays 8–4:30.*

★ ⑫   **Coconut Island.** This small (approximately 1 acre) island, just offshore from Lili'uokalani Gardens, was a place of healing in ancient times. Today children play in the tide pools while fisherfolk try their luck. The island is accessible via a footbridge. ⊠ *Lili'uokalani Gardens, Banyan Dr.*

③   **Haili Church.** This church was originally constructed in 1859 by New England missionaries, but the church steeple was rebuilt in 1979 following a fire. Haili Church is known for its choir, which sings hymns in Hawaiian during services. ⊠ *211 Haili St.* ☎ *808/935–4847.*

★ ⑨   **Hilo Farmers' Market.** An abundant and colorful market draws farmers and shoppers from all over the island. Two days a week, bright orchids, anthuriums, and birds-of-paradise create a feast for the eyes, while exotic vegetables, tropical fruits, and baked goods create a feast for the stomach. ⊠ *Mamo and Kamehameha Sts.* ⊙ *Wed. and Sat. 6:30 AM–2:30 PM.*

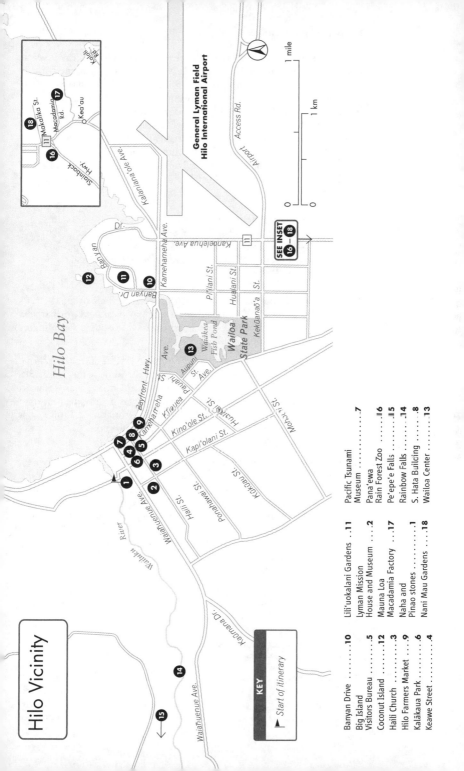

Hilo Vicinity

Hilo Bay

Waiākea River

Wailuku River

General Lyman Field
Hilo International Airport

0   1 km
0   1 mile

SEE INSET 16 — 18

KEY

▲ Start of itinerary

Banyan Drive **10**
Big Island
Visitors Bureau **5**
Coconut Island **12**
Haili Church **3**
Hilo Farmers Market . . . **9**
Kalākaua Park **6**
Keawe Street **4**

Lili'uokalani Gardens . . **11**
Lyman Mission
House and Museum . . . **2**
Mauna Loa
Macadamia Factory . . . **17**
Naha and
Pinao stones **1**
Nani Mau Gardens . . . **18**

Pacific Tsunami
Museum **7**
Pana'ewa
Rain Forest Zoo **16**
Pe'epe'e Falls **15**
Rainbow Falls **14**
S. Hata Building **8**
Wailoa Center **13**

6 Kalākaua Park. King Kalākaua, who revived the hula, was the inspiration for Hilo's Merrie Monarch Festival. The park is named in his honor. A bronze statue, sculpted in 1988, depicts the king with a taro leaf in his left hand to signify the Hawaiian peoples' bond with the land. In his right hand the king holds an *ipu*, a symbol of Hawaiian culture, chants, and hula. The park also features a huge spreading banyan tree and small fishponds, but no picnic or recreation facilities. In a local tradition, families that have held recent funerals for loved ones often set up leftover floral displays and funeral wreaths along the fishpond walkway as a way of honoring and celebrating the deceased. It makes for a unique and colorful display. ✉ *Kalākaua and Kino'ole Sts.*

need a break? For breads and sandwiches, mouthwatering apple pies, croissants, and biscotti, **O'Keefe & Sons Bread Bakers** (✉ 374 Kino'ole St. ☎ 808/934–9334) is the place to go. Their tiny retail shop is filled with specialties such as five-grain sourdough, banana bread, and cinnamon toast.

4 Keawe Street. Buildings here have been restored to their original 1920s and '30s plantation styles. Although most shopping is along Kamehameha Avenue, the ambience on Keawe Street offers a nostalgic sampling of Hilo as it might have been 80 years ago.

★ 11 Lili'uokalani Gardens. Fish-filled ponds, unique Japanese stone lanterns, half-moon bridges, pagodas, and a ceremonial teahouse make this 30-acre park a favorite Sunday destination for residents. It was designed to honor Hawai'i's first Japanese immigrants. The surrounding area used to be a busy residential neighborhood until a tsunami in 1960 swept the buildings away, taking the lives of 60 people in the process. ✉ *Banyan Dr. at Lihiwai St.* ☎ 808/961–8311.

2 Lyman Mission House and Museum. Built in 1839 by David and Sarah Lyman, Congregationalist missionaries, Lyman House is the oldest frame building on the island. In the adjacent museum, dedicated in 1973, the Earth Heritage Gallery includes a realistic magma chamber and displays the Earth's formation and the arrival of life, with a section on Hawaiian flora and fauna. You can view unique artifacts of Hawaiian and other major ethnic groups in the Island Heritage Gallery. The gift shop sells a map of the tsunami flows in the Hilo area. ✉ *276 Haili St.* ☎ *808/935–5021* ⊕ *www.lymanmuseum.org* 🎟 *$10* ☉ *Mon.–Sat. 9–4:30.*

★ 17 Mauna Loa Macadamia Factory. Acres of macadamia trees lead to a processing plant with viewing windows. A videotape depicts the harvesting and preparation of the nuts, and there are free samples in the visitor center. Children can run off their energy on the nature trail. Feel free to bring your own picnic lunch. ✉ *Macadamia Rd. off Hwy. 11, 5 mi south of Hilo* ☎ *808/966–8618* ⊕ *www.maunaloa.com* ☉ *Daily 8:30–5:30.*

▶ 1 Naha and Pinao stones. These two huge, oblong stones are legendary. The Pinao stone is purportedly an entrance pillar of an ancient temple built near the Wailuku River. Kamehameha I is said to have moved the 5,000-pound Naha stone when he was still in his teens. Legend decreed

IF TREES COULD TALK

THE HISTORY OF THE TREES lining Hilo's Banyan Drive is one of the Big Island's most interesting and least-known stories. Banyan Drive was named for these trees, which were planted by VIP visitors to Hilo. Altogether, some 50 or so banyans were planted between 1933 and 1972.

The majority are Chinese banyans, and each one is marked with a sign naming the VIP who planted it and the date on which it was planted. The first trees were planted on October 20, 1933, by a Hollywood group led by director Cecil B. DeMille, who was in Hilo making the film *Four Frightened People*. Soon after, on October 29, 1933, another banyan was planted by the one and only George Herman "Babe" Ruth, who was in town playing exhibition games.

President Franklin D. Roosevelt planted a tree on his visit to Hilo on July 25, 1934.

And in 1935, famed aviatrix Amelia Earhart put a banyan in the ground just days before she became the first person to fly solo across the Pacific Ocean.

Trees continued to be planted along Banyan Drive until World War II. The tradition was then revived in 1952 when a young and aspiring U.S. senator, Richard Nixon of California, planted a banyan tree. Nixon's tree was later toppled by a storm and was replanted by his wife, Pat, during a Hilo visit in 1972. On a bright, sunny day, strolling down Banyan Drive is like going through a green, shady tunnel. The banyans form a regal protective canopy over Hilo's own "Walk of Fame."

---

that he who did so would become king of all the islands. The building they're in front of is the Hilo Public Library. ⊠ *300 Waiānuenue Ave.*

★ ⑱ **Nani Mau Gardens.** Theme gardens (a Hawaiian garden and a palm garden among them) are spread over 20 acres, showcasing several varieties of fruit trees and hundreds of varieties of ginger, orchids, anthuriums, and other exotic plants. A botanical museum details the history of Hawaiian flora. Guided tours by tram are available. ⊠ *421 Makalika St., off Hwy. 11* ☎ *808/959–3500* ⊕ *www.nanimau.com* ✑ *$10, tram tour $15* ⊙ *Daily 8–5.*

★ ❼ **Pacific Tsunami Museum.** A memorial to all those who lost their lives in the tragedies that have struck this side of the island, this small museum offers a poignant history of tsunamis. In a 1931 C. W. Dickey-designed building—former home of the First Hawaiian Bank—you'll find an interactive computer center, a science room, a theater, a replica of Old Hilo Town, a *keiki* (children's) corner, and a knowledgeable, friendly staff. In the background, a striking quilt tells a silent story. ⊠ *130 Kamehameha Ave.* ☎ *808/935–0926* ⊕ *www.tsunami.org* ✑ *$7* ⊙ *Mon.–Sat. 9–4.*

 ⑯ **Pana'ewa Rain Forest Zoo.** Children enjoy the monkeys and the white tiger in this quiet, often wet zoo, which also hosts native Hawaiian species such as the state bird—the nēnē. It's the only rain-forest zoo in the United States. Trails have been paved, but you should take an umbrella for protection from the frequent showers. ⊠ *Stainback Hwy. off Hwy. 11* ☎ *808/959–7224* ⊕ *www.hilozoo.com* 🖾 *Free* ⊙ *Daily 9–4.*

⑮ Pe'epe'e Falls. Four separate streams fall into a series of circular pools, forming the Pe'epe'e Falls. The resulting turbulent action—best seen after a good rain when the water is high—has earned this stretch of the Wailuku River the name Boiling Pots. Caution! There is no swimming allowed in these pools due to extremely hazardous currents. ⊠ *3 mi northwest of Hilo on Waiānuenue Ave.; keep to the right when road splits and look for a green sign.*

★ ⑭ Rainbow Falls. After a Hilo rain, these falls thunder into Wailuku River gorge. If the sun peeks out in the morning hours, rainbows form above the mist. Caution! There is no swimming allowed anywhere in the Wailuku River due to dangerous currents and undertows. ⊠ *Take Waiānuenue Ave. west of town 1 mi; when road forks, stay on right of Waiānuenue Ave.; look for Hawaiian warrior sign.*

⑧ S. Hata Building. Erected as a general store in 1912 by Sadanosuke Hata and his family, this historic structure now houses shops, restaurants, and offices. During World War II the Hatas were interned and the building confiscated by the U.S. government. When the war was over, a daughter repurchased it for $100,000. A beautiful example of Renaissance-revival architecture, it won an award from the state for the authenticity of its restoration. ⊠ *308 Kamehameha Ave., at Mamo St.*

need a break? Wander inside the S. Hata Building and get a table at **Café Pesto** (⊠ 308 Kamehameha Ave. ☎ 808/969–6640 ⊕ www.cafepesto. com). Enjoy lunch or dinner from a menu of creative Italian fare including pastas, sandwiches, and the house special: wood-fired pizzas scented with native 'ōhi'a and guava hardwoods.

⑬ Wailoa Center. This circular exhibition center, adjacent to Wailoa State Park, has shows by local artists that change monthly. There's also a photographic exhibit of the 1946 and 1960 tidal waves. Just in front of the center is a 12-foot-high bronze statue of King Kamehameha I, made in Italy in the late 1980s. Check out his gold Roman sandals. ⊠ *Pi'opi'o St. off Kamehameha Ave.* ☎ *808/933–0416* ⊙ *Mon. and Tues., Thurs. and Fri. 8:30–4:30, Wed. noon–4:30, Sat. 9:30–3.*

PUNA

The Puna District includes the southeast section of the Big Island. It's an area of open lava lands, rugged coastline, quiet villages, and rain-forest slopes leading up to Hawai'i Volcanoes National Park, which straddles the Puna border. Before you head off to Hawai'i Volcanoes National Park, take some time to explore Puna, where farmers grow everything from orchids and anthuriums to papayas, bananas, and macadamia nuts; numerous farms and orchards are located throughout the Puna District. Several of the island's larger, rural residential subdivisions are located between Kea'au and Pāhoa, including Hawaiian Paradise Park, Orchidland Estates, Hawaiian Acres, Hawaiian Beaches, and others. Tide pools and natural springs dot the coastal area here.

a good drive

Heading out from Hilo, turn left at Kea'au—or take the new bypass road (Highway 130) just south of this little town—and drive about 11 mi; then take the turnoff to **Pāhoa** ⑲ ▶.

At the bypass intersection of Pāhoa, continue on Highway 132 in the direction of Kapoho. Take a break at **Lava Tree State Park** ⑳. Just south of the park entrance is the intersection of the highway and Pāhoa-Pohoiki Road. Continue southeast on Highway 132, passing papaya and orchid farms. As you near the coast, you'll pass through recent lava flows that cover the former town of Kapoho. The highway intersects with the coastal road, Highway 137, which turns south along the Kapoho–Opihikao coast, linking up with Highway 130 in the Kalapana area to complete the loop back to Pāhoa.

When it crosses Highway 137, Highway 132 terminates and becomes a gravel road that leads straight to the coast and **Cape Kumukahi Lighthouse** ㉑. After visiting the lighthouse, return to Highway 137 and go southwest along the coast, stopping for a dip in the pond at **Ahalanui Park** ㉒.

From Ahalanui Park, continue driving southwest along Highway 137. This proves to be a narrow winding coastal road with some magnificent views of rugged coastline, plus relaxing stops at **Isaac Hale Beach Park** ㉓, **MacKenzie State Recreation Area** ㉔, and **Kehena Beach** ㉕. After passing through the settlements of Pohoiki and Opihikao on the coast, the road links up with Highway 130 at the Kaimu-Kalapana area. This area marks the eastern expanse of lava flows of the early 1990s, which covered the Kalapana residential area and several fine black-sand beaches and parks. Take Highway 130 north back towards Pāhoa, stopping at **Star of the Sea Painted Church** ㉖, about a mile north of the intersection of Highways 130 and 137.

TIMING The Pāhoa to Kapoho and Kalapana coast drive is a loop that's about 25 mi long; driving times are from two to three hours, depending on the number of stops you make and the length of time at each stop.

What to See

㉒ **Ahalanui Park.** This park was established with a federal grant in the mid-1990s to replace parks lost to the lava flows at Kalapana. It's 2½ mi south of the intersection of Highways 132 and 137 on the Kapoho Coast, southeast of Pāhoa town. There is a half-acre pond fed by thermal freshwater springs mixed with seawater which makes for a relaxing warm-saltwater swim or soak. However, there have been recent reports of occasional bacterial contamination; the health department has been monitoring the situation. Check with on-duty lifeguards and follow any posted advisory signs. Facilities include portable rest rooms, outdoor showers, and picnic tables; no drinking water is available. ⊠ *Hwy. 137, Puna District.*

㉑ **Cape Kumukahi Lighthouse.** The lighthouse, 1½ mi east of the intersection of Highways 132 and 137, was miraculously unharmed during the

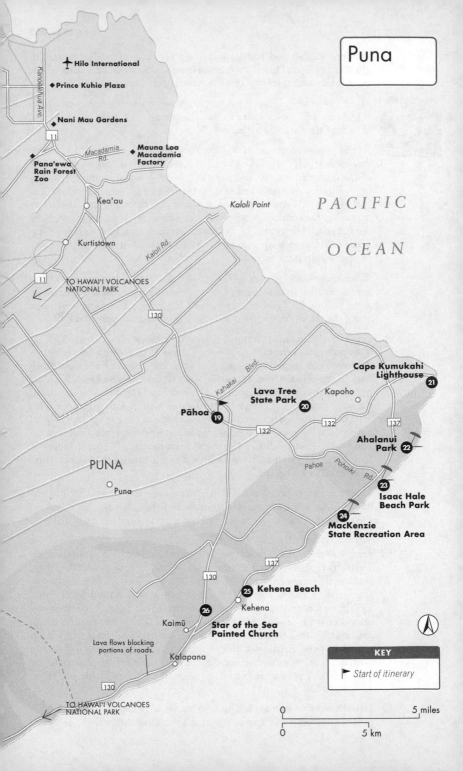

1960 volcano eruption here that destroyed the town of Kapoho. The lava flowed directly up to the lighthouse's base but instead of pushing it over, actually flowed around it. According to Hawaiian legend, Pele, the volcano goddess, protected the Hawaiian fisherfolk by sparing the lighthouse. The lighthouse itself is a simple metal frame structure with a light on top, similar to a tall electric line transmission tower. Seeing the hardened lava flows skirting directly around the lighthouse is worth the visit. ⊠ *Past the intersection of Hwys. 132 and 137, Kapoho.*

❷❸ **Isaac Hale Beach Park.** This beach park on Highway 137, south of Cape Kumukahi, has a busy boat-launching ramp used by local commercial fisherfolk. The bay is also used for water sports like body boarding, surfing, and swimming. The beach has small pebbles and rocks—no fine sand. The Pohoiki Warm Springs is a natural warm-water bathing pool behind the beach area. Rest rooms and showers are available. ⊠ *Hwy. 137, Puna District.*

❷❺ **Kehena Beach.** This is a nice black-sand crescent beach just off the highway; it's reached via a steep, rough trail down the cliff face. The beach is good for sunning, but swimming is dangerous due to strong currents. No facilities are available; there is a parking area at the Kehena Lookout. ⊠ *Hwy. 137, Puna District.*

❷⓪ **Lava Tree State Park.** Tree molds that rise like blackened smokestacks formed here in 1790 when a lava flow swept through the ʻōhiʻa forest. Some reach as high as 12 feet. The meandering trail provides close-up looks at some of Hawaii's tropical plants and trees. There are rest rooms and a couple of picnic pavilions and tables. Mosquitoes like to live here in abundance, so be sure to bring repellant. ⊠ *Hwy. 132, Puna District* ☎ 808/974–6200 ☞ *Free* ☉ *Daily 30 mins before sunrise–30 mins after sunset.*

❷❹ **MacKenzie State Recreation Area.** This is a coastal park located on rocky shoreline cliffs in a breezy, cool ironwood grove. There are picnic tables, rest rooms, and a tent-camping area; bring your own drinking water. The park is significant for the restored section of the old "King's Highway" trail system, which circled the island along the coast in the days before Hawaiʻi was discovered by the Western world. In those pre-Western-contact times, the Hawaiian tribal kings and chiefs used these trails to connect the coastal villages, allowing them to collect taxes and maintain control over the common people. Short hikes of an hour or less are possible along the existing sections of the rough rocky trail. There are views of rugged coast, rocky beach, and coastal dry forest. ⊠ *Hwy. 137, Puna District.*

❶⑨ **Pāhoa.** This little town still has wooden boardwalks and rickety buildings reminiscent of the Wild West. The secondhand stores, tie-dye clothing boutiques, and art galleries in quaint old buildings are fun to wander through. Pāhoa's main street boasts several island eateries including **Luquin's Mexican Restaurant, Paolo's Bistro** and **The Godmother.** ⊠ *Turn southeast onto Hwy. 130 at Keaʻau, drive 11 mi to right turn marked Pāhoa.*

★ ㉖ **Star of the Sea Painted Church.** This historic church, now a community center, was moved to its present location in 1990 just ahead of the advancing lava flow that destroyed the Kalapana area. The church, which dates from the 1930s, was built by a Belgian Catholic missionary priest, Father Everest Gielen, who also did the detailed paintings of religious scenes on the interior. The building has several lovely stained-glass windows. ⊠ *Hwy. 130, 1 mi north of Kalapana.*

HAWAI`I VOLCANOES NATIONAL PARK

The most popular attraction on the Big Island, Hawai`i Volcanoes National Park holds the active Kīlauea Volcano. The 359-square-mi park, established in 1916, provides an unmatched volcanic experience. The current eruption has been ongoing since January 3, 1983, primarily from a vent called Pu`u O`o. The lava flows are steady and slow, appearing and disappearing from view. Even when there is no fiery display or lava flowing, you'll have plenty to see in the park, which includes the summit caldera and the gently sloping northeast flank of 13,677-foot Mauna Loa volcano. With more than 150 mi of trails passing tree ferns, tropical plants such as *ohia lehua, ohelo berry,* and *pukeawe,* lava tubes, cinder cones, odd mineral formations, steam vents, and the vast barren craters along Chain of Craters Road, this is the ultimate ecotour. Don't forget to take a sweater (or a jacket in winter), as temperatures can get nippy at the park's 4,000-foot elevation. Also take a flashlight if you plan to visit the shoreline lava flow around sunset.

Before setting out on any hike in the eruption area, check with the park staff for the latest lava flow and eruption information. Be sure to follow all rules and posted signs and markers, stay on the marked trails, and don't wander off by yourself. The risk of injury from falling into a lava crack is real, as is the threat of becoming disoriented and lost due to volcanic fumes, smoke, and haze clouds.

Yellow, acrid-smelling sulfur banks and gaping vents emitting warm steam are found throughout the cool environs of the park. Pregnant women and anyone with heart or respiratory problems should avoid both the sulfur banks and the noxious fumes. The park and Chain of Craters Road are open 24 hours a day, but you must obtain a backcountry hiker's permit to remain in the park area overnight. Admission is $10 per car for seven days.

a good tour

From Hilo take Highway 11, Kanoelehua Avenue, which takes you directly to the park, 30 mi to the southwest. The drive is uphill all the way, through the towns of Kurtistown, Mountain View, and Volcano. **Dan Deluz Woods** ㉗ ►, just past mile marker 12, is a perfect place to buy handmade hardwood crafts. Just ½ mi past mile marker 22 you'll find **Akatsuka Orchid Gardens** ㉘.

About 1½ mi west past the turnoff to Volcano Village is the entrance sign to the park. Stop first at the **Kīlauea Visitor Center** ㉙ to get the latest information on volcanic activity and hiking trails. Across the street is **Volcano House** ㉚.

You can drive the crater's circumference via the 11-mi **Crater Rim Drive** ㉛. Scenic stops include the yellow, acrid-smelling sulfur banks; steam vents; and the park's **Thomas A. Jaggar Museum** ㉜, on the edge of Kīlauea Caldera. You'll find several easy walks along the way: Halema'uma'u Overlook (a 10-minute walk), Devastation Trail (30 minutes), and Thurston Lava Tube (20 minutes).

If you have time, drive from the center of the park down **Chain of Craters Road** ㉝. A sign midway down on the left marks a trail across the lava to **Pu'u Loa Petroglyphs** ㉞, a field of lava etchings left by early Hawaiians. It's about a 25-minute walk to the petroglyph field.

Chain of Craters Road stops abruptly after about 22 mi. Turn around and head back, making one last stop in the park at **Volcano Art Center** ㉟. Exiting the park, turn left onto Highway 11, then take a right at the first crossroads toward the Volcano Golf & Country Club. Less than a mile beyond the club you'll find the **Volcano Winery** ㊱.

Back on Highway 11 drive southwest to the next right and turn onto Mauna Loa Road. You'll see a sign marked TREE MOLDS. Each chimneylike formation was created when molten lava hardened around a tree, burning it away in the process. About 2 mi in, you can take a self-guided mile-long walk around **Kīpuka Puaulu** ㊲.

Head back toward Hilo via the Old Volcano Highway, which passes through Volcano Village before linking back up with Highway 11.

TIMING Open daily, this is a national park, ideal for families and therefore busier during the summer months, holidays, and weekends. Count on spending at least three-quarters of a day at the park, and keep in mind that a round-trip from Kona or the resorts takes four to six hours. You may want to plan an overnight stay at one of the charming B&Bs tucked into the fern forest.

It'll take you about 45 minutes to drive the distance from Hilo to the park. Allow two hours for the trip up and back down the 22 mi of the Chain of Craters Road. Check with park staff on the latest lava-flow viewing conditions and accessibility. You may need to allow two or three extra hours to walk to any active lava-flow sites.

What to See

㉘ **Akatsuka Orchid Gardens.** This is one of the largest collections of orchids in Hawai'i. The greenhouse includes a covered garden where you can take a self-guided tour and enjoy the beauty of hundreds of orchids and exotic tropical flowers. The cool Volcano climate provides the ideal conditions for orchid cultivation. The floral shop sells orchid plants and cut flowers and can pack and ship to anywhere in the world. ⌑ *Hwy. 11, just past mile marker 22, Volcano* ☎ *808/967–8234, toll-free 888-967–6669,* ⊕ *www.akatsukaorchid.com* ⌑ *Free* ☉ *Daily 8:30–5.*

★ ㉝ **Chain of Craters Road.** No food, water, or gasoline is available along this road, which descends 3,700 feet in 22 mi to the Kalapana Coast. You'll pass barren lava deserts and thick 'ōhi'a forests, which are quite stirring when in full blossom. At road's end (where a portable ranger's in-

formation booth and portable toilets are usually available), you may be able to walk to where the lava flows into the ocean; ask at the Kīlauea Visitor Center before starting out, but be forewarned: It's a long, hot trek, often over very difficult and dangerous terrain, and there are limited or no facilities. ⊠ *Begins in Hawai'i Volcanoes National Park.*

★ ㉛ **Crater Rim Drive.** This scenic 11-mi drive provides panoramic vistas of the national park's vast lava deserts, steaming craters, and forests. Start from the visitor center and drive southwest past the sulfur banks and turn off to the overlook for Kīlauea Caldera at the Thomas A. Jaggar Museum. The museum features natural history and scientific displays on the volcano. The overlook provides a panoramic view of Kīlauea Caldera. From the museum, continue the drive across a huge, open lava desert and old lava flows to a turnout to view Halema'uma'u Crater. It's a ¼-mi hike from the road to the crater overlook. The drive continues past other craters into the forest, past Devastation Trail, Thurston Lava Tube, and Kīlauea Iki Crater, before coming full circle back at the visitor center.

⚑ ㉗ **Dan Deluz Woods.** This country craftshop is the place to stop for hand-made native Hawaiian hardwood crafts. The shop features fine wood-work crafts including bowls, carvings, picture frames, furniture, jewelry and jewelry boxes, and a variety of accessory items made from koa, monkeypod, mango, kiawe, and other fine local hardwoods. Dan's wife, Mary Lou, operates the Koa Shop Kaffee restaurant next to the woodshop. ⊠ *17-4003 Ahuahu Pl. (Hwy. 11), at mile marker 12, Mountain View* ☎ *808/968–6607* ☉ *Daily 9–5.*

Devastation Trail. This trail was created after a 1959 eruption, when fiery lava from the adjacent Kīlauea Iki Crater burned the surrounding 'ohi'a forest. The 30-minute walk on a paved path off Crater Rim Drive is self-guided and gives visitors a close-up look at the lava-cindered forest with hundreds of stark tree skeletons protruding from the mounds of volcanic cinders and pumice. It's like a walk through an eerie abstract painting.

Kīlauea Caldera. Halema'uma'u Crater is the steaming pit within this gaping caldera in the national park. You can hike around or into the crater. Trails leading from the visitor center and the Volcano House Hotel on the rim crisscross the caldera and link up with other park trails. You can also drive around the crater's 11-mi circumference to **Halema'uma'u Overlook** for another view of the crater.

> **need a break?** For a decent meal, a drink, or Internet access, head to **Lava Rock Café** (⊠ Old Volcano Hwy., behind Kīlauea General Store ☎ 808/967–8526), which serves breakfast and lunch daily and dinner Tuesday through Saturday in a breezy, pinewood-lattice setting. You'll find a variety of dishes, from chicken salad to New York steak, cappuccino to wine.

Kīlauea Iki Crater. If you're in the park for a full day or more, you could venture on an exhilarating hike into Kīlauea Iki (*iki* means little). It takes less than a half day, but get information and maps first at the Kīlauea Visitor Center. On the 4-mi loop you'll descend 400 feet through rain forest and cross the crater floor. A 20-minute walk will take you 450 feet into **Thurston Lava Tube,** a natural tunnel about 10 feet high that formed when the cooling top and sides of a lava flow hardened and the lava inside drained away.

29 Kīlauea Visitor Center. The visitor center lies just beyond the park's entry booth. You can learn about park wildlife and vegetation and get updates on the flow. If you can't see a real eruption, don't miss the movie shown on the hour from 9 to 4. Hikers can obtain information about trails, ranger-escorted scenic walks, and camping permits at the center. ⊠ *Hawai'i Volcanoes National Park, Volcano 96785* ☎ *808/985–6010* ⊕ *www.nps.gov/havo* ⊙ *Daily 7:45–5.*

★ ☺ **37 Kīpuka Puaulu.** A *kīpuka* is a forested island surrounded by a sea of lava. This unique and diverse 100-acre mesic forest is also known as Bird Park, although its real beauty lies in its rare flora. Native birds, such as the 'apapane and the 'elepaio, call from their hiding places in the thick canopy. A written guide is available at the Kīlauea Visitor Center in Hawai'i Volcanoes National Park. ⊠ *Hawai'i Volcanoes National Park, Mauna Loa Rd.*

34 Pu'u Loa Petroglyphs. It's a 25-minute walk across the lava to this spot where etchings of people, boats, and animals made by early Hawaiians are spread over a vast area of black lava. The round depressions are thought to be *piko* holes, where umbilical cords of newborns were buried. ⊠ *Hawai'i Volcanoes National Park, Chain of Craters Rd., on left past mile marker 16.*

☺ **32 Thomas A. Jaggar Museum.** Children can enjoy hands-on fun at this free museum at the edge of Kīlauea Caldera. Seismographs that measure the Earth's movement will also record a child's footfall. Fascinating film-strips document current and previous eruptions. ⊠ *Crater Rim Dr., Volcano* ☎ *808/985–6010* ⬚ *Free* ⊙ *Daily 8:30–5.*

★ **35 Volcano Art Center.** This celebrated gallery displays the work of Big Island photographers, artists, and craftspeople. The building was originally constructed in 1877 to be the Volcano House (the current Volcano House is across the street), replacing a thatch-roof hut built in 1846. ⊠ *Hawai'i Volcanoes National Park, Crater Rim Dr., Volcano 96785* ☎ *808/967–7565* ⊕ *www.volcanoartcenter.org* ⊙ *Daily 9–5.*

30 Volcano House. This old lodge, with its huge stone fireplace, 42 rooms, the Ka 'Ōhelo Dining Room, and a snack bar, dates from 1941. The windows in the dining room overlook Kīlauea, and, in the center of the caldera, you'll see Halema'uma'u Crater. The dining room is busy with tour groups for the buffet lunch, but dinner can be a quieter experience. ⊠ *Hawai'i Volcanoes National Park, Crater Rim Dr.* ☎ *808/967–7321* ⊕ *www.nps.gov/havo/pphtml/lodging.html.*

★ **36 Volcano Winery.** Have a tasting and shop at this unusual winery, which creates white table wines from Symphony grapes grown nearby. Also offered are honey wines, a red Pele Delight, Guava or Passion Chablis, and Volcano Blush. Experiments with traditional varietals such as pinot noir are underway. ⊠ *35 Pi'imauna Dr., Volcano 96785* ☎ *808/967–7772* ⊕ *www.volcanowinery.com* ⊙ *Daily 10–5:30.*

need a break? Coffee and a steaming bowl of saimin (ramen noodle soup) at **Volcano Golf & Country Club Restaurant** (✉ Volcano Golf & Country Club, 35 Pi'imauna Dr., Volcano ☎ 808/967–8228) can be a soul-saving meal on a cool, wet day.

HĀMĀKUA COAST

The Hilo–Hāmākua Heritage Coast leads past green cliffs and gorges, jungle vegetation, open emerald fields, and stunning ocean scenery along Highway 19, which runs north-northwest from Hilo. Brown signs featuring a sugarcane tassel point out this area's history: thousands of acres of sugar land are now idle, as the area's sugar mills all went out of business by the late 1990s. "King Sugar," which once dominated daily life here, is no longer the economic backbone of the Hāmākua Coast community. The 45-mi drive winds through little plantation towns— Pāpa'ikou, Laupāhoehoe, and Pa'auilo among them. It veers to the right at Honoka'a, taking you to the end of the road bordering Waipi'o Valley. The isolated valley floor has maintained the ways of old Hawai'i, with taro patches, wild horses, and a handful of houses. This is a great drive if you're on your way from Hilo to one of the resorts along the Kohala Coast. To Kailua-Kona, count on a total of 95 mi via this shorter of the two coastal routes from Hilo.

a good drive Seven miles north of Hilo, turn right off Highway 19 onto a 4-mi scenic drive to reach **Hawai'i Tropical Botanical Garden** ❸ ►. After the scenic drive rejoins Highway 19, turn left toward **Honomū** ❸. At Honomū, travel 4 mi inland to **'Akaka Falls State Park** ❹. Continue north on Highway 19 and stop at **Kolekole Beach Park** ❹: it's a nice place for a picnic, and it has facilities. Keep heading north on Highway 19 and turn left to visit the 300-acre, still-growing **World Botanical Gardens** ❹. From here you'll see stunning views of triple-tiered Umauma Falls, one of the prettiest waterfalls on the isle.

Continue north on Highway 19 and enjoy the ride through sleepy little villages with music in their names: Wailea, Hakalau, Ni'nole, Pāpa'aloa, and Laupāhoehoe. The **Laupāhoehoe Train Museum** ❹ takes you back to the time when sugar reigned along the Hāmākua Coast.

Just beyond the museum is **Laupāhoehoe Point Park** ❹, which is good for fishing but not swimming. About 13 mi farther inland, hikers will enjoy the nature walk through the cool upland forest of **Kalōpā State Park** ❹.

Next, you'll reach the turnoff to **Honoka'a** ❹. Secondhand and antiques stores, with dusty dishes, fabrics, and crafts, line Honoka'a's main street along with a few cafés and island-style eateries.

Just before the road (Route 240) ends, 8 mi beyond Honoka'a, a sign directs you to the right to Kukuihaele, a small, quiet plantation village on a coastal loop with no name. Here, at the Last Chance building and Waipi'o Valley Artworks gallery, you can make arrangements for tours to explore the 6-mi-deep Waipi'o Valley. The once heavily populated valley is a tropical Eden bounded by 2,000-foot cliffs. There are spectac-

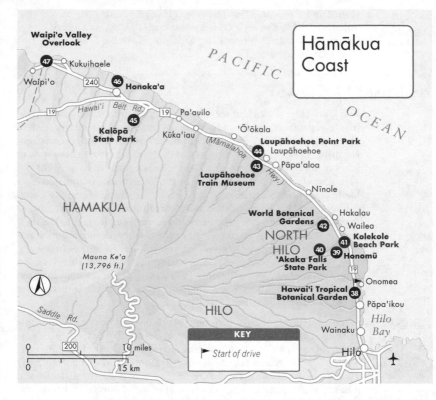

ular views of the valley and coast from the **Waipi'o Valley Overlook** ㊼, located at the very end of Route 240.

TIMING If you've stopped to explore the quiet little villages with wooden board-walks and dogs dozing in backyards, or if you've spent several hours in Waipi'o Valley, night will undoubtedly be falling by the time you complete this journey. Don't worry: the return to Hilo via Highway 19 only takes about an hour, or you can continue on the same road to stop for dinner in Waimea (30 minutes) and head to the Kohala Coast resorts (another 25 to 45 minutes).

What to See

★ ㊵ **'Akaka Falls State Park.** A meandering 20-minute loop trail takes you to the best spots to see the two falls, **'Akaka** and **Kahuna.** The 400-foot Kahuna Falls is on the lower end of the trail. The majestic upper 'Akaka Falls drops more than 442 feet, tumbling far below into a pool drained by Kolekole Stream amid a profusion of fragrant white, yellow, and red torch ginger. ✉ *4 mi inland off Hwy. 19, near Honomū* ☎ *808/974–6200* 💲 *Free* ⊙ *Daily 7–7.*

▸ ★ ㊳ **Hawai'i Tropical Botanical Garden.** Eight miles north of Hilo, stunning coastline views appear around each curve of the 4-mi scenic jungle drive that accesses the privately owned, nonprofit, 17-acre nature preserve beside Onomea Bay. Paved pathways lead past waterfalls, ponds, and more than 2,000 species of plants and flowers, including palms, bromeliads, ginger, heleconia, orchids, and ornamentals. ⊠ *27-717 Old Māmalahoa Hwy., Pāpaʻikou* ☎ *808/964–5233* ⊕ *www.hawaiigarden. com* ⊡ *$15* ⊘ *Daily 9–4.*

46 Honokaʻa. In 1881, Australian William Purvis planted the first macadamia-nut trees in Hawaiʻi in what is now this funky little town. But the macadamia-nut-processing factory has long since closed. Honokaʻa's true heyday came when sugar thrived, in the early and mid-1900s. During World War II, this was also the place for soldiers stationed around Waimea to cut loose. Its historic buildings are home today to little eateries and stores crammed with knickknacks, secondhand goods, and antiques. ⊠ *Mamane St. (Hwy. 240).*

need a break? A quick stop at **Tex Drive-In** (⊠ 45-690 Pakalana St. and Hwy. 19 ☎ 808/775–0598) will give you a chance to taste the snack it is famous for: *malasada,* a puffy, doughy Portuguese doughnut (sans hole), deep-fried and rolled in sugar and best eaten hot. They also come in cream-filled versions, including vanilla, chocolate, and coconut. For mouthwatering pastries and a strong espresso in Honokaʻa, stop in at **Mamane Street Bakery** (⊠ Mamane St. ☎ 808/775–9478), where residents from as far as Waimea and Hilo gladly shop. **Café il Mondo** (⊠ 45-3626 Mamane St. ☎ 808/775–7711) serves stone oven–baked pizzas and calzones until 9 PM.

39 Honomū. A plantation past is reflected in the wooden boardwalks and tin-roof buildings of this small, struggling town. It's fun to poke through old, dusty shops such as Glass from the Past, where you'll find an assortment of old bottles. The Woodshop Gallery/Café showcases fine local art. ⊠ *2 mi inland from Hwy. 19 en route to ʻAkaka Falls State Park.*

★ ☙ **45 Kalōpā State Park.** Past the old plantation town of Paʻauilo, at a cool elevation of 2,000 feet, lies this 100-acre state park. There is a lush forested area with picnic tables and rest rooms, and an easy ¾-mi loop trail with additional paths in the adjacent forest reserve. Small signs identify some of the plants. Cabins are available. ⊠ *12 mi north of Laupāhoehoe and 3 mi inland off Hwy. 19* ☎ *808/775–8852* ⊡ *Free* ⊘ *Daily 7–7 or by permit.*

41 Kolekole Beach Park. This rocky beach at the mouth of the Kolekole River is not safe for inexperienced swimmers, but when the river runs low, it might just make for a chilly, refreshing dip. Facilities at the park include rest rooms, barbecue pits, and covered picnic areas. A scenic drive takes you from the top of the park through the old town of Wailea back to Highway 19. ⊠ *Off Hwy. 19* ☎ *808/961–8311* ⊡ *Free* ⊘ *Daily 7 AM–sunset.*

44 Laupāhoehoe Point Park. Come here to watch the surf pound the jagged black rocks at the base of the stunning point, but remember that this is not a safe place for swimming. Still vivid in the minds of longtime area residents is the 1946 tragedy in which 21 schoolchildren and three teachers were swept to sea by a tidal wave. The park has bathrooms, picnic tables, and stone barbecue pits. ⊠ *On northeast coastline, Hwy. 19, makai side, north of Laupāhoehoe* ☏ *808/961–8311* ✉ *Free* ☉ *Daily 7 AM–sunset.*

㊸ Laupāhoehoe Train Museum. Behind the stone loading platform of the once-famous Hilo Railroad, constructed around the turn of the 20th century, the former manager's house is a poignant display of the era when sugar was king. The railroad, one of the most expensive built in its time, was washed away by the tidal wave of 1946. Today, one of the old engines is running again on a short Y-track at the museum. ⊠ *Hwy. 19, Laupāhoehoe, mauka side* ☏ *808/962–6300* ✉ *$3* ☉ *Weekdays 9–4:30, weekends 10–2.*

Fodor'sChoice **Mauna Kea.** Mauna Kea is the antithesis of the typical island experience.
★ Freezing temperatures and arctic conditions are common at the summit, and snowstorms can occur year-round. It's also home to Lake Waiau, one of the highest lakes in the world. The summit—at 13,796 feet—is reputedly the clearest place in the world for viewing the night sky; it's also an outstanding place to see the sun rise and set. If you're driving to the summit on your own, stop in first at the **Onizuka Center for International Astronomy Visitor Information Station** (☏ 808/961–2180 ⊕ www.ifa. hawaii.edu/info/vis), at a 9,300-foot elevation, open from 9 AM to 10 PM daily. (Technically it can be reached in a standard automobile, but you'll need four-wheel drive to get to the summit.) To reach this station from Hilo, which is about 34 mi away, take Highway 200 (Saddle Road), and turn right at mile marker 28 onto the John A. Burns Way which is the access road to the summit. The observatory patio here is the best amateur observation site on Earth, with three telescopes and a knowledgeable staff, so you might not need to go farther. However, free summit tours are also available at the center. Whether you're hiking or driving to the summit, take the change in altitude seriously—don't overexert yourself, especially at the top. Note that scuba divers must wait at least 24 hours before attempting a trip to the summit to avoid getting the bends.

off the beaten path **WAIPI'O VALLEY –** Though completely off the grid today, Waipi'o was once the center of Hawaiian life; somewhere between 4,000 and 20,000 people made it their home between the 13th and 17th centuries. In 1780, Kamehameha I was singled out here as a future ruler by reigning chiefs. In 1791 he fought Kahekili in his first naval battle at the mouth of the valley. In 1823, the first white visitors found 1,500 people living in this Eden-like environment amid fruit trees, banana patches, taro fields, and fishponds. The 1946 tidal wave drove most residents to higher ground. Now, as then, waterfalls frame the landscape, but the valley has become one of the most isolated places in the state. To preserve this pristine part of the island, commercial transportation permits are limited—only four outfits offer organized valley trips—and Sunday the valley rests. The walk down into the valley is less than a mile—start at the four-wheel-drive road leading down from the lookout point—but keep in mind, the climb back up is strenuous in the hot sun.

★ **47** **Waipiʻo Valley Overlook.** Bounded by 2,000-foot cliffs, the Valley of the Kings—Waipiʻo—was once a favorite retreat of Hawaiian royalty. Waterfalls drop 1,200 feet from the Kohala Mountains to the valley floor. Sheer cliffs make access difficult. Only four-wheel-drive vehicles should attempt the steep road from the overlook. A handful of families still cultivate taro in the pastoral valley, a few residents find refuge here, and horses roam narrow trails and rocky streams. A crescent of black sand makes it a popular spot for surfers, but the beach is not safe for swimming due to strong currents and undertows. Caution! Continued overuse of the beach area and lack of sanitary facilities have caused serious unhealthy conditions to persist since mid-2003 at Waipiʻo's beach. Landowners and government officials are working to resolve the problem. ⊠ *Follow Hwy. 240 8 mi northwest of Honokaʻa.*

42 **World Botanical Gardens.** About 300 acres of former sugarcane land are slowly giving way to a botanical center, which includes native Hawaiian plants such as orchids, palms, gingers, hibiscus, heliconias, and more. In the 10-acre arboretum children love to wind their way through a maze of 5-foot shrubs. From within the gardens you have access to splendid views of one of the prettiest waterfalls on the isle, triple-tiered **Umauma Falls.** ⊠ *Hwy. 19, from Hilo just past mile marker 16* ☎ *808/ 963–5427* ⊕ *www.wbgi.com* ⊠ *$8* ☉ *Mon.–Sat. 9–5:30.*

KAILUA-KONA

The touristy seaside village of Kailua-Kona, at the base of the 8,271-foot Mt. Hualalai, has many historic sites tucked among the open-air shops and restaurants that line Aliʻi Drive, its main oceanfront street. This is where King Kamehameha I died in 1819 and where his successor, Liholiho, broke the *kapu* (taboo) system, a rigid set of laws that had provided the framework for Hawaiian government. The following year, on April 4, 1820, the first Christian missionaries from New England came ashore at Kailua-Kona.

The easiest place to park your car (fee $3) is at King Kamehameha's Kona Beach Hotel. Some free parking is available: when you enter Kailua via Palani Road (Highway 190), turn left onto Kuakini Highway; drive for a half block, and turn right (into the small marked parking lot). Walk makai on Likana Lane a half block to Aliʻi Drive and you'll be in the heart of Kailua-Kona town.

a good walk

This ½-mi walk follows Aliʻi Drive south. Begin at **King Kamehameha's Kona Beach Hotel 48** ➤ at the northern end of town. The hotel, which borders the last residency of King Kamehameha I, **Kamakahonu 49**, offers free tours of a replica of the king's temple, Ahuʻena Heiau. You can also wander around the two stone platforms at the ocean's edge to view the site on your own. Next, investigate **Kailua Pier 50**. Walk a short distance and take in **Huliheʻe Palace 51**, on your right, and **Mokuʻaikaua Church 52**, on your left. Tackle a plethora of shops in the block-long **Kona Inn Shopping Village 53**. End your walk at **St. Michael's Church 54**, on your left, across the street from the wooden restaurant complex known as Waterfront Row, or continue another block past the Ali'i Sunset Plaza to the Coconut Grove Marketplace.

If you have a car, return to it to complete your historical tour; drive to the end of Ali'i Drive past Disappearing Sands Beach Park, the tiny blue-and-white St. Peter's Catholic Church, the ruins of a heiau, and Kahalu'u Beach Park. There, a jagged lava lake on the edge of a bay outlines the **Kuamo'o Battlefield and Lekeleke Burial Grounds** 55.

TIMING You can walk the whole ½-mi length of "downtown" Kailua-Kona and back again in an hour, or else spend an entire day here, taking time to browse in the shops, do the historical tours, and have lunch. The drive to the Kuamo'o Battlefield and Lekeleke Burial Grounds takes less than 10 minutes. If you want to know more about Kailua's fascinating past, arrange for a guided tour by the Kona Historical Society.

Kailua-Kona enjoys year-round sunshine—except for the rare deluge. Mornings offer cooler weather, smaller crowds, and more birds singing in the banyan trees, but afternoon outings are great for cool drinks while gazing out over the ocean.

What to See

off the beaten path

ASTRONAUT ELLISON S. ONIZUKA SPACE CENTER – This informative museum 7 mi north of Kailua-Kona, at the airport, was opened as a tribute to Hawai'i's first astronaut, who was killed in the 1986 *Challenger* disaster. The space center has computer-interactive exhibits. You can launch a miniature rocket and rendezvous with an object in space, feel the effects of gyroscopic stabilization, participate in hands-on science activities, and view educational films. ⊠ *Keāhole–Kona International Airport, Kailua-Kona* ☎ *808/329–3441* ⊕ *www.planet-hawaii.com/astronautonizuka* 🎫 *$3* ⊙ *Daily 8:30–4:30.*

★ 51 **Hulihe'e Palace.** Fronted by a wrought-iron gate decorated with the royal crest, Hulihe'e Palace is one of only three royal palaces in America. The two-story residence was built of lava, coral, koa wood, and 'ōhi'a timber in 1838 by the island's governor, John Adams Kuakini, a year after he completed Moku'aikaua Church. During the 1880s it served as King David Kalākaua's summer palace. The oversize doors and koa-wood furniture bear witness to the size of some of the Hawaiian people. On weekday afternoons hula schools rehearse on the grounds. ⊠ *75-5718 Ali'i Dr.* ☎ *808/329–1877* ⊕ *www.huliheepalace.org* 🎫 *$5* ⊙ *Weekdays 9–4, weekends 10–4.*

50 **Kailua Pier.** Though most fisherfolk use Honokōhau Harbor, north of Kailua-Kona, Kailua Pier, built in 1918, is still a hub of ocean activity. Outrigger canoe teams practice, and tour boats depart. Each October close to 1,500 international athletes swim 2.4 mi from the pier to begin the grueling Ironman Triathlon competition.

Along the **seawall** fisherfolk and children daily cast their lines. For youngsters, a bamboo pole and hook are easy to come by, and plenty of locals are willing to give pointers. ⊠ *Next to King Kamehameha's*

Kona Beach Hotel; the seawall is between Kailua Pier and Hulihe'e Palace on Ali'i Dr.

★ ❹❾ **Kamakahonu.** King Kamehameha I chose to spend his last years, from 1812 until his death in 1819, in this area, just outside what is now King Kamehameha's Kona Beach Hotel, adjacent to the little beach and lagoon. Part of what was once a 4-acre homestead complete with several houses and religious sites has been swallowed by Kailua Pier, but a replica of the temple, **Ahu'ena Heiau,** keeps history alive. Free tours start from King Kamehameha's Kona Beach Hotel. ✉ *75-5660 Palani Rd.* ☎ *808/ 329–2911* 💲 *Free* ☺ *Tours weekdays at 1:30.*

⚑ ❹❽ **King Kamehameha's Kona Beach Hotel.** Stroll through the high-ceiling lobby of this Kailua-Kona fixture, built in the mid-'70s, to view displays of Hawaiian artifacts and mounted marlin from Hawaiian International Billfish tournaments (from when Kailua Pier was still the weigh-in point). One tournament winner, a marlin that weighed in at 1,062 pounds, hangs on a wall. An even larger, 1,166-pound record-setter is a floor display. These "granders," marlin weighing 1,000 pounds or more, are the big attraction for Kona fisherfolk. Classes in Hawaiian arts and crafts take place regularly. ✉ *75-5660 Palani Rd.* ☎ *808/329–2911, toll-free 800/367–6060* ⊕ *www.konabeachhotel.com.*

KONA BREWING COMPANY & BREWPUB – A few blocks mauka of King Kamehameha's Kona Beach Hotel, Kona Brewing Company offers thirst-quenching tours and tastings. Its wheat ale, flavored with liliko'i, is a staple of the pub here, which is eclectic in its architecture, with a koa-wood bar, driftwood benches, and a historic tin roof. The pub uses local and organic produce for its pizzas. For nondrinkers, an exquisite sparkling ginger ale hits the spot. ⊠ *North Kona Shopping Center, 75-5629 Kuakini Hwy.* ☎ *808/334–2739* ⊕ *www. konabrewingco.com* ⊙ *Mon.–Thurs. 11–10, Fri. and Sat. 11–11, Sun. 4–10.*

53 Kona Inn Shopping Village. This shopping arcade, fronting Kailua Bay, was once the Kona Inn, a hotel built in 1928 to attract a new wave of wealthy travelers. As new vacation condos and resorts opened along the Kona and Kohala coasts, the old Kona Inn lost much of its appeal and finally closed in 1976. The former hotel was renovated into a shopping complex with dozens of clothing boutiques, art stores, gift shops, and island-style eateries. Prior to the construction of the inn, the personal heiau of King Liholiho was on this shore. Today, shops and restaurants line the boardwalk. Broad lawns with coconut trees on the ocean side are lovely for afternoon picnics. ⊠ *75-5744 Ali'i Dr.*

While visiting the Kona Inn Shopping Center, enjoy a break on the lānai and relax with a cup of Kona's famed brew. Sample some 100% pure Kona coffee at the **Kona Coffee Café** (⊠ 75-5744 Ali'i Dr. ☎ 808/329–7131). If it's late afternoon, it's time to imbibe a tropical libation and unwind from the day's events. For cocktails at sunset head to the **Kona Inn Restaurant** (⊠ 75-5744 Ali'i Dr. ☎ 808/329–4455), a traditional favorite.

55 Kuamo'o Battlefield and Lekeleke Burial Grounds. In 1819, an estimated 300 Hawaiians were killed on this vast, desolate black-lava field now filled with terraced graves. After the death of his father, King Kamehameha I, Liholiho became king; shortly thereafter King Liholiho ate at the table of women, thereby breaking an ancient kapu. Chief Kekuaokalani, vying for the throne and with radically different views about traditions and religion, unsuccessfully challenged King Liholiho in battle. In breaking the ancient kapu, Liholiho forced a final battle not just between him and his opponent but, more importantly, between traditional and new religious beliefs in Hawai'i. ⊠ *South end of Ali'i Dr.*

★ **52 Moku'aikaua Church.** The earliest Christian church on the Islands was founded here as a thatch hut by Hawai'i's first missionaries in 1820. The present incarnation of the church was built in 1836 with black stone from an abandoned heiau. The stone was mortared with white coral and topped by an impressive steeple. Inside, at the back, behind a panel of gleaming koa wood, is a model of the brig *Thaddeus.* ⊠ *75-5713 Ali'i Dr.* ☎ *808/329–0655.*

54 St. Michael's Church. The site of the first Catholic church built in Kona, in 1840, is marked by a small thatch structure to the left of the present

(handwritten margin notes: Kaiwa pawai / right after Firestone)

church, which dates from 1850. In front of the church a coral grotto shrine holds 2,500 coral heads, harvested in 1940, when preservation was not yet an issue. ⊠ *75-5769 Ali'i Dr.* ☎ *808/326–7771.*

need a break? **Island Lava Java** (⊠ 75-5799 Ali'i Dr. ☎ 808/327–2161), in the Ali' Sunset Plaza, a popular, laid-back café, has live light jazz Friday and Saturday evenings, and oldies music in the mornings. Sip a cappuccino, munch on oven-fresh pastries, or sample the salad bar. Locals hang out here to read the paper, play board games, or just watch the surf.

SOUTH KONA & KA'U

South of Kailua-Kona, Highway 11 hugs splendid coastlines, leaving busy streets behind. Cradled against the slopes of Mauna Loa, coffee plantations alternate with arid landscapes in the surreal emptiness of the most southern part of the United States. The 50-mi drive to windswept South Point, where the first Polynesians came ashore as early as AD 750, passes a national historic park, Pu'uhonua O Hōnaunau, the only remaining Hawaiian place of refuge, as well as a whimsically painted church. Below the highway shimmers Kealakekua Bay, where Captain James Cook arrived in 1778, bringing radical change to Hawai'i. Narrow, steep roads off the main highway lead to isolated fishing towns where life unfolds far removed from the modern world. To the east of Highway 11, an 11,000-acre development overgrown with ohelo berries, Ocean View Estates, testifies to the struggle it takes to survive in this land crisscrossed by lava flows. Mark Twain, however, wrote some of his finest prose in the southerly Ka'u district, and macadamia-nut farms, fine beaches, and tiny villages offer as-yet largely undiscovered beauty.

a good drive From Kailua-Kona, drive south on Highway 11, also known as Hawai'i Belt Road or Māmalahoa Highway, to historic **Kainaliu** ㊱ ㆑. Just outside the town, on your right, you'll find the **Greenwell Site** ㊲, now headquarters of the Kona Historical Society. Pick up brochures and guides here and arrange for a tour of the Kona Coffee Living History Farm.

At the junction in the town of Captain Cook, turn right and follow the steep descent along Nāpō'opo'o Road to **Kealakekua Bay** ㊸. Park your car and walk to the nearby **Hikiau Heiau** ㊹. A moderately difficult three-hour hike on a rough trail from the top of Nāpō'opo'o Road takes you to **Captain Cook Monument** ㊵. Dip into the calm, dolphin-friendly waves that lap onto rocky Nāpō'opo'o Beach before taking Route 160, which hugs the coast, to **Pu'uhonua O Hōnaunau** ㊶. Plan to spend some time walking around this ancient Hawaiian sanctuary. Visit the restored royal Hale-o-Keawe Heiau, built circa 1650, and wander to the tide pools south of the park. Back in your car, head mauka on Route 160 toward Kēōkea, and turn left at Painted Church Road to visit the whimsical **St. Benedict's Painted Church** ㊷.

Continue south on Highway 11; after about 2 mi, you'll pass the turnoff to Ho'okena Beach Park, a busy steamer port in the 19th century. About

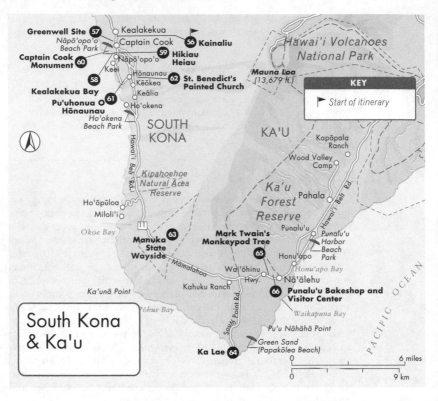

South Kona & Ka'u

KEY

▶ *Start of itinerary*

57 Greenwell Site
Kealakekua
Nāpō'opo'o Beach Park
Captain Cook
56 Kainaliu
60 Captain Cook Monument
Nāpō'opo'o
59 Hikiau Heiau
Keei
Hōnaunau
Kēōkea
62 St. Benedict's Painted Church
58 Kealakekua Bay
Keālia
61 Pu'uhonua O Hōnaunau
Ho'okena
Ho'okena Beach Park
SOUTH KONA
KA'U
Mauna Loa (13,679 ft.)
Hawai'i Volcanoes National Park
Kapāpala Ranch
Wood Valley Camp
Kipahoehoe Natural Area Reserve
Ka'u Forest Reserve
Pahala
Ho'ōpūloa
Miloli'i
Okoe Bay
63 Manuka State Wayside
Mark Twain's Monkeypod Tree
Punalu'u
65 Honu'apo
Honu'apo Bay
Punalu'u Harbor / Beach Park
Māmalahoa
Wai'ōhinu
Hwy.
Nā'ālehu
Kahuku Ranch
Ka'unā Point
66 Punalu'u Bakeshop and Visitor Center
Pōhue Bay
Waikapuna Bay
Pu'u Nāhāhā Point
64 Ka Lae
Green Sand (Papakōlea Beach)
PACIFIC OCEAN
0 ___ 6 miles
0 ___ 9 km

12 mi farther south, at mile marker 88, the infamous Mauna Loa lava flow of 1926 destroyed an entire Hawaiian fishing village. Turn left here for a 2-mi scenic drive along the old Māmalahoa Highway; then take a break at **Manuka State Wayside** 63.

Drive another 12 mi on Māmalahoa Highway to reach the windswept South Point Road, which leads to the southernmost part of the United States, **Ka Lae** 64. No vehicles are allowed on the coastal trail beyond road's end to Green Sand Beach. Hikers need a permit for the exhilarating 5-mi round-trip hike to this remote, isolated area.

For the last leg of this drive, head east on Highway 11 to the wetter, windward towns of Wai'ōhinu and Nā'ālehu, small communities struggling in the aftermath of sugar-plantation closures. Be sure to stop first at **Mark Twain's Monkeypod Tree** 65 for inspiration, then at **Punalu'u Bakeshop and Visitor Center** 66.

TIMING   Start your day early, as it takes 2½ hours from Kona just to get to the southern end of the island. You may want to make this a two-day excursion and stay in one of the many cozy B&Bs at Hawai'i Volcanoes National Park—a short 45-minute drive away from Nā'ālehu. Fill up on gasoline and pack some snacks, as there are few amenities along the way. Chances are it'll be close to dinnertime by the time you've completed this tour, but eateries in Kona remain open late.

What to See

★ ⑥ **Captain Cook Monument.** No one knows for sure what happened on February 14, 1779, when English explorer Captain James Cook was killed here. He chose Kealakekua Bay as a landing place in November 1778 and initiated Hawai'i's dramatic change. Cook was welcomed at first, arriving during the celebration of Makahiki, the harvest season. Some Hawaiians saw him as an incarnation of the god Lono, and he was received with great reverence. Cook's party reprovisioned and sailed away in February 1779. But a freak storm off the Kona Coast forced him back to Kealakekua Bay for repairs. The Hawaiians were not so welcoming this time, and various confrontations arose between them and Cook's sailors. The theft of a longboat brought Cook and an armed party ashore to reclaim the boat. One thing led to another: shots were fired, daggers and spears were thrown, and Captain Cook fell, mortally wounded. Suffice it to say, Captain James Cook and his party introduced the Hawaiian Islands to the world. Soon after, Western influences arrived on Hawai'i's shores: whalers, sailors, traders, missionaries, and more, and they brought with them crime, debauchery, alcohol, disease, and a world unknown to the Hawaiians. A 27-foot-high obelisk marks the spot where Captain Cook died on the shore of Kealakekua Bay. The three-hour 2½-mi hike to get to the monument begins at the trailhead 100 yards off Highway 11 on Nāpō'opo'o Road. Look for the downslope trail opposite three large royal palm trees.

⑤ **Greenwell Site.** Established in 1850, the homestead of Henry N. Greenwell served as cattle ranch, sheep station, post office, store complex, and family home all in one. Now, all that remains is the 1875 stone store, which is listed on the National Register of Historic Places. It is headquarters for the **Kona Historical Society** which has a fascinating museum, including ranching and coffee-farming photographs and exhibits. ✉ *81-6551 Māmalahoa Hwy.* ☎ *808/323–3222* ⊕ *www.konahistorical. org* 🎫 *Donations accepted* ⊘ *Weekdays 9–3.*

⑤ **Hikiau Heiau.** The remains you see of the stone platform and walls were once an impressive state temple, a large and sacred site enclosed by stone walls, dedicated to the god Lono. When Captain Cook arrived in 1778, ceremonies in his honor were held here. ✉ *Bottom of Nāpō'opo'o Rd.*

★ ⑥ **Ka Lae.** Windswept Ka Lae, the southernmost point of land in the United States, has a few abandoned structures once used in the 19th and early 20th centuries to lower cattle and produce to ships anchored below the cliffs. It is thought that the first Polynesians came ashore here. Check out the old canoe-mooring holes that are carved through the rocks, possibly by settlers from Tahiti as early as AD 750. Some artifacts, thought to have been left by early voyagers who never settled here, date to AD 300. Driving down the 12-mi road, you pass Kama'oa Wind Farm; although the rows of windmill turbines are still working, fueled by the nearly constant winds sweeping across this coastal plain, the equipment and facilities are falling into disrepair due to neglect. Some of the windmills are no longer working at all. ⊠ *Turn right just past mile marker 70 on Māmalahoa Hwy. and drive for 12 mi down South Point Rd.*

▶ ⑤ **Kainaliu.** It doesn't seem like much, this ribbon of funky old stores, but Kainaliu hosts a wealth of traditional Japanese family–operated shops. Browse around Heritage Stores such as Oshima's, established in 1926, and Kimura's, established in 1927, to find authentic Japanese goods beyond tourist trinkets. When times were tough, these stores survived by accepting coffee as tender. Peek into Aloha Theatre, built in 1932, where community-theater actors might be practicing a Broadway revue. Also check out the Aloha Angel Cafe for quick refreshments. ⊠ *Hwy. 11, mile markers 112–114.*

★ ⑤ **Kealakekua Bay.** Before the arrival of Captain Cook in the late 18th century, this now tranquil state marine park and sanctuary with its old steamer landing lay at the center of Hawaiian life. Historians consider Kealakekua Bay to be the birthing ground for the postcontact era. ⊠ *Bottom of Nāpō'opo'o Rd.*

need a break?

Treat yourself to awesome views of Kealakekua Bay at the **Coffee Shack** (⊠ 83-5799 Māmalahoa Highway ☎ 808/328–9555 ⊕ www.coffeeshack.com), a deli and pizza place with just nine tables on an open, breezy lānai. The bread is home-baked, the sandwiches are generous, and the staff is friendly.

☾ ⑥ **Manuka State Wayside.** This is a dry, upland native forest spread across several lava flows. It has a well-maintained arboretum. A rugged trail follows a 2-mi loop past a pit crater and winds around ancient trees such as *hau* and *kukui*. Kids love the trees, so large you can't get your arms around them, but pathways aren't well maintained. Rest rooms, picnic areas, and telephones are available. ⊠ *Hwy. 11, north of mile marker 81* ☎ 808/974–6200 ⊡ *Free* ☉ *Daily 7–7.*

⑥ **Mark Twain's Monkeypod Tree.** Legend has it that Mark Twain, who gained inspiration for some of his writings during his travels in this area, planted this robust, gnarled tree in 1866. In the 1950s a storm blew the tree down. New shoots have since developed into an impressive tree again. Watch for the Hawaiian warrior marker sign. ⊠ *Hwy. 11, just before mile marker 64, in Wai'ohinu.*

off the beaten path

PAHALA – About 16 mi east of Na'lehu, beyond Punalu'u Beach Park, Highway 11 flashes past this little town. You'll miss it if you blink. Pahala is a perfect example of a sugar-plantation town. Behind it, along a wide cane road, you enter Wood Valley, once a prosperous community, now a mere road heavily scented by night-blooming jasmine, coffee blossoms, and eucalyptus trees. Here you'll find **Wood Valley Temple** (☎ 808/928–8539), a quiet Tibetan Buddhist retreat that welcomes guests who seek serenity and solitude.

⑥ **Punalu'u Bakeshop and Visitor Center.** They say it's the best sweetbread—of course, it's the only sweetbread—in this area. While here, browse for rare *pohā*-berry (gooseberry) jam, look up at the old tamarind tree outside, and be sure to take some of that sweetbread home. The expanded snack shop offers daily light lunches, sandwiches, pastries, and more. ✉ *Māmalahoa Hwy. at Kaalaiki Rd., Na'alehu* ☎ *808/929–7343* ⊙ *Daily 9–5.*

★ ⑥ **Pu'uhonua O Hōnaunau.** This 180-acre National Historic Park, about 20 mi south of Kailua-Kona, was, in early times, a place of refuge and healing. It was a safe haven for women in times of war as well as for kapu breakers, criminals, and prisoners of war—anyone who could get inside the 1,000-foot-long wall, which was 10 feet high and 17 feet thick, was safe and could avoid punishment. **Hale-o-Keawe Heiau,** built in 1650 as the burial place of King Kamehameha I's ancestor Keawe, has been restored. South of the park, tide pools offer another delight. Demonstrations of Hawaiian skills, games, poi pounding, canoe making, and more are scheduled occasionally. ✉ *Rte. 160* ☎ *808/328–2288* ⊕ *www.nps.gov* 🖃 *$3–$5* ⊙ *Park grounds Mon.–Thurs. 6 AM–8 PM, Fri.–Sun. 6 AM–11 PM; visitor center daily 8 AM–4:30 PM.*

★ ⑥ **St. Benedict's Painted Church.** Whimsical, bright, and creative, the ceiling, columns, and walls of this Roman Catholic church depict Bible scenes through the paintbrush of Belgian-born priest Father Velghe. Mass is still held every weekend. The view of Kealakekua Bay from the entrance is amazing. ✉ *Painted Church Rd., off Hwy. 160* ☎ *808/328–2227.*

THE KOHALA DISTRICT

Along the roadside of Highway 19, brightly colored bougainvillea stands out in relief against the chunky black-lava landscape that stretches as far as the eye can see. Most of the lava flows, spreading from the mountain to the sea, are from the last eruptions of Mt. Hualālai, in 1800–01. They are interrupted only by the green oases of irrigated golf courses surrounding the glamorous luxury resorts rising along the Kona-Kohala Coast. The landscape along this long stretch of coastline changes considerably, from the cool 2,500-foot altitude of the cowboy town of Waimea to the green rolling fields that compose much of North Kohala. During the winter months, glistening humpback whales cleave the waters just offshore. On the coast you'll see ancient stone heiau and the remains of a fishing village, moving legacies of the Hawaiian people who still inhabit the area.

a good drive

If you're staying in Kona or at a Kohala Coast resort, begin this tour early in the morning by driving north on Queen Ka'ahumanu Highway 19 along the base of Mt. Hualālai. When you get to the split in the road 33 mi from Kailua-Kona, turn left on Highway 270 toward Kawaihae and stop at **Pu'ukoholā Heiau National Historic Site** ⑥ ⌐. Go straight when Highway 270 veers sharply to the right to continue on to **Kawaihae Harbor** ⑥. Here, in 1793, British captain George Vancouver brought on land the cattle that would proliferate beyond control and draw the first paniolo.

Rejoin Highway 270 to drive north through an arid landscape. The sweeping coastline offers great places to spot whales. Just after mile marker 6, you'll see the red warrior sign for **Pua Mau Botanical Garden** ⑥.

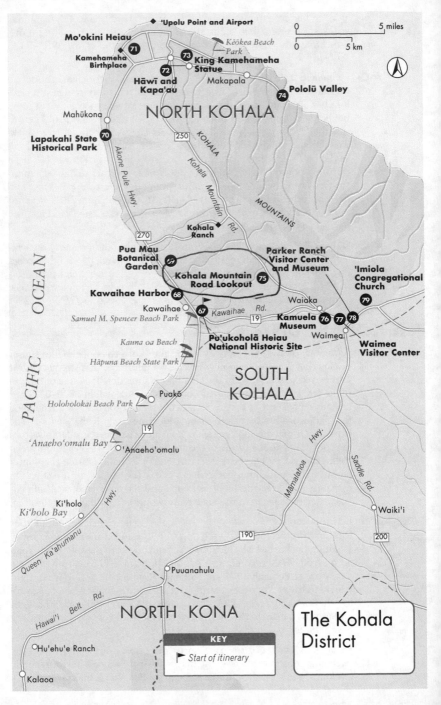

'Upolu Point and Airport

Mo'okini Heiau

71

Kēōkea Beach Park

73

Kamehameha Birthplace

King Kamehameha Statue

72

Hāwī and Kapa'au

Makapala

Pololū Valley

74

Mahūkona

NORTH KOHALA

Lapakahi State Historical Park

70

250

KOHALA

Kohala Mountain Rd.

MOUNTAINS

Akone Pule Hwy.

270

Kohala Ranch

Pua Mau Botanical Garden

65

Kohala Mountain Road Lookout

75

Parker Ranch Visitor Center and Museum

'Imiola Congregational Church

79

Kawaihae Harbor

68

Kawaihae

67

Kawaihae Rd.

Waiaka

19

Kamuela Museum

76 **77** **78**

Samuel M. Spencer Beach Park

Pu'ukoholā Heiau National Historic Site

Waimea

Waimea Visitor Center

Kauna oa Beach

Hāpuna Beach State Park

SOUTH KOHALA

PACIFIC OCEAN

Holoholokai Beach Park

Puakō

19

'Anaeho'omalu Bay

'Anaeho'omalu

Māmalahoa Hwy.

Saddle Rd.

Ki'holo

Ki'holo Bay

Queen Ka'ahumanu Hwy.

Waiki'i

190

200

Puuanahulu

Hawai'i Belt Rd.

NORTH KONA

The Kohala District

Hu'ehu'e Ranch

KEY

► Start of itinerary

Kalaoa

Continue north on Highway 270 for seven or eight miles to **Lapakahi State Historical Park** ⑳. A 1-mi trail meanders through the site of once-prosperous Koai'e, an ancient fishing village. Back on the highway, past Māhukona Beach Park and Kapa'a Beach Park, turn left at the sign for the remote, old 'Upolu Airport. At the bottom of the paved road you'll need a four-wheel-drive vehicle or good hiking shoes to traverse a 1½-mi dirt lane to **Mo'okini Heiau** ㉑. About 1,000 yards away from the heiau is King Kamehameha I's birthplace.

Continue north on the highway. Your next stops are in the old sugar-plantation villages of **Hāwī and Kapa'au** ㉒. Browse through the many galleries and gift shops, have some lunch, and be sure to visit the original **King Kamehameha Statue** ㉓. Highway 270 ends farther east at an overlook with a stunning view of **Pololū Valley** ㉔. A rugged, steep hiking trail leads down into the valley. Drive back toward Hāwī to complete the loop via Highway 250, better known as Kohala Mountain Road.

This scenic ride across high elevations and through ironwood trees that act as windbreaks along a narrow, twisting road passes an exclusive country-home subdivision called Kohala Ranch as well as active working ranches such as Kahuā. Take a break at **Kohala Mountain Road Lookout** ㉕ for a view of the entire coastline, including the protective breakwater, directly below. The road slopes down toward Waimea. Where the road bumps into Highway 19, take a sharp right and turn into the first open gate on your left to visit **Kamuela Museum** ㉖.

Next, head for Waimea, a bustling, affluent town with a cowboy heritage. Behind the shops of High Country Traders on your right on Highway 19, **Waimea Visitor Center** ㉗ offers detailed information on the cultural and historic sites of Kohala. On the other side of the traffic lights are the **Parker Ranch Visitor Center and Museum** ㉘ and the recently renovated Parker Ranch Shopping Center. In the parking lot, there's a handsome sculpture of famous Parker Ranch cowboy, Ikua Purdy, roping a steer. Purdy won the roping event at a national rodeo years ago and brought fame to the Hawaiian paniolo.

Drive northeast on Highway 19. On the left lies Church Lane—stop to peek into the cream-color **'Imiola Congregational Church** ㉙ to see its unique koa-wood interior. Be sure to browse through Cook's Discoveries at the third traffic light for exquisite local-theme gifts.

Reverse directions and head west on Highway 19; follow the road down to get back to the resorts along the coast.

TIMING   This is an all-day excursion covering many miles over ground that ranges from lava-covered flatlands with glorious seaside views to lush mountain pastures. If you're short on time, head either straight for Waimea to shop and dine and to visit the Parker Ranch Museum or drive to Hāwī and Kapa'au via Highway 270 to see the dramatic history of these sugar towns. Allow a half day or more for the abbreviated trip.

What to See

 Hāwī and Kapa'au. These two neighboring villages thrived during plantation days. There were hotels, saloons, and theaters—even a railroad.

Today, both towns are blossoming once again, honoring their past. Old historic buildings have been restored and now hold shops, galleries, and eateries. In Kapaʻau, browse through the Hawaiian collection of **Kohala Book Shop** (✉ 54-3885 Akoni Pule Hwy. ☎ 808/889–6400 ⊕ www.kohalabooks.com), the second-largest bookstore in the state. ✉ *Highway 270, Kapaʻau, Kohala.*

need a break? It can get hot and humid in North Kohala. A great place to feel the breeze is on the lawn of the **Nanbu Courtyard** (✉ Kapaʻau ☎ 808/889–5546), behind the historic Old Nanbu Hotel. Open as early as 6:30 on weekdays, this friendly espresso shop serves toasted bagels, salads, and grilled sandwiches along with soft ice cream. If you're looking for something sweet, head to **Kohala Coffee Mill** (✉ Akone Pule Hwy. ☎ 808/889–5577), a café in bustling Hāwī that whips up Kona coffee, espresso drinks, and luscious iced *chai* (Indian tea).

⑳ ʻImiola Congregational Church. Stop here to admire the dark koa interior and the unusual wooden calabashes hanging from the ceiling. Be careful not to walk in while a service is in progress, as the front entry of this church, which was established in 1832 and rebuilt in 1857, is behind the pulpit. ✉ *Off Hwy. 19, along Waimea's famous "church row,"* Waimea ☎ 808/885–4987.

off the beaten path **FIRE HOUSE GALLERY –** Walk across the Parker Ranch Shopping Center parking lot to a historic 77-year-old fire station, now a gallery, to glimpse what the artists in Hāmākua and Kohala are up to. The Waimea Arts Council sponsors free *kaha kiʻis* (one-person shows). ✉ *Near main stoplight in Waimea, toward Kailua-Kona on Hwy. 190* ☎ 808/887–1052.

⑳ Kamuela Museum. This small private museum has a fascinating collection of artifacts from Hawaiʻi and around the world. The eclectic collection includes Hawaiian weapons and a satiny-smooth koa table that once graced ʻIolani Palace in Honolulu. There are also period furniture pieces, artwork, and military and war memorabilia. ✉ *Hwys. 19 and 250, Waimea* ☎ 808/885–4724 🖭 *$5* ⊗ *Daily 8–4.*

⑳ Kawaihae Harbor. This commercial harbor, where in 1793 the first cattle came on land, setting the course of the Big Island's ranching history, is a hub of activity, especially on weekends, when paddlers and local fishing boats seek the waves. Second in size only to Hilo Harbor on the east coast, the harbor is often home to the *Makaliʻi*, one of three Hawaiian sailing canoes. King Kamehameha I and his men launched their canoes from here when they set out to conquer the island chain. ✉ *Kawaihae Harbor Rd. off Hwy. 270.*

⑳ Kohala Mountain Road Lookout. The lookout here provides a splendid view of the Kohala Coast and Kawaihae Harbor far below. On clear days, you can see well beyond the resorts. It's one of the most scenic spots on the island and great for a picnic. Often, thick mists drift in, casting an eerie feeling. ✉ *Kohala Mountain Rd. (Hwy. 250).*

73 King Kamehameha Statue. This is the original of the statue in front of the Judiciary Building on King Street in Honolulu. It was cast in Florence in 1880 but lost at sea when the German ship transporting it sank near the Falkland Islands. A replica was shipped to Honolulu. Two years later an American sea captain found the original in a Port Stanley (Falkland Islands) junkyard and brought it to the Big Island. The legislature voted to erect it near Kamehameha's birthplace. Every year, on King Kamehameha Day (June 11), a magnificent abundance of floral lei adorns the image of Hawai'i's great king. Located in front of the old Kohala Courthouse next to the highway. ⊠ *Hwy. 270, Kapa'au.*

need a break? **Kohala Rainbow Cafe** (☎ 808/889–0099), across from the King Kamehameha statue in Kapa'au, serves wraps, salads, smoothies, and sandwiches all day long. Try the Kamehameha wrap—filled with Hawaiian-style kalua pork, organic greens, tomatoes, onions, cheeses and Maui onion dressing. Open weekdays, except Tues., 10–6, weekends 11–5.

★ **76 Lapakahi State Historical Park.** A self-guided, 1-mi walking tour leads through the ruins of the once-prosperous fishing village Koai'e, which dates as far back as the 15th century. Displays illustrate early Hawaiian fishing, salt gathering, legends, games, shelters, and crops, and a park guide is often on-site to answer questions. Since the shores off Lapakahi are now mostly a Marine Life Conservation District, and part of the site itself is considered sacred, swimming is discouraged. ⊠ *Makai side of Hwy. 270, between Kawaihae and Māhukona, North Kohala* ☎ 808/974–6200 or 808/882–6207 💲 *Free* ☉ *Daily 8–4.*

★ **77 Mo'okini Heiau.** This National Historic Landmark, an isolated *luakini* (sacrificial) heiau, is so impressive in size it may give you goose bumps. Its foundations date to about AD 480, but the high priest Pa'ao from Tahiti built the heiau in earnest several centuries later to sacrifice people to please his gods. You can still see the lava slab. A nearby sign marks the place where Kamehameha I was born in 1758. The area is now part of the Kohala Historical Sites State Monument. ⊠ *Turn off Hwy. 270 at sign for 'Upolu Airport, near Hāwī, and hike or drive in a four-wheel-drive vehicle 1½ mi southwest* ☎ 808/974–6200.

78 Parker Ranch Visitor Center and Museum. The center chronicles the life of John Palmer Parker (and his descendants), who founded Parker Ranch in 1847. Parker married the granddaughter of King Kamehameha and bought 2 acres of land from the king for the sum of $10. Purchase your tickets here for the **Parker Ranch Historic Homes,** a couple of miles south of town. The original family residence, Mānā, is built entirely from native koa-wood. Pu'ōpelu, added to the estate in 1879, was the residence of Richard Smart, a sixth-generation Parker who expanded the house to make room for his European art collection. On Friday, Hawaiian crafts demonstrations take place at the homes. A wagon ride allows you a comfortable, albeit old-fashioned, visit to the pastures. Also available are horseback rides and walking tours. ⊠ *Parker Ranch Shopping Center, 67-1185 Māmalahoa Highway, Waimea* ☎ 808/885–7655 or 808/885–

5433, toll-free 800/262-7290 ⊕ *www.parkerranch.com* 🖾 *Museum $6.50, homes $8.50, both $14* ⊙ *Museum daily 9–5, homes daily 10–5.*

need a break?

At the **Little Juice Shack** (✉ Parker Ranch Shopping Center, off Hwy. 19 ☎ 808/885–1686), you can treat yourself to fresh juices made with carrots, beets, or even watermelon. Add a shot of wheatgrass juice from the crop grown in the windows. Sample an organic spinach salad or turkey sandwich on six-grain bread, or, on a cold day, try the thick and spicy five-pepper chowder.

74 Pololū Valley. A steep trail leads into this once heavily populated valley, which edges a rugged coastline ribboned by silver waterfalls. The valleys beyond provide water for the Kohala Ditch, the ingenious project that used to bring water to the sugar plantation. Some of the former ditch trails have become inaccessible and dangerous. A kayak cruise through the old irrigation ditch, a mule ride, and a ditch-trail hike, offered by tour operators and outfitters, reveal more of this dramatic part of Kohala history. ✉ *End of Hwy. 270.*

69 Pua Mau Botanical Garden. Virgil and Irina Place are slowly transforming 45 acres of arid land into a desert garden of everblooming plants, plumeria trees, and bronze sculptures modeled after Kohala's desert bugs. A maze of 200-plus hibiscus varieties leads to a magic circle—in accordance with Celtic traditions, a configuration of stones placed to follow the path of the sun through the seasons. Self-guided tours pass inviting picnic spots with sweeping coastal views. ✉ *Kohala Estates, 10 Ala Kahua Dr., off Hwy. 270 at mile marker 6, Kawaihae* ☎ *808/882–0888* ⊕ *www. puamau.com* 🖾 *$5* ⊙ *Wed.–Sun. 10–5.*

★ ▶ 67 Pu'ukoholā Heiau National Historic Site. In 1790 a prophet told King Kamehameha I to build a heiau on top of Pu'ukoholā (Hill of the Whale) and dedicate it to the war god Kūkā'ilimoku by sacrificing his principal Big Island rival, Keōua Kūahu'ula. By doing so the king would achieve his goal of conquering the Hawaiian Islands. The prophecy came true in 1810. A short walk over arid landscape leads from the visitor center to **Pu'ukoholā Heiau** and to **Mailekini Heiau,** constructed about 1550. An even older temple, dedicated to the shark gods, lies submerged just offshore. The center organizes Hawaiian arts-and-crafts programs on a regular basis. ✉ *Hwy. 270, Kawaihae* ☎ *808/882–7218* ⊕ *www. nps.gov* 🖾 *Free* ⊙ *Daily 7:30–4.*

77 Waimea Visitor Center. The old Lindsey House—a restored ranch cabin built in 1909 and now listed on the Hawai'i Register of Historic Places—serves as a visitor center. Part of the Waimea Preservation Association, it offers detailed information on Kohala's many historic and cultural sites. (Note: technically, the name of the Waimea post office is Kamuela, and the name of the town is Waimea. Therefore, you'll see Kamuela in many addresses. Some say the post office is named for the son of the founder of Parker Ranch.) ✉ *65-1291 Kawaihae Rd., behind High Country Traders, Waimea* ☎ *808/885–6707* ⊕ *www.northhawaii.net* ⊙ *Mon.–Sat. 9:30–4:30.*

need a break? At **Aioli's** (✉ 'Opelo Plaza, Hwy. 19 and 'Opelo Rd., Waimea ☎ 808/885–6325) you can pick up ready-to-go box lunches or opt for a custom-made sandwich. **Tako Taco Taqueria** (✉ 65-1271 Kawaihae Rd. next to Parker Sq., Waimea ☎ 808/887–1717) serves superb fresh, organic Mexican fare. If you're in the mood for a mug of steaming caffe latte with a hot croissant, stop by **Waimea Coffee & Company** (✉ Parker Sq., 65-1279 Kawaihae Rd., Waimea ☎ 808/ 885–4472).

BEACHES

Don't believe anyone who tells you the Big Island lacks beaches. It actually has 80 or more, and new ones appear—and disappear—regularly. In 1989 a black-sand beach, Kamoamoa, formed when molten lava shattered as it hit cold ocean waters. Kamoamoa was the largest of the black-sand beaches, more than ½ mi long and 25 yards wide, until it was closed by new lava flows in 1992. Some beaches are just a little hard to get to—several are hidden behind elaborate hotels or down unmarked roads.

Note that many beaches have dangerous undertows—rip currents and pounding shore breaks may cause serious risk anywhere at any time. The surf tends to get rough in winter. To be safe, swim only when you see other visitors swimming in the area. Local surfers are not an indication that the area is safe. Few public beaches have lifeguards.

That said, the most beautiful, swimmable white-sand beaches stretch along the Kohala coastline. The beaches below are listed in a counterclockwise direction around the island, starting from the northern tip. For overnight permits, necessary at all parks, contact the Department of Land and Natural Resources for state parks and the Department of Parks and Recreation for county parks.

Kēōkea Beach Park. Driving back from the end of Highway 270 at the Pololū overlook to the north, you'll see a curvy road angle off to the right. Follow it for a mile, past the cemetery with the weathered old stones, and you'll come upon the green lawns and large picnic pavilion of Kēōkea Beach Park. You can fish from the black boulders, but heavy surf makes this a hazardous swimming beach. This is a popular weekend destination for local folks. ⌖ *Off Hwy. 270, near Pololū overlook* ☎ 808/961–8311.

Māhukona Beach Park. Next to the abandoned Port of Māhukona, in the Kohala District, where sugar was once shipped by rail to be loaded on boats, Māhukona Beach's old docks and buildings are a treat for photographers. You can still view remnants of shipping machinery in the clear water, but heavy surf makes swimming dangerous at times. It's a pleasant picnicking spot, with rest rooms and showers, but no sandy beach. ✉ *Off Hwy. 270, Māhukona* ☎ 808/961–8311.

★ **Spencer Beach Park.** This spot is popular with local families because of its reef-protected, gently sloping white-sand beach. It's safe for swimming year-round. Close to large shade trees are cooking facilities, showers, and a large pavilion with electrical outlets. You can walk from here

CloseUp

HAWAIIAN MYTHS & LEGENDS

THE BEST-KNOWN DEITY in Hawaiian lore is Pele, the beautiful volcano goddess. Although visitors are warned not to remove lava rocks from Pele's domain without her permission, some do and find themselves dogged by bad luck until they return the stolen items. The Hawai'i Volcanoes National Park Service often receives packages containing chunks of lava along with letters describing years of misfortune.

Tales of Pele's fiery temper are legendary. She battled Poli'ahu, ruler of snowcapped Mauna Kea on the Big Island, in a fit of jealousy over the snow goddess's extraordinary beauty. She picked fights with her peace-loving sister, Hi'iaka, turning the younger goddess's friends into pillars of stone. And her recurring lava-flinging spats with suitor Kamapua'a, a demigod who could change his appearance at will, finally drove him into the sea, where he turned into a fish to escape her wrath.

But Pele can be kind if the mood suits her. It is said that before every major eruption, she appears in human form as a wrinkled old woman walking along isolated back roads. Those who offer her a ride return home to find a river of boiling magma abruptly halted inches from their property or diverted around their houses. Those who pass her by find their homes devastated by molten lava. Many hula hālau still make pilgrimages to the rim of Kīlauea—Pele's home on the Big Island—where they honor the fickle goddess with prayers, chants, and offerings of gin and flower lei.

In addition to battling the elements and each other, gods were thought to have intervened in the daily lives of early Hawaiians. Storms that destroyed homes and crops, a fisherman's poor catch, or a loss in battle were blamed on the wrath of angry gods. And according to legend, an industrious race of diminutive people called menehune built aqueducts, fishponds, and other constructs requiring advanced engineering knowledge unavailable to early Hawaiians. Living in remote hills and valleys, these secretive workers toiled only in darkness and completed complex projects in a single night. Their handiwork can still be seen on all the Islands.

Also at night, during certain lunar periods, a traveler might inadvertently come across the Night Marchers—armies of dead warriors, chiefs, and ancestral spirits whose feet never touch the ground. They float along the ancient highways, chanting and beating their drums, pausing only to claim the spirits of their brethren who died that night. It was believed that such an encounter would bring certain death unless a relative among the marchers pleaded for the victim's life.

to the Pu'ukoholā and Mailekini heiaus. ☒ *Entry road off Hwy. 270, uphill from Kawaihae Harbor* ☎ *808/961–8311.*

★ **Kauna'oa Beach at Mauna Kea Beach Hotel.** It's a toss-up whether this or neighboring Hāpuna is the most beautiful beach on the island. Kauna'oa unfolds like a white crescent, and it slopes very gradually. It's a great place for snorkeling. In winter, however, the powerful waves can be dangerous. Amenities are hotel-owned. Public parking places are limited. ☒ *Entry through gate to Mauna Kea Beach Resort, off Hwy. 19.*

Fodor'sChoice **Hāpuna Beach State Recreation Area.** This beach, part of a 61-acre park, ★ forms a ½-mi crescent of glistening sand guarded by rocky points at either end. The surf can be hazardous in winter, but in summer the gradual slope of the beach can stretch as wide as 200 feet into a perfectly blue ocean—ideal for swimming, snorkeling, and bodysurfing. State cabins are available. There's even a small concession stand. Lifeguards are not always on duty, so be careful. ☒ *Adjacent to and below the Hāpuna Beach Prince Hotel, off Hwy. 19* ☎ *808/974–6200.*

Holoholokai Beach Park. This rocky beach of black-lava formations and white-coral clinkers, with bathrooms, picnic tables, barbecue grills, and a small grassy area nearby, makes for a pleasant afternoon of snorkeling and sunbathing. Just before the beach park, you can explore historic Puakō Petroglyph Park: Malama Trail meanders 7/10 mi through brush and *kiawe* trees to an area of lava covered with ancient etchings of Hawaiian figures and animals. ☒ *Off Hwy. 19 next to the Fairmont Orchid Hawai'i.*

Fodor'sChoice **'Anaeho'omalu Beach, at Waikoloa Beach Marriott.** This expansive beach ★ on the west coast, also known as A-Bay, is perfect for swimming, windsurfing, snorkeling, and diving. Some equipment is for rent at the north end. Be sure to wander around the ancient fishponds and petroglyph fields. ☒ *Follow Waikoloa Beach Dr. to the Kings' Shops, then turn left at signs to the park; parking lot and beach right-of-way just south of Marriott.*

★ **Kiholo Bay.** A 20-minute hike across lava leads to an oceanfront with private homes but no public facilities. The huge, spring-fed Luahinewai Pond anchors the south end of the bay, and the three black-pebble beaches are fine for swimming in calm weather. At the northern end, Wainānāli'i Pond (a 5-acre lagoon) is a feeding site for green sea turtles. The two ponds are off-limits to swimmers. Kamehameha I had a well-stocked fishpond here that was destroyed by lava in 1859. ☒ *Hwy. 19, mile marker 81, unmarked trail.*

Kekaha Kai State Park. Beyond the park's entrance, at the end of separate, unpaved roads, about 1½ mi each, you'll find two sandy beaches, Mahai'ula to the south, and Kua Bay to the north. In calm weather, they are great for swimming. You can hike along a historic 4½-mi trail from one to the other, but be prepared for the heat and bring lots of drinking water. Mahai'ula has a picnic area and portable toilets. ☒ *Sign about 2 mi north of Keāhole–Kona International Airport, off Hwy. 19, marks rough 1½-mi road to beach* ☎ *808/327–4958 or 808/974–6200.*

★ **Kaloko–Honokōhau National Historical Park.** Part of a 1,160-acre park, two beaches, rich in archaeology and good for swimming, are down the road from Honokōhau Harbor. 'Alula is a slip of white sand, a short walk over lava to the left of the harbor entrance. Honokōhau Beach, a ¾-mi stretch with ruins of ancient fishponds, is north of the harbor. At the north end of the beach, a historic trail leads mauka across the lava to a freshwater pool. A Hawaiian settlement until the 19th century, the park is being developed as a cultural and historical site. For information about the park, visit its headquarters, a 5- to 10-minute drive away. ⌧ *Park Headquarters and Main Gate, off Highway 19 opposite Kaloko Industrial Park between mile markers 96 and 97* ☎ *808/329–6881* ⊕ *www.nps.gov* ⊘ *Park road gate 8 AM–3:30 PM.*

Old Kona Airport State Recreation Area. The unused runway—great for jogging—is still visible above this beach at Kailua Park, which has picnic tables, showers, bathroom facilities, tennis courts, and palm trees strung along the shore. The beach has a sheltered, sandy inlet with tide pools for children, but for adults it's better for snorkeling than swimming. An offshore surfing break known as Old Airport is popular with Kona surfers. ⌧ *North end of Kuakini Hwy., Kona* ☎ *808/327–4958 or 808/974–6200.*

★ **White Sands, Magic Sands, or Disappearing Sands Beach Park.** Now you see it, now you don't. Overnight, winter waves wash away this small white-sand beach on Ali'i Drive just south of Kailua-Kona. In summer you'll know you've found it when you see the body- and board surfers. Rest rooms, showers, a lifeguard tower, and a coconut grove create a convenient summer hangout, but this isn't a great beach for swimming. ⌧ *4½ mi south of Kailua-Kona on Ali'i Dr.* ☎ *808/961–8311.*

★ **Kahalu'u Beach Park.** This spot was a favorite of King Kalākaua, whose summer cottage is on the grounds of the Ohana Keauhou Beach Resort next door. Kahalu'u is popular with commoners, too, and on weekends there are too many people. This is, however, one of the best snorkeling spots—it's a good place to see reef fish up close, as the fish are used to snorkelers. But beware: a strong riptide during high surf pulls swimmers away from shore. Facilities include a pavilion, rest rooms, showers, a lifeguard tower, and limited parking. A narrow path takes you directly to the resort's beach bar, which serves sandwiches and plate lunches. ⌧ *5½ mi south of Kailua-Kona on Ali'i Dr.* ☎ *808/961–8311.*

Ho'okena Beach Park. You'll feel like an adventurer when you come upon Ho'okena, at the northern end of Kauhakō Bay. When Mark Twain visited, 2,500 people populated the busy seaport village. You can still find gas lampposts dating from the early 1900s. This dark-gray coral-and-lava-sand beach offers good swimming, snorkeling, and bodysurfing. Rest rooms, showers, and picnic tables are available at the park. The access road is narrow and bumpy. ⌧ *2-mi drive down road bordered by ruins of stone wall off Hwy. 11, 23 mi south of Kailua-Kona* ☎ *808/961–8311.*

Nāpō'opo'o Beach Park. The best way to enjoy this marine preserve is to take a snorkel, scuba, or glass-bottom boat tour from Keauhou Bay.

A 27-foot white obelisk indicates where Captain James Cook was killed in 1779. Although this 6-acre beach park has a picnic pavilion, the beach consists of rocks, making access to the water difficult. ⊠ *End of Nāpō'opo'o Road, off Highway 11, Kealakekua Bay* 🕾 *808/961–8311.*

★ **Green Sand (Papakōlea) Beach.** You need a permit, good hiking shoes, and a four-wheel-drive vehicle to get to this green crescent, one of the most unusual and prettiest beaches on the island. The beach lies at the base of Pu'u o Mahana, at Mahana Bay, a cinder cone formed during an early eruption of Mauna Loa. The greenish tint is caused by an accumulation of olivine that forms in volcanic eruptions. Swimming is dangerous in this windy, remote area, and there are no facilities. Still, in calm water close to the shore, the aquamarine surf feels great and you find yourself in a surreal grass-plain landscape. Follow the trail 2 to 3 mi along the shoreline. Permits can be obtained from **Hawaiian Homelands** (⊠ 160 Baker Ave., Hilo 96720 🕾 808/974–4250). There you can get a key to the gate for a $25 deposit. ⊠ *2½ mi northeast of South Point, off Hwy. 11.*

★ **Punalu'u Beach Park.** The endangered Hawaiian green sea turtle nests in the black sand of this beautiful and easily accessible beach. You can see the turtles feeding on the seaweed along the surfbreak. Fishponds are just inland. At the northern end of the beach near the boat ramp lie the ruins of a heiau and a flat sacrificial stone. This used to be a sugar and army port until the tidal wave of 1946 destroyed the buildings. Offshore rip currents are extremely dangerous, though you'll see a few local surfers riding the waves. There are rest rooms across the road. Inland is a memorial to Henry Opukaha'ia. In 1809, when he was 17, Opukaha'ia swam out to a fur-trading ship in the harbor and asked to sail as a cabin boy. When he reached New England, he entered the Foreign Mission School in Connecticut, but he died of typhoid fever in 1818. His dream of bringing Christianity to the Islands inspired the American Board of Missionaries in 1820 to send the first Protestant missionaries to Hawai'i. ⊠ *Hwy. 11, 27 mi south of Hawai'i Volcanoes National Park* 🕾 *808/961–8311.*

MacKenzie State Recreation Area. This 13-acre park shaded by ironwoods is good for picnicking. You can't swim here, but there are rest rooms and a few picnic table pavilions. ⊠ *Off Hwy. 137, 9 mi northeast of Kaimū, Puna District* 🕾 *808/974–6200.*

Isaac Hale Beach Park. Oceanfront park facilities include rest rooms and picnic areas. This is a good place for an afternoon nap but is dangerous for swimming. ⊠ *Off Hwy. 137, about 10 mi northeast of Kaimū, Puna District* 🕾 *808/961–8311.*

Ahalanui Park. This 3-acre beach park, also known as Pū'āla'a, has a ½-acre pond heated by volcanic steam. There's nothing like swimming in this warm pool, but the nearby ocean is rough. Note: since mid-2003, the thermal pool has had bacterial-contamination problems; check with the lifeguard/attendant on safety and heed all posted signs. Drinking water and a few tables are available for picnicking, and there are portable rest rooms. ⊠ *Southeast of Pāhoa, 2½ mi south of junction of Hwys. 132 and 137, Puna District* 🕾 *808/961–8311.*

★ **Leleiwi Beach Park and Richardson Ocean Park.** Along Hilo's Keaukaha shoreline—laced with bays, inlets, lagoons, and pretty parks—these two beaches lie adjacent to one another. The grassy area is ideal for picnics. The beaches are rocky and dangerous for swimming, though you can dip your feet in the shallow areas. ⊠ *2349 Kalaniana'ole Ave.; follow Kalaniana'ole Ave. along the water about 4 mi east of Hilo* ☎ *808/ 961–8311.*

Onekahakaha Beach Park. A protected, white-sand beach makes this a favorite for Hilo families with small children. Lifeguards are on duty. The park has picnic pavilions, rest rooms, and showers. ⊠ *Follow Kalaniana'ole Ave. 3 mi east of Hilo* ☎ *808/961–8311.*

Reeds Bay Beach Park. Rest rooms, showers, drinking water, calm and safe swimming, and proximity to downtown Hilo are the enticements of this cove. Cold freshwater springs seep from the bottom of a nearby pond and rise in the saltwater. ⊠ *Banyan Dr. and Kalaniana'ole Ave., Hilo* ☎ *808/961–8311.*

WHERE TO EAT

Updated by
John Penisten

Choosing a place to eat in the western part of the Big Island is difficult, as there are many good, established restaurants and ethnic eateries. All along Ali'i Drive in Kailua-Kona, sunny little cafés with indoor-outdoor seating serve numerous international cuisines as well as American and Hawaiian regional food. Hotels along the Kohala Coast invest in top chefs to match their opulent settings; diners are rarely disappointed. Kawaihae Harbor offers some fun choices, and Upcountry Waimea—just a 40-minute drive inland from the resorts—also has a variety of popular restaurants. Although Hilo's dining scene may seem less exciting, restaurants are often inexpensive family places where good, substantial food makes up for lack of atmosphere.

Hilo

American/Casual

$$–$$$ ✕ **Harrington's.** A great view and a daily happy hour make this steak-and-seafood restaurant on Reed's Bay a popular place. You can't go wrong with either the catch of the day served in a tangy citrus-wasabi beurre blanc or the New York peppercorn steak. The garlic-laced Slavic steak is a specialty. For lunch try the Harrington's Burger, served with cream cheese aioli. ⊠ *135 Kalaniana'ole Ave.* ☎ *808/961–4966* ▭ *MC, V.*

$$–$$$ ✕ **Seaside Restaurant.** The Nakagawa family has been running this home-based eatery and aquafarm since the early 1920s. The decor is bare-bones, with plastic chairs and wooden tables, but Seaside serves some of the best and freshest fish on the island. Locals travel far for the fried *āholehole* (young Hawaiian flagtail). Not a fish eater? Try the grilled lamb chops, pasta, chicken, or prime rib. Arrive before sunset and request a table on the patio for a view of fishponds and egret roosting. ⊠ *1790 Kalaniana'ole Ave.* ☎ *808/935–8825* ▭ *AE, DC, MC, V* ⊘ *Closed Mon. No lunch.*

$–$$ ✗ **Uncle Billy's Restaurant.** Uncle Billy's is pure Hawaiian kitsch—right out of 1930s Hollywood—but the thatch roofs, tinkling Capiz-shell wind chimes, and Tahitian-print curtains add to the fun, as does a free nightly hula show. Choose from mahimahi meunière, teriyaki chicken, pastas, soup and salad, and local specialties. ⊠ *Hilo Bay Hotel, 87 Banyan Dr.* ☎ *808/935–0861* ⊟ *AE, D, DC, MC, V* ⊙ *No lunch.*

$ ✗ **Ken's House of Pancakes.** For years this 24-hour coffee shop between the airport and the Banyan Drive hotels has been a gathering place for Hilo residents. As its name implies, Ken's serves good pancakes but there are about 180 items to choose from on the menu. Wednesday is paniolo prime-rib night. ⊠ *1730 Kamehameha Ave.* ☎ *808/935–8711* ⊟ *AE, D, DC, MC, V.*

Chinese

$–$$ ✗ **Ting Hao.** This Mandarin restaurant on the edge of Hilo Bay emphasizes fresh island fish with offerings that change daily. Entrées include spicy Szechuan and Hunan dishes and scrumptious specialties from Taiwan and Beijing. The special slow-roasted Peking duck, wrapped in a Mandarin pastry layer and served with plum sauce, must be ordered a day in advance. ⊠ *Hawai'i Naniloa Resort, 93 Banyan Dr.* ☎ *808/935–8888* ⊟ *AE, D, DC, MC, V* ⊙ *Closed Tues.*

Eclectic

★ $$–$$$$ ✗ **Restaurant Kaikodo.** Hilo's newest upscale fine-dining room blends East-West cuisines and decor. For appetizers, try the Chinese dumplings, Big Island sushi roll, stir-fried Hawaiian peppers and mushrooms, or wok-seared crispy tofu. Seafood rules here, so sample the gomashio-seared 'ahi tuna, lemongrass-steamed *'ōpakapaka* (blue snapper), or shrimp with green and white pasta ribbons. There are lamb, beef, and chicken selections as well, and scrumptious desserts to top off the meal. A long Victorian bar graces the lounge area. ⊠ *60 Keawe St.* ☎ *808/961–2558* ⊟ *AE, D, DC, MC, V.*

Hawaiian

¢–$ ✗ **Kūhiō Grille.** There is no ambience to speak of, and your water is served in unbreakable plastic, but if you're searching for local fare—that eclectic and undefinable fusion of ethnic cuisines—Kūhiō Grille is a must. Sam Araki serves a 1-pound *laulau* (a steamed bundle made with Waipi'o Valley–grown taro leaves and pork), alongside "loco" plate lunches and grilled meats. This diner at the edge of Hilo's largest shopping mall opens as early as 6 AM. ⊠ *Prince Kūhiō Shopping Plaza, 111 E. Puainako St., at Hwy. 11* ☎ *808/959–2336* ⊟ *AE, MC, V.*

Italian

$$–$$$ ✗ **Pescatore.** With dim lights, stately high-backed chairs, and dark wood, Pescatore serves traditional Italian cuisine. The menu features several types of pasta, pizza, and items like cioppino, lasagne, chicken marsala, eggplant, chicken or veal parmigiana and more. Lunch consists of Italian-style sandwiches; breakfast, on weekends only, features Italian omelettes and crepes. Families love the pastas made to please choosy children. ⊠ *235 Keawe St., at Haili St.* ☎ *808/969–9090* ⊟ *AE, D, DC, MC, V.*

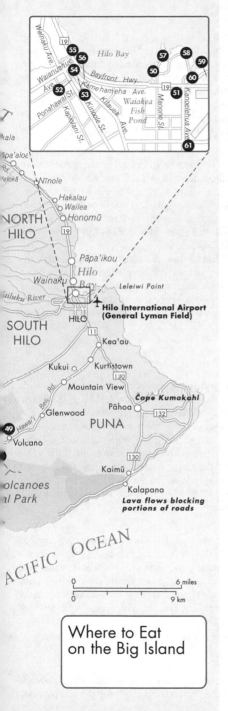

Where to Eat
on the Big Island

Japanese

$$–$$$ ✕ **Nihon Restaurant.** This open, airy dining room has a scenic view of Hilo Bay and is adjacent to the Lili'uokalani Gardens and the Banyan Drive hotels along the bayfront. Servers are dressed in colorful kimonos, and Japanese art and music add to the ambience. The menu offers a wide choice of authentic Japanese cuisine including beef, pork, chicken, and seafood. Try the soba noodles, butterfish misoyaki, and teriyaki steak. A sushi bar provides a full range of wonderful and varied sushi. ✉ *123 Lihiwai St.* ☎ *808/969–1133* ▭ *AE, MC, V* ☾ *Closed Sun.*

Thai

$ ✕ **Naung Mai.** This restaurant in downtown Hilo is nothing more than five tables, three booths, and owner-chef Alisa Rung Khongnok hard at work in the visible kitchen. It's hard to find, but a colorful exterior, a cozy interior with mellow music and original art on the walls, and fresh, reasonably priced meals greet intrepid customers. It may be the best Thai food on the island. ✉ *86 Kīlauea Ave.* ☎ *808/934–7540* ▭ *MC, V* ☾ *Closed Sun. No lunch Wed. or Sat.*

$ ✕ **Royal Siam.** A downtown Hilo fixture, this authentic Thai eatery offers little ambience in its straightforward dining room. But you don't need a dramatic view when you can choose from a menu that includes five curries and plenty of stir-fry—the tangy stir-fried garlic shrimp with coconut milk and wild mushrooms is particularly good. ✉ *70 Mamo St.* ☎ *808/961–6100* ▭ *AE, D, DC, MC, V* ☾ *Closed Sun.*

Volcano

Contemporary

★ $$–$$$ ✕ **Kīlauea Lodge.** Chef Albert Jeyte combines contemporary trends with traditional cooking styles from the mainland, France, and his native Hamburg, Germany. Built in 1937 as a YMCA camp, the restaurant still has the original "Friendship Fireplace" made from stones from around the world. The roaring fire, koa tables, and warm lighting create a lodge feel inside the sunny main building. Entrées include venison, duck à l'orange with an apricot-mustard glaze, and authentic hasenpfeffer (braised rabbit served with Jeyte's signature sauerbraten) to name a few. ✉ *Old Volcano Hwy., Volcano Village* ☎ *808/967–7366* ⊕ *www.kilauealodge. com* ▭ *AE, MC, V* ☾ *No lunch.*

Continental

$$–$$$ ✕ **Ka 'Ōhelo Dining Room.** Eat here just for the incomparable views of Kīlauea Caldera. During the day this old, well-worn locale serves up breakfast and luncheon buffets primarily for tour groups. Roast prime rib, king crab legs, lamb chops, seafood, and pasta are on the dinner menu. Art aficionados appreciate several magnificent early-19th-century oil paintings of the volcano. ✉ *Volcano House, Hawai'i Volcanoes National Park* ☎ *808/967–7321* ▭ *AE, D, DC, MC, V.*

Kailua-Kona & South Kona

American/Casual

$$$ ✕ **Beachcomber's & Paradise Lounge.** Many come to this casual, oceanfront restaurant at the far end of Waterfront Row for the happy hour

(5 to 7) drinks, pūpū, and sunset views. The menu features a crunchy coconut-shrimp appetizer. Steak, seafood, and prime-rib entrées include the popular salad bar. ✉ *75-5770 Ali'i Dr., Kailua-Kona* ☎ *808/329–2451* ▤ *AE, MC, V* ⊘ *No lunch.*

$$$ ✕ **Jameson's by the Sea.** Sit outside next to the ocean or just inside the picture windows for glorious sunset views over Magic Sands Beach. You can choose between three or four daily fish specials, some prepared Cajun-style. Sautéed scallops with lemon butter and capers, and Jameson's special creamy clam chowder are popular as well. Hawaiian music accompanies dinner five nights a week. ✉ *77-6452 Ali'i Dr., Kailua-Kona* ☎ *808/329–3195* ▤ *AE, D, DC, MC, V* ⊘ *No lunch weekends.*

$$–$$$ ✕ **Kona Beach Restaurant at King Kamehameha's Kona Beach Hotel.** The buffet-style meals at this Kailua-Kona hotel are themed and great for families: Monday it's Hawaiian, Tuesday and Thursday feature crab dishes and tempura, and Friday and Saturday are for prime rib and seafood. Tables overlook a torch-lighted lawn. Beyond is the beach, with outrigger canoes and a thatch house built on a restored heiau. A Sunday champagne brunch is served from 9 to 1. ✉ *75-5660 Palani Rd., Kailua-Kona* ☎ *808/329–2911* ▤ *AE, D, DC, MC, V.*

$$–$$$ ✕ **Kona Inn Restaurant.** In the historic Kona Inn, this open-air restaurant, which faces a wide lawn with the ocean beyond, has been a longtime favorite for cocktails at sunset in the café. A more formal menu is served in the main dining area; fresh fish—'ahi and mahimahi—and beef entrées are consistently delectable. ✉ *75-5744 Ali'i Dr., Kailua-Kona* ☎ *808/329–4455* ▤ *AE, MC, V.*

$ ✕ **Manago Hotel.** Manago offers a time-warp experience: a vintage neon sign identifies the hotel, and Formica tables, ceiling fans, and venetian blinds add to the flavor of this film noir spot. Pork chops are popular, but the *ono* (an albacore-like fish) is the best deal. The restaurant is about 20 minutes south of Kailua-Kona. ✉ *82-6155 Māmalahoa Hwy., Captain Cook* ☎ *808/323–2642* ⊕ *www.managohotel.com* ▤ *D, DC, MC, V* ⊘ *Closed Mon.*

¢–$ ✕ **Ocean View Inn.** To those on a tight budget, this local hangout facing the pier at Kailua Bay has been a lifesaver for breakfast, lunch, and dinner since the 1920s. Chinese and American food are on the plate-lunch menu, and you can get Hawaiian specialties à la carte. The atmosphere is pure old-time diner, with a funky full bar. Note that the "ocean view" is across the road. ✉ *75-5683 Ali'i Dr., Kailua-Kona* ☎ *808/329–9998* ▤ *No credit cards* ⊘ *Closed Mon.*

¢ ✕ **Bubba's.** If you're hankering for a burger but don't want the chain variety, try Bubba's. Their menu lists a bunch of them plus other sandwiches, salads, sides, and more. For something different, try the corn dog or local-style chili rice. The atmosphere is casual and fun, as shown by their slogan: "We cheat tourists, drunks and attorneys." ✉ *75-5705 Kuakini Highway Kailua-Kona* ☎ *808/329–2966* ⊕ *www.bubbaburger.com* ▤ *MC, V.*

Contemporary/Hawaiian

$–$$$ ✕ **Huggo's.** Open windows extend out over the rocks at the ocean's edge, and at night you can almost touch the manta rays drawn to the spotlights. Relax with a Kīlauea cocktail for two, or feast on fresh local

THE PLATE LUNCH TRADITION

To experience island history first-hand, take a seat at one of Hawai'i's ubiquitous "plate lunch" eateries, and order a segmented Styrofoam plate piled with rice, macaroni salad, and maybe some fiery pickled vegetable condiment. On the sugar plantations, native Hawaiians and immigrant workers from many different countries ate together in the fields, sharing food from their "kaukau kits," the utilitarian version of the Japanese bento lunchbox. From this "melting pot" came the vibrant language of pidgin and its equivalent in food: the plate lunch.

At beaches and events, you'll probably see a few tiny kitchens-on-wheels, another excellent venue for sampling plate lunch. These portable restaurants are descendants of "lunch wagons" that began selling food to plantation workers in the 1930s. Try the deep-fried chicken katsu (rolled in Japanese panko flour and spices). The marinated beef teriyaki is

another good choice, as is miso butterfish. The noodle soup, saimin, with its Japanese fish stock and Chinese red-tinted barbecue pork, is a distinctly local medley. Koreans have contributed spicy barbecue kal-bi ribs, often served with chili-laden kimchi (pickled cabbage). Portuguese bean soup and tangy Filipino adobo stew are also favorites. The most popular Hawaiian contribution to the plate lunch is the laulau, a mix of meat and fish and young taro leaves, wrapped in more taro leaves and steamed.

If you are reluctant to try a corner lunch wagon, go to local franchises Zippy's or L&L Drive-In for large, reasonably priced portions. For nouveau (and less carb-packed) plate lunches, check out Tex Drive-In at Honoka'a on the Big Island or Kaka'ako Kitchen in Ward Centre, near downtown Honolulu.

---

seafood. **Huggo's on the Rocks,** next door, has become Kailua-Kona's hot spot for drinks, wraps, sandwiches, pizza, and burgers. Lawn tables are right next to the water. ⊠ *75-5828 Kahakai Rd., off Ali'i Dr., Kailua-Kona* ☎ *808/329–1493* ⊕ *www.huggos.com* ⊟ *AE, D, DC, MC, V.*

$–$$ ✕ **Ke'ei Café.** This casual restaurant is in a plantation-style building 15 minutes south of Kona. Delicious dinners with Brazilian, Asian, and European flavors utilize fresh ingredients provided by local farmers. Try the Thai red curry or wok-seared 'ahi accompanied by a selection from the extensive wine list. ⊠ *Hwy. 11, ½ mi south of Kainaliu, Hōnaunau* ☎ *808/328–8451* ⚹ *Reservations essential* ⊟ *No credit cards* ⊗ *Closed Sun.*

¢–$ ✕ **Sam Choy's Kaloko Restaurant.** Locals come here to fuel up on the huge breakfast, *loco moco* (rice, gravy, and grilled onions topped with 13 choices ranging from Spam to teriyaki chicken), and home-style plate lunches. The restaurant is cavernous and cafeteria-like and is adorned with photos of celebrity visitors. It's in the Kaloka Light Industrial Park, off Highway 19, between Kona and the airport. ⊠ *73-5576 Kauhola St., Kailua-Kona* ☎ *808/326–1545* ⊟ *MC, V* ⊗ *No dinner.*

¢ ✕ **Kona Mix Plate.** Don't be surprised if you find yourself rubbing elbows with lots of hungry locals at this inconspicuous Kona lunch spot.

The antithesis of a tourist trap, this casual island favorite with fluorescent lighting and stark wooden tables is all about the food. Try the teriyaki chicken, shrimp tempura, or the *katsu*—a chicken breast fried with Japanese bread crumbs and served with a sweet, rich sauce. ⊠ *341 Palani St., Kailua-Kona* ☎ *808/329–8104* ▭ *No credit cards* ⊙ *Closed Sun.*

Continental

$–$$$ ✕ **Tropics Café at Royal Kona Resort.** From the open-air dining room, you'll have a lovely view of boats bobbing in Kailua Bay, outlined by the sun. The restaurant serves daily breakfast buffets and is open nightly for à la carte dinners, but the place is best known for its ample seafood and prime-rib buffets on Tuesday, Friday, and Saturday nights, a good-value feast for big eaters. The resort is within walking distance of central Kailua-Kona. ⊠ *75-5852 Ali'i Dr., Kailua-Kona* ☎ *808/329–3111* ▭ *AE, D, DC, MC, V.*

Eclectic

$$$–$$$$ ✕ **Edward's at Kanaloa.** What is essentially a covered patio next to the pool of a condo complex also happens to be (weather permitting) a fabulous restaurant overlooking the ocean. Real tablecloths, fresh flowers, and candles on the tables make this a romantic spot as well. The Mediterranean menu includes wild game, fresh fish, rack of lamb, pork tenderloin, and a 16-ounce T-bone steak. Edward's is discreetly tucked away inside a residential community just south of the Keahou Shopping Center; it's a good idea to call for directions. Reservations are recommended. ⊠ *Kanaloa at Kona, 78-261 Manukai St., Kailua-Kona* ☎ *808/324–1434* ▭ *MC, V.*

$$–$$$ ✕ **Oodles of Noodles.** Chef Amy Ferguson-Ota combines Southwestern flavors with Hawaiian regional cuisine and a touch of French cooking. There are noodles of all types, in all shapes, from all ethnic backgrounds—be they as delicate spring rolls, a crisp garnish to an exquisite salad, or as orecchiette with wok-seared spiced 'ahi and shiitake cream. ⊠ *Crossroads Shopping Center, 75-1129 Henry St., Kailua-Kona* ☎ *808/329–9222* ▭ *AE, D, DC, MC, V.*

French

$$$–$$$$ ✕ **La Bourgogne.** A genial husband-and-wife team owns this relaxing, country-style restaurant with dark-wood walls and private, romantic booths. The traditional French menu has classics such as beef fillet with a cabernet sauvignon sauce, escargots, rack of lamb with roasted garlic and rosemary, and a less-traditional venison with a pomegranate glaze. ⊠ *Kuakini Plaza S on Hwy. 11, 77-6400 Nālani St., Kailua-Kona* ☎ *808/329–6711* ⌖ *Reservations essential* ▭ *AE, D, DC, MC, V* ⊙ *Closed Sun. and Mon. No lunch.*

Indonesian

$$ ✕ **Sibu.** This restaurant is inside a tiny shopping mall (and nearly hidden by a large stone fountain) close to the pier in central Kailua-Kona. Try the shrimp satay flavored with coconut milk and red chili and served with peanut sauce. Be forewarned: the tasty Ayum Panggang Pedis (spicy grilled chicken fillets with black and red pepper) really packs a

punch! ✉ *75-5695 Ali'i Dr., Kailua-Kona* ☎ *808/329–1112* 🖃 *No credit cards.*

Italian

\$\$ - \$\$\$ ✕ **Michaelangelo's Italian & Seafood Restaurant.** This dining room has a lovely upstairs location, with great waterfront views, in the Waterfront Row complex of shops and eateries. The menu features traditional Italian fare prepared with creative local flavors. Favorite entrées include lasagna, chicken cacciatore, and macadamia-nut sea scallops. The crusted mozzarella planks or fried calamari are excellent appetizers. Dress is casual, but reservations are recommended. ✉ *75-5770 Ali'i Dr., Kailua-Kona* ☎ *808/329–4436* 🖃 *AE, D, MC, V.*

Japanese

\$–\$\$ ✕ **Teshima's.** Locals show up at Teshima's whenever they're in the mood for sashimi, beef *hekka* (beef and vegetables cooked together in an iron pot), or puffy shrimp tempura at a reasonable price. You might also want to try a *teishoku* (tray) of assorted Japanese delicacies. Service is laid-back and friendly. The restaurant is 15 minutes south of Kailua-Kona. ✉ *Māmalahoa Hwy., Honalo* ☎ *808/322–9140* 🖃 *No credit cards.*

Mexican

¢ ✕ **Tacos El Unico.** At last, Mexican food at the right price on the Big Island. You'll find an array of soft taco choices (beef, chicken, and more), burritos, *tortas*, great homemade tamales, quesadillas, and *taquitos*. Order at the counter, take a seat outside at one of a dozen yellow tables with blue umbrellas, and enjoy all the good flavors served up in those red plastic baskets. ✉ *Kona Marketplace, 75-5729 Ali'i Dr., Kailua-Kona* ☎ *808/326–4033* 🖃 *No credit cards.*

Thai

\$–\$\$ ✕ **Orchid Thai Cuisine.** This reasonably priced, family-run restaurant is off the beaten track in a small strip mall in Kona's old industrial area. It's cheerfully decorated with purple and gold Thai fabrics, and orchids (real and fake) abound. Entrées range from barbecue hen with lemongrass and garlic to basic curries (red, green, yellow, and "evil"); don't miss the summer rolls. Top off your meal with mango and sticky rice. ✉ *77-5563 Kaiwi St., Suite B 27-28, Kailua-Kona* ☎ *808/327–9437* 🖃 *MC, V* ☉ *Closed Sun.*

\$–\$\$ ✕ **Thai Rin Restaurant.** The Thai chef-owner at this old-timer in Ali'i Sunset Plaza is likely to take your order, cook it, and bring it to your table himself. The menu includes five curries, a green-papaya salad, and a popular Thai Rin platter, which combines spring rolls, satay, *tom yum* (lemongrass soup), and beef salad. ✉ *75-5799 Ali'i Dr., Kailua-Kona* ☎ *808/329–2929* 🖃 *AE, D, DC, MC, V.*

Kohala Coast

American/Casual

\$\$–\$\$\$\$ ✕ **Big Island Steak House.** The walls here are adorned with Hawaiian kitsch dating from the '30s, '40s, and '50s—'ukuleles, steamer trunks, and a zany grass-skirted gorilla. As the name implies, the place serves steak—large portions in different styles, straight from the grill and without much fanfare. Also on the menu are local fish (charbroiled, sautéed, or blackened) and live lobster. There's an outdoor dining area overlooking the golf course lake. The Merry Wahine Bar serves tropical libations. ✉ *King's Shops, Waikoloa Resort, 250 Waikoloa Beach Dr., Kohala Coast* ☎ *808/886–8805* ▭ *AE, D, MC, V* ⊘ *No lunch.*

$–$$$ ✕ **Kawaihae Harbor Grill and Seafood Bar.** This popular little restaurant is always packed—the enticing aromas alone would draw anyone in. Both the Harbor Grill and the new hot spot, the Seafood Bar (upstairs in a separate building), are housed in historic buildings from the 1850s. Errol Flynn was here—a life preserver off his yacht hangs in the thatched bar along with old records, hula skirts, a surfboard, and other vintage Hawaiiana. The bar is a good place to wait before your table is ready, or you can just feast from the all-pūpū menu. Fresh island fish (charbroiled, sautéed, and Cajun-style), ribs, chicken, and more are served at the equally atmospheric restaurant. ✉ *Kawaihae Harbor, Hwy. 270, Kawaihae* ☎ *808/882–1368* ▭ *MC, V.*

$$–$$$ ✕ **The Village Steak House.** Sunset views overlooking the golf course and steaks are the highlights here. Start with pūpū like Togarashi skewered shrimp, crab cakes Kohala or, Hawaiian-Chinese mushrooms. Steaks come in all sizes and include filet, tenderloin shiitake, New York strip, T-bone, and porterhouse. Other features range from fresh island fish, to chicken Ka'u with orange sauce, baby back ribs with passion fruit-hoisin sauce, pork chops pineapple, curry coconut prawns, and more. There is a quiet, comfortable clubhouse atmosphere. Dress is casual, but reservations are recommended. ✉ *68-1792 Melia St., Waikoloa* ☎ *808/883–9644* ▭ *AE, D, MC, V* ⊘ *Closed Mon.*

Chinese

$–$$$ ✕ **Grand Palace Chinese Restaurant.** A reasonable alternative in a land of high-price hotel dining, this restaurant offers dishes from most regions, including such standards as egg foo yung, wonton soup, chicken with snow peas, and beef with broccoli. More adventurous dishes include sautéed local seafood, lobster, and sizzling shrimp with garlic sauce. Etched-glass panels are a nice embellishment. ✉ *King's Shops, Waikoloa Resort, 250 Waikoloa Beach Dr., Kohala Coast* ☎ *808/886–6668* ▭ *AE, DC, MC, V.*

Contemporary/Hawaiian

★ $$$$ ✕ **Hale Samoa at Kona Village Resort.** Formal and romantic, this Kona Village restaurant has a magical atmosphere, especially at sunset. In a Samoan setting with tapa screens and candles, you can feast on five-course prix-fixe dinners that change daily. Specialties may include papaya-and-coconut bisque, duck stuffed with andouille sausage, or wok-charred prime strip loin. Reservations can be made only on the day you want to dine. ✉ *Kona Village, 12 mi north of Kailua-Kona on Hwy. 19, North Kona Coast* ☎ *808/325–5555* ⬥ *Reservations essential* ▭ *AE, DC, MC, V* ⊘ *Closed Wed., Fri., and 1st wk in Dec.*

★ $$$–$$$$ ✕ **The Batik at Mauna Kea Beach Hotel.** For the hotel's elegant signature restaurant—with its glass-enclosed, split-level waterfront dining room—executive chef Thomas Woods combines French-Mediterranean elements with Indonesian influences to create dazzling dishes such as a macadamia-nut-crusted ono with lemongrass-coconut emulsion. Most of the staff has been here for 15 years, so the service is seamless. ⊠ 62-100 Mauna Kea Beach Dr., Kohala Coast ☎ 808/882–5810 ⊟ AE, D, DC, MC, V ☺ Closed nights vary. No lunch.

★ $$$–$$$$ ✕ **Coast Grille at Hāpuna Beach Prince Hotel.** This spacious, high-ceiling restaurant has a lānai overlooking the ocean. Oyster lovers should head straight to the oyster bar. The creative Pacific Rim menu has such seafood dishes as pan-seared *opah* (moonfish) in cardamom sauce and, when available, delicate farm-raised *moi*, in ancient times enjoyed only by chiefs. Don't overlook the appetizer sampler with seared 'ahi and tempura sushi, and save room for warm Valrhona chocolate cake. ⊠ *Hāpuna Beach Prince Hotel, 62-100 Kauna'oa Dr., Kohala Coast* ☎ *808/880–3192* ⊟ *AE, D, DC, MC, V* ☺ *No lunch.*

★ $$$–$$$$ ✕ **CanoeHouse at the Mauna Lani Bay Hotel and Bungalows.** This award-winning, open-air beachfront restaurant is among Hawai'i's best. Its cuisine is Pacific Rim the way it used to be: a matching of pure Asian and Western flavors in imaginative entrées such as Shanghai lobster, spiced lacquered tofu with Chinese greens and jasmine rice, and the popular seafood salad. ⊠ *68-1400 Mauna Lani Dr., Kohala Coast* ☎ *808/885–6622* ⊟ *AE, D, DC, MC, V.*

$$$–$$$$ ✕ **Hawai'i Calls at Waikoloa Beach Marriott.** With its retro art, Hawai'i Calls offers a nostalgic taste of the past, from the '20s to the '50s. The menu, however, is contemporary and fresh, changing seasonally, with specialties such as moi, seared crispy and served with coconut rice, pickled ginger, and spicy cucumber salad. Don't miss the macadamia-chocolate tart with vanilla ice cream. The spacious outdoor setting is lovely—ask for a table near the koi pond and waterfall—and a great place to watch the sun set as tiki torches light up the gardens. The adjacent Clipper Lounge serves tropical drinks and features a bistro menu. ⊠ *69-275 Waikoloa Beach Dr., Kohala Coast* ☎ *808/886–6789* ⊟ *AE, D, DC, MC, V.*

$$$–$$$$ ✕ **Kamuela Provision Company at the Hilton Waikoloa Village.** Quiet guitar music, tables along a breezy lānai, and a sweeping view of the Kohala-Kona coastline are the perfect accompaniments to KPC's elegant yet down-to-earth Hawai'i regional cuisine. Popular are the bouillabaisse with nori crostini and the Parker Ranch rib-eye steak with green peppercorn sauce. KPC is a great place to sip cocktails—the adjacent Wine Bar makes for a romantic evening in itself, with an appetizer menu and more than 40 labels available by the glass. ⊠ *425 Waikoloa Beach Dr., Kohala Coast* ☎ *808/886–1234* ⊟ *AE, D, DC, MC, V* ☺ *No lunch.*

$$$–$$$$ ✕ **Pahu i'a at Four Seasons Resort Hualālai.** The English translation for
FodorsChoice *pahu i'a* is "aquarium," and the 9- by 4-foot aquarium in the entrance
★ casts a dreamy light through this exquisite restaurant. Presentation is paramount—tables are beautifully set, with handblown glassware—and the food tastes as good as it looks. Asian-influenced dishes on the menu stand out for their layers of flavor. Don't miss the three sashimi and three caviar appetizers, or the crispy whole moi served with Asian slaw, black beans, and sweet chili-lime vinaigrette. Reserve a table on the patio and you may be able to spot whales while dining. ⊠ *Four Sea-*

sons Resort Hualālai, 100 Kaʻūpūlehu Dr., North Kona Coast ☎ *808/ 325–8000* ▭ *AE, D, DC, MC, V* ⊙ *No lunch.*

$$–$$$ ✕ **Bamboo Restaurant.** It's out of the way, but the food is good and the service has a country flair. Creative entrées feature fresh island fish prepared several ways. Thai-style fish, for example, combines lemongrass, kaffir lime leaves, and coconut milk—best washed down with a passion-fruit margarita or passion-fruit iced tea. Bamboo finishes, bold artwork, and an old unfinished wooden floor make the restaurant cozy. Local musicians entertain on Friday and Saturday night. ⊠ *Old Takata Store, Hwy. 270, Hāwī* ☎ *808/889–5555* ▭ *MC, V* ⊙ *Closed Mon. No dinner Sun.*

★ **$$–$$$** ✕ **Roy's Waikoloa Bar and Grill.** You can easily fill up on the enormous selection of appetizers at Roy Yamaguchi's cool and classy place overlooking a golf course lake. If you want a full meal, try the blackened island ʻahi with spicy soy-mustard-butter sauce, or jade-pesto steamed Hawaiian whitefish with cilantro, ginger, garlic, and peanut oil. An extensive wines-by-the-glass list offers good pairing options. Be forewarned that the place tends to get noisy. ⊠ *King's Shops, Waikoloa Resort, 250 Waikoloa Beach Dr., Kohala Coast* ☎ *808/886–4321* ⊕ *www. roysrestaurant.com* ▭ *AE, D, DC, MC, V.*

Eclectic

★ **$$$–$$$$** ✕ **Brown's Beach House at the Fairmont Orchid.** The gorgeous torchlighted setting at this waterfront restaurant makes this the quintessential splurge. The restaurant combines a casual beach vibe with elegant resort dining at night. Wok-seared Kona lobster, farm-raised on the island and served with lobster ravioli in a wasabi-butter sauce, is rich and delicious. Leave room for the chocolate hazelnut soufflé. ⊠ *1 N. Kanikū Dr., Kohala Coast* ☎ *808/885–2000* ▭ *AE, D, DC, MC, V* ⊙ *No lunch.*

★ **$$$–$$$$** ✕ **The Grill at the Fairmont Orchid.** With a superb wine list and menu, this steak restaurant has earned its stellar reputation. Rich koa-wood paneling and a piano next to a small dance floor give it an old-world vibe. Entrées include robust dishes such as filet mignon of certified black Angus beef, wild game, and whole Keāhole-Maine lobster. Open-air seating is available, and the service is impeccable. ⊠ *The Fairmont Orchid, 1 N. Kanikū Dr., Kohala Coast* ☎ *808/885–2000* ⚏ *Reservations essential* ▭ *AE, D, DC, MC, V.*

$–$$$ ✕ **Café Pesto.** Both branches of Café Pesto—in the quaint harbor town of Kawaihae and in Hilo—are equally popular. Fresh local seafood, exotic pizzas (with chili grilled shrimp, shiitake mushrooms, and cilantro crème fraîche, for example), and Asian-inspired pastas and risottos reflect the ethnic diversity of the island. Local microbrews and a full-service bar make this a good place to end the evening. ⊠ *Kawaihae Shopping Center, Kawaihae* ☎ *808/882–1071* ⊠ *S. Hata Bldg., 308 Kamehameha Ave., Hilo* ☎ *808/969–6640* ⊕ *www.cafepesto.com* ▭ *AE, D, DC, MC, V.*

Italian

$$$–$$$$ ✕ **Donatoni's at the Hilton Waikoloa Village.** This romantic restaurant overlooking the boat canal resembles an Italian villa and serves scrumptious dishes with the subtle sauces of northern Italy. From mahimahi with marinated artichokes to fettuccine with Hawaiian lobster, this intimate place sets out to please. Be sure to look over the Italian wine and champagne list. ⊠ *425 Waikoloa Beach Dr., Kohala Coast* ☎ *808/886–1234* ⊟ *AE, D, DC, MC, V* ☉ *No lunch.*

Japanese

★ **$$$–$$$$** ✕ **Hakone Steakhouse and Sushi Bar at Hāpuna Beach Prince Hotel.** It's hard not to start whispering in this tranquil and graceful restaurant. Choose from exquisite Japanese sukiyaki, shabu shabu (thin slices of beef cooked in broth), and an elaborate sushi bar. The broad selection of sake (try a sakitini, a martini made with sake) is guaranteed to enliven your meal. ⊠ *Hāpuna Beach Prince Hotel, 62-100 Kaunaʻoa Dr., Kohala Coast* ☎ *808/880–3192* ⊟ *AE, D, DC, MC, V* ☉ *No lunch.*

★ **$$$–$$$$** ✕ **Imari at the Hilton Waikoloa Village.** This elegant restaurant, complete with waterfalls and a teahouse, serves sukiyaki and tempura aimed to please mainland tastes. Beyond the impressive display of Imari porcelain at the entrance, you'll find *teppanyaki* (beef or shrimp cooked table-side), shabu shabu, and an outstanding sushi bar. Impeccable service by kimono-clad waitresses adds to the quiet refinement. ⊠ *425 Waikoloa Beach Dr., Kohala Coast* ☎ *808/886–1234* ⊟ *AE, D, DC, MC, V* ☉ *No lunch.*

Mexican

$–$$ ✕ **Tres Hombres Beach Grill.** This casual restaurant serves the usual Mexican combination plates (enchiladas, tacos, chiles rellenos) as well as burgers and sandwiches at lunch. Dinner items include bean-and-rice combinations, fresh fish, salads, and steaks. The separate bar is known for its Mexican beer and tequila selection. The restaurant has two locations, one in Kawaihae and one in Kailua-Kona. ⊠ *Kawaihae Shopping Center, Kawaihae* ☎ *808/882–1031* ⊠ *75-5864 Wālua Rd. (just above Aliʻi Dr.), Kailua-Kona* ☎ *808/329–2173* ⊟ *MC, V.*

Waimea

American/Casual

$$–$$$ ✕ **Koa House Grill.** In the heart of cowboy country, this bar and grill has developed into a busy stop for Waimea's residents. Local Parker Ranch Angus beef is a favorite, and a full salad bar has fresh Waimea greens. Large windows open out onto the Keck Observatory headquarters. ⊠ *Waimea Shopping Center, 65-1144 Māmalahoa Hwy.* ☎ *808/885–2088* ⊟ *AE, D, MC, V.*

$$–$$$ ✕ **Parker Ranch Grill.** With cowhides serving as wallpaper and riding boots as doorknobs, this popular restaurant is not shy about its paniolo identity and Parker Ranch heritage. In front of a blazing fire, the koa tables are a perfect setting for, of course, Parker Ranch beef entrées. A separate bar area offers a variety of pūpū. ⊠ *Parker Ranch Shopping Center, 67-1185 Māmalahoa Hwy.* ☎ *808/887–2624* ⊕ *www.parkerranchgrill.com* ⊟ *AE, D, MC, V.*

Contemporary

$$$–$$$$ ✕ **Daniel Thiebaut.** Underneath 11-foot ceilings, the space once known as the historic Chock In Store (built in 1900) has been transformed into seven dining areas. Collectibles abound, such as antique porcelain, original bar stools, and a long redwood community dining table, once the store's countertop. Chef Daniel Thiebaut's French-Asian creations include an amazing appetizer of sweet-corn crab cake with a lemongrass, coconut, and lobster sauce. Other signature dishes include Hunan-style rack of lamb served with eggplant compote, and Big Island goat cheese. ⊠ *65-1259 Kawaihae Rd.* ☎ *808/887–2200* ⊕ *www.danielthiebaut.com* ⊟ *AE, D, DC, MC, V.*

★ **$$$** ✕ **Merriman's.** This is the signature restaurant of Peter Merriman, one of the pioneers of Hawai'i regional cuisine. Merriman's is the home of the original wok-charred 'ahi, usually served with buttery Wainaku corn. If you prefer meat, try the Kahuā Ranch lamb, raised to the restaurant's specifications, or opt for the prime Kansas City Cut steak, grilled to order. The wine list includes 22 selections poured by the glass, and the staff is refreshingly knowledgeable. ⊠ *'Opelo Plaza, Hwy. 19 and 'Opelo Rd. 65-1227 'Opelo Road, Waimea/* ☎ *808/885–6822* ⊕ *www. merrimanshawaii.com* ⌔ *Reservations essential* ⊟ *AE, MC, V.*

Continental

$$$–$$$$ ✕ **Edelweiss.** Faithful local diners and visitors alike flock to this relaxed, family-oriented restaurant with rustic redwood furnishings. The rack of lamb is always excellent. Soup, salad, and coffee or tea are included in dinner prices. A varied menu includes 15 to 20 daily specials (such as a sausage platter and fresh seafood), many rich and with a German flavor. ⊠ *Hwy. 19, entering Waimea* ☎ *808/885–6800* ⌔ *Reservations essential* ⊟ *MC, V* ☾ *Closed Sun. and Mon. and Sept.*

WHERE TO STAY

You'll almost always be able to find a room on the Big Island, but you might not get your first choice if you wait until the last minute. Make reservations six months to a year in advance if you're visiting during the winter season (December 15 through April 15). The week after Easter Sunday, when the Merrie Monarch Festival is in full swing, all of Hilo's rooms are taken. Kailua-Kona bursts at the seams in mid-October during the Ironman World Triathlon Championship. (Even tougher than trying to find a room at these times is trying to find a rental car.)

Hotel package deals are often available in all price categories and may include a rental car, meals, spa treatments, golf, and other activities. Children under 17 can sometimes stay for free. Check with a travel agent or visit the listed Web sites. All rooms have air-conditioning, a TV, and a phone unless otherwise indicated.

If you choose a B&B, inn, or an out-of-the-way hotel, explain your expectations fully and ask plenty of questions before booking. Be clear about your travel and location needs. Some places require stays of two or three days. Many B&Bs close to Hawai'i Volcanoes National Park are not the best locations for beach and sun worshipers; rain forests come with the price of humid conditions. When booking, ask about car-rental arrangements, as many B&B networks offer discounted rates.

Hilo

$$$–$$$$ 🖼 **The Palms Cliff House Inn.** This handsome Victorian-style mansion is perched on the sea cliffs 150 feet above the crashing surf of the tropical Hamakua Coast, 15 mi north of Hilo. Eight beautifully appointed suites, with ocean views from private lānai, offer secluded, quiet, tropical elegance. Guests can stroll the lush grounds and pick tropical fruit and macadamia nuts from the gardens of the 3½-acre estate. High tea is served English-style on Saturday from 3 to 5. ✉ *28-3514 Māmalahoa Hwy., Honomū, 96728-0189* ☎ *808/963–6076* 🖷 *808/963–6316* ⊕ *www.palmscliffhouse.com* 🛏 *8 suites* ♨ *Cable TV, Internet; no a/c in some rooms, no kids under 12, no smoking* ⊟ *AE, D, DC, MC, V* ⑩ *BP.*

★ **$$–$$$$** 🖼 **Hilo Hawaiian Hotel.** With large bay-front rooms offering spectacular views of Mauna Kea and Coconut Island, this is one of the most pleasant lodgings on Hilo Bay. Streetside rooms overlook the golf course. Most accommodations have private lānai, and kitchenettes are available in some one-bedroom suites. Views of the bay are showcased in the Queen's Court dining room, and the Wai`oli Lounge has entertainment Thursday through Saturday. ✉ *71 Banyan Dr., 96720* ☎ *808/935–9361, 800/367–5004 from the mainland, 800/272–5275 interisland* 🖷 *808/ 961–9642* ⊕ *www.hilohawaiian.com* 🛏 *286 rooms, 6 suites* ♨ *Restaurant, some kitchenettes, refrigerators, pool, bar, meeting room* ⊟ *AE, D, DC, MC, V.*

★ **$$$** 🖼 **Shipman House Bed & Breakfast Inn.** You'll have a choice between one of three rooms in the main house—a 100-year-old turreted "castle"— or one of two rooms in a separate cottage unit. The B&B is on 5½ verdant acres on Reed's Island; the house is furnished with antique koa and period pieces, some dating from the days when Queen Lili`uokalani came to tea. On Tuesday night, an authentic hula school practices Hawai`i's ancient dances in the house. ✉ *131 Kaiulani St., 96720* ☎ *808/934– 8002 or 800/627–8447* 🖷 *808/934–8002* ⊕ *www.hilo-hawaii.com* 🛏 *3 rooms, 2 cottage rooms* ♨ *Fans, refrigerators, library; no a/c, no room phones, no room TVs, no smoking* ⊟ *AE, MC, V* ⑩ *CP.*

$$ 🖼 **Hilo Bay Hotel, Uncle Billy's.** Don't expect more than a casual, inexpensive place to stay at this friendly, easygoing hotel—a popular stopover for Neighbor Islanders who enjoy proprietor Uncle Billy Kimo's Hawaiian hospitality. A nightly hula show and entertainment during dinner are part of the fun. ✉ *87 Banyan Dr., 96720* ☎ *808/935–0861, 800/ 367–5102 from the mainland, 800/442–5841 interisland* 🖷 *808/935– 7903* ⊕ *www.unclebilly.com* 🛏 *145 rooms* ♨ *Restaurant, some kitchenettes, refrigerators, pool, bar, laundry facilities, Internet, meeting room, free parking* ⊟ *AE, D, DC, MC, V.*

$–$$ 🖼 **Hale Kai.** On a bluff above Hilo Bay, just 2 mi from downtown Hilo, this 5,400-square-foot modern home has four impeccable rooms with patios and a private loft that is ideal for families—all with grand ocean views and within earshot of lapping waves. Fresh flowers add a warm, European touch. The Norwegian-Hawaiian hosts, Evonne and Paul Bjornen, serve a delightful breakfast—fruits, breads, and special egg dishes—on an outdoor deck or in the kitchen's bay-window dining area. ⊠ *111 Honoli'i Pali St., 96720* ☎ *808/935–6330* 🖷 *808/935–8439* ⊕ *www.halekaihawaii.com* ⇆ *4 rooms, 1 suite* ⚭ *Fans, pool, hot tub, laundry service, no smoking* ☰ *No credit cards.*

$–$$ 🏨 **Waterfalls Inn Bed & Breakfast.** This elegant old family home is located in the exclusive Reed's Bay neighborhood, just a few blocks from downtown Hilo. Relaxation is the key here. Bounded on two sides by tropical streams and forest, there is no traffic and no noise except the gentle gurgle of the stream. The 1916-era home has been carefully restored, retaining the original light fixtures, fine 'ōhi'a wood flooring, antique furniture, and some original bath fixtures. You'll find lots of room to unwind in the expansive glassed-in lānai; breakfast is served in the large dining room. Business travelers enjoy easy access to town, government offices, and the University of Hawai'i at Hilo. ⊠ *240 Kaiulani St., 96720* ☎ *808/969–3407* ⊕ *www.waterfallsinn.com* ⇆ *4 large suites* ⚭ *Cable TV with movies, Internet, meeting room; no a/c* ☰ *AE, MC, V.*

$ 🏨 **Dolphin Bay Hotel.** True, the units are modest, but they are clean and inexpensive, and the staff has plenty of aloha. Coffee and fresh fruit are offered daily. Just four blocks from Hilo Bay, in a residential area called Pu'ue'o, the hotel borders a verdant 2-acre Hawaiian garden with jungle trails and shady places to rest. The owner loves the Volcano and the camera: stunning lava pictures adorn the common area. Guests of the hotel return repeatedly, and it's ideal for families who seek a home base. ⊠ *333 'Iliahi St., 96720* ☎ *808/935–1466* 🖷 *808/935–1523* ⊕ *www. dolphinbayhotel.com* ⇆ *13 rooms, 4 1-bedroom units, 1 2-bedroom unit* ⚭ *Fans, kitchens, kitchenettes, microwave; no a/c, no room phones, no room TVs* ☰ *MC, V.*

$ 🏨 **The Inn at Kulaniapia.** With an awesome view of Hilo Bay 4 mi below, as well as access to a magnificent 120-foot waterfall that tumbles into a 300-foot-wide swimming pond, this inn is an oasis of beauty and tranquility. Trails meander to the river, and Hilo is just a 15-minute drive away over sugarcane roads. Hosts Jane and Len Sutton added Asian accents, koa, and eucalyptus wood floors to the inn. Complete breakfasts are served, and you can cook an informal dinner on the barbecue. ⬤ *Box 11338, 96721* ☎ *808/935–8088 or 888/838–6373* 🖷 *808/935–8088* ⊕ *www.waterfall.net* ⇆ *4 rooms* ⚭ *No a/c, no smoking* ☰ *AE, MC, V.*

¢–$$ 🏨 **Arnott's Lodge.** Owner Doug Arnott runs a budget lodge for backpackers that manages to combine the joy of oceanside wilderness with the convenience of being just minutes away from the airport. You can choose to tent on the lawn or stay in dormitory-style bunk beds, semiprivate rooms, or private accommodations. Four rooms in an adjacent house have private tile bathrooms. There's a shared kitchen and a separate video gazebo for all. Young travelers take advantage of guided activities provided by the lodge. Arnott's latest addition is an Internet café. ⊠ *98 'Apapane Rd., 96720* ☎ *808/969–7097* 🖷 *808/961–9638* ⊕ *www. arnottslodge.com* ⇆ *12 semiprivate units, 6 private units, 36 bunks* ⚭ *Some microwaves, hair salon, bicycles, hiking, laundry facilities, Internet, airport shuttle, travel services; no a/c in some rooms, no room phones, no room TVs* ☰ *AE, D, DC, MC, V.*

Where to Stay
on the Big Island

¢–$$ ⊞ **Hilo Seaside Hotel.** This is as close to the airport as you can get, which means it can get noisy during the day. It's also a friendly, laid-back, and otherwise peaceful place, with neutral rooms that have private lānai. The nicest ones overlook the koi-filled lagoon, or are around the pool. The staff is friendly, the restaurant serves local fare, and the tropical foliage around you gives you a sense of old Hawai'i. ⊠ *126 Banyan Way, 96720* ☎ *808/935–0821 or 800/560–5557* 🖷 *808/969–9195* ⊕ *www.hiloseasidehotel.com* ➥ *135 rooms* ♿ *Restaurant, fans, some kitchenettes, refrigerators, pool, laundry facilities* ☰ *AE, D, DC, MC, V.*

Puna

$$–$$$$ ⊞ **Kalani Oceanside Retreat.** An unusual tropical getaway, Kalani is an out-of-the-way retreat with healthful cuisine, nearby thermal springs, a yoga retreat center, and Watsu-therapy (water shiatsu) training, as well as programs on Hawaiian culture, healing, and gay relationships. Accommodations include campsites; shared rooms; cottage units with shared kitchen; lodge rooms; and private, luxurious tree-house units. Bathing suits are optional both on the nearby beach and at the Olympic-size pool. Full meal plans are available at an additional charge. ⊠ *Pāhoa-Beach Rd. (Hwy. 137), R.R. 2 (Box 4500), Pāhoa 96778* ☎ *808/965–7828 or 800/800–6886* 🖷 *808/965–0527* ⊕ *www.kalani.com* ➥ *24 rooms with shared bath, 9 cottages, 4 tree-house units, 3 guest-house rooms* ♿ *Fans, some refrigerators, tennis court, pool, hair salon, hot tub, sauna, laundry facilities, laundry service, no-smoking room; no a/c, no room TVs* ☰ *AE, D, MC, V.*

$–$$$ ⊞ **Yoga Oasis.** This center, on 26 tropical acres, isn't your average vacation rental: with an expensive design of Mexican tiles, finished redwood, Balinese doorways, and imported art, it draws those who seek rejuvenation, and perhaps a free yoga lesson or two. You're close to hot springs and black-sand beaches; the Volcano is a 45-minute drive away. Bathrooms are shared. A 1,600-square-foot state-of-the-art yoga and gymnastics space, with 18-foot ceilings, crowns this friendly retreat. ⊠ *Pohoiki Rd. (Box 1935), Pāhoa 96778* ☎ *808/965–8460 or 800/274–4446* ⊕ *www.yogaoasis.org* ➥ *5 rooms with shared bath, 4 bungalows, 1 cottage* ♿ *Some fans, massage, laundry service; no a/c, no room phones, no room TVs, no smoking* ☰ *MC, V.*

★ ¢–$$ ⊞ **Bed & Breakfast Mountain View.** This modern home is surrounded by rolling forest and farmland. The secluded 4-acre estate has extensive floral gardens and a fishpond. Owners Linus and Jane Chao are longtime Big Island art educators and have an art studio on the lower level, where they conduct ongoing classes. Inquire about special packages that include art lessons. The house itself is a virtual art gallery with varied displays in oil, acrylic, watercolor, and Oriental brush paintings. ⊠ *South Kulani Rd., Kurtistown 96760* ☎ *808/968–6868 or 888/698–9896* 🖷 *808/968–7017* ⊕ *www.bbmtview.com* ➥ *4 rooms, 2 with shared bath* ♿ *Pond, fishing, billiards, laundry facilities; no a/c* ☰ *MC, V.*

Volcano/South Point

¢–$$$$ 🏠 **Chalet Kīlauea Collection.** The Collection comprises five inns and lodges and five vacation houses in and around Volcano Village; the theme rooms, suites, and vacation homes range from no-frills dorm-style bedrooms in a funky old house to a plantation mansion with its own six-person Jacuzzi. Best known is the Inn at Volcano, a "boutique resort." The two-story Treehouse Suite, with wraparound windows, a marble wet bar, and a fireplace, gives one the impression of floating on the tops of the trees. Afternoon tea is served before a fireplace. A candlelit breakfast under a glittering chandelier adds a touch of elegance. ⊠ *Wright Rd., Volcano Village 96785* ☎ *808/967–7786 or 800/937–7786* 🖷 *808/ 967–8660* ⊕ *www.volcano-hawaii.com* 🛏 *11 rooms, 9 suites, 5 houses* ⚷ *Some kitchens, some microwaves, cable TV with movies; no a/c, no phones in some rooms.* ☰ *AE, D, DC, MC, V.*

$$–$$$ 🏠 **Kīlauea Lodge.** A mile from the Hawai'i Volcanoes National Park en-
Fodor'sChoice   trance, this country inn is possibly the most elegant place to stay in the
★   area. The original building dates from the 1930s, and rooms have rich quilts, Hawaiian photographs, and European antiques, as well as their own wood-burning fireplaces. Two cottages off the main property include the two-bedroom Tutu's Place, and Pii Mauna House on the 6th fairway of the Volcano Golf Course. On property, a charming one-bedroom cottage with a gas fireplace and a deluxe honeymoon room with a private balcony are perfect for romance. ⊠ *Old Volcano Hwy. about 1 mi northeast of Volcano Store* 🖃 *Box 116, Volcano Village 96785* ☎ *808/967–7366* 🖷 *808/967–7367* ⊕ *www.kilauealodge.com* 🛏 *11 rooms, 3 cottages* ⚷ *Restaurant, dining room, hot tub, shop; no a/c, no smoking* ☰ *AE, MC, V.*

$–$$$ 🏠 **Carson's Volcano Cottages.** You can choose the privacy of a romantic hideaway with a full kitchen and a hot tub in the midst of hapu ferns; a deluxe oceanfront cottage down at Kapoho, an hour away; or the intimate rooms and cottages around the property itself. Each unit has its own theme decor, from country-style to Hawaiian. Elaborate breakfasts in the main house's cozy dining room include home-baked breads and such dishes as spinach quiche and poi doughnuts. 🖃 *Box 503, Volcano 96785* ☎ *808/967–7683 or 800/845–5282* 🖷 *808/967–8094* ⊕ *www. carsonscottage.com* 🛏 *5 rooms, 6 cottages* ⚷ *Dining room, no-smoking room; no a/c, no phones in some rooms* ☰ *AE, D, MC, V.*

$–$$$ 🏠 **Volcano House.** The rooms look a bit tired with their old-fashioned white wallpaper and faded, flowered carpets, but they're clean, and bright teal-and-peach quilts and gorgeous koa rocking chairs add some class. Besides, nothing beats the view of the crater from the higher-end rooms: the Volcano House, built in 1941, perches on the edge of Kīlauea Caldera. The Ka 'Ōhelo Dining Room is convenient after a day of hiking, and a drink in front of the 'ohi'a-wood fire in the lobby's stone fireplace is great on a cold, misty day. ⊠ *Crater Rim Dr. (Box 53), Hawai'i Volcanoes National Park 96718* ☎ *808/967–7321* 🖷 *808/967–8429* 🛏 *42 rooms* ⚷ *Restaurant, snack bar, shops; no a/c* ☰ *AE, D, DC, MC, V.*

★ $$ 🏠 **Hale Ohia Cottages.** This peaceful estate was built in 1931 as a vacation home for the Dillingham family. It has a Japanese hot tub surrounded by ancient trees and glorious gardens. Antique furnishings, stained glass, unique collectibles, and fireplaces abound. The luxurious Ihilani Cottage is an octagonal hideaway with a private garden. Another luxury unit, prosaically named Number 44 but poetic as can be with skylights and a see-through fireplace, has a bedroom that incorporates an old water tank. ⊠ *Hale Ohia Rd. off Hwy. 11 (Box 758), Volcano Village 96785* ☏ *808/967–7986 or 800/455–3803* 📠 *808/967–8610* ⊕ *www.haleohia.com* ⌦ *4 suites, 4 cottages* ⚭ *Some microwaves, refrigerators, hot tub; no a/c, no room phones, no room TVs, no smoking* ▭ *D, DC, MC, V.*

$$ 🖽 **Hydrangea Cottage & Mountain House.** You'll find this landscaped jungle estate about a mile from Hawai'i Volcanoes National Park. The private one-bedroom cottage has a wraparound covered deck and floor-to-ceiling windows looking out over giant tree ferns. The Mountain House has three bedrooms with antique furnishings, each with its own bath. Both units have a kitchen and breakfast fixings are provided. ⌂ *Reservations: Pacific Islands Reservations, 571 Pauku St., Kailua-Kona 96734* ☏ *808/262–8133* 📠 *808/262–5030* ⊕ *www.aloha.com/~pir/hydcott. html* ⌦ *1 3-bedroom house, 1 cottage* ⚭ *Kitchen, cable TV, in-room VCRs, laundry facilities; no a/c* ▭ *No credit cards.*

$–$$ 🖽 **Volcano Inn I & II.** Nestled among tree ferns within a rain forest, Volcano Inn offers a choice of four private cedar cottages with enormous picture windows, four rooms in the original main building (which is a 15-minute walk from the center of Volcano Village), three rooms in the newly added 1928-era plantation-style home, or a one-room private cottage. Wherever you stay, the owners provide a breakfast every morning that includes fresh eggs and whole-grain breads. Guests have access to a pay phone. ⊠ *19-3820 Old Volcano Hwy., Volcano Village* ⌂ *Box 490, Volcano 96785* ☏ *808/967–7293 or 800/997–2292* 📠 *808/985–7349* ⊕ *www.volcanoinn.com* ⌦ *7 rooms, 1 one-room cottage* ⚭ *Some microwaves, cable TV with movies; no a/c, no room phones, no smoking* ▭ *AE, D, DC, MC, V* ⏍ *BP.*

¢–$$ 🖽 **My Island Bed & Breakfast Inn.** Gordon, Joann, and daughter Ki'i Morse opened their historic century-old home and 7-acre botanical estate to visitors in 1985. The house is the oldest in Volcano, built in 1886 by the Lyman missionary family. Three rooms, sharing two baths, are available in the main house. Scattered around the area are five fully equipped guest houses and another three rooms in private garden apartments. You won't start the day hungry after a deluxe all-you-can-eat breakfast. ⊠ *19-3896 Old Volcano Hwy., Volcano Village* ⌂ *Box 100, Volcano 96785* ☏ *808/967–7216 or 808/967–7110* 📠 *808/967–7719* ⊕ *www.myislandinnhawaii.com* ⌦ *6 rooms, 3 with bath; 5 guest houses* ⚭ *No a/c, no phones in some rooms, no TV in some rooms* ▭ *MC, V.*

$ 🖽 **Bougainvillea Bed & Breakfast.** This large country home is off Highway 11 at Ocean View Estates (between mile markers 77 and 78). The remote, quiet area is close to South Point and the rural charm of Ka'u District and within easy distance of Hawai'i Volcanoes National Park, hiking, and black- and green-sand beaches. Breakfast is served on the lānai. There are restaurants, a Laundromat, a grocery store, and a gas station nearby. ⌂ *Box 6045, Ocean View 96737* ☏ *808/929–7089 or*

800/688–1763 ⊕ *hi-inns.com/bouga* ⤴ *3 rooms* ⚬ *Pool, hot tub, massage, lounge* ⊟ *MC, V.*

Upcountry Kona District

$$$–$$$$ 🏨 **Hōlualoa Inn.** Six spacious rooms are available in this cedar home on a 40-acre Upcountry orchard estate with glorious coastal views, 4 mi above Kailua Bay. The artists' town of Hōlualoa is steps away. Each room has an island theme. The premium Balinese suite has wraparound windows with stunning views. A lavish breakfast includes estate-grown coffee as well as homemade breads and macadamia-nut butter. Rooftop gazebos inspire quiet, relaxing moments, and for stargazers there's a telescope. ⊠ *76-5932 Māmalahoa Hwy. (Box 222), Hōlualoa 96725* ☎ *808/324–1121 or 800/392–1812* ⧠ *808/322–2472* ⊕ *www.holualoainn.com* ⤴ *6 rooms* ⚬ *Fans, pool, hot tub, billiards; no a/c, no room TVs, no kids under 13, no smoking* ⊟ *AE, D, DC, MC, V.*

$–$$ 🏨 **Hale Maluhia.** This expansive country home occupies a quiet tree-shaded plot above Kailua-Kona. Choose from several guest rooms or opt for the private cottage. There's a Japanese gazebo with a hot tub for relaxing. Kailua-Kona's restaurants and shops are minutes away. ⊠ *76-770 Hualalai Rd., Kailua-Kona 96740* ☎ *808/329–1123, 808/329–5773, or 800/559–6627* ⧠ *808/326–5487* ⊕ *www.hawaii-inns.com/hi/kna/hmh* ⤴ *5 rooms, 1 cottage* ⚬ *Billiards, library, recreation room; no a/c* ⊟ *MC, V.*

Kailua-Kona & South Kona

★ $$$$ 🏨 **Horizon Guest House.** About 30 mi south of Kona, at an elevation of 1,100 feet on 40 acres overlooking the Kona Coast, this private luxury retreat offers tranquility, comfort, sweeping views, and a state-of-the-art solar-heated pool. Hawaiian quilts, collectibles, and antiques give personality and warmth to the four spacious suites, all with private lānai. Host Clem Classen's generous breakfast starts your day. The estate borders the native forests of the 15,000-acre McCandless Ranch. ⌂ *Box 268, Hōnaunau 96726* ☎ *808/328–2540 or 888/328–8301* ⧠ *808/ 328–8707* ⊕ *www.horizonguesthouse.com* ⤴ *4 suites* ⚬ *Refrigerators, pool, hot tub, library, Internet; no a/c, no kids under 14, no smoking* ⊟ *MC, V.*

$$$–$$$$ 🏨 **Aston Kona by the Sea.** Complete modern kitchens, tile lānai, and a washer-dryer can be found in every suite of this comfortable oceanfront condo complex. Despite being near the bustling town of Kailua-Kona, this four-story place is quiet and relaxing. The nearest sandy beach is 2 mi away, but the pool is next to the ocean. ⊠ *75-6106 Ali'i Dr., Kailua-Kona 96740* ☎ *808/327–2300 or 800/922–7866* ⧠ *808/922–8785* ⊕ *www.aston-hotels.com* ⤴ *37 1-bedroom units, 41 2-bedroom units* ⚬ *Kitchens, pool, hot tub, spa* ⊟ *AE, D, DC, MC, V.*

$$$–$$$$ 🏨 **Kona Bali Kai.** Though slightly older, with rattan furnishings and a basic layout, these condominium units do have a pretty good location, just a couple of minutes from Kailua-Kona and popular White Sands beach. And they are great for families. Kitchens are fully equipped, and there's a little convenience store. If you can afford it, choose an

oceanfront unit for the luxury of quiet sunsets. ✉ 76-6246 *Ali'i Dr., Kailua-Kona 96740* ☏ *808/329–9381 or 800/535–0085* 🖨 *808/326–6056* ⊕ *www.marcresorts.com* ➣ *62 condominiums (13 studios, 25 1-bedroom, 24 2-bedroom)* ♦ *Fans, kitchens, in-room VCRs, pool, hair salon, hot tub, laundry facilities; no a/c in some rooms* ▤ *AE, D, DC, MC, V.*

$$$–$$$$ 🏨 **Royal Kona Resort.** The spacious Royal Kona Resort, a steady downtown landmark, remains ever popular with travelers. Rooms, all with lānai, have natural stone, sand, and green tones. The resort is within walking distance of Kailua and right across from shops and restaurants. Little artificial streams and a private lagoon with a sandy beach create an ambience of carefree tropical living. The resort hosts a weekly lū'au with Polynesian entertainment. ✉ *75-5852 Ali'i Dr., Kailua-Kona 96740* ☏ *808/329–3111 or 800/222–5642* 🖨 *808/329–9532* ⊕ *www. royalkona.com* ➣ *452 rooms, 8 suites* ♦ *Restaurant, in-room data ports, in-room safes, refrigerators, 4 tennis courts, pool, health club, spa, beach, bar, meeting room* ▤ *AE, D, DC, MC, V.*

★ **$$–$$$$** 🏨 **Kanaloa at Kona.** The 16-acre grounds provide a verdant background for this low-rise condominium complex bordering the Keauhou-Kona Country Club. Large one-, two-, and three-bedroom apartments have koa-wood cabinetwork and washer-dryers; oceanfront villas have private hot tubs. Edward's at Kanaloa Restaurant serves excellent Mediterranean cuisine. ✉ *78-261 Manukai St., Kailua-Kona 96740* ☏ *808/322–9625, 808/322–2272, or 800/688–7444* 🖨 *808/322–3818* ⊕ *www. outrigger.com* ➣ *166 units* ♦ *Restaurant, kitchenettes, 2 tennis courts, 3 pools* ▤ *AE, D, DC, MC, V.*

★ **$$–$$$$** 🏨 **Ohana Keauhou Beach Resort.** This oceanfront hotel with sage-green rooms is just 5 mi south of Kailua-Kona. It has won awards for the preservation of its unique history: its grounds include a heiau, a sacred fishpond, and a replica of the summer home of King David Kalākaua. Consider a nightcap at the Verandah, a bar just a few feet away from lapping waves and turtles. The hotel is adjacent to Kahalu'u, one of the Big Island's best snorkeling beaches; the rooms on that side may get noisy. ✉ *78-6740 Ali'i Dr., Kailua-Kona 96740* ☏ *808/322–3441 or 800/462–6262* 🖨 *808/322–3117* ⊕ *www.ohanahotels.com* ➣ *311 rooms, 6 suites* ♦ *Restaurant, 6 tennis courts, pool, health club, beach, bar, meeting room* ▤ *AE, D, DC, MC, V.*

$$–$$$ 🏨 **King Kamehameha's Kona Beach Hotel.** Rooms are not particularly special here (the fifth- and sixth-floor oceanfront rooms are best), but what you get instead of the luxury of upscale Kohala resorts is a great central Kailua-Kona location with a small white-sand family beach and a calm swimming bay, right next to Kailua Pier. There are several resort shops in the lobby. Visitors can explore the grounds and Ahu'ena Heiau, which King Kamehameha I had reconstructed in the early 1800s. The hotel serves an ample champagne brunch every Sunday and hosts a fabulous beachfront Polynesian lū'au several nights a week. ✉ *75-5660 Palani Rd., Kailua-Kona 96740* ☏ *808/329–2911 or 800/367–6060* 🖨 *808/329–4602* ⊕ *www.konabeachhotel.com* ➣ *455 rooms* ♦ *2 restaurants, tennis courts, pool, hot tub, sauna, beach, 2 bars* ▤ *AE, D, DC, MC, V.*

$–$$ ⊞ **Kona Seaside Hotel.** If you're on a budget, want a central location, and don't need resort extras, spacious rooms, or lavish bathrooms, you'll feel at home in this casual hotel. It's on a busy intersection, right across the street from Kailua Bay. Rooms nearest the main street are built around a private pool. The staff is very friendly. ⊠ *75-5646 Palani Rd., Kailua-Kona 96740* ☎ *808/329–2455 or 800/560–5558* 🖶 *808/329–6157* ⊕ *www.konaseasidehotel.com* ⬗ *223 rooms, 1 suite* ♦ *Refrigerators, 2 pools, bar, laundry facilities, meeting room* ⊟ *AE, D, DC, MC, V.*

$ ⊞ **Kona Bay Hotel, Uncle Billy's.** These two- and four-story motel-type units are right in the center of town, across the street from the ocean. The mood is friendly and casual, with relaxed open-air dining around the pool. Some rooms have kitchenettes. The place is owned and managed by the same local family that owns the Hilo Bay Hotel, Uncle Billy's. ⊠ *75-5739 Ali'i Dr., Kailua-Kona 96740* ☎ *808/329–1393 or 800/367–5102* 🖶 *808/935–7903* ⊕ *www.unclebilly.com* ⬗ *146 rooms* ♦ *Restaurant, refrigerators, pool, bar* ⊟ *AE, D, DC, MC, V.*

$–$$ ⊞ **Kona Magic Sands.** Cradled between two small beach parks, one of which is Magic Sands, this condo complex is great for swimmers and sunbathers in summer (the sand washes away in winter). Units vary because they are individually owned, but all are oceanfront, spacious, and light. Some units have enclosed lānai, and all have an ocean view. ⊠ *77-6452 Ali'i Dr., Kailua-Kona 96740* ☎ *808/329–9393 or 800/622–5348* 🖶 *808/326–4137* ⊕ *www.konahawaii.com* ⬗ *37 rooms* ♦ *Restaurant, kitchens, kitchenettes, pool, bar; no a/c in some rooms* ⊟ *MC, V.*

¢–$ ⊞ **Kona Tiki Hotel.** The best thing about this three-story walk-up budget hotel, about a mile south of Kailua-Kona, is that all the units have lānai right next to the ocean. The rooms are modest but pleasantly decorated. You can sunbathe by the seaside pool, where a Continental breakfast is also served. Some would call this place old-fashioned; others would say it's local and the best deal in town, with glorious sunsets no different from those at the resorts. ⊠ *75-5968 Ali'i Dr., Kailua-Kona 96745* ☎ *808/329–1425* 🖶 *808/327–9402* ⊕ *www.wheretostay.com* ⬗ *15 rooms* ♦ *BBQ, fans, refrigerators, pool; no a/c, no room phones, no room TVs* ⊟ *No credit cards* ⃝ *CP.*

¢–$ ⊞ **Manago Hotel.** You'll get a great ocean view high above the Kona Coast in the newer wing of this family-run three-story hotel, the oldest operating hotel in the area. To honor his grandparents, Kinzo and Osame Manago, who built the main hotel in 1917, Dwight Manago has maintained one Japanese-style room with tatami mats and a *furo*, a traditional Japanese bath. The other rooms are nothing special, but the hotel has an authentic old Hawai'i vibe, especially in the bar and local-style restaurant. ⊠ *81-6155 Māmalahoa Hwy. (Box 145), Captain Cook 96704* ☎ *808/323–2642* 🖶 *808/323–3451* ⊕ *www.managohotel.com* ⬗ *64 rooms, 42 with bath* ♦ *Restaurant, bar; no a/c, no room TVs* ⊟ *D, MC, V.*

Kohala Coast & Waikoloa

★ **$$$$** ⊞ **The Fairmont Orchid Hawai'i.** This elegant hotel, with its romantic botanical gardens and waterfall ponds, stretches along 32 beachfront acres.

Rooms are refined and luxurious; marble bathrooms and fluffy robes are just part of the pampering. The Spa Without Walls incorporates traditional and contemporary treatments, including Tibetan yoga, body and facial rejuvenations, and massage practices ranging from Swedish to Hawaiian. The resort offers 2½-hour voyages aboard an authentic Polynesian double-hulled sailing canoe, the *Hahalua Lele,* or "Flying Manta Ray." ⊠ *1 N. Kanikū Dr., Kohala Coast 96743* ☎ *808/885–2000 or 800/845–9905* 🖹 *808/885–8886* ⊕ *www.fairmont.com* ⤶ *486 rooms, 54 suites* ♿ *3 restaurants, 2 18-hole golf courses, 10 tennis courts, pool, health club, sauna, spa, beach, snorkeling, boating, 4 bars, children's programs (ages 5–12)* ☰ *AE, D, DC, MC, V.*

$$$$
Fodor's Choice
★
🏨 **Four Seasons Resort Hualālai.** Slate floors, Hawaiian artwork, warm earth and cool white tones, and spacious bathrooms create peaceful retreats, tucked into four clusters of oceanfront bungalows. Ground-level rooms have outdoor garden showers. Natural ponds dot the property. The on-siteHawaiian Cultural Center honors the grounds' spiritual heritage, and the Sports Club and Spa offers guests top-rate health and fitness options. Hualālai's golf course hosts the Senior PGA Tournament of Champions. ⊠ *100 Ka'ūpūlehu Dr., Ka'ūpūlehu/Kona* ⤓ *Box 1269, Kailua-Kona 96745* ☎ *808/325–8000, 800/819–5053, or 888/340–5662* 🖹 *808/325–8200* ⊕ *www.fourseasons.com* ⤶ *243 rooms, 31 suites* ♿ *3 restaurants, 18-hole golf course, 8 tennis courts, 5 pools, health club, spa, beach, recreation room, babysitting, children's programs (ages 5–11), laundry service, concierge, Internet, business services, meeting rooms, airport shuttle* ☰ *AE, DC, MC, V.*

★ $$$$
🏨 **Hāpuna Beach Prince Hotel.** This luxury hotel—a glitzy beauty with floors of slate tile—fronts white-sand Hāpuna, one of the best beaches in the United States. Spacious, with marble bathrooms and private lānai, all rooms have at least a partial ocean view. Meandering pathways lead to restaurants, beach facilities, and a spectacular golf course. The showpiece of the hotel is the 8,000-square-foot, four-bedroom Hāpuna Suite, with its own swimming pool and 24-hour butler service. A hiking trail and a frequent shuttle connect Hāpuna with its partner, the Mauna Kea Beach Hotel. ⊠ *62-100 Kauna'oa Dr., Kohala Coast 96743* ☎ *808/880–1111 or 800/882–6060* 🖹 *808/880–3112* ⊕ *www. princeresortshawaii.com* ⤶ *314 rooms, 36 suites* ♿ *5 restaurants, refrigerators, 18-hole golf course, 13 tennis courts, pool, health club, hair salon, hot tub, spa, 2 bars, children's programs (age 5–12), Internet, business services, convention center, meeting rooms* ☰ *AE, D, DC, MC, V.*

★ $$$$
🏨 **Kona Village Resort.** Without phones, TVs, or radios, it's easy to feel like you are part of an extended Polynesian *ohana* (family), with your own thatch-roof *hale* (house) near the resort's sandy beach. Built on the grounds of an ancient Hawaiian village, the modern bungalows reflect styles of South Seas cultures—Tahitian, Samoan, Tongan, Maori, Fijian, or Hawaiian. The extra large Royal rooms have private hot tubs. Rates include meals, an authentic Polynesian Friday-night lū'au, ground tours, tennis, sports activities, and rides in the resort's glass-bottom boat. ⊠ *Queen Ka'ahumanu Hwy. (Box 1299), Kailua-Kona 96745* ☎ *808/ 325–5555 or 800/367–5290* 🖹 *808/325–5124* ⊕ *www.konavillage.*

com ↝ *125 bungalows* ⅋ *2 restaurants, fans, 3 tennis courts, 2 pools, health club, hot tub, beach, boating, 3 bars, children's programs (ages 6–17; not available in May or Sept.), meeting room, airport shuttle; no a/c, no room phones, no room TVs* ▭ *AE, DC, MC, V* ⋈ *FAP.*

★ $$$$ ▦ **Mauna Kea Beach Hotel.** The Mauna Kea Beach is the grande dame of Kohala Coast hotels. Opened in 1965, it has long been regarded as one of the world's premier vacation resort hotels. It borders one of the islands' finest white-sand beaches. Rare works of art, such as a 7th-century Buddha, enhance walkways and open spaces. The rooms have a natural look with pastel tones and natural woods. Shuttles operate between the Mauna Kea and the adjacent Hāpuna Beach Prince Hotel, allowing guests to use the facilities at both hotels. ✉ *62-100 Mauna Kea Beach Dr., Kohala Coast 96743* ☎ *808/882–7222 or 800/882–6060* 🖷 *808/880–3112* ⊕ *www.princeresortshawaii.com* ↝ *300 rooms, 10 suites* ⅋ *5 restaurants, in-room safes, refrigerators, 2 18-hole golf courses, 13 tennis courts, pool, health club, hair salon, beach, children's programs (age 5–12), Internet* ▭ *AE, D, DC, MC, V.*

★ $$$$ ▦ **Mauna Lani Bay Hotel and Bungalows.** Ninety percent of the spacious rooms in this elegant hotel have ocean views, and all have a large lānai. Comfortable furnishings grace rooms with natural fabrics and teak. The resort is known for its two spectacular golf courses. The new Mauna Lani Spa offers mud wraps with volcanic ash, hot-stone therapies, massage, and more. Some of the best Pacific Rim cuisine is served at the oceanfront CanoeHouse. ✉ *68-1400 Mauna Lani Dr., Kohala Coast 96743* ☎ *808/885–6622 or 800/367–2323* 🖷 *808/885–1484* ⊕ *www. maunalani.com* ↝ *335 rooms, 10 suites, 5 bungalows* ⅋ *6 restaurants, in-room safes, refrigerators, in-room VCRs, 2 18-hole golf courses, 16 tennis courts, pool, spa, 5 bars, children's programs (ages 5–12), Internet* ▭ *AE, D, DC, MC, V.*

$$$$ ▦ **Mauna Lani Point Condominiums.** Surrounded by the emerald greens of a world-class oceanside golf course, spacious two-story suites offer a private, independent home away from home. The privately owned units, individually decorated according to the owners' tastes, have European cabinets and oversize soaking tubs in the master bedrooms. The pool sports a little waterfall. You're just a few steps away from the Mauna Lani Bay Hotel and Bungalows, where you have access to golf, tennis, spa facilities, and restaurants. ✉ *68-1050 Mauna Lani Point Dr., Kohala Coast 96743* ☎ *808/885–5022 or 800/642–6284* 🖷 *808/885–5015* ⊕ *www.classicresorts.com* ↝ *24 1-bedroom units, 37 2-bedroom units* ⅋ *Some kitchens, some kitchenettes, pool, hot tub, sauna* ▭ *AE, DC, MC, V.*

$$$–$$$$ ▦ **Aston the Shores at Waikoloa.** These red-tile-roof villas are set amid landscaped lagoons and waterfalls at the edge of the championship Waikoloa Village Golf Course. The spacious villas and condo units—the ground floor and upper floor are available separately—are privately owned, so all furnishings are different. Sliding glass doors open onto large lānai. Large picture windows look out on rolling green fairways. Units have complete kitchens with washer-dryer and come with maid service. ✉ *69-1035 Keana Pl., Waikoloa 96738* ☎ *808/886–5001 or 800/922–7866* 🖷 *808/922–8785* ⊕ *www.aston-hotels.com* ↝ *75 1- and*

2-bedroom units ⚄ *Fans, kitchens, putting green, 2 tennis courts, pool, hot tub, shop* ☐ *AE, D, DC, MC, V.*

★ **$$$–$$$$** ⛱ **Hilton Waikoloa Village.** Shaded pathways pass by artifacts from a multimillion-dollar Pacific Island art collection to connect the three tall buildings that make up this 62-acre resort. Trams and boats shuttle you around if you don't want to walk. The pool has a 175-foot water slide and a meandering river that connects smaller pools. A man-made sand beach borders a 4-acre lagoon, a playground for dolphins. The Kohala Spa has some of the finest fitness facilities on the island. ✉ *425 Waikoloa Beach Dr., Waikoloa 96738* ☎ *808/886–1234 or 800/445–8667* 📠 *808/ 886–2900* ⊕ *www.hiltonwaikoloavillage.com* ☝ *1,240 rooms, 57 suites* ⚄ *9 restaurants, 2 18-hole golf courses, putting green, 8 tennis courts, 3 pools, health club, spa, beach, 7 bars, shops, children's programs (ages 5–12), Internet* ☐ *AE, D, DC, MC, V.*

★ **$$$–$$$$** ⛱ **Waikoloa Beach Marriott.** The most affordable of the Kohala Coast resorts, this hotel covers 15 acres, and encompasses ancient fishponds, historic trails, and petroglyph fields. All rooms have Hawaiian art and bamboo-type furnishings. The oversize cabana rooms overlook the lagoon. Reliable dining is available at the Hawai'i Calls restaurant. The Hawaiian Rainforest Salon & Spa offers a full range of treatments. Bordering the white-sand beach of 'Anaeho'omalu Bay, the hotel has a range of ocean activities, including wedding-vow renewals on a catamaran. ✉ *69-275 Waikoloa Beach Dr., Waikoloa 96738* ☎ *808/886– 6789 or 800/688–7444* 📠 *808/886–1554* ⊕ *www.outrigger.com* ☝ *524 rooms, 21 suites* ⚄ *Restaurant, refrigerators, 2 18-hole golf courses, 6 tennis courts, pool, health club, hair salon, 2 hot tubs, sauna, spa, beach, 2 bars, children's programs (ages 5–12), laundry facilities, Internet, business services, meeting rooms* ☐ *AE, D, DC, MC, V.*

$–$$ ⛱ **Hale Ho'onanea.** The Hawaiian translation of this comfortable home's name is "House of Relaxation." It sits on 3 acres in the Kohala Estates hills, above the ocean. From here you can watch the sun rise over Mauna Kea and set over the Pacific, and view the sparkling beauty of Hawai'i's night sky. It's minutes away from dining and shopping at Waimea and the attractions of the Kohala Coast resorts. ✉ *Kohala Estates, 59-513 Ala Kahua Dr., Waimea 96743* ☎ *808/882–1653 or 877/ 882–1653* 📠 *808/882–1653* ⊕ *www.houseofrelaxation.com* ☝ *3 suites* ⚄ *Kitchenettes, library; no a/c* ☐ *No credit cards* ⓘ⓵ *CP.*

¢–$$ ⛱ **Kohala's Guest House.** In rural North Kohala, the birthplace of King Kamehameha, contemporary comforts and the aloha style of old meet in the tropical orchard property of Don and Nani Svendsen. The cozy studio and 3-bedroom rental house, adorned with Svendsen's flowers, are minutes away from Pololū Valley. It's just 30 minutes to the white-sand beaches of the resorts. Close to the shops, eateries, and activities in Hāwī and Kapa'au, but sheltered from heavy tourism, you can live like the locals here. ⓓ *Box 172, Hāwī 96719* ☎ *808/889–5606* 📠 *808/ 889–5572* ⊕ *home1.gte.net/svendsen* ☝ *1 studio, 1 three-bedroom house (for families or rented as separate room units)* ☐ *No credit cards.*

¢–$ ⛱ **Kohala Village Inn.** Located in the heart of Hāwī town in the rural far-north peninsula of the Big Island, this budget no-frills country lodge offers clean and simple rooms. It's perfect for backpackers or those seeking the opposite of the resort experience. Some rooms accommodate up to six. It's steps away from Hāwī dining and shops. There's easy access to Pololū Valley, Kapaʻau, Moʻokini Heiau, King Kamehameha's birthplace, and whale-watching spots. ⊠ *55-514 Hāwī Rd. (Box 74), Hāwī 96719* ☎ *808/889–0404* ⊕ *www.kohalavillageinn.com* ⥲ *17 rooms* ⌂ *Cable TV; no a/c* ⊟ *MC, V* ⧉ *CP.*

Waimea/Hāmākua Coast

$$$–$$$$ ▦ **Waianuhea.** Located two miles above Honokaʻa town in a forested pasture area upslope on the Hāmākua Coast. This gorgeous country home is fully self-contained with solar electric power, cell phones, and more. The four guest rooms and large suite, all with private baths, are lavishly furnished with tasteful color schemes, and contemporary artwork throughout. The large common room and lava-rock fireplace are big attractions, especially at the wine tasting hour each evening. Stroll the flower garden and fruit orchards, and soak up the ambience of genuine Hawaiian country. Waianuhea defines Hawaiian country elegance. ⊠ *45-3503 Kahana Dr., Honokaʻa, 96727* ☎ *888/775–2577 or 808/775–1118* 🖷 *888/296–6302* ⊕ *www.waianuhea.com* ⥲ *5 rooms* ⌂ *Room TVs with movies, Internet, meeting room; no a/c, no smoking.* ⊟ *AE, D, MC, V* ⧉ *BP.*

★ **$$** ▦ **Cook's Discoveries Waimea Suite.** Patti Cook, owner of the well-known Cook's Discoveries arts-and-crafts shop in Waimea, has opened her elegant Waimea country home to guests. The Waimea Suite is a private lower apartment unit that opens onto an expansive lawn with beautiful trees framing views of Mauna Kea. The common living room has beautiful antique furniture and decorative artwork. The double and twin bedrooms are tastefully furnished. Make a direct booking and receive a $20 gift certificate to Cook's Discoveries; stay six nights and you get the seventh night free. ⊠ *64-5246 Lokua St.,(Hwy. 19 at Kamamalu St.), Waimea 96743* ☎ *808/937–2833* 🖷 *808/885–9691* ⊕ *www. hawaii-island.com/cooks.htm* ⥲ *2 rooms* ⌂ *Kitchen; no a/c* ⊟ *AE, D, MC, V.*

$–$$$$ ▦ **Jacaranda Inn.** Built in 1897, this sprawling, historic estate was once the home of the Parker Ranch manager; it has been completely restored in raspberry and lavender colors, with lots of koa wood and Upcountry Victorian elements. The units are booked under two separate plans. Plan A includes daily maid service, full breakfasts, and a bottle of wine; Plan B is simpler, with Continental breakfast and less service. The Jacaranda is close to Waimea shops as well as to beaches. ⊠ *65-1444 Kawaihae Rd., Waimea 96743* ☎ *808/885–8813* 🖷 *808/885–6096* ⊕ *www.jacarandainn.com* ⥲ *8 suites, 1 cottage* ⌂ *Some in-room hot tubs, recreation room; no a/c, no room TVs, no smoking* ⊟ *MC, V* ⧉ *CP.*

★ **$–$$$** ▦ **Kamuela Inn.** The rooms in this unpretentious, peaceful inn, just 20 minutes from the island beaches, are basic but clean. Small lānai look out over the inn's gardens. Depending on your needs, you can choose anything from a no-nonsense single bedroom to two connecting penthouse suites with a lānai and full kitchen. ⊠ *65-1300 Kawaihae Rd. (Box 1994), Kamuela 96743* ☎ *808/885–4243 or 800/555–8968* 🖷 *808/885–8857* ⊕ *www.kamuelainn.com* ⥲ *20 rooms, 11 suites*

  ⚠ *Some kitchenettes; no a/c, no phones in some rooms* ▤ *AE, D, DC, MC, V* ⊙ *CP.*

★ **$–$$** ▦ **Waimea Country Lodge.** In the heart of cowboy country, next door to the Paniolo Country Inn, this quiet, modest lodge offers views of the green, rolling slopes of Mauna Kea yet is close to the activity of busy Waimea town. The rooms are adequate and clean, with Hawaiian quilts lending them a personal touch. You can arrange to charge meals at Merriman's restaurant and the Paniolo Country Inn to your room. ✉ *65-1210 Lindsey Rd., Waimea* ⊕ *Box 2559, Kamuela 96743* ☎ *808/885–4100 or 800/367–5004* 🖷 *808/885–6711* ⊕ *www.castleresorts.com/wcl* 🛏 *21 rooms* ⚠ *Some kitchenettes; no a/c* ▤ *AE, D, DC, MC, V* ⊙ *CP.*

$–$$ ▦ **Waipi'o Wayside.** Nestled amid avocado and kukui trees, on a plantation estate, this serene inn provides a retreat close to Waipi'o Valley. Hostess Jacqueline Horne has given each room its own character with, for example, rare Chinese antiques or patchwork quilts. A sprawling garden with an orchid-covered deck and a little gazebo has hammocks to help you indulge your lazy side. ✉ *Waipi'o Valley Rd. (Hwy. 240), Honoka'a 96727* ☎ *808/775–0275 or 800/833–8849* 🖷 *808/775–0275* ⊕ *www.waipiowayside.com* 🛏 *5 rooms* ⚠ *Snack bar; no a/c, no room phones, no room TVs, no smoking* ▤ *MC, V* ⊙ *CP.*

¢–$ ▦ **Hotel Honoka'a Club.** This basic bargain hotel is 45 minutes from Hilo and close to Waipi'o Valley. Rustic rooms range from lower-level dormitory-style hostel units—bring your own sleeping bag—with shared bathrooms to upper-story rooms with private bath, queen-size beds, an ocean view, and a complimentary Continental breakfast. ✉ *45-3480 Māmane St. (Box 247), Honoka'a 96727* ☎ *808/775–0678 or 800/808–0678* ⊕ *www.hotelhono.com* 🛏 *13 rooms, 5 hostel rooms* ⚠ *Restaurant; no a/c, no room phones, no TV in some rooms, no smoking* ▤ *MC, V.*

NIGHTLIFE & THE ARTS

If you're the sort of person who doesn't come alive until after dark, you're going to be pretty lonely on the Big Island. Blame it on the plantation heritage. People did their cane-raising in the morning.

Clubs & Cabarets

Honu Bar. This elegant spot at the Mauna Lani Bay Hotel and Bungalows on the Kohala Coast has a nice dance floor for weekend revelers; the music varies, so call ahead. Regardless, appetizers, imported cigars, and fine cognacs make this a popular, upscale gathering spot. ✉ *68-1400 Mauna Lani Dr., Kohala Coast* ☎ *808/885–6622.*

Ho'omalimali Lounge. This lounge and dance club at the Hawai'i Naniloa Resort in Hilo competes with the crashing surf on Friday and Saturday night with live music from 9 to midnight. ✉ *93 Banyan Dr., Hilo* ☎ *808/969–3333.*

Huggo's. Jazz, country, and even rock bands perform at this popular restaurant, so call ahead of time to find out what's on. Outside, people often dance in the sand to Hawaiian songs. ✉ *75-5828 Kahakai Rd., at Ali'i Dr., Kailua-Kona* ☎ *808/329–1493.*

Koa House Grill. A popular hangout for Waimea's residents, this old-fashioned bar has live music Friday and Saturday night—until 2 in the morning at times. ⊠ *Waimea Shopping Center, 65-1144 Māmalahoa Hwy., Waimea* ☎ *808/885–2088.*

Lulu's. A young crowd gyrates until 1:30 AM Friday and Saturday to hot dance music—hip-hop, R&B, and rock—spun by a professional DJ. ⊠ *75-5819 Ali'i Dr., Kailua-Kona* ☎ *808/331–2633.*

Michaelangelo's. On the second level of the Waterfront Row complex, this Italian restaurant starts rocking after 10 every night with a live DJ. ⊠ *75-5770 Ali'i Dr., Waterfront Row, Kailua-Kona* ☎ *808/329–4436.*

Film

Recorded **showtime information** (☎ 808/961–3456 or 808/327–0444) is available for all movie houses.

Hilo

Kress Cinemas (⊠ 174 Kamehameha Ave. ☎ 808/961–3456) screens selected art films. After decades of being closed, the historic **Palace Theatre** (⊠ 38 Haili St. ☎ 808/934–7010), built in 1925, now shows movies. First-run films are shown regularly at the state-of-the-art **Prince Kūhiō Stadium Cinemas** (⊠ Prince Kūhiō Plaza, 111 E. Puainako St. ☎ 808/959–4595).

Kailua-Kona

Keauhou 7 Cinemas (⊠ Keauhou Shopping Center, 78-6831 Ali'i Dr. ☎ 808/324–7200) is a splendid seven-theater complex. The 10-screen **Makalapua Stadium Cinemas** (⊠ Makalapua Ave., next to Big Kmart ☎ 808/327–0444) has stadium seating and digital surround sound.

Around the Island

Aloha Theatre (⊠ Hwy. 11, Kainaliu ☎ 808/322–2323) shows plays and movies in a 320-seat historic arts center built in 1923. **Honoka'a Peoples Theaters** (⊠ Māmame St., Honoka'a ☎ 808/775–0000) screens movies on weekends only. **Kahilu Theatre** (⊠ Parker Ranch Shopping Center, Hwy. 19, Waimea ☎ 808/885–6868) occasionally shows best-selling or foreign movies on weekends.

Hula

★ For hula lovers, the biggest show of the year and the largest event of its kind in the world is the annual **Merrie Monarch Hula Festival** (⊠ Hawai'i Naniloa Resort, 93 Banyan Dr., Hilo 96720 ☎ 808/935–9168). Honoring the legacy of King David Kalākaua, Hawai'i's last king, the festival is staged in Hilo at the spacious Edith Kanaka'ole Stadium during the first week following Easter Sunday. Hula hālau compete in various classes of ancient and modern dance styles. You need to reserve accommodations and tickets up to a year in advance.

Lū'au & Polynesian Revues

Kailua-Kona

★ **King Kamehameha's Kona Beach Hotel's Island Breeze Lū'au.** Witness the arrival of the Royal Court by canoe and have pictures taken at this beach-

CloseUp
HAWAI'I'S HIPPY HIPPY SHAKE

LEGENDS IMMORTALIZE LAKA as the goddess of hula, portraying her as a gentle deity who journeyed from island to island, sharing the dance with all who were willing to learn. Laka's graceful movements, spiritual and layered with meaning, brought to life the history, the traditions, and the genealogy of the islanders. Ultimately taught by parents to children and by kumu (teachers) to students, the hula preserved without a written language the culture of these ancient peoples.

Some legends trace the origins of hula to Moloka'i, where a family named La'ila'i was said to have established the dance at Ka'ana. Eventually the youngest sister of the fifth generation of La'ila'i was given the name Laka, and she carried the dance to all the Islands in the Hawaiian chain.

Another legend credits Hi'iaka, the volcano goddess Pele's youngest sister, as having danced the first hula in the hala groves of Puna on the Big Island. Hi'iaka and possibly even Pele were thought to have learned the dance from Hōpoe, a mortal and a poet also credited as the originator of the dance.

In any case, hula thrived until the arrival of puritanical New England missionaries, who with the support of Queen Ka'ahumanu, an early Christian convert, attempted to ban the dance as an immoral activity throughout the 19th century.

Though hula may not have been publicly performed, it remained a spiritual and poetic art form, as well as a lively celebration of life presented during special celebrations in many Hawaiian homes. David Kalākaua, the popular "Merrie Monarch" who was king from 1874 to 1891, revived the hula. Dancers were called to perform at official functions.

Gradually, ancient hula, called kahiko, was replaced with a lively, updated form of dance called 'auana (modern). Modern costumes of fresh ti-leaf or raffia skirts replaced the voluminous pa'u skirts made of kapa (cloth made of beaten bark), and the music became more melodic, as opposed to earlier chanted routines accompanied by pahu (drums), 'ili 'ili (rocks used as castanets), and other percussion instruments. Such tunes as "Lovely Hula Hands," "Little Grass Shack," and the "Hawaiian Wedding Song" are considered hula 'auana. Dancers might wear graceful holomu'u with short trains or ti-leaf skirts with coconut bra tops.

In 1963 the Merrie Monarch Festival was established in Hilo on the Big Island and has since become the most prestigious hula competition in the state. It's staged annually the weekend after Easter, and contestants of various halau (hula schools) from Hawai'i and the mainland compete in the categories of Miss Aloha Hula, hula kahiko (ancient), and hula 'auana (modern). For more information, contact the **Merrie Monarch Hula Festival** (✉ Hawai'i Naniloa Resort, 93 Banyan Dr., Hilo 96720 ☎ 808/935–9168).

Moloka'i stages its own Ka Hula Piko festival every May to celebrate the birth of hula. Singers, musicians, and dancers perform in a shaded glen at Pāpōhaku Beach State Park. During the week preceding the festival, John Kaimikaua, the founder, and his halau present hula demonstrations, lectures, and storytelling at various Moloka'i sites. For more information, contact the **Moloka'i Visitors Association** (✉ Box 960, Kaunakakai 96748 ☎ 808/553–3876 or 800/800–6367 ⊕ www.molokai-hawaii.com).

front event, which includes a 22-item buffet, an open bar, and a show. ⊠ *75-5660 Palani Rd.* ☎ *808/326–4969 or 808/329–8111* ⊕ *www. islandbreezeluau.com* ⊠ *$55* ⊗ *Tues.–Thurs. and Sun. 5:30–8:30.*

★ **Kona Village Resort.** In its utter isolation, the lū'au here is one of the most authentic and traditional on the Islands. As in other lū'au, activities include the steaming of a whole pig in the *imu* (ground oven). A Polynesian show on a stage over a lagoon is magical. ⊠ *6 mi north of Kona International Airport, off Queen Ka'ahumanu Hwy., Kailua-Kona* ☎ *808/325–5555 or 808/325–4273* ⊕ *www.konavillage.com* ⊠ *$76, including open bar* ⊗ *Fri. from 5; walking tour at 5:30, imu ceremony at 6:30, dinner at 7, show at 8.*

Royal Kona Resort. This resort lights lū'au torches for a full Polynesian show and a Hawaiian-style oceanfront buffet three times a week. ⊠ *75-5852 Ali'i Dr.* ☎ *808/329–3111 Ext. 4* ⊕ *www.konaluau.com* ⊠ *$57, including beer and wine* ⊗ *Mon., Wed., Fri., and Sat. at 5.*

Kohala Coast & Waikoloa

Hilton Waikoloa Village. The Hilton seats 400 people outdoors at the Kamehameha Court, where the acclaimed Polynesian group Tihati performs a lively show. A buffet dinner provides samplings of Hawaiian food as well as fish, beef, and chicken to appeal to all tastes. ⊠ *425 Waikoloa Beach Dr., Waikoloa* ☎ *808/886–1234* ⊕ *www.hiltonwaikoloavillage. com* ⊠ *$68* ⊗ *Fri. at 6.*

Mauna Kea Beach Hotel. Once a week, on the gracious North Pointe Lū'au Grounds of the Mauna Kea Beach Hotel, you can sample the best of Hawaiian cuisine while listening to the enchanting songs of Nani Lim. Every Tuesday, chefs come together here to create a traditional Hawaiian *pa'ina* (dinner feast), which includes the classic *kalua* (roasted in an underground oven) pig. ⊠ *62-100 Mauna Kea Beach Dr., Kohala Coast* ☎ *808/882–7222* ⊕ *www.maunakeabeachhotel.com* ⊠ *$76* ⊗ *Tues. at 6.*

Waikoloa Beach Marriott. The Marriott offers a great-value lū'au at the Lū'au Grounds, where entertainment includes a Samoan fire dance as well as songs and dances of various Pacific cultures. Traditional Hawaiian dishes are served alongside more familiar fare. ⊠ *69-275 Waikoloa Beach Dr., Waikoloa* ☎ *808/886–6789* ⊕ *www.outrigger.com* ⊠ *$67, including open bar* ⊗ *Wed. and Sun. 5–8:30.*

Sunset Cruises

★ **Captain Beans' Polynesian Dinner Cruise.** This is the ever-popular standby in sunset dinner cruises. You can't miss it—as the sun sets in Kailua, look out over the water and you'll see a big gaudy boat with distinctive orange sails. This cruise is corny, and dinner is nothing great, but it's an experience, with unlimited drinks and a Hawaiian show. This is for adults only. ⊠ *Kailua Pier, Kailua-Kona* ☎ *808/329–2955, 800/831–5541* ⊕ *www.robertshawaii.com* ⊠ *$55–$66, including dinner, entertainment, and open bar* ⊗ *Tues.–Sun. at 5:15.*

◔ **Island Grill Dinner Cruise.** The *Kona Dream*, a comfortable modern trimaran, takes you on a fabulous sunset cruise along the scenic Kona Coast from Kailua-Kona Pier. Enjoy tropical libations and indulge in a spectacular island grilled dinner served pūpū-style while relaxing to the sounds of contemporary island music. This two-hour cruise includes the best of Kona's famed beautiful blazing sunsets. ⊠ *Kailua-Kona Pier, Ali'i Dr. at Palani Rd., Kailua-Kona* ☎ *808/326–6000 or 800/400–7300* ⊕ *www.dream-cruises.com* ☎ *$55* ⊙ *Daily, 5:30–7:30.*

Theater

Aloha Performing Arts Center. Local talent stages musicals and Broadway plays at this center near Kailua-Kona. ⊠ *Aloha Theatre Café, 79-7384 Māmalahoa Highway, Kainaliu* ☎ *808/322–2122.*

Hilo Community Players. This group stages plays on an occasional basis. ⊠ *141 Kalākaua Ave., Hilo* ☎ *808/935–9155.*

Kahilu Theater. For legitimate theater, the little town of Waimea is your best bet. The Kahilu Theater hosts regular internationally acclaimed performances. ⊠ *Parker Ranch Center, 67-1185 Māmalahoa Highway, Waimea* ☎ *808/885–6868.*

University of Hawai' at Hilo Theater. A full concert series of varied performances, acts, musical groups, and plays is held from September through May each year. ⊠ *200 W. Kawili St., Hilo* ☎ *808/974–7310.*

SPORTS & THE OUTDOORS

Airplane & Helicopter Tours

There's nothing quite like the aerial view of a waterfall that drops a couple thousand feet into multiple pools. You can also fly above the lava lake on Kīlauea, then follow the flow to the ocean, where clouds of steam billow into the air. (The lava flow has been changing locations and sometimes goes underground, so ask exactly what you'll see when you book your flight.) For a fee, some tour companies will record your flight as a souvenir if you wish. You can go in small planes that carry three to nine passengers or helicopters that carry up to six passengers. Expect to pay anywhere from $75 to $150 for 50-minute flights, and $325-plus for two hours; make reservations in advance, discounts are often available if you book online.

Big Island Air (⊠ Kona International Airport ☎ 808/329–4868 or 800/303–8868) operates 1½- to 2-hour plane tours out of Kona International Airport.

Blue Hawaiian Helicopters (⊠ Hilo International Airport or Waikoloa Helipad ☎ 808/961–5600 or 800/786–2583 ⊕ www.bluehawaiian.com) offers 45-minute and 2-hour group tours. Private tours are also available.

Island Hoppers Hawai'i (⊠ Hilo and Kona International Airports ☎ 808/969–2000, 808/329–0018, or 800/538–7590 ⊕ www.fly-hawaii.com/above) has operated plane tours over the Big Island since 1986. Fifty-minute tours are available from Hilo Airport, and 2- and 2-½- hour tours from Kona.

Mokulele Flight Service (✉ Kona International Airport ☎ 808/326–7070 or 866/260–7070 ⊕ www.mokulele.com) was started by Kawehi Inaba, a native of the island and a female pilot. The company offers 45-minute volcano/waterfall plane tours from Hilo; and 2-hour Circle Isle tours from Kona.

Sunshine Helicopters (✉ Helipad at the Hāpuna Beach Prince Hotel and Hilo International Airport ☎ 808/882–1223, 808/969–7506 or 800/469–3000 ⊕ www.sunshinehelicopters.com) offers 30-minute, 45-minute, and 2-hour group tours.

Tropical Helicopters (✉ Hilo International Airport ☎ 808/961–6810 ⊕ www.tropicalhelicopters.com) is pilot-owned and operated. Tours range from 35 minutes to two hours.

Biking

Backroads Bicycle Touring. This company has been pushing pedaling in Hawai'i since 1985. One six-day biking trip on the southern part of the island includes a day of hiking in Hawai'i Volcanoes National Park. The other choice, also six days, allows for kayaking and snorkeling. Lodgings alternate between luxury resorts and old Hawaiian inns. Fees starting at $2,500 include meals and accommodations, but bicycles and airfare are extra. ✉ *801 Cedar St., Berkeley, CA 94710-1800* ☎ *510/527–1555 or 800/462–2848* ⊕ *www.backroads.com.*

Bicycle Adventures, Inc. Eight-day tours of the Big Island accommodate both easygoing bikers and hard-core enthusiasts. You'll enjoy beach time, snorkeling, hiking excursions, comfortable accommodations, and fine dining, in addition to visits to Kīlauea Volcano and Pu'uhonua O Hōnaunau. The cost of $2,500 doesn't include bicycle rental or airfare. ✉ *Box 11219, Olympia, WA 98508* ☎ *360/786–0989 or 800/443–6060* ⊕ *www.bicycleadventures.com.*

C&S Outfitters. These folks in Waimea have a wealth of knowledge about the island's biking trails. They have a shop for accessories and repair needs, plus they rent kayaks and can equip you for paintball and archery sports held at a nearby range. ✉ *64-1066 Māmalahoa Hwy. (Box 2338), Kamuela 96743* ☎ *808/885–5005.*

Kona Coast Cycling Tours. Kona Coast leads a number of bike tours all over the Big Island. See the Island's wonders up close on a tour including the Kohala Coast, Hāmākua Coast, historical Māmalahoa Highway, Kona coffee country, and backcountry Mauna Kea via the Mana Road. Custom tours are also available. Rates for standard tours range from $50 to $150. ✉ *74-5588 Pawai Pl., Suite 1, Kailua-Kona 96740* ☎ *808/327–1133 or 877/592–2453* ⊕ *www.cyclekona.com.*

Mauna Kea Mountain Bikes, Inc. Daily tours down the upper slopes of Mauna Kea—chances are you'll start out in the snow—and downhill along the Kohala Mountains, as well as bike rentals are offered by this company. Tour prices range from $50 to $115. ✉ *Box 44672, Kamuela 96743* ☎ *808/883–0130 or 888/682–8687* ⊕ *www.bikehawaii.com/maunakea.*

Vermont Bicycle Tours. Bruce Starbuck, your experienced guide, has biked every road and trail on the Big Island. His eight-day winter tours cruise mostly downhill and visit Hawai'i's cultural sites, including Hawai'i Volcanoes National Park, Pu'uhonua O Hōnaunau, and Parker Ranch. Tour fees start at $1,800. ⊠ *614 Monkton Rd. (Box 711), Bristol, VT 05443* ☎ *802/453–4811 or 800/245–3868* ⊕ *www.vbt.com.*

BIKE RENTAL If you want to strike out on your own, there are several rental shops in Kailua-Kona and a couple in Waimea and Hilo. Resorts rent bicycles that can be used around the properties. Most outfitters listed can provide a bicycle rack for your car.

B&L Bike and Sports (⊠ 75-5699 Kopiko Pl., Kailua-Kona ☎ 808/329–3309), in downtown Kailua-Kona, rents various bikes, with prices for mountain bikes starting around $30 for 24 hours.

Upcountry, close to trails that flank the slopes of Mauna Kea, **C&S Outfitters** (⊠ 64-1066 Māmalahoa Hwy., Waimea ☎ 808/885–5005) has both road and mountain bikes.

Dave's Bike & Triathlon Shop (⊠ 75-5669 Ali'i Dr., Kailua-Kona ☎ 808/329–4522) specializes in road and race bikes.

Hawaiian Pedals (⊠ Kona Inn Shopping Village, 75-5744 Ali'i Dr. ☎ 808/329–2294 ⊕ www.hpbikeworks.com) rents road and mountain bikes, starting at $15 for five hours or $20 for the whole day.

Hilo Bike Hub (⊠ 318 E. Kawili St., Hilo ☎ 808/961–4452) caters to bike enthusiasts ready to explore Volcano and its surroundings.

Experienced riders will find rugged mountain bikes at **HP BikeWorks** (⊠ 74-5599 Luhia St., Suite F-3, Kailua-Kona ☎ 808/326–2453 ⊕ www.hpbikeworks.com) for $35 a day for front-suspension bikes and $45 a day for full-suspension bikes.

Fitness & Spa Centers

Several health clubs around the island offer inexpensive day passes for your routine workout; they have showers and lockers. With 10 spas encircling the island, you can find rejuvenation easily. Six of the major hotels have spa facilities that may be used by nonguests.

The Club. High-tech fitness facilities, with a pool and sauna, are available here for a daily rate of $15. ⊠ *75-5699 Kopiko Rd., Kailua-Kona* ☎ *808/326–2582.*

The Fairmont Orchid Hawai'i. The Spa Without Walls program offers an ever-expanding choice of treatments, indoors and outdoors. Ancient Hawaiian techniques, fragrant herbal wraps, and Hawaiian-coffee and vanilla scrubs are just a sampling of what's available. The fitness center and hot tubs are free for hotel guests only. ⊠ *1 N. Kanikū Dr., Kohala Coast* ☎ *808/885–2000.*

Four Seasons Resort Hualālai. This may well be the most beautiful spa on the island, but you have to be a guest of the hotel to indulge in the top-rate health and fitness options. ⊠ *100 Ka'ūpūlehu Dr., Ka'ūpūlehu Kona* ☎ *808/325–8000.*

Hāpuna Beach Prince Hotel. The hotel offers $15 day-passes for its Fitness Center at the Clubhouse. Herbal treatments and massages, including a soothing poi body wrap, are available. ✉ *62-100 Kauna'oa Dr., Waimea* ☎ *808/880–1111.*

Hawai'i Naniloa Resort. Nonguests can use the spa and fitness center for $15. ✉ *93 Banyan Dr., Hilo* ☎ *808/969–3333.*

Hilton Waikoloa Village. The hotel lays claim to the well-known and recently renovated Kohala Spa ($33 daily), where you can even find a healthful smoothie at the Spa Café. ✉ *425 Waikoloa Beach Dr., Kohala Coast* ☎ *808/886–1234.*

Kona Village Resort. Kona Village remains true to its secluded, romantic, and luxurious isolation with a health club open to resort guests only. ✉ *Queen Ka'ahumanu Hwy., Kailua-Kona* ☎ *808/325–5555.*

Mauna Kea Beach Hotel. A state-of-the-art fitness center for guests only is in the hotel's private beachfront building. ✉ *62-100 Mauna Kea Beach Dr., Kohala Coast* ☎ *808/882–7222.*

Mauna Lani Spa. This indoor-outdoor spa is a combination of Hawaiian gardens, thatch hales, and slate-floor state-of-the-art treatment rooms. The "Fire & Ice" theme influences the treatments, which include, among others, mud wraps using volcanic ash and hot-stone therapies. Facilities are available to nonguests; a minimum 60-minute treatment is required. ✉ *68-1400 Mauna Lani Dr., Kohala Coast* ☎ *808/881–7922.*

Ohana Keauhou Beach Resort. At the Kalona Salon & Spa you can opt for spa or beauty treatments and gardenside massages. The resort's fitness room is for hotel guests only. ✉ *78-6740 Ali'i Dr., Kailua-Kona* ☎ *808/322–3441.*

Pacific Coast Fitness. This fitness center in Waimea offers daily classes and has state-of-the-art equipment; the fee is $8 daily. ✉ *65-1298 A Kawaihae Rd., Waimea* ☎ *808/885–6270.*

Spencer Health and Fitness Center. Exercise addicts can try this $10-a-day health club in Hilo. ✉ *197 Keawe St., Hilo* ☎ *808/969–1511.*

Waikoloa Beach Marriott. The Hawaiian Rainforest Salon & Spa features traditional Hawaiian healing arts as well as the latest spa therapies and aromatherapy facials. The spa facilities are for hotel guests only. ✉ *69-275 Waikoloa Beach Dr., Waikoloa* ☎ *808/886–7727.*

Golf

If there is one thing the Big Island is known for, it's beautiful golf courses. Five of the courses—two at the Mauna Kea Resort, two at the Mauna Lani Resort, and the course at the Four Seasons Resort Hualālai—are repeatedly chosen by golfing magazines as the best in the country.

Big Island Country Club. At a 2,500-foot elevation, this 18-hole course has a dramatic layout and stunning views. Formerly a private-membership course, it's now open to the public. ✉ *71-1420 Māmalahoa Hwy., Kailua-Kona* ☎ *808/325–5044* ✎ *Greens fee $85, twilight (after 11 AM) $55.*

★ **Francis H. I'i Brown Golf Course at the Mauna Lani Hotel.** This demanding and beautiful course was redesigned by Nelson Wright Haworth and now has two 18-hole courses (North and South). The men's tee at the 15th hole of the South Course is famous among golfers because they must carry their tee shot over a stretch of open ocean to reach the green. ✉ 68-1310 Mauna Lani Dr., Kohala Coast ☎ 808/885–6655 ☞ Greens fee for either course $185 nonguests, cart included.

★ **Hāpuna Golf Course.** Landscaped with indigenous plants, trees, and grasses, this course at the Hāpuna Beach Prince Hotel aims to be environmentally sensitive. It's also one of the best on the island, a challenging par-72 course designed by Arnold Palmer and Ed Seay. Both the 1st and 18th holes are within easy walking distance of Mauna Kea Beach Hotel. ✉ 62-100 Kauna'oa Dr., Waimea ☎ 808/880–3000 ☞ Greens fee $145, twilight $105, cart included.

Hilo Municipal Golf Course. On the east side of the island is this 18-hole, inexpensive course with four sets of tees. It's in an older residential area upslope of town and the airport. Bring an umbrella for sudden passing showers. ✉ 340 Haihai St., Hilo ☎ 808/959–7711 ☞ Greens fee $30 weekdays, $35 weekends.

★ **Hualālai Golf Course.** Designed by Jack Nicklaus, this 18-hole course is a masterpiece. Players can see the ocean from every hole. Play here is a treat reserved for Four Seasons Resort Hualālai guests and resort residents, so the course is seldom crowded. ✉ 100 Ka'ūpūlehu Dr., Ka'ūpūlehu/Kona ☎ 808/325–8480 ☞ Greens fees $175.

Kona Country Club. Choose from two Kailua-Kona 18-hole courses, both with awesome views of the Kona Coast: the **Ali'i Course** (Mountain Course) or the **Ocean Course**. The pros try to avoid the lava. ✉ 78-7000 Ali'i Dr., Kailua-Kona ☎ 808/322–2595 ☞ Greens fee $130 for Ocean Course (twilight $85), $115 for Mountain Course (twilight $75).

Mākālei Hawai'i Country Club. On the cool slopes of Hualālai Mountain, the 18-hole course climbs from 1,800 to 2,800 feet and is interrupted by peacocks, wild turkeys, and pheasants that wander across the bentgrass greens. ✉ 72-3890 Hawai'i Belt Rd., Kailua-Kona ☎ 808/325–6625 ☞ Greens fee $110, twilight $50, cart included.

★ **Mauna Kea Beach Resort Golf Course.** This extremely challenging championship par-72, 18-hole course receives award after award from golf magazines. It was designed by Robert Trent Jones Sr. ✉ 62-100 Mauna Kea Beach Dr., Kohala Coast ☎ 808/882–5400 ☞ Greens fee $195, twilight $160.

Naniloa Country Club Golf Course. The Naniloa is a 9-hole course convenient to Hilo's major hotels. For one fee you may take the course twice. ✉ 120 Banyan Dr., Hilo ☎ 808/935–3000 ☞ Greens fee weekday $25, weekend $30; cart $8.

Sea Mountain Golf Course. This course overlooks the shores of a black-sand beach about 30 mi south of Volcano Village. The 18-hole, par-72 course stretches from the Pacific coast up the slopes of Mauna Loa. ✉ Hwy. 11, Ninole Loop Rd., Punalu'u ☎ 808/928–6222 ☞ Greens fee weekdays $42, weekend $45, cart included.

★ **Volcano Golf & Country Club.** This 18-hole, par-72 course perches near the rim of Kīlauea Volcano, at an elevation of 4,000 feet. It is comfortably cool, and on clear days you'll have glamorous views. It was originally built in 1922. Three grass bunkers and a pond have been added since. ✉ Hawai'i Volcanoes National Park ☎ 808/967–7331 ☞ Greens fee $63, twilight $50, cart included.

★ **Waikoloa Beach Golf Course.** Designed by Robert Trent Jones, Jr., in 1981, this course sprawls over historical grounds at the two Waikoloa resorts. An 18-hole, par-70 course with three sets of tees, it wends through lava formations and has beautiful ocean views. ⊠ *1020 Keana Place, Waikoloa* ☎ *808/886–6060* ⛳ *Greens fee $165 nonguests for 18 holes, twilight $75, cart included.*

★ **Waikoloa King's Golf Course.** This par-72, 18-hole course, designed by Tom Weiskopf and Jay Morrish, has four large lakes and four sets of tees and is adjacent to the Hilton Waikoloa Village. ⊠ *600 Waikoloa Beach Dr., Waikoloa* ☎ *808/886–7888* ⛳ *Greens fee $165 nonguests for 18 holes, twilight $75, cart included.*

Waikoloa Village Golf Club. You'll have beautiful views at this 1,000-foot elevation. The club is 6 mi up from the resorts and is the second of the two Waikoloa courses designed by Robert Trent Jones Jr. ⊠ *68-1792 Melia St., Waikoloa Village* ☎ *808/883–9621* ⛳ *Greens fee $100, twilight $55, cart included.*

Waimea Country Club. Wedged inside a eucalyptus forest is this 18-hole, bent-grass-greens, par-72 course. It lies in the cool, misty highlands on the Hilo side of Waimea and often gets rainy in the afternoon. ⊠ *47-5220 Māmalahoa Hwy., Waimea* ☎ *808/885–8053* ⛳ *Greens fee $65, twilight $50, cart included; call for reduced rates for senior citizens or for golfers who want to walk.*

ON THE SIDELINES | Ample celebrity-spotting is possible at golf tournaments held at resort golf courses in the Kohala area. The biggest and best is the **MasterCard Championship** (☎ 800/417–2770 ⊕ www.pga.com), a Senior PGA Tour event hosted by the **Four Seasons Resort Hualālai** (☎ 808/325–8000) in January.

Hiking & Camping

For the fit adventurer, hiking is a great way to explore the Big Island's natural beauty. If you're eager to learn as you hike through pristine wilderness, you may want to book a guided nature trek with experienced naturalists and bird-watchers.

Trails crisscross the slopes of **Mauna Kea.** Hiking up here is particularly rigorous because of the change in altitude. Hikers should be sure they have plenty of water and warm clothes—sunscreen, sunglasses, and a compass are also good items to bring. The most popular hike is up to the summit, a difficult, four-hour journey that rewards the stalwart with glimpses of endangered species and amazing views. The trail begins at the Onizuka Center and makes a stop at Lake Waiau before bringing you to the summit.

The best—but also the most dangerous—overnight backcountry hikes follow the steep, isolated trails in **Hawai'i Volcanoes National Park.** Conditions are often extremely hazardous, and you must register to obtain a free permit at Kīlauea Visitor Center first. One trek leads to the top of 13,677-foot **Mauna Loa;** it's 20 mi one-way, with overnight stops at two cabins, one at 10,000 feet and the other at the summit. You should count on spending three to four days on this hike, which is possibly the hardest in the Hawaiian Islands, with arctic conditions. The **Nāpau Trail** takes you through the Kīlauea rain forest to a campsite close to the percolating stream around Pu'u O'o cone, itself active and therefore extremely dangerous. The **Coastal and East Rift Backcountry** descends to isolated beach sites that hide sea turtles but are not safe for swimming. ⊠ *Hawai'i Volcanoes National Park, Kīlauea Visitor Center, Volcano 96785* ☎ *808/ 985–6000* ⊕ *www.nps.gov* ⊗ *Daily 7:45–5.*

Dozens of trails at the center of Hawai'i Volcanoes National Park make for great day hikes. A ranger will be happy to help you choose according to your fitness level and time frame. Consider staying at the inexpensive **Nāmakani Paio Cabins**, at a 4,000-foot elevation, managed by Volcano House, a concession of the National Park Service. Each cabin has a double bed, two bunk beds, and electric lights. Bring extra blankets, as it gets cold in these basic units. Each cabin also has a grill outside, but you must bring your own firewood. ☎ *Volcano House, Box 53, Hawai'i Volcanoes National Park, 96718* ☎ *808/967–7321* ☎ *808/967–8429* ☎ *Single or double $40; a $32 refundable deposit allows guests to pick up bedding and keys (for cabins and separate bath facilities) at Volcano House.*

For information about the Big Island's state parks, including Hāpuna Beach and Kalopa Park, contact the **Department of Land and Natural Resources, State Parks Division** (⊠ 75 Aupuni St., Hilo 96720 ☎ 808/974–6200 ⊕ www.hawaii.gov).

For general hiking information, topographic and other maps, as well as up-to-date hiking guides, contact the **Hawai'i Geographic Society** (☎ Box 1698, Honolulu 96806 ☎ 800/538–3950).

For information on camping at county parks, including Spencer Beach Park, contact the **Department of Parks and Recreation** (⊠ 25 Aupuni St., Hilo 96720 ☎ 808/961–8311 ⊕ www.hawaii-county.com).

Horseback Riding

In addition to the companies listed below, the Mauna Kea Beach Hotel maintains stables in Waimea.

King's Trail Rides O'Kona, Inc. Riders take a 4½-hour excursion to Captain Cook Monument in Kealakekua Bay. The trip includes snorkeling and lunch for $135 to $150. Custom rides can also be arranged. ⊠ *Hwy. 11, mile marker 111, (Box 270), Kealakekua* ☎ *808/323–2388* ⊕ *www. konacowboy.com.*

Kohala Na'alapa. Here, adjacent to the white fence of Kohala Ranch, riders of all levels are invited to take open-pasture rides on historic Kahuā Ranch. Forested areas alternate with splendid panoramic views. Excursions range from $55 to $75. ⊠ *Kohala Mountain Rd. (Hwy. 250)* ☎ *808/ 889–0022.*

Paniolo Riding Adventures. Trail rides for beginners to buckaroos pass through lush Kohala ranch land. You'll never be nose-to-tail on these rides. A 1½-hour ride costs $63, a 2½-hour ride costs $89, and a 4-hour adventure costs $130. Custom rides are available. ⊠ *Kohala Mountain Rd. (Hwy. 250)* ☎ *808/889–5354* ⊕ *www.panioloadventures.com.*

Waipiʻo Naʻalapa Trail Rides. Deep in Waipiʻo Valley, riders meander past waterfalls and rivers over lush, secluded trails on these twice-daily rides. Expeditions cost $75 and depart from Waipiʻo Valley Artworks in Kukuihaele. ⊠ *Waipiʻo Valley Artworks, off Hwy. 240, Kukuihaele* ☎ *808/775–0419 for information about trail rides, 808/775–0958 for Artworks.*

Waipiʻo on Horseback and Taro Farm. Only two riding outfits venture into the green jungle of the valley floor. Waipiʻo on Horseback takes you to an authentic taro farm. Rides depart twice daily from the Last Chance Store and cost $78. ⊠ *Last Chance Store, off Hwy. 240, Kukuihaele* ☎ *877/775–7291 or 808/775–7291.*

Waipiʻo Ridge Stables. Two different rides around the rim of Waipiʻo are offered—a 2½-hour trek for $75 and a 5-hour hidden-waterfall adventure for $145. Riders meet at Waipiʻo Valley Artworks. ⊠ *Waipiʻo Valley Artworks, off Hwy. 240, Kukuihaele* ☎ *808/775–1007, 877/757–1414 for information about trail rides, 808/775–0958 for Artworks* ⊕ *www.topofwaipio.com.*

Paragliding

Paragliding is a relatively new sport in Hawaiʻi. Not quite hang gliding and not quite parachuting, it's an exciting way to take in the isle's beauty from above.

Paraguides Hawaiʻi. You need to be certified to soar swiftly above grassy mountains and over deep valleys. This outfitter provides guide services for $100, and will help you become a paraglide pilot. Expect to pay $175 for your first day, or $1,200 for the complete training (five days). ✍ *Box 1954, Kamuela 96743* ☎ *808/887–8359* ⊕ *www.paraguideshawaii.com.*

Polo

Matches sponsored by the **Mauna Kea Polo Club** (⊠ Waikiʻi Ranch, off Saddle Rd., 6½ mi from Māmalahoa Hwy. ☎ 808/960–5098) are scheduled every Sunday, October through mid-December.

Skiing

Skiing on Mauna Kea is for experienced skiers only. Currently the ski area has no lodge, lifts or facilities of any kind.

Ski Guides Hawaiʻi. Christopher Langan of Mauna Kea Ski Corporation is the only outfitter licensed to furnish transportation, guide services, and ski equipment on Mauna Kea. Snow can fall from Thanksgiving through June, but the most likely months are February and March. Langan charges $450 per person for a daylong experience that includes refreshments, lunch, ski or snowboard equipment, guide service, transportation from Waimea, and four-wheel-drive shuttle back up the mountain after each ski run. He also offers a $250 mountain ski service without the frills and ski or snowboard rentals. ✍ *Box 1954, Kamuela 96743* ☎ *808/885–4188, 808/884–5131 off-season* ⊕ *www.skihawaii.com.*

Tennis

School and park courts are free and open to anyone who wishes to play, though students have first priority during school hours at high school courts. Listed below are the most popular courts. Resort courts often rent rackets, shoes, and balls. Nonguests can play for a fee at the **Royal Kona Resort,** at the **Ohana Keauhou Beach Resort,** and at the **King Kamehameha's Kona Beach Hotel. Waikoloa Beach Marriott, Hilton Waikoloa Village, Mauna Kea Beach Hotel,** and the **Fairmont Orchid Hawai'i** also have superb courts you can book as a nonguest. Contact the **Department of Parks and Recreation** (✉ 25 Aupuni St., Hilo 96720 ☎ 808/961–8311 ⊕ www.hawaii-county.com) for a full list of all public Big Island tennis courts.

On the Hilo side, the eight courts (three lighted for night play) at **Hilo Tennis Stadium** (✉ Ho'olulu County Park, Pi'ilani and Kalanikoa Sts., Hilo ☎ 808/961–8720) require a small fee. There are four free (two lighted) courts at **Lincoln Park** (✉ Kino'ole and Ponahawai Sts., Hilo). You will find well-maintained courts at the **University of Hawai'i–Hilo** (✉ 200 Kawili St., Hilo ☎ 808/974–7520). **Waiākea Racquet Club** (✉ 400 Hualani St., Hilo ☎ 808/961–5499) is open to the public for a reasonable fee.

In Kailua-Kona, you can play for free at the **Kailua Playground** (✉ 75-5794 Kuakini Hwy., Kailua-Kona). Tennis courts are available at the **Old Kona Airport** (✉ north end of Kuakini Hwy., Kailua-Kona).

There are two free, lighted courts at **Waimea Park** (✉ Kawaihae and Lindsey Rds., Waimea). Courts at **Colony One at Sea Mountain** (✉ 95-789 Ninole Loop Rd., turn off Hwy. 11 at Punalu'u, Punalu'u ☎ 808/928–6200 or 800/344–7675) are available at an hourly charge.

ON THE SIDELINES   The world's best players compete in January in the **USTA Challenger** (✉ Kohala Coast ☎ 518/274–1674 ⊕ www.tesports.com) on the courts of **Hilton Waikoloa Village** (☎ 808/886–1234).

Triathlon

Fodor'sChoice ★   The highly popular **Ironman Triathlon** (☎ 808/329–0063 ⊕ www.ironmanlive.com), with a $430,000 purse, is limited to 1,500 competitors, who swim 2.4 mi, bicycle 112 mi, and run a 26.2-mi marathon. Entrants must qualify through other international competitions. The grueling event begins with the ocean swim from Kailua Pier at 7 AM, usually on the third Saturday in October. Close to 7,000 volunteers along Ali'i Drive, Queen Ka'ahumanu Highway, and the turnaround in Hāwī provide encouragement and much-needed water to the world's top athletes.

Water Sports

DEEP-SEA FISHING   Along the Kona Coast you'll find some of the world's most exciting "bluewater" fishing. Although July, August, and September are peak months, with a number of tournaments, charter fishing goes on year-round. You don't have to compete to experience the thrill of landing a big Pacific blue marlin or other game fish. More than 60 charter boats, averaging

26 to 58 feet, are available for hire, most of them out of **Honokōhau Harbor,** just north of Kailua. Prices for a full day of fishing range from $350 for shared charters to $900 for private trips. Half-day charters are also available in the $225 to $600 range. Tackle, bait, and ice are furnished, but you'll have to bring your own lunch. Most boats do not allow you to keep your entire catch, although if you ask, many captains will send you home with a few fish fillets. In addition, be sure to describe your expectations when you book your charter so the booking agent can match you with a captain and a boat you will like.

Make arrangements for deep-sea fishing at your hotel activities desk or stop by at the **Charter Desk** (⊠ Kailua-Kona ☎ 808/329–5735 ⊕ www. charterdesk.com) at Honokōhau Harbor; you can pick up a lunch-to-go for the trip at the **Fish Dock Deli & Store** (☎ 808/329–8389) next door.

With its varied fleet, the **Charter Locker** (☎ 808/326–2553 ⊕ www. charterlocker.com) has been in business since 1964. **Charter Services Hawai'i** (☎ 808/334–1881 or 800/567–2650 ⊕ www.konazone.com) represents nine boats ranging from 33 to 46 feet. **Kona Activities Center** (☎ 808/329–3171 or 800/367–5288 ⊕ www.konaactivitiescenter.com) provides bookings and information for several charter companies. Book charters directly or get information about tournaments at **Kona Charter Skippers Association** (☎ 808/329–3600 or 800/762–7546 ⊕ www. konabiggamefishing.com). **Notorious Sport Fishing** (☎ 808/322–6407, 800/ 545–5662 ⊕ www.interpac.net/-jackc) favors small groups of up to six people. For the true fishing enthusiast, **Reel Action Light-Tackle Sportfishing** (☎ 808/325–6811) runs an open-center console boat and offers light tackle fishing, including fly fishing.

The biggest of the fishing competitions is the five-day **Hawaiian International Billfish Tournament** (⊡ Box 4800, Kailua-Kona 96745 ☎ 808/ 329–6155 ⊕ www.konabillfish.com), held annually in August since 1959. Tournament results can serve as a helpful guide in choosing which boat to charter.

Big fish are weighed in daily at **Honokōhau Harbor's Fuel Dock.** Try to be there in the afternoon between 4 and 5 to watch the weigh-in of the day's catch. It might just be another "grander" (more than 1,000 pounds).

JET SKIING Kailua Bay in Kona has generally calm waters that are perfect for jet skiing. At the present time, there is only one jet ski outfitter. **Aloha Jet Ski Rentals** (⊠ Kailua Pier, Ali'i Dr. at Palani Rd., Kailua-Kona ☎ 808/ 329–2754) charges $75 per hour for up to three riders.

KAYAKING Kayaks are great for observing Hawai'i's diverse marine life and serene shores. When you venture out, however, be sure to respect Hawai'i's waters: 30% of marine mammals are unique to the Big Island, and coral reefs are endangered; as a result, many bays are protected marine preserves. A reputable kayak shop can point out friendly locations, as currents can be dangerous.

Ocean Eco Tours (⊠ Honokōhau Harbor, 74-425 Kealekehe Pkwy., Kailua-Kona ☎ 808/324–7873 ⊕ www.oceanecotours.com) provides kayak sales and rentals, complete with gear and coolers, as well as guided tours. A tandem kayak costs $45 for the day. Daily tours are $125 per person.

Ocean Safari's Kayak Adventures (⊠ end of Kamehameha III Rd. [Box 515], Keauhou, Kailua-Kona ☎ 808/326–4699 ⊕ www. oceansafariskayaks.com) offers a variety of snorkeling and kayaking expeditions to sea caves and the Kealakekua Bay marine preserve on the Kona Coast. Guided kayak adventures range from $60 to $75.

SAILING AND PARASAILING

Ralph Blancato and Kalia Potter of **Maile Charters** (⊠ Kawaihae Harbor, Kawaihae ☎ 808/326–5174 or 800/726–7245 ⊕ www.adventuresailing. com) offer unique around-the-Islands sailing adventures that range from half-day to five-day journeys. Island-cuisine meals, itineraries, and activities are custom-designed. Private cabins and hot showers keep you comfortable. Fees start at $575 for six passengers for a half day.

Parasailers sit in a harness attached to a parachute that lifts off from the boat deck and sails aloft. Passengers can choose to glide 7 or 10 minutes at 400-, 800-, or 1,200-foot heights. Call **UFO Parasail** (⊠ 75-5669 Ali'i Dr., across the street from Kailua Pier, Kailua-Kona ☎ 808/325–5836 or 800/359–4836 ⊕ www.ufoparasailing.com) to make arrangements. Costs range from $42 to $57.

SCUBA DIVING & SNORKELING

Two-tank dives average $100 to $150, depending on whether you're certified and whether you're diving from a boat or from the shore. Many dive outfits have underwater cameras for rent. Instruction with PADI, SDI, or TDI certification in three to five days is $400 to $650. The Kona Coast has calm waters for diving, and dive operators are helpful about suggesting dive sites as far south as Pu'uhonua O Hōnaunau. Some companies also teach surfing, and most rent out dive equipment, snorkel gear, and other water toys. A few organize otherworldly manta-ray dives at night or whale-watching cruises in season.

A reputable scuba charter in Kailua-Kona is **Big Island Divers** (⊠ 75-5467 Kaiwi St., Kailua-Kona ☎ 808/329–6068 or 800/488–6068 ⊕ www. bigislanddivers.com). **Body Glove Cruises** (⊠ Kailua Pier, Kailua-Kona ☎ 808/326–7122 or 800/551–8911 ⊕ www.bodyglovehawaii.com) has a 55-foot catamaran that sets off from the Kailua Pier daily for a 4½-hour dive and snorkel cruise, which includes breakfast and a buffet lunch. Children are welcome. **Eco-Adventures Dive** (⊠ at the Lighthouse, 75-5614 Palani Rd., Kailua-Kona ☎ 808/329–7116 or 800/949–3483 ⊕ www.eco-adventures.com) creates daylong experiences with three dives as well as discovery trips, packages that include snorkeling and kayaking, and charter vacations. **Kohala Divers Ltd** (⊠ Kawaihae Shopping Center, downstairs, Kawaihae ☎ 808/882–7774 ⊕ www. kohaladivers.com) offers complete diving services. **Kona Coast Divers** (⊠ Honokōhau Harbor, 74-425 Kealekehe Pkwy., Kailua-Kona ☎ 808/329–8802 or 800/562–3483 ⊕ www.konacoastdivers.com) is a reputable, friendly outfit that has been around a long time. **Ocean Eco Tours** (⊠ Honokōhau Harbor, 74-425 Kealekehe Pkwy., Kailua-Kona ☎ 808/324–7873 ⊕ www.oceanecotours.com) is an ecofriendly, full-service outfit eager to share a wealth of knowledge. At 'Anaeho'omalu Bay, at

 the Hilton Waikoloa Village on the Kohala Coast, **Red Sail Sports** (⊠ 425

Waikoloa Beach Dr. ☎808/886–2876 ⊕www.redsail.com) certifies divers and organizes dives from the 38-foot *Lani Kai*. **Sandwich Isle Divers** (✉ 75-5729 Ali'i Dr., Kailua-Kona ☎ 808/329–9188 or 888/743–3483 ⊕ www.sandwichisledivers.com) is central and well established.

Colorful tropical fish frequent the lava outcroppings along many Big Island shorelines, so it's easy to arrange a do-it-yourself snorkeling tour by renting masks and snorkels from any of the many diving outfits in Kona or at the resorts. If you are island-hopping and want to drop off your equipment on O'ahu, Maui, or Kaua'i, consider **Snorkel Bob's** (✉ 75-5831 Kahakai Rd., next to the Royal Kona Resort, Kailua-Kona ☎ 808/329–0770 or 800/262–7725 ⊕ www.snorkelbob.com), where prices start at $9 to $10 a week for a simple set.

Many snorkel cruises are available. Shop for prices at kayak, scuba, and sailing outfitters; ask about the size of the boat, and be sure you know what is included and how much the extras, such as underwater cameras, cost.

Among the Big Island's wet-and-wild offerings is the **Captain Zodiac Raft Expedition** (✉ Honokōhau Harbor, Kailua-Kona ☎ 808/329–3199 ⊕ www.captainzodiac.com). The exciting four-hour 14-mi trip on this inflatable raft takes you along the Kona Coast to explore gaping lava-tube caves, search for dolphins and turtles, and drift through Kealakekua Bay for snorkeling. The cost is $80.

★ At Keauhou Bay **Fair Wind Snorkel and Orca Raft Adventures** (✉ 78-7130 Kaleiopapa St. Keauhou Bay, Kailua-Kona ☎ 808/322–2788 or 800/677–9461 ⊕ www.fair-wind.com) offers 4½-hour morning and 3½-hour afternoon excursions as well as special tours and packages. *Fair Wind* is a 60-foot double-decker catamaran with a 15-foot water slide and a dive tower. Gear includes prescription masks. Morning sails feature a barbecue lunch. The *Orca,* a 28-foot inflatable raft, cleaves the waves in a high-thrill, fast-pace ride not for the weak at heart. It also makes time for snorkeling and gentler floating opportunities. Morning sails cost around $87 on the *Fair Wind* and $73 on the *Orca*; afternoon trips are around $55 for both vessels.

WINDSURFING One of the best windsurfing locations on the Big Island is at 'Anaeho'omalu Bay, at the beach in front of the Waikoloa Beach Marriott. Call **Ocean Sports** (☎ 808/886–6666) to obtain information.

SHOPPING

Residents like to complain that there isn't much to shop for on the Big Island, but unless you're searching for winter coats or high-tech toys, you'll find plenty to deplete your pocketbook. Kailua-Kona has a range of souvenirs from far-flung corners of the globe. Resorts along the Kohala Coast have high-quality exclusive clothing, art, and accessories. Galleries and boutiques, many with the work of local artists, fill historic buildings in Waimea and North Kohala.

In general, stores and shopping centers on the Big Island open at 9 or 10 AM and close by 6 PM. Hilo's Prince Kūhiō Shopping Plaza stays open until 9 weekdays. In Kona, most shops in shopping plazas that are geared toward tourists remain open until 9. Big outlets such as KTA (a supermarket in Kona Coast Shopping Center) or Wal-Mart on Henry Street are open until midnight.

Shopping Centers

HāMāKUA COAST Developed for local consumers, **Kaloko Industrial Park** (☒ off Hwy. 19 and Hina Lani St., near Keāhole-Kona International Airport) has outlets such as Costco Warehouse and Home Depot. It's useful for industrial shopping, off-the-beaten-path finds, and wholesale prices.

HILO In Hilo the most comprehensive mall, similar to mainland malls, is **Prince Kūhiō Shopping Plaza** (☒ 111 E. Puainako St., at Hwy. 11). Here you'll find Macy's for fashion, Safeway for food, and Longs Drugs for just about everything else, along with several other shops and boutiques. The older **Hilo Shopping Center** (☒ Kekuanaoa St. at Kīlauea Ave.) has several air-conditioned shops and restaurants. Great cookies, cakes, and baked goodies are at Lanky's Pastries. And there's plenty of free parking. Hilo's **Waiakea Center** (☒ Maka'ala St. and Kanoelehua Ave., across from Prince Kūhiō Shopping Plaza, at Hwy. 11) has a Borders Books & Music, Island Naturals, a food court, and a Wal-Mart.

KAILUA-KONA **Coconut Grove Plaza** (☒ 75-5795–75-5825 Ali'i Dr.), just south of Kona Inn Shopping Village, hides coffee shops, boutiques, ethnic restaurants, and an exquisite gallery in its meandering labyrinth of airy buildings.

Shopping in Kailua-Kona has begun to go the way of mainland cities with Wal-Mart, a huge Safeway, Borders Books & Music, and an eclectic collection of restaurants at **Crossroads Shopping Center** (☒ 75-1000 Henry St.). **Keauhou Shopping Center** (☒ 78-6831 Ali'i Dr.) 5 mi south of Kailua-Kona town has a variety of stores and boutiques including KTA Superstore, Long's Drugs, and Alapaki's Hawaiian Gifts and a few island-style eateries.

On the makai side of Ali'i Drive in the heart of Kailua-Kona, extending for an entire block along Kailua Bay, is **Kona Inn Shopping Village** (☒ 75-5744 Ali'i Dr. ☎ 808/329–6573), crammed with boutiques selling bright pareus (beach wraps) and knickknacks. Here **Island Salsa** (☎ 808/329–9279) has great tropical toppers and T-shirts, and **Honolua Surf Company** (☎ 808/329–1001) is filled with cool beachwear. In Kailua-Kona, head north on **Palani Road** from Kailua Pier toward the intersection with Highway 19; **Kopiko Plaza** and **Lanihau Center,** on your right, house Longs Drugs, gift stores such as Kathryn's of Kona, sandwich shops, and a budget-friendly Sack 'n Save Foods. On your left, you'll find **North Kona Center** and **Kona Coast Shopping Center.**

Just north of Kona, off Highway 19, islanders find bargains at Big Kmart in the **Makalapua Center** (☒ Makalapua Ave.). Of more interest might be the large Macy's; although a mainland chain, it keeps nice selections in apparel and gifts from local vendors.

KOHALA   The harborside **Kawaihae Center** (✉ Hwy. 270, Kawaihae) houses restaurants, a dive shop, a bathing-suit store, and art galleries, including the Harbor Gallery.

King's Shops (✉ 250 Waikoloa Beach Dr., Waikoloa ☎ 808/886–8811) houses fine stores such as Under the Koa Tree, with its upscale gift items by artisans. You'll also find high-end outlets such as DFS Galleria and Louis Vuitton and several other specialty resort shops and boutiques.

WAIMEA   **Parker Ranch Center** (✉ 67-1185 Māmalahoa Highway, Waimea,) sports a newly renovated ranch-style motif. Anchors include a Foodland supermarket, Starbucks Coffee, and a natural foods store called Healthways II. Other shops in the mix are clothing boutiques and food outlets. The Parker Ranch Store and Parker Ranch Visitor Center and Museum are also here.

In Waimea, browse around boutiques in **Parker Square** (✉ 65-1279 Kawaihae Road, Waimea ☎ 808/331–1000) and in the adjacent **High Country Traders,** where you may find hand-stitched Hawaiian quilts. **Waimea Center** (✉ 65-1158 Māmalahoa Highway, Waimea,) has an eclectic mix of stores, including a large KTA supermarket, an unusual San Francisco–style gift shop, and a travel service, Without Boundaries.

Specialty Stores

Books & Maps
Basically Books (✉ 160 Kamehameha Ave., Hilo ☎ 808/961–0144 or 800/903–6277 ⊕ www.basicallybooks.com) stocks one of Hawai'i's largest selections of maps and charts, including USGS, topographical, and raised relief maps. It also has Hawaiiana books, with great choices for children. **Kohala Book Shop** (✉ 54-3885 Akoni Pule Hwy., Kapa'au ☎ 808/889–6400 ⊕ www.abebooks.com/home/kohalawind) in the historic Old Nanbu Hotel is the largest used-book store in the state, with one of the most complete Hawaiian and Pacific collections in the nation and rare first editions. **Middle Earth Bookshoppe** (✉ 75-5719 Ali'i Dr., Kailua-Kona ☎ 808/329–2123) is an independent bookstore with superb maps and an esoteric collection of literary works.

Candies & Chocolates
★ The chocolate factory **Big Island Candies** (✉ 585 Hinano St., Hilo ☎ 808/935–8890 ⊕ www.bigislandcandies.com) lets you tour and taste before you buy. **Kailua Candy Company** (✉ 74-5563 Kaiwi St., Kailua-Kona ☎ 808/329–2522) sells chocolate made with locally grown cacao beans from the Original Hawaiian Chocolate Factory. Of course, tasting is part of the fun. Through a glass wall you can watch the chocolate artists at work.

Hawaiian Art & Crafts

HAWAI'I
VOLCANOES
NATIONAL PARK

On your way to Hawai'i Volcanoes National Park, be sure to visit the workshop of **Dan DeLuz's Woods, Inc.** (⊠ 17-4003 Ahuahu Pl.,Hwy. 11, mile marker 12, Mountain View ☎808/968–6607 ⊠ 64-1013 Māmalahoa Hwy., Waimea ☎ 808/885–5856), where master bowl-turner Dan DeLuz creates works of art from 50 types of exotic wood grown on the Big Island.

★ In Hawai'i Volcanoes National Park, **Volcano Art Center** (☎ 808/967–7565) remains a favorite with everyone. The Art Center represents more island artists than any other gallery and carries a selection of fine art prints and oils as well.

HILO
Step into **Dragon Mama** (⊠ 266 Kamehameha Ave. ☎ 808/934–9081 ⊕ www.dragonmama.com) to find authentic Japanese fabrics, futons, and antiques. You'll find exquisite ceramics, Japanese tea sets, and affordable bamboo ware at **Ets'ko** (⊠ 35 Waiānuenue Ave. ☎ 808/961–3778). Hilo's **Most Irresistible Shop** (⊠ 256 Kamehameha Ave. ☎ 808/935–9644 ⊠Prince Kūhiō Plaza, 111 E. Puainako St., at Hwy. 11, ☎808/959–6515) lives up to its name with unique gifts from the Pacific, be it coconut-flavored butter or a whimsical wind chime.

If you're driving north from Hilo, take time to browse through **Hoaloha** (⊠ Last Chance Store, off Hwy. 240, Kukuihaele ☎ 808/775–0502) and pick up a colorful pareu or accessory. In the remote **Waipi'o Valley Artworks** (⊠ off Hwy. 240, Kukuihaele ☎ 808/775–0958) you'll find finely crafted wooden bowls, koa furniture, paintings, and jewelry—all made by local artists.

KAILUA-KONA
For hula instruments, intricate feather headbands, and other original art, head to **Alapaki's Hawaiian Gifts** (⊠ Keauhou Shopping Village, 78-6831 Ali'i Dr. ☎ 808/322–2007). Geared toward cruise-ship passengers
★ with little time, **Made on the Big Island** (⊠ King Kamehameha's Kona Beach Hotel, 75-5660 Palani Rd., at Kailua Pier ☎ 808/326–4949) is one-stop shopping for traditional Big Island gifts. You'll find quite a few treasures here, such as koa boxes and bonsai trees that may be exported. At **Rift Zone** (⊠ Coconut Plaza, 75-5801 Ali'i Dr. ☎ 808/331–1100), owned by ceramist Robert Joiner and his wife, Kathy, you'll not only find ceramics but also exquisite jewelry, bowls, ornaments, and hand-blown glass.

KOHALA
Cook's Discoveries (⊠ 64-1066 Māmalahoa Hwy., Waimea ☎ 808/885–
★ 3633) is one of the best places in the state to shop for high-end Hawaiian gifts. In the **Gallery of Great Things** (⊠ 65-1279 Kawaihae Rd., Waimea ☎ 808/885–7706) at Parker Square, you might fall in love with the Ni'ihau shell leis ($150–$7,000) it occasionally carries. More affordable perhaps are koa mirrors and other high-quality artifacts from all around the Pacific basin. For fine art, furniture, and decorative pieces made with koa and other native woods, be sure to stop in Kawaihae and visit the **Harbor Gallery** (⊠ Kawaihae Shopping Center, Kawaihae ☎ 808/882–1510). **Mauna Kea Galleries** (⊠ 65-1298 Kawaihae Rd.,

Waimea ☎ 808/887–2244) specializes in rare vintage collectibles, including hula dolls, prints, and koa furniture.

Upcountry of Kailua-Kona, in the little coffee town of Hōlualoa, several galleries crowd the narrow street. **Hōlualoa Gallery** (✉ 76-5921 Māmalahoa Hwy., Hōlualoa ☎ 808/322–8484) has stunning *raku* (Japanese lead-glazed pottery). Men can pick up an authentic *lauhala* hat ★ for some top-level sun protection at **Kimura's Lauhala Shop** (✉ Māmalahoa Hwy., Hōlualoa ☎808/324–0053). The **Kona Arts Center** (✉Māmalahoa Hwy., Hōlualoa) has drawn an entire community of artists; feel free to drop in if the doors are open.

Remote North Kohala has dozens of artists and hosts a remarkable number of galleries in its old restored plantation buildings. At **Ackerman Gallery** (✉ Akoni Pule Hwy., Kapa'au ☎ 808/889–5971), painter Gary Ackerman; his wife, Yesan; and their daughter, Camille, have a fine and varied collection of gifts for sale in two locations near the King Kamehameha statue. Be sure to stop at the Old Nanbu Hotel, a historic building constructed in 1898. Here, working in the front window of his store, **Elements** (✉ 54-3885 Akoni Pule Hwy., Kapa'au ☎ 808/889–0760), John Flynn creates exquisite jewelry such as delicate, silver-maile lei and gold waterfalls. The shop also showcases carefully chosen gift items, including unusual ceramics and glass. Inside the Bamboo Restaurant in Hāwī, the **Gallery at Bamboo** (✉ Hāwī Rd., Hāwī ☎ 808/889–1441) seduces visitors with koa-wood pieces such as rocking chairs and writing desks. It also has a wealth of gift items such as boxes, jewelry, and Hawaiian wrapping paper.

Nanbu Gallery (✉ 54-3885 Akoni Pule Hwy., Kapa'au ☎ 808/889–0997) shows the paintings of owner Patrick Sweeney and other island artists. Watercolorist and oil painter Patrick Louis Rankin runs **Rankin Gallery** (✉ 53-4380 Akoni Pule Hwy., Kapa'au ☎ 808/889–6849) in the old Wo On Store, next to the Chinese community and social hall, the Tong Wo Society. Resident artist Sue Swerdlow owns the **Sue Swerdlow Art Gallery** (✉ 54-3862 Akoni Pule Hwy., Kapa'au ☎ 808/889–0002). It's worth a stop to browse the tropically-inspired artworks.

Vintage & Resort Wear
Hotel shops generally offer the most attractive and original resort wear, but prices run higher than elsewhere.

HILO **Hilo Hattie** (✉ Prince Kūhiō Plaza, 111 E. Puainako St., Hilo ☎ 808/
★ 961–3077 ✉ 75-5597 Palani Rd., Kopiko Plaza, Kailua-Kona ☎ 808/
329–7200) matches his-and-her aloha wear and carries a huge selection of casual clothes, slippers, jewelry, and souvenirs. Call for free trans-
★ portation from selected hotels. The well-known **Sig Zane Designs** (✉ 122 Kamehameha Ave., Hilo ☎ 808/935–7077) sells distinctive island wearables with bold colors and motifs.

KAILUA-KONA For rare vintage clothing and authentic antique jewelry, browse through the selection at **Flamingo's** (✉ Kona Inn Shopping Village, 75-5744 Ali'i Dr. ☎ 808/329–4122). In **Keauhou Shopping Center** (✉ 76-6831 Ali'i Dr.)

in Kailua-Kona, stop in at **Borderlines** (☎ 808/322–5003) for colorful women's apparel. **Laneke Boutique** (☎ 808/322–9100) carries a great variety of aloha attire and resort wear.

KOHALA At **Adasa** (✉ 3 Opelo Plaza, Waimea ☎ 808/887–0997), designer Donna Lore carries high-end couture, her own designs, and matching accessories. Custom design is also possible. In North Kohala, in the historic 1932 Toyama Building, **As Hāwī Turns** (✉ Akoni Pule Hwy., Hāwī ☎ 808/889–5023) adds a sophisticated touch to breezy resort wear, pareos, and hand-painted silk clothing. There are vintage and secondhand treasures, crafts, and gifts as well. If you'd like to take home some of Hawai'i's splashy material, stop in at **Kimura's Fabrics** (✉ Māmalahoa Hwy. 11, Kainaliu ☎ 808/322–3771). Upcountry on the one-street town of Kainaliu—and in Kailua-Kona's shopping centers—**Paradise Found** (✉ Māmalahoa Hwy. 11 ☎ 808/322–2111 ✉ Lanihau Center, Kailua-Kona ☎ 808/329–2221 ✉ Keauhou Shopping Center, Kailua-Kona ☎ 808/324–1177) has contemporary silk and rayon clothing.

Tropical Flowers & Produce

★ You can buy tropical blooms at **Akatsuka Orchid Gardens** (✉ Hwy. 11, Volcano ☎ 808/967–8234) and have them shipped home. The nursery is in Volcano, a 10-minute drive from Hawai'i Volcanoes National Park. At **Ali'i Gardens Market Place** (✉ 75-6129 Ali'i Dr., 1½ mi south of Kona Inn Shopping Village, Kailua-Kona ☎ 808/334–1381), open Wednesday through Sunday, individual entrepreneurs sell everything from tropical flowers to Kona coffee, baskets, souvenirs, and crafts. It's more of a flea market than a farmers' market. In addition to selling and shipping miniature *brassaia lava* plantings and other bonsai plants, **Fuku-Bonsai Cultural Center** (✉ Ola'a Rd., Kurtistown ☎ 808/982–9880 ⊕ www.fukubonsai.com), which is on the way to Volcano, has free educational exhibits of different ethnic styles of pruning.

★ At **Hilo Farmers Market** (✉ Kamehameha Ave. and Mamo St., Hilo) farmers sell a profusion of tropical flowers, high-quality produce, and macadamia nuts. This colorful, open-air market—the most popular in the state—takes place on Wednesday and Saturday from 6:30 AM to 2:30 PM. The low-key **Kona Inn Farmers' Market** (✉ 75-7544 Ali'i Dr., Kona Inn Shopping Village parking lot, Kailua-Kona) is filled with colorful tropical flowers and locally grown produce, including macadamia nuts and coffee. It takes place Wednesday and Saturday from 7 AM until 3 PM.

In North Kohala, **Na Pua O Kohala** (✉ 55-3413 Akoni Pule Hwy. ☎ 808/889–5541 or 877/889–5571 ⊕ www.kohalaflowers.com) you can order leis or let owner Johanna Bard help you create a memorable bouquet. She'll ship your selections for you. The old stone **Volcano Store** (✉ Old Volcano Hwy., Volcano Village ☎ 808/967–7210), near Hawai'i Volcanoes National Park, has excellent bargains in cut flowers such as anthuriums and will ship them for you.

THE BIG ISLAND A TO Z

To research prices, get advice from other travelers, and book travel arrangements, visit www.fodors.com.

AIR TRAVEL

Several domestic and international airlines serve the Big Island's two airports from the mainland as well as from the other islands. Charters around the Islands are available from any airport location through Pacific Wings, a charter and scheduled airline serving all airports in Hawai'i with twin-engine Cessna 402C-8 passenger aircraft. For information call 888/575-4546 or 808/873-0877, or visit www.pacificwings.com.

CARRIERS Both national and local airlines offer daily flights to several cities on the mainland. Connections of airlines listed are direct, but keep in mind that you can fly from anywhere as long as you're willing to transfer on O'ahu or Maui. Hawaiian Airlines, for example, now serves San Diego, San Francisco, Portland, Phoenix, Las Vegas, Los Angeles, and Seattle from Honolulu. Aloha Airlines has daily trips connecting Oakland, Orange County, Burbank, Phoenix, Vancouver, and Las Vegas with the Islands.

United offers daily direct and seasonal flights from San Francisco and Los Angeles to Kona International Airport.

Between the Neighbor Islands, Aloha and Hawaiian airlines offer frequent jet flights that take about 40 minutes from Honolulu to either Hilo or Kona. Fares are approximately $160 to $220.

Aloha Airline's sister commuter carrier Island Air provides frequent, direct flights from Kona to Hawai'i's resort and smaller community destinations, including Lāna'i, Moloka'i, and Kapalua.
🛧 **Aloha Airlines** ☎ 800/367-5250 or 808/935-5771 ⊕ www.alohaairlines.com. **Big Island Air** ☎ 808/329-4868 or 800/303-8868. **Hawaiian Airlines** ☎ 800/882-8811 in Hawai'i, 800/367-5320 from the mainland ⊕ www.hawaiianair.com. **Island Air** ☎ 800/652-6541 in Hawai'i, 800/323-3345 from the mainland ⊕ www.islandair.com. **United** ☎ 800/241-6522 ⊕ www.ual.com.

AIRPORTS

The Big Island has two main airports: Kona International Airport, near Kailua-Kona, and Hilo International Airport. Visitors whose accommodations are on the west side of the island normally fly into Kona. If you're staying on the eastern side, in Hilo or near Volcano, fly into Hilo. Midway between Hilo and Kailua-Kona, a small airstrip is used primarily by residents of Waimea. In North Kohala a deserted airstrip, Upolo Point, services small private planes only.
🛧 **Hilo International Airport** ✉ General Lyman Field ☎ 808/934-5838 for visitor information. **Kona International Airport** ☎ 808/329-3423 for visitor information. **Waimea-Kohala Airport** ☎ 808/887-8126.

Kona International Airport is about 7 mi (a 10-minute drive) from Kailua-Kona. The Keauhou resort area stretches another 6 mi to the south beyond Kailua. It takes about 30 to 45 minutes by car to reach the upscale resorts along the North Kona-Kohala Coast.

Hilo International Airport is just 2 mi from Hilo's Banyan Drive hotels. If you have chosen a B&B closer to Hawai'i Volcanoes National Park, plan on a 40-minute drive south from Hilo International Airport.

If you have booked accommodations in the Waimea area, expect an hour's drive north from either the Kona or Hilo airport.

Limousine service with a chauffeur who will act as your personal guide averages $100 and up an hour, with a two-hour minimum. A few have all the extras—TV, bar, and narrated tours, plus Japanese-speaking guides.

There is no regularly scheduled shuttle service from either main airport, although private service is offered by the Kohala Coast resorts to the north of Kona International Airport. The rates for this service vary depending on the distance but are less than taxi fare. Check-in is at the Kohala Coast Resort Association counters at the Aloha and Hawaiian airlines arrival areas. SpeediShuttle arranges shared rides from Kona International Airport and may be less expensive than a taxi, but you must call ahead of time.

If you're staying in Kailua or at the Keauhou resort area to the south of the airport, check with your hotel upon booking to see if shuttle service is available.

Taxis are on hand for plane arrivals at both major airports. Taxis from Hilo International Airport to Hilo's Banyan Drive hotels charge about $10 to $12 for the 2-mi ride. At Kona International Airport, fares start at about $20 for transport to King Kamehameha's Kona Beach Hotel and are slightly more expensive for other Kailua-Kona hotels and condos. Taxi fares to Kohala Coast resorts range from $45 to $65. Several taxis offer guided tours.

🚩 In Hilo:**A-1 Bob's Taxi** ☎ 808/959-4800. **Hilo Harry's Taxi** ☎ 808/935-7091.

🚩 In Kona:**Aloha Taxi** ☎ 808/325-5448. **Elsa Taxi** ☎ 808/887-6446. **Luana Limousine** ☎ 808/326-5466. **Kona Airport Taxi** ☎ 808/329-7779. **Paradise Taxi** ☎ 808/329-1234. **SpeediShuttle** ☎ 808/329-5433.

BOAT & FERRY TRAVEL

Many luxury cruise ships visit the Islands throughout the year. Currently only Norwegian Cruise Lines sails its luxury vessel among the Islands exclusively, pausing in Hilo on the Big Island. Point of departure and of final return is Honolulu. The interisland cruises also stop on Maui and Kaua'i and at Fanning Island, Kiribati in Micronesia, south of Hawai'i. Costs for seven-day cruises begin at about $1,100, depending on your choice of cabin and the time of year. Longer cruises are more.

Starting in 2004, Norwegian brings two new ships online in Hawai'i, the *Pride of America* and *Pride of Aloha*. These new ships will greatly expand cruise capacity and schedules for the interisland cruises.

🚩**Norwegian Cruise Lines:** *Norwegian Star* ☎ 800/327-7030 🌐 www.ncl.com.

BUS TRAVEL

Hele-On Bus operates Monday through Saturday between Hilo and Kailua-Kona, for $6 each way. The once-daily connection takes about three hours each way and stops in numerous locations. An additional $1 is charged for luggage and backpacks that do not fit under the seat. The Hele-On operates in the Hilo and Kailua-Kona town areas themselves for 75¢ and up; exact fare is required. The bus also services the regions of North Kohala, Waimea, and Ka'u. The county Web site shows complete schedules, additional services, and fees.

The Ali'i Shuttle operates a bus service in the Kona resort area between Keauhou Bay and Kailua-Kona town Monday through Saturday, 8:30 AM to 7 PM. The shuttle connects all major hotels, condos, attractions, and shopping centers along Ali'i Drive. The cost is $3.

Ali'i Shuttle ☎ 808/938-1112. **Hele-On Bus** ☎ 808/961-8744 ⊕ www.hawaii-county.com/mass_transit/transit_main.htm.

CAR RENTAL

To get the best rate on a rental car, book it in conjunction with an interisland Hawaiian or Aloha Airlines flight, or ask your travel agent to check out room-and-car packages. Drivers must be 25 years or older. Note that dropping off a rental at a different airport from where you originally rented may cost you as much as $85 extra.

Most agencies make you sign an agreement that you won't drive on Saddle Road between Hilo and Waimea: it's a bumpy route that can be dangerous, and there are no gas stations or emergency phones. On the other hand, if you're thinking about stargazing, you'll have to take the road up to Mauna Kea off Saddle Road for the clearest views. Alamo, Budget, Dollar, and Harper Rentals let you do this in their four-wheel-drive vehicles. You might consider a four-wheel-drive vehicle anyway to reach rugged shoreline sights.

Two companies on the island rent RVs. Island RV gives you a ready-to-go vacation that includes a complete itinerary, equipment rentals, and customized care; Harper Rentals just gets you the RV as is. Linens are available at both outfits.

Major Agencies:Alamo ☎ 877/603-0615. **Avis** ☎ 800/321-3712. **Budget** ☎ 800/527-7000. **Dollar** ☎ 800/800-4000. **Enterprise** ☎ 800/736-8222. **Hertz** ☎ 800/654-3011. **National** ☎ 888/868-6207. **Thrifty** ☎ 800/847-4389.

Local Agencies:Harper Car and Truck Rental ☎ 808/969-1478 or 800/852-9993 ⊕ www.harperhawaii.com. **Island RV** ☎ 808/334-0464 or 800/406-4555 ⊕ www.islandrv.com.

CAR TRAVEL

You need a car to see the sights of the Big Island in any reasonable amount of time. Even if you're solely interested in relaxing at your self-contained megaresort, you may still want to rent a car, simply to travel to Kailua-Kona or to the restaurants in Waimea.

Though there are several car-rental companies from which to choose, cars can be scarce during holiday weekends, special events, and peak seasons—from mid-December through mid-March. It is best to book well in advance.

EMERGENCIES

Dial **911** in an emergency to reach the police, fire department, or an ambulance. Call one of the hospitals listed for a doctor or dentist close to you. The Volcano Update Hotline provides 24-hour recorded information.

🚹 Emergency Services: **Police** ☎ 808/935-3311. **Poison Control Center** ☎ 800/362-3585. **Volcano Update Hotline** ☎ 808/985-6000.

🚹 Hospitals: **Hilo Medical Center** ✉ 1190 Waiānuenue Ave., Hilo ☎ 808/974-4700. **Kona Community Hospital** ✉ Hwy. 11 at Hau Kapila St., Kealakekua ☎ 808/322-9311. **Kona-Kohala Medical Associates** ✉ 75-137 Hualalai Rd., Kailua-Kona ☎ 808/329-1346. **North Hawai'i Community Hospital** ✉ 67-1125 Māmalahoa Hwy., Waimea ☎ 808/885-4444.

LODGING

B & BS Members of the Big Island–based Hawai'i Island Bed and Breakfast Association are listed with phone numbers and rates in a comprehensive online brochure from the Hawai'i Island Bed and Breakfast umbrella organization. Or you can go with several network booking agencies that try to meet your needs on an individual basis.

🚹 **Bed & Breakfast Honolulu (Statewide)** ☎ 800/288-4666 🖷 808/595-7533 ⊕ www.hawaiibnb.com. **Go Native Hawai'i** ☎ 800/662-8483 ⊕ www.gonativehi.com. **Hawai'i Island Bed and Breakfast Association** ⊕ www.stayhawaii.com. **Hawai'i's Best Bed and Breakfasts** ☎ 808/985-7488 or 800/262-9912 🖷 808/967-8610 ⊕ www.bestbnb.com.

MOTORCYCLE TRAVEL

Scooters and motorcycles can be rented in Hilo and Kailua-Kona. Some words of warning: Big Island roads often have narrow shoulders, and the drafts from oversize tour buses swooping by can unexpectedly double the excitement of a simple Sunday ride. Helmets are advised but not mandatory in Hawai'i.

🚹 **DJ's Rentals** ✉ 75-5563A Palani Rd., Kailua-Kona ☎ 808/329-1700 or 800/993-4647 ⊕ www.harleys.com. **Hilo Harley Davidson** ✉ 100 Kanoelehua Ave., Hilo ☎ 808/934-9090. **Kona Harley Davidson** ✉ 74-5615 Luhia St., Kailua-Kona ☎ 808/326-9887.

TAXIS

Several companies advertise guided tours by taxi, but it is an expensive way to travel, with a trip around the island totaling about $350.

SIGHTSEEING TOURS

ALL-TERRAIN-VEHICLE TOURS A different way to experience the Big Island's rugged coastline and wild ranch lands is through an off-road adventure. At higher elevations, weather can be nippy and rainy, but views can be awesome. You can ride in your own all-terrain vehicle or share a Hummer. Protective gear is provided. Prices range from $85 to $125 per person, depending on tour length and specifics.

🚹 **ATV Outfitters Hawai'i** ✉ Old Sakamoto Store, Hwy. 270, Kapa'au ☎ 808/889-6000 or 888/288-7288 ⊕ www.outfittershawaii.com. **HMV Tours** ✉ Hwy. 250, Hāwī ☎ 808/

889-6922 or 877/449-6922 ⊕ www.hmvtours.com. **Kahuā Ranch ATV Rides** ⊠ Hwy. 250, 10 mi north of Waimea ☎ 808/882-7954 or 808/882-4646 ⊕ www.kahuaranch. com. **Kukui ATV & Adventures** ⊠ Pickup from Waipi'o Valley Artworks, Kukuihaele ☎ 808/775-1701 or 877/757-1414 ⊕ www.topofwaipio.com.

BOAT TOURS A voyage on a traditional double-hulled sailing canoe is available on the *Hahalua Lele* along the Kohala shores near the Fairmont Orchid Hawai'i. The crew spices up the tour with Hawaiian history and legends. Expect to pay $100.

Unique among the abundance of water adventures is the *Atlantis IV* one-hour submarine tour from Kailua Pier, across from King Kamehameha's Kona Beach Hotel in Kona. A large glass dome in the bow and 13 viewing ports on the sides allow clear views of the watery world. Children must be at least 3 feet tall. Fees for adults range from $75 to $90.
🚢 *Atlantis IV* Submarine ☎ 808/329-6626 or 800/548-6262 ⊕ www.atlantisadventures. com. **Hahalua Lele** ☎ 808/885-2000 ⊕ www.fairmont.com.

BUS TOURS Local tour-bus operators conduct volcano tours and circle-island tours, with pickup at the major resorts. Costs range from $38 to $68, depending on pickup location.
🚌 **Jack's Tours** ☎ 808/329-2555 in Kona, 808/961-6666 in Hilo, 800/442-5557 ⊕ www. jackstours.com. **Polynesian Adventure Tours** ☎ 808/329-8008 in Kona, 800/622-3011 ⊕ www.polyad.com. **Roberts Hawai'i** ☎ 808/329-1688 in Kona, 808/966-5483 in Hilo, 800/831-5541 ⊕ www.robertshawaii.com.

COFFEE-FARM TOURS Several coffee farms around the South Kona and Upcountry Kona coffee-belt area from Hōlualoa to Hōnaunau welcome visitors. You'll learn about the whole process, from green beans to packaging. Often, macadamia nuts are for sale, and the brew, of course, is always ready. Some tours are self-guided, and most are free. The exception is the Kona Coffee Living History Farm (known as the D. Uchida Farm), unique in its heritage of coffee pioneers. The site, which has been preserved and restored by the Kona Historical Society, includes a 1913 farmhouse surrounded by coffee trees, a Japanese bathhouse, Kuriba (coffee processing mill), and Hoshidana (traditional drying platform). Tours of the farm are available by reservation only and cost $20.
🚜 **Bay View Farms** ⊠ ½ mi past St. Benedict's Painted Church, 83-5249 Painted Church Rd., Hōnaunau ☎ 808/328-9658. **Greenwell Farms** ⊠ 81-6581 Māmalahoa Hwy., Kealakekua ☎ 808/323-2862. **Holualoa-Kona Coffee Company** ⊠ 77-6261 Old Māmalahoa Hwy. (Hwy. 180), Hōlualoa ☎ 808/322-9937 or 800/334-0348. **Kona Coffee Living History Farm** ⊠ Kona Historical Society, 81-6551 Māmalahoa Hwy., Kealakekua ☎ 808/323-3222 ⊕ www.konahistorical.org. **Royal Kona Coffee Museum and Coffee Mill** ⊠ 83-5427 Māmalahoa Hwy., next to tree house in Hōnaunau ☎ 808/328-2511.

GARDEN TOURS Several botanical gardens across the island welcome you to meander along the trails and study the diversity of the local flora. Often overlooked is the Amy B. H. Greenwell Ethnobotanical Garden, with its wealth of Hawaiian cultural traditions. On 12 acres, it has 250 types of plants, including food and fiber crops, that were typical in an early Hawaiian *ahupua'a,* a pie-shape land division that ran from the mountains to the sea. Call to find out about guided tours or drop in between 8:30 AM and 5 PM.

🔢 **Amy B. H. Greenwell Ethnobotanical Garden** ✉ 82-6188 Māalahoa Hwy., Captain Cook ☎ 808/323-3318 ⊕ www.bishopmuseum.org/greenwell.

MAUNA KEA ASTRONOMY TOURS — On the weekend, the Onizuka Center offers an escorted summit tour using four-wheel-drive vehicles. Departure is at 1 PM, and reservations are not required. You must be 16 or older, in good health, and not pregnant. **Onizuka Center for International Astronomy Visitor Information Station** (✉ Summit Access Rd. ☎ 808/961–2180 ⊕ www.ifa.hawaii.edu/info/vis).

As an easier alternative, book a tour with a reliable company. Tour operators usually provide parkas, as well as telescopes, snacks, and meals when appropriate. They pick you up at convenient locations, including the resorts. Excursion fees range from about $75 to $155.

🔢 **Arnott's Lodge & Hiking Adventures** ☎ 808/969-7097 ⊕ www.arnottslodge.com. **Hawai'i Forest & Trail** ☎ 808/331-8505 or 800/464-1993 ⊕ www.hawaii-forest.com. **Paradise Safaris** ☎ 808/322-2366 or 888/322-2366 ⊕ www.maunakea.com.

RANCH TOURS — Three historic, working ranches have opened their lands to guided activities. The verdant Kohala Mountains land stretches down to the sea from the rim of Pololū Valley high in the rain forest and holds legendary stories about King Kamehameha and his troops. Here, the owners of the 8,000-plus acres of Kahuā Ranch—known for its lamb, beef, and hydroponic vegetables—provide horseback riding, operations tours, ATV adventures, mountain biking, hiking, and clay shooting. There is even a guest house.

Paniolo Riding Adventures offers horseback rides, mountain-bike tours, and guided hikes in Ponoholo Ranch, an 11,000-acre cattle ranch that shelters prehistoric sites and ancient ruins.

A covered wagon pulled by a pair of draft horses leads you through a portion of the 225,000-acre Parker Ranch. If you are a reasonably experienced horseback rider, you can also participate in a two-hour trek that includes a cattle drive. Hiking tours and other adventures are available as well.

🔢**Kahuā Ranch Tours** ✉Kahuā Ranch, Hwy. 250 ☎808/882-4646 ⊕www.kahuaranch.com. **Paniolo Riding Adventures** ✉ Hwy. 250, close to mile marker 13, Kohala Mountain Rd. ☎808/889-5354 ⊕www.panioloadventures.com. **Parker Ranch** ✉Parker Ranch Visitor Center, Hwy. 19, Waimea ☎ 808/885-7655 ⊕ www.parkerranch.com.

VALLEY TOURS — Although you certainly can hike down into the Waipi'o and Pololū valleys that frame the Kohala Mountains, a horseback-riding tour might be more fun. Or consider a guided tour around Waipi'o rim by a four-wheel-drive vehicle and around Pololū by mule. You'll be treated to breathtaking views along historic trails, and experienced guides are happy to recount the ancient history of this land. Costs range from about $40 to $145 depending on the tour.

🔢 **Four-Wheel, Wagon, Shuttle Tours: Waipi'o Rim Backroad Adventures** ☎ 808/775-1122 or 877/757-1414 ⊕ www.topofwaipio.com. **Waipi'o Valley Shuttle** ☎808/775-7121. **Waipi'o Valley Wagon Tours** ☎ 808/775-9518.

🔲 Horseback Riding Tours: **Waipiʻo on Horseback** ☎ 808/775-7291. **Waipiʻo (Naʻalapa) Stables** ☎ 808/775-0419.

🔲 Mule Tours: **Hawaiʻi Forest and Trail** ☎ 808/331-8505 or 800/464-1993 ⊕ www. hawaii-forest.com.

WALKING &
HIKING TOURS

Maps and brochures for self-guided walking tours in historic areas or parks are often available on-site or at locations listed below. In Kailua-Kona, interpretive guides from the Kona Historical Society conduct various guided tours for a small fee.

As for nature hikes, to get to some of the best trails and places, it's worth going with a skilled guide. Costs range from $75 to $180, and hikes include picnic meals and gear such as binoculars, ponchos, and walking sticks. The outfitters mentioned here also offer customized adventure tours. Expert naturalist guides from Hawaiʻi Forest and Trail take you to 500-foot Kalopa Falls in North Kohala and on bird-watching expeditions. They, as well as Hawaiʻi Volcanoes National Park rangers, also offer tours into lava tubes and through normally inaccessible areas of Hawaiʻi Volcanoes National Park and rain forests. Hawaiian Walkways conducts several tours—waterfall hikes, coastal adventures, flora and fauna explorations, and jaunts through Hawaiʻi Volcanoes National Park—as well as custom-designed trips.

🔲 Historic Tours: **Big Island Visitors Bureau** ✉ 250 Keawe St., Hilo ☎ 808/961-5797 ✉ King's Shops, 250 Waikoloa Beach Dr., Suite B 15, Waikoloa ☎ 808/886-1655. **Kona Historical Society** ✉ 81-6551 Māmalahoa Hwy., Kealakekua ☎ 808/323-3222 ⊕ www. konahistorical.org. **Lyman House Memorial Museum** ✉ 276 Haili St., Hilo ☎ 808/ 935-5021 ⊕ www.lymanmuseum.org.

🔲 Nature Hikes: **Hawaiʻi Forest and Trail** ☎ 808/331-8505 or 800/464-1993 ⊕ www. hawaii-forest.com. **Hawaiʻi Volcanoes National Park** ☎ 808/985-6010. **Hawaiian Walkways** ☎ 808/775-0372 or 800/457-7759 ⊕ www.hawaiianwalkways.com.

WHALE-
WATCHING
TOURS

Most Hawaiian whale-watching cruises focus on the migratory humpbacks that are seen here only from December through April. You can contact any one of the many snorkeling, scuba diving, sailing, and kayaking companies as well: in season they adapt their adventures. Captain Dan McSweeney's offers three-hour trips year-round to find six other species of whales that rarely stray far from the Kona Coast. The cost is about $55.

🔲 **Captain Dan McSweeney's Year-Round Whale Watching Adventures** ✉ Honokōhau Harbor, Kailua-Kona ☎ 808/322-0028 or 888/942-5376 ⊕ www.ilovewhales.com.

WATER-SPORTS
TOURS

You can sail, cruise the ocean, fish, and snorkel to your heart's content on the Big Island, but two unique water tours stand apart from the others. One is an $89 kayak adventure down the pitch-black, eerie tunnels of the 22½-mi Kohala Ditch—irrigation ditches, built in 1905 by Japanese workers. You'll emerge now and then to pristine rain forests. "Flumin the ditch" in an inner tube used to be a dangerous and exciting pastime for sugar-plantation children. The other tour, provided by Hawaiian Adventure Tours, is a land-and-water package that combines hiking, swimming, snorkeling, and kayaking in 7-day ($1,750) or 10-day ($2,100) adventures on two or three Islands. **Flumin' Da Ditch** ✉ 55-519 Hāwī Rd. (Hwy. 250), Hāwī ☎ 808/889-6922 or 877/449-6922 ⊕ www.flumindaditch.com. **Hawaiian Adventure Tours** ✉ Kapa'au ☎ 808/889-0227 or 800/659-3544 ⊕ www.hawaiianadventuretours.com.

VISITOR INFORMATION

You can find lots of information and brochures at the Big Island Visitors Bureau (BIVB) booths at Big Island airports and at the offices in Hilo and King's Shops at Waikoloa. If you rent a car, be sure to get a "Drive Guide " from the rental agency. These handy booklets have all the maps you'll probably need to navigate the island. The state, county, and resort organizations and Web sites listed below are invaluable.

Visit the bookstores below for detailed street maps, and call the weather hot line for daily reports. **Basically Books** ✉ 160 Kamehameha Ave., Hilo ☎ 808/961-0144. **Borders Books & Music** ✉ 75-1000 Henry St., Kailua-Kona ☎ 808/331-1668 ✉ 301 Maka'ala, Hilo ☎ 808/933-1410. **Middle Earth Bookshoppe** ✉ 75-5719 Ali'i Dr., Kailua-Kona ☎ 808/329-2123.

Big Island Visitors Bureau ✉ 250 Keawe St., Hilo 96720 ☎ 808/961-5797 🖶 808/961-2126 ✉ 250 Waikoloa Beach Dr., B12, King's Shops, Waikoloa 96738 ☎ 808/886-1655 ⊕ www.bigisland.org. **Destination Hilo** ✉ 2109F Kaiwiki Rd., Hilo 96720 ☎ 808/935-5294. **Destination Kona Coast** ⌔ Box 2850, Kailua-Kona 96745 ☎ 808/329-6748 ⊕ www.destinationkonacoast.com. **Hawai'i Island's Magazine online** ⊕ www.hawaii-island.com. **Hawai'i Visitors and Convention Bureau** ⊕ www.gohawaii.com. **Kohala Coast Resort Association** ✉ 69-275 Waikoloa Beach Dr., Waikoloa 96743 ☎ 808/886-4915 or 800/318-3637 ⊕ www.kkra.org. **Weather** 🖶 808/961-5582.

KAUA'I
THE GARDEN ISLE

HIKE INTO PURE ADVENTURE
on the Kalalau Trail ⇨*p.301*

REACH FOR THE SKY
with a helicopter tour ⇨*p.343*

SNORKEL IN THE DEEPEST LAGOON
at Tunnels Beach ⇨*p.313*

SLURP THE BEST NOODLES
at Hamura Saimin, in Līhu'e ⇨*p.322*

SWING, BABY, SWING!
at some of the world's best golf courses ⇨*p.341*

Updated by
Maggie
Wunsch

NICKNAMED THE GARDEN ISLE, Kaua'i is Eden epitomized. The mountains and valleys here are raw, wild, and green with untamed beauty just waiting to tempt you. In Kōke'e, lush swamps ring with songs of rare birds; in Hā'ena, the aroma of ginger blossoms sweetens the rain forests. Time carved the elegant spires along the remote northwestern shore known as Nā Pali (The Cliffs) Coast as seven coursing rivers gave life to the valleys where ancient Hawaiians once dwelled. Today you can explore this Pacific paradise by land, sea, and air—hiking along the Kalalau Trail, kayaking up the Hanalei River, or hovering in a helicopter high above 5,148-foot Wai'ale'ale, the wettest spot on earth.

The Garden Isle is a laid-back, restful retreat—an island of unmatched physical beauty that beckons those who love the outdoors. You can take a boat trip up Nā Pali Coast to snorkel in azure waters; ride a horse-drawn coach around a plantation-era sugar estate; or play golf on the world-class greens of Princeville Resort, where a majestic mountain peak, nicknamed Bali Hai, rises just beyond the fairways. To take the path less traveled, you might want to saddle up and go horseback riding into the steep ridges and ravines of Waimea Canyon.

One road runs almost all the way around the island but dead-ends on either side of a 15-mi stretch of the rugged Nā Pali Coast. Driving from one end to the other takes you past lustrous green stands of sugarcane, which are gradually being replaced with coffee and macadamia-nut orchards. Dating from 1835, when Hawai'i's first sugar mill was built in Kōloa, sugar was a key economic force on the island until the early 1990s. Patches of taro are found around Hanalei Valley. This longtime staple of the Hawaiian diet is grown for its root (to make poi, a puddinglike accompaniment for fish and meat) as well as its leaves (used to wrap and cook food).

Kaua'i, an almost circular island located on the northernmost tip of Hawaii's major Islands, is the fourth-largest island in the Hawaiian chain and has its capital in Līhu'e, the island's commercial center. Līhu'e's collection of businesses—a handful of banks, a library, a school, a museum, some family-run restaurants, and hotels—is small enough to keep the pace unhurried.

On the south coast, the sunny beaches and clear skies around Po'ipū have spawned a crop of condos and resorts. The area has also come into its own as a golf destination, and several fine restaurants have found a home here as well. Head west, beneath the slopes of the Hoary Head Mountains, to encounter such storybook plantation villages as Hanapēpē, Kalāheo, and Waimea—where Captain James Cook first landed back in 1778. Beyond Waimea lies Polihale Beach, an idyllic stretch of golden sand sprawled beneath the cool highlands of Kōke'e State Park.

From the southwestern part of Kaua'i you can see the island of Ni'ihau 17 mi off the coast. Until 1987 no uninvited guests were allowed to visit this family-owned island. Most people who live in Hawai'i still consider Ni'ihau off-limits, but its mysteries can now be breached by helicopter.

Numbers in the text correspond to numbers in the margin and on the Kaua`i map.

If you have
4 days

Spend the first day exploring **Līhu`e** ⑮. Get a feeling for Kaua`i's history at the **Kaua`i Museum** ⑯ and then drive south to **Kōloa** ㉑ for some leisurely shopping. Have lunch and soak up some rays on the beach in **Po`ipū** ㉒.

A drive to **Waimea** ㉝ and Kōke`e on the second day will allow time for a hike, lunch, and gallery hopping in **Hanapēpē** ㉙. The third day should be devoted to Kaua`i's North Shore. Head to **Kīlauea Lighthouse and Kīlauea Point National Wildlife Refuge** ⑧. Then stop in Hanalei for lunch before stretching out at **Ke`e Beach State Park** ⑭. Along the way, you can check out **Maniniholo Dry Cave** ⑪, **Limahuli Gardens** ⑫, and **Waikapala`e and Waikanaloa Wet Caves** ⑬.

On your fourth day stick close to Kapa`a. In the morning, make the Fern Grotto your destination, either going aboard one of the Wailua river boats or renting a kayak. Then drive up Mā`alo Road to see the **Pōhaku-ho`ohānau and Pōhaku Piko** ④ and **`Ōpaeka`a Falls** ⑤. If you follow the road nearly to its end, you come upon the Keāhua Forestry Arboretum, where you can picnic before you head back.

If you have
6 days

Consider splitting your vacation between two hotels, spending the first two nights on the South Shore and the last three on the North Shore. On the first day, explore the **Waimea Canyon** ㉟, stopping at **Ft. Elisabeth** ㉛, or the main street (one block off the highway) of **Hanapēpē** ㉙. Leave the afternoon for a boat trip out of Port Allen.

Spend the morning of the second day in **Līhu`e** ⑮, touring **Grove Farm Homestead** ⑲ and the **Kaua`i Museum** ⑯. In the afternoon take time to explore **Kōloa** ㉑ and see **Spouting Horn** ㉕.

Pack and get away early on the third day so you can take in the Fern Grotto, the **Pōhaku-ho`ohānau and Pōhaku Piko** ④, and **`Ōpaeka`a Falls** ⑤. Alternatively, you could take a helicopter tour.

On day four, you might simply want to revel in your north-shore surroundings: play golf, paddle a kayak up Hanalei River, or soak in the pool. For hikers, the fifth day could involve a several-hour-long trek along the Kalalau Trail to Hanakāpī`ai Beach. If you prefer a less strenuous stroll, investigate the grounds at **Limahuli Gardens** ⑫. In any case, this fifth afternoon is the time to drive to the end of the road at Hā`ena, visiting **Maniniholo Dry Cave** ⑪ and **Waikapala`e and Waikanaloa Wet Caves** ⑬ along the way.

Reserve your sixth and final day to see sights you missed along the northeast shore or just relax.

North of Līhu'e the climate turns cooler and wetter, and everything sparkles green. In Wailua and Kapa'a, resort complexes huddle along a picturesque shoreline called the Royal Coconut Coast, for its abundance of palms. As you head farther north to Anahola, Kīlauea, Princeville, and Hanalei, vines and flowers flourish. At the end of the road, in Hā'ena, you encounter a misty otherworldliness conjuring up the legends of the ancients.

More myths are attached to the natural landscape of Kaua'i than to any other Hawaiian island. A favorite among locals is the legend of the Menehune, a community of diminutive yet industrious workers said to have lived on Kaua'i before the Polynesians. Few people actually saw the Menehune because they worked in privacy at night—practicing, it seems, their impressive stoneworking skills. There are bridges, walls, fishponds, and other solid constructions attributed to the engineering skill of these mysterious mythical stonemasons.

Kaua'i is the oldest of the Hawaiian Islands, and its 552 square mi are rich in natural history and the resonance of the past. A sense of relaxation and natural beauty calmly welcomes all who step off the plane at the Līhu'e Airport and wraps them in a lei of traditional Hawaiian hospitality. Many feel that Kaua'i's people are the friendliest in all the Islands.

Exploring Kaua'i

The main road tracing the island's perimeter takes you past easily explored landscapes and attractions. There are magical mountains, cascading waterfalls, mist-shrouded caves, a fern grotto, and a lighthouse designated a National Historic Landmark. All around the island are highway overlooks where you can take in the view.

Directions on the island are often referred to as *mauka* (toward the mountains) and *makai* (toward the ocean).

About the Restaurants

Sugar plantations of 19th-century Kaua'i brought together a universe of cultures as workers from other countries sought new jobs in Hawai'i. With these influences came an array of foods and preparations that constitute a purely Hawaiian style of cuisine, known to some as Pacific Rim. This style is typified by fresh local seafood prepared with hints of Asian cooking. Into this melting pot, add a bit of Mexican, Italian, French, and American influence to both food choice and cooking technique. The hallmark of Hawaiian regional cuisine is *poke,* fresh raw tuna, marinated with combinations of sesame oil, soy sauce, onions, and pickled seaweed. No trip to Kaua'i is complete without it.

When it's time for a snack, look for the carryout wagons that are often parked at major beaches. They serve local foods, such as the ubiquitous plate lunch.

About the Hotels

Part of the appeal of the Garden Isle is its range of accommodations— from swanky resorts to rustic cabins. In the older, low-budget locations,

4

Beaches The island is surrounded by stretches of magnificent ivory sand, many with breathtaking mountain backdrops. Pay attention to the surf conditions, and heed any warnings. Some beaches are just perfect for swimming, and some are just perfect for looking. Check which one you are at before diving in.

Hitting the Links Princeville Resort's stunning Robert Trent Jones Jr.–designed Prince Course is rated the second-most difficult course in Hawai'i. The resort's (and Jones's) neighboring Makai Course is also beautiful, with the so-called Zen bunker (a boulder in the middle of a huge sand trap) and an 8th hole played across an ocean chasm. As you play the four closing holes of Jones's Po'ipū Bay course you will hear the crashing surf on your left. Kiahuna Plantation, Jones's fourth design on Kaua'i, is a challenging inland course that winds over streams, through woods, and past lava formations.

Jack Nicklaus's Kiele course, adjoining the Kaua'i Marriott Resort & Beach Club, has many greens positioned diagonally to the fairway. His Mokihana course is less dramatic and wider. Endangered wildlife, such as the nēnē goose, monk seal, and sea turtle, can often be spotted from the course.

Hiking Kaua'i is best known to hikers for the challenging north-shore Kalalau Trail. Trails at Kōke'e State Park cover all skill levels and overlook the green ramparts of the Nā Pali coastline or Waimea Canyon. For easy excursions, visit Keāhua Forestry Arboretum, Limahuli Gardens, and other tropical gardens.

Horseback Riding Kaua'i offers possibly the broadest selection of equestrian outings of all the Islands. You can saddle up to ride along the rim of Waimea Canyon, to a secluded waterfall, along the edge of a moonlit beach, or through green mountain pastures.

Water Sports Safe yet exciting water adventures are possible through companies that rent equipment or have guided excursions. Kayaking is big here—this is the only island where you have the choice of kayaking on rivers, in ancient fishponds, or on the ocean. Fishing and snorkel guides are quick to locate the spots where the biggest or most colorful fish hang out. Surfing and windsurfing instructors can help you get on the waves in no time.

There are three great dive sites on the North Shore's Cannon's Reef, which drops quickly from the shoreline, forming a long ledge permeated with lava tubes. Plate coral is found here, turtles are a common sight, and you may come across white-tip sharks. General Store, at Kukui'ula, is the site of a 19th-century shipwreck. The horseshoe-shape ledge and two caverns teem with lemon butterfly fish that follow divers around. There's also black coral at this site which runs to depths of 65 to 80 feet. Sheraton Caverns, off Po'ipū, are formed by three immense, parallel lava tubes. There is a lobster nursery in one cavern, sea turtles swim in all three, and the occasional white-tip shark cruises by. Depths range from 35 to 60 feet.

what you lose in modernity you gain in authenticity. They can be kitschy and outdated, filled with bamboo and tikis, but they really give you the feeling of old Hawai'i. Bed-and-breakfasts and vacation rentals reflect current island life, with peaceful settings and plenty of aloha welcome. The major hotels have numerous activities and amenities, often catering to families.

Sunseekers head south to the condo-studded shores of Po'ipū, where three- and four-story complexes line the coast and the surf is ideal for swimming. Po'ipū has more condos than hotels, with prices in the moderate to expensive range, though several oceanfront cottages are in demand with budget travelers.

Interested in the history of the Islands? Stay on the east coast near the Wailua River, where Kaua'i's first inhabitants resided. Many of the lodgings here place an emphasis on the legends and lore of the area. The beaches are so-so for swimming but nice for sunbathing. Farther north are the swanky hotels and condominiums of Princeville Resort; golfers should head here. There are lots of B&Bs and rentals hiding out in the jungles of the North Shore. They can be an attractive option if you're looking for a more settled-in and residential experience. A good booking service can be a big help.

WHAT IT COSTS				
$$$$	**$$$**	**$$**	**$**	**¢**
RESTAURANTS over $30	$20–$30	$12–$20	$7–$12	under $7
HOTELS over $200	$150–$200	$100–$150	$60–$100	under $60

Restaurant prices are for a main course. Lodging prices are for two people in a standard double room, including tax and service.

TIMING   Kaua'i is beautiful in every season; however, if you prefer hot beach weather, you might want to schedule your visit for some time between June and October, when rainfall is at its lightest. The northern coast of Kaua'i receives more precipitation than the rest of the island, particularly from December through February. Sometimes it can be downright drenched. To avoid family crowds, plan your visit for months when school is in full session, May or October, for example, when the weather is generally fine and plenty of rooms are available.

THE NORTH SHORE

Traveling north from Līhu'e, you encounter green pastureland and valleys of Kīlauea, an area rich in history and legend. It was one of the first communities of the Polynesians who settled here more than 1,000 years ago. As the road turns west, tracing the island's shore, you time-travel through historic plantation towns, then past Princeville, winding up in the mist-shrouded primeval wilds around Ke'e Beach and Nā Pali Coast State Park.

a good drive

Head north out of Līhuʻe on Route 56, the main artery that traces the eastern and northern coasts of Kauaʻi. For an early scenic side trip turn left on Māʻalo Road (Route 583) before you reach Kapaʻa. Then drive 4 mi to **Wailua Falls ❶ ▐**. Backtrack to Route 56 and continue north. A short drive will take you to **Lydgate County Park ❷**.

On the mauka side of Route 56, follow the sign directing you to Wailua Marina, where cruise boats depart for the Fern Grotto. Continue north on Route 56. You can head up to **Wailua ❸** for a bite to eat or some shopping, or you can turn left past the mouth of the Wailua River onto Kuamoʻo Road (Route 580). Just beyond Wailua River State Park on your left is one of seven revered *heiau* (stone platforms that were the site of worship) and the royal birthing stones, **Pōhaku-hoʻohānau and Pōhaku Piko ❹**. Farther up Kuamoʻo Road, you reach the most intact of the stone temples, Poliʻahu, complete with storyboards. On clear days you can see Waiʻaleʻale, the misty peak that is the source of the Wailua River. Across the road is the spectacular **ʻŌpaekaʻa Falls ❺**. Drive farther to get to the viewing area.

You can follow Kuamoʻo Road another 7 or 8 mi to its end in Keāhua Forestry Arboretum for a picnic.

Head back to Route 56 and drive north toward Waipouli. On your left you pass a mountain ridge resembling the mythical **Sleeping Giant ❻**. Follow the highway along the eastern coast to Kapaʻa, Kauaʻi's largest town.

To the north you pass Keālia and the turnoff to Anahola Beach Park. Seven miles farther is **Kīlauea ❼**, another former plantation town. Turn right on Kolo Road when you see the Menehune Foodmart next to Christ Memorial Episcopal Church. Take the first left onto Kīlauea Road, and follow it to the end for **Kīlauea Lighthouse and Kīlauea Point National Wildlife Refuge ❽**.

After Kīlauea, continue west on Route 56 and enjoy the view of Kalihi Wai Valley. Drive farther along and pass Princeville Airport (on the mauka side of the road) to reach **Hanalei Valley Overlook ❾**, across the street from the Princeville Shopping Center. From here you can look out across acres of taro fields in the valley below. The road descends and comes to a rustic, one-lane bridge dating from 1912, then heads into the town of Hanalei and the 19th-century **Waiʻoli Mission House ❿**.

West of Hanalei the highway (now labeled 560 on street signs) winds its way between the mountains and the sea and crosses a series of old one-lane bridges. When the road rises and curves left, and you see hosts of rental cars on the side of the road, you've reached Lumahaʻi Beach.

As you continue west, past mile marker 8, there's a right turn through a grove of trees. This takes you to Tunnels Beach. A little farther, on the mauka side, is **Maniniholo Dry Cave ⓫**. A few miles farther, on the mauka side, is **Limahuli Gardens ⓬**. Less than ½ mi up the highway, a five-minute walk uphill takes you to **Waikapalaʻe and Waikanaloa Wet Caves ⓭**. At the end of Route 560 in Hāʻena, the Kalalau trailhead is near **Keʻe Beach State Park ⓮**.

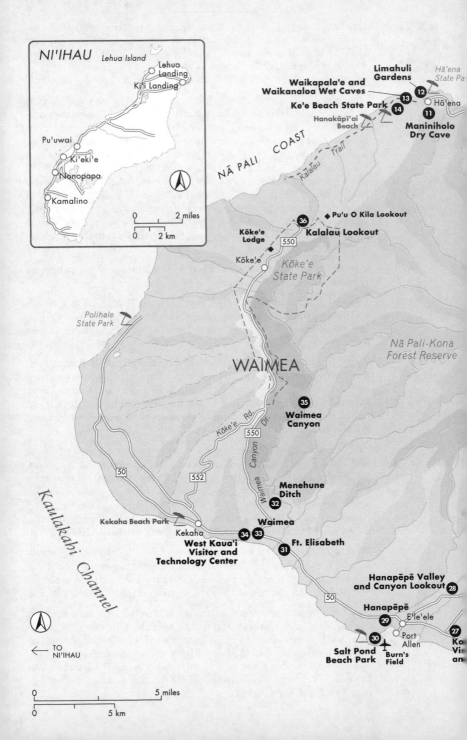

NI'IHAU

Lehua Island

Lehua Landing

Ki'i Landing

Pu'uwai

Ki'eki'e

Nonopapa

Kamalino

0   2 miles

0   2 km

Limahuli Gardens

Waikapala'e and Waikanaloa Wet Caves

Ke'e Beach State Park

Hā'ena State Pa

Hanakāpī'ai Beach

13 **12**

14 Hā'ena

11

Maniniholo Dry Cave

NĀ PALI COAST

Kalalau Trail

36

Pu'u O Kila Lookout

Kōke'e Lodge

550

Kalalau Lookout

Kōke'e

Kōke'e State Park

Polihale State Park

Nā Pali-Kona Forest Reserve

WAIMEA

Kōke'e Rd.

35

Waimea Canyon

550

Waimea Canyon Dr.

Menehune Ditch

50

552

32

Kekaha Beach Park

Kekaha

34 **33** Waimea

West Kaua'i Visitor and Technology Center

31 Ft. Elisabeth

Kaulakahi Channel

Hanapēpē Valley and Canyon Lookout

28

50

Hanapēpē

29

E'le'ele

27

Ka Vis an

Port Allen

TO NI'IHAU

30

Salt Pond Beach Park

Burn's Field

0   5 miles

0   5 km

TIMING   Without stopping, you can drive the 40 mi from Līhu'e to Hā'ena in less than 90 minutes if you avoid traveling during rush hour. Including meal breaks, allow a full day to stop and explore the sights along the way and take a short hike or swim.

What to See

Fern Grotto. A 3-mi boat ride up the Wailua River culminates at a yawning lava tube covered with enormous fishtail ferns. You can rent a kayak, hire a boat and captain, or take one of the popular boat tours to this site, which is approachable only via the river. ⊠ *Depart from Wailua Marina on mauka side of Rte. 56* ☎ *808/821–6892.*

GUAVA KAI PLANTATION – Come have a look around the orchard, and sample all kinds of guava goodies—jellies, juices, and marinades—at the visitor center. This 480-acre farm is one of the most productive guava plantations in the world. Here you can see how guava is grown and processed and ends up on your table. Self-guided tours are available. ⊠ *Rte. 56, north of mile marker 23 on Kūhiō Hwy.; turn mauka onto Kuawa Rd., near Kīlauea, and follow signs* ☎ *808/828–6121* ☜ *Free* ⊙ *Daily 9–5.*

⑨ Hanalei Valley Overlook. Mountains form the backdrop to a 900-acre National Wildlife Refuge for endangered waterfowl. In the 1850s Robert Wyllie attempted to establish a coffee plantation below. After that failed the Chinese farmed rice in the valley until the early 1900s. Now, the valley floor is a patchwork of more than ½ mi of taro ponds. ⊠ *Rte. 56, Princeville.*

★ ⑭ Ke'e Beach State Park. The stunning beach here is also the trailhead for Nā Pali's **Kalalau Trail.** Hikers taking the Kalalau Trail must obtain a permit from the Department of Land and Natural Resources if they plan to camp or hike beyond Hanakapiai Beach. Another path leads from the sand to an open, grassy meadow with a stone altar called **Lohi'au's Hula Platform,** which is still revered for its historical and spiritual *mana* (power). It's said that Laka, goddess of the hula, originated her dancing on this very spot. Hula practitioners sometimes leave offerings for her. ⊠ *Drive to western end of Rte. 560.*

⑦ Kīlauea. A former plantation town, Kīlauea is known today for its aquacultural successes, especially with prawns. It has also distinguished itself in guava cultivation. One of Kīlauea's most notable buildings, **Christ Memorial Episcopal Church** on Kolo Street, dates from 1941. The church is constructed of native lava rock, and its stained-glass windows came from England. Also in town is the Kong Lung Center, which houses the unique Kong Lung Co. boutique and Kīlauea Bakery and Pau Hana Pizza, known for its pizza and tropical pastries. ⊠ *Take Rte. 56, 25 mi north of Līhu'e.*

★ ⑧ Kīlauea Lighthouse and Kīlauea Point National Wildlife Refuge. A beacon for passing air and sea traffic since it was built in 1913, and a National Historic Landmark, this lighthouse has the largest clamshell lens of any lighthouse in the world. The Kīlauea Wildlife Refuge surrounds the lighthouse, and several species of seabirds, some endangered, roost here. Two-hour guided hikes are conducted through the refuge from Monday through Thursday; reserve ahead. ⊠ *Kīlauea Lighthouse Rd., Kīlauea* ☎ *808/828–0168* ⊕ *www.kilauea-point.com* ⊠ *$3* ⊙ *Daily 10–4.*

need a break? **Banana Joe's Tropical Fruit Stand** (⊠ 5-2719 Kūhiō Hwy., Kīlauea ☎ 808/828–1092) occupies a rustic yellow shelter on the mauka side of Route 56, past the turnoff to Kīlauea. Sample the Kaua'i-grown fruit here (fresh, dried, or in smoothies and salads). It's the perfect tropical energy booster. Banana Joe's also sells fresh corn and other vegetables in season.

★ ⓬ **Limahuli Gardens.** Early Hawaiians lived in this area known for its mana. Today the botanical garden here focuses on preserving the integrity, appearance, and environment of the native flora and fauna. Several endangered plants call Limahuli home. The gardens are an archaeological site, and restoration projects are underway. The agricultural areas and taro patches are, in fact, actual working farms in the ancient Hawaiian tradition. Picnicking is not allowed. You must call for reservations to join the guided tour, which starts at 10 AM. ⊠ *Rte. 560, Hā'ena* ☎ *808/ 826–1053* ⊕ *www.ntbg.org* ⊠ *Self-guided tour $10, guided tour $15* ⊙ *Tues.–Fri. and Sun. 9:30–4.*

☾ ❷ **Lydgate County Park.** The park, named for the Reverend J. M. Lydgate, founder of the Līhu'e English Union Church, has an imaginative children's playground and is the start of a 2.6-mi bike path. It also houses the remains of a heiau. In pre–Captain Cook days, the area was a city of refuge for Hawaiians who had violated one of the religious *kapu* (taboos). If they made their way to this beachfront haven, they could escape banishment or death by remaining until their families arranged for their forgiveness. ⊠ *Before mouth of Wailua River turn makai off Rte. 56 onto Lehu Dr. and left onto Nalu Rd.* ⊠ *Free* ⊙ *Daily.*

⓫ **Maniniholo Dry Cave.** An ancient place of worship, this cave was said to have been dug by a Menehune chief searching for an evil spirit. Don't be spooked; one or another Hawaiian goddess removed the traces of evil that lurked here long ago, most likely Laka and her hula followers. Across the highway from Maniniholo Dry Cave is **Hā'ena State Park,** a fine beach for swimming when there's no current. The well-protected **Tunnels Beach** adjoins Hā'ena State Park. ⊠ *Rte. 560, Hā'ena.*

off the beaten path **NĀ PALI COAST AND STATE PARK –** This park contains Kaua'i's ultimate adventure hike: the Kalalau Trail. Even if you plan to complete only the first 2 mi of the 11-mi trek—from Ke'e Beach to Hanakāpī'ai Beach—start early, wear rugged shoes, carry a picnic lunch, and don't forget plenty of drinking water. Note that swimming is extremely dangerous due to strong currents and surf conditions at the white-sand beach at the head of Hanakāpī'ai Valley. If you're in good shape you may want to follow an unmaintained trail which takes you the additional 2 mi to the waterfall and freshwater river pool at the back of the valley. The permit waiting list for the Hanakāpī'ai campsite is long.

Serious backpackers can continue along the entire 11-mi coastal trail. The hike crosses streams that bisect a series of valleys and then passes waterfalls and wild fruit trees until, after 4 mi, you reach another campsite at Hanakoa Valley. Hanakoa Falls, ⅓ mi inland, provides a refreshing, cool shower.

The last 5 mi of the trail culminate at Kalalau Valley and Beach. Nearby, after the final stream crossing, a red-dirt trail leads uphill to an old heiau. A nearby campsite can be crowded in fine weather, when many adventurers seek out Kalalau's legendary beauty.

Backpackers headed to Kalalau must obtain permits from the Department of Land and Natural Resources and are limited to five nights in Nā Pali State Park. Hiking the trail during the rainy winter season should not be attempted, as flash floods are a danger. Tour boats no longer take passengers along Nā Pali shore from Hanalei on the north side of the island, but in the summer months, when the ocean is calm, boats run from Port Allen on the west coast, and kayakers can take a guided tour or explore the coastline in their own rental kayaks. ⊠ *Department of Land and Natural Resources, 3060 Eiwa St., Līhu'e 96766* ☎ *808/274–3444* ⊕ *www.kauai-hawaii.com.*

★ ❺ **'Ōpaeka'a Falls.** A dramatic waterfall plunges hundreds of feet to the pools below. 'Ōpaeka'a means "rolling shrimp," which refers to the little creatures that are said to have been so abundant at one time that they could be seen tumbling in the falls to the pool below. ⊠ *Rte. 580 (Kuamo'o Rd.), Wailua.*

❹ **Pōhaku-ho'ohānau and Pōhaku Piko.** These two rocks make Wailua one of the most sacred sites in all Hawai'i, as it was here that all the royal births of Kaua'i took place. An expectant royal mother supported her back against the birthing stone Pōhaku-ho'ohānau. After the newborn's umbilical cord fell off, it was wrapped in *kapa* (cloth made from bark) and deposited in the crevices of the Pōhaku Piko for safekeeping. Just up the road is Poli'ahu Heiau, where storyboards tell about the heiau, the Wailua River area, and its former inhabitants. ⊠ *Rte. 580 (Kuamo'o Rd.), Wailua.*

off the beaten path

SUNSHINE MARKETS – If you want to rub elbows with the locals and get an eyeful of homegrown produce and flowers, head for one of these **County of Kaua'i outdoor markets** (☎ 808/241–6303 ⊕ www.kauaigov.org), held once a week at five locations around the island, including sessions in Kapa'a and Kīlauea. Hours and locations change frequently.

❻ **Sleeping Giant.** Puni, a mythical giant, is said to be represented in this formation on Mt. Nounou. His back outlining the mountain ridge, he has dozed here undisturbed since hungry villagers fed him stones after he ate all their taro and fish. ⊠ *Rte. 56, about 1 mi north of Wailua River.*

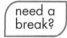 **Smith's Tropical Paradise.** Right next to Wailua Marina in the lush Wailua Valley, this 30-acre botanical and cultural garden offers a glimpse at exotic foliage, rare birds like the "singing tree ducks," fruit orchards, bamboo rain forest, and tropical lagoons. Take the tram and enjoy a narrated tour or stroll along the mile-long pathways. A lū'au and show are held Monday, Wednesday, and Friday from 5 to 9, and there is free shuttle service from Wailua area hotels. Reservations are essential for the evening events and shuttle. ✉ *174 Wailua Rd., Kapa'a* ☎ *808/821–6895* 🎟 *$5.25, lū'au and show $61* ⊙ *Daily 8:30–4.*

⑬ Waikapala'e and Waikanaloa Wet Caves. Said to have been dug by Pele, goddess of fire, these watering holes used to be clear, clean, and great for swimming. Now stagnant, they're nevertheless a photogenic example of the many haunting natural landmarks of Kaua'i's north shore. Waikanaloa is visible right beside the highway. Acorss the road from a small parking area, a five-minute uphill walk leads to Waikapala'e. ✉ *Western end of Rte. 560.*

❸ Wailua. Kaua'i's first communities were built along the Wailua River. Among Wailua's historic treasures, tucked away along the riverbanks, are remnants of important heiau. The town was the island's early capital. Its name means "two waters." ✉ *Rte. 56, 7 mi north of Līhu'e.*

need a break? The jukebox at **Beezers** (✉ 1380 Kūhiō Hwy., Kapa'a ☎ 808/822–4411) plays '50s songs you can sing to. Pictures of Marilyn and Elvis adorn the walls. On the way north to Wailua, stop in and drink a malt or a root-beer float or have a chocolate brownie topped with ice cream, hot fudge, whipped cream, and nuts.

▶ **❶ Wailua Falls.** You may recognize this impressive cascade from the opening sequences of the *Fantasy Island* television series. Kaua'i has plenty of picturesque waterfalls, but this one surpasses most. ✉ *End of Rte. 583 (Ma'alo Rd.), 4 mi west of Rte. 56.*

⑩ Wai'oli Mission House. This 1837 mission was once the home of teachers Lucy and Abner Wilcox. Its tidy architecture feels as if it belongs back in New England, and the prim and proper koa-wood furnishings epitomize missionary Hawai'i. Half-hour guided tours are available. ✉ *Kūhiō Hwy., Hanalei* ☎ *808/245–3202* 🎟 *Donations accepted* ⊙ *Tues., Thurs., and Sat. 9–3.*

LĪHU'E & THE SOUTH SHORE

As you follow the main road south from Līhu'e the air heats up and dries out. This is one way to tell you're nearing the region called Po'ipū, named after the south-shore resort town that is its unofficial center. The sun shines steadily on the condo- and hotel-lined beaches, and there are plenty of water sports to engage in.

a good drive

Begin in **Līhu'e ⑮** ▶ and visit the **Kaua'i Museum ⑯**. Head southeast on Rice Street, the town's main road, until it drops you off at **Nāwiliwili ⑰**, Kaua'i's major port. From Wa'apā Road, turn right onto Hulemalu Road and follow the Hulē'ia River to view **Menehune Fishpond ⑱**.

Return to Nāwiliwili, take a left on Nāwiliwili Road (Route 58), and look on your right for **Grove Farm Homestead ⑲**. At the intersection of Nāwiliwili Road and Route 50, turn left and head west on Route 50. Two miles farther on the right is the entrance to **Kilohana Plantation ⑳**.

Continuing west on Route 50, you pass the majestic slopes of the Hoary Head Mountains. On the top of the range to your right is a formation called Queen Victoria's Profile, indicated by a Hawaiian-warrior marker. When you get to the intersection of Routes 50 and 520, you have reached Kōloa Gap, a natural pass between Mt. Wai'ale'ale on your right and the Hoary Heads on your left. Turn left onto Route 520 (Maluhia Road), also known as the Tunnel of Trees because of the eucalyptuses that border the road to form a canopy overhead.

Route 520 takes you to **Kōloa ㉑**, site of Kaua'i's first sugar mill, dating from 1835. Head south on Route 520, which is also called Po'ipū Road locally. At the fork stay to the left.

From here turn right onto Hoowili Road, which takes you through the heart of sunny **Po'ipū ㉒**. On the makai side of the road are Po'ipū Beach Park and Brennecke's Beach, prime spots for sunbathers and body-surfers. Return to Po'ipū Road and follow it past the stunning Hyatt Regency Kaua'i, which fronts Shipwreck Beach. The road abruptly turns to dirt, but 2 mi farther awaits beautiful Māhā'ulepū Beach. To reach it, follow the road to the T intersection, turn right, stop at the gates to sign in (this is private property, open daily from 7:30 AM to 6 PM), and park at the end of the dirt road to walk to the beach. Explorers willing to search can find an interesting cave site at the far end of this beach if they hike inland beside a little stream.

When you head back on Po'ipū Road, instead of turning to Kōloa go left onto Lāwa'i Road just after you cross the bridge over Waikomo Stream. You soon come to **Prince Kūhiō Park ㉓**. Beyond the park is the visitor center for the **National Tropical Botanical Gardens ㉔**. At the end of this beachfront road is **Spouting Horn ㉕**. Its rising plume signals your drive's end.

TIMING   From Līhu'e to Po'ipū is only 14 mi, but since there is plenty to see, you can easily devote a day or two to this itinerary. If you have only a half day, be sure to watch the sunset from Brennecke's Beach. The bodysurfers on this legendary beach are something to see.

What to See

⑲ **Grove Farm Homestead.** One of Kaua'i's oldest plantation estates, founded in 1864, now offers a look at 19th-century life on Kaua'i. On the 80 acres composing this living museum are the original family home filled with turn-of-the-20th-century memorabilia, workers' quarters, and elaborate tropical flower gardens. The homestead is accessible only by tour, offered twice a day, three days per week. Note that the tours last two hours which may be too long for young children. There's a six-person limit per tour; reservations are essential. ⊠ *Rte. 58 (Nāwiliwili Rd.), Līhu'e* ☏ *808/245–3202* 🎫 *$5* ⊙ *Tours Mon., Wed. and Thurs. at 10 and 1.*

⓰ Kaua'i Museum. A permanent display, "The Story of Kaua'i," provides an overview of the Garden Isle and Ni'ihau, tracing its mythology and its geological and cultural history. A highlight is the 30-minute aerial-view movie. Works by local artists are on display in the Mezzanine Gallery, and the gift shop carries impressive Ni'ihau shell lei and ethnic textiles—including clothing, scarves, rugs, wall hangings—and wooden bowls. ⊠ *4428 Rice St., Līhu'e* ☏ *808/245–6931* 🎫 *$5* ⊙ *Weekdays 9–4, Sat. 10–4.*

★ ⓴ Kilohana Plantation. This 35-acre estate, site of the old Wilcox sugar plantation, dates from 1935. It's a beautiful showpiece from earlier days. At one time, it was the most expensive manor built on the island and was originally filled with furnishings brought in from Gump's of San Francisco. Today the 16,000-square-foot Tudor mansion is host to specialty shops and art galleries, as well as Gaylord's, a courtyard restaurant with an island-wide reputation for excellent contemporary food. Tours of the sugarcane fields and carriage rides are available. ⊠ *3-2087 Kaumuali'i Hwy. (Rte. 50), Līhu'e* ☏ *808/245–5608* 🎫 *Free* ⊙ *Mon.–Sat. 9:30–9:30, Sun. 9:30–5.*

㉑ Kōloa. Kaua'i's first sugar mill began operating in this town in 1835. You can see the remains of the old stone smokestack on the right side of the road. A sculpture depicting the various ethnic groups that made their mark on the sugar industry on Kaua'i sits on a small green nearby. The main street of Kōloa is lined with old plantation-style buildings that have been preserved to house boutiques, a general store, and a selection of restaurants. Placards outside each building describe the original tenants and tell about life in the old mill town. Here you'll find Kōloa Fish Market, which offers poke and sashimi takeout; and Kōloa One Hour Photo for quick processing of your vacation snaps. ⊠ *Rte. 520.*

need a break?

Pizzetta (⊠ 5408 Kōloa Rd., Kōloa ☏ 808/742–8881), located in the historic Asahi Soda Building, concocts the best mai tai cocktail on the island. A rustic wood-panel room at the back, with an open deck, makes up the bar area. When you're ready for dinner, order a pizza, try a Hawaiian calzone, or chill out with a cold Panini sandwich served with pasta salad.

★ ▶ ⓯ Līhu'e. The commercial and political center of Kaua'i County, which includes the islands of Kaua'i and Ni'ihau, Līhu'e is home to the island's major airport and harbor. The main thoroughfare, Rice Street, offers a short, pleasant stroll from the War Memorial and Convention Hall (Rice and Hardy streets), past government offices, to the Līhu'e Shopping Center (Rice Street and Route 50). ⊠ *Rtes. 56 and 50.*

⓲ Menehune Fishpond. A diminutive race of ancient Hawaiians is said to have built this intricate aquaculture structure for a princess and prince.

Today the 4-foot-thick and 5-foot-high walls, also known as 'Alekoko, still contain placid waters where mullet thrive and kayakers glide. ⊠ *Hulemalu Rd., Niumalu.*

㉔ National Tropical Botanical Gardens. Tucked away beneath the cliffs of the Lāwa'i Valley, these gardens were once a favorite of Hawai'i's Queen Emma. Today they contain a 252-acre scientific research center (McBryde Gardens) and a 100-acre estate property (Allerton Gardens) dedicated to preserving Hawai'i's natural flora. Tours of McBryde Gardens are self-guided and require no reservations. Visits to the Allerton Gardens are restricted—you must make advance reservations for a guided tour, offered three times a day, every day except Sunday. At Allerton, kids enjoy getting a close-up view of the *Jurassic Park* trees, otherwise known as Moreton Bay Figs. ⊠ *Lāwa'i Rd., across from Spouting Horn parking lot, Po'ipū* ☎ *808/742–2623* ⊕ *www.ntbg.org* ⊠ *Self-guided tour (McBryde) $15, guided tour (Allerton) $30* ☉ *McBryde Gardens Mon.–Sat. 9:30–5, Allerton Gardens tours Mon.–Sat. at 9, 10, 1, and 2, Sun. at 10 and 1:30.*

⑰ Nāwiliwili. Numerous fishing and private boats come and go at Kaua'i's major port. Tour boats also set out for snorkeling and sightseeing adventures along the coast. This is a port of call for container ships, U.S. Navy vessels, and passenger cruise lines. Nearby there's protected swimming at **Kalapakī Beach.** ⊠ *Makai end of Wa'apā Rd., Līhu'e.*

㉒ Po'ipū. The major resort destination of the South Shore remains irrepressibly sunny. Anchored by the Sheraton Kaua'i Resort and a half dozen condominiums, including Kiahuna Plantation, Po'ipū is famous for its golden sandy beaches—some say Poipu Beach is the best beach in America. ⊠ *Rte. 520.*

㉓ Prince Kūhiō Park. The park behind the Prince Kūhiō Condominium honors the birthplace of one of Hawai'i's most beloved congressional representatives, Prince Jonah Kūhiō Kalaniana'ole, a man who might have become Hawai'i's king if Queen Lili'uokalani had not been overthrown in 1893. ⊠ *Lāwa'i Rd., Po'ipū.*

★ ㉕ Spouting Horn. This ocean waterspout shoots up like Old Faithful from an ancient lava tube. Follow the paved walkways around; avoid the rocks which can be slippery and have caused people to fall in. Vendors sell inexpensive souvenirs and costume jewelry, in addition to one of the best selections of rare and treasured Ni'ihau shell necklaces. When purchasing a Ni'ihau shell lei, ask for a certificate of authenticity and an address in case you need to reorder or repair your purchase at a later date. ⊠ *Lāwa'i Bay, Lāwa'i Rd., Po'ipū.*

THE WEST SIDE

Heading west along Kaua'i's South Shore, you'll pass through old plantation towns and historical sites, each with a story to tell: Hanapēpē, whose salt ponds have been harvested since ancient times; Ft. Elisabeth, from which an enterprising Russian tried to take over the island in the

KAUA'I: UNDERCOVER MOVIE STAR

Though Kaua'i has played itself in the movies (you may remember Nicolas Cage frantically shouting "Is it Kapa'a or Kapa'a-a?" into a pay phone in Honeymoon in Vegas [1992]), most of its screen time has been as a stunt double for a number of tropical paradises. The island's remote valleys and waterfalls portrayed a Costa Rican dinosaur preserve in Steven Spielberg's Jurassic Park (1993). Spielberg was no stranger to Kaua'i, having filmed Harrison Ford's escape via seaplane from Menehune Fishpond in Raiders of the Lost Ark (1981). The fluted cliffs and gorges of Kaua'i's rugged Nā Pali Coast play the misunderstood beast's island home in King Kong (1976), and a jungle dweller of another sort, in George of the Jungle (1997), frolicked on Kaua'i. Harrison Ford returned to the island for 10 weeks during the filming of Six Days, Seven Nights (1998), a romantic adventure set in French Polynesia.

early 1800s; and Waimea, home of the Menehune Ditch, supposedly built by the legendary race of little people.

From Waimea town you can drive along the rim of magnificent Waimea Canyon to reach the crisp, cool climate of Kōke'e, which ranges from 3,200 to 4,200 feet above sea level. The staff at a mountain lodge here welcomes guests with old-style warmth and hospitality.

a good drive

The west side of the island offers a look at the sleepiest—as well as the most dramatic—sections of Kaua'i. Begin this tour by heading west on Route 50 out of Līhu'e. The first town you come to is tiny Lāwa'i, which once housed the Kaua'i Pineapple Cannery. In its wake, Lāwa'i has emerged as a significant producer of tropical fruits and plants. The next town along Route 50 is Kalāheo. Turn left on Pāpālina Road to make the climb to **Kukui o Lono Park** ㉖ ▶.

Beyond Kalāheo, a left turn onto Route 540 takes you to the **Kaua'i Coffee Visitor Center and Museum** ㉗. Route 540 loops back to Route 50. You'll pass acres of shiny-leaf coffee trees, but if you travel the loop, you'll miss the **Hanapēpē Valley and Canyon Lookout** ㉘. Backtrack to Route 50 to see this dramatic divide, which holds a place in Hawaiian history as the site of Kaua'i's last battle, in 1824.

Hanapēpē ㉙ lies west of the lookout. At the fork turn right to drive down Hanapēpē's dusty main street and visit a surprising number of galleries or pick up a plate lunch. If you want to bypass Hanapēpē, angle left and follow Route 50 past the town. Then turn makai on Lele Road to reach **Salt Pond Beach Park** ㉚. Nearby is Burns Field, Kaua'i's first airfield. Just around the bend and across the bay from the airstrip is Port Allen, the shipping center for the west side of the island and home base for snorkeling excursions.

Head west again on Route 50 and look on the makai side of the road for the Hawaiian-warrior marker to **Ft. Elisabeth** ③. Cross the Waimea River Bridge and take your first right on Menehune Road, which leads you 2½ mi up Waimea Valley to **Menehune Ditch** ③. As you enter **Waimea** ③ you might spot the statue commemorating Captain Cook's arrival here in 1778. The remains of a missionary church built in 1846 should hold your interest as well. On the right, **West Kaua'i Visitor and Technology Center** ③ has information on Kaua'i.

Route 50 meanders through the sugar town of Kekaha. Eventually it passes the Pacific Missile Range Facility. Take the right fork after you pass the missile range and you can follow Route 50 to where it ends near Polihale State Park. The park is accessible only by a long, bumpy dirt road through sugarcane fields. During or after heavy rain—or if you're more inclined to smooth, pleasant rides—you might want to skip it. At the end of the road is a long, arching beach with few people. It's quiet, striking, and private, and a good place to watch the sunset, but not well suited for swimming. Be careful not to get your car stuck in the sand or you could be seeing the sunrise from here, too.

You have two choices for visiting **Waimea Canyon** ③. Kōke'e Road (Route 55) makes a steep climb from Kekaha. The other, more scenic option is Waimea Canyon Drive (Route 550), which you pick up near the western edge of Waimea, by the church. It's narrow but well paved and climbs quickly for immediate views of the town and ocean below. A few miles up, the roads converge and continue the steep ascent with spectacular bird's-eye views out over the canyon. Be sure to stop at the Pu'u-ka-Pele and Pu'u-hinahina lookouts for the most appealing views. As the road rises to 4,000 feet, it passes through Kōke'e State Park, with its Natural History Museum and cozy Kōke'e Lodge. The road out of the park leads past the NASA Tracking Station.

Waimea Canyon Drive ends 4 mi above the park at the **Kalalau Lookout** ③. This is the beginning of a beautiful hiking trail that passes Pu'u-o-Kila Lookout. Be sure to bring a jacket for the cooler weather here.

TIMING The 36-mi drive from Līhu'e to Waimea Canyon can take 60 to 90 minutes without stops at the botanical gardens, beaches, or quaint little towns. If you want to spend a half day or more hiking in the canyon, you might save south-shore sightseeing for another day. In winter be prepared for chilly temperatures in the heights above the canyon, especially in the early morning.

What to See

★ ③ **Ft. Elisabeth.** The ruins of this stone fort, built in 1816 by an agent of the imperial Russian government named Anton Scheffer, are reminders of the days when Scheffer tried to conquer the island for his homeland. King Kaumuali'i eventually chased him off the island. The crumbling walls of the fort are not particularly interesting, but the informative placards are. ⊠ *Rte. 50, Waimea.*

② **Hanapēpē.** This quiet farming town on the south coast supplies Kaua'i with much of its produce and all of the Islands with Lappert's famous ice cream. **Hanapēpē Road** had a featured role (as an Australian town) in the television miniseries *The Thorn Birds*. Today shops sell koa-wood crafts and other artwork. Every Friday night the town's handful of art galleries open their doors for Art Night. There's usually live music and one gallery will offer snacks and beverages. Just to the east is the main boat-excursion departure point, **Port Allen.** The harbor is still the shipping center for the west side of Kaua'i and headquarters of the McBryde Company, which has replaced sugarcane fields with coffee trees. If you want further proof that Hanapēpē was once a power center, check out 'Ele'ele **Shopping Center** on Lele Road. It was the first "modern" shopping center built on Kaua'i. ⊠ *Rte. 50.*

need a break?
You can sit at the spiffy black-and-white bar for a quick espresso or relax at one of a dozen tables while you dine on vegetarian food with French-Italian flair at **Hanapēpē Café and Espresso** (⊠ 3830 Hanapēpē Rd., Hanapēpē ☎ 808/335–5011).

㉘ Hanapēpē Valley and Canyon Lookout. This dramatic divide once housed a thriving Hawaiian community, and some remains of its taro patches still exist. Hanapēpē is a historic canyon: it's the site of Kaua'i's last battle, led in 1824 by Humehume, son of the island's King Kaumuali'i. ⊠ *Rte. 50.*

★ **㊱ Kalalau Lookout.** Near the end of the road, high above Waimea Canyon, Kalalau Lookout marks the start of a challenging one-hour, 2-mi hike to **Pu'u-o-Kila Lookout.** On a clear day at either spot you can gaze right down into the gaping valley at sawtooth ridges and waterfalls. But stick around for a few minutes if clouds are obscuring the view. Winds are strong up here and might blow away the clouds so you can snap a photo. If you turn your back to the valley and look to the northwest, you might pick out the shining sands of Kalalau Beach, gleaming like a tiny golden thread against the Pacific. ⊠ *Waimea Canyon Dr., 4 mi north of Kōke'e State Park.*

㉗ Kaua'i Coffee Visitor Center and Museum. Two restored camp houses, dating from the days when sugar was the main agricultural crop on the Islands, have been converted into a museum, visitor center, and gift shop. About 3,400 acres of McBryde sugar land have become Hawai'i's largest coffee plantation. You can walk among the trees, view old grinders and roasters, watch a video to learn how coffee is processed, sample various estate roasts, and check out the gift store. On the way to Waimea Canyon in 'Ele'ele, take Highway 50 and veer right onto Highway 540, west of Kalāheo. The center is 2½ mi from the Highway 50 turnoff. ⊠ *870 Halawili Rd.,* ☎ *808/335–3237* ⊕ *www.kauaicoffee.com* ☞ *Free* ⊙ *Daily 9–5.*

Kōke'e State Park. At the north end of Waimea Canyon, this park rises 4,000 feet above sea level. Here, the air is cool and crisp, and the vegetation turns to evergreens and ferns. This 4,345-acre wilderness park is filled with wild fruit, flowers, and colorful rare birds that make these forests their home. A 45-mi network of hiking trails takes you to some of Kaua'i's most remote places. Before you set off, ask about trail conditions. **Kōke'e Natural History Museum** has displays of plants, native birds, and other wildlife, as well as a weather exhibit that describes the formation of hurricanes. ✉ *Rte. 550* ☎ *808/335–9975* ✉ *Donations accepted* ⊙ *Daily 10–4.*

need a break? Treat yourself to a cup of coffee or a sandwich at the rustic mountaintop inn, **Kōke'e Lodge** (✉ Kōke'e State Park, 3600 Kōke'e Rd., mile marker 15 ☎ 808/335–6061). Peruse the gift shop for T-shirts, postcards, or other Kōke'e memorabilia.

▶ ㉖ **Kukui o Lono Park.** Translated as "light of the god Lono," Kukui o Lono has serene Japanese gardens and a display of significant Hawaiian stones, including an anchor stone and salt pan, collected by Walter McBryde, the sugar-plantation heir who founded the estate in the 1900s. Spectacular panoramic views make this one of Kaua'i's most scenic park areas and an ideal picnic spot. There's also a golf course. ✉ *Pāpālina Rd., Kalāheo* ☎ *808/332–9151* ✉ *Free* ⊙ *Daily 6:30–6:30.*

㉜ **Menehune Ditch.** Archaeologists claim that this aqueduct was built before the first Hawaiians lived on Kaua'i, and it is therefore attributed to the industrious hands of the legendary, tiny Menehune. The way the flanged and fitted cut-stone bricks are stacked and assembled indicates a knowledge of construction that is foreign to Hawai'i, and the ditch is inscribed with mysterious markings. Until someone comes up with a better suggestion, the Menehune retain credit for this engineering feat. ✉ *Menehune Rd., Waimea Valley.*

㉚ **Salt Pond Beach Park.** Hawaiians harvested salt for almost 200 years here. They let the sun evaporate the seawater in mud-lined drying beds, then gathered the salt left behind. This is a safe area for swimming. ✉ *Lele Rd., Hanapēpē.*

㉝ **Waimea.** This is the town that first welcomed Captain James Cook to the Sandwich Islands in 1778. An easy-to-miss monument on the mauka side of the road commemorates his landing, as does a statue near the entry to town. Waimea was also the place where Kaua'i's King Kaumuali'i ceded his island to the unifying efforts of King Kamehameha. Waimea played host to the first missionaries on the island, and you can still see what's left of the old **Waimea Christian Hawaiian and Foreign Church** on Mākeke Road. Constructed in 1846, the church was made of huge timbers brought down from the mountains 8 mi away, as well as limestone blocks from a nearby quarry. The church suffered severe damage from Hurricane 'Iniki in 1992, but the beautiful stonework of its front and side walls is worth a photo. ✉ *Rte. 50.*

㉟ **Waimea Canyon.** Created by an ancient fault in the Earth's crust, the canyon has been eroding over the centuries due to weather, wind, and the water of its rivers and streams. The "Grand Canyon of the Pacific" is 3,600 feet deep, 2 mi wide, and 10 mi long. The earth's deep reds, greens, and browns are ever changing in the light. Be sure to allow time to soak up the views from **Pu'u-ka-Pele** and **Pu'u-hinahina** lookouts.

③④ **West Kauaʻi Visitor and Technology Center.** Local photos and informational computers with touch screens bring the island's history and attractions to life. ⊠ *9565 Kaumualiʻi Hwy. (Rte. 50), Waimea* ☎ *808/338–1332* ⊕ *www.kauaivisitorscenter.com* ✉ *Free* ⊙ *Mon.–Sat. 9–5, Sun. 9–2.*

BEACHES

The waters that hug the island are clean, clear, and inviting, but be careful to go in only where it's safe. All beaches on Kauaʻi are free and open to the public; none have phone numbers.

The North Shore has some of the most spectacular beaches on the island, but they can be treacherous in winter. Many of these beaches require a hike in or walk down, but are worth the effort. There's great snorkeling here in summer.

The South Shore has the softest, sandiest, most consistently sunny beaches with excellent snorkeling and swimming. You may come across endangered monk seals or turtles basking on the beach—don't touch or disturb these creatures in any way.

The beaches fronting the hotels and condos along the eastern shore are conducive to seaside strolling but not swimming. The strong surf and rip currents of the winter months are unpredictable, and it's often windy.

If you want wide-open spaces, drive to the west coast beyond Waimea where many locals go to fish and swim. Plus, you can catch the best sunsets from this side. Waimea has a black-sand beach, and a dazzling white-sand beach starts beneath the cliffs at Polihale. The current at Polihale can be tricky.

Beaches along the northwest shore are inaccessible except to those who hike the rugged Nā Pali trail from the opposite end of the road at Hāʻena or who book a boat tour. After a 2-mi hike, it's tempting to dive into the water at Hanakāpīʻai Beach, but the memorial to those lost at sea while swimming here might convince you that a dip in the river is a better option.

For general information about beaches around the island, call the **County Department of Parks and Recreation** (☎ 808/241–6670).The **Department of Land and Natural Resources** (☎ 808/274–3445) is the source for beach-camping permits.

The list of beaches below starts from the western end of Route 50 and goes counterclockwise around the island to the end of the road on the North Shore.

Fodor's Choice **Polihale Beach Park.** This large-grain sand beach stretches almost 15 mi
★ from the town of Kekaha to the 140-acre Polihale State Park. The wide beach, with mountains ⅓ mi away in the distance, is beautiful for sunbathing, beachcombing, and surf casting, but the rip currents and crashing waves can be too rough for swimming, and there are no lifeguards. Locals dune-buggy here on weekends. The road here is rough and

rugged; many first-timers turn around before finishing the 35-minute drive from the end of Route 50. Be careful not to get stuck. Bring your own drinking water. ☒ *Drive to end of Rte. 50 and turn left at Hawaiian warrior marker onto dirt road, which leads several mi through sugarcane fields; turn left at small national park sign.*

Kekaha Beach Park. On the South Shore, this miles-long strip of sand brings to mind the endless beaches of southern California. Dune-buggying is popular. If you don't like the noise, stay away. There is a lifeguard stand, as well as port-a-potties and showers. ☒ *Take Rte. 50 west of Kekaha.*

Salt Pond Beach Park. The protected bay at Salt Pond is particularly safe for swimmers, so its crescent-shape beach is popular with families. There are picnic tables under covered pavilions, showers, rest rooms, lifeguards, and a large grassy lawn. Camping is allowed with a permit from the Kaua'i County Parks Department. The beach derives its name from the ancient salt ponds that can still be seen to the left as you enter the park. ☒ *Follow Lele Rd., on makai side off Rte. 50 in Hanapēpē.*

Po'ipū Beach Park. A popular bodysurfing and swimming spot, Po'ipū Beach has clean white sand. It's a fun place for a picnic or a barbecue under the palm trees. There are lifeguards, a children's playground, showers, rest rooms, and a take-out deli across the street. A stroll on the beach takes you past a half dozen condominiums to the Sheraton Kaua'i Resort, which has an inviting cocktail lounge overlooking the beach. ☒ *Po'ipū Rd. on South Shore, opposite Ho'ōne and Pane Rds.*

Brennecke's Beach. A steady stream of small- to medium-size waves makes this a bodysurfer and boogie-boarder heaven. Waves are bigger here in summer than in winter. Showers, rest rooms, and lifeguards are on hand, and there are food stands nearby. It's also a great place to catch a glimpse of sea turtles. ☒ *Po'ipū Rd. on South Shore.*

Shipwreck Beach. Nicknamed for an old wooden boat that wrecked on the 2-mi stretch of sand fronting the Hyatt Regency, this beach, also known as Keoneloa, is popular with surf casters who fish from Makawehi Point on the east side. Sea turtles and monk seals like the coves, but strong rip currents and shore breaks can make swimming dangerous. The winds here are a magnet for windsurfers, who head to the beach's east end. Rest rooms and showers are available. ☒ *Turn into Hyatt Regency Kaua'i Resort, drive along the east side of the hotel, and turn right.*

Kalapakī Beach. This sheltered bay is ideal for swimming, surfing, and windsurfing in the small waves, and offers a magnificent view of cruise ships plying Nāwiliwili Harbor. It fronts the Kaua'i Marriott Resort & Beach Club. Rest rooms, lifeguards, showers, and concessions are steps away. ☒ *Off Wapa'a Rd., which runs from Līhu'e to Nāwiliwili.*

Fodor'sChoice
★ **Lydgate Beach Park.** One of the island's busiest beach parks, Lydgate sits at the mouth of the Wailua River and offers two fishponds and an ironwood-tree grove in addition to its oceanfront setting. A rock wall protects the swimming area here, and there are lifeguards at this family-friendly beach. Picnic under the covered pavilion or send the kids

to romp on the large playground. Rest rooms and showers are available. ⊠ *Before mouth of Wailua River, turn makai off Rte. 56 onto Lehu Dr. and left onto Nalu Rd.*

Anahola Beach Park. A grassy park on the east end of the beach offers sometimes-calm waters for swimming and snorkeling. The Makalena Mountains are your backdrop here. There are rest rooms and showers but no lifeguards. ⊠ *After mile marker 13 on Rte. 56, turn makai on Anahola Rd.*

★ **'Anini Beach County Park.** The safest of the north-shore beaches, this 3-mi stretch of golden sand lies beside a reef-protected blue lagoon, making it ideal for beginning windsurfers, snorkelers, and swimmers. A beachside park, polo field, campground (permit required), public rest rooms, showers, grills, and picnic tables keep families happy year-round. There are no lifeguards. Sunsets here can be spectacular. ⊠ *Turn makai off Rte. 56 onto Kalihi Wai Rd. on Hanalei side of Kalihi Wai Bridge; road angles left along beach onto 'Anini Rd.*

Hanalei Bay Beach Park. This perfectly curved beach, officially named Black Pot Park, is a marvel of natural beauty. Views of the Nā Pali Coast and tree-shaded picnic tables attract plenty of beach bums, but swimming here can be treacherous, even in summer months, due to strong currents. Stay near the old pier, where the water is a bit calmer. There are rest rooms, showers, and lifeguards. ⊠ *In Hanalei turn makai at Aku Rd. and right at dead end.*

Lumaha'i Beach. Lumaha'i is flanked by high mountains and lava rocks. In the movie *South Pacific,* this is where Mitzi Gaynor sang "I'm Gonna Wash That Man Right Outta My Hair." There are no lifeguards, showers, or rest rooms. The currents here have a habit of sweeping people out to sea. ⊠ *On winding section of Rte. 56 west of Hanalei between mile markers 4 and 5. Park on makai side of road and walk down a steep path to the beach.*

★ **Tunnels Beach.** Kaua'i's best-protected, big, deep lagoon for swimming and snorkeling is surrounded by a gently sloping beach shaded with ironwood trees. There are no lifeguards, showers, or rest rooms. ⊠ *½ mi past mile marker 8 on Rte. 56. Turn makai onto dirt road that runs through grove of trees. If parking lot is full, continue ½ mi to Hā'ena Beach Park and walk back.*

Hā'ena Beach Park. This beach on Maniniholo Bay was once a popular site for net fishing. Today it is good for swimming but only in summer when the surf is down. There are rest rooms, showers, camping facilities, picnic tables, and food wagons, but no lifeguards. ⊠ *On North Shore near end of Rte. 56 across from lava-tube sea caves.*

★ **Ke'e Beach.** In summer this is a fine swimming beach, with a reef lagoon made for snorkeling. In winter, big waves wash away the sand, so stay out of the water and enjoy the views of Nā Pali Coast. This is where the Kalalau Trail begins. Changing facilities are available, as are showers and rest rooms, but there are no lifeguards. ⊠ *Northern end of Rte. 56, 7 mi west of Hanalei.*

Hanakāpī'ai Beach. It's a 2-mi hike to this crescent of beach, which changes length and width throughout the year as fierce winter waves rob the shoreline of sand and summer's calm returns it. Be very careful swimming

CloseUp
SEAL-SPOTTING ON THE SOUTH SHORE

W HEN SIGHTSEEING or strolling on one of Kaua`i's magnificent beaches, don't be surprised if you find yourself in some unusual company. Although it is thought that there are fewer than 1,500 Hawaiian monk seals in existence today, which lands this animal on the endangered species list, the seals have been known to come ashore to rest after a night of catching food and swimming, and impromptu sightings are not uncommon. Heavy rains also tend to bring them out.

If you see a monk seal, keep your distance and do not attempt to assist the seal back into the water. They are usually not sick or injured but just resting or happily digesting a big meal (the monk seal can eat up to 10 percent of its own body weight per day). It is illegal to capture or harass these wonderful creatures, and you can incur heavy fines if you do so. If you do have concerns about the health or safety of a seal—or just want more information about these creatures—contact the **Kaua`i Monk Seal Watch Program** (⌂ Box 1898, Koloa 96756 ☎ 808/938–5715 ⊕ www.kauaimonkseal.com) to report seal harassment.

Hawaiian monk seals are usually sighted on the leeward (southwest) shores of Hawai`i's northwestern islands. If you are lucky enough to see one, enjoy the view and let them be. After all, monk seals got their name not only because they have round, shiny heads but also because they are solitary creatures who like to lead a "monklike" existence at sea.

here in summer, and don't even think of going in during the winter swells. Hike an additional 2 mi inland beside the adjacent stream and you'll find Hanakāpī'ai Falls, which splashes into a freshwater pool perfect for a photo opportunity or a cool dip. ⊠ *Mi 2 of Kalalau Trail, which begins near Ke'e Beach, at northern end of Rte. 56.*

WHERE TO EAT

In addition to preparing all kinds of ethnic dishes, restaurateurs use local produce and seafood to create regional dishes. Dining out can be costly, and the menus begin to blur after a while, but you can find some interesting, inspired cuisine. Romance is a big part of Kaua'i dining, with oceanfront dining rooms, orchids, tiki torches as decorations, and elaborate food presentation. Reservations are always a good idea if you'd like a table with a view.

The East Side

American/Casual

$–$$ ✕ **The Eggbert's.** If you're big on breakfasts, try Eggbert's, in the Coconut Marketplace, which serves breakfast items until 3 PM daily. This family-friendly restaurant, with a sunny soft-yellow interior, lots of windows, and lānai seating, is a great spot for omelettes, banana pancakes, and eggs Benedict in five styles. Lunch and dinner selections include club sandwiches, stir-fry, pot roast, and fresh fish. Take-out orders are also available ⊠ *Coconut Marketplace, 4-484 Kūhiō Hwy., Kapa'a* ☎ *808/822–3787* ⊟ *MC, V.*

Contemporary

★ **$$$** ✕ **A Pacific Cafe.** Chef Jean-Marie Josselin, one of the creators of the cuisine known as "Hawaiian Regional cuisine," serves up distinctive menu choices in a setting of cool white calm amid a busy shopping center. Here, Asian cooking styles fuse with Hawaiian seafood and *kiawe* wood-burning grill specialities. The menu changes daily. Josselin might present a wok-charred mahimahi with a garlic sesame crust, Asian stir-fried vegetables, and a lime-ginger beurre blanc; or a crispy Salmon Firecracker—a signature dish. ⊠ *Kaua'i Village Shopping Center, 4-831 Kūhiō Hwy., Kapa'a* ☎ *808/822–0013* ⊟ *AE, D, DC, MC, V* ☺ *No lunch.*

$–$$ ✕ **Caffé Coco.** A restored plantation cottage set back off the highway and surrounded by a riot of tropical foliage is the setting for this island café. You'll know it by its bright lime-green storefront. An attached black-light art gallery and a vintage apparel shop called Bambulei make this a fun stop for any meal. Occasional live music attracts a laid-back local crowd. Pot stickers filled with tofu and chutney, 'ahi wraps, Greek and organic salads, fresh fish and soups, along with a daily list of specials are complemented by a full espresso bar and outdoor seating in the vine-covered gardens. ⊠ *4-369 Kūhiō Hwy., Wailua* ☎ *808/822–7990* ⊟ *MC, V* ☺ *Closed Mon.*

Eclectic

$–$$ ✕ **Wailua Family Restaurant.** The 25,000 Christmas lights along the roof might catch your attention, as will the "bars"—as in the all-you-can-eat hot-and-cold salad bar; tostada, taco, and pasta bar; sushi bar; and dessert bar. Steaks, chops, and seafood fill out the menu. Emphasis is on low price rather than high quality, so it's a good place to come with children or if your wallet needs a break. Breakfast buffets on the weekend mornings include eggs Benedict, a mahimahi and eggs combo, fresh tropical fruit, and corn-bread muffins, among other things. ⊠ *4-361 Kūhiō Hwy., Kapa'a* ☎ *808/822–3325* ⊟ *AE, D, MC, V.*

¢–$ ✕ **Ono Family Restaurant.** A cross between a country diner and a Hawaiian plantation home, Ono's has faded yellow walls, wooden booths and tables, and local antiques. Breakfast packs 'em in with specialties such as eggs Canterbury (poached eggs, ham, turkey, jack cheese, tomato, hollandaise sauce, and mushrooms on an English muffin), banana macadamia-nut pancakes, and a breakfast burrito. The lunch menu has burgers, meat-loaf sandwiches, salads, fish, and stir-fries. Try the Portuguese bean soup. You have a choice of indoor or outdoor seating. ⊠ *4-1292 Kūhiō Hwy., Kapa'a* ☎ *808/822–1710* ⊟ *AE, D, DC, MC, V* ☺ *No dinner.*

Japanese

$$ ✕ **Restaurant Kintaro.** Come find out what the locals know: Kintaro's has a great sushi menu. Try the Bali Hai, a roll of eel and smoked

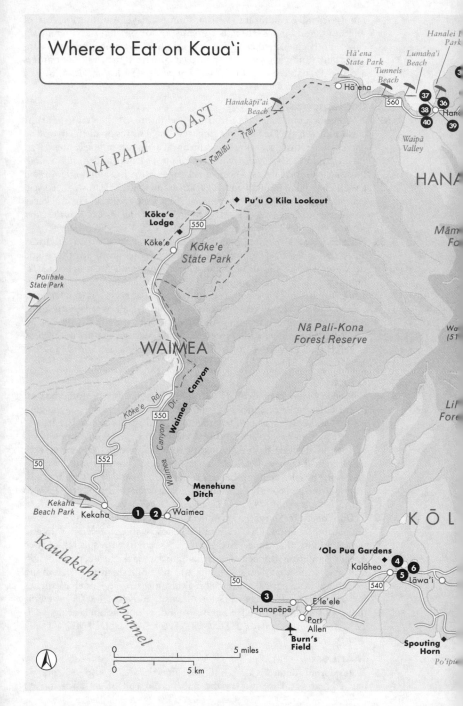

Where to Eat on Kaua'i

salmon, baked and topped with wasabi mayonnaise. For an "all-in-one-dish" meal, consider the *Nabemono,* a one-pot dish filled with a healthy variety of seafood and vegetables. teppanyaki (grilled) dinners include tender hibachi shrimp sautéed in lemon butter and served with bean sprouts and steamed rice. Tatami-mat seating is available behind shoji screens, as is lots of black-lacquered table seating by a giant fish tank. ⊠ *4-370 Kūhiō Hwy., Kapa'a* ☎ *808/822–3341* ⊟ *AE, D, DC, MC, V* ⊗ *Closed Sun. No lunch.*

Pan-Asian

$$–$$$ ✕ **Lemongrass Grill, Seafood and Sushi Bar.** The owner of this two-story restaurant is of Chinese heritage and raised in Laos. His food is inventive and exciting, combining elements of Burmese, Chinese, Lao, and Japanese cuisine with those of Thai cooking. The focus is on seafood and includes the fresh fish of the day on Thai spiced eggplant, fried Kaua'i prawns, and salmon grilled with lemongrass and ginger. Orders from the sushi bar are presented on tiny surfboards that make their way to you via a waterway that surrounds the bar. The dining room is rich with Asian art, sculptures, and fresh orchids. ⊠ *4-885 Kūhiō Hwy., Kapa'a* ☎ *808/821–2888* ⊟ *AE, D, DC, MC, V* ⊗ *No lunch.*

Steak & Seafood

$$–$$$ ✕ **Bull Shed.** The A-frame design of this popular restaurant imparts a distinctly rustic feel, but the interior is brightened by light-color walls and unobstructed ocean views. Although it's known especially for its prime rib, Australian rack of lamb, and fresh fish, its "surf and turf" dinner platter combos combine the best of both worlds for hungry diners. The view of the surf as it hits the rocks is magnificent. Arrive early, before dinner service begins at 5:30, for your best chance at getting a window seat. ⊠ *796 Kūhiō Hwy., Kapa'a* ☎ *808/822–3791 or 808/822–1655* ⊟ *AE, D, DC, MC, V* ⊗ *No lunch.*

$–$$$ ✕ **Wailua Marina On the River.** Boats chug along the Wailua past the riverview lānai of this marina restaurant, a great stop on the way to or from Fern Grotto. For the large number of people it serves, the restaurant has a surprisingly sophisticated menu and generous portions. Stuffed chicken is baked in plum sauce, and the 'ahi is stuffed with crab. There's a good choice of steak and fresh seafood dishes as well. ⊠ *Wailua River State Park, Wailua Rd., Wailua* ☎ *808/822–4311* ⊟ *AE, DC, MC, V* ⊗ *Closed Mon.*

Thai

$–$$ ✕ **Mema Thai Chinese Cuisine.** Sophisticated and intimate, Mema Thai serves its dishes on crisp white linens accented by tabletop orchid sprays. Menu items such as broccoli with oyster sauce and cashew chicken reveal Chinese origins, but the emphasis is on Thai dishes. A host of curries—red, green, yellow, and house—made with coconut milk and kaffir lime leaves runs from mild to mouth-searing. The traditional green-papaya salad adds a cool touch for the palate. ⊠ *Wailua Shopping Plaza, 369 Kūhiō Hwy., Kapa'a* ☎ *808/823–0899* ⊟ *AE, D, DC, MC, V* ⊗ *No lunch weekends.*

Vegetarian

¢–$ ✕ **Papaya's.** This well-stocked natural foods market dedicates a corner area to its vegetarian café which is open for breakfast, lunch, and dinner. Begin your day with a tofu scrambler served with brown rice. Lunch and dinner specialties run the gamut from baked tofu to a homemade spinach and herb lasagna. The café is usually crowded but you can find a bit of solitude to go with your smoothies outside in the Village's courtyards. ⊠ *Kaua'i Village Shopping Center, 4-831 Kūhiō Hwy., Kapa'a* ☎ *808/823–0190* ⊟ *AE, D, MC, V* ⊘ *Closed Sun.*

The North Shore

American/Casual

$–$$$ ✕ **Hanalei Gourmet.** Located in Hanalei's restored old school house, this North Shore spot offers diners dolphin-free tuna, low sodium meats, fresh baked breads, and homemade desserts as well as a casual atmosphere where both families and the sports-watching crowds can feel equally comfortable. Lunch and dinner menus begin with pūpū (appetizer) platters, burgers, and pan-fried crab cakes. They also will prepare a picnic and give it to you in an insulated backpack for hiking treks, the beach, or tailgate parties at the Kaua'i Polo Club. ⊠ *5-5161 Kūhiō Hwy., Hanalei* ☎ *808/826–2524* ⊟ *D, DC, MC, V.*

$–$$$ ✕ **Kīlauea Bakery and Pau Hana Pizza.** The bakery has garnered tons of press for its Hawaiian sourdough loaf made with guava starter, and such pizzas as the Billie Holliday (smoked ono, roasted onions, Gorgonzola-rosemary sauce, and mozzarella). To begin your day on a sweet note, check out the tropical Danish assortment with fillings that include mango, guava, and macadamia nut. Open at 6:30 AM, the bakery serves as "coffee central" in Kīlauea, with outdoor seating under large umbrellas for those who like to linger, sip, and read. ⊠ *Kong Lung Center, 2490 Keneke St., Kīlauea* ☎ *808/828–2020* ⊟ *MC, V.*

Contemporary

$$$–$$$$ ✕ **Cafe Hanalei and Terrace.** You're in for a very romantic evening here: the view from the Princeville Resort overlooking Hanalei Bay is mesmerizing, and the attention to detail and service is superb. The Sunday brunch and the daily breakfast buffet are enormous feasts. Lunch includes Japanese specialties, lobster bisque, Cobb salad, and sandwiches. For dinner, the Kaua'i coffee rack of lamb and lemongrass 'ahi are two popular items. On Friday nights, opt for the seafood buffet. Save room for the decadent "Tower of Passion," a chocolate tower filled with passion-fruit mousse. ⊠ *Princeville Resort, 5520 Ka Haku Rd., Princeville* ☎ *808/826–2760* ⌂ *Reservations essential* ⊟ *AE, D, DC, MC, V.*

$$–$$$ ✕ **Lighthouse Bistro.** Tucked into the heart of Kīlauea, next to the Kong Lung store but with no real view of the Kīlauea Lighthouse, this North Shore bistro has terra-cotta floors, bamboo chairs, and open-air dining, reminiscent of the plantation era. Some entrées, like seafood linguine or tortellini, have an Italian flair. Others, such as stuffed shrimp in phyllo or mango-cherry chicken are more Pacific Rim. There's live music Sunday through Wednesday evenings. ⊠ *2484 Keneke St., at Lighthouse Rd., Kīlauea* ☎ *808/828–0480* ⊟ *MC, V.*

★ **$$–$$$** ✕ **Postcards Cafe.** With its postcard artwork, beamed ceilings, and light interiors, this plantation-cottage restaurant has a menu consisting mostly of organic, additive-free vegetarian foods. But don't get the wrong idea—this isn't simple cooking: specials might include carrot-ginger soup, fish tacos, taro fritters, or fresh fish served with peppered pineapple-sage sauce. Their signature breakfast is a seven-grain English muffin topped with sautéed greens, tempeh strips, and hollandaise—all dairy free. Desserts are made without refined sugar. ⊠ *5-5075A Kūhiō Hwy., Hanalei* ☎ *808/826–1191* ☰ *AE, MC, V* ☉ *No lunch.*

$–$$ ✕ **Bamboo Bamboo.** Locally grown produce, island fish, and homemade desserts are served in this restaurant that features a cappuccino bar and outdoor courtyard seating in a bamboo garden overlooking Hanalei's lush green taro fields. 'Ahi spring rolls, potato-crusted mahimahi, and Kīlauea-goat-cheese salad are choices to fit any appetite. Save room for the blackberry cheesecake. ⊠ *Hanalei Center, 5-5161 Kūhiō Hwy., Hanalei* ☎ *808/826–1177* ☰ *AE, MC, V.*

Eclectic

$$–$$$ ✕ **Zelo's Beach House.** Call the menu eclectic—what else could you say about its Hawaiian-American-Thai-Mexican leanings? The decor, however, is strictly South Seas tropical. A bamboo bar, *lau hala* (pandanus leaf) mats on the walls, a kayak overhead, and Tahitian-print bar stools add to the relaxed family atmosphere. Zelo's signature "macho nachos," burgers, and tequila seafood tostadas are served on an open-air deck. For dinner, large salads, fresh fish, pasta, steak, and crab stuffed ono wrapped in shredded phyllo fit the bill. ⊠ *5-5156 Kūhiō Hwy., Hanalei* ☎ *808/826–9700* ☰ *MC, V.*

Italian

$$$–$$$$ ✕ **La Cascata.** Terra-cotta floors, hand-painted murals, and trompe l'oeil paintings give La Cascata a Tuscan-villa flair, and picture windows offer dazzling views of Hanalei Bay. The menu emphasizes light sauces, plenty of pastas, fresh seafood, beef, and lamb. Savor Brodetto di Pesce (Kaua'i prawns, snapper, scallops, and clams with Arrabbiata sauce served over linguine), or seared 'ahi with artichoke cannelloni, carmelized onion broth and toasted pine nuts. Come early for sunset views of Bali Hai. Stay late for a nightcap and hand-rolled cigar. ⊠ *Princeville Resort, 5520 Ka Haku Rd., Princeville* ☎ *808/826–2761* ⚑ *Reservations essential* ☰ *AE, D, DC, MC, V* ☉ *No lunch.*

Steak & Seafood

$$$–$$$$ ✕ **Bali Hai.** Views of the bay are as memorable as the cuisine at this open-air restaurant, richly appointed with natural wood. Specialties include the Kaua'i-onion soup topped with melted provolone cheese; the "Namolokama Platter," a combo of watermelon-barbecued pork ribs, chicken skewers, and tiger prawns with sweet chili sauce; and pan-seared fresh fish served over a crispy crab cake. Breakfast includes poi pancakes, fried taro, and eggs. ⊠ *Hanalei Bay Resort, 5380 Honoiki Rd., Princeville* ☎ *808/826–6522* ☰ *AE, D, DC, MC, V.*

$$–$$$ ✕ **Sushi Blues.** If you'd like a little jazz with that roll, check out these second-story digs with copper table tops and photos of some of the world's jazz greats lining the staircase. Sushi Blues hits a high note with its full sashimi and sushi menu along with views of the lush Hanalei waterfalls and nightly jazz entertainment. You can definitely gamble on the Las Vegas Roll filled with tuna, yellowtail, and avocado, made crispy by a tempura batter coating. For those who opt out of sushi, there are steaks and seafood. A full sake menu is also featured. ⊠ *Ching Young Village, 5-5190 Kūhiō Hwy., Hanalei* ☎ *808/826–9701* ▭ *AE, D, DC, MC, V.*

Līhu'e

American/Casual

$–$$ ✕ **JJ's Broiler.** Overlooking Kalapakī Bay, this spacious, low-key local favorite has two levels: downstairs is a bar and lānai with hearty American fare including a hefty clam bucket with 2 pounds of steamer clams bathed in white wine garlic and herbs; upstairs you can feast on fancier Pacific Rim dishes, including sugarcane shrimp and Peking chicken tacos in a garlic oyster sauce. The house specialty is Slavonic steak, a broiled sliced tenderloin dipped in a buttery wine sauce. While many eateries on the island close early, this one is open until 11 PM. ⊠ *Anchor Cove, 3146 Rice St., Nāwiliwili* ☎ *808/246–4422* ▭ *D, MC, V.*

$–$$ ✕ **Līhu'e Barbecue Inn.** The menu at this local-style hangout ranges from classic American fare to Asian. Try the baby back ribs, the macadamia-nut chicken, or the Cajun seafood medley with king crab. If you can't make up your mind, the Inn's tri-sampler is a good compromise. This venue is family-owned and has been a mainstay on Kaua'i since 1940. ⊠ *2982 Kress St., Līhu'e* ☎ *808/245–2921* ▭ *No credit cards.*

Eclectic

$$$–$$$$ ✕ **Gaylord's.** Located in what was at one time Kaua'i's most expensive plantation estate, Gaylord's pays tribute to the elegant dining rooms of 1930s society. Candlelit tables on a cobblestone patio overlook a wide lawn with a fountain creating a romantic ambience. The menu pairs classic American cooking with an island twist. Try wonton-wrapped prawns with a wasabi plum sauce, New Zealand venison, or blackened prime rib. For breakfast, Gaylord's serves up a traditional lei greeting for the ladies, live Hawaiian music, and hula entertainment along with its breakfast offerings of mango muffins, eggs, and Kilohana French toast. A lavish Sunday brunch has innovative dishes like sweet-potato hash and Cajun 'ahi in addition to the standard omelettes and pancakes. You can also arrange for a pre- or postmeal horse-drawn carriage ride of the plantation. ⊠ *Kilohana Plantation, 3-2087 Kaumuali'i Rd., Līhu'e* ☎ *808/245–9593* ▭ *AE, D, DC, MC, V.*

$$$–$$$$ ✕ **Kukui's Restaurant and Bar.** With an imaginative menu that focuses on healthful choices and cross-cultural flavors, Kukui's epitomizes the casual, open-air oceanfront dining experience. For lunch, try the blackened Pacific salmon with grilled-pineapple-scallion salsa, the *kālua* (roasted) pork quesadillas, or the Thai-chicken pizza. Dinner is more formal, with an island-influenced menu that includes a shrimp boat buffet, served from a real island canoe. On Friday and Saturday nights there's also a prime rib and king crab buffet. At breakfast the temptations are

twofold: a buffet or a full à la carte menu. ⊠ *Kaua'i Marriott Resort & Beach Club, 3610 Rice St., Līhu'e* ☎ *808/245–5050* ⊟ *AE, D, DC, MC, V.*

Hawaiian

¢–$ ✕ **Dani's Restaurant.** Kaua'i residents often frequent this big and bare come-as-you-are eatery near the Līhu'e Fire Station. Dani's is a good place to try lū'au food without commercial lū'au prices. You can order Hawaiian-style *laulau* (pork wrapped in ti leaves and steamed) or kālua pig and rice. Other island-style dishes include Japanese-prepared *tonkatsu* (pork cutlet) and teriyaki beef, and there's always the all-American New York steak. Breakfast omelets are whipped up with fish cake, *kalua* pig, or seafood. ⊠ *4201 Rice St., Līhu'e* ☎ *808/245–4991* ⊟ *No credit cards* ⊙ *Closed Sun. No dinner.*

¢ ✕ **Hamura Saimin.** It doesn't look like much from the outside, but in-
FodorśChoice side this old plantation diner each day the Hiraoka family serves 1,000
★ orders of saimin, a steaming bowl of broth and noodles with varying garnishes. This little landmark also turns out tasty chicken and beef grilled on barbecue sticks, as well as *liliko'i* (passion fruit) chiffon pie. Open till 11 PM on week nights and midnight on weekends, this spot is favored by night owls. ⊠ *2956 Kress St., Līhu'e* ☎ *808/245–3271* ⊟ *No credit cards.*

Italian

$$–$$$ ✕ **Café Portofino.** Since moving into his new "restaurant row" location on the Kalapakī Promenade of the Kaua'i Beach Marriott, owner Giuseppe Avocadi has created a menu that continues to garner a host of culinary awards. The cuisine is northern Italian. The fresh 'ahi carpaccio, along with pasta, scampi, and veal dishes, each enhanced by sauces "with an Italian soul," have drawn raves from dining critics. Dine with a view of Kalapakī Bay and watch the luxury liners as they make their way into and out of Nāwiliwili Harbor. ⊠ *Kaua'i Marriott & Beach Club 3610 Rice St., Līhu'e* ☎ *808/245–2121* ⊟ *AE, D, DC, MC, V* ⊙ *No lunch.*

Japanese

$–$$ ✕ **Hanamā'ulu Restaurant, Tea House, Sushi Bar, and Robatayaki.** An island tradition, this old-time Japanese restaurant is spartan; it's not the furnishings but the food that is popular. Traditional Japanese fare such as sashimi; sushi; *teishoku* (set meal) platters with miso soup, tempura shrimp, fish, and vegetables; chicken *katsu*; and *robatayaki* (grilled seafood and meat) is the main attraction. Call ahead to reserve one of the private teahouse dining rooms for soothing views of the Japanese garden and ponds. ⊠ *1-4291 Kūhiō Hwy. (Rte. 56), Hanamā'ulu* ☎ *808/245–2511* ⊟ *MC, V* ⊙ *Closed Mon.*

Seafood

$–$$$ ✕ **Duke's Canoe Club.** Surf legend Duke Kahanamoku would be proud of this bi-level beachfront restaurant replete with indoor garden and waterfall, the high-energy, good-time Barefoot Bar (a bar menu is available), and the biggest salad bar on the island. For lunch, try the stir-fry cashew chicken or the fish burger. The best order here is the fresh catch of the day—prepared as you like it, from broiled to Thai-chili-glazed. Strolling musicians are a fun accompaniment, as is the view of Kalapakī Bay and Nāwiliwili Harbor at sunset. ✉ *Kaua'i Marriott & Beach Club, Līhu'e* ☎ *808/246–9599* ⊟ *AE, D, DC, MC, V.*

The South Shore & The West Side

American

$–$$ ✗ **Camp House Grill.** A simple plantation-style camp house with squeaky wooden floors has become a simple, down-home restaurant. The food is basic: hamburgers, chicken, pork ribs, and fresh fish aimed to please families. Barbecued specialties include chicken marinated in a blend of Chinese, Cajun, and Hawaiian spices. Huge sandwiches are served at lunchtime. Large breakfasts are available, and pies are baked fresh daily; you can eat a slice on the premises or take home an entire pie for a late-night craving. As you enter Kalāheo heading west toward Waimea Canyon, look for the blue building on the right. ✉ *Kaumuali'i Hwy. (Rte. 50), Kalāheo* ☎ *808/332–9755* ✉ *Kaua'i Village, Kūhiō Hwy., Kapa'a* ☎ *808/822–2442* ⊟ *AE, D, MC, V.*

Contemporary

★ $$$ ✗ **The Beach House.** This restaurant may have the best ocean view of any on the South Shore, and the cuisine is equally impressive. The menu changes often as does the work of local artists displayed on the walls. Dishes might include sea scallops on a green-papaya salad with white truffle vinaigrette and cranberry essence, Local Boy paella, fire-roasted 'ahi, or seared macadamia-nut-crusted mahimahi with citrus *aki* miso sauce. A coconut-butter *mochi* (doughy Japanese rice cake) sundae or the Kahlua-taro cheesecake is a sweet finale. ✉ *5022 Lāwa'i Rd., Kōloa* ☎ *808/742–1424* ⊟ *AE, D, DC, MC, V* ☽ *No lunch.*

$–$$$ ✗ **Tomkats Grille.** Tropical ponds, a waterfall, a large bar area, and a porch overlooking an inner courtyard give this grill its casual island ambience. You can have the blackened "katch of the day" with tropical salsa, or homemade chili and a burger. Wash it down with a glass of wine or one of 35 ales, stouts, ports, and lagers. Plenty of Tomkats' Nibblers—buffalo wings, stuffed mushrooms, sautéed shrimp—enliven happy hour from 3 to 6. ✉ *Old Kōloa Town, 5402 Kōloa Rd., Kōloa* ☎ *808/742–8887* ⊟ *DC, MC, V.*

$$ ✗ **Waimea Brewing Company.** Housed within the Waimea Plantation Cottages, this brewpub-restaurant is spacious, with hardwood floors and open-air decks. Dine indoors amid rattan furnishings or at a bar decorated with petroglyphs and colored with Kaua'i red dirt. Smoked-chicken quesadillas, grilled portobellos, hamburgers, *kal-bi* beef short ribs, and fresh fish are highlights. Entrées come in two sizes (small and big!) and are reasonably priced. It's a good place to pick up a picnic basket on the way to the West End's Waimea Canyon. ✉ *9400 Kaumuali'i Hwy., Waimea* ☎ *808/338–9733* ⊟ *MC, V.*

Eclectic

★ $$$–$$$$ ✗ **Roy's Po'ipū Bar & Grill.** Hawai'i's culinary superstar Roy Yamaguchi created a sleek restaurant style to showcase what he calls "Hawaiian Fusion" cuisine. Who but Roy would turn smoked duck into *gyoza* (Japanese dumplings), or present a spiny lobster tail with sautéed garlic glass noodles, laid out on your plate like a fiery dragon? The menu here changes daily with 15 to 20 (or more) specials nightly. ⊠ *Po'ipū Shopping Village, 2360 Kiahuna Plantation Dr., Po'ipū Beach* ☎ *808/742–5000* ▭ *AE, D, DC, MC, V* ⊗ *No lunch.*

$$–$$$ ✕ **Green Garden.** Once a family plantation manager's home, this historic building was transformed into a restaurant at about the same time Hawai'i was transformed from a U.S. territory into a state. Surrounded by tropical greenery that seems to hug its very foundation, Green Garden is very low-key: servers treat you like longtime friends, and the food is solid, no-frills fare. Dinner includes some 30 items of native Hawaiian, Asian, and American influence. Mahimahi, scallops, oysters, and shrimp are key ingredients along with kiawe broiled rack of lamb and steak. The homemade desserts are the best part of a meal here, particularly the liliko'i chiffon pie. ⊠ *Hwy. 50, Hanapēpē* ☎ *808/335–5422* ▭ *AE, MC, V* ⊗ *Closed Tues.*

Italian

$$$–$$$$ ✕ **Dondero's.** Inlaid marble floors, ornate tile work, and Italianate murals inside compete with the cliff-side ocean setting here, and make it difficult to choose between indoor and outdoor dining. Chef Vincent Pecoraro combines Old World techniques with new energy in creating menu selections as enticing as the surroundings. Porcini-mushroom crepes with Parmesan sauce, a perfectly seasoned Caesar salad, and lobster piccata with pistachio fettuccine tempt the palate along with sweet endings like traditional tiramisu and chocolate crème brûlée with fresh raspberries. ⊠ *Hyatt Regency Kaua'i Resort and Spa, 1571 Po'ipū Rd., Po'ipū Beach* ☎ *808/742–1234* ▭ *AE, D, DC, MC, V* ⊗ *No lunch.*

$$–$$$ ✕ **Casa di Amici.** Tucked away in a quiet neighborhood above Po'ipū Beach, this "House of Friends" is worth seeking out. Entrées from the internationally eclectic menu include a saffron-vanilla paella risotto made with black tiger prawns, fresh fish, chicken breast and homemade Italian sausage; or a laulau Borsettino (spinach pasta purses stuffed with kālua pork served with a smoked portobello sauce). For dessert, take the plunge with a baked Hawai'i created from a chocolate-macadamia-nut brownie topped with coconut and passion-fruit sorbet and flambéed Italian meringue. There's live classical piano music on the weekends and the outside deck is open to sweeping beach views. ⊠ *2301 Nalo Rd., Po'ipū* ☎ *808/742–1555* ▭ *AE, D, DC, MC, V* ⊗ *No lunch.*

$$–$$$ ✕ **Plantation Gardens.** A former plantation manager's residence, this historic home now serves Italian food in a Polynesian atmosphere—an interesting mix. There are torch-lit orchid gardens, koi and lotus ponds, cherrywood floors, and veranda dining. Chef Brenda Morando takes fish right off the boat and utilizes fresh herbs and produce—straight from the plantation's gardens—to create such menu delights as shrimp and wasabi ravioli, seafood *laulau* (seafood wrapped in ti leaves and steamed) served with mango chutney, and tender osso buco served with saffron risotto. ⊠ *Kiahuna Plantation, 2253 Po'ipū Rd., Kōloa* ☎ *808/742–2216* ▭ *AE, DC, MC, V* ⊗ *No lunch.*

$-$$ ✕ **Pomodoro Ristorante Italiano.** Begin with prosciutto and melon, and then proceed directly to the multi-layered meat lasagna, a favorite of the chefs—two Italian-born brothers. Highlights include eggplant or veal parmigiana, chicken saltimbocca, and scampi in a garlic, caper, and white wine sauce. Two walls of windows brighten this intimate second-story restaurant in the heart of Kalāheo. ✉ *Upstairs at Rainbow Plaza, Kaumuali'i Hwy. (Rte. 50), Kalāheo* ☎ *808/332–5945* ▭ *MC, V* ☽ *No lunch.*

Steak & Seafood

$$$–$$$$ ✕ **Tidepools.** The Hyatt Regency Kaua'i has three superb restaurants, but this one delivers the most. Dine in one of the grass-thatch huts that float on a koi-filled pond, and enjoy views of the romantic torch-lit grounds and starry Po'ipū skies. A major advocate of Hawai'i regional cuisine, which utilizes Kaua'i-grown products, the chef prepares fish with local flavors. Specialties include macadamia-crusted fish, prime rib, and filet mignon. Start the evening with the local favorite—Kimo's crab cake—and end your meal with the popular ginger crème brûlée. ✉ *Hyatt Regency Kaua'i Resort and Spa, 1571 Po'ipū Rd., Po'ipū Beach* ☎ *808/742–1234 Ext. 4260* ▭ *AE, D, DC, MC, V* ☽ *No lunch.*

$$–$$$ ✕ **Kalāheo Steak House.** Prime rib, tender top sirloin, Cornish game hen in citrus marinade, Kalāheo shrimp, Alaskan king crab legs, and Portuguese bean soup bring in the locals. The interior is Upcountry casual with weathered wood furnishings and artifacts that pay tribute to the paniolo cowboys. It's a room designed to stand up to hearty eating. Fresh-baked rum cake comes with Lappert's ice cream (made at a factory up the road). Wines range from $8 to $25 a bottle. ✉ *4444 Pāpālina Rd., Kalāheo* ☎ *808/332–9780* ▭ *D, MC, V* ⌣ *Reservations not accepted* ☽ *No lunch.*

$$–$$$ ✕ **Keoki's Paradise.** Built to resemble a dockside boathouse, this is an active, boisterous place that fills up quickly on weekend nights because of live music. Ocean-originating appetizers span the tide from sashimi to Thai shrimp sticks. The day's fresh catch is available in half a dozen styles and sauces. And there's a sampling of beef, chicken, and pork-rib entrées for the committed carnivore. A lighter menu is available at the bar. ✉ *Po'ipū Shopping Village, 2360 Kiahuna Plantation Dr., Po'ipū Beach* ☎ *808/742–7534* ▭ *AE, D, DC, MC, V.*

$$–$$$ ✕ **Shells Steak and Seafood.** Chandeliers made from big shells light the way for a tropically influenced meal. Prime cuts of steak and fresh fish, prepared with spices and sauces with a distinctly Island flair, highlight this menu. Friday evenings there is a bountiful seafood buffet. Shells is one of three signature restaurants in the Sheraton's Oceanfront Galleria. Each of these restaurants has been designed to embrace the view of the Pacific Ocean from sunrise to starlight. ✉ *Sheraton Kaua'i Resort, 2440 Ho'onani Rd., Po'ipū Beach, Kōloa* ☎ *808/742–1661* ▭ *AE, D, DC, MC, V* ☽ *No lunch.*

$$–$$$ ✕ **Wrangler's Steakhouse.** Denim-cover seating, decorative saddles, and a stagecoach in a loft helped to transform the historic Ako General Store in Waimea into a west-side steak house. You can eat under the stars on the deck out back. The 16-ounce steak comes sizzling with either garlic, capers, peppers, or teriyaki. Those with smaller appetites might

consider the vegetable tempura or the 'ahi served on penne pasta. Local folks love the tin lunch: soup, rice, beef teriyaki, and shrimp tempura served in a three-tier lunch pail (the kind that sugar-plantation workers once carried). A gift shop has local crafts (and sometimes a craftsperson). ☒ *9852 Kaumuali'i Hwy., Waimea* ☎ *808/338–1218* ▭ *AE, MC, V* ⊙ *Closed Sun.*

$–$$$ ✕ **Brennecke's Beach Broiler.** Brennecke's is decidedly casual and fun, with a busy bar, windows overlooking the beach, and a cheery blue-and-white interior. It specializes in big portions of kiawe-broiled foods such as New York steak, spiny lobster, and the fresh catch of the day. Seafood kebabs, jumbo shrimp skewers, New Zealand green-lipped mussels, pasta, and deluxe fish sandwiches are other options. There's a take-out deli downstairs. ☒ *2100 Ho'ōne Rd., Po'ipū* ☎ *808/742–7588* ▭ *AE, D, DC, MC, V.*

WHERE TO STAY

Make reservations in advance, whether you choose to stay at a plush Po'ipū resort or a condo on the South Shore; at the posh Princeville Resort on the North Shore; at a Coconut Coast guest house on the east side; or at a rustic cabin on Kaua'i's west side. Peak months are February, August, and October. When booking your accommodations, ask about such extras as tennis, golf, honeymoon, and room-and-car packages.

BED-AND-BREAKFASTS   There are two B&B reservation services based in Kaua'i. Liz Hay's **Bed and Breakfast Kaua'i** (☒ 105 Melia St., Kapa'a 96746 ☎ 808/822–1177 or 800/822–1176 🖷 808/826–9292 ⊕ www.bnb-kauai.com) has been in operation on the Garden Isle for many years and offers visitors a personalized approach for all lifestyles and budgets, as well as a network of more than 200 cottages, condos, and B&Bs.

Island-wide reservations services, such as **Hawaii's Best Rentals** (⌂ Box 790450, Paia 96779 ☎ 808/929–9557 or 866/772–5642 ⊕ www.hawaiisbestrentals.com), can book B&B rooms and exclusive vacation hideaways for either a Kaua'i vacation or a multi-island getaway. Although its name is **Bed and Breakfast Honolulu** (☒ 3242 Kā'ohinani Dr., Honolulu 96817 ☎ 808/595–7533 or 800/288–4666 🖷 808/595–2030 ⊕ www.hawaiibnb.com), this agency represents more than 400 host homes covering all the major islands and can assist with interisland airfares and car rental.

The North Shore

$$$$ 🏠 **Kīlauea Lakeside Estate.** Imagine having your own private island retreat where the amenities and activities are custom-designed to meet your every vacation dream. This is what you'll find at Kīlauea Lakeside Estate. The proprietors can arrange for personal chefs, windsurfing lessons, lakeside spa treatments, and on-site weddings. A private 20-acre freshwater lake teeming with bass and catfish awaits your fishing pole. You'll also have your own par-three golf hole and putting green, and 3 acres of botanical gardens to stroll through. The modern three-bedroom house includes a romantic master suite and bath. ✉ *4613 Waiakalua Rd., Kīlauea 96754* ☎ *310/379–7842* 🖷 *310/379–0034* ⊕ *www. kauaihoneymoon.com* ➷ *1 house △ BBQ, fans, kitchen, cable TV, in-room VCRs, putting green, lake, beach, fishing, laundry facilities; no a/c* ☰ *AE, D, MC, V.*

$$$$ 🏨 **Princeville Resort.** Built into the cliffs overlooking Hanalei Bay,
Fodor'sChoice Princeville's views of "Bali Hai" frame the beauty that made the Gar-
★ den Island film *South Pacific* famous. Guest rooms are spacious and de-
signed in primary colors to match those of Kaua'i's abundant yellow
hibiscus, red 'ōhi'a flower, and dark green *mokihana* berry. The luxury
of the resort is completed by attention to the little details that make a
difference, like lighted closets, dimmer switches on all lamps, original
artwork, and door chimes. Bathrooms feature height-adjustable show-
erheads and a privacy window—flip a switch and it goes from clear to
opaque. A sunset drink in the Living Room is an event complete with
a traditional Hawaiian ceremony. A poolside lū'au is held Monday and
Thursday evenings year-round. There are two top-ranked golf courses
on the resort grounds; a spa and tennis center can be reached by shut-
tle. ✉ *5520 Ka Haku Rd. (Box 3069), Princeville 96722* ☎ *808/826–
9644 or 888/488–3535* 🖷 *808/826–1166* ⊕ *www.starwood.com/hawaii*
➷ *201 rooms, 51 suites △ 4 restaurants, room service, minibars, 2 18-
hole golf courses, 8 tennis courts, pool, gym, health club, massage, spa,
beach, 2 bars, children's programs (ages 5–12), dry cleaning, laundry
service, concierge, business services, meeting rooms, travel services*
☰ *AE, D, DC, MC, V.*

$$$$ 🏨 **Secret Beach Hideaway.** Revel in a romance or write the great Amer-
ican novel—anything seems possible at these three sumptuous one-bed-
room, one-bath retreats. The cottages feature custom furniture and
flooring in island-hewn hardwoods, gourmet kitchens with European
appliances, indoor-outdoor garden showers, and picture windows de-
signed to offer the most stunning ocean and mountain views. Each unit
has a washer-dryer, two phone lines for Internet access, and a private
outdoor hot tub with an ocean view. Four private paths lead down to
Secret Beach. Catered meals as well as other services, like massage, can
be arranged upon request. ✉*2884 Kauapea Rd. (Box 781), Kīlauea 96754*
☎ *808/635–6184 or 800/820–2862* 🖷 *808/828–0899* ⊕ *www.
secretbeachkauai.com* ➷ *3 cottages △ Fans, in-room fax, kitchens,
microwaves, cable TV, in-room VCRs, hot tub, beach; no a/c.*

$$$–$$$$ 🏨 **Hanalei Bay Resort.** Three-story buildings angle down the cliffs over-
looking Hanalei Bay and the famed Bali Hai. Units are extremely spa-
cious, with high, sloping ceilings and large private lānai. Rattan furniture
and island art add a casual feeling to rooms. Studios have small kitch-
enettes not meant for serious cooking. The resort's upper-level pool has
lava-rock waterfalls, an open-air hot tub, and a kid-friendly sand
"beach." Guests have golf privileges at Princeville Resort. More than
half the units on this property are now dedicated to vacation owner-
ship rentals. ✉ *5380 Honoiki Rd., Princeville 96722* ☎ *808/826–6522
or 800/827–4427* 🖷 *808/826–6680* ⊕ *www.hanaleibayresort.com*
➷ *134 units △ Restaurant, in-room safes, kitchenettes, refrigerators,
cable TV, 8 tennis courts, 2 pools, hot tub, massage, beach, lobby*

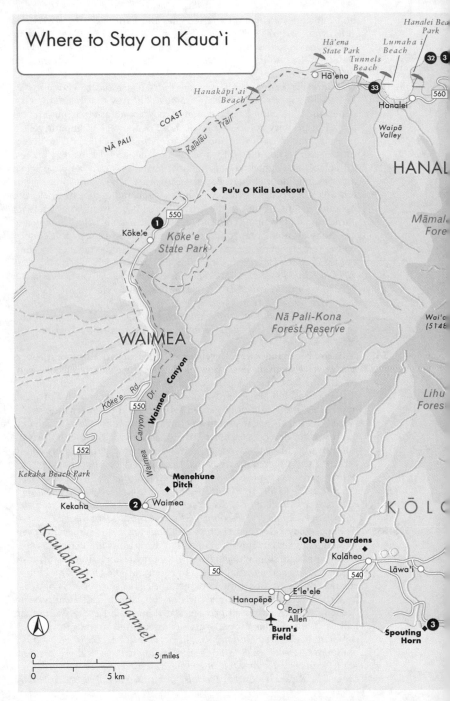

Where to Stay on Kaua`i

Hanalei Bea Park

Hā`ena State Park

Lumaha`i Beach

Tunnels Beach

Hā`ena

32 **3**

33

560

Hanalei

Hanakāpī`ai Beach

Waipā Valley

NĀ PALI

COAST

Kalalau Trail

HANAL

Māmal Fore

◆ Pu`u O Kila Lookout

550

1

Kōke`e

Kōke`e State Park

Nā Pali-Kona Forest Reserve

Wai`c (5148

Lihu Fores

WAIMEA

Kōke`e Rd.

Waimea Canyon

Canyon Dr.

550

Waimea Canyon

552

Kekaha Beach Park

Menehune Ditch ◆

Kekaha

2 Waimea

KŌLO

`Olo Pua Gardens ◆

Kalāheo

Lāwa`i

50

540

E`le`ele

Hanapēpē

Port Allen

Kaulakahi

Channel

⚓ **Burn's Field**

◆ **Spouting Horn**

3

0 — 5 miles

0 — 5 km

lounge, shop, babysitting, children's programs (ages 5–12), laundry facilities $\equiv$ *AE, D, DC, MC, V.*

\$\$\$–\$\$\$\$ 🖾 **Hanalei Colony Resort.** This 5-acre property is a laid-back, go-barefoot kind of place sandwiched between towering mountains and the sea. The only true beachfront resort on Kaua'i's North Shore, its charm is in its simplicity. Here, there are no phones in the rooms, and no stereos or TVs. Each of the two-bedroom condominium units can sleep a family of four. The units are well maintained, with Hawaiian-style furnishings, full kitchens, and lānai. Amenities, like cocktail receptions and cultural activities, vary by the season. There is an art gallery with coffee bar on-site. ⊠ *5-7130 Kūhiō Hwy. (Box 206), Hā'ena 96714* 🕾 *808/ 826–6235 or 800/628–3004* 🖶 *808/826–9893* ⊕ *www.hcr.com* 🖙 *48 units* ♻ *BBQs, fans, kitchens, pool, hot tub, beach, shop, laundry facilities; no a/c, no room phones, no room TVs* $\equiv$ *AE, MC, V.*

The East Side

\$\$\$\$ 🖾 **Aloha Beach Resort Kaua'i.** This is a sprawling jewel on the eastern shore. The short walk from the resort on Wailua Bay to Lydgate Park and the beach helps make this a great place for families. It's also close to shops and restaurants. Rooms are in two wings and have beach, mountain, or ocean views. The resort also offers one-bedroom beach cottages with kitchenettes. ⊠ *3-5920 Kūhiō Hwy., Kapa'a 96746* 🕾 *808/823– 6000 or 888/823–5111* 🖶 *808/823–6666* ⊕ *www.abrkauai.com* 🖙 *188 rooms, 2 suites, 24 beach cottages* ♻ *Restaurant, snack bar, in-room data ports, in-room safes, 2 tennis courts, 2 pools, gym, hot tub, shuffleboard, volleyball, lobby lounge* $\equiv$ *AE, D, DC, MC, V.*

\$\$\$\$ 🖾 **Outrigger Lae nani.** Ruling Hawaiian chiefs once returned from ocean voyages to this spot, now host to condominiums comfortable enough for minor royalty. An oceanside heiau and hotel-sponsored Hawaiiana programs, with a booklet for self-guided historical tours, are nice extras. Units are all decorated differently, with bright, full kitchens and expansive lānai. Your view of landscaped grounds is interrupted only by a large pool before ending at a sandy, swimmable beach. You'll find plenty of dining and shopping at the adjacent Coconut Marketplace. ⊠ *410 Papaloa Rd., Kapa'a 96746* 🕾 *808/822–4938 or 800/688–7444* 🖶 *808/822–1022* ⊕ *www.outriggerlaenani.com* 🖙 *84 condominiums (52 rentals)* ♻ *BBQs, picnic area, fans, in-room safes, kitchens, microwaves, cable TV, tennis court, pool, beach, laundry facilities; no a/c* $\equiv$ *AE, D, DC, MC, V.*

\$\$\$–\$\$\$\$ 🖾 **Aston Islander on the Beach.** The eight three-story buildings of this pleasant 6-acre beachfront property have a low-key Hawai'i-plantation look. Rooms have showers but not tubs. The dark carpeting is brightened by the light from glass doors leading to the lānai and lovely green lawns outside. A free-form pool sits next to a golden-sand beach, and you can take the lounge chairs to the ocean's edge. ⊠ *4-484 Kūhiō Hwy., Kapa'a 96746* 🕾 *808/822–7417 or 877/977–6667* 🖶 *808/822–1947* 🖙 *194 rooms, 2 suites* ♻ *Restaurant, in-room safes, cable TV, tennis court, pool, hair salon, hot tub, volleyball, bar, laundry facilities, meeting room* $\equiv$ *AE, D, DC, MC, V.*

$$$–$$$$ 🏨 **Kaua'i Coast Resort at the Beachboy.** On an uncrowded stretch of Waipouli Beach, the resort is a quick drive to Kapa'a and the Wailua Municipal Golf Course, and within walking distance of the Coconut Marketplace. The three-building, three-story condominium consists of fully furnished one- and two-bedroom units, some of which are time-share. They are decorated in rich woods with tropical prints and Hawaiian-quilt designs. Each unit has a kitchen and private lānai. The 8 acres feature a heated pool with waterscapes, a children's pool, a day spa, and an oceanside hot tub. ✉ *520 Aleka Loop, Kapa'a 96746* ☎ *808/822–3441 or 877/977–4355* 🖷 *808/822–0843* 🌐 *www. shellhospitality.com* ⇨ *108 1- and 2-bedroom condos* 🍴 *Restaurant, in-room safes, in-room data ports, kitchens, microwaves, refrigerators, tennis court, 2 pools, gym, hot tub, spa, lobby lounge, concierge.* 🚭 *AE, D, DC, MC, V.*

$$$–$$$$ 🏨 **Kaua'i Coconut Beach Resort.** Considered the most authentic by many, this resort's nightly lū'au and free hula and sunset torch-lighting show perpetuate the true native spirit. Modern rooms have plantation-style furnishings and floral bedspreads. Set back from the highway amid 11 acres of coconut grove and on Waipouli Beach, this resort is centrally located between north- and south-shore attractions and within walking distance of three major shopping centers. ✉ *Coconut Plantation on Kūhiō Hwy. (Box 830), Kapa'a 96746* ☎ *808/822–3455 or 800/222–5642* 🖷 *808/822–0035* 🌐 *www.kcb.com* ⇨ *307 rooms, 2 suites* 🍴 *Restaurant, room service, in-room safes, refrigerators, 3 tennis courts, pro shop, pool, hot tub, shuffleboard, lobby lounge, meeting room, no-smoking rooms.* 🚭 *AE, D, DC, MC, V.*

$$$ 🏨 **Best Western Plantation Hale Suites.** These attractive plantation-style one-bedroom units have fully equipped kitchens and garden lānai. Rooms are clean and pretty, with white rattan furnishings and pastel colors. You couldn't ask for a more convenient location for dining, shopping, and sightseeing: it's across from Waipouli Beach and near Coconut Marketplace. Request a unit on the makai side, away from Kūhiō Highway. ✉ *484 Kūhiō Hwy., Kapa'a 96746* ☎ *808/822–4941 or 800/775–4253* 🖷 *808/822–5599* 🌐 *www.plantation-hale.com* ⇨ *145 units* 🍴 *BBQs, in-room safes, cable TV with movies and video games, kitchens, kitchenettes, microwaves, putting green, 3 pools, hot tub, shuffleboard, laundry facilities.* 🚭 *AE, D, DC, MC, V.*

$$ 🏨 **Kapa'a Sands.** An old rock etched with kanji, Japanese characters, reminds you that the site of this condominium gem formerly contained a Shinto temple. Two-bedroom rentals—equipped with full kitchens and private lānai—are a fair deal. Studios feature pull-down Murphy beds to create more daytime space. Ask for an oceanfront room to get the breeze. ✉ *380 Papaloa Rd., Kapa'a 96746* ☎ *808/822–4901 or 800/ 222–4901* 🖷 *808/822–1556* 🌐 *www.kapaasands.com* ⇨ *20 condominiums* 🍴 *Fans, kitchens, microwaves, cable TV, in-room VCRs, pool; no a/c* 🚭 *MC, V.*

$$ 🏨 **Kaua'i Sands.** Hawaiian owned and operated, this oceanfnt inn is a real example of Hawai'i before the arrival of megadevelopers. Think ideal-roadside-motel-chic with a location on the Royal Coconut Coast that serves as a central launching point for island-wide sightseeing. The carpets are sea-foam green, the bedspreads floral prints, the furniture spare and simple. It's so retro it's unintentionally hip. A big grassy courtyard opens to the beach. For dining and shopping, the Coconut Marketplace is adjacent. ✉ *420 Papaloa Rd., Kapa'a 96746* ☎ *808/822–4951 or 800/560–5553* 🖷 *808/822–0978* 🌐 *www.kauaisandshotel. com* ➭ *250 rooms, 2 suites* ♻ *Some kitchenettes, cable TV, 2 pools, gym, lobby lounge, laundry facilities, no-smoking rooms.* 🖃 *AE, D, DC, MC, V.*

¢–$ 🏨 **Hotel Coral Reef.** Coral Reef has been in business since the 1960s and is something of a beachfront landmark. The well-maintained, no-frills hotel sits right on the sand's edge. Upper units have carpeting, while ground-level rooms are done in terrazzo tile with patios that lead out to the beach and barbecue grills. Rooms have showers only, no tubs. There are two two-room units, good for families. ✉ *1516 Kūhiō Hwy., Kapa'a 96746* ☎ *808/822–4481 or 800/843–4659* 🖷 *808/822–7705* 🌐 *www.hotelcoralreef.com* ➭ *24 rooms, 2 suites* ♻ *Picnic area, some refrigerators, cable TV, beach, laundry facilities, free parking; no a/c, no room phones* 🖃 *MC, V* ❤ *CP.*

¢–$ 🏨 **Rosewood Bed and Breakfast.** This charming B&B on a macadamia-nut plantation estate offers four separate styles of accommodations, including a two-bedroom Victorian cottage, a little one-bedroom grass-thatch cottage, a bunkhouse with three rooms and a shared bath, and the traditional main plantation home. The bunkhouse and thatched cottage feature outside hot/cold private shower areas hidden from view by a riot of tropically scented foliage. ✉ *872 Kamalu Rd., Kapa'a 96746* ☎ *808/822–5216* 🖷 *808/822–5478* 🌐 *www.rosewoodkauai. com* ➭ *3 cottages, main home with 1 room* ♻ *Kitchens, some cable TV; no a/c, no room phones, no smoking* 🖃 *No credit cards.*

Līhu'e

$$$$ 🏨 **Kaua'i Marriott Resort & Beach Club.** An elaborate tropical garden,
Fodor'sChoice   waterfalls right off the lobby, and an enormous 26,000-square-foot
★   swimming pool characterize the grand scale of this resort, which is oceanfront on stunning Kalapakī Bay. This resort has it all, with fine dining, shopping, spa, golf, tennis, water activities of all kinds, and Hawaiian-cultural activities that embrace the island's revered heritage. Rooms are appointed with tropical touches, and most have expansive ocean views. ✉ *3610 Rice St., Kalapakī Beach, Līhu'e 96766* ☎ *808/245–5050 or 800/220–2925* 🖷 *808/245–5148* 🌐 *www. marriotthotels.com* ➭ *356 rooms, 11 suites, 232 time-share units* ♻ *2 restaurants, room service, minibars, 2 18-hole golf courses, 7 tennis courts, pool, health club, outdoor hot tub, spa, beach, boating, lobby lounge, children's programs (ages 5–12), airport shuttle* 🖃 *AE, D, DC, MC, V.*

$$$$ 🏨 **Radisson Kaua'i Beach Hotel.** A low-rise, horseshoe-shape hotel, the Radisson surrounds a pool complex with rock-sculpted slopes, waterfalls, tropical flowers, and a cave resembling the Fern Grotto. The sand-bottom swimming pool makes up for the rough coastline. There are lots of little extras here, such as the 5 PM complimentary mai tai happy hour, followed by a torch-lighting ceremony and live Hawaiian music. Guest

rooms are attractive in rich tones with maroon accents and dark wood. The lānai have views of mountains, gardens, or the sea. ⊠ *4331 Kauaʻi Beach Dr., Līhuʻe 96766* ☎ *808/245–1955 or 888/805–3843* 🖷 *808/ 246–9085* ⊕ *www.radissonkauai.com* ⟿ *347 rooms, 8 suites* ♨ *2 restaurants, room service, in-room safes, some refrigerators, cable TV, in-room VCRs, 18-hole golf course, 4 tennis courts, 2 pools, wading pool, health club, hot tub, beach, lobby lounge, pub, Internet, airport shuttle* ⊟ *AE, D, DC, MC, V.*

$–$$ ▥ **Garden Island Inn.** This handy three-story inn, near Kalapakī Beach and Anchor Cove shopping center, is a bargain. From here you can walk across the street and enjoy the majesty of Kalapakī Beach or check out the facilities and restaurant of the Marriott. The orchid suites on the top floor, and tropical rooms on the second, have lānai and glimpses of the bay. Budget accommodations are on the ground floor and offer views of the inn's garden setting. The innkeepers lend out boogie boards and snorkeling and golf equipment and give away fruit from their trees. ⊠ *3445 Wilcox Rd., Kalapakī Beach 96766* ☎ *808/245–7227 or 800/ 648–0154* 🖷 *808/245–7603* ⊕ *www.gardenislandinn.com* ⟿ *21 rooms, 2 suites, 1 condominium* ♨ *Fans, some kitchens, some kitchenettes, microwaves, refrigerators, cable TV; no a/c in some rooms, no smoking* ⊟ *AE, DC, MC, V.*

The South Shore

★ $$$$ ▥ **Gloria's Spouting Horn Bed & Breakfast.** The most elegant oceanfront B&B on Kauaʻi, this cedar home was built specifically for guests. The comfortable common room has a soaring A-frame ceiling and deck. Waves dash the black rocks below, while just above the ocean's edge, the beach invites sunbathers. All three bedrooms have four-poster beds with canopies created from koa, willow, or bamboo woods, oceanside lānai, and bathrooms with deep soaking tubs and separate showers. You will be treated to a full breakfast each morning and in late afternoon, there is an open bar with pūpū, timed to the setting of the sun. ⊠ *4464 Lāwaʻi Rd., Poʻipū* ☎ *808/742–6995* 🖷 *808/742–6995* ⊕ *www. gloriasbedandbreakfast.com* ⟿ *3 rooms* ♨ *Fans, refrigerators, cable TV, in-room VCRs, pool; no a/c.* ⊟ *No credit cards* ⫶◉ *BP.*

★ $$$$ ▥ **Hyatt Regency Kauaʻi Resort and Spa.** Step into this superbly designed and dramatically handsome, classic Hawaiian low-rise, built right into the cliffs overlooking Shipwreck Beach. Spacious rooms, two-thirds with ocean views, have a plantation theme with bamboo and wicker furnishings and island art. Five acres of meandering fresh- and saltwater-swimming lagoons are beautifully set amid landscaped grounds. While adults enjoy treatments at the Anara Spa, kids can check out Camp Hyatt's activities created especially with the *keiki* (child) in mind. ⊠ *1571 Poʻipū Rd., Kōloa 96756* ☎ *808/742–1234 or 800/633–7313* 🖷 *808/ 742–1557* ⊕ *www.kauai.hyatt.com* ⟿ *565 rooms, 37 suites* ♨ *6 restaurants, room service, in-room safes, in-room data ports, minibars, refrigerators, cable TV with movies, 18-hole golf course, 4 tennis courts, pro shop, pool, health club, hot tub, massage, spa, beach, horseback riding, 4 bars, 6 lounges, nightclub, shops, babysitting, children's programs (ages 5-12), concierge* ⊟ *AE, D, DC, MC, V.*

$$$$ ⊞ **Outrigger Kiahuna Plantation.** Forty-two plantation-style low-rise buildings arc around a large, grassy field leading to the beach at this 35-acre oceanfront condominium resort. The individually decorated one- and two-bedroom units vary in style, but all are comfortable and clean, have lānai, and get lots of ocean breezes. This is a popular destination for families who take advantage of the swimmable beach and the lawn, for picnics and games. Great sunset and ocean views are available from some units. The Sheraton is next door, and there are facility-use agreements between the two locations. ⊠ *2253 Po'ipū Rd., Kōloa 96756* ☎ *808/742–6411 or 800/688–7444* 🖷 *808/742–1698* ⊕ *www. outrigger.com* ⊅ *333 condominiums* ⌂ *Restaurant, fans, in-room data ports, some kitchens, some kitchenettes, microwaves, cable TV, in-room VCRs, 18-hole golf course, 6 tennis courts, pool; no a/c* ⊟ *AE, DC, MC, V.*

$$$$ ⊞ **Po'ipū Kapili.** Spacious one- and two-bedroom condo units are minutes from Po'ipū restaurants. White-frame exteriors and double-pitched roofs complement the tropical landscaping. Interiors include full kitchens and entertainment centers. There are garden and across-the-street ocean views to choose from. Three deluxe 2,600-square-foot penthouse suites have enormous lānai, private elevators, and cathedral ceilings. You can mingle at a weekly coffee hour held beside the ocean-view pool, grab a good read from the resort library, or get your seasonings fresh from the herb garden for meals you grill on the BBQ, located poolside. In winter, you can whale-watch as you cook. ⊠ *2221 Kapili Rd., Kōloa 96756* ☎ *808/742–6449 or 800/443–7714* 🖷 *808/742–9162* ⊕ *www. poipukapili.com* ⊅ *57 condominiums, 3 penthouse suites* ⌂ *Fans, kitchens, microwaves, cable TV, in-room VCRs, 2 tennis courts, pool, library; no a/c* ⊟ *MC, V.*

$$$$ ⊞ **Po'ipū Shores.** Sitting on a rocky point above pounding surf, this is a perfect spot for whale- or turtle-watching. Weddings are staged on a little lawn beside the ocean, and a sandy swimming beach is a 10-minute walk away. There are three low-rise buildings, with a pool in front of the middle one. Condo units are individually owned and decorated, but all have large windows and many of them have bedrooms on the ocean side; they either share a sundeck or have a lānai. ⊠ *1775 Pe'e Rd., Kōloa 96756* ☎ *808/742–7700 or 800/367–5004* 🖷 *808/ 742–9720* ⊕ *www.castle-group.com* ⊅ *39 condominiums* ⌂ *Fans, kitchens, kitchenettes, microwaves, cable TV, pool, laundry facilities; no a/c* ⊟ *AE, MC, V.*

$$$$ ⊞ **Sheraton Kaua'i Resort.** The ocean wing accommodations here are so close to the water you can practically feel the spray of the surf as it hits the rocks below. Beachfront rooms have muted sand and eggshell colors and are as soothing as the comfortable lounge seating. Brighter palettes enliven the garden rooms. Dining rooms, king beds, and balconies differentiate the suites. Hawaiian artisans stage crafts demonstrations under a banyan tree in the central courtyard. The dining Galleria was designed so that all restaurants take advantage of the endless ocean horizon. ⊠ *2440 Ho'onani Rd., Po'ipū Beach, Kōloa 96756* ☎ *808/742–1661 or 888/488–3535* 🖷 *808/742–9777* ⊕ *www.starwood. com/hawaii* ⊅ *399 rooms, 14 suites* ⌂ *4 restaurants, room service, in-*

room safes, some minibars, refrigerators, cable TV, 3 tennis courts, 2 pools, 2 wading pools, gym, massage, beach, bar, babysitting, children's programs (ages 5–12), laundry facilities, concierge, Internet, meeting rooms ☱ *AE, D, DC, MC, V.*

$$$$ 🖻 **Whalers Cove.** All of the two-bedroom condos face the water and share a swimming pool, which is almost near enough to the surf to cast out a fishing line. The rocky beach is good for snorkeling, and a short drive or brisk walk will get you to a sandy stretch. A handsome koa-bedecked reception area offers services for the plush units. Two barbecue areas, big picture windows, spacious living rooms, lānai, and modern kitchens with washer-dryers make this a home away from home. ☒ *2640 Pu'uholo Rd., Kōloa 96756* ☎ *808/742–7400 or 800/367–8020* 🖷 *808/ 742–9121* ⊕ *www.suiteparadise.com* ⟲ *30 condominiums* ⟁ *Fans, in-room data ports, some kitchens, some kitchenettes, microwave, cable TV with movies, in-room VCRs, pool, hot tub, laundry facilities; no a/c* ☱ *AE, MC, V.*

$$$–$$$$ 🖻 **Makahuena at Po'ipū.** Large, tastefully decorated one-, two- and three-bedroom suites with white tile and sand-color carpets are housed in white wood buildings on well-kept lawns. Each unit has a kitchen and washer and dryer; there is also a small pool and shared barbecue area on the property. Situated close to the center of Po'ipū, on a rocky point over the ocean, the Makahuena is near Shipwreck and Po'ipū beaches. ☒ *1661 Pe'e Rd., Po'ipū 96756* ☎ *808/742–2482 or 800/ 367–5004* 🖷 *808/742–2379* ⊕ *www.castleresorts.com* ⟲ *79 suites* ⟁ *BBQs, fans, in-room VCR, kitchenettes, tennis court, pool, hot tub, free parking; no a/c.* ☱ *AE, MC, V.*

$$–$$$$ 🖻 **Suite Paradise Po'ipū Kai.** Condominiums, many with cathedral ceilings and all with big windows overlooking the lawns, give this property the feeling of a spacious, quiet retreat inside and out. Large furnished lānai have views to the ocean and across the 110-acre grounds. All the condos are furnished with modern kitchens. Some units are two-level; some have sleeping lofts. Three-, four-, and five-bedroom units are also available. A two-night minimum stay is required. Walking paths connect to both Brennecke's and Shipwreck Beaches. ☒ *1941 Po'ipū Rd., Kōloa 96756* ☎ *808/742–6464 or 800/367–8020* 🖷 *808/742–9121* ⊕ *www.suite-paradise.com* ⟲ *130 1- and 2-bedroom condominiums* ⟁ *Restaurant, fans, in-room data ports, in-room safes, kitchens, cable TV, in-room VCRs, 9 tennis courts, 6 pools, hot tub; no a/c in some rooms* ☱ *AE, D, DC, MC, V.*

$$–$$$ 🖻 **Garden Isle Cottages.** Tropical fruit trees and flower gardens surround these spacious oceanside accommodations. Contemporary Hawaiian furnishings include some rattan; the best part of the cottages is the ocean view. All four units have kitchens with microwaves, ceiling fans, and washers and dryers. It's a five-minute walk to the restaurants of nearby Po'ipū. ☒ *2660 Pu'uholo Rd., Kōloa 96756* ☎ *808/742–6717 or 800/ 742–6711* ⊕ *www.oceancottages.com* ⟲ *4 cottages* ⟁ *Fans, kitchens, microwaves, laundry facilities; no a/c* ☱ *No credit cards.*

$$–$$$ 🖻 **Po'ipū Plantation Resort.** Plumeria, ti, and other tropical foliage fill the 1-acre grounds of this resort, which has one B&B–style plantation home and nine one- and two-bedroom cottage apartments. All

cottage units have vaulted ceilings and full kitchens and are decorated in light, airy shades. The 1930s plantation home has three rooms with private baths and one suite. A full complimentary breakfast is served daily for those staying in the main house. A minimum three-night stay is required, but rates decrease with the length of stay. ⊠ *1792 Pe'e Rd., Kōloa 96756* ☎ *808/742–6757 or 800/634–0263* ⊜ *808/742–8681* ⊕ *www.poipubeach.com* ⇲ *3 rooms, 9 cottages* ⚿ *BBQs, fans, kitchens, in-room VCRs, hair salon, hot tub, laundry facilities* ⊟ *D, MC, V* ⊺⊙⊺ *BP.*

$–$$ ⊞ **Kaua'i Cove Cottages.** Three modern studio cottages sit side by side at the mouth of Waikomo Stream, beside an ocean cove that offers super snorkeling. The studios, with complete kitchens, have airy tropical decor under cathedral ceilings. Private patios on the ocean side have their own gas barbecue grills. There is a $25 cleaning fee for stays of fewer than three nights. VCRs are available upon request. ⊠ *2672 Pu'uholo Rd., Po'ipū 96756* ☎ *808/742–2562 or 800/624–9945* ⊕ *www.kauaicove. com* ⇲ *3 cottages* ⚿ *BBQs, fans, kitchens, cable TV, snorkeling, laundry facilities; no a/c* ⊟ *D, MC, V.*

$–$$ ⊞ **Kōloa Landing Cottages.** You'll be treated like family here. Kōloa Landing has five cottages, including a studio that's about a five-minute walk to a swimming beach. The cottages are also across the street from Kōloa Landing, a popular location for diving, snorkeling, and fishing. Accommodations sleep two to eight; all cottages have showers only. Open-beam ceilings and fans keep the interiors cool. Book well in advance. ⊠ *2704-B Ho'onani Rd., Kōloa 96756* ☎ *808/742–1470 or 800/779–8773* ⊕ *www.koloa-landing.com* ⇲ *5 cottages, 2 rooms* ⚿ *BBQs, fans, some kitchens, some kitchenettes, laundry facilities; no a/c* ⊟ *No credit cards.*

The West Side

$$–$$$$ ⊞ **Waimea Plantation Cottages.** Tucked into a coconut grove, these reconstructed oceanfront sugar-plantation cottages, near the stunning Waimea Canyon on the secluded west-end side, make for a laid-back vacation experience. The one- to five-bedroom cottages are rustic but spacious and all have porches. Plantation-era furnishings are updated with modern kitchens and cable TV. Barbecue grills, hammocks, porch swings, a gift shop, a spa, and a museum are on the property. Complimentary wireless Internet access is available in the main building; in-room data ports are available upon advance request. Swimming waters here are sometimes murky, depending on weather conditions. ⊠ *9400 Kaumuali'i Hwy. (Box 367), Waimea 96796* ☎ *808/338–1625 or 800/ 992–4632* ⊜ *808/338–2338* ⊕ *www.waimea-plantation.com* ⇲ *48 cottages* ⚿ *Restaurant, fans, some kitchens, pool, beach, horseshoes, bar, concierge, Internet; no a/c* ⊟ *AE, D, DC, MC, V.*

¢ ⊞ **Kōke'e Lodge.** If you're an outdoor enthusiast, you can appreciate Kaua'i's mountain wilderness from this lodge. Wood-burning stoves in the 12 rustic cabins ward off any chill from the mountain air (wood is a few dollars extra). If you aren't partial to dormitory-style sleeping, request the cabins with two bedrooms; both styles sleep six. The lodge restaurant serves a light breakfast and lunch between 9 and 3:30 daily.

Many locals fill up Kōke'e on the weekend, so make your reservations early. ☒ *3600 Kōke'e Rd., mile marker 15, Kekaha* ✆ *Box 819, Waimea 96796* ☏ *808/335–6061* ⌨ *12 cabins* ♿ *Restaurant, hiking, shops; no a/c, no room phones, no room TVs.* ▭ *D, DC, MC, V.*

NIGHTLIFE & THE ARTS

People on Kaua'i embrace the natural beauty and legends of their island's unique cultural heritage and enjoy sharing their traditions with those who come to call. As a result, on the Garden Isle you will find more traditional Hawaiiana and less glitz than on neighboring O'ahu.

Most of the island's dinner and lū'au shows take place within a hotel or resort. Hotel lounges and restaurant bars offer live music with no cover charge. True to Kaua'i's agricultural roots of "early to bed, early to rise," most evening events around the island, outside of major hotels, wrap up by 9 PM.

Check the local newspaper, the *Garden Island Times,* for listings of weekly happenings. Free publications such as *Kaua'i Gold, This Week on Kaua'i,* and *Kaua'i Beach Press* also list entertainment events. You can pick them up at the Kaua'i Visitors Bureau and at Līhu'e Airport at kiosks located by the baggage claim area.

Bars & Clubs

Nightclubs that stay open to the wee hours are rare on Kaua'i, and the bar scene is pretty limited. The major resorts generally host their own live entertainment and happy hours. All bars and clubs that serve alcohol must close at 2 AM, except those with a cabaret license, which allows them to close at 4 AM.

Duke's Barefoot Bar. Contemporary Hawaiian music is performed in the beachside bar on Thursday and Friday, and upstairs a traditional Hawaiian trio plays nightly for diners, making this bar one of the liveliest on Kalapakī Beach. The bar closes at 11 most nights. ☒ *Kalapakī Beach, Līhu'e* ☏ *808/246–9599.*

Hanalei Gourmet. The sleepy North Shore stays awake—until 10:30, that is—each evening in this small, convivial setting inside Hanalei's restored old school building. The emphasis here is on local live jazz, rock, and folk music. ☒ *5-5161 Kūhiō Hwy., Hanalei Center, Hanalei* ☏ *808/826–2524.*

Happy Talk Lounge. Hawaiian entertainment takes center stage Monday through Saturday evenings in this lounge at the Hanalei Bay Resort. Come Sunday, this joint is swinging to the sounds of jazz in jam sessions that run from 3 to 7 PM. ☒ *5380 Honoiki Rd., Princeville* ☏ *808/826–6522.*

Rob's Good Times Grill. Let loose at this sports bar which also houses Kaua'i's hottest DJs spinning Thursday through Saturday from 9 PM to 2 AM. Wednesday you can kick up your heels with country line dancing from 7:30 PM to midnight. Sunday, Monday and Tuesday evenings are open mic for karaoke enthusiasts. ☒ *4303 Rice St., Līhu'e* ☏ *808/246–0311.*

Tropics. A sports bar on the weekends, this funky hangout presents live island-style music several nights a week. It closes at 11 PM. ⊠ *4-1330 Kūhiō Hwy., at Kauwila St., Kapa'a* ☎ *808/822–7330.*

Lū'au

Drums of Paradise Lū'au. More than music and dance, the Hyatt lū'au displays Hawaiian artwork and includes the dances of Polynesia, the traditional fire dance, and a contemporary menu to suit all tastes. ⊠ *Hyatt Regency Kaua'i Resort and Spa, 1571 Po'ipū Rd., Po'ipū Beach* ☎ *808/742–1234* ⌨ *$65* ☉ *Thurs. and Sun. 6–8:30.*

Kaua'i Aloha Lū'au. Performers from the celebrated "Rohotu" dance company take the stage at these lū'au festivities held each Monday evening on the grounds of the Radisson Kau'i Beach Resort. ⊠ *4331 Kau'ai Beach Dr., Līhu'e* ☎ *808/335–5828* ⌨ *$60* ☉ *Mon. 5:15–8:30.*

Kaua'i Coconut Beach Resort Lū'au. The evening begins with a traditional *imu* (underground oven) ceremony. After dark, Polynesian culture comes to life on a musical voyage of discovery. Traditional dances, including the Samoan fire dance, tell the stories of the islands from Tahiti to the Hawaiian Isles. ⊠ *Coconut Plantation, Kūhiō Hwy., Kapa'a* ☎ *808/822–3455 Ext. 651* ⌨ *$57* ☉ *Mon.–Sat. 6–9.*

Lū'au Kilohana. This lū'au—on an old sugar plantation, with 35-acre grounds, gardens, workers' homes, and a 16,000-square-foot Tudor mansion—has a kick: all guests arrive at the feast by horse-drawn carriage (reservations are staggered to prevent lines). Families especially seem to enjoy the food and fun here. The evening's theme is the history of sugar on the Islands. ⊠ *3-2087 Kaumuali'i St., Līhu'e* ☎ *808/245–9593* ⌨ *$61* ☉ *Tues. and Thurs. wagon rides begin at 5:15, dinner at 6, show at 6:30.*

Pa'ina o Hanalei. The blowing of the conch calls revelers to the beach at Hanalei Bay for a gourmet lū'au feast. Entertainment includes a celebration of the songs and dances of the islands of the South Pacific. ⊠ *Princeville Resort, 5520 Ka Haku Rd.* ☎ *808/826–2788* ⌨ *$68* ☉ *Mon. and Thurs. at 6.*

Smith's Tropical Paradise Lū'au. Amid 30 acres of tropical flora and fauna, this lū'au begins with the traditional blowing of the conch shell and imu ceremony, followed by cocktails, an island feast, and an international show in the amphitheater overlooking a torch-lighted lagoon. ⊠ *174 Wailua Rd., Kapa'a* ☎ *808/821–6895* ⌨ *$58* ☉ *Mon., Wed., and Fri. 6–9:15.*

Tahiti Nui Lū'au. This venerable institution in sleepy Hanalei is a welcome change from the standard commercial lū'au. It's intimate (about 40 guests), casual, and put on by an Island family that really knows how to throw a party. The all-you-can-eat buffet includes kālua pig that has been slow-roasted in an imu, and the show has plenty of dancing, music, and laughs. ⊠ *Kūhiō Hwy., Hanalei* ☎ *808/826–6277* ⌨ *$62* ☉ *Wed. at 5.*

Music

Check the local papers for outdoor reggae and Hawaiian-music shows, or one of the numbers listed below for more formal performances.

Kaua'i Community College Performing Arts Center (✉ 3-1901 Kaumuali'i Hwy., Līhu'e ☎ 808/245–8270) provides a venue for Hawaiian music and dance as well as visiting performers. **Kaua'i Concert Association** (✉ 3-1901 Kaumuali'i Hwy., Līhu'e ☎ 808/245–7464) offers a seasonal program at the arts center. The **Līhu'e Public Library** (✉ 4344 Hardy St., Līhu'e ☎ 808/241–3222) sometimes plays host to storytelling, music, and arts-and-crafts events.

Film & Theater

The **Kaua'i Community Players** (✉ Līhu'e Parish Hall, 4340 Nāwiliwili Rd., Līhu'e ☎ 808/245–7700) is a talented local group that presents plays throughout the year.

Kaua'i Village Theatre (✉ Kaua'i Village Shopping Center, 4831 Kūhiō Hwy., Kapa'a ☎ 808/823–6789) presents six shows per season plus concerts and feature films in a 62-seat, air-conditioned theater.

The tiny **Kīlauea Theater and Community Event Center** (✉ 2490 Keneke St., Kīlauea ☎ 808/828–0438) is the site of north-shore live concert events, first-run movies, and art films.

SPORTS & THE OUTDOORS

Biking

Kaua'i Adventure Trek. This 4½-hour bike, hike, and beach adventure follows an old cane road through Grove Farm Plantation, stops for a tour of the island's first sugar mill, then heads for Māhā'ulepū Beach, where a picnic lunch is served. Trips are geared to novice and intermediate-level bikers. This is one of the few bike companies to furnish electric bikes for riders who prefer to take the easy way. Vans carry bikers back to Kilohana Plantation, which has upscale shops and Gaylord's restaurant. ✉ *3-2087 Kaumuali'i Hwy., Līhu'e 96766 ☎ 808/245–3440 or 808/635–8735 ⊕ www.kauaiadventuretrek.com.*

Outfitters Kaua'i. Ride right out the door to tour Po'ipū on a rented bike or get information on how to do a self-guided tour of Kōke'e State Park and Waimea Canyon. The company also leads sunrise coasting tours (under the name Canyon to Coast) from Waimea Canyon (100 percent downhill and a 12-mi trek) to the island's west-side beaches. Rentals cost between $20 and $40. ✉ *2827-A Po'ipū Rd., Po'ipū 96756 ☎ 808/742–9667or 888/742–9887 ⊕ www. outfitterskauai.com.*

Pedal 'n' Paddle. This company rents single-speed beach cruisers, tandem, and mountain bicycles for $10–$20 a day. Motorized scooter rentals can be found here for those with a valid driver's license. Hourly and weekly rates are available. ✉ *Ching Young Village, 5-5190 Kūhiō Hwy., Hanalei ☎ 808/826–9069 ⊕ www.pedalnpaddle.com.*

CloseUp

THE FORBIDDEN ISLE

SEVENTEEN MILES *and a world away from Kaua'i across the Kaulakahi Channel sits one of the most Hawaiian islands of all, the* privately owned Ni'ihau. It's commonly called the "Forbidden Isle," because access is limited to the 200 residents who live and work here and their guests.

Ni'ihau was bought from King Kamehameha in 1864 by a Scottish widow, Eliza Sinclair, who was looking for a quiet place to raise her family. Sinclair was introduced to the island after an unusually wet winter; she saw nothing but green pastures and thought it would be an ideal place to raise cattle. The cost was $10,000. It was a real deal, or so Sinclair thought.

Unfortunately, Ni'ihau's usual rainfall is about 12 inches a year, and the land soon returned to its normal desertlike state. Regardless, Sinclair did not abandon her venture and today the island and ranching operation are owned by Bruce Robinson, Eliza Sinclair's great-great-grandson. What makes this island so unique is that here, the traditions of ancient Hawai'i are still observed. The 200 residents speak Hawaiian, and there is no indoor plumbing or electricity. Bikes and horses are the preferred modes of transportation. Everyone who lives on the island works on the ranch and lives in the single town of Pu'uwai.

Although visits to the island are still restricted, the Robinson family operates Ni'ihau Helicopter flightseeing tours.

Bruce Robinson started the tours in 1984 in order to supplement the cost of medical evacuation via helicopter for residents. Tours avoid the western coastline, especially the village of Pu'uwai, where the island's 200 residents live. Flights depart from and return to Kaumakani. There's a four-passenger minimum for each flight, and reservations are essential. Ground transportation is not available. A picnic lunch on a secluded Ni'ihau beach is included along with time for swimming, beachcombing, and snorkeling along the island's pristine shoreline. The half-day tour is $280 per person.

For more information contact: **Ni'ihau Tours** ✉ *Ni'ihau Helicopters, Box 690370, Makaweli 96769* ☎ *808/335–3500 or 877/441–3500* ⊕ *www.niihau.us*

MOUNTAIN BIKING	The 12-mi Power Line Trail, which begins in the mountains above Wailua in Keāhua Forestry Arboretum and ends mauka of Princeville Resort, is a challenge even for the seasoned biker. It's a muddy, difficult ride, but you have views of Wai'ale'ale that are usually seen only from the air. Be sure your mountain bike is in top condition, take plenty of water and energy bars, and let someone know when and where you are

going. If you rent a mountain bike, explain what you've got in mind and heed any advice offered by the experts.

Fitness & Spa Centers

Alexander Day Spa at the Kaua'i Marriott. This sister spa of Alexander Simson's Beverly Hills spa offers body treatments utilizing the Epicuren Discovery skin-care line, including a Kaua'i honey mask facial and a green-tea-and-ginger sea-enzyme body wrap. The spa also provides facials, salon services, beachside massage, and wedding-day and custom spa packages. ⊠ *Kaua'i Marriott Resort & Beach Club, 3610 Rice St., Lihu'e* ☎ *808/246–4918* ⊕ *www.alexanderspa.com.*

Anara Spa. Twenty-five thousand square feet of luxurious pampering await you at this spa and fitness facility. Indulge in Anara's signature coco mango facial or brush body treatment featuring ground coffee, orange peel, and vanilla bean. An open-air lava rock shower, hot tub, and a fitness center which features massage, yoga, and fitness training complete the setting. Spa cuisine is available for breakfast and lunch at Kupono Café next door. ⊠ *Hyatt Regency Kaua'i Resort and Spa, 1571 Po'ipū Rd., Po'ipū* ☎ *808/742–1234* ⊕ *www.anaraspa.com.*

Yoga Hanalei. More than 20 classes are offered weekly in Ashtanga, Bikram, and Hatha yoga in this second-story studio overlooking Hanalei's waterfalls and taro patches. Begin your day with sunrise yoga or refresh yourself with an evening meditation class. The studio also houses a boutique and can arrange customized yoga retreat vacation packages. ⊠ *Hanalei Center, 5-5161 Kūhiō Hwy. Hanalei* ☎ *808/826–9642* ⊕ *www.yogahanalei.com.*

Kaua'i Athletic Club. This centrally located facility offers a $15 day pass that grants you access to wet-dry saunas, handball, racquetball, aerobics classes, swimming, cardio-fitness instruction, and a hot tub. ⊠ *4370 Kukui Grove, Lihu'e* ☎ *808/245–5381.*

Princeville Health Club & Spa. State-of-the-art workout equipment, saunas, and hot tubs are surrounded by inspiring views of mountains, sea, and sky; a day pass is $20. The King's facial tends to the special skin-care needs of men while the massage "sampler" is an introduction to a blend of massage techniques. Body treatments include a body polish with aromatherapy wrap. A round of golf at a Princeville course entitles you to a complimentary admission to the spa. ⊠ *Princeville Resort, 53-900 Kūhiō Hwy., Princeville* ☎ *808/826–5030* ⊕ *www.princeville.com.*

Golf

Greens fees vary according to season, time of day, whether you're a Hawai'i resident, and whether you are a guest of a particular hotel. Playing in the afternoon and staying at a partner hotel can save you a bundle of money—up to 60 percent.

Kaua'i Lagoons Golf Club. Two Jack Nicklaus–designed, par-72 courses adjoin the Kaua'i Marriott Resort & Beach Club. The championship Kiele course challenges golfers of all levels. The links-style Mokihana's greens hug the magnificent ocean cliffs. Forty acres of tropical lagoons provide breathtaking views. A shared cart and the same-day use of the practice facility are included. Golf instruction, daily clinics, and equipment rentals are also available. ⊠ *3351 Ho'olaulea Way, Līhu'e* ☎ *808/ 241–6000* ⊕ *www.kauailagoonsgolf.com* ⊠ *Greens fee $170 for Kiele, $120 for Mokihana.*

Kiahuna Plantation Golf Club. On the southern side of the island is this Robert Trent Jones Jr.–designed 18-hole course. This course could be the longest short course you've ever had the pleasure to play on. It includes unique archaeological features like a Hawaiian heiau, a lava-tube entrance, a crypt, and an ancient pigpen—as well as the usual water hazards, 68 bunkers, and the challenge of playing to prevailing tradewinds. There are equipment rentals, a driving range, pro shop, restaurant, and bar. A shared cart is included in the greens fee. At press time, a $3 million renovation was underway. ⊠ *2545 Kiahuna Plantation Dr., Po'ipū* ☎ *808/742–9595* ⊠ *Greens fee $75.*

Kukuiolono Golf Course. You can play 9 holes or a full round here on a peaceful wooded hilltop setting with spectacular views of Kaua'i's eastern shore. A cart is $6 for 9 holes; club rental is $6. ⊠ *854 Pu'u Rd., Kalāheo* ☎ *808/332–9151* ⊠ *Greens fee $7.*

Po'ipū Bay Resort Golf Course. This 18-hole links-style course has been the site of the PGA Grand Slam for almost a decade. It's next to the Hyatt Regency Kaua'i, and many of the distractions on this course come not only from its Robert Trent Jones Jr. design, but also from its naturally inspiring location on Po'ipū Bay. Amenities like in-cart satellite navigation systems, on-course beverage carts and cold "refresh" towels are included in this golf experience. A shared cart is included in the price. ⊠ *2250 'Ainakō St., Po'ipū Beach* ☎ *808/742–8711 or 800/858–6300* ⊕ *www.kauai-hyatt.com/golf.html* ⊠ *Greens fee $125 Hyatt Regency guests, $185 nonguests.*

Princeville Resort Makai Course. This is Kaua'i's best-known golf facility. The Makai Course, designed by Robert Trent Jones Jr. features an ocean 9, lakes 9, and woods 9 that combine the best of human ingenuity with Princeville's natural beauty. The facility includes a pro shop, driving range, practice area, lessons, club rental and storage, tennis facilities, and a snack bar. ⊠ *Off Rte. 56, at Princeville Resort, 5520 Ka Haku Rd., Princeville* ☎ *808/826–2727* ⊕ *www.princeville.com* ⊠ *Greens fee $110 Princeville guests, $125 nonguests.*

Princeville Resort Prince Course. Spectacular ocean and mountain views are some of the delights at this 18-hole, Robert Trent Jones Jr.–designed course. It is also rated Kaua'i's toughest course, with a USGA course rating of 75.3 and a 145 slope. A restaurant and bar are open for breakfast and lunch. A shared cart, a pass to the Princeville Spa, and use of the driving range are included in the fee. ⊠ *Off Rte. 56, at Princeville Resort, 5520 Ka Haku Rd., Princeville* ☎ *808/826–2727* ⊕ *www. princeville.com* ⊠ *Greens fee $125 Princeville guests, $175 nonguests.*

Puakea Golf Course. Developed on the lush lands of the former Grove Farm Homestead sugar plantation, Kaua'i's youngest course is a challenging 18-hole beauty by golf architect Robin Nelson. Puakea also offers food and beverage services, a pro shop, a natural-grass practice facility, and lessons. A cart is included in the greens fee. ⊠ *4150 Nohou Rd., Līhu'e* ☎ *808/245–8756 or 886/773–5554* ⊕ *www.puakeagolf.com* ☜ *Greens fee $125.*

Wailua Municipal Golf Course. This municipal course sits next to the Wailua River and beach and has a pro shop, driving range, instruction, and restaurant. Its 18 holes have hosted national tournaments, and golfers here play to undulating fairways and the sounds of the ocean, which borders four of the greens. Carts cost $14. ⊠ *3-5351 Kūhiō Hwy., Wailua* ☎ *808/241–6666* ☜ *Greens fee $25 weekdays, $35 weekends.*

Helicopter Tours

From the air, the Garden Isle blossoms with views you cannot see by land, foot, or sea. In an hour you can see waterfalls, craters, and places that are inaccessible even by hiking trails. If you plan to take a helicopter tour, it's a good idea to take it when you first arrive, rather than saving it for the end of your trip. It will help you visualize what's where on the island and it may help you decide what you want to see from a closer point of view during your stay.

Expect to pay $195 or more per person for the longest, most comprehensive tours, but call around for itineraries. A shorter, less-expensive flight might suit your needs. Don't be afraid to ask about the pilot's experience and safety record. Most, but not all, companies use top-of-the-line equipment, and the operators listed below have reliable flight experience. There are 20 companies flying on Kaua'i, so if you don't like what you see, keep looking. Ask about special discounts sometimes available with coupons from free visitors' pamphlets. For both safety and comfort, single passengers weighing 250 pounds or more, or couples with a combined weight of 450 pounds or more, are required to purchase an additional seat.

Air Kaua'i (⊠ 3651 Ahukini Rd., Līhu'e 96766 ☎ 808/246–4666 or 800/972–4666 ⊕ www.airkauai.com) has A-Star choppers with all-glass doors for amazing views.

Island Helicopters (⊠ Līhu'e Airport, Līhu'e 96766 ☎ 808/245–8588 or 800/829–5999 ⊕ www.islandhelicopters.com) operates 60-minute tours out of the Līhu'e Airport. A free video of your tour is included in the price.

Jack Harter Helicopters (⊠ 4231 Ahukini Rd., Līhu'e 96766 ☎ 808/245–3774 or 888/245–2001 ⊕ www.helicopters-kauai.com) is the originator of heli-tours on Kaua'i. In the air since the early 1960s, it has an outstanding safety record and a modern fleet and offers both 60- and 90-minute air tours.

South Sea Tour Co. (✉ 4480 Ahukini Rd., Suite 204, Līhu'e 96766 ☎ 808/245–2222 or 800/367–2914 ⊕ www.southseashelicopters.com) has a choice of tours available from Līhu'e.

Will Squyres Helicopter Tours (✉ 3222 Kūhiō Hwy., Līhu'e 96766 ☎ 808/245–8881 or 888/245–4354 ⊕ www.helicopters-hawaii.com) offers group rates and charters from Līhu'e Airport.

Hiking & Camping

For your safety, wear sturdy shoes, bring plenty of water, never hike alone, stay on the trail, and avoid hiking when it's wet and slippery. All hiking trails on Kaua'i are free.

Before planning any hike or camping trip on Kaua'i, contact the **Department of Land and Natural Resources** for information on trail conditions and camping permits. ✉ *State Parks Division, 3060 'Eiwa St., Room 306, Līhu'e 96766 ☎ 808/274–3445.*

Kalalau Trail. Kaua'i's prize hike begins at the western end of Route 56 and proceeds 11 mi to Kalalau Beach. With hairpin turns, sometimes very muddy conditions, and constant ups and downs, this hike is a true test of endurance and can't be tackled round-trip in one day. For a good taste of it, hike the first 2 mi to Hanakāpī'ai Beach. For the best trail and weather conditions, hike Kalalau between May and September.

If you plan to hike beyond Hanakāpī'ai Beach to Kalalau, a camping permit must be obtained from the Department of Land and Natural Resources. Permits must also be obtained to camp at Miloli'i, Kōke'e, and Polihale. Permits, which are issued for five nights maximum, are free and can be requested up to a year in advance. There is a $10 charge for campsites along the Kalalau Trail, $5 for other locations. ✉ *Western end of Rte. 56 ☎ No phone.*

Kōke'e State Park. The park contains a 45-mi network of hiking trails of varying difficulty that take you through acres of native forests, home to many rare species of birds. The Kukui Trail leads down the side of Waimea Canyon. Awa'awapuhi Trail descends 4 mi to a spectacular overlook into the canyons of the North Shore. Pleasant, shaded campsites can be reserved through the Parks Department. All hikers should register at Kōke'e Park headquarters, which offers trail maps and information. Camping permits from the land department are $5 per night. Seasonal plum picking and trout fishing is available. ✉ *Kōke'e Rd., 20 mi north of Hwy. 50, Kekaha ☎ 808/335–6061 for Kōke'e Lodge, 808/274–3445 for camping permits.*

Polihale Beach Park. Tent camping is permitted here, at the westernmost beach in the United States. Three sets of numbered campsites have rest rooms, outdoor showers, picnic shelters, and barbecues. Swimming can be dangerous when the waves are rough. Permits are $5 per night. ✉ *Drive to end of Rte. 50 and turn left at Hawaiian-warrior marker onto dirt road, which leads several mi through sugarcane fields; turn left at small national park sign ☎ 808/274–3446.*

Waimea Canyon State Park. Four tent campsites are hidden along the Kukui Trail, on the floor of Waimea Canyon near the Waimea River. The Kukui trailhead is along Waimea Canyon Road. You may want to hike beyond the first campsite to Lonomea Camp, about 6 mi in, where there are pit toilets, roofed shelters, and a picnic table. Near Hipalau Camp are two waterfall-fed pools worth hiking to even if you don't camp at the site. There's no fee to camp in Waimea. Group cabin rates are $50 per night. ⊠ *Drive 7½ mi north on Waimea Canyon Rd., then hike approximately 6 mi on Kukui Trail* ☎ *808/274–3433.*

Horseback Riding

Exploring by horseback is a great way to get an up-close look at rolling green pastures, sandy shorelines, and the hidden spots of Kaua'i. Escorted rides often provide meals or a snack and guides who are full of local lore.

CJM Country Stables. This company in Kōloa, on the South Shore, charges $75 to $95 for each of three guided rides: a 2-hour ranch ride with ocean scenery, a 3-hour hidden-valley beach breakfast ride, and a 3½-hour swim and picnic ride. Children age seven and older are permitted to ride, and two weekends a month, CJM sponsors rodeo events that are free and open to the public. ⊠ *1731 Kekaukia St., 1½ mi from Hyatt Regency Kaua'i Resort and Spa at east end of Po'ipū Rd., Kōloa* ☎ *808/742–6096* ⊕ *www.cjmstables.*

Esprit de Corps. In Kapa'a, Esprit de Corps offers private lessons, pony parties for children, and half-day horse camps, as well as trail rides that range from three-hour jaunts at sunrise for $112 to eight-hour island excursions for $350 that include lunch. The six-hour spiritual exploration ride includes stops for guided meditations. Group trail rides require some experience, as they allow trotting and cantering. Weddings on horseback can be arranged, and custom rides for less-experienced riders are available. ⊠ *Wailua Homesteads, end of Kualapa Pl., Kapa'a* ☎ *808/822–4688* ⊕ *www.kauaihorses.com.*

Princeville Ranch Stables. Guided horseback tours from this very professional operation take riders into the less-explored northern reaches of the island. A 90-minute country ride is $65 per person. A three- or four-hour waterfall picnic ride is $125 to $170, including lunch. Join a 90-minute cattle-drive ride with Princeville's working paniolo for $120. Individual tours and riding times are available. ⊠ *5-4430 Kūhiō Hwy., Princeville* ☎ *808/826–6777* ⊕ *www.princevilleranch.com.*

Silver Falls Ranch. You can take a private lesson at this Kīlauea ranch, join a two-hour Hawaiian Discovery ride with refreshments ($80), or try a three-hour Silver Falls ride ($110) that includes picnicking by a waterfall and a swim in a secluded freshwater pool. ⊠ *2818 Kamookoa Rd., Kīlauea* ☎ *808/828–6718* ⊕ *www.sfrkauai.com.*

Tennis

Kaua'i has 20 lighted public tennis courts and more than 70 private courts at hotels and resorts.

Hanalei Bay Resort. Nonguests pay $8 per hour to play at Hanalei Bay; there are eight courts and a pro shop. ⊠ *5380 Honoiki Rd., Princeville* ☎ *808/826–6522.*

Hyatt Regency Kaua'i Resort and Spa. The Hyatt has four courts, a pro shop, and a tennis pro. The cost is $20 per hour. ⊠ *1571 Po'ipū Rd., Po'ipū Beach* ☎ *808/742–1234.*

Kaua'i Coconut Beach Resort. Guests play for free and nonguests pay $10 to use the three courts at this resort. ⊠ *Coconut Plantation, Kūhiō Hwy., Kapa'a* ☎ *808/822–3455.*

Kiahuna Swim and Tennis Club. Ten newly paved tennis courts, a pro shop, swimming pool, jet spa, and outdoor café make up this facility across the street from Kaihuna Plantation. The hourly court fee is $10. ⊠ *Kiahuna Plantation Po'ipū* ☎ *808/742–9533.*

Princeville Tennis Center. The six courts here cost $12 for resort guests and $15 for nonguests for 90 minutes (you can extend your play as long as the courts are not in demand). Weekly rates and tennis lessons are available. A full-service pro shop is on-site. ⊠ *4080 Lei-o-papa Rd., Princeville* ☎ *808/826–1230.*

The Tennis Club at the Kaua'i Lagoons. The island's only tennis stadium is here, as well as seven courts for mere mortals. An hour of court time costs $20. Private lessons, lessons for two, and a daily clinic are available. ⊠ *3351 Ho'olaulea Way, Līhu'e* ☎ *808/244-3323.*

Water Sports

FISHING   Kaua'i waters are home to marlin, tuna, and mahimahi, with many charter boats berthed at Nāwiliwili Harbor. No matter which company you choose for ocean fishing, plan to spend $135 to $165 for almost a full day of charter fishing on a shared basis, $100 on up for a half day on a shared basis, and $495 to $1,500 for exclusive charters ranging from half-day excursions to 10-hour trips fishing off Ni'ihau.

For freshwater fishing, head for the bass- and trout-filled streams near Kōke'e and Waimea Canyon. A seven-day visitor license for $10 or a 30-day license for $20 must be obtained from the **Department of Land and Natural Resources–Division of Aquatic Resources,** any fishing supply store, or online from the Web address listed below. ⊠ *3060 'Eiwa St., Līhu'e 96766* ☎ *808/274–3344* ⊕ *www.ehawaiigov.org/fish/exe/fish/cgi.*

'Anini Fishing Charters. Skipper Bob Kutkowski completed his 33-foot sport cruiser, *Sea Breeze V,* himself for sport- or bottom-fishing charters, as well as Nā Pali Coast tours. The boat launches from Princeville. ✉ *Box 594, Kīlauea 96754* ☎ *808/828–1285.*

Sportfishing Kaua'i. This outfitter runs 33-foot and 38-foot six-passenger custom sportfishers for shared or private charters for half-, three-quarter-, or full-day trips. ✉ *Box 1195, Kōloa 96756* ☎ *808/639–0013* ⊕ *www.fishing-kauai-hawaii.com.*

True Blue. True Blue offers charters on a roomy 55-foot Delta, the *Konane Star,* which features some of the luxuries of home, like a microwave oven, television, and hot and cold running showers. This vessel is certified to carry 32, but fishing trips are limited to 10 anglers. ⊠ *Nāwiliwili Harbor entrance, Slip 112* 🕭 *Box 1722, Kalapakī Beach, Līhu'e 96766* 🕿 *808/246–6333* ⊕ *www.truebluecharters.com.*

KAYAKING
Fodor'sChoice
★

Guided kayak trips are ideal for novices; renting a kayak for ocean journeys is more popular with experienced paddlers. Rentals include roof padding and straps for your car. Be sure to inquire with an outfitter about weather conditions and trips suitable for your ability. Nā Pali trips are for experienced, seaworthy paddlers only, unless accompanied by a knowledgeable guide.

Aloha Canoes and Kayaks. This Hawaiian-owned and -operated company offers guided Hawaiian double-hull canoe and kayak trips, with guides whose families have lived here for generations. Adventures lasting 3½ hours take you up the Wailua River to a mountain pool, including lunch. One tour combines helicopter sightseeing, a kayak trip up the Hulē'ia River, and a hike through tropical forestland on Kipu Ranch. For the extreme enthusiast, there is a six-hour open ocean kayak, snorkel, and swim package. Tours range from $60 to $199, depending on the activity. ⊠ *3366 Wa'apa Rd., Suite 106, Līhu'e 96766* 🕿 *808/ 246–6804 or 877/473–5446* ⊕ *www.hawaiikayaks.com.*

Island Adventures. These one-way, guided kayak trips up the Hulē'ia River lead to the heart of a national wildlife refuge and Papakolea Falls, which is only accessible by this river trip. The 2½-hour excursion ($59) includes a snack and ends with a hike and van transportation back to civilization. ⊠ *Take Hwy. 58 to Wilcox St. Continue past main pier to opening of Nāwiliwili Small Boat Harbor* 🕭 *Box 3370, Līhu'e 96766* 🕿 *808/245–9662* ⊕ *www.kauaibykayak.com.*

Kayak Kaua'i. In addition to renting kayaks, this outfit also offers professionally guided half- and full-day tours along the Nā Pali Coast and up the Hanalei and Wailua rivers. Snorkeling is included in the Hanalei excursion. These guys are the favored choice for *National Geographic* excursions. One-day tours range from $60 to $175; six-night, seven-day packages are $1,750, including accommodations, transportation, boats, and meals. They also rent camping equipment, surfboards, bicycles, canoes, and kayaks. It's the third building to your right as you enter Hanalei, 1 mi west of the Hanalei Bridge. 🕭 *Box 508, Hanalei 96714* 🕿 *808/826–9844 or 800/437–3507* ⊕ *www. kayakkauai.com.*

Outfitters Kaua'i. This company runs guided kayak excursions for novices as well as longer Nā Pali Coast and jungle-stream paddles. If you're an experienced paddler, you can rent a kayak, grab a plastic-coated map, and discover a romantic waterfall on your own. For a family adventure, consider the Kipu Falls Safari ($119), which includes a short kayak trip up a jungle stream, a ¾-mi hike, a covered-wagon ride, a picnic at a swimming hole with a waterfall, and a double-hull canoe ride back to civilization. Other guided tours range from $80 to $165, and kayak rentals cost $30 to $65. ⊠ *2827-A Po'ipū Rd., Po'ipū 96756* ☎ *808/742–9667 or 888/742–9887* ⊕ *www.outfitterskauai.com.*

Paradise Outdoor Adventures. Paradise provides topographical maps, powerboat and kayak rentals, and guided excursions. A half-day guided Wailua Jungle-River Safari includes a hike to a waterfall and lunch for $85. Tour vessels range from one-person kayaks to six-person Boston Whaler powerboats. A two-person kayak costs $50 per day. ⊠ *1-561 Kūhiō Hwy., Kapa'a 96746* ☎ *808/822–1112 or 877/422–6287* ⊕ *www. kayakers.com.*

Wailua Kayak Adventures. Rent a kayak that holds two adults and two small children, bring your own picnic lunch, and follow the map to your own adventure. It's the most convenient place to get a kayak for use on the river. These folks also specialize in guided tours to Wailua's Secret Falls. A guided tour is $85; kayak rentals are $25 to $50. ⊠ *411 Kaholalele St., Kūhiō Hwy., Kapa'a 96746* ☎ *808/822–5795.*

SCUBA DIVING **Dive Kaua'i Scuba Center.** Introductory, half-day scuba excursions are $98 at Dive Kaua'i. Two-tank shore dives for certified divers cost $135, a refresher course is $89, and a three- to five-day PADI (scuba-diving certification) course is $425. A boat dive with two tanks costs $100, including equipment. Excursions to dive locations on each of Kaua'i's coastlines are available. ⊠ *1038 Kūhiō Hwy., Kapa'a 96746* ☎ *808/822–0452 or 800/828–3483* ⊕ *www.divekauai.com.*

Seasport Divers. This full-service PADI, NAUI, and SSI training facility's dive options range from daily shore dives to dives off Ni'ihau, from beginner lessons and introductory dives to private charters. It also offers equipment rental and repair service, as well as SASY (Supplied Air Snorkeling for Youths) programs for children ages five and older. ⊠ *2827 Po'ipū Rd., Kōloa 96756* ☎ *808/742–9303 or 800/685–5889* ⊕ *www. kauaiscubadiving.com.*

SNORKELING & WHALE- WATCHING Snorkeling cruises run along the South Shore and Nā Pali Coast. Most trips depart from Port Allen. Whale-watching is possible during the winter months, and curious dolphins are a regular sight. Inquire about sunset and dinner cruises as well.

Captain Andy's Sailing Adventures. Captain Andy's can accommodate up to 49 passengers on its 55-foot catamaran *Spirit of Kaua'i*; cruises depart from Port Allen and Kukui'ula Harbor in Po'ipū. The rate for the four-hour morning snorkel-picnic tour is $109, including gear and lunch. Whale-watching excursions run during the winter months. Seasonal Nā Pali Coast tours are offered that include Continental breakfast, lunch, snorkeling gear, and instruction for $109—or try the $59 afternoon Nā Pali sunset snorkel excursion that includes snack and buffet. ⊠ *'Ele'ele Shopping Center, 4469 Waialo Rd., 'Ele'ele* ☎ *808/335–6833 or 800/535–0830* ⊕ *www.sailing-hawaii.com.*

Catamaran Kahanu. This Hawaiian-owned and -operated company has been in business since 1985. It offers a 4½-hour Nā Pali Coast cruise on a 36-foot power catamaran. The trip includes snorkeling, whale- or dolphin-watching, buffet lunch, and a bit of Hawaiian history and culture. The price is $105 for adults, and cruises depart from Port Allen. ⊠ *43 Waialo Rd., 'Ele'ele* ☎ *808/335–3577 or 888/213-7711* ⊕ *www.catamarankahanu.com.*

Hanalei Watersports. You can take scuba and surfing lessons in addition to guided kayak and snorkel tours. Accommodating guides can craft a full day's land-and-sea adventure to suit your whims. There's also an idyllic $85 sunset cruise from the Princeville Resort aboard a Hawaiian outrigger canoe equipped with a traditional sail and a paddling canoe. Prices run the gamut. ⊠ *Princeville Resort, 5520 Ka Hoku Rd., Princeville* ☎ *808/826–7509.*

HoloHolo Charters. A deluxe snorkel cruise with this charter takes in the majesty of the Nā Pali Coast and anchors off the private island of Ni'ihau. Continental breakfast and a deluxe lunch buffet are served on the 61-foot power catamaran during the seven-hour excursion. Wine, beer, soda, and juice are included in the $156 fee. Three other shorter (and less expensive) excursions are offered on the 48-foot sailing catamaran *Leila* and the 61-foot high-speed Power Cat *HoloHolo*. Complimentary shuttle transportation is offered from many hotel locations. ⊠ *'Ele'ele Shopping Center, Rte. 541 at Waialo Rd., 'Ele'ele* ☎ *808/335–0815 or 800/848–6130* ⊕ *www.holoholocharters.com.*

Kaua'i Sea Tours. During the winter Kaua'i Sea Tours runs marine-ecology whale-watching tours; it also has year-round snorkeling tours on Power Cats and rigid-hull inflatable rafts. Narrated sightseeing trips range from $89 to $140 and take from two hours to a full day. Longer cruises include snorkeling gear, Continental breakfast, lunch, and cold drinks. ⊠ *4610 Waialo Rd., 'Ele'ele* ☎ *808/826–7254 or 800/733–7997* ⊕ *www.kauaiseatours.com.*

SURFING & WINDSURFING Just about any of the outfitters who handle kayaking and snorkeling also arrange surfing and windsurfing lessons and excursions. Below is one of the real specialists.

Margo Oberg Surfing School. Seven-time world surfing champion Margo Oberg furnishes surfboards, and she and her staff give dry-land and wave instruction to beginning surfers. Lessons are $48 for 1½ hours. The surf shop is next to Brennecke's Beach Broiler, between Kiahuna Plantation and the Sheraton Kaua'i. ⊠ *Nukumoi Surf Shop, Po'ipū Beach* ☎ *808/332–6100 or 888/742–6924.*

SHOPPING

Along with one major shopping mall, Kaua'i has some really delightful mom-and-pop shops and family-run boutiques with loads of character.

Kaua'i also offers one-of-a-kind options for souvenirs. For instance, the famous shell jewelry from nearby Ni'ihau is sometimes sold on Kaua'i for less than it is on other islands. For such a small island, there is an abundance of art galleries that showcase the creative works of the many artisans who live here. The Garden Isle is also known for its regular outdoor markets where you can find bargain prices on various souvenirs and produce and get a chance to mingle with island residents.

A few mainland-style discount and department stores reached Kaua'i years ago, carrying an all-inclusive selection of moderately priced merchandise. Kaua'i's shopping centers are open daily from 9 or 10 to 5, although some stay open until 9. Stores are basically clustered around the major resort areas and Līhu'e.

Department Stores

Big Kmart (⊠ Kukui Grove Center, 3-2600 Kaumuali'i Hwy., Līhu'e ☎ 808/245–7742) has groceries, film, flip-flops, a souvenirs section, beach items, sunscreen products, and more. **Sears** (⊠ Kukui Grove Center, 3-2600 Kaumuali'i Hwy., Līhu'e ☎ 808/246–8301) sells electronics and housewares, plus a line of casual clothes. **Wal-Mart** (⊠ 3-3300 Kūhiō Hwy., Līhu'e ☎ 808/246–1599) has Hawaiian-print tropical-style clothing and a variety of Hawaiian souvenir items ranging from books to stationery to food products.

Shopping Centers

Ching Young Village. In the heart of Hanalei, Ching Young draws people to its Village Variety Store with cheap prices on beach towels, macadamia nuts, film and processing, wet suits—you name it. There's also the well-stocked Hanalei Natural Foods store, and a few steps away is Evolve Love Artists Gallery, where you can find work by local artisans. A florist, bank, and activity booking services can also be found here. ⊠ 5-1590 Kūhiō Hwy., Hanalei ☎ 808/826–7222.

Coconut Marketplace. This tourist-oriented complex is centrally located on the busy Coconut Coast near resort hotels. Here 60 shops sell everything from snacks and slippers to scrimshaw. There are also two movie theaters with first-run features, restaurants open from breakfast to evening, and a free nightly Polynesian show at 5. ⊠ 4-484 Kūhiō Hwy., Kapa'a ☎ 808/822–3641.

'Ele'ele Shopping Center. Kaua'i's west side has a scattering of stores, including those at this no-frills strip-mall shopping center where several tour-boat companies have offices. It's a good place to rub elbows with local folk or to grab a quick bite to eat at the casual Grinds Cafe or McDonald's. ⊠ Rte. 50 near Hanapēpē, 'Ele'ele ☎ 808/246–0634.

Hanalei Center. Listed on the Historic Register, the old Hanalei School has been refurbished and rented out to boutiques and restaurants. After you dig through '40s and '50s vintage clothing and memorabilia in the Yellow Fish Trading Company or search for that unusual gift at Sand People, you can grab a shaved ice (the Hawaiian version of a snow cone) or catch a class at the Hanalei Yoga studio. ⊠ 5-5161 Kūhiō Hwy., Hanalei ☎ 808/826–7677.

Kaua'i Village Shopping Center. The buildings of this Kapa'a shopping village are in the style of 19th-century plantation towns. ABC Discount Store sells sundries; Safeway carries groceries and alcoholic beverages and has a pharmacy; Kaua'i One-Hour Photo provides speedy film processing. Worth a look is the Kaua'i Heritage Center, which sponsors cultural workshops and displays authentic crafts for sale. For children, there is the Kaua'i Children's Discovery Museum which, in addition to interactive exhibits, offers children's day-camp programs. ✉ *4-831 Kūhiō Hwy., Po'ipū Beach* ☎ *808/822–4904.*

Kilohana Plantation. This 35-acre parcel of a former sugar plantation is buttressed by a 16,000-square-foot Tudor mansion, which now contains five art galleries and a restaurant. There is a craft shop and a Hawaiian-clothing shop in restored plantation quarters as well. The house itself is worth a look, filled with antiques from its original owner. Gaylord's restaurant is located in the house. Horse-drawn carriage rides are available, with knowledgeable guides reciting the history of sugar on Kaua'i. ✉ *3-2087 Kaumuali'i Hwy., 1 mi west of Līhu'e* ☎ *808/245–7818.*

Kinipopo Shopping Village. Kinipopo is on Kūhiō Highway in Kapa'a, across from Wailua Family Restaurant. The Goldsmith's Gallery sells handcrafted Hawaiian-style gold jewelry, and Tin Can Mailman bookstore is filled with an eclectic collection of books, Hawaiiana, and paper ephemera. You can also rent water skis and beach paraphernalia here at Kaua'i Water Ski, or dig in at Korean Barbeque. ✉ *4-356 Kūhiō Hwy., Kapa'a* ☎ *No phone.*

Kukui Grove Center. This is Kaua'i's largest mall. Besides Sears and Kmart, it offers a Longs Drugs and Star Market for groceries. Island-inspired garb is for sale at Hawaiian Islands Creations, Kaua'i-made gifts at Kaua'i Products Store, and girls' and women's surfwear at Chicks Who Rip Clothing. Restaurants range from fast food and deli takeout to La Bamba Mexican and Ho's Chinese. ✉ *3-2600 Kaumuali'i Hwy., west of Līhu'e* ☎ *808/245–7784.*

Po'ipū Shopping Village. Convenient to nearby hotels and condos on the South Shore, the two dozen shops here sell resort wear, gifts, souvenirs, and art. The upscale Black Pearl Kaua'i shop and the Hale Manu store, with "gifts for the spirited," are particularly appealing. Restaurants within include Roy's, Po'ipū Tropical Burgers, and Pattaya Asian Cafe. A Polynesian Revue performs in the open-air courtyard Tuesday and Thursday at 5. ✉ *2360 Kiahuna Plantation Dr., Po'ipū Beach* ☎ *808/742–2831.*

Princeville Shopping Center. A busy little gathering of shops includes Kaua'i Kite and Hobby Shop, Princeville Music, and JM's Jewels. Stock up on groceries and a bottle of wine at Foodland. Eateries include Bourbon Street Cafe, Chuck's Steakhouse, and Lappert's Ice Cream and Coffee. You'll also find a post office, gas station, and two banks here. ✉ *5-4280 Kūhiō Hwy., Princeville* ☎ *808/826–7513.*

Waimea Canyon Plaza. The little town of Kekaha is proud of its tidy complex of shops selling local foods, souvenirs, and island-made gifts for all ages. It is also the last stop for supplies before heading up to Waimea Canyon. ✉ *Kōke'e Rd. at Rte. 50, Kekaha* ☎ *No phone.*

Waipouli Town Center. On the east coast of the island in Kapa'a is a modest collection of 10 shops. Buy a T-shirt at Waipouli Variety, pick up a video at Blockbuster, and then grab a good-value plate lunch or other local food at Waipouli Restaurant. Libations and a grill menu can be found at the Lizard Lounge Bar and Grill. ✉ *4-901 Kūhiō Hwy., Kapa'a* ☎ *808/524–2023.*

Specialty Stores

Books

Borders Books & Music. Here, you'll find a large section of books focused on Hawai'i, plus plenty of magazines for beach reading, a music section, and a café. There are definite "rush" hour lines for coffee drinks. ⊠ *Kukui Grove Shopping Center, 4303 Nāwiliwili Rd., Līhu'e* ☎ *808/ 246–0862.*

Kaua'i Museum. The gift shop at the museum sells some fascinating books, maps, and prints. ⊠ *4428 Rice St., Līhu'e* ☎ *808/245–6931.*

Tin Can Mailman Books and Curiosities. Both new and used books can be found here, along with an extensive collection of Hawaiian and South Pacific literature. The shop also houses stamps and coins, rare prints, and vintage maps. ⊠ *Kinipopo Shopping Village, 4-356 Kūhiō Hwy., Kapa'a* ☎ *808/822–3009.*

Clothing

Bambulei. Two 1930s-style plantation homes have been transformed into this unique boutique featuring vintage and contemporary clothing, antiques, jewelry, and accessories. ⊠ *4-369 Kūhiō Hwy., Wailua* ☎ *808/ 823–8641.*

Crazy Shirts. This chain has a wide variety of shirts, from classy to genuinely crazy designs. It's a good place for active wear. ⊠ *Po'ipū Shopping Village, 2360 Kiahuna Plantation Dr., Po'ipū Beach* ☎ *808/742– 9000* ⊠ *Anchor Cove, 3416 Rice St., Līhu'e* ☎ *808/245–7073* ⊠ *Kaua'i Village Shopping Center, 4-831 Kūhiō Hwy., Kapa'a* ☎ *808/823–6761* ⊠ *5356 Kōloa Rd., Kōloa* ☎ *808/742–7161.*

Kilohana Clothing Company. This store, located in the guest cottage by Gaylord's restaurant, offers vintage Hawaiian clothing as well as contemporary styles using traditional Hawaiian designs. The store also features a wide selection of home products in vintage fabrics. ⊠ *Kilohana Plantation, 3-2087 Kaumuali'i Hwy., Līhu'e* ☎ *808/246–6911.*

Macy's. High-quality designer labels usually found in this store's mainland counterparts are sold here, along with labels from top Hawaiian designers. ⊠ *Kukui Grove Center, 3-2600 Kaumuali'i Hwy., Līhu'e* ☎ *808/245–7751.*

M. Miura Store. This mom and pop operation has a great assortment of clothes for outdoor fanatics, including tank tops, visors, swimwear, and Kaua'i-style T-shirts. ⊠ *4-1419 Kūhiō Hwy., Kapa'a* ☎ *808/ 822–4401.*

Paradise Sportswear. This is the retail outlet of the folks who invented Kaua'i's popular "red dirt" shirts, which are dyed and printed with the characteristic local soil. Do let the salesperson tell you the charming story behind these shirts. Sizes from infants up to 5X are available. ⊠ *4350 Waialo Rd., Port Allen* ☎ *808/335–5670.*

ISLAND WEAR **Hilo Hattie Fashion Factory.** This is the big name in aloha wear for tourists throughout the Islands. You can visit the factory, a mile from Līhu'e Airport, to pick up cool, comfortable aloha shirts and muʻumuʻus in bright floral prints, as well as other souvenirs. While there, check out the line of Hawaiian-inspired home furnishings. ⊠ *3252 Kūhiō Hwy., Līhuʻe* ☎ *808/245–3404*.

Coconut Republic. Come here for the beautiful clothing embroidered by local artists. There's also a selection of the island's unique "red dirt" T-shirts. ⊠ *Poʻipū Shopping Village, 2360 Kiahuna Plantation Dr., Poʻipū Beach* ☎ *808/742–6691*.

Flowers

Kauaʻi Tropicals. You can have this company ship heliconia, anthuriums, ginger, and other tropicals directly from its flower farm in 5-foot-long boxes. ⊠ *3870 Waha Rd., Kalāheo* ☎ *808/332–9071 or 800/303–4385*.

Food

Kauaʻi produces more coffee than any other island in the state, and the local product, somewhat milder than the Big Island's better-known Kona coffee, makes a worthy souvenir.

Kauaʻi Coffee Visitor Center and Museum. Coffee can be purchased from the source at the grower's visitor center. ⊠ *870 Halawili Rd., off Rte. 50, west of Kalāheo* ☎ *808/335–0813 or 800/545–8605*.

Kauaʻi Fruit and Flower Company. Near Līhuʻe you can buy fresh sugar-loaf pineapple, sugarcane, ginger, coconuts, local jams, jellies, and honey, plus Kauaʻi-grown papayas, bananas, and mangos in season. Special gift packs are available, pre-inspected and certified for shipment out of the state. ⊠ *3-4684 Kūhiō Hwy., Kapaʻa* ☎ *808/245–1814 or 800/ 943–3108*.

Kauaʻi Products Council. They'll tell you the best places to find Kauaʻi Kookies, taro chips, Kauaʻi boiled peanuts, salad dressings, and jams and jellies made from locally grown fruit, as well as nonfood items handcrafted on the island. ⊕ *Box 3660, Līhuʻe 96788* ☎ *808/823–8714*.

Kauaʻi Products Fair. Open weekends, this outdoor market features craftspeople, artisans, fresh produce, tropical plants and flowers, aloha wear, collectibles, and food along with wellness practitioners who will give you a massage right on the spot. ⊠ *Outside next to 4-1621 Kūhiō Hwy., in Kapaʻa* ☎ *808/246–0988*.

Lappert's Ice Cream. Don't forget to try a scoop of Hawaiʻi's own ice cream. Created by Walter Lappert of Hanapēpē in 1983, it's now a favorite on all the Islands. Lappert shops also sell locally produced coffees, which are easier to ship home than the ice cream. ⊠ *1-3555 Kaumualiʻi Hwy., Hanapēpē* ☎ *808/335–6121* ⊠ *Coconut Marketplace, 4-484 Kūhiō Hwy., Kapaʻa* ☎ *808/822–0744* ⊠ *5242 Kōloa Rd., Kōloa* ☎ *808/742– 1272* ⊠ *Princeville Shopping Center, 5-4280 Kūhiō Hwy., Princeville* ☎ *808/826–7393*.

Star Market. Some of the best prices on Hawai'i's famous macadamia nuts are available at Star Market. ⊠ *Kukui Grove Center, 3-2600 Kaumuali'i Hwy., Līhu'e* ☎ *808/245–7777.*

Gifts

Hilo Hattie Fashion Factory. This is the place where you can buy all the hats, baskets, inexpensive shell jewelry, rubber slippers, golf towels, and other trinkets you need to carry home to friends and family. The location is perfect for a last-minute stop en route to Līhu'e Airport. If you don't have room in your luggage for your purchases, worldwide shipping services are available. ⊠ *3252 Kūhiō Hwy., Līhu'e* ☎ *808/ 245–3404.*

Kong Lung Co. Sometimes called the Gump's of Kaua'i, this gift store combines elegant clothing, exotic glassware, ethnic books, gifts, and artwork mainly of Asian heritage. There's a working artists' studio upstairs where you can purchase works fresh off the easel. The shop is housed in a beautiful 1892 stone structure on the way to the lighthouse in Kīlauea. ⊠ *2490 Keneke St., Kīlauea* ☎ *808/828–1822.*

Lee Sands' Eelskin. You can buy the popular eel skin wholesale here at this rural spot at the Hawaiian Trading Post. It's an unusual store, with other skin lines such as sea snake, chicken feet, and frog. A lizard card case is available for about $12. ⊠ *Rte. 50 at Kōloa Rd., Lāwa'i* ☎ *808/ 332–7404.*

Village Variety Store. How about a fun beach towel for the folks back home? That's just one of the gifts you can find here, along with shell leis, Kaua'i T-shirts, macadamia nuts, and other great souvenirs at low prices. ⊠ *Ching Young Village, Kūhiō Hwy., Hanalei* ☎ *808/826– 6077.*

Hawaiian Arts & Crafts

Art Shop. This intimate gallery in Līhu'e sells original oils, photos, and sculptures. ⊠ *3196 'Akahi St., Līhu'e* ☎ *808/245–3810.*

Kahn Galleries. You can purchase the works of many local artists—including seascapes by George Sumner and Roy Tabora—at this gallery's locations. ⊠ *Coconut Marketplace, 4-484 Kūhiō Hwy., Kapa'a* ☎ *808/822–3636* ⊠ *Kilohana Plantation, 3-2087 Kaumuali'i Hwy., Līhu'e* ☎ *808/246– 4454* ⊠ *Kaua'i Village Shopping Center, 4-831 Kūhiō Hwy., Kapa'a* ☎ *808/822–4277* ⊠ *Kōloa Rd., Old Kōloa Town* ☎ *808/742–2277* ⊠ *Hanalei Center, 5-5161 Kūhiō Hwy., Hanalei* ☎ *808/826–6677.*

Kapaia Stitchery. Quilts and other fabric arts are featured in this cute little red plantation-style structure. The starter kits are great gifts for crafters. ⊠ *Kūhiō Hwy., in red building ½ mi north of Līhu'e* ☎ *808/ 245–2281.*

Kaua'i Heritage Center. Authentic reproductions of old (and new) Hawaiian crafts by Kaua'i artisans are displayed here: feather hatbands, nose flutes, *konane* (a Hawaiian game similar to checkers) boards and playing pieces, calabashes, and woven lau hala hats and pocketbooks. Sales help to support the center's cultural workshops and programs, which sometimes take place in the courtyard by the clock tower. ⊠ *Kaua'i Village, 4-831 Kūhiō Hwy., No. 838, Kapa'a* ☎ *808/821–2070.*

Kaua'i Products Store. Every seed lei, every finely crafted koa-wood box, every pair of tropical-flower earrings, and every other item in this boutique is handcrafted on Kaua'i. Other gift options include koa oil lamps, pottery, hand-painted silk clothing, sculpture, and homemade fudge. ⊠ *Kukui Grove Center, 3-2600 Kaumuali'i Hwy., Līhu'e* ☎ *808/ 246–6753.*

★ **Kebanu Gallery.** Original works by Island artists at this stunning space definitely lean toward the contemporary. Words can't do justice to the rare wood sculptures, whimsical ceramics, beaded jewelry, and colorful glassware. The Kebanu may just be the artistic pinnacle of your trip. ⊠ *Hee Fat Marketplace, 4-1354 Kūhiō Hwy., Kapa'a* ☎ *808/823–6820* ⊕ *www.aloha.net/~kebanu.*

★ **Piece of Paradise Gallery.** Fine art, koa-wood clocks and sushi platters, carved island tikis, handblown glass, and unique jewelry are available here, all designed by talented Kaua'i-based artisans. ⊠ *Radisson Kaua'i Beach Hotel, 4331 Kaua'i Beach Dr., Līhu'e* ☎ *808/246–2834* ⊕ *www. apieceofparadise.org.*

Ye Olde Ship Store & Port of Kaua'i. Scrimshaw-decorated pocket and army knives, boxes, and other gift items are available at this store in the Coconut Marketplace. The shop carries the work of nearly 40 scrimshaw artists and sponsors an annual contest celebrating the art form. ⊠ *Coconut Marketplace, 4-484 Kūhiō Hwy., Kapa'a* ☎ *808/822–1401.*

Jewelry

Jim Saylor Jewelers. Jim Saylor has been designing beautiful keepsakes for more than 20 years on Kaua'i. Gems from around the world appear in his unique settings, including black pearls and diamonds. ⊠ *1318 Kūhiō Hwy., Kapa'a* ☎ *808/822–3591.*

Kaua'i Gold. A wonderful selection of the rare Ni'ihau shell lei ranges in price from $20 to $200. Ask about how these remarkable necklaces are made to appreciate the craftsmanship, understand the sometimes high prices, and learn to care for and preserve them. The store also sells a selection of 14-karat gold jewelry. ⊠ *Coconut Marketplace, 4-484 Kūhiō Hwy., Kapa'a* ☎ *808/822–9361.*

Remember Kaua'i. Pick up a memento of your trip in the form of jewelry, Ni'ihau shell necklaces, or other gift items here. The shop also runs a booth at Po'ipū Spouting Horn. ⊠ *Radisson Kaua'i Beach Hotel, 4331 Kaua'i Beach Dr., Līhu'e* ☎ *808/639–9622.*

KAUA'I A TO Z

To research prices, get advice from other travelers, and book travel arrangements, visit www.fodors.com.

AIR TRAVEL

Several short daily flights can take you from Honolulu to Kaua'i, and there is limited service from Los Angeles and San Francisco.

CARRIERS Two main carriers, Aloha Airlines and Hawaiian Airlines, offer daily round-trip flights from Honolulu and Neighbor Islands to Līhu'e Airport. Rates fluctuate from $80 to $100 one-way. It's generally a 20- to 40-minute flight, depending on where you start. United Airlines has a daily direct flight from Los Angeles and San Francisco to Līhu'e Airport; American Airlines has a daily flight from Los Angeles to Līhu'e Airport. ✈ **Aloha Airlines** ☎ 808/245-3691 or 800/367-5250 ⊕ www.alohaairlines.com. **American Airlines** ☎ 800/433-7300 ⊕ www.aa.com. **Hawaiian Airlines** ☎ 808/838-1555 or 800/882-8811 ⊕ www.hawaiianair.com. **United Airlines** ☎ 800/241-6522 ⊕ www.ual.com.

AIRPORTS

The Līhu'e Airport is 3 mi east of the town of Līhu'e. There's a Visitor Information Center outside each baggage-claim area.

Used primarily by private planes, the Princeville Airport is a tiny strip on the North Shore, set within rolling ranches and sugarcane fields. It's a five-minute drive from the Princeville Resort and condo development, and a 10-minute drive from the shops and accommodations of Hanalei. ✈ **Līhu'e Airport** ☎ 808/246-1488, 888/697-7813 for Visitor Information Center. **Princeville Airport** ☎ 808/826-3040.

AIRPORT TRANSFERS Līhu'e Airport is a five-minute drive from Līhu'e. If you're staying in Wailua or Kapa'a, your driving time from Līhu'e is 15 minutes; to Princeville and Hanalei it's about 45 minutes. A charter flight into Princeville might save you a few minutes, but it's not worth the additional cost.

To the south, it's a 30-minute drive from Līhu'e to Po'ipū, the major resort area. To Waimea it takes one hour, and if you choose the rustic accommodations in the hills of Kōke'e, allow a good hour and a half of driving time from Līhu'e.

Check with your hotel or condo to see if it offers free shuttle service from the airport.

For luxurious transportation between the airport and your accommodations, contact Custom Limousine Service. Rates are $75 per hour, with a two-hour minimum. It also has packages that include lei greetings, wedding arrangements, and tours. North Shore Limousine specializes in service in the Hanalei and Princeville areas; it can pick you up at Princeville Airport.

Taxi fares around the island are $2 at the meter drop plus $2 per mile. That means a taxicab from Līhu'e Airport to Līhu'e town runs about $6 and to Po'ipū about $32, excluding tip. Akiko's Taxi offers its services from the east side of the island. Po'ipū Taxi will take you to Līhu'e and Po'ipū. Scotty Taxi provides quick service around the airport and Līhu'e. From the Princeville Airport to Hanalei, you pay about $14 when you ride with the North Shore Cab Company, which serves only the northeast portion of the island. ✈ **Akiko's Taxi** ☎ 808/822-7588. **Custom Limousine Service** ☎ 808/246-6318. **North Shore Cab Company** ☎ 808/826-6189. **North Shore Limousine** ☎ 808/826-6189. **Po'ipū Taxi** ☎ 808/639-2042 or 808/639-2044. **Scotty Taxi** ☎ 808/245-7888 or 808/639-9807.

BIKE TRAVEL

A two-wheeler is an exciting way to cruise around the Garden Isle. Kaua'i's country roads are generally uncrowded, so you can ride along at your own pace and enjoy the views. There are few designated bike lanes, but as long as you exercise caution on the busier thoroughfares, you should be fine. You can rent bikes from the activities desks of certain hotels and at sports outfitters.

CAR RENTAL

Unless you plan to do all of your sightseeing as part of guided tours, you will want a rental car on Kaua'i, since the attractions are sprinkled from one end of the island to the other. Reserve your vehicle in advance, especially during the peak seasons of summer, the Christmas holidays, and February.

Right across from the baggage claim at Līhu'e Airport are several rental-car counters, as well as vans that will shuttle you to rental offices nearby. Rental companies also have desks at Princeville Airport. Prices for a car from the major-name companies begin at $40 per day, unless you qualify for a discount rate through AAA, AARP, or by other means. A fly-drive deal can sometimes reduce costs, and many hotels—and even some condos—offer packages that include rental cars. There is a $3 daily surcharge on all rentals.

Several companies operate small reservation desks at major hotels, but spur-of-the-moment rentals will cost you more than pre-arranged ones. Alamo, Avis, Budget, Dollar, Hertz, National, and Thrifty have offices at the Līhu'e Airport. Avis has offices at the Hyatt Regency.

You may get a good deal on a car if you book with one of Kaua'i's local budget or used-car rental companies. Westside U-Drive, which rents cars and jeeps, is reliable. It keeps its vehicles in good shape and offers free delivery and pickup of your car at your hotel or condo in Po'ipū.

Major Agencies: Alamo ☒ Līhu'e Airport ☎ 808/246-0646 or 800/327-9633 ⊕ www.alamo.com. **Avis** ☒ Līhu'e Airport ☎ 808/245-3512 or 800/831-8000 ⊕ www.avis.com ☒ Hyatt Regency Kaua'i Resort and Spa, 1571 Po'ipū Rd., Kōloa ☎ 808/742-1627. **Budget** ☒ Līhu'e Airport ☎ 808/245-1901 or 800/527-0700 ⊕ www.budget.com. **Dollar** ☒ Līhu'e Airport ☎ 808/245-3651 or 800/342-7398, 800/800-4000 from outside HI ⊕ www.dollar.com. **Hertz** ☒ Līhu'e Airport ☎ 808/245-3356 or 800/654-3011 ⊕ www.hertz.com. **National** ☒ Līhu'e Airport ☎ 808/245-5636 or 800/227-7368 ⊕ www.nationalcar.com. **Thrifty** ☒ Līhu'e Airport ☎ 808/246-6252 or 800/847-4389 ⊕ www.thrifty.com.

Local Agency: Westside U-Drive ☒ 4552 Ehako St., Kalaheo ☎ 808/332-8644.

CAR TRAVEL

Although Kaua'i is relatively small, its sights stretch across the island. You can walk to the stores and restaurants in your resort area, but major attractions are not within walking distance.

It's easy to get around on Kaua'i—it has one major road almost encircling the island. Your rental-car company will supply you with a map with enlargements of each area of the island. The traffic on Kaua'i is pretty light most of the time, except in the Līhu'e and Kapa'a areas during rush hour (6:30 AM to 8:30 AM and 3:30 PM to 5:30 PM), and heading south to Po'ipū. Major attractions are indicated by road signs depicting King Kamehameha wearing a red cape.

Although Kaua'i looks like paradise, it has its fair share of crime. Lock your car wherever you park it. Don't leave valuables in the car, even in the trunk. Pay attention to parking signs, particularly in Līhu'e.

CRUISE TRAVEL

A romantic way to visit Kaua'i for a short time is to book passage on an interisland cruise ship. Norwegian Cruise Lines now has four vessels deployed in Hawaiian waters, including two of its new Project America liners, which offer three- and four-day interisland cruises. These ships join the luxurious *Norwegian Sky* and *Norwegian Wind* liners, which offer 7-, 10-, and 11-day sailings. Departures are weekly with varied island itineraries of five Hawaiian islands. Sightseeing and shore excursions are available at each port. On Kaua'i, the ships dock at Nāwiliwili on the southeast coast. Optional extension packages allow you to add a hotel stay before or after the cruise in the port of your choice.

🛈 **Norwegian Cruise Lines** ✉ 7665 Corporate Center Dr., Miami, FL 33126 ☎ 800/343-0098 ⊕ www.ncl.com.

EMERGENCIES

To reach the police, ambulance, or fire department in case of any emergency, dial **911.**

Kaua'i's Wilcox Memorial Hospital is one of the top 100 in the country. Its Kaua'i Medical Clinic (KMC) has a staff with 32 different specialties. It has lab and X-ray facilities, physical therapy, optometry, and emergency rooms. The main clinic is in Līhu'e. Other KMC clinics are in Kīlauea, Kukui Grove, 'Ele'ele, Kōloa, and Kapa'a. Major emergency cases are often airlifted to O'ahu. West Kaua'i Medical Center serves the area from Po'ipū to Kekaha.

Except for Longs Drugs, which often stays open until 9, most pharmacies close about 5 PM on Kaua'i. The Kaua'i Medical Clinic has a well-stocked pharmacy at its main clinic.

🛈 **Doctors: Kaua'i Medical Clinic** ✉ 3420-B Kūhiō Hwy., Līhu'e ☎ 808/245-1500, 808/245-2471 for pharmacy, 808/245-1831 for 24-hr on-call physicians, 808/338-9431 for after-hours emergencies ✉ North Shore Clinic, Kīlauea and Oka Rds., Kīlauea ☎ 808/828-1418 ✉ 4392 Waialo Rd., 'Ele'ele ☎ 808/335-0499 ✉ 5371 Koloa Rd., Kōloa ☎ 808/742-1621 ✉ 4-1105 Kūhiō Hwy., Kapa'a ☎ 808/822-3431.

🛈 **Hospitals: West Kaua'i Medical Center** ✉ 4643 Waimea Canyon Dr., Waimea ☎ 808/338-9431. **Wilcox Memorial Hospital** ✉ 3420 Kūhiō Hwy., Līhu'e ☎ 808/245-1010.

🛈 **Pharmacies: Longs Drugs** ✉ Kukui Grove Center, Rte. 50, Līhu'e ☎ 808/245-8871. **Safeway Food and Drug** ✉ Kaua'i Village Shopping Center, 4-831 Kūhiō Hwy., Kapa'a ☎ 808/822-2191. **Shoreview Pharmacy** ✉ 4-1177 Kūhiō Hwy., Suite 113, Kapa'a ☎ 808/822-1447. **Westside Pharmacy** ✉ 1-3845 Kaumuali'i Hwy., Hanapēpē ☎ 808/335-5342.

SIGHTSEEING TOURS

There are three major methods for getting a good guided look at the Garden Isle: by land, by sea, and by air. You can book these tours through the travel desk of your hotel or call directly.

Tour companies use big air-conditioned buses as well as smaller, more personalized vans. When making reservations, ask what vehicle it is and which tours let you get off and look around. Guides are friendly and generally know their island inside out—tip them $10 or more per person for their efforts.

If you're interested in a north-shore sea excursion, be forewarned that big winter waves often cause trips to be canceled, so call first to find out if the company you're interested in is operating.

BOAT TOURS A great way to take a look at Kaua'i is by boat, including kayak rentals and half-day tours. Intrepid explorers can traverse mountains, rivers, and ocean on a Kayak Kaua'i Discovery Tour. For $1,750 (including accommodations, ground transportation, and meals), you get a seven-day paddling and hiking adventure with six nights spent in out-of-the-way inns and cottages.

Cruise boats depart Wailua Marina at the mouth of the Wailua River for the Fern Grotto. Round-trip excursions, on 150-passenger flat-bottom riverboats, take an hour and a half, including time to walk around the grotto and environs. During the boat ride, guitar and 'ukulele players regale you with Hawaiian melodies and tell the history of the river. The 3-mi upriver trip culminates at a yawning lava tube that is covered with enormous fishtail ferns. Two companies offer several trips daily to Fern Grotto. Wai'ale'ale Boat Tours is well known for its Fern Grotto expedition ($16). Smith's Motor Boat Services ($16) tours get passengers involved in singing and learning hula while on board.

Captain Andy's Sailing Adventures' 55-foot catamaran *Spirit of Kaua'i* takes passengers on a two-hour sunset sail along the South Shore. Hors d'oeuvres and beverages are included in the $59 cost. Captain Andy also offers a five-hour Nā Pali Coast cruise from Port Allen with breakfast and lunch for $109. This is Kaua'i's best-known boat operator, famous for big buffet meals.

Liko Kaua'i Cruises tour the northern coastline in a 49-foot powered catamaran while captains share Hawaiian history and legends. Boats depart for four-hour tours—with time for snorkeling, a deli lunch, and whale-watching in season—from Kīkīaola Harbor in Kekaha for $110.

Nā Pali Explorer departs at 7:30 AM from Kīkīaola Harbor in Kekaha to tour the Nā Pali Coast (weather permitting) in a 48-foot adventure craft with an onboard toilet, freshwater shower, and shade canopy. Scenic 3½-hour cruises include a snack; longer snorkel trips include Continental breakfast and a picnic lunch, snorkel gear, and a Hawaiian cultural specialist to answer questions. Zodiac boat trips make a Nā Pali beach landing. Rates range from $79 to $118, and charters are available.

🅕 **Captain Andy's Sailing Adventures** ⬡ Box 876, 'Ele'ele 96705 ☎ 808/335–6833 or 800/535–0830 ⊕ www.captainandys.com. **Kayak Kaua'i** ⬡ Box 508, Hanalei 96714

☎ 808/826-9844 or 800/437-3507 ⊕ www.kayakkauai.com. **Liko Kaua'i Cruises** ✉ 9875 Waimea Rd., Waimea 96796 ☎ 808/338-0333 or 888/732-5456 ⊕ www.liko-kauai.com. **Nā Pali Explorer** ✉ 9935 Kaumuali'i Hwy., Waimea 96796 ☎ 808/338-9999 or 877/335-9909 ⊕ www.napali-explorer.com. **Smith's Motor Boat Services** ✉ 174 Wailua Rd., Kapa'a 96746 ☎ 808/821-6892 ⊕ www.smithskauai.com. **Wai'ale'ale Boat Tours** ✉ 6455 Makana Rd., Kapa'a 96746 ☎ 808/822-4908.

ALL-TERRAIN-VEHICLETOURS You get *way* off the beaten track on Aloha Kaua'i Tours' four-wheel-drive van excursions into Kōke'e, along the rugged side of Waimea Canyon, to the top of Kilohana Crater, or into the rain forests and the crater of Wai'ale'ale. Also offered are a half-day back-roads tour, bike and hike tours, and a "SeaFun" snorkeling tour. Prices range from $60 to $125.

You must be 16 or older to operate your own ATV, but Kaua'i ATV Tours also offers its "Mud Hog" six-passenger dune-buggy vehicle that can accommodate families with kids age five and older with the option of having a guide in the driver's seat. The $99 three-hour jaunt takes you through a private sugar plantation and historic cane-haul tunnel. The $145 four-hour tour visits secluded waterfalls and includes lunch. The longer excursion includes a hike through a bamboo forest and a swim in a freshwater pool at the base of the falls.
🛈 **Aloha Kaua'i Tours** ✉ 1702 Haleukana St., Līhu'e 96766 ☎ 808/245-6400 or 800/452-1113 ⊕ www.alohakauaitours.com. **Kaua'i ATV Tours** ✉ 3412 Weliweli Rd., Kōloa 96756 ☎ 808/742-2734 or 877/707-7088 ⊕ www.kauaiatv.com.

NI'IHAU TOUR It takes only 12 minutes to fly from Kaua'i to an island that few out-siders have set foot on since 1864. This 72-square-mi island 17 mi from Kaua'i is now run by the Robinson family, who raise cattle and sheep on the barren land. Bruce Robinson initiated Ni'ihau Helicopters in 1984 in order to supplement the cost of medical evacuation via helicopter for residents. Tours avoid the western coastline, especially the village of Pu'uwai, where the island's 200 residents live. Flights depart from and return to Kaumakani. There's a four-passenger minimum for each flight, and reservations are essential. Ground transportation is not available. A picnic lunch on a secluded Ni'ihau beach is included along with time for swimming, beachcombing, and snorkeling along the island's pris-tine shoreline. The half-day tour is $280 per person.
🛈 **Ni'ihau Tours** 🖘 Ni'ihau Helicopters, Box 690370, Makaweli 96769 ☎ 808/335-3500 or 877/441-3500 ⊕ www.niihau.us.

ORIENTATION TOURS The Round-the-Island Tour, sometimes called the Wailua River/Waimea Canyon Tour, gives a good overview of the island including Ft. Elisa-beth, 'Ōpaeka'a Falls, and Menehune Fishpond. Guests are transported in air-conditioned 17-passenger minivans. The $59 trip includes a boat ride up the Wailua River to Fern Grotto, and then a drive around the island to lookouts above Waimea Canyon. Companies offering Round-the-Island ground tours include Roberts Hawai'i Tours.

The Best of Kaua'i is a whirlwind daylong tour, sponsored by Kaua'i North Shore Limousine and Tours, for $240 per person. It includes a visit to Kilohana, a refurbished plantation mansion in Līhu'e; a boat ride to the Fern Grotto; a tour of Kīlauea Lighthouse; and a helicopter tour.

Ground transportation is in 15-passenger, air-conditioned vans. They will pick you up at Līhu'e Airport or at your hotel if it's on the north or east side of the island.

Kaua'i Island Tours will arrange charter tours around Kaua'i in anything from a passenger car to a 57-person motorcoach.

Kaua'i Island Tours ✉ 2960 Aukele St., Līhu'e 96766 ☎ 808/245–4777 or 800/733–4777. **Kaua'i North Shore Limousine and Tours** ✆ Box 109, Kīlauea 96754 ☎ 808/826–6189 or 808/634–7260. **Roberts Hawai'i Tours** ✆ Box 3389, Līhu'e 96766 ☎ 808/245–9101 or 800/831–5541 ⊕ www.robertshawaii.com.

THEME TOURS   Gay and Robinson can take you on a sugar plantation, field, and factory tour. Venturing into where the cane is grown, you learn about the history of sugar in Hawai'i; then you head to Kaua'i's last working sugar mill to see the refining process. Tours are offered weekdays at 8:45 and 12:45 for $35. Another option is the sugar and ranch-land tour, which revisits old ranch roads and Waimea Canyon destinations that were popular prior to World War II. The views include the rugged Olokele Canyon. The cost is $65, including lunch.

Hawai'i Movie Tours' minibuses with in-van television monitors let you see the actual scenes of films while visiting the real locations used for the filming of *Jurassic Park, Raiders of the Lost Ark, South Pacific, Blue Hawaii, Gilligan's Island,* and more. One stop is for a picnic lunch at 'Anini Beach. The standard land tour is $95. The four-wheel-drive Off Road Tour is $113 and takes you to film locations located on the private Kipu Ranch, usually not open for public viewing.

Gay and Robinson Tours ✉ 423 Kaumakani Ave., Kaumakani 96747 ☎ 808/335–2824 ⊕ www.gandrtours-kauai.com. **Hawai'i Movie Tours** ✉ 356 Kūhio Hwy., Kapa'a 96746 ☎ 808/822–1192 or 800/628–8432 ⊕ www.hawaiimovietour.com.

WALKING TOURS   History buffs curious about Kapa'a's sugarcane-, pineapple-, and rice-growing past and the World War II years will enjoy Kapa'a History Tour's 90-minute laid-back stroll from the Pono Kai Resort at the gateway of Kapa'a town. This insider's look led by locals tells the story of Kapa'a's Japanese stone lantern. Tours take place on Tuesday, Thursday, and Saturday at 10 AM and 4 PM and cost $15.

To see a rapidly vanishing lifestyle, take the unique, volunteer-led Plantation Lifestyles Walking Tour through the residential housing of a real mill camp. In the shadow of the old sugar mill, the dirt lanes of the 70-year-old camp are shaded by fruit trees and tropical gardens, and sometimes elderly residents come out to say aloha. Reservations are needed for the $10 1½-hour to 2-hour tours that begin at 9 AM every Tuesday, Thursday, and Saturday at Waimea Plantation Cottages.

Kapa'a History Tour–Kaua'i's Historical Society ✉ 4-1250 Kūhio Hwy., Kapa'a 96746 ☎ 808/245–3373. **Plantation Lifestyles Walking Tour** ✆ Box 1178, Waimea 96796 ☎ 808/335–2824 ⊕ www.gandrtours-kauai.com.

TAXIS

Cabs can be costly on Kaua'i. Each mile is $2, after a $2 meter drop; from Līhu'e to Po'ipū the price is $32; from Līhu'e to Princeville it's $60, excluding tip. Use a cab for short distances only (to a restaurant, for instance).

Akiko's Taxi operates from Kapa'a and offers minivans in its fleet. City Cab is a reliable taxi company with island-wide services; it uses Līhu'e as a home base. Based in Princeville, the North Shore Cab Company provides complete ground handling services for the north and east sections of the island.

🚖 **Akiko's Taxi** ✉ 5258 Laipo Rd. ☎ 808/822-7588 or 808/634-6018. **City Cab** ✉ 2979 Ohiohi St. ☎ 808/245-3227 or 808/639-7932. **North Shore Cab Company** ✉ 4480 Ka Haku Rd. ☎ 808/826-4118 or 808/639-7829.

VISITOR INFORMATION

The Kaua'i Visitors Bureau, the local island chapter of the Hawai'i Visitors and Convention Bureau, is on Rice Street, Līhu'e's main thoroughfare, near the Kaua'i Museum.

Activity centers such as Activity Warehouse with locations at Po'ipū, Kapa'a, and Princeville, will help you book tours with more than 200 activity vendors. They also offer recreational gear, convertibles, mopeds, and motorcycles for rent.

Po'ipū Beach Resort Association is the central source of information about the South Shore. You can make online reservations through the organization's Web site, and maps and brochures can be mailed to you on request.

🚖 **Activity Warehouse** ✉ 4-788 Kūhiō Hwy., Kapa'a 96746 ☎ 808/822-4000. **Kaua'i Visitors Bureau** ✉ 4334 Rice St., Suite 101, Līhu'e 96766 ☎ 808/245-3971 or 800/262-1400 🖷 808/246-9235 ⊕ www.kauaivisitorsbureau.com. **Po'ipū Beach Resort Association** ✎ Box 730, Kōloa 96756 ☎ 808/742-7444 or 888/744-0888 🖷 808/742-7887 ⊕ www.poipu-beach.org.

MOLOKA'I
THE FRIENDLY ISLE

5

Updated by
Paul Wood

MOLOKA'I'S ROUGH-AND-TUMBLE LANDSCAPE—much of it inaccessible by conventional means—spans climatic zones from rain forest to desert, encompassing misty mountain peaks and parched, windblown ranch land. Beaches are untrammeled and often empty enough to call your own. The Kalaupapa Peninsula, home to a former colony of leprosy patients, is guarded by the tallest sea cliffs in the world. Mountain bikers ply the dry open pastures of the west end. Divers revel in black coral reefs.

Pulling out of Moloka'i's Ho'olehua Airport you see a hand-painted sign that reads ALOHA! SLOW DOWN, THIS IS MOLOKA'I. It doesn't refer just to road speed but also to your internal pace and expectations. Heeding this advice is the best way to enjoy the island on its own terms.

Moloka'i residents strongly resist the unchecked growth of neighboring islands, even at the expense of the economy, and struggles with the influence of development are common. The 7,000 or so inhabitants focus more on family, community, and the retention of Hawaiian culture than on the eradication of the past for a high-rise future. Because of this, some areas can seem outdated and stuck in the past. But as you sit quietly on a deserted west-end beach looking at the lights of Honolulu twinkling across the channel 25 mi away, you realize that being lost in time can be a beautiful thing.

Exploring Moloka'i

Moloka'i is long and shaped like a slipper, with the "heel" facing west and the "toe" pointing to the east. Two dormant volcanoes are connected by a long plain. The imaginary dividing line is the town of Kaunakakai, in the center of the island's southern shore. West, Central, and East Moloka'i are used as natural divisions in this chapter.

Nature is the main attraction—waterfalls, valleys, cliffs, and the like. A rental car is the best way to explore at your own pace.

Directions on the island are often referred to as *mauka* (toward the mountains) and *makai* (toward the ocean).

About the Restaurants

During a week's stay, you might easily hit all the dining spots worth a visit, then return to your favorites for a second round. The dining scene is fun because it's a microcosm of Hawai'i's diverse cultures. You can find locally grown vegetarian foods, spicy Filipino cuisine, and Hawaiian fish with a Japanese influence—such as 'ahi or *aku* (types of tuna), mullet, and moonfish grilled, sautéed, or sliced, mixed with seaweed and eaten raw as poke (marinated raw fish). Most eating establishments are on Ala Mālama Street in Kaunakakai, with pizza, pasta, and ribs only a block away. What's more, the price is right.

About the Hotels

Moloka'i appeals more to travelers who appreciate genuine Hawaiian hospitality than to those who like swanky digs. Hotel and condominium properties range from adequate to funky. Kaunakakai's accommodations

Numbers in the text correspond to numbers in the margin and on the Moloka'i map.

If you have
1 day

Book a **Moloka'i Mule Ride** ❹ and a tour of **Kalaupapa** ❻ prior to leaving home. Fly into Ho'olehua Airport and drive to Kala'e, where the steep, 26-switchback mule trail begins. The tour of the former leper colony, where some 43 people live with the now manageable illness currently known as Hansen's disease, is the most emotionally moving experience on Moloka'i. If you ask nicely, you might be able to persuade your driver to stop at **Pālā'au State Park** ❺ for a photo of the Phallic Rock before you head back to the airport in the afternoon. For less-adventurous souls, flights directly to Kalaupapa can be arranged, thereby eliminating the grueling hike or mule ride.

5

If you have
2 days

Maunaloa ❸ on West Moloka'i makes a good starting point, particularly because there are many places to stay in the area. Spend a little time poking through the jumble of treasures at the Big Wind Kite Factory and Plantation Gallery, and you've just about seen the town. The Lodge at Moloka'i Ranch, and its activities base, is also here. You can enjoy skeet shooting, a kayak ride, world-class mountain-biking trails, or maybe a horseback trip on the 58,000-acre ranch. By afternoon, head for the nearest beach. This could be the former Kaluako'i Hotel and Golf Club's own Kawākiu Beach (the hotel is closed, but the beach is open). Or, if you prefer privacy, try **Pāpōhaku Beach** ❷, just a few miles southwest of the hotel. Reserve the second day for the **Moloka'i Mule Ride** ❹ and a tour of **Kalaupapa** ❻, taking in Pala'au State Park ❺ and the Phallic Rock afterward. If you're up to it after the ride, you can stop by **Moloka'i Coffee Plantation** ❽, **R. W. Meyer Sugar Mill and Moloka'i Museum** ❼, or **Purdy's Macadamia Nut Farm** ❾. If not, pause for some island-style corned beef hash or a burger with the locals at the Kamuela's Cookhouse before heading back to your hotel.

If you have
4 days

Follow the itinerary above for your first two days, then visit **Kaunakakai** ⓬ on your third day to pick up souvenirs, sample ethnic foods, and stop at the Kanemitsu Bakery, a local institution, for a loaf of its famous Moloka'i sweet bread, pastries, or snacks for the road. Check out **Kaunakakai Wharf** ⓭; you might set out on a fishing or scuba excursion from here. Otherwise, continue on a leisurely drive to Moloka'i's east end. Along the way, sightseeing points include **Kaloko'eli Fishpond** ⓮, St. Joseph's Church near **Kamalō** ⓯, and 'Ili'ili'ōpae Heiau. Turn around for the return drive when you reach **Hālawa Valley** ⓳. Your final day should be reserved for your own pleasures—perhaps a morning game of golf, an easy hike, a return to the beach, or a drive to see anything you might have missed.

are ideal if you're on a tight budget and want a central location. There's also a handful of bed-and-breakfasts around the island.

WHAT IT COSTS				
	$$$$	**$$$**	**$$**	**$**	**¢**
RESTAURANTS	over $30	$20–$30	$12–$20	$7–$12	under $7
HOTELS	over $200	$150–$200	$100–$150	$60–$100	under $60

Restaurant prices are for one main course at dinner. Hotel prices are for two people in a standard double room in high season, including tax and service.

Timing

Moloka'i's weather is good year-round. There are seldom crowds, but the island gets an influx of visitors during festivals. For a real taste of Hawaiian culture, you might want to visit during event weekends anyway. Be sure you make reservations for accommodations and a rental car well in advance if you schedule a trip during any major holiday.

WEST MOLOKA'I

The region is largely made up of the 53,000-acre Moloka'i Ranch. The rolling pastures and farmlands are presided over by Maunaloa, a sleepy little plantation town with a dormant volcano of the same name. West Moloka'i has another claim to fame: Pāpōhaku, the island's best beach.

a good drive

This driving tour focuses on two of Moloka'i's tourist areas. If you're approaching the west end from Kaunakakai on Route 460 (also called Maunaloa Highway), turn right at mile marker 15 down Kaluako'i Road and right again at the sign for **Kaluako'i Hotel and Golf Club ❶ ▶**. Take time to enjoy the grounds and the beach.

Back behind the wheel, turn right out of Kaluako'i Hotel and Golf Club and follow Kaluako'i Road 2 mi west until it dead-ends. This shoreline drive takes you past a number of lovely parks, including **Pāpōhaku Beach ❷**, the largest white-sand beach on the island. Look for a big sign on the side of the road.

Turn around and follow Kaluako'i Road back past the resort entrance, and continue uphill to the intersection with Route 460. Turn right and drive 2 mi on Route 460 (Maunaloa Highway) to **Maunaloa ❸**, a former plantation town that was torn down and replaced with—guess what—buildings resembling a plantation town. Much controversy surrounds development in this area. Landowners in favor of large-scale development come up against residents who resist the loss of their lifestyle. Raise this subject with locals, and you may hear a lively debate.

TIMING If you follow this excursion at a leisurely Moloka'i pace, it will take you the better part of a day, particularly if your accommodations are not on the west end of the island. A walk around Kaluako'i Hotel and Golf Club can take an hour or more.

5

Festivals & Seasonal Events

The year kicks off with the Ka Moloka'i Makahiki Festival in January, a day when islanders and visitors get together to compete in ancient Hawaiian games. In May, Moloka'i Ka Hula Piko, an annual daylong event, brings performances by some of the state's best hula troupes, musicians, singers, lecturers, and storytellers. It's all in tribute to Kā'ana, on the slopes of Maunaloa Mountain, which is reputed to be the birthplace of the hula. Late September's Aloha Week has live music, hula, and fashion shows in front of the town library. It tops off with a big (by Moloka'i standards) parade down Ala Mālama Street. The autumn Moloka'i-to-O'ahu Canoe Race is the world's major long-course outrigger canoeing event. It begins near the harbor of Haleolono. After paddling across the rough Kaiwi Channel, participants finish at Ft. DeRussy Beach in Waikīkī. The event takes place each September (women) and October (men). The Moloka'i year closes with the December Festival of Lights, featuring an Electric Light Parade down the main street of Kaunakakai.

Sports & the Outdoors

Moloka'i's beauty, sunny skies, and fragrant winds beckon. A mule ride down a narrow 1,664-foot cliff over a 3-mi, 26-switchback trail leads to Kalaupapa National Historical Park. At Kamakou Preserve, a Hawai'i Nature Conservancy property protecting endangered plants and birds, you can embark on a challenging trek. Arrange for a fishing charter, a sailing-snorkeling-scuba outing, or a whale-watching cruise at Kaunakakai Wharf. Mokuho'oniki Island, at the east end of the island, is a great dive spot. It was once a military bombing target, and artifacts from World War II are scattered throughout its many pinnacles and drop-offs. The area is home to barracuda and gray reef sharks. Black coral grows in depths ranging from 30 to 100 feet.

Another hour can fly by at Pāpōhaku Beach as you dig your toes in its sands and picnic on its shady grassy area. Allow one hour for exploring Maunaloa's main street to shop for souvenirs and chat with local shop owners. Don't try to do your shopping on Sunday, or you may find many CLOSED signs on the doors.

What to See

▶ ❶ **Kaluako'i Hotel and Golf Club.** This late-1960s resort passed through several owners, and the hotel itself is now closed, awaiting its next incarnation. Some very nice condos are still operating here, however. Stroll the grounds—an impressive 6,700 acres of beachfront property, including the newly revived golf course and 5 mi of coastline. ⊠ *Kaluako'i Rd., Maunaloa* ☎ *808/552–2555 or 888/552–2550.*

★ ❸ **Maunaloa.** This sleepy town was developed in 1923 to support the island's pineapple plantation. Although the fields of golden fruit have gone fallow, some of the workers' dwellings still stand, anchoring the west end of Moloka'i. Colorful local characters run the half-dozen businesses (including a kite shop and an eclectic old market) along the town's short main street. This is also the headquarters for Moloka'i Ranch that has an outfitters center, rodeo arena, and luxury lodge. ⊠ *Western end of Maunaloa Hwy. (Rte. 460).*

② **Pāpōhaku Beach.** The most splendid stretch of white sand on Moloka'i, Pāpōhaku is also the island's largest beach—it stretches 3 mi along the western shore. Even on busier days you're likely to see only a handful of other people. If the waves are up, swimming is dangerous. ⊠ *Kaluako'i Rd.; 2 mi beyond Kaluako'i Hotel and Golf Club, look for sign on makai side of road.*

CENTRAL MOLOKA'I

The center of the island is where the action is, relatively speaking. If you opt to do the Moloka'i Mule Ride in the morning and still feel up to exploring afterward, you can make quick stops at the places along the drive that follows. Central Moloka'i has the shops and eateries of Kaunakakai, water sports based at Kaunakakai Wharf, and the attractions and natural beauty of the central highlands.

a good drive

If you have reserved the **Moloka'i Mule Ride ④**, go directly to Kala'e, north on Route 470. Otherwise, drive north on Route 470 until it ends at **Pālā'au State Park ⑤** ▶, where you can admire knockout views of **Kalaupapa ⑥** and the Kalaupapa Peninsula. Bring along a light jacket for cooler upland weather in the fall and winter.

On the way back down the hill on Route 470, stop at the **R. W. Meyer Sugar Mill and Moloka'i Museum ⑦** to see photos and machinery from earlier times. Then turn right on Farrington Highway to visit the little town of Kualapu'u, where **Moloka'i Coffee Plantation ⑧** has a plantation store and espresso bar and offers tours of its coffee fields and processing plant. A five-minute drive west takes you to **Purdy's Macadamia Nut Farm ⑨** in Ho'olehua.

Head back on Farrington Highway, and then take a right onto Route 470; go down the rest of the hill and turn left on Route 460. Near the ocean on Route 460 are two stops of note that are practically right across the road from each other: **Kapuāiwa Coconut Grove ⑩** and **Church Row ⑪**. Follow Route 460 east to reach **Kaunakakai ⑫**, Moloka'i's "big city." **Kaunakakai Wharf ⑬** is the home base for deep-sea fishing excursions and other aqua adventures.

TIMING   Allow at least a day to explore. If you take the Moloka'i Mule Ride, many shops in Kaunakakai may be closed by the time you get there. If you save the ride for another day, there's no need to rush. During your tour of the highlands, take an hour to visit the sugar museum and another hour or more for the macadamia-nut farm and plantation store. Once you hit Kaunakakai, indulge yourself: take an hour or two to stroll around town and *talk story* (chat) with the locals. Be sure to save a half hour for snacks at the Kanemitsu Bakery, a local institution.

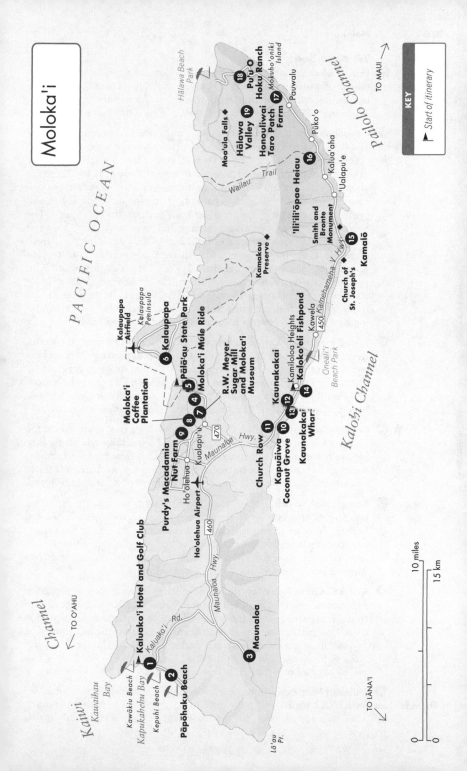

Moloka'i

PACIFIC OCEAN

Kaiwi Channel

TO O'AHU

Kawaikiu Bay

Kapukahehu Bay

Kawākiu Beach

Kepuhi Beach

❶ **Kaluako'i Hotel and Golf Club**

❷ **Pāpōhaku Beach**

Lā'au Pt.

Kaluako'i Rd.

Maunaloa Hwy.

Ho'olehua Airport

❸ **Maunaloa**

TO LĀNA'I

Maunaloa Hwy.

460

Purdy's Macadamia Nut Farm

Ho'olehua

Moloka'i Coffee Plantation

Kualapu'u

470

Maunaloa Hwy.

❾ ❽ ❼ ❹ ❺

R.W. Meyer Sugar Mill and Moloka'i Museum

Moloka'i Mule Ride

Pālā'au State Park ❻

Kalaupapa Peninsula

Kalaupapa Airfield

Kalaupapa

Wailau Trail

Kamakou Preserve

❶❶ **Church Row**

❶❶ **Kapuāiwa Coconut Grove**

❶❷ ❶❸ **Kaunakakai**

Kaunakakai Wharf

❶❹

Kamiloloa Heights

Kalokoʻeli Fishpond

Kawela

Oneali'i Beach Park

450

Kamehameha V Hwy.

Smith and Bronte Monument

'Ili'ili'ōpae Heiau ❶❻

❶❺ **Kamalō**

Church of St. Joseph's

'Ualapu'e

Kalua'aha

Pūko'o

Kalohi Channel

Honouliwai Taro Patch ❶❼

Pauwalu

Hālawa Valley ❶❾

Moa'ula Falls ◆

Hālawa Beach Park

❶❽ **Pu'u O Hoku Ranch**

Mōkuho'oniki Island

Pailolo Channel

TO MAUI

0 | 10 miles

0 | 15 km

What to See

⓫ Church Row. Standing cheek by jowl along the highway are several houses of worship with primarily native Hawaiian congregations. Notice the unadorned, boxlike style of architecture so similar to missionary homes. ⊠ *Mauka side of Rte. 460, 5½ mi southwest of airport.*

❻ Kalaupapa. The Kalaupapa Peninsula was once a community of about **Fodor'sChoice** 1,000 victims of Hansen's disease (leprosy) who were banished from ★ other parts of Hawai'i. Father Damien committed himself to the care of the afflicted until he died here of the same disease in 1889. There are about 40 patients still living in Kalaupapa—now by choice, as the disease is controlled by drugs and patients are no longer carriers. You will probably not see any patients other than perhaps the tour guide. The history of the community is fascinating and heart wrenching. Views of the peninsula from Kalaupapa Lookout in Pālā'au State Park are a standout. Note that no one under the age of 16 is allowed to visit Kalaupapa. Whether you hike down, take a mule ride down, or fly in, you must be part of a tour to visit. You can book through Moloka'i Mule Ride, or through **Damien Tours** (☎ 808/567–6171) if you want to hike or fly in. Book before getting to the island. Hikers need to start walking by 8 AM to connect with a tour. ⊠ *North end of Rte. 470.*

❿ Kapuāiwa Coconut Grove. At first glance this looks like a sea of coconut trees. Close-up you'll see that the tall, stately palms are planted in long rows leading down to the sea. This is one of the last surviving royal groves planted by Prince Lot, who ruled Hawai'i as King Kamehameha V from 1863 until his death in 1872. Watch for falling coconuts; protect your head and your car. ⊠ *Makai side of Rte. 460, 5½ mi south of airport.*

★ ⓬ Kaunakakai. Kaunakakai looks like an Old West movie set. Along the one-block main drag is a cultural grab bag of restaurants and shops. People are friendly and willing to supply directions. The preferred dress is shorts and a tank top, and no one wears anything fancier than a mu'umu'u or aloha shirt. ⊠ *Rte. 460, about 3 blocks north of Kaunakakai Wharf.*

⓭ Kaunakakai Wharf. Docks, once bustling with watercraft exporting pineapples, now host boats shipping out potatoes, tomatoes, baby corn, herbs, and other produce. The wharf is also the starting point for excursions, including deep-sea fishing, sailing, snorkeling, whale-watching, and scuba diving. ⊠ *Rte. 450 and Ala Mālama St.; drive makai on Kaunakakai Pl., which dead-ends at the wharf.*

❽ Moloka'i Coffee Plantation. Take a 45-minute walking tour of the coffee production process "from bean to cup," after which you can head over to the espresso bar for a fresh-brewed cup of java and *liliko'i* (passion fruit) cheesecake. Or, buy roasted beans to go from the gift shop. The Muleskinner is a great, low-acid, dark roast. ⊠ *Farrington Hwy., off Rte. 470, Kualapu'u* ☎ *800/709–2326, 808/567–9023* ⊕ *www. molokaicoffee.com* ⊠ *$7* ⊗ *Tours Mon.–Sat. 9:30 and 11:30 AM.*

❹ Moloka'i Mule Ride. Mount a friendly mule and wind along a 3-mi, 26- **Fodor'sChoice** switchback trail to reach the town of Kalaupapa. The path was built in ★ 1886 as a supply route for the settlement below. Once in Kalaupapa, you'll take a guided tour of the town and have a picnic lunch. The trail is very steep, down some of the highest sea cliffs in the world. Only those in good shape should attempt the ride, as two hours each way on a mule can take its toll. The entire event takes seven hours. It's wise to make reservations ahead of time, as spots are limited. The same outfit can also arrange for you to hike down or fly in, or some combination of a hike in and fly out. ⊠ *100 Kala'e Hwy. (Rte. 470), Kualapu'u* ☎ *808/567–6088* ⊕ *www.muleride.com* ✆ *$150* ⊙ *Mon.–Sat. 8–3:30.*

★ ▶ ❺ **Pālā'au State Park.** One of the island's few formal recreation areas, this cool retreat covers 233 acres at a 1,000-foot elevation. A short path through a heady pine forest leads to **Kalaupapa Lookout,** a magnificent overlook with views of the town of Kalaupapa and the 1,664-foot-high sea cliffs protecting it. Informative plaques have facts about leprosy, Father Damien, and the colony itself. The park is also the site of **Phallic Rock,** known as Kauleonānāhoa to the ancient Hawaiians. It's said that if women sit by this large rock formation they will become more fertile. The park is well maintained, with camping facilities, rest rooms, and picnic tables. ⊠ *Take Rte. 460 west from Kaunakakai and then head mauka on Rte. 470, which ends at the park* ☎ *No phone* ✆ *Free* ⊙ *Daily dawn–dusk.*

❾ **Purdy's Macadamia Nut Farm.** Moloka'i's only working macadamia-nut farm is open for educational tours hosted by the knowledgeable and entertaining owner. A family business on Hawaiian homestead land in Ho'olehua, the farm takes up 1½ acres with a flourishing grove of some 50 trees more than 70 years old. Taste a delicious nut right out of its shell, or fresh macadamia-blossom honey; then buy some at the shop on the way out. Look for Purdy's sign behind Moloka'i High School. ⊠ *Lihipali Ave., Ho'olehua* ☎ *808/567-6601* ✆ *Free* ⊙ *Weekdays 9:30–3:30, Sat. 10–2.*

❼ **R. W. Meyer Sugar Mill and Moloka'i Museum.** Built in 1877, this old mill has been reconstructed to signify Moloka'i's agricultural history. The equipment is still in working order, including a mule-driven cane crusher, redwood evaporating pans, some copper clarifiers, and a steam engine. A museum with changing exhibits on the island's early history and a gift shop are on-site as well. The facility serves as a campus for Elderhostel programs. ⊠ *Rte. 470, 2 mi southwest of Pālā'au State Park, Kala'e* ☎ *808/567-6436* ✆ *$2.50* ⊙ *Mon.–Sat. 10–2.*

EAST MOLOKA'I

On the beautifully undeveloped eastern end of Moloka'i, you'll find ancient fishponds, a magnificent coastline, splendid ocean views, and a gaping valley that's been inhabited for centuries. The east is flanked by Mt. Kamakou, the island's highest point at 4,961 feet, and home to The Nature Conservancy's Kamakou Preserve. Miles of rain forests burgeon with tropical fruit, mist hangs over waterfall-filled valleys, and ancient lava cliffs jut out from the sea.

a good drive

The journey east from Kaunakakai, on Route 450, is 30 mi long. The farther you drive, the wilder the coastline, changing from white sandy beaches to rocky shores. Much of the road hugs the shore as it twists and turns. Be forewarned: it's fraught with bumps, blind curves, and potholes. There are, however, several bays beside which you can stop and take a breather. Keep your eyes open for mile markers: at times, they're the only references for locating sights.

Six miles east of Kaunakakai, look offshore to see **Kaloko'eli Fishpond** ⓔ ▶, surrounded by the most picturesque of Moloka'i's historic rock walls. After another 5 mi you reach the natural harbor of **Kamalō** ⓕ. En route is the stark white Church of St. Joseph's, built in 1876. It's one of four houses of worship built by Father Damien. The statue of him here is frequently adorned with flower lei. At mile marker 15, a hidden trail leads to the enormous **'Ili'ili'ōpae Heiau** ⓖ. Close to mile marker 20 at a small but deeply curved bay, an unpaved road leads a short distance off the highway to **Honouliwai Taro Patch Farm** ⓗ. After that the road climbs and winds through **Pu'u O Hoku Ranch** ⓘ, a vast Upcountry expanse with sparkling ocean panoramas.

The road east dead-ends at the beach in the lush **Hālawa Valley** ⓙ. If you're interested in exploring trails, contact a local tour outfitter first for a map. Landowners here are known to chase away unsuspecting hikers on the wrong trail.

TIMING   Give yourself a full day for this meandering drive, especially if you want to break it up with a picnic at one of the beach parks. From Kaunakakai, you can complete the tour in a half day; allow a full day if you're going to visit the Kamakou Preserve. The sights on the east end of the island are natural, so opening hours don't apply. You might want to save this excursion for a weekend and visit the shops and attractions of East and Central Moloka'i during the week, when they're open.

What to See

ⓙ **Hālawa Valley.** As far back as AD 650 a busy community lived in this valley, the oldest recorded habitation on Moloka'i. Hawaiians grew fruit and taro and fished here until 1946, when a fierce tidal wave struck. Now much of the valley is overrun with lush vegetation, though you can still see the remains of house platforms and garden walls. There's a nice beach at the end of the road. An accessible 3-mi trail leads back to Moa'ula Falls, a 250-foot cascade. Residents prefer that hikers come only with an authorized tour guide. ⊠ *Eastern end of Rte. 450.*

ⓗ **Honouliwai Taro Patch Farm.** Jim and Lee Callahan have revived the curious form of agriculture that sustained the pre-discovery Hawaiians, taro farming. The stream here, fed by a spring, provides a year-round supply of fresh water which flows through cleverly designed taro ponds (or *lo'i*). The owners provide 1½-hour educational tours so visitors can experience all phases of taro farming, from planting to eating. Lee was born and raised in Thailand, so she uses a traditional southeast Asian farm device—a docile, plow-pulling water buffalo named Bigfoot. Tours are available every day, but you must call for an appointment. ⊠ *East of mile marker 20, mauka side, where the sign says "Honouliwai Is A*

Beautiful Place To Be." ☎ *808/558–8922* ⊕ *www.angelfire.com/film/chiangmai/index.html.*

⑯ 'Ili'ili'ōpae Heiau. Human sacrifices once took place at this hidden *heiau*. As long as a football field, it's a well-preserved example of Hawai'i's ancient outdoor shrines. This revered site is still said to hold great power. Please act with respect by speaking in a soft voice. The sacrifices were introduced by Tahitian immigrants who came between AD 1090 and 1240, but the heiau could have existed before then—as early as AD 650, the time of the first island habitation. The trail is on private property, but the owners don't object to people simply visiting the heiau. Permission should be requested by phone. ⊠ *15 mi east of Kaunakakai and ½ mi inland of Rte. 450; park on the side of road, look for Wailau Trail sign, and walk about 10 minutes mauka until you see sign on left for heiau* ☎ *808/558–8380.*

★ ▶ ⑭ Kaloko'eli Fishpond. With its narrow rock walls connecting two points of the shore, Kaloko'eli is typical of the numerous fishponds that define southern Moloka'i. Many of them were built around the 13th century. This early type of aquaculture, particular to Hawai'i, exemplifies the ingenuity of precontact Hawaiians. One or more openings were left in the wall, where gates called *makaha* were installed. These gates allowed seawater and tiny fish to enter the enclosed pond but kept larger predators out. The tiny fish would then grow too big to get out. At one time there were 62 fishponds around Moloka'i's coast. ⊠ *Rte. 450, about 6 mi east of Kaunakakai.*

★ Kamakou Preserve. Tucked away on the slopes of Mt. Kamakou, Moloka'i's highest peak, the 2,774-acre preserve is a dazzling wonderland full of wet *'ōhi'a* (hardwood trees of the myrtle family, with red blossoms called lehua flowers) forests, rare bogs, and native trees and wildlife. Monthly guided hikes, limited to eight people, are held on Saturday. Reservations are required well in advance. You can visit the park without a tour, but you need a good four-wheel-drive vehicle, and the Nature Conservancy requests that you sign in at the office and get directions first. ⊠ *The Nature Conservancy, 23 Pueo Pl., Kualapu'u* ☎ *808/553–5236* 🖅 *Free; donation suggested for guided hike, $10 members, $25 nonmembers (includes one-year membership).*

⑮ Kamalō. A natural harbor used by small cargo ships during the 19th century, this is also the site of the **Church of St. Joseph's,** a tiny white church built by Father Damien in the 1880s. ⊠ *Rte. 450, about 11 mi east of Kaunakakai, on makai side.*

⑱ Pu'u O Hoku Ranch. A 14,000-acre private spread in the highlands of East Moloka'i, Pu'u O Hoku was developed in the '30s by wealthy industrialist Paul Fagan. Route 450 cuts right through this rural gem with its green pastures and grazing horses and cattle. As you drive along, enjoy the splendid views of Maui and Lāna'i. The small island off the coast is Mokuho'oniki, where the military practiced bombing techniques during World War II. ⊠ *Rte. 450 about 20 mi east of Kaunakakai* ⊕ *www.puuohoku.com.*

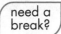

The best place to grab a snack or stock up on picnic supplies is the **Neighborhood Store 'N Counter** (⊠ Rte. 450, 16 mi east of Kaunakakai, Puko'o ☎ 808/558–8498). It's the last store on your drive east from Kaunakakai. There's no pay phone here, or in the neighborhood, in case you're looking.

BEACHES

Moloka'i has numerous beaches, many of them quite remote and undisturbed. The largest and most beautiful beaches are along the west coast, but steer clear of their high winter waves. Beaches fronting the Kaunakakai hotels and condominiums are narrow and the shore is not appealing for swimmers, yet the shallow waters are almost always calm for a beginning kayak trip. At the extreme east end of the island is the beach fronting Hālawa Valley, a nice place to relax after the long drive.

Island beaches are free and open to the public. None have telephones or lifeguards. They're all under the jurisdiction of the **Department of Parks, Land and Natural Resources** (✉ Box 153, Kaunakakai 96746 ☎ 808/567–6083).

The beaches below are listed counterclockwise.

West Moloka'i

Kawākiu Beach. Seclusion is the reason to come to this remote beach, accessible only by four-wheel drive or a 45-minute walk. The white-sand beach is beautiful, but rocks and undertow make swimming really dangerous. Head past the Ke Nani Kai condominiums, and look for the dirt road off to the right. Park here and hike in. ⊠ *Kaluako'i Rd.*

Kapukahehu Bay. Locals like to surf just out from this bay in a break called Dixie's or Dixie Maru. The sandy protected cove is usually completely deserted during the weekdays but can fill up when the surf is up. There are no facilities. ⊠ *Drive about 3½ mi beyond Pāpōhaku Beach to end of Kaluako'i Rd. on northwest end of island; beach-access sign on makai side of road points to parking lot.*

Kepuhi Beach. Ideal for strolling, sunbathing, and watching the sunset, this white-sand beach stretches about a half mile in front of Kaluako'i Hotel and Golf Club. It's fairly windy here, which makes the swimming somewhat dangerous during high tide. There are outdoor showers at the resort and a few shops selling snacks and beachwear. ⊠ *Kaluako'i Hotel and Golf Club, Kaluako'i Rd.*

Fodor'sChoice ★ **Pāpōhaku Beach.** One of the most sensational beaches in Hawai'i, Pāpōhaku is a 3-mi-long strip of white sand, the longest of its kind on the island. Some places are too rocky for swimming; look carefully before entering the water and go in only when the waves are small (generally in summer). Between the parking lot and the beach are outdoor showers, picnic facilities, and a rest room. ⊠ *Kaluako'i Rd.; 2 mi beyond Kaluako'i Hotel and Golf Club, look for sign on makai side of road.*

Central Moloka'i

Oneali'i Beach Park. Smashing views of Maui and Lāna'i across the Pailolo Channel dominate this, the only decent beach park on the island's south-central shore. A narrow and long stretch of sand, Oneali'i has adequate swimming in calm waters year-round, along with rest rooms, outdoor showers, and tree-shaded picnic tables. ⊠ *Rte. 450, east of Hotel Moloka'i.*

East Moloka'i

Hālawa Beach Park. The long drive to Hālawa Valley is worth it, in part because it culminates in this pretty, curving beach flanked by cliffs. Swimming is safe only during the summer. Watch out for hazardous currents and high surf in winter. ⊠ *Drive east on Rte. 450 until it dead-ends.*

WHERE TO EAT

West Moloka'i

★ $$–$$$ ✕ **Maunaloa Room.** Order haute cuisine appetizers such as coconut-crusted shrimp, Moloka'i 'opihi (a crunchy limpet), or *lumpia* (egg roll) stuffed with *kālua* duck (roasted in an underground oven). Entrées follow a steak-and-seafood theme, and the catch of the day can be prepared with *alae* (a pale-orange salt found in Moloka'i and Kaua'i). Inside, wagon-wheel chandeliers with electric candles typify the hotel restaurant's ranch fixtures. A dinner on the outside deck can't be beat. ⊠ *The Lodge at Moloka'i Ranch, 8 Maunaloa Hwy., Maunaloa* ☎ *808/ 660–2725* ☱ *AE, MC, V.*

¢ **Paniolo Cafe.** The only other restaurant in Maunaloa town is this casual place that specializes in "plate lunches"—hearty fare with scoops of rice and macaroni salad accompanying an island-style main dish such as chicken *katsu* (breaded cutlet), kālua pork, or teriyaki beef. The servings are generous. Technically the café doesn't serve dinner. But they stay open till 7:30, so if you find yourself wondering where to dine, especially at the west end, come here for take-out boxes. ⊠ *Maunaloa town right next to the movie theater.* ☎ *808/552–2625* ☱ *No credit cards.*

Central Moloka'i

$$ ✕ **Oceanfront Dining Room.** This is *the* place to hang out on Moloka'i. Locals relax at the bar listening to live music on weekends, or they come in for theme-night dinners (posters around town tell you what's in store for the week). Prime-rib specials on Friday and Saturday nights draw a crowd. Try the broiled baby back ribs smothered in barbecue sauce. Every Friday from 4 to 6 PM Moloka'i's *kūpuna* (old-timers) bring their instruments here for a lively Hawaiian jam session, a wonderful experience of grassroots aloha spirit. ⊠ *Hotel Moloka'i, Kamehameha V Hwy., Kaunakakai* ☎ *808/553–5347* ☱ *AE, D, DC, MC, V.*

$–$$ ✕ **Moloka'i Pizza Cafe.** A cheerful, busy restaurant, Moloka'i Pizza is a popular gathering spot for families. Pizza, sandwiches, salads, pasta, fresh fish, and homemade pies are simply prepared and tasty. Kids keep busy on a few little coin-operated rides. ⊠ *Kaunakakai Pl. on Wharf Rd., Kaunakakai* ☎ *808/553–3288* ⚎ *Reservations not accepted* ☱ *No credit cards.*

$ ✕ **Oviedo's.** This spare lunch counter specializes in *adobos* (stews) with traditional Filipino spices and sauces. Try the tripe, pork, or beef adobo for a real taste of tradition. The locals say that Oviedo's makes the best roast pork in the state. You can eat in or take out. ⊠ *145 Ala Mālama St., Kaunakakai* ☎ *808/553–5014* ▭ *No credit cards* ⊘ *No dinner.*

¢–$ ✕ **Kamuela's Cookhouse.** Kamuela's is the only eatery in rural Kualapu'u. This laid-back diner looks like a little plantation house; paintings of hula dancers and island scenes enhance the green-and-white furnishings. Typical fare is a plate of chicken or pork *katsu* served with rice. They shut down the grill by 6 PM, so unless you order takeout ahead of time, this is not a dinner option. It's located across the street from the Kualapu'u Market. ⊠ *Farrington Hwy., 1 block west of Rte. 470, Kulapūu* ☎ *808/567–9655* ▭ *No credit cards* ⊘ *Closed Mon. No dinner.*

¢–$ ✕ **Kanemitsu Bakery and Restaurant.** Come here for a taste of *lavosh*, a
Fodor'sChoice   pricey flatbread flavored with sesame, taro, Maui onion, Parmesan
★   cheese, or jalapeño. Or try the round Moloka'i bread—a sweet, pan-style white loaf that makes excellent cinnamon toast. ⊠ *79 Ala Mālama St., Kaunakakai* ☎ *808/553–5855* ▭ *No credit cards* ⊘ *Closed Tues.*

¢–$ ✕ **Moloka'i Drive Inn.** Fast food Moloka'i-style is served at a walk-up counter. Hot dogs, fries, and sundaes are on the menu, but residents usually choose the foods they grew up on, such as saimin, plate lunches, shaved ice (snow cone with flavored syrup), and the beloved *loco moco* (rice topped with a hamburger and a fried egg, covered in gravy). ⊠ *857 Ala Mālama St., Kaunakakai* ☎ *808/553–5655* ▭ *No credit cards.*

¢–$ ✕ **Sundown Deli.** This clean little rose-color deli focuses on freshly made take-out food. Sandwiches come on half a dozen types of bread, and the Portuguese bean soup and chowders are rich and filling. Specials, which might include the likes of vegetarian quiche, change daily. The deli sells vitamins and local-theme T-shirts. ⊠ *145 Ala Mālama St., Kaunakakai* ☎ *808/553–3713* ▭ *AE, MC, V* ⊘ *Closed Sun. No dinner.*

¢   ✕ **Outpost Natural Foods.** The heart of Molokai's health-food community, Outpost is a well-stocked store. At the counter you can get fresh juices and delicious sandwiches geared toward the vegetarian palate. It's a great place to pick up local produce and all the ingredients you need for a picnic lunch. ⊠ *70 Makaena St., Kaunakakai* ☎ *808/553–3377* ▭ *No credit cards* ⊘ *Closed Sat. No dinner.*

WHERE TO STAY

Several of the lodging establishments listed in this chapter arrange outdoor excursions and have sports facilities that aren't accessible to nonguests and are hard to find elsewhere.

West Moloka'i

$$$$ ▥ **Hale Aloha.** This spacious four-bedroom, three-bath vacation rental is on 12 secluded acres, has ocean views, and is surrounded by an orchard and woodlands. Wood floors stretch the length of the house, connecting the two kitchens. A wraparound porch leads to a gazebo-covered hot tub. Rooms are open and simple, with wood-beam ceilings. The managers of this property, 1-800-Molokai, also have other rentals in the area.

⊠ *Kaluako'i Rd. (Box 20), Maunaloa 96770* ☎ *800/665–6524* ⊕ *www.1-800-molokai.com* ⤳ *1 house* ⌂ *Fans, kitchen, cable TV, in-room VCRs, pool, hot tub; no a/c* ⊟ *AE, MC, V.*

★ $$$$ ▦ **The Beach Village at Moloka'i Ranch.** This dream-come-true campground consists of one- and two-unit canvas bungalows, mounted on wooden platforms. Don't let the presence of ecotravelers fool you—the rooms are unexpectedly luxurious, with queen-size beds, self-composting flush toilets, and private outdoor showers. Breakfast, lunch and dinner are served family-style in an open-air pavilion. Extensive activities, including snorkeling, kayaking, clay shooting, and mountain biking, are available. ⊠ *Maunaloa Hwy. (Box 259), Maunaloa 96770* ☎ *888/627–8082* ⊕ *www.molokairanch.com* ⤳ *100 tents* ⌂ *Restaurant, fans, beach, snorkeling, boating, mountain bikes, hiking, horseback riding, airport shuttle; no a/c, no room phones, no room TVs* ⊟ *AE, D, MC, V.*

$$$$ ▦ **The Lodge at Moloka'i Ranch.** Moloka'i's plushest accommodation is
Fodor's Choice this Old West–style lodge. Ranching memorabilia and local artwork
★ adorn guest-room walls, with each of the 22 suites individually decorated. All rooms have private lānai and some have skylights. An impressive stone fireplace warms up the central Great Room, and there's a games room for pleasant socializing during cool Moloka'i evenings. Pathways and a greenhouse delineate the grounds. Spa facilities include massage rooms, a juice bar, and men's and women's saunas. ⊠ *Maunaloa Hwy. (Box 259), Maunaloa 96770* ☎ *888/627–8082* ⊕ *www.molokairanch.com* ⤳ *22 rooms* ⌂ *Restaurant, in-room data ports, in-room safes, refrigerators, pool, gym, massage, sauna, spa, beach, boating, fishing, mountain hikes, billiards, hiking, horseback riding, horseshoes, bar, lounge, library, recreation room, children's programs (ages 5–12)* ⊟ *AE, D, MC, V.*

★ $$–$$$$ ▦ **Paniolo Hale.** Perched high on a ledge overlooking the beach, Paniolo Hale is one of Moloka'i's best condominium properties. Some units have spectacular ocean views. Studios and one- or two-bedroom units all have beautiful screened lānai and kitchens; some have hot tubs for an additional charge. Kitchens are well equipped, and the rooms are tidy and simple. Adjacent to the Kaluako'i Golf Course and a stone's throw from the Kaluako'i Hotel and Golf Club, the property is some times a playground for wild turkeys and deer at night. ⊠ *Lio Pl. (Box 190), Maunaloa 96770* ☎ *808/552–2731 or 800/367–2984* 🖷 *808/552–2288* ⊕ *www.paniolohaleresort.com* ⤳ *77 condominiums (22 rentals)* ⌂ *Kitchens, microwaves, 18-hole golf course, golf privileges, pool, paddle tennis* ⊟ *AE, MC, V.*

$$$ ▦ **Ke Nani Kai.** These pleasant one- and two-bedroom condo units have ocean views and use of the facilities at the former Kaluako'i Hotel and Golf Club. Furnished lānai have flower-laden trellises, and the spacious interiors are decorated with rattans and pastels. Each unit has a washer-dryer and a fully equipped kitchen. The beach is a five-minute walk away. ⊠ *Kaluako'i Rd. (Box 289), Maunaloa 96770* ☎ *808/552–2761 or 800/535–0085* 🖷 *808/552–0045* ⊕ *www.marcresorts.com* ⤳ *120 condominiums (22 rentals)* ⌂ *Fans, kitchens, cable TV, 18-hole golf course, 2 tennis courts, pool, laundry facilities; no a/c* ⊟ *AE, D, DC, MC, V.*

$$–$$$ ⊞ **Kaluako'i Villas.** Studios and one-bedroom ocean-view suites are dec-
orated in blue and mauve, with island-style art, rattan furnishings, and
private lānai. Units are spread out in 21 two-story buildings covering
29 acres, adjacent to the now defunct Kaluako'i Resort. The view
toward the ocean looks across the newly revived golf course. The seclusion and sunsets make this a great find. ⊠ *1131 Kaluako'i Rd. (Box 200),
Maunaloa 96770* ☎ *808/552–2721 or 800/367–5004* 🖶 *808/552–
2201* ⊕ *www.castleresorts.com* ⇨ *36 rooms, 11 suites, 2 1-bedroom
cottages* ⚅ *Fans, kitchens, in-room VCRs, 18-hole golf course, pool,
beach, shops; no a/c* ⊟ *AE, MC, V.*

Central Moloka'i

$$ ⊞ **Moloka'i Shores.** Every room in this oceanfront, three-story condo-
minium complex has a view of the water. One-bedroom, one-bath units
or two-bedroom, two-bath units all have full kitchens and furnished lānai,
which look out on 4 acres of manicured lawns with picnic tables. There's
a great view of Lāna'i in the distance. ⊠ *450 Kamehameha V Hwy. (Box
1037), Kaunakakai 96748* ☎ *808/553–5954 or 800/535–0085* 🖶 *800/
633–5085* ⇨ *100 units* ⚅ *Fans, kitchens, cable TV, pool, shuffleboard;
no a/c* ⊟ *AE, D, MC, V.*

$–$$ ⊞ **Hotel Moloka'i.** Friendly staff members here embody the aloha spirit.
Fodor'sChoice Low-slung Polynesian-style buildings with wood roof shingles are set
★ waterside. Simple, tropical furnishings with white rattan accents fill the
rooms, and a basket swing awaits on the lānai. The Oceanfront Dining
Room serves breakfast, lunch, dinner, and libations—with entertainment
on weekend nights. Ask about deals in conjunction with airlines and
rental-car companies when you make your reservation. ⊠ *Kamehameha
V Hwy. (Box 1020), Kaunakakai 96748* ☎ *808/553–5347 or 800/367–
5004* 🖶 *808/553–5047* ⊕ *www.hotelmolokai.com* ⇨ *45 rooms*
⚅ *Restaurant, fans, some kitchenettes, cable TV, pool, lounge, laundry
facilities; no a/c* ⊟ *AE, D, DC, MC, V.*

¢–$ ⊞ **A Hawaiian Getaway.** If you want to learn about Moloka'i's history
and culture, consider staying here: gracious hosts Lawrence and Catherine Aki have an extensive library and also conduct cultural hikes. Two
rooms in the home are available. Small and simply decorated, both have
double beds and one has a TV and VCR. Guests use the same entrance,
bathroom, and living room as the proprietors. It's within walking distance of Kaunakakai town. ⊠ *270 Kaiwi St., Kaunakakai 96748* ☎ *808/
553–9803 or 800/274–9303* ✉ *mcai@aloha.net* ⇨ *2 rooms with
shared bath* ⚅ *Fans, some cable TV, some in-room VCRs, hair salon,
library, laundry facilities; no a/c* ⊟ *No credit cards.*

East Moloka'i

$$–$$$ ⊞ **Pu'u O Hoku Ranch.** At the east end of Moloka'i, near mile marker
25, are three ocean-view accommodations on 14,000 isolated acres of
pastures and forest. One country cottage has two bedrooms, basic
wicker furnishings, and *lau hala* matting on the floors. An airy four-bedroom cottage has a small deck and a somewhat Balinese air. The lodge,
which has 11 rooms and seven bathrooms, is similarly decorated. Groups

can book the full lodge for $1,100 nightly. Inquire about horseback riding on the property. ⊠ *Rte. 450 (Box 1889), Kaunakakai 96748* ☎ *808/ 558–8109* 🗗 *808/558–8100* ⊕ *www.puuohoku.com* 🗗 *1 2-bedroom cottage, 1 4-bedroom cottage, 11 rooms in lodge* ⚬ *Kitchens, pool, hiking, horseback riding; no a/c* ⊟ *No credit cards.*

$$ ⊞ **Dunbar Beachfront Cottages.** These two spotlessly clean two-bedroom, one-bath cottages with complete kitchens—each with its own secluded beach—are set near the ocean, about ¼ mi apart. The beach is good for swimming and snorkeling during the summer months and great for whale-watching during the winter. Covered lānai have panoramic vistas of Maui, Lānaʻi, and Kahoʻolawe across the ocean. ⊠ *King Kamehameha V Hwy., mile marker 18 (HC01, Box 901), Kauanakakai 96748* ☎ *808/ 558–8153 or 800/673–0520* 🗗 *808/558–8153* ⊕ *www.molokai-beachfront-cottages.com* 🗗 *2 cottages* ⚬ *Fans, kitchens, in-room VCRs, beach; no a/c* ⊟ *No credit cards.*

$–$$ ⊞ **Kamalō Plantation Cottage and Moanui Beach House.** Both of these Polynesian-style cottages have a fully equipped kitchen, living room, dining room, and deck. Kamalō, with one king-size bed, is at the base of a mountain. Moanui has two king-size beds, a TV, and a VCR. It's on a good snorkeling beach and has great views from its huge deck. Home-grown fruit and fresh-baked bread are provided for breakfast. ⊠ *East of Kaunakakai off Rte. 450* 🗗 *HC 01, Box 300, Kaunakakai 96748* ☎🗗 *808/558–8236* ⊕ *www.molokai.com/kamalo* 🗗 *2 cottages* ⚬ *Fans, kitchens; no a/c* ⊟ *No credit cards* ⎮⊚⎮ *BP.*

$–$$ ⊞ **Wavecrest.** This oceanfront condominium complex is convenient if you want to explore the east side of the island—it's 3 mi east of Kaunakakai. Individually decorated one- and two-bedroom units have full kitchens. Each has a furnished lānai, some with views of Maui and Lānaʻi. Be sure to ask for an updated unit when you make your reservation. The shallow water here is bad for swimming but good for fishing. ⊠ *Rte. 450 near mile marker 13* 🗗 *Friendly Isle Realty, 75 Ala Mālama, Kaunakakai 96748* ☎ *808/553–3666 or 800/600–4158* 🗗 *808/553– 3867* ⊕ *www.molokairealty.com* 🗗 *126 1- and 2-bedroom condominiums (10 rentals)* ⚬ *Fans, kitchens, 2 tennis courts, pool, beach, shuffleboard; no a/c* ⊟ *V.*

$ ⊞ **Honomuni House.** One acre of tropical garden is complemented by waterfalls and a freshwater stream. Inside the rental are a kitchen, one bedroom, one bath, and a large living-dining room with pullout couch. An outdoor shower with hot water is an added bonus. It's 17 mi east of Kaunakakai on Route 450. ⊠ *Rte. 450 (HC 1, Box 700), Kaunakakai 96748* ☎ *808/558–8383* 🗗 *1 house* ⚬ *Kitchen; no a/c, no room TVs* ⊟ *No credit cards.*

NIGHTLIFE & THE ARTS

Local nightlife consists mainly of gathering with friends and family, sipping a few cold ones, strumming ʻukuleles and guitars, singing old songs, and talking story. Still, there are a few ways to kick up your heels for a festive night out. Pick up a copy of the weekly *Molokaʻi Dispatch*—and see if there's a church supper or square dance. The bar at the Hotel

Moloka'i is always a good place to drink by the tiki torches. Most nights they have some kind of live music by island performers. The "Aloha Friday" weekly gathering here, 4–6 PM, always attracts a couple dozen old-timers with guitars and 'ukuleles. This impromptu, feel-good event is a peak experience for any Moloka'i trip.

Film

Maunaloa Town Cinemas. Folks from all around Moloka'i come here nightly for current blockbusters. ⊠ *Maunaloa Hwy., Maunaloa* ☎ *808/ 552–2707.*

SPORTS & THE OUTDOORS

Fitness & Spa Centers

The **Spa Venture** is Moloka'i's closest thing to a full-service spa. With natural-wood decor lending a rustic feeling to locker rooms and saunas, the spa fits right in with the low-key ranch hotel. A swimming pool and an exercise room are here, and massages are available. ⊠ *The Lodge at Moloka'i Ranch, Maunaloa Hwy., Maunaloa* ☎ *808/660–2710* ▣ *Free admittance for lodge guests or nonguests with massage appointment.*

Turning Point Therapeutic Massage has herbal remedies, and the staff offers nutritional advice to keep you at the top of your form. Allana Noury has been studying natural medicine for more than 30 years and is a licensed massage therapist, herbalist, and naturopathic physician. Ask for a traditional Hawaiian *lomi lomi* treatment. A 30-minute massage is $30; one hour is $50. It's just across the street from the Friendly Market in Kaunakakai. ⊠ *107 Ala Mālama., Kaunakakai* ☎ *808/553–8034.*

Golf

Compared with the more commercialized Neighbor Islands, Moloka'i has a relatively mellow golf scene.

Although west-end Kaluako'i Hotel remains closed, the **Kaluako'i Golf Club** has reopened with enthusiasm and with the boost of drought-ending rains. In the basking heat, golfers can look out over the Kaiwi Channel, with O'ahu in the background. The 9-hole course includes a driving range and rentals of clubs, shoes, and pull carts. ⊠ *Kaluako'i Rd., Maunaloa* ☎ *808/552–0255* ▣ *Greens fee $35, cart $20.*

The **Ironwood Hills Golf Club** in Upcountry Kala'e is a public 9-hole course. This was pastureland until the Del Monte Corporation turned it into a golf course for plantation workers in 1928. It gets windy in the afternoons, so plan for a morning tee time. ⊠ *Turn off Rte. 460 onto 470 and go north uphill 3½ mi; dirt road to golf course is on left side, Kualapu'u* ☎ *808/567–6000* ▣ *Greens fee $14, cart $14.*

Hiking

You can make a day of hiking to Kalaupapa and back along the 3-mi, 26-switchback trail that is also used for the Moloka'i Mule Ride. The trail is well maintained by the **National Park Service** (🖃 Box 2222, Kalaupapa 96742 ☎ 808/567–6802). You need a confirmed reservation with **Damien Tours** (☎ 808/567–6171) to see Kalaupapa village.

Historical Hikes of West Moloka'i has six guided hikes, ranging from two to six hours. The outings focus on Moloka'i's cultural past taking you to sites such as an ancient quarry, an early fishing village, or high sea cliffs where Hawaiian chiefs played games during the Makahiki season. Backpacks are provided, as is lunch on intermediate and advanced hikes. Guides Lawrence and Catherine Aki also run A Hawaiian Getaway vacation rental. 🖃 *The Lodge at Moloka'i Ranch Activity Desk, Maunaloa Hwy., Maunaloa* ☎ *808/552–2797, 808/553–9803, or 800/274–9303* ⊕ *www.molokai-aloha.com/hikes* 🖃 *$45–$125.*

Horseback Riding

Set on the prow of the island's Maui-facing east end, **Pu'u O Hoku Ranch** keeps a stable of magnificent, amiable horses that are available for trail rides starting at $55 an hour. The peak experience is a four-hour beach ride ($120) that culminates at a secluded cove where the horses are happy to swim, rider and all. Bring your own lunch. 🖃 *Rte. 450, 20 mi east of Kaunakakai* ☎ *808/558–8109* ⊕ *www.puuohoku.com.*

Water Sports

FISHING The six-passenger, 31-foot cruiser *Alyce C.* (🖃 Kaunakakai Wharf ☎ 808/558–8377) runs excellent sportfishing excursions. The cost is $400 for a nine-hour trip, $300 for five to six hours. Shared charters are available.

Fun Hogs Hawai'i (🖃 Kaunakakai Wharf ☎ 808/567–6789) takes out the 27-foot *Ahi* for half-day ($350), six-hour ($400), and full-day ($450) sportfishing. Full-day bottom-fishing trips, all equipment furnished, are $500.

SAILING The 42-foot Cascade sloop *Satan's Doll* is your craft with **Moloka'i Charters** (🖃 Kaunakakai Wharf ☎ 808/553–5852). The company arranges two-hour sails for $40 per person. Half-day sailing trips cost $50 per person, including soft drinks and snacks. A minimum of four people is required, but shared charters can be arranged.

KAYAKING **Moloka'i Fish and Dive** (🖃 61 Ala Mālama St., Kaunakakai ☎ 808/553–5926) offers guided kayak excursions along the island's south shore, where you'll paddle through a dense mangrove forest and explore a huge, hidden ancient fishpond. The fee is $80 for the half-day trip. Check at the store (located on Ala Mālama Street) for numerous other outdoor activities. To rent a kayak for your own purposes, go to **Moloka'i Outdoors** (🖃 in the Hotel Moloka'i lobby ☎ 808/553–4227), or **Moloka'i Rentals & Tours** (☎ 800/553–9071, 808/658–1717 ⊕ www.molokai-rentals.com).

Spectacular north-shore sightseeing trips with **Fun Hogs Hawai'i** (✉ Kaunakakai Wharf ☎ 808/567–6789) cost $500 and are only for the sea hardy. Whale-watching trips from December to April take 2½ hours, depart at 8 and 10:30, and cost $65 per person. Bring your own snacks and drinks. You can also book a snorkeling excursion or a custom cruise.

Moloka'i Charters (✉ Kaunakakai Wharf, Kaunakakai 96748 ☎ 808/553–5852) takes people via sailboat on full-day snorkeling excursions to the island of Lāna'i for $90 per person. Soft drinks and a picnic lunch are included.

Tim and Susan Forsberg, owners of **Moloka'i Fish and Dive** (✉ 61 Ala Mālama St., Kaunakakai ☎ 808/553–5926), can fill you in on how to find the best snorkel and dive sites, rent you the gear, or hook you up with one of their PADI-certified dive guides to take you to the island's best underwater spots. They know the island's best blue holes and underwater cave systems, and they can take you swimming with hammerhead sharks.

SHOPPING

Moloka'i has one main commercial area: Ala Mālama Street in Kaunakakai. There are no department stores or shopping malls, and the clothing available is typical island wear.

Most stores in Kaunakakai are open Monday through Saturday between 9 and 6. In Maunaloa most shops close by 4 in the afternoon and all day Sunday.

West Moloka'i

A handful of family-run businesses line the main drag of Maunaloa, a rural plantation town.

Arts & Crafts

The **Big Wind Kite Factory and Plantation Gallery** (✉ 120 Maunaloa Hwy., Maunaloa ☎ 808/552–2364) has custom-made appliquéd kites you can fly or display. Designs range from hula girls to tropical fish. Also in stock are kits, paper kites, minikites, and wind socks. Ask to go on the factory tour, or take a free kite-flying lesson. The gallery is intermingled with the kite shop and carries everything from locally made crafts to Hawaiian books and CDs, sunglasses, and incense.

Grocery Store

Victuals and travel essentials are available at the **Maunaloa General Store** (✉ 200 Maunaloa Hwy., Maunaloa ☎ 808/552–2346). Open Monday–Saturday 8–6, it's convenient for guests staying at the nearby condos of the Kaluako'i Resort area, who shop here for meat, produce, dry goods, drinks, and all the little things you find in a general store.

Central Moloka'i

You can walk from one end of Kaunakakai's main street, Ala Mālama, to the other in about five minutes—unless you like to browse, of course.

Ho'olehua has just one must-shop stop, the Plantation Store, next to Coffees of Hawai'i.

Arts & Crafts
Kamakana Fine Arts Gallery (✉ 110 Ala Mālama St., Kaunakakai ☎ 808/553–8520) only represents artists who live on the island, including world-class talent in photography, wood carving, ceramics, and Hawaiian musical instruments. This business actively supports the local community by showcasing talents that might otherwise go undiscovered. It's above American Savings Bank.

Clothing
Casual, knockabout island wear is sold at **Imports Gift Shop** (✉ 82 Ala Mālama St., Kaunakakai ☎ 808/553–5734), across from Kanemitsu Bakery. **Moloka'i Island Creations** (✉ 62 Ala Mālama St., Kaunakakai ☎ 808/553–5926) carries exclusive swimwear, beach cover-ups, sun hats, and tank tops. **Moloka'i Surf** (✉ 130 Kamehameha V Hwy., Kaunakakai ☎ 808/553–5093) is known for its wide selection of Moloka'i T-shirts, swimwear, and sports clothing.

Grocery Stores
Friendly Market Center (✉ 93 Ala Mālama St., Kaunakakai ☎ 808/553–5595) is the best-stocked supermarket on the island. Its slogan—"Your family store on Moloka'i"—is truly credible: hats, T-shirts, and sun-and-surf essentials keep company with fresh produce, meat, groceries, liquor, and sundries. Locals say the food is fresher here than at the other major supermarket in town. It's open weekdays 8:30–8:30 and Saturday 8:30–6:30.

Misaki's Inc. (✉ 78 Ala Mālama St., Kaunakakai ☎ 808/553–5505) is a grocery with authentic island allure. It has been in business since 1922. Pick up housewares and beverages here, as well as your food staples, Monday–Saturday 8:30–8:30 and Sunday 9–noon.

Don't let the name **Moloka'i Wines 'n' Spirits** (✉ 77 Ala Mālama St., Kaunakakai ☎ 808/553–5009) fool you. Along with a surprisingly good selection of fine wines and liquors, the store also carries gourmet cheeses and snacks. It's open Sunday–Thursday 9 AM–10 PM, Friday and Saturday until 10:30.

Island Goods
The **Plantation Store** (✉ Kualapu'u Base Yard, Farrington Hwy., Ho'olehua ☎ 808/567–9023) has Moloka'i-made products, including Moloka'i-grown coffee, local artwork, jewelry, homemade jellies and jams, island soaps, pen-and-ink drawings of Moloka'i landscapes, and handcrafted pottery.

Jewelry
Imports Gift Shop (✉ 82 Ala Mālama St., Kaunakakai ☎ 808/553–5734) sells a decent collection of 14-karat-gold chains, rings, earrings, and bracelets, plus a jumble of Hawaiian quilts, pillows, books, and postcards. It also carries Hawaiian heirloom jewelry, unique replicas of popular Victorian pieces. These stunning gold pieces are made to order with your Hawaiian name inscribed on them.

Moloka'i Island Creations (✉ 62 Ala Mālama St., Kaunakakai ☎ 808/553–5926) carries its own unique line of jewelry, including sea opal, coral, and sterling silver, as well as other gifts and resort wear.

Sporting Goods

Moloka'i Bicycle (✉ 80 Mohala St., Kaunakakai ☎ 808/553–5740, or 800/709–2453 ⊕ www.bikehawaii.com/molokaibicycle) rents and sells mountain and road bikes as well as jogging strollers, kids' trailers, helmets, and racks. It supplies maps and information on biking and hiking and will drop off and pick up equipment for a fee nearly anywhere on the island. Call or stop by to arrange what you need.

Moloka'i Fish and Dive (✉ 61 Ala Mālama St., Kaunakakai ☎ 808/553–5926) is *the* main source for your sporting needs, from snorkeling rentals to free and friendly advice. These folks handle all activities for The Lodge at Moloka'i Ranch. This is also a good place to pick up original-design Moloka'i T-shirts and gifts.

MOLOKA'I A TO Z

To research prices, get advice from other travelers, and book travel arrangements, visit www.fodors.com.

AIR TRAVEL

If you're flying in from the mainland United States, you must first make a stop in Honolulu. From there, it's a 25-minute trip to the Friendly Isle.

CARRIERS Hawaiian Airlines flies its DC-9 jet aircraft daily between O'ahu and Moloka'i. A round-trip ticket can cost up to $200 per person. Island Air, the puddle-jumper arm of Aloha Airlines, provides daily flights between Molokai and O'ahu or Maui on its 18-passenger de Haviland Dash-8 Twin Otters. Pacific Wings flies an eight-passenger Cessna daily between O'ahu and Moloka'i.

Pacific Wings also flies from Honolulu to Ho'olehua Airport and from Honolulu to the airstrip in Kalaupapa. Your arrival there should coincide with one of the authorized ground tours of the area. Otherwise you'll be asked to leave. Paragon Air runs commuter and charter flights and trips to Kalaupapa. Moloka'i Air Shuttle flies from Honolulu to Kalaupapa.

🛪 **Hawaiian Airlines** ☎ 800/367–5320 ⊕ www.aa.com. **Island Air** ☎ 800/323–3345 ⊕ www.islandair.com. **Moloka'i Air Shuttle** ☎ 808/567–6847 in Honolulu. **Pacific Wings** ☎ 808/873–0877 or 888/575–4546 ⊕ www.pacificwings.com. **Paragon Air** ☎ 808/244–3356 or 800/428–1231 ⊕ www.paragon-air.com.

AIRPORTS

Moloka'i's transportation hub is Ho'olehua Airport, a tiny airstrip 8 mi west of Kaunakakai and about 18 mi east of Maunaloa. An even smaller airstrip serves the little community of Kalaupapa on the north shore.

🛪 **Ho'olehua Airport** ☎ 808/567–6140. **Kalaupapa Airfield** ☎ 808/567–6331.

AIRPORT From Ho'olehua Airport, it takes about 10 minutes to reach Kau-
TRANSFERS nakakai and 25 minutes to reach the condominiums of Kaluako'i Hotel

by car. Since there's no rush hour, traffic won't be a problem. There's no public bus.

Shuttle service for two passengers costs about $18 from Ho'olehua Airport to Kaunakakai and about $18 to Kaluako'i Hotel and Golf Club. A trip to Moloka'i Ranch costs $28, divided by the number of passengers. For shuttle service via a car or a van, call Moloka'i Off-Road Tours and Taxi or Molokai Outdoors.

🚩 **Moloka'i Off-Road Tours and Taxi** ☎ 808/553-3369. **Molokai Outdoors** ☎ 808/553-4227 ⊕ www.molokai-outdoors.com.

FERRY   The Moloka'i Ferry crosses the channel every day between Lahaina (Maui) and Kaunakakai, making it easy for West Maui visitors to put Moloka'i on their itineraries. The 1½-hr trip takes passengers but not cars, so arrange ahead of time for a car rental or tour at the arrival point.

🚩 **Moloka'i Ferry** ☎ 800/275-6969 ⊕ www.molokaiferry.com.

CAR RENTAL

Budget maintains a counter near the baggage claim area at the airport. Dollar also has offices at Ho'olehua Airport, and your rental car can be picked up in the parking lot. Expect to pay from $30 to $50 per day for a standard compact and from $36 to $55 for a midsize car. Rates are seasonal and may run higher during the peak winter months. It's best to make arrangements in advance. If you're flying on Island Air or Hawaiian Airlines, see whether fly-drive package deals are available—you might luck out on a less-expensive rate. Hotels and outfitters might also offer packages.

Locally owned Island Kine Rent-a-Car offers airport or hotel pickup and sticks to one rate year-round for vehicles ($35 to $50 per day) in a broad spectrum from two- and four-wheel drives to 15-passenger vans. The same is true for Moloka'i Rentacar, located right on the main street in Kaunakakai. Another option is to contact Moloka'i Rentals & Tours, a company that provides customized solutions to Moloka'i visitors' specific needs.

🚩 **Major Agencies: Budget** ☎ 808/451-3600 or 800/527-7000 ⊕ www.budget.com. **Dollar** ☎ 808/567-6156 or 800/367-7006 ⊕ www.dollar.com.

🚩 **Local Agencies: Island Kine Rent-a-Car** ☎ 808/553-5242 ⊕ www.molokai-aloha.com/cars. **Moloka'i Rentacar** ✉ 82 Ala Mālama, Kaunakakai ☎ 808/553-3929 🖷 808/553-9808. **Moloka'i Rentals & Tours** ☎ 808/658-1717 or 800/553-9071 ⊕ www.molokai-rentals.com.

CAR TRAVEL

If you want to explore Moloka'i from one end to the other, it's best to rent a car. With just a few main roads to choose from, it's a snap to drive around here.

The gas stations are in Kaunakakai and Maunaloa. When you park your car, be sure to lock it—thefts do occur. Drivers must wear seat belts or risk a $42 fine. Children under three must ride in a federally approved child passenger restraint device, easily leased at the rental agency. Ask your rental agent for a free *Moloka'i Drive Guide*.

EMERGENCIES

Round-the-clock medical attention is available at Moloka'i General Hospital. Severe cases or emergencies are often airlifted to Honolulu.

⚡ Emergency Services Ambulance and general emergencies ☎ 911. **Coast Guard** ☎ 808/552-6458 on O'ahu. **Fire** ☎ 808/553-5601 in Kaunakakai, 808/567-6525 at Ho'olehua Airport. **Police** ☎ 808/553-5355.

⚡ Hospital Moloka'i General Hospital ✉ 280A Puali St., Kaunakakai ☎ 808/553-5331.

TOURS

ADVENTURE TOURS
Walter Naki is a friendly, knowledgeable guide who custom-designs tours through his Moloka'i Action Adventures. One of his most popular excursions is a north-shore cruise aboard a 21-foot Boston Whaler. He is also a competent guide for year-round fishing and hunting trips.

Moloka'i Outdoors is a "one-stop shop" provider of customized visits to this unusual island. The company will shuttle you from the airport, set you up with one of its own rental cars, rent you a bike or kayak, and guide you where you want to go—with particular emphasis on the east end of the island.

If you want a smart island resident to set you up with a unique vacation rental, a car to drive, a kayak tour, private cooking, and personalized help with tours of any kind, you should call Moloka'i Rentals & Tours. It's like having a close friend on the island.

⚡ Moloka'i Action Adventures ☎ 808/558-8184. **Moloka'i Outdoors** ☎ 808/553-4477 ⊕ www.molokai-outdoors.com. **Moloka'i Rentals & Tours** ☎ 808/658-1717 or 800/553-9071 ⊕ www.molokai-rentals.com.

BIKE TOURS
Moloka'i Fish and Dive runs the activity desk of The Lodge at Moloka'i Ranch in Maunaloa, which has a well-stocked rental shop for mountain bikes and related two-wheel gear. This is the gateway to one of the best mountain-biking facilities in the world, compared favorably by enthusiasts to Moab and Hood River. Guides will take you on the network of single-track biking trails that branches out from Maunaloa. Excursions can be super-challenging or as easy as a mild gravity ride to the coast, with van transport back. The guides take extremists on a gorgeous but challenging adventure in Na'iwa—the remote central mountains—for convoluted forest courses, daredevil verticals (if you want), and exhilarating miles at the brink of the world's tallest sea cliffs.

Moloka'i Bicycle will take mountain-bikers out to two-wheel the expansive east-end spread of Pu'u O Hoku Ranch. You might ride along an eastern ridge rimming Hālawa Valley to four waterfalls and a remote pool for swimming, or pedal on sea cliffs to a secluded beach. Daily tours for a minimum of two people cost $45 per person for a half day and $65 for a full day, including lunch.

⚡ Moloka'i Bicycle ☎ 808/553-3931. **Moloka'i Fish and Dive** ✉ 61 Ala Mālama St., Kaunakakai ☎ 808/553-5926.

KALAUPAPA TOURS
Tours of this former leper colony are led through Damien Tours by long-time residents of Kalaupapa, who are well versed in its history. The four-hour van tour begins and ends at Kalaupapa Airfield if you arrive by

air, or at the foot of the 3-mi trail if you hike down the mountain. Tours depart at 10:15 Monday–Saturday and cost $30. Reservations are essential. No one under 16 is allowed. Bring your own lunch and water.

You can contact Damien Tours directly, and it can arrange everything including flights. Moloka'i Mule Ride can also make all your arrangements—transport, flight or mule ride, and tour. Moloka'i Air Shuttle also offers packages, or flights can be arranged separately for the tour through several airlines.

7 Damien Tours ☎ 808/567-6171. **Moloka'i Air Shuttle** ☎ 808/567-6847 in Honolulu. **Moloka'i Mule Ride** ☎ 808/567-6088.

VAN TOURS   Visit Hālawa Valley, Kalaupapa Lookout, Maunaloa town, and other points of interest in the comfort of an air-conditioned van on four- or six-hour tours. At Moloka'i Off-Road Tours and Taxi, Pat and Alex Pua'a are your personal guides. They'll even help you mail a coconut back home. Tours cost $36 to $49 and begin at 9 AM. Charters are also available.

Moloka'i Outdoors, based in the lobby of the Hotel Moloka'i, can organize island van tours with experienced guides who focus on local culture, customs, and history. It can also arrange trips to Kamakou Preserve.

7 Moloka'i Off-Road Tours and Taxi ☎ 808/553-3369. **Molokai Outdoors** ☎ 808/553-4227 ⊕ www.molokai-outdoors.com.

VISITOR INFORMATION

There's tourist information available in kiosks and stands at the airport in Ho'olehua or at the Moloka'i Visitors Association. The Maui Visitors Bureau has travel information for Maui County, of which Moloka'i is a part.

Molokaievents.com, Inc., has information on island events and can help you plan your own events on the island.

Car-rental agencies distribute the free *Moloka'i Drive Guide* along with maps and other up-to-date information.

7 Maui Visitors Bureau ⌂ On Maui: Box 580, Wailuku 96793 ☎ 808/244-3530 ⊕ www.visitmaui.com. **Molokaievents.com, Inc.** ☎ 808/567-6789 ⊕ www.molokaievents.com. **Moloka'i Visitors Association** ⊠ 10 Kamehameha V Hwy. (Box 960), Kaunakakai ☎ 808/553-3876 or 800/800-6367 ⊕ molokai-hawaii.com.

LĀNA‘I

TAKE THE ULTIMATE PLUNGE
at the Cathedrals dive site ⇨*p.402*

GO FOR THE GLOW AT SUNSET
in the Garden of the Gods ⇨*p.395*

MAKE LIKE ROBIN HOOD
at Lāna‘i Pine archery range ⇨*p.402*

BEAT IT TO A MOUNTAIN RETREAT
at the secluded Lodge at Kō‘ele ⇨*p.399*

GET SHELL SHOCKED
at Shipwreck Beach, the best spot
for beachcombers ⇨*p.397*

Updated by
Shannon
Wianecki

LĀNAʻI WELCOMES VISITORS with its rustic charm, but it hasn't always been so amiable. The earliest Polynesians believed it to be haunted by evil ghosts who gobbled up unsuspecting souls. In 1836, a pair of missionaries named Dwight Baldwin and William Richards came and went after failing to convert the locals to Christianity. In 1854, a group of Mormons tried to create the City of Joseph here, but they were forced to abandon their mission after a drought in 1857.

With the Mormons came Walter Gibson, who managed to acquire ownership of much of the land and transformed Lānaʻi into a ranching colony: by 1892 close to 50,000 sheep grazed the dry hillsides, competing for food with goats and cattle. Eighteen years later a New Zealander, George Munro, was hired by an investment group that later formed the Lānaʻi Company to reforest the land, which marked the first effort to protect Lānaʻi's eroding watershed. The hundreds of Cook pines that define the profile of Lānaʻi today form part of his legacy.

There were also attempts to grow sugar, but they never took hold in Lānaʻi: on the east side, the ruins of a boat landing and an abandoned church tell the story of this ill-fated crop.

In 1922, American-born Jim Dole's Hawaiian Pineapple Company bought the island for $1.1 million, thus marking a time of great transition for Lānaʻi. Hundreds of people, mostly of Asian descent, moved to the island. To accommodate them, Dole built Lānaʻi City on the flatlands beneath Lānaʻihale. He also planned the harbor at Kaumalapau, from which his pineapples would be shipped. Four years later, as he watched the first harvest sail away to Honolulu, the entrepreneur could safely say Dole Plantation was a success.

For decades, Lānaʻi was known as the Pineapple Island, with hundreds of acres filled with the golden fruit. But in the late 1980s pineapples ceased to be profitable. The solution? Dole's Lānaʻi Company, currently known as Castle & Cooke Resorts, built two sophisticated resorts and developed a now thriving tourism industry.

Lānaʻi City, the island's only population center, with about 2,800 residents, remains an old plantation town with a few family-run shops, diner-style eateries, and an art center. Tall Cook pines shade streets filled with tiny, colorful houses with tin roofs, and tidy gardens.

Lānaʻi is home to many natural wonders. To the northwest lies the Garden of the Gods, where wind-sculpted boulders punctuate a crimson landscape. Adjacent is a trail through the Kānepuʻu Preserve, a dryland forest with some 48 native species, including the endangered Hawaiian gardenia. On the southern tip, at Hulopoʻe Beach, you can see turquoise and jade fish within a minute of snorkeling. After ascending the summit of Lānaʻihale, a 3,370-foot-high windswept perch in the eastern reaches, you'll see the profile of nearly every Hawaiian island.

Though Castle & Cooke still owns 98% of this 141-square-mi island, pineapple fields have given way to championship golf courses and an open wilderness. Despite the changes, Lānaʻi remains remote and intimate, earning its new nickname, Hawaiʻi's Most Secluded Island.

Exploring Lāna'i

Most of Lāna'i's sights are out of the way—rent a four-wheel-drive vehicle, ask for a road map, be sure you have a full tank, and bring a snack. Don't stray from marked paths, and ask your hotel's concierge about road conditions before you set out.

The main road in Lāna'i, Route 440, refers to both Kaumalapau Highway and Mānele Road.

On the Islands, the directions *mauka* (toward the mountains) and *makai* (toward the ocean) are often used.

About the Restaurants

Lāna'i has developed its own version of Hawai'i regional cuisine. The upscale menus at the Lodge at Kō'ele and Mānele Bay Hotel draw on the bounty provided by local hunters and fisherfolk—everything from 'ahi to venison. Lāna'i City's eclectic fare ranges from local-style plate lunches to Louisiana ribs and pizza.

About the Hotels

Though Lāna'i has few properties, it does have a range of price options. The Lodge at Kō'ele and Mānele Bay Hotel are luxury resorts, which their rates reflect. If you're on a budget, seek out a bed-and-breakfast or consider the Hotel Lāna'i. House rentals, a great option for families, give you a taste of everyday life on the island.

WHAT IT COSTS				
	$$$$	**$$$**	**$$**	**$**	**¢**
RESTAURANTS	over $30	$20–$30	$12–$20	$7–$12	under $7
HOTELS	over $200	$150–$200	$100–$150	$60–$100	under $60

Restaurant prices are for one main course at dinner. Hotel prices are for two people in a standard double room in high season, including tax and service.

Weather

Lāna'i has an ideal climate year-round, hot and sunny at the sea and a few delicious degrees cooler Upcountry. In Lāna'i City, the nights and mornings can be almost chilly when a mystic fog settles in.

SOUTH & WEST LĀNA'I

Pineapples once blanketed the Pālāwai Basin, the flat area south of Lāna'i City. Today it's primarily a wilderness traversed by hunters and botanists, and holds historic treasures. You'll need a four-wheel-drive vehicle to explore this rugged area.

a good drive

Start at the Lodge at Kō'ele to get a glimpse of early ranching history. The lone **Norfolk Pine ❶** ▶ in front of the Lodge, planted in 1875, was the source of inspiration for the island's current watershed of pines. On the left stands **Ka Lokahi o Ka Mālamalama Church ❷**.

If you have 1 day

If you can squeeze in just one day of exploring, rent a four-wheel-drive vehicle and get to know the back roads, where the landscape's power and beauty are immutable. If you're staying at or close to the Lodge at Kō'ele, take a look here at the solitary **Norfolk Pine ❶** and the little historic **Ka Lokahi o Ka Mālamalama Church ❷** before heading out to swim at Hulopo'e Beach at **Mānele Bay ❹**. Stop to find the **Lu'ahiwa Petroglyphs ❺** on your way back up to **Lāna'i City ❸**. After lunch in town, drive to **Garden of the Gods ❿** and the **Kānepu'u Preserve ❾**. If you're a guest at the Mānele Bay Hotel, reverse the morning itinerary.

If you have 3 days

On the first day, follow the above itinerary. On the second day, take an adventurous tour of the undeveloped east shore. Pack a picnic lunch and start the day with a drive to **Shipwreck Beach ⓬** for a morning walk. Then drive along a bumpy coastal road to explore **Keōmuku ⓭**, **Kahe'a Heiau ⓯**, **Naha ⓰**, and Lōpā Beach. Start your third day with a cool morning hike up the **Munro Trail ⓫** to Lāna'ihale. A drive out to **Kaumalapau Harbor ❽**, stopping to explore **Kaunolū ❼** and **Halulu Heiau ❻**, gives you a fascinating glimpse into Lāna'i's ancient cultural past and its bygone pineapple days.

If you have 5 days

Follow the three-day itinerary above and dedicate the fourth day to the sport of your choice. On the fifth day, rent a jeep to drive out to spectacular Polihua Beach or take a half-day fishing trip or snorkeling–scuba diving expedition.

Pause in **Lāna'i City ❸** for an espresso, and then drive south on Route 440 until you reach a major intersection. Turn left on Highway 440 East, and drive down the long, steep hill. At the bottom awaits **Mānele Bay ❹** and the island's only true swimming area, Hulopo'e Beach. Backtrack up the hill. After about five miles you'll see a stop sign and a dirt road on the right, leading to the **Lu'ahiwa Petroglyphs ❺**.

Return to the Highway 440 intersection, this time turning toward the airport. Drive 4 mi south to where the road veers left. Venture onto unpaved Kaupili Road; then navigate your jeep down to the well-preserved archaeological sites of **Halulu Heiau ❻** and **Kaunolū ❼**. Returning to the paved highway, follow it west to **Kaumalapau Harbor ❽**, the island's main seaport and a great sunset spot.

TIMING   You could explore this small area in just half a day, but if you like water sports, you may indulge in a few hours at Hulopo'e Beach. The wind often picks up in the afternoon, so it's best to swim early. The south is sunny, clear, and warm, so wear sunscreen and find shade at midday.

What to See

❻ **Halulu Heiau.** The carefully excavated remains of an impressive heiau, which was actively used by Lāna'i's earliest residents, attest to this spot's sacred history. As late as 1810, this hilltop sight was also considered a place of refuge, where those who had broken *kapu* (taboos) were forgiven and where women and children could find safety in times of war. ✉ *From*

Lāna'i City follow Hwy. 440 (Mānele Rd.) south; when road makes sharp left, continue straight on Kaupili Rd.; turn makai onto fourth dirt road.

② **Ka Lokahi o Ka Mālamalama Church.** This picturesque church was built in 1938 to provide Hawaiian services for Lāna'i's growing population—for many people, the only other Hawaiian church, in coastal Keōmuku, was too far away. Typical of plantation days, the church had to be moved from its original Lānāi Ranch location when the Lodge at Kō'ele was built. Services are still held, in Hawaiian and English. ⊠ *Left of entrance to Lodge at Kō'ele.*

⑧ **Kaumalapau Harbor.** Built in 1926 by the Hawaiian Pineapple Company, which later became Dole, this is Lāna'i's principal seaport. The cliffs that flank the western shore are as much as 1,000 feet tall. Water activities aren't allowed here, but it's a dramatic sunset spot. On Thursdays you can witness the arrival of the barge: the island depends on its weekly deliveries. ⊠ *From Lāna'i City follow Hwy. 440 (Kaumalapau Hwy.) west as far as it goes.*

⑦ **Kaunolū.** Atop the island's highest cliffs, Kaunolū was once a prosperous fishing village. This important archaeological site includes terraces, stone floors, and platforms. The impressive 90-foot drop to the ocean is called **Kahekili's Leap.** The ramparts of a shrine to Halulu, a deity who takes the shape of a colossal bird, guard the cliff edge. Warriors would make the death-defying jump into the mere 12 feet of water below to show their courage to Hawai'i's King Kamehameha I, who used the island as his summer hideaway. ⊠ *From Lāna'i City follow Hwy. 440 (Kaumalapau Hwy.) west; at the second stop sign, turn onto unpaved Kaupili Rd.; head makai after 2 mi.*

③ **Lāna'i City.** This tidy plantation town was built in 1924 by Jim Dole. It reflects his wish to create a model plantation village: a simple grid of roads lined with tall Cook pines and all the basic services a person might need. Visit the **Lāna'i Arts & Cultural Center** to get a glimpse of this island's creative abundance. ⊠ *339 7th Ave.*

⑤ **Lu'ahiwa Petroglyphs.** On a steep slope overlooking the Pālāwai Basin are 34 boulders with carvings. Drawn in a mixture of ancient and historic styles dating to the late 1700s and early 1800s, the simple stick-figure illustrations depict life on Lāna'i. Some of the stones are believed to possess the spiritual power of rain gods. ⊠ *From Lāna'i City follow Hwy. 440 (Mānele Rd.) south 2 mi to unmarked dirt road leading left through fallow pineapple fields; at road's end, walk up unmarked trail to petroglyphs.*

④ **Mānele Bay.** The site of a Hawaiian village dating from AD 900, Mānele Bay is flanked by lava cliffs that are hundreds of feet high. Though a Marine Life Conservation District, it's the island's only public boat harbor and was the location of most post-contact shipping until Kaumalapau Harbor was built in 1926. The ferry to and from Maui also pulls in here.

Just offshore you can catch a glimpse of **Pu'upehe.** Often called Sweetheart Rock, the isolated 80-foot-high islet carries a sad Hawaiian legend. The rock is named after Pehe, a woman so beautiful that her

Hitting the Links

Lāna'i has two championship golf courses. The pine-covered fields of the Experience at Kō'ele stretch across hills punctuated by lakes, streams, and waterfalls. At the Challenge at Mānele, the Pacific Ocean makes a daunting water hazard: dolphins and whales have been known to distract even the most serious golfer.

Hiking & Biking

Only 30 mi of Lāna'i's roads are paved. But red-dirt roads and trails, ideal for hiking and mountain biking, will take you to abandoned villages with historic *heiau* (stone altars), isolated beaches, and forest preserves. Follow a self-guided walk through Hawai'i's largest native dryland forest, explore the Munro Trail over Lāna'ihale with views of plunging canyons, or participate in a guided hike along an old, coastal fisherman trail or across Koloiki Ridge.

Snorkeling & Scuba Diving

When you have a dive site such as Cathedrals—with pinnacle formations and mysterious caverns—it's no wonder that snorkeling and scuba diving buffs consider exploring the waters off Lāna'i akin to having a religious experience. For the best underwater viewing, try Hulopo'e Beach, a Marine Conservation Area, or go on an excursion with Trilogy or the Adventure Lāna'i Eco Centre.

---

husband, afraid that others would steal her away, kept her hidden in a sea cave. One day, while Pehe was alone, the surf surged into the cave and she drowned. With the help of the gods, her grief-stricken husband buried her offshore on the summit of this rock and then jumped to his own death. ⊠ *From Lāna'i City follow Hwy. 440 (Mānele Rd.) south to bottom of hill and look for harbor on your left.*

▶ ❶ **Norfolk Pine.** More than 100 feet high, this majestic pine tree was planted here, at the former site of the manager's house, in 1875. Almost 30 years later, George Munro, then the ranch manager, would observe how, in foggy weather, water collected on its foliage, forming a natural rain. This drip led to the planting of Cook pines along the ridge of Lāna'ihale and across town. ⊠ *Entrance of Lodge at Kō'ele.*

NORTH & EAST LĀNA'I

The north and east sections of Lāna'i are wild and untouched. A ghost town and deserted heiau are the only traces of civilization. Four-wheel drive is a must to explore this side of the isle, and be prepared for hot, rough conditions. Pack a picnic lunch and bring plenty of drinking water.

a good drive

Set out north of the Lodge at Kō'ele on Keōmuku Highway: turn left on the road between the Stables at Kō'ele and the tennis courts. Follow the dirt road a couple of miles and turn right at the crossroads onto Polihua Road, which heads north through the dryland forest of **Kānepu'u Preserve** ❾ ▶ and, 1½ mi beyond, the **Garden of the Gods** ❿.

Return to Keōmuku Highway and head east. After about 1 mi, make a right onto the only road in sight, Cemetery Road, and you're on your way to the **Munro Trail** ⑪, a 9-mi route that runs over the top of Lānaʻihale, the mountain that rises above Lānaʻi City.

Back on Keōmuku Highway, head makai—at an unofficial scenic point between mile markers 4 and 5 you'll find awesome views of Molokaʻi, Maui, and Kahoʻolawe and a first glimpse of the stranded World War II oiler at **Shipwreck Beach** ⑫.

If you feel adventurous, head southeast at the fork in the road where the beach starts, and follow the dirt road along the coast. The landscape changes from coastal dunes to *kiawe* forest (kiawe is a mesquite-type wood; watch for thorns!). Along the way, you'll come across abandoned Hawaiian homesteads. Five miles later, dozens of tall coconut trees announce the site of the old village **Keōmuku** ⑬, once a bustling sugar-mill town. Pause at the **Japanese Cemetery** ⑭. Nearby are the ruins of a temple called **Kaheʻa Heiau** ⑮, but you may need an experienced guide to find it. The road passes the often-deserted Lōpā Beach and ends 3 mi later at the remnants of an old Hawaiian fishpond at **Naha** ⑯.

TIMING Give yourself a day to tour the island's northern and eastern reaches. Keep your eye on the sky: the highlands tend to attract heavy fog. If you're a hiker, you'll want a day just to enjoy the journey up to Lāna'ihale. Since many of the roads are bumpy, it takes more time to reach sights than it does to actually experience them. But getting there is half the fun.

What to See

⑩ Garden of the Gods. This preternatural plateau is scattered with boulders of different sizes, shapes, and colors, the products of a million years of wind erosion. Time your visit for sunset, when the rocks begin to glow—from rich red to purple—and the fiery globe sinks to the horizon. Magnificent views of the Pacific Ocean, Moloka'i, and, on clear days, O'ahu provide the perfect backdrop for photographs.

FodorsChoice ★

The ancient Hawaiians shunned Lana'i for hundreds of years, believing the island was the inviolable home of spirits. Standing beside the oxide-red rock spires of this strange, raw landscape, you might be tempted to believe the same. This lunar savannah still has a decidedly eerie edge; but the shadows disappearing on the horizon are those of escaped game animals—mouflon sheep and axis deer—not the fearsome man-eating bird spirits of lore. According to tradition, the spirits were vanquished by Kā'ulula'au, a chief's son who was exiled here for destroying his father's prize breadfruit groves. The clever boy outwitted and exhausted the spirits, and announced the island's liberation with a giant bonfire. ⊠ *From The Stables at Kō'ele, follow dirt road through hay fields 2 mi; turn right at crossroads and head through ironwood forest 1½ mi.*

⑭ Japanese Cemetery. In 1899, sugar came to this side of Lāna'i. A plantation took up about 2,400 acres and seemed a profitable proposition, but that same year, disease wiped out the labor force. This authentic Buddhist shrine commemorates the Japanese workers who died. ⊠ *6½ mi southeast from where Keōmuku Hwy. dead-ends at Shipwreck Beach, on dirt road running along north shore.*

⑮ Kahe'a Heiau. What was once a central place of worship for the people of Lāna'i may now be hard to find through the kiawe overgrowth. Equally hidden are the remaining stone platforms of the **Halepaloa Landing,** a wharf used by the Maunalei Sugar Company (1899) to ship cane. Some say that the company failed because attempted construction of a railroad disturbed the sacred stones of the heiau, which angered the gods, who then turned the drinking water salty, forcing closure in 1901. ⊠ *6½ mi southeast from where Keōmuku Hwy. dead-ends at Shipwreck Beach, on dirt road running along north shore.*

▶ **⑨ Kānepu'u Preserve.** The 590 acres of this native dryland forest are under the stewardship of the Nature Conservancy of Hawai'i. Kānepu'u contains the largest remnant of this rare forest type. More than 45 native species of plants, including the endangered Hawaiian gardenia, grow in the shade of such rare trees as Hawaiian sandalwood, olive, and ebony. A short self-guided loop trail, with eight signs illustrated by local artist Wendell Kaho'ohalahala, reveals this ecosystem's beauty and the challenges it faces. ⊠ *Polihua Rd., 6 mi north of Lāna'i City* ☎ *808/537–4508* ⊙ *Daily 9–4.*

⑬ **Keōmuku.** There's an eerie beauty about Keōmuku, with its crumbling, weed-choked stone walls and homes. During the late 19th century, this busy Lāna'i community of some 900 to 2,000 residents served as the headquarters of Maunalei Sugar Company. After the company failed, the land was used for ranching, but by 1954 the area lay abandoned. Its church, **Ka Lanakila O Ka Mālamalama**, the oldest on the island, was built in 1903. It has been partially restored by volunteers. Among the worn stone walls you may find a Portuguese beehive-shaped communal bread oven, or the remains of a windmill. ⊠ *5 mi along unpaved road southeast of Shipwreck Beach.*

★ ⑪ **Munro Trail.** This 9-mi jeep trail along a pine-covered ridge was named after George Munro, manager of the Lāna'i Ranch Co., who began a reforestation program in the 1950s to provide a much-needed watershed. The trail climbs **Lāna'ihale** (House of Lāna'i), which, at 3,370 feet, is the island's highest point; on clear days you'll be treated to a panorama of canyons and almost all of the Hawaiian Islands. Be careful: the roads get very muddy, and trade winds can be strong. This is a difficult hike in general: it's steep, the ground is uneven, and there is little shade. ⊠ *From Lodge at Kō'ele head north on Keōmuku Hwy. for 1¼ mi, then turn right onto dirt road; trailhead is ½ mi past cemetery on right.*

⑯ **Naha.** An ancient rock-walled fishpond—visible at low tide—lies here, where the sandy shorelines end and the cliffs begin their rise along the island's shores. The beach is a frequent resource for local fisherfolk, but the treacherous tides make this a dangerous place for swimming. ⊠ *East side of Lāna'i, at end of dirt road that runs from end of Keōmuku Hwy. along eastern shore.*

★ ⑫ **Shipwreck Beach.** The rusting World War II tanker may be a clue that the waters off this 8-mi stretch of sand aren't friendly. Strong trade winds have propelled innocent vessels onto the reef since at least 1824, when the first shipwreck was recorded. Some believe that the unknown oiler you see stranded today, however, was merely abandoned. ⊠ *End of Keōmuku Hwy. heading north.*

BEACHES

Though all of Lāna'i's beaches provide peaceful strolls, sunbathing, and, of course, sunsets, only Hulopo'e Beach is safe for swimming. To reach most of the beaches, you will need a four-wheel-drive vehicle; note that it is illegal to go four-wheeling on the beaches themselves.

Fodor'sChoice **Hulopo'e Beach.** A five-minute walk from the Mānele Bay Hotel, Hulopo'e
★ is one of the best beaches in all Hawai'i. The sparkling crescent of this Marine Life Conservation District beckons with clear waters safe for swimming, great snorkeling reefs, tide pools, and, often, spinner dolphins. Shady grassy expanses are perfect for picnics, and there are showers, rest rooms, and changing facilities. ⊠ *From Lāna'i City follow Hwy. 440 (Mānele Rd.) south to bottom of hill; road dead-ends at beach's parking lot.*

Lōpā Beach. A popular surfing spot for locals, Lōpā is also an ancient fishpond. With majestic views of West Maui and Kaho'olawe, this remote, white-sand beach is a great place for a picnic. Don't let the sight of surfers fool you: the channel's currents are too strong for swimming. ⊠ *East side of Lāna'i, 7 mi down dirt road that runs from end of Keōmuku Hwy. along eastern shore.*

Polihua Beach. This often-deserted beach should get a star for beauty with its long, wide stretch of white sand and the clear views of Moloka'i. The drive to get here isn't easy, though, and frequent high winds whip up sand and waves. Strong currents and a sudden drop in the ocean floor make swimming extremely dangerous. ⊠ *Northwest shore, 11 mi from Lāna'i City, past Garden of the Gods.*

★ **Shipwreck Beach.** Beachcombers come to this windswept area for shells and washed-up treasures; photographers for great shots of Moloka'i, just across the 9-mi wide Kalohi Channel; and walkers for the broad, 8-mi stretch of sand. Kaiolohia, as it's also called, is not, however, for swimmers. ⊠ *North shore, 10 mi north of Lāna'i City at end of Keōmuku Hwy.*

WHERE TO EAT

Although Lāna'i's restaurant choices are limited, the menus are wide-ranging. Dine at the Lodge at Kō'ele or Mānele Bay Hotel, and you'll be served top-notch cuisine in sumptuous surroundings. Lāna'i City's restaurants are unpretentious, with simple fare. A lesser-known alternative is the clubhouse at the Challenge golf course, open seasonally until 9 PM.

South & West Lāna'i

★ **$$$$** ✕ **'Ihilani.** The Mānele Bay Hotel's dining room shimmers with crystal and silver as light filters through the glass ceiling. Executive chef Pierre Bellon prepares fresh island ingredients in the tradition of the Mediterranean, in particular southern France. Sterling choices on the menu include the crispy whole *moi*, a fish once reserved for Hawaiian royalty, and a lavender-honey-glazed Muscovy duck breast. You can opt for a five-course food-and-wine pairing menu. ⊠ *Mānele Bay Hotel* 🕾 *808/565–7700* ⌖ *Reservations essential* ▭ *AE, DC, MC, V* ☽ *No lunch.*

North & East Lāna'i

$$$$ ✕ **Formal Dining Room.** Reflecting the Lodge's elegant, old-world atmoFodor'sChoice sphere, this romantic octagonal restaurant is one of the best in the state. ★ Intimate tables sit close to a roaring fireplace. An expansion of Hawai'i regional cuisine, the changing menu includes specialties such as pancetta-wrapped roasted Lāna'i venison loin and seared Hawaiian snapper with gingered crab. Visiting chefs and a master sommelier provide exclusive wine-pairings, and service is flawless. ⊠ *Lodge at Kō'ele* 🕾 *808/565–7300* ⌖ *Reservations essential* 🏛 *Jacket required* ▭ *AE, DC, MC, V* ☽ *No lunch.*

$$$–$$$$ ✕ **Henry Clay's Rotisserie.** With the only bar and comparatively fine dining in Lāna'i City, this is a busy spot, right at the Hotel Lāna'i. Louisiana-style ribs, Cajun-style shrimp, and gumbo add up to what chef Henry Clay Richardson calls "American country," but he brings it back home with island venison and locally caught fish. A fireplace and paintings by local artists add to the country feel. ✉ *Hotel Lāna'i, 828 Lāna'i Ave., Lāna'i City* ☎ *808/565–7211* ▭ *MC, V.*

$–$$ ✕ **Pele's Other Garden.** Mark and Barbara Zigmond's dynamic little eatery is a deli and bistro all in one. For lunch, mile-high sandwiches and fresh-baked breads are a great reward after an arduous hike. You can also order picnic lunches served in a convenient cooler bag. At night, the tiny spot turns into an intimate tablecloth-dining bistro, complete with soft jazz music. Bring your own wine, start with bruschetta, then choose from a selection of pasta dishes or pizzas. ✉ *811 Houston St., Lāna'i City* ☎ *808/565–9628 or 888/764–3354* ▭ *AE, DC, MC, V.*

¢–$ ✕ **Blue Ginger Café.** This cheery blue-and-white-painted eatery is a Lāna'i City institution. The wonderful owner, Georgia Abilay, turned this place, with its bare floor and plastic tablecloths, into one of the town's most popular hangouts. For breakfast, try the Portuguese sausage omelet with rice or fresh pastries. Lunchtime selections range from burgers and pizza to Hawaiian staples such as saimin and *Spam musubi* (fried Spam on rice). Try a stir-fry with mahimahi for dinner. ✉ *409 7th Ave., Lāna'i City* ☎ *808/565–6363* ▭ *No credit cards.*

¢–$ ✕ **565 Café.** This is a convenient stop for pizza, plate lunches, and hot and cold subs. Fresh cookies and breads are baked on the premises. If you happen to need a helium balloon for a festive occasion, you can find that here, too. ✉ *408 8th St., Lāna'i City* ☎ *808/565–6622* ▭ *D, DC, MC, V.*

¢ ✕ **Lāna'i Coffee.** Just around the corner from Lana'i City square, you can sit outside, sip cappuccinos, and munch on lox bagels. Who would have thought this remote island would have blended espresso shakes and gourmet ice cream! ✉ *604 Ilima St., Lāna'i City* ☎ *808/565–6962* ☾ *Closed Sunday.*

WHERE TO STAY

For years the island's only accommodation was the no-fuss Hotel Lāna'i in Lāna'i City. Today, you can choose among classy resorts, pleasant B&Bs, and a few rental houses.

South & West Lāna'i

★ **$$$$** ⊞ **Mānele Bay Hotel.** This ornate property has spectacular views of Lāna'i's coastline and beyond. Courtyard gardens, breezeways, and bridges connect guest-room buildings. The architecture combines Mediterranean and South Pacific elements. Chinese warrior robes, vases, and carved ivory tusks decorate the common areas. The crescent of Hulopo'e Bay is just minutes away, and a *keiki* (children's) program focuses on the island's cultural and environmental heritage, with petroglyph walks, crab hunting, 'ukulele playing, and more. ✑ *Box 310, Lāna'i City 96763* ☎ *808/565–7700 or 800/321–4666* 🖷 *808/565–3868* ⊕ *www.manelebayhotel.com* ➫ *222 rooms, 28 suites* ♗ *4 restaurants, room* *service, in-room safes, minibars, cable TV with movies and video games, 18-hole golf course, 6 tennis courts, pool, health club, spa, billiards, bar, library, babysitting, children's programs (ages 5–13), Internet, convention center* ☲ *AE, DC, MC, V.*

North & East Lāna'i

$$$$ ⊞ **Captain's Retreat.** This private two-story cedar home is always popular. Within walking distance of town, it provides a great family or friends' getaway, with 3,000 square feet, four bedrooms (including one master suite with private bath and patio), a redwood deck, an outside shower, and a roomy kitchen. The house accommodates 10 comfortably; single-room bookings aren't available. ⊠ *Okamoto Realty, 730 Lāna'i Ave., Lāna'i City 96763* ☎ *808/565–7519 or 888/565–6106* ⊕ *www. lanairental.com* ⤳ *1 4-bedroom unit* ☲ *MC, V.*

$$$$ ⊞ **Lodge at Kō'ele.** In the highlands edging Lāna'i City, this grand country estate exudes luxury and romance. Secluded by old pines, 1½ mi of
Fodor's Choice paths meander through gardens with a pond and an orchid greenhouse.
★ Afternoon tea served beneath the beamed ceilings and immense stone fireplaces of the magnificent Great Hall has an old-world feel. The music room lounge is a relaxing haven after a day on the Lodge's golf course or shooting range. The porch looks out on a rolling green expanse with spectacular sunsets. ⌂ *Box 310, Lāna'i City 96763* ☎ *808/ 565–7300 or 800/321–4666* ☏ *808/565–3868* ⊕ *www.lodgeatkoele. com* ⤳ *88 rooms, 14 suites* ⌕ *3 restaurants, room service, in-room safes, minibars, cable TV with movies and video games, 18-hole golf course, tennis courts, pool, health club, archery, croquet, horseback riding, bar, children's programs (ages 5–12), Internet* ☲ *AE, DC, MC, V.*

$–$$ ⊞ **Hotel Lāna'i.** Built in 1923 to house visiting plantation executives, this 10-room inn was once the only accommodation on the island. The rooms, with country quilts, light pine woods, and watercolors by a local artist, make you feel like you're staying in someone's home. Rooms with patios overlooking the garden and Lāna'i City are especially nice. A Continental breakfast with fresh-baked breads is included in the rate. ⊠ *828 Lāna'i Ave., Lāna'i City 96763* ☎ *808/565–7211 or 800/795–7211* ☏ *808/565–6450* ⊕ *www.hotellanai.com* ⤳ *10 rooms, 1 cottage* ⌕ *Restaurant; no a/c, no room TVs, no smoking* ☲ *AE, MC, V.*

$ ⊞ **Dreams Come True.** Michael and Susan Hunter rent out a four-bedroom, four-bathroom plantation home in the heart of Lānai City, available in its entirety or as individual guest rooms. Some rooms have canopy beds, and each has its own marble bath. Tropical fruits from the yard and freshly squeezed passion-fruit juice make breakfast a special occasion. Susan is a trained massage therapist and provides in-house massage for $50 an hour. Vehicle rental is also available. ⊠ *1168 Lāna'i St., Lāna'i City 96763* ☎ *808/565–6961 or 800/566–6961* ☏ *808/565–7056* ⊕ *www.circumvista.com/dreamscometrue.html* ⤳ *3 rooms* ⌕ *Massage, car rental; no a/c, no room phones, no room TVs, no smoking* ⦾ *CP* ☲ *AE, D, MC, V.*

NIGHTLIFE & THE ARTS

Nightlife

Lāna'i is certainly not known for its nightlife. Fewer than a handful of places stay open past 9 PM. At the resorts, excellent piano music or light live entertainment makes for a quiet, romantic night.

At the **Hotel Lāna'i** (☎ 808/565–7211), a lively bar stays open until the last dinner guest leaves. The cozy cocktail lounge at the **Lodge at Kō'ele** (☎ 808/565–7300) stays open until 11 PM. The lodge also features music in its Great Hall every evening from 7 to 10. Hale Aheahe (House of Gentle Breezes), the classy lounge at the **Mānele Bay Hotel** (☎ 808/ 565–7700), offers entertainment every evening from 5:30 to 9:30.

The Arts

A surprising number of talented artists have made Lāna'i their home. Their work enhances both resorts and restaurants in town and is for sale in gift stores.

The **Visiting Artist Program** (☎ 800/321–4666), at either the Lodge at Kō'ele or the Mānele Bay Hotel, brings internationally renowned authors, chefs, and musicians to Lāna'i for intimate presentations. Participants are often famous chefs, such as Tim and Liza Goodell, the team behind four nationally acclaimed restaurants, including Newport Beach's Aubergine. Other celebrity visits have included Hiroshima, Clint Eastwood, and Ellen Goodman.

Lāna'i Arts and Cultural Center (✉ 337 7th Ave., Lāna'i City ☎ 808/565– 7503) is the dynamic center for local artists to practice and display their crafts. Workshops in the pottery, photography, woodworking, and painting studios can be booked via the resorts.

Film

The 153-seat **Lāna'i Theater and Playhouse** (✉ 465 7th Ave., Lāna'i City ☎ 808/565–7500), a '30s landmark, presents first-run movies.

SPORTS & THE OUTDOORS

Camping

Camping isn't encouraged outside Lāna'i's one official campground at Hulopo'e: the isle's ecosystem is fragile; islanders are keen on privacy; and, unless you know about tides, winds, and undertows, camping on the beach can be hazardous. The companies below will help you play it safe and be respectful of the island.

Adventure Lāna'i Eco Centre (☎ 808/565–7373 ⊕ www.adventurelanai. com) in town can set you up with complete camping packages and provide a wealth of inside tips. **Castle & Cooke Resorts** (☎ 808/565–3982 for permits) operates the great little campground at Hulopo'e Beach with clean rest rooms, fire pits, and showers. Call first to obtain a permit. **Destination Lāna'i** (☎ 808/565–7600 or 800/947–4774) can help you locate no-frills campsites.

Fitness & Spa Centers

The Fitness Center at the Lodge at Kō'ele. The center provides state-of-the-art equipment and yoga classes. In conjunction with the Spa at Mānele, specialty treatments and massages are available. A heated pool keeps you agreeably warm. ⊠ *Lodge at Kō'ele* ☎ *808/565–7300.*

The Spa at Mānele. With granite stone floors, eucalyptus steam rooms, and private beachside cabanas, this spa offers a delicious menu of state-of-the-art pampering. The popular Ali'i Banana Coconut Scrub and Pineapple Citrus Polish treatments have inspired their own cosmetic line. Massages, starting at $110, can be booked in cabanas steps away from crashing surf. An on-site fitness center, open 24 hours, offers cardiovascular equipment and free weights. ⊠ *Mānele Bay Hotel, Lāna'i City* ☎ *808/565–7700.*

Golf

Cavendish Golf Course. This 9-hole course in the pines is free, but a donation for upkeep is requested. Call the Lodge at Kō'ele concierge for information and directions. Bring your own clubs. ☎ *808/565–7300.*

Challenge at Mānele. Jack Nicklaus designed this award-winning, 18-hole course close by the sea—so close, in fact, one hole must be shot 200 yards across the ocean to the opposing sea cliff. The clubhouse serves lunch and, in the busier season, light dinners as well. ⊠ *Mānele Bay Hotel* ☎ *808/565–2222* 🖼 *Greens fee $165 for guests of the Lodge at Kō'ele or Mānele Bay Hotel, $205 for nonguests; cart included.*

Experience at Kō'ele. The Lodge at Ko'ele has a championship 18-hole course designed by Greg Norman. The signature 17th hole drops stunningly into a lush valley with a lake. There's an 18-hole executive putting course, and the clubhouse serves lunch. ⊠ *Lodge at Kō'ele* ☎ *808/565–4653* 🖼 *Greens fee $165 guests, $205 nonguests; cart included.*

Hiking

Lāna'i's remote trails snake through dryland forest, over rugged grasslands, and along splendid shores. Be sure to get a good map before setting out.

Koloiki Ridge, a wide, easy trail of about 2 ½ mi behind the Lodge at Kō'ele, overlooks the island's north side. Ask the concierge at the Lodge about guided, interpretive hikes.

The **Lāna'i Fisherman Trail** takes about an hour and follows the oceanside perimeter of Mānele Bay Hotel, along cliffs bordering the golf course. Mānele Spa offers early morning fitness hikes along the trail; if you're lucky, you may see dolphins leaping offshore.

★ The **Munro Trail,** a strenuous 9-mi trek that commences in the forest behind the Lodge, is the island's most popular hike. There is an elevation gain of 1,400 feet, leading you to the lookout at Lāna'i's highest point, Lāna'ihale.

Horseback Riding

The **Stables at Kō'ele** (☎ 808/565–4424) is your starting point for scenic high-country trails. The corral is full of well-groomed horses for riders of all ages and skill levels. Your options include sunset rides, private saunters, and four-hour adventures. Prices start at $50 for one hour. You can also arrange lessons or customized daylong rides.

Mountain Biking

John, the friendly owner of **Adventure Lāna'i Eco Centre** (☎ 808/565–7373 ⊕ www.adventurelanai.com), rents 21-speed mountain bikes for $25 per day. He and his team also offer downhill bike treks for $89 and multi-treks ($129) that get you into a variety of island sports.

Sporting Clays & Archery

★ **Lāna'i Pine Sporting Clays and Archery Range** (⊠ off Keōmuku Hwy. ☎ 808/559–4600) has outstanding rustic terrain, challenging targets, and a well-stocked pro shop, all of which make this sporting-clays course top-flight in the expert's eyes. Sharpshooters can complete the meandering 14-station course in an hour, by golf cart. Group tournaments and even kids can enjoy skilled instruction at the archery range and compressed air rifle gallery. The $45 archery introduction includes an amusing "pineapple contest"—contestants are given five arrows with which to hit a pineapple. The winner takes home a lovely crystal prize.

Water Sports

DEEP-SEA FISHING Jeff Menzie captains the *Kila Kila* (☎ 808/565–2387 or 808/565–4555), a 53-foot fishing vessel with a spacious cockpit and the comforts of a luxury ship. Its heritage includes world records for sportfishing in Florida and Kona. A four-hour deep-sea-fishing trip with up to six passengers costs $825; a full day run is $1,200. Book your expedition with the concierges at the resorts.

Sherry Menzie (Captain Jeff's wife) pilots **Spinning Dolphin Fishing Charters** (☎ 808/565–6613); charters are somewhat hard to book, as she's also the island's harbor mistress. Make advance reservations for her 28-foot diesel-powered Omega sportfisher, which handles both heavy- and light-tackle fishing. Half-day ($400) and full-day ($600) charters out of Mānele Bay are private, with a six-person maximum. Bring your own lunch. Juice and ice are provided.

SNORKELING & SCUBA DIVING **Hulopo'e Beach** is an outstanding snorkeling destination. Several companies offer snorkeling tours, and the hotels rent equipment as well.

★ Some say scuba diving doesn't get better than off the south shores of Lāna'i. The boat dive site **Cathedrals** gets its name from the spacious caverns created by numerous pinnacles rising from depths of 60 feet to just below the water's surface. In these beautiful chambers lurk spotted moray eels, lobster, and ghost shrimp. **Sergeant Major Reef**, is made up of three parallel lava ridges, a cave, and an archway, with rippled sand valleys between the ridges. Depths range from 15 to 50 feet.

Carey Lasiter (☎ 808/565–0121 ⊕ www.divecenter.com), a retired Delta Special Forces officer, can introduce you to the underwater world. Scuba dive trips typically last 3 hours, are geared for families, and count toward PADI certification. Thrilling night dives are an option for experienced divers.

Adventure Lānaʻi Eco Centre (☎ 808/565–7373 ⊕ www.adventurelanai. com) offers unique kayaking and snorkeling adventures in remote locations, often excellent whale-watching spots. The four-hour excursions cost around $89. You can also opt for surf safaris and learn to navigate wooden long boards.

Spinning Dolphin Fishing Charters (☎ 808/565–6613) offers private snorkeling and sightseeing tours. When the whales are here (December through April), three-hour whale-watching tours are available.

Trilogy Oceansports Lānaʻi (☎ 808/667–7721 or 888/628–4800 ⊕ www. sailtrilogy.com) offers a daily four-hour morning snorkel sail on a 51-foot catamaran with lessons, equipment, and meals included. It charters two-tank dives on their catamarans for experienced divers for $160—ask about the availability of introductory dives. You can also sign up for ocean kayaking adventures or book a blue-water dolphin watch, a whale-watching sail, or a sunset cruise. It's best to book trips through your hotel concierge.

SHOPPING

Except for the high-end resort boutiques and pro shops, the island's only shopping is on 7th and 8th streets in Lānaʻi City. Friendly general stores are straight out of the '20s. Most shops close on Sunday and after 5.

General Stores

International Food and Clothing Center. You may not find everything the name implies, but this old-fashioned emporium does stock items for your everyday needs, from fishing gear to beer. ✉ 833 ʻIlima Ave., Lānaʻi City ☎ 808/565–6433.

Lānaʻi City Service. In addition to being a gas station and car-rental operation, this outfit sells sundries, T-shirts, and island crafts in the **Plantation Store**. ✉ 1036 Lānaʻi Ave., Lānaʻi City ☎ 808/565–7227.

Pine Isle Market. One of Lānaʻi City's two supermarkets, you can get everything from cosmetics to canned vegetables here. It's a great place to buy fresh fish. ✉ 356 8th St., Lānaʻi City ☎ 808/565–6488.

Richard's Shopping Center. Richard Tamashiro founded this store in 1946, and the Tamashiro clan continues to run the place. Along with groceries, the store has a fun selection of Lānaʻi T-shirts. ✉ 434 8th St., Lānaʻi City ☎ 808/565–6047.

Clothing

Local Gentry. This tiny, classy store has clothing for every need, from casual men's and women's beachwear to evening resort wear, shoes, jewelry, and hats. A small selection of children's apparel is also available. ✉ 363 7th St., Lānaʻi City ☎ 808/565–9130.

Crafts

Gifts with Aloha. Hand-painted clothing and casual resort wear is sold alongside a great collection of Hawaiiana books and the work of local artists, including ceramic ware, *raku* (Japanese-style lead-glazed pottery), fine handblown glass, and watercolor prints. ✉ *811-B Houston St., Lāna'i City* ☎ *808/565-6589.*

Lāna'i Arts and Cultural Center. The center's gift shop sells original art and unique Lāna'i handicrafts. ✉ *337 7th St., Lāna'i City* ☎ *808/565-7503.*

LĀNA'I A TO Z

To research prices, get advice from other travelers, and book travel arrangements, visit www.fodors.com.

AIR TRAVEL

You can reach Lāna'i from O'ahu's Honolulu International Airport, Maui's Kahului Airport, or the Big Island's Keāhole-Kona International Airport. The flight takes about a half hour. Round-trip tickets start at $170.

CARRIERS Hawaiian Airlines offers two round-trip flights daily on DC-9 jets. Island Air offers several flights daily on 18-passenger Dash-6s and 37-seat Dash-8s.

🛪 **Hawaiian Airlines** ☎ 800/882-8811 ⊕ www.hawaiianair.com. **Island Air** ☎ 808/484-2222 or 800/323-3345 ⊕ www.islandair.com.

AIRPORTS

The small Lāna'i Airport is in the southwest area of the island. There's a federal agricultural inspection station so that guests departing to the mainland can check luggage directly.

🛪 **Lāna'i Airport** ☎ 808/565-6757.

AIRPORT Lāna'i Airport is a 10-minute drive from Lāna'i City. If you're staying
TRANSFERS at the Hotel Lāna'i, the Lodge at Kō'ele, or the Mānele Bay Hotel, you'll be met by a shuttle for a $25 round-trip. If you're staying elsewhere in Lāna'i City, make arrangements with your hosts or hire a taxi. If you want to travel in style, splurge on a private limousine—$42 to the Lodge at Kō'ele or $81 to Mānele Bay Hotel.

🛪 **Rabaca's Limousine Service** ☎ 808/565-6670.

BOAT & FERRY TRAVEL

Ferries cross the channel five times daily, departing from Lahaina on Maui and Mānele Bay Harbor on Lāna'i. The crossing takes 45 minutes and costs $25 each way. Lāna'i City Service offers a $10 shuttle service to the harbor.

🛪 **Expeditions** ☎ 808/661-3756 or 800/695-2624 ⊕ www.go-lanai.com. **Lāna'i City Service** ✉ Lāna'i Ave. at 11th St. ☎ 808/565-7227 or 800/533-7808.

CAR RENTAL

Renting a jeep is expensive but essential. A free shuttle transports hotel guests only between the Hotel Lāna'i, the Lodge at Kō'ele and the Mānele Bay Hotel. To explore beyond these destinations, a four-wheel-drive vehicle is required. Make reservations far in advance of your trip, because Lāna'i's fleet of vehicles is limited. Lāna'i City Service, a subsidiary of Dollar Rent A Car, is open daily 7–7. Jeep Wranglers go for $130 a day, and compact cars are about $60. Adventure Lāna'i Eco Centre offers Safari Jeep Wranglers (with dashboard hula dancers!) for $104 per day; weekly rentals are available. You can also rent four-wheel-drive vehicles from the proprietors of Dreams Come True.

🚗 **Local Agencies Adventure Lāna'i Eco Centre** ☎ 808/565-7373 ⊕ www.adventurelanai.com. **Dreams Come True** ☎ 808/565-6961 or 800/566-6961. **Lāna'i City Service** ✉ Lāna'i Ave. at 11th St. ☎ 808/565-7227 or 800/533-7808.

CAR TRAVEL

There are only 30 mi of paved road on the island. Keōmuku Highway runs north to Shipwreck Beach and Mānele Road (Highway 440) runs south down to Mānele Bay and Hulopo'e Beach. Kaumalapau Highway (also Highway 440) heads west to Kaumalapau Harbor. The rest of your driving takes place on bumpy, muddy, secondary roads which generally aren't marked.

The island doesn't have traffic lights, and you'll never find yourself in a traffic jam, but it's easy to get lost; before heading out ask for a map at your hotel desk, and verify that you're headed in the right direction. People still drive slow here, wave, and pull over to give each other lots of room. The only gas station on the island is in Lāna'i City, at Lāna'i City Service.

EMERGENCIES

In an emergency, dial **911** to reach an ambulance, the police, or the fire department. The Lāna'i Community Hospital is the island's health-care center. It has 24-hour ambulance service and a pharmacy.

🚑 **Lāna'i Community Hospital** ✉ 628 7th St., Lāna'i City ☎ 808/565-6411.

SIGHTSEEING TOURS

Adventure Lāna'i Eco Centre's popular 4x4 Adventure Trek takes you to the island's most scenic places, stopping where and when you want. Guides "talk story" about local history and flora and fauna. They even provide binoculars, snorkeling gear, snacks, and drinks. Expect to pay around $90. Kayak adventures and bike treks also start at around $90.

Rabaca's Limousine Service offers four-wheel-drive tours that start at $50 per hour, with a three-hour minimum.

🚐 **Adventure Lāna'i Eco Centre** ☎ 808/565-7373 ⊕ www.adventurelanai.com. **Rabaca's Limousine Service** ☎ 808/565-6670.

VISITOR INFORMATION

Destination Lāna'i, the island's visitors bureau, is your best bet for general information and maps. Feel free to stop in, but be aware that opening hours are erratic. The Maui Visitors Bureau also has some information on the island.

ℹ️ **Destination Lāna'i** ✉ 730 Lāna'i Ave., Suite 102, Lāna'i City 96763 ☎ 808/565-7600 ⊕ www.aloha.net/~dlanai. **Maui Visitors Bureau** ☎ 808/244-3530 ⊕ www.visitmaui.com.

UNDERSTANDING HAWAI'I

THE ALOHA SHIRT: A COLORFUL SWATCH OF ISLAND HISTORY

ELVIS PRESLEY had an entire wardrobe of them in the '60s films *Blue Hawaii* and *Paradise, Hawaiian Style*. During the '50s, entertainer Arthur Godfrey and bandleader Harry Owens often sported them on television shows. John Wayne loved to lounge around in them. Mick Jagger felt compelled to buy one on a visit to Hawai'i in the 1970s. Dustin Hoffman, Steven Spielberg, and Bill Cosby avidly collect them.

The roots of the aloha shirt go back to the early 1930s, when Hawai'i's garment industry was just beginning to develop its own unique style. Although locally made clothes did exist, they were almost exclusively for plantation workers and were constructed of durable palaka or plain cotton material.

Out of this came the first stirrings of fashion: Beachboys and schoolchildren started having sport shirts made from colorful Japanese kimono fabric. The favored type of cloth was the kind used for children's kimonos—bright pink and orange floral prints for girls; masculine motifs in browns and blues for boys. In Japan, such flamboyant patterns were considered unsuitable for adult clothing, but in the Islands such rules didn't apply, and it seemed the flashier the shirt, the better—for either sex. Thus, the aloha shirt was born.

It was easy and inexpensive in those days to have garments tailored to order; the next step was moving to mass production and marketing. In June 1935, Honolulu's best-known tailoring establishment, Musa-Shiya, advertised the availability of "Aloha shirts—well tailored, beautiful designs and radiant colors. Ready-made or made to order . . . 95¢ and up." This is the first known printed use of the term that would

soon refer to an entire industry. By the following year, several local manufacturers had begun full-scale production of "aloha wear." One of them, Ellery Chun of King-Smith, registered as local trademarks the terms "Aloha Sportswear" and "Aloha Shirt" in 1936 and 1937, respectively.

These early entrepreneurs were the first to create uniquely Hawaiian designs for fabric as well—splashy patterns that would forever symbolize the Islands. A 1939 *Honolulu Advertiser* story described them as a "delightful confusion [of] tropical fish and palm trees, Diamond Head and the Aloha Tower, surfboards and leis, 'ukuleles and Waikīkī beach scenes."

The aloha wear of the late 1930s was intended for—and mostly worn by—tourists, and interestingly, a great deal of it was exported to the mainland and even Europe and Australia. By the end of the decade, for example, only 5% of the output of one local firm, the Kamehameha Garment Company, was sold in Hawai'i.

World War II brought this trend to a halt, and during the postwar period, aloha wear really came into its own in Hawai'i itself. A strong push to support local industry gradually nudged island garb into the workplace, and kama'āina began to wear the clothing that previously had been seen as attire for visitors.

In 1947, for example, male employees of the City and County of Honolulu were first allowed to wear aloha shirts "in plain shades" during the summer months. Later that year, the first observance of Aloha Week started the tradition of "bankers and bellhops . . . mix[ing] colorfully in multihued and tapa-designed Aloha shirts every day," as a local newspaper's Sunday

"The Aloha Shirt: A Colorful Swatch of Island History" first appeared in ALOHA *magazine. Reprinted with permission of Davick Publications.*

magazine supplement noted in 1948. By the 1960s, "Aloha Friday," set aside specifically for the wearing of aloha attire, had become a tradition. In the following decade, the suit and tie practically disappeared as work attire in Hawai`i, even for executives.

Most of the Hawaiian-theme fabric used in manufacturing aloha wear was designed in the Islands, then printed on the mainland or in Japan. The glowingly vibrant rayons of the late '40s and early '50s (a period now seen as aloha wear's heyday) were at first printed on the East Coast, but manufacturers there usually required such large orders, local firms eventually found it impossible to continue using them. By 1964, 90% of Hawaiian fabric was being manufactured in Japan—a situation that still exists today.

Fashion trends usually move in cycles, and aloha wear is no exception. By the 1960s, the "chop suey print" with its "tired clichés of Diamond Head, Aloha Tower, outrigger canoes [and] stereotyped leis" was seen as corny and garish, according to an article published in the *Honolulu Star-Bulletin*. But it was just that outdated aspect that began to appeal to the younger crowd, who began searching out old-fashioned aloha shirts at the Salvation Army and Goodwill thrift stores. These shirts were dubbed "silkies," a name by which they're still known, even though most of them were actually made of rayon.

Before long, what had been 50¢ shirts began escalating in price, and a customer who had balked at paying $5 for a shirt that someone had already worn soon found the same item selling for $10—and more. By the late 1970s, aloha-wear designers were copying the prints of yesteryear for their new creations.

The days of bargain silkies are now gone. The few choice aloha shirts from decades past that still remain are offered today by specialized dealers for hundreds of dollars apiece, causing many to look back to the time when such treasures were foolishly worn to the beach until they fell apart. The best examples of vintage aloha shirts are now rightly seen as art objects, worthy of preservation for the lovely depictions they offer of Hawai`i's colorful and unique scene.

— DeSoto Brown

THESE VOLCANIC ISLES

DAWN AT THE CRATER ON HORSE-BACK. It's cold at 10,023 feet above the warm Pacific—maybe 45°F. The horses' breath condenses into smoky clouds, and the riders cling to their saddles. It's eerily quiet except for the creak of straining leather and the crunch of volcanic cinders underfoot, sounds that are absurdly magnified in the vast empty space that yawns below.

This is Haleakalā, the "house of the sun." It's the crown of east Maui and the largest dormant volcanic depression in the world. The park encompasses 28,665 acres, and the valley itself is 21 mi in circumference and 19 square mi in area. At its deepest, it measures 3,000 feet from the summit, and could fit all of Manhattan. What you see here isn't actually a crater at all but something called a caldera, formed by the collapsing of the main cone, the result of eons of wind and rain wearing down what was once a small dip at the original summit peak. The small hills within the valley are volcanic cinder cones, each the site of an eruption.

Every year thousands of visitors drive the world's steepest auto route to the summit of Haleakalā National Park. Sunrise is extraordinary here. Mark Twain called it "the sublimest spectacle" he had ever witnessed.

But sunrise is only the beginning.

Hiking Haleakalā is like walking on the moon, with thirty-two miles of trails weaving around volcanic rubble, crater cones, frozen lava flows, vents, and tubes. The colors are muted yet dramatic—black, yellow, russet, orange, lavender, brown, even a pinkish blue—and change throughout the day.

This ecosystem sustains the surefooted mountain goat; the rare nēnē goose (no webbing between its toes, the better to negotiate this rugged terrain); and the strange, delicate silversword. A spiny, metallic-leaf plant, the silversword once grew abundantly on Haleakalā's slopes. Today it survives in small numbers at Haleakalā and at high elevations on the Big Island of Hawai'i. The plants live up to 40 years, bloom only once, scatter their seeds, and die.

It's not difficult to see this place as a bubbling, sulfurous cauldron, a direct connection to the core of the earth. Haleakalā's last—and probably final—eruption occurred in 1790, a few years after a Frenchman named Jean-François de Galaup, Comte de La Pérouse, became the first European to set foot on Maui. The rocky area on the southwest side of east Maui known as La Pérouse Bay is the result of that flow.

Large and small, awake or sleeping, volcanoes are Hawai'i's history and heritage. Behind their beauty is the story of the flames that created this ethereal island chain. The islands in the Hawaiian archipelago are actually the upper bodies of immense mountains rising from the bottom of the sea. Formed by molten rock known as magma, the islands have slowly grown from the earth's volatile mantle, lava forced through a "hot spot" in the thin crust of the ocean floor. The first ancient eruptions cooled and formed pools on the Pacific bottom. Then as magma spilled from the vents over millions of years, the pools became ridges and grew into crests. The latter built upon themselves over the eons, until finally they towered above the surface of the sea. This type of volcano, with its slowly formed, gently sloping sides, is known as a shield volcano. All of the Hawaiian Islands were created this way.

As the Islands cooled in the Pacific waters, the lava slopes slowly bloomed, over centuries, with colorful flora. About once every 35,000 years, a seed, spore, bird, or insect arrived here on the winds or waves. They found a fertile, sun-and-rain–drenched home, free of predators. Over time, these migrants developed into highly specialized organisms. A land with no predatory species breeds a population of plants and animals devoid of biological protections, making them especially fragile and vulnerable to foreign species and human development. Today Hawai'i suffers from one of the world's highest species extinction rates; eighty percent of native Hawaiian birds are now gone.

But for all the talk of geology, Hawaiian myth casts a different history of the islands. Pele, the beautiful and tempestuous daughter of Haumea, the Earth Mother, and Wakea, the Sky Father, is the Hawaiian goddess of fire, the maker of mountains, melter of rock, eater of forests—a creator and a destroyer. Legend has it that Pele came to the Islands long ago to flee from her cruel older sister, Na Maka o Kahai, goddess of the sea. Pele ran first to the small island of Ni'ihau, making a crater home there with her digging stick. But Na Maka found her and destroyed her hideaway, so Pele again had to flee. On Kaua'i she delved deeper, but Na Maka chased her from that home as well. Pele ran on—from O'ahu to Moloka'i, Lāna'i to Kaho'olawe, Molokini to Maui—but always Na Maka pursued her.

Pele came at last to Halema'uma'u, the vast fire-pit crater of Kīlauea, and there, on the Big Island, she dug deepest of all. There she is said to remain, all-powerful, quick to rage, and often unpredictable; the mountain is her impenetrable fortress and domain—a safe refuge, at least for a time, from Na Maka o Kahai.

The chronology of the old tales of Pele's flight from isle to isle closely matches the reckonings of modern volcanologists regarding the ages of the various craters. Today, the Big Island's Kīlauea and Mauna Loa retain the closest links with the earth's superheated core and are active and volatile. The other volcanoes have been carried beyond their magma supply by the movement of the Pacific Plate. Those on Kaua'i, O'ahu, and Moloka'i are completely extinct. Those at the southeasterly end of the island chain—Haleakalā, Mauna Ke'a, and Hualālai—are dormant and slipping away, so that the implacable process of volcanic death has begun. As erosion continues, the islands will someday melt back into the sea.

The largest island of the archipelago, the Big Island of Hawai'i rises some 13,796 feet above sea level at the summit of Mauna Ke'a. Mauna Loa is nearly as high at 13,667 feet. Geologists believe it required more than 3 million years of steady volcanic activity to raise these peaks up above the waters of the Pacific. From their bases on the ocean floor, these shield volcanoes are the largest mountain masses on the planet.

Mauna Loa's little sister, Kīlauea, at about 4,077 feet, is the most active volcano in the world. Between the two volcanoes, they have covered nearly 200,000 acres of land with their red-hot lava flows over the past 200 years. In the process, they have ravished trees, fields, meadows, villages, and more than a few unlucky humans. For generations, Kīlauea, in a continually eruptive state, has pushed molten lava up from the earth's magma at 1,800°F and more. But as active as she and Mauna Loa are, their eruptions are comparatively safe and gentle, producing continuous small flows rather than large bursts of fire and ash. The exceptions were two explosive displays during recorded history—one in 1790, the other in 1924. During these eruptions, Pele came close to destroying the Big Island's largest city, Hilo.

It is around these major volcanoes that the island's Hawai'i Volcanoes National Park was created. A sprawling natural preserve, the park attracts visitors from around the world for the unparalleled opportunity to view lava up-close and personal. Geology experts and volcanologists have been coming for a century or more to study and to improve methods for predicting the times and sites of eruptions.

Thomas Augustus Jaggar, preeminent volcanologist and student of Kīlauea, built his home on stilts wedged into cracks in the volcanic rock of the crater rim. Harvard-trained and universally respected, he was the driving force behind the establishment of the Hawaiian Volcano Observatory at Kīlauea in 1912. When he couldn't raise research funds from donations, public and private, he raised pigs to keep the scientific work going. After Jaggar's death, his wife scattered his ashes over the great fiery abyss.

The park is on the Big Island's southeastern flank, about 30 minutes out of Hilo on the aptly named Volcano Highway. Wear sturdy walking shoes and carry a warm sweater. It can be a long hike across the lava flats to see Pele in action, and at 4,000 feet above sea level, temperatures can be brisk, however hot the volcanic activity. So much can be seen at close range along the road circling the crater that Kīlauea has been dubbed the "drive-in volcano."

At the park's visitor center sits a large display case. It contains dozens of lava-rock "souvenirs"—removed from Pele's grasp and then returned, accompanied by letters of apology. They are sent back by visitors who say they regret having broken the *kapu* (taboo) against removing even the smallest grain of native volcanic rock from Hawai'i. A typical letter might say: "I never thought Pele would miss just one little rock, but she did, and now I've wrecked two cars . . . I lost my job, my health is poor, and I know it's because I took this stone." The letters can be humorous, or poignant and remorseful, requesting Pele's forgiveness.

It is surprisingly safe at the crater's lip. Unlike Japan's Mount Fuji or Washington State's Mount Saint Helens, Hawai'i's shield volcanoes spew their lava downhill, along the sides of the mountain. Still, the clouds of sulfur gas and fumes produced during volcanic eruptions are noxious and heady and can make breathing unpleasant, if not difficult. It has been pointed out that the chemistry of volcanoes—sulfur, hydrogen, oxygen, carbon dioxide—closely resembles the chemistry of the egg.

It's an 11-mi drive around the Kīlauea crater via the Crater Rim Road, and the trip takes about an hour. But it's better to walk a bit. There are at least eight major trails in the park, ranging from short 15-minute strolls to the three-day, 18-mi (one way) Mauna Loa Trail. An easy, comfortable walk is Sulfur Banks, with its many steaming vents creating halos of clouds around the rim of Kīlauea. The route passes through a forest of sandalwood, flowers, and ferns.

Just ahead is the main attraction: the center of Pele's power, Halema'uma'u. This yawning pit of flame and burning rock measures some 3,000 feet wide and is a breathtaking sight. When Pele is in full fury, visitors come in droves, on foot and by helicopter, to see her crimson expulsions coloring the dark earth and smoky sky. Kīlauea's most recent violent activity has occurred at mountainside vents instead of at the summit crater. Known as rift zones, they are lateral conduits that often open in shield volcanoes.

Kīlauea has two rift zones, one extending from the summit crater toward the southwest, through Kau, the other to the east-northeast through Puna, past Cape Kumakahi, into the sea. In the last two decades, repeated eruptions in the east rift zone have blocked off 12 mi of coastal road—some under more than 300 feet of rock—and have covered a total of 10,000 acres with lava. Where the flows entered the ocean, roughly 200 acres have been added to the Big Island.

Farther along the Crater Rim Road is the Thurston Lava Tube, an example of a strangely beautiful volcanic phenomenon common on the Islands. Lava tubes form when lava flows rapidly downhill. The sides and top of this river of molten rock cool, while the fluid center flows on. Most formations are short and shallow, but some measure 30 to 50 feet high and hundreds of yards long. Lava tubes were often used to store remains of the ancient Hawaiian royalty—the *ali'i*. The Thurston Lava Tube sits in a beautiful prehistoric fern forest.

Throughout the park, new lava formations are continually being created. These volcanic deposits exhibit the different types of lava produced by Hawai'i's volcanoes: *'a'ā*, the dark, rough lava that solidifies as cinders of rock; and the more common *pāhoehoe*, the smooth, satiny lava that forms the vast plains of black rock in ropy swirls known as lava flats, which in some areas go on for miles. Other terms that help identify what may be seen in the park include *caldera*, which are the open, bowl-like lips of a volcano summit; *ejecta*, the cinders and ash that float through the air around an eruption; and *olivine*, the semiprecious chrysolite (greenish in color) found in volcanic ash.

But this volcanic landscape isn't all fire and flash, cinders, and devastation. Hawai'i Volcanoes National Park is also the home of some of the most beautiful of the state's black-sand beaches; forest glens full of lacy butterflies and colorful birds such as the dainty flycatcher, called the *'elepaio*; and exquisite grottoes sparked with bright wild orchid sprays and crashing waterfalls. Even as the lava cools, still bearing a golden, glassy skin, lush, green native ferns—*ama'uma'u, kupukupu,* and *'ōkupukupu*—spring up in the midst of Pele's fallout, as if defying her destructiveness or simply confirming the fact that after fire she brings life.

Some 12 centuries ago, in fact, Pele brought humans to her verdant islands: the fiery explosions that lit Kīlauea and Mauna Loa probably guided the first explorers to Pele's side from the Marquesas Islands, some 2,400 mi away across the ocean.

Once settled, they worshiped her from a distance. Great numbers of religious *heiau* (outdoor stone platforms) dot the landscapes near the many older and extinct craters scattered throughout Hawai'i, demonstrating the reverence the native islanders have always held for Pele and her creations. But the ruins of only two heiau are to be found near the very active crater at Halema'uma'u. There, at the center of the capricious Pele's power, native Hawaiians caution one even today to "step lightly, for you are on holy ground."

In future ages, when mighty Kīlauea is no more, this area will still be a volcanic isle. Beneath the blue Pacific waters, fiery magma flows and new mountains form and grow. Off the south coast of the Big Island, a new island is forming. Still ½ mi below the water's surface, it won't be making an appearance any time soon, but already has a name: Lōihi.

— Gary Diedrichs

BOOKS & MOVIES

Books

If you like your history in novel form, you'll enjoy James A. Michener's *Hawaii* for its overall perspective. Captain James Cook's *A Voyage to the Pacific Ocean,* one of the first guidebooks to the Islands, contains many valid insights; *Shoal of Time,* by Gavan Daws, chronicles Hawaiian history from Cook's time to the 1960s. History also comes to life in the pages of *Travels in Hawaii,* by Robert Louis Stevenson. To gain familiarity with the gods and goddesses who have also had a hand in this land's development, read *Hawaiian Mythology* by Martha Beckwith. *Hawai'i's Story by Hawai'i's Queen,* the tale of the overthrow of the Hawaiian monarchy in Queen Lili'uokalani's own words, is poignant and thought-provoking. For a truly Hawaiian perspective, *Voices of Wisdom: Hawaiian Elders Speak* by M. J. Harden shares interviews with some of Hawai'i's most respected elders. Albert J. Schütz's *All About Hawaiian* is a good introduction to the language of the Islands and efforts to preserve it.

Paul Wood's essays, collected in *Four Wheels, Five Corners: Facts of Life in Upcountry Maui,* are quirky tales of life on a rock in the middle of the Pacific. Writers Paul Theroux, Barbara Kingsolver, and Maxine Hong Kingston are among those who share stories about the Islands in *Hawai'i: True Stories of the Island Spirit,* a collection edited by Rick and Marcie Carroll. *Call for Hawaiian Sovereignty,* by Michael Kioni Dudley, traces the growing movement for a sovereign Hawaiian nation. *Kamehameha and the Warrior Kekūhoaupi'o* is a classical Hawaiian epic, translated by Naomi Sodetani. For kids, pick up *Beautiful Hawaiian Day,* by Henry Kapono, a story about a little girl who finds a seashell that takes her back through the history of Hawai'i.

The *Handbook of Hawaiian Fishes,* by W. A. Gosline and Vernon Brock, is great for snorkelers. *Hawai'i's Birds,* put out by the Hawai'i Audubon Society, is perfect for bird-watchers. *Hawaiian Hiking Trails,* by Craig Chisholm, is just the guide for day hikers and backpackers. *Surfing: The Ultimate Pleasure,* by Leonard Lueras, covers everything about the sport. Geographers greatly appreciate the maps, social and geological history, and biology in *Atlas of Hawai'i,* by Sonia Juvik.

The New Cuisine of Hawaii, by Janice Wald Henderson, features recipes from the 12 chefs credited with defining Hawai'i regional cuisine. One of these pioneers, celebrity chef Roy Yamaguchi, provides an in-depth taste of the Islands with his cookbook *Roy's Feasts from Hawaii. Hawaiian Country Tables* by Kaui Philpotts spotlights vintage Island recipes and dishes.

For swaying musicologists, there's *Hula Is Life, The Story of Maiki Aiu and Hālau Hulo o Maiki,* by Rita Aryioshi; it's the definitive book on hula's origins and development. Hawaiian-music lovers might take note of the ideas presented in *Strains of Change: Impact of Tourism on Hawaiian Music* by Elizabeth Tatar.

Instead of just taking home a lei, learn how to make one: *Hawaiian Lei Making,* by Laurie Shimizu Ide, offers a photographic guide for making floral leis.

Movie buffs enjoy *Made in Paradise: Hollywood's Films of Hawaii and the South Seas,* by Luis Reyes. It points out movie locations and pokes gentle fun at some of the misinformation popularized by Tinseltown's version of Island life. Guided tours of Kaua'i locations used in filming are provided by **Hawai'i Movie Tours** (☎ 800/628–8432).

Movies

For a preview of your vacation, take a look at *Forever Hawaii,* a video portrait of Hawai'i's six major islands.

The video *Hawaii on Foot,* with Robert Smith, gives hikers a peek at some of the best trails on O'ahu, Maui, the Big Island, and Kaua'i. It is available from **H.O.A. Publications** (✉ 102-16 Kaui Pl., Kula 96796 ☎ 808/678–2664 ⊕ www.maui. net/~hionfoot). Hula comes alive in the *1999 Merrie Monarch Festival Highlights.* The video is available from ⊕ *www. BooklinesHawaii.com* ☎ 877/828–4852.

Most people automatically think of Elvis when the words "Hawai'i" and "movie" are mentioned in the same sentence. Elvis Presley's Hawaiian-filmed movies are *Girls! Girls! Girls!* (1962), *Paradise, Hawaiian Style* (1966), and *Blue Hawaii* (1962), which showcases O'ahu's picturesque Hanauma Bay and Kaua'i's Coco Palms Resort.

Films such as Shirley Temple's *Curly Top* (1935); *Waikiki Wedding* (1937), with Bing Crosby; and *Gidget Goes Hawaiian* (1962) feature Hawai'i's beaches, palm trees, and hula dancers. The Islands' winter waves have taken center stage in a legion of hang-ten films of which only *North Shore* (1987) is on video.

Mitzi Gaynor washed that man right out of her hair on Kaua'i's Lumaha'i Beach in *South Pacific* (1958). And the tempestuous love scene between Burt Lancaster and Deborah Kerr in *From Here to Eternity* (1954) took place on O'ahu's Halona Cove beach.

Military-theme movies filmed in Hawai'i include *Mister Roberts* (1955), starring Henry Fonda, Jack Lemmon, and James Cagney; and *Lt. Robin Crusoe, USN* (1966), with Dick Van Dyke. *Tora! Tora! Tora!* (1971) re-created the December 7, 1941, bombing of Pearl Harbor. For *Flight of the Intruder* (1991), director John Milius turned taro farms at the base of Kaua'i's Mount Wai'ale'ale into the rice paddies of Southeast Asia.

The film version of James A. Michener's story *Hawaii* (1967) chronicles the lives of the Islands' missionary families. *Picture Bride* (1995) tells the story of a young Japanese girl who arrives on the Islands to face harsh realities as the wife of a sugar-plantation laborer.

Other movies with Hawai'i settings include *Black Widow* (1987), in which journalist Debra Winger travels to the Big Island's lava fields to prevent a murder; *Honeymoon in Vegas* (1992); *Under the Hula Moon* (1995); *Blue Crush* (2002); Disney's animated *Lilo & Stitch* (2002); and, of course, *Pearl Harbor* (2001).

CHRONOLOGY

ca. AD 500–750 The first humans to set foot on Hawaiian shores are Polynesians, who travel 2,400 mi in 60- to 80-foot canoes in search of a land revered in ancient mythology. Researchers today believe they were originally from Southeast Asia and that they discovered the South Pacific islands of Tahiti and the Marquesas before ending up in Hawai'i.

ca. 750–1200 The Islands are well populated with well-defined social and political structures brought by the Polynesians. Ali'i (chiefs) own the land, and the citizens tend to it and are taxed. Kahuna (priests) are the link between the gods; their oracular advice is sought for matters of all types.

ca. 1200 Tahitian voyagers arrive, bringing with them rituals of human sacrifice, as well as highly developed ecosystem-management techniques for livestock and agriculture.

ca. 1758 Kamehameha, the Hawaiian chief who unifies the Islands, is born.

1778 In January, Captain James Cook, commander of the H.M.S. *Resolution* and the consort vessel H.M.S. *Discovery,* lands on the island of Kaua'i. He arrives during a festival honoring the god Lono, and he himself is revered as a god prophesied to appear. He names the archipelago the Sandwich Islands after his patron, the Earl of Sandwich. In November, he returns to the Islands for the winter, anchoring at Kealakekua Bay on the Big Island.

1779 In February, Cook is killed in a battle with Hawai'i's indigenous people at Kealakekua.

1785 The isolation of the Islands ends as British, American, French, and Russian fur traders and New England whalers come to Hawai'i. Tales spread of thousands of acres of sugarcane growing wild, and farmers come in droves from the United States and Europe.

1790 Kamehameha begins his rise to power with a series of bloody battles.

1791 Kamehameha builds Pu'ukoholā Heiau (temple) on the Big Island and dedicates it by sacrificing a rival chief, Keoua Kuahu'ula, whom he has killed.

1795 Using Western arms, Kamehameha wins a decisive confrontation on O'ahu. Except for Kaua'i, which he tries to invade in 1796 and 1804, this completes his military conquest of the Islands.

1810 The chief of Kaua'i acknowledges Kamehameha's rule, giving him suzerainty over Kaua'i and Ni'ihau. Kamehameha becomes known as King Kamehameha I, and he rules the unified Kingdom of Hawai'i with an iron hand.

1819 Kamehameha I dies, and his oldest son, Liholiho, rules briefly as Kamehameha II, with Ka'ahumanu, Kamehameha I's favorite wife, as co-executive. Ka'ahumanu persuades the new king to abandon old religious *kapu* (taboos), including those that forbade women to eat with men or to hold positions of power. The first whaling ships land at Lahaina on Maui.

1820   By the time the first missionaries arrive from Boston, Hawai'i's social order is beginning to break down. First, Ka'ahumanu and then Kamehameha II defy kapu without attracting divine retribution. Hawaiians, disillusioned with their own gods, are receptive to the ideas of Christianity. The influx of Western visitors also introduces Western diseases, liquor, and what some view as moral decay.

1824   King Kamehameha II and his favorite wife die of measles during a visit to England. Honolulu missionaries give both royals a Christian burial outside Kawaiaha'o Church, inspiring many Hawaiians to convert to the Protestant faith. The king's younger brother, Kau'ikea'ōuli, becomes King Kamehameha III, a wise and gentle sovereign who reigns for 30 years with Ka'ahumanu as regent.

1832   Ka'ahumanu is baptized and dies a few months later.

1840   The Wilkes Expedition, sponsored by the U.S. Coast and Geodetic Survey, pinpoints Pearl Harbor as a potential naval base.

1845   Kamehameha III and the legislature move Hawai'i's seat of government from Lahaina, on Maui, to Honolulu, on O'ahu.

1849   Kamehameha III turns Hawai'i into a constitutional monarchy, and the United States, France, and Great Britain recognize Hawai'i as an independent country.

1850   The Great Mahele, a land commission, reapportions the land to the crown, the government, chiefs, and commoners, introducing for the first time the Western principle of private ownership. Commoners are now able to buy and sell land, but this great division becomes the great dispossession. By the end of the 19th century, white men own 4 acres for every 1 owned by a native Hawaiian. Some of the commission's distributions continue to be disputed to this day.

1852   As Western diseases depopulate the Islands, a labor shortage occurs in the sugarcane fields. For the next nine decades, a steady stream of foreign labor pours into Hawai'i, beginning with the Chinese. The Japanese begin arriving in 1868, followed by Filipinos, Koreans, Portuguese, and Puerto Ricans.

1872   Kamehameha V, the last descendent of the king who unified the Islands, dies without heirs. A power struggle ensues between the adherents of David Kalākaua and William Lunalilo.

1873   Lunalilo is elected Hawai'i's sixth king in January. The bachelor rules only 13 months before dying of tuberculosis.

1874   Kalākaua vies for the throne with the Dowager Queen Emma, the half-Caucasian widow of Kamehameha IV. Kalākaua is elected by the Hawai'i Legislature, against protests by supporters of Queen Emma. American and British marines are called in to restore order, and Kalākaua begins his reign as the "Merrie Monarch."

1875   The United States and Hawai'i sign a treaty of reciprocity, assuring Hawai'i a duty-free market for sugar in the United States.

1882 King Kalākaua builds ʻIolani Palace, an Italian renaissance–style structure, on the site of the previous royal palace.

1887 The reciprocity treaty of 1875 is renewed, giving the United States exclusive use of Pearl Harbor as a coaling station. Coincidentally, successful importation of Japanese laborers begins in earnest (after a false start in 1868).

1891 King Kalākaua dies and is succeeded by his sister, Queen Liliʻuokalani, the last Hawaiian monarch.

1893 After a brief two-year reign, Liliʻuokalani is removed from the throne by American business interests led by Lorrin A. Thurston (grandson of the missionary and newspaper founder Asa Thurston). Liliʻuokalani is imprisoned in ʻIolani Palace for nearly eight months.

1894 The provisional government converts Hawaiʻi into a republic and proclaims Sanford Dole president.

1898 With the outbreak of the Spanish-American War, President William McKinley recognizes Hawaiʻi's strategic importance in the Pacific and moves to secure the Islands for the United States. On August 12, Hawaiʻi is officially annexed by a joint resolution of Congress.

1901 Sanford Dole is appointed first governor of the territory of Hawaiʻi. The first major tourist hotel, the Moana (now called the Sheraton Moana Surfrider), is built on Waikīkī Beach.

1903 James Dole, a cousin of Sanford Dole, produces nearly 2,000 cases of pineapple, marking the beginning of Hawaiʻi's pineapple industry. Pineapple eventually surpasses sugarcane as Hawaiʻi's number one crop.

1907 Fort Shafter Base on Oʻahu, headquarters for the U.S. Army, becomes the first permanent military post in the Islands.

1908 Dredging of the channel at Pearl Harbor begins.

1919 Pearl Harbor is formally dedicated by the U.S. Navy. Representing the Territory of Hawaiʻi in the U.S. House of Representatives, Prince Jonah Kūhiō Kalanianaʻole—the adopted son of Kapiʻolani, the wife of Kalākaua, and with his brother one of the designated heirs to the throne of the childless Liliʻuokalani—introduces the first bill proposing statehood for Hawaiʻi.

1927 Army lieutenants Lester Maitland and Albert Hegenberger make the first successful nonstop flight from the mainland to the Islands. Hawaiʻi begins to increase efforts to promote tourism, the industry that eventually dominates development of the Islands. The Matson Navigation Company builds the Royal Hawaiian Hotel as a destination for its cruise ships.

1929 Hawaiʻi's commercial interisland air service begins.

1936 Pan American World Airways introduces regular commercial passenger flights to Hawaiʻi from the mainland.

1941 At Pearl Harbor the U.S. Pacific Fleet is bombed by the Japanese, forcing U.S. entry into World War II. Nearly 4,000 men are killed in the surprise attack.

1942 James Jones, with thousands of others, trains at Schofield Barracks on O'ahu. He later writes about his experience in *From Here to Eternity*.

1959 Congress passes legislation granting Hawai'i statehood. In special elections the new state sends to the U.S. House of Representatives its first American of Japanese ancestry, Daniel Inouye, and to the U.S. Senate its first American of Chinese ancestry, Hiram Fong. Later in the year, the first Boeing 707 jets make the flight from San Francisco in a record five hours. By year's end 243,216 tourists visit Hawai'i, and tourism becomes Hawai'i's major industry.

1986 Hawai'i elects its first native Hawaiian governor, John Waihe'e.

1992 Hurricane 'Iniki, the most devastating hurricane to hit Hawai'i, tears through Kaua'i on September 11. The island's people, infrastructure, gardens, and tourism industry have happily all since recovered.

1993 After native Hawaiians commemorate the 100th anniversary of the overthrow of Queen Lili'uokalani with a call for sovereignty, Congress issues an apology to the Hawaiian people for the annexation of the Islands.

1997 After 34 years of planning, construction, and endless litigation, O'ahu's H-3 "Trans-Koolau" freeway linking Pearl Harbor to the windward side of O'ahu finally opens. Opposition to the highway centered on the route through the Hālawa and Haiku valleys, areas of historical and religious significance to native Hawaiians. The price tag for this scenic roadway with a million-dollar view? More than 1 billion in state and federal tax dollars.

1998 The USS *Missouri* comes to her final resting place in Pearl Harbor. The battleship, on whose decks the Japanese signed their surrender agreement in World War II, is now a floating museum, permanently docked at Ford Island.

2001 Kīlauea Volcano on the Big Island of Hawai'i reaches the 19th year of its current eruptive phase and the longest phase of such activity in recorded volcanic history.

2004 Kīlauea is still at it.

HAWAI'I AT A GLANCE

Fast Facts

Nickname: Aloha State
Capital: Honolulu
State song: "Hawai'i Pono'i"
State bird: The Nēnē, an endangered land bird and variety of goose
State flower: Yellow Hibiscus Brackenridgii
State tree: Kukui (or candlenut), a Polynesian-introduced tree
Administrative divisions: There are four counties with mayors and councils: City and County of Honolulu (island of O'ahu), Hawai'i County (Hawai'i Island), Maui County (islands of Maui, Moloka'i, Lāna'i and Kahoolawe), and Kaua'i County (islands of Kaua'i and Ni'ihau)
Entered the Union: August 21, 1959, as the 50th state
Population: 1,334,023
Life expectancy: Female 82, male 76
Literacy: 81%

Ethnic groups: Hawaiian/part Hawaiian 22.1%; Caucasian 20.5%; Japanese 18.3%; Filipino 12.3%; Chinese 4.1%
Religion: Roman Catholic 22%; Buddhist, Shinto and other East Asian religions 15%; Mormon 10%; Church of Christ 8%; Assembly of God and Baptist 6% each; Episcopal, Jehovah's Witness and Methodist 5% each
Language: English is the first language of the majority of residents; Hawaiian is the native language of the indigenous Hawaiian people and an official language of the state; other languages spoken include Samoan, Chinese, Japanese, Korean, Spanish, Portuguese, Filipino, and Vietnamese

The loveliest fleet of islands that lies anchored in any ocean.

Mark Twain

Geography

Land area: An archipelago of 137 islands encompassing a land area of 6,422.6 square mi in the north-central Pacific Ocean, (about 2,400 mi from the west coast of the continental U.S.).
Coastline: 750 mi
Terrain: Volcanic mountains, tropical rain forests, verdant valleys, sea cliffs, canyons, deserts, coral reefs, sand dunes, sandy beaches
Natural resources: Dimension limestone, crushed stone, sand and gravel, gemstones
Natural hazards: Hurricanes, earthquakes, tsunamis
Flora: More than 2,500 species of native and introduced plants throughout the islands.
Fauna: Native mammals include the hoary bat, Hawaiian monk seal and

Polynesian rat. The Humpback Whale migrates to Hawaiian waters every winter to mate and calve. More than 650 fish and 40 different species of shark live in Hawaiian waters. Freshwater streams are home to hundreds of native and alien species. The Humuhumunukunukuapuaa (Hawaiian triggerfish) is the unofficial state fish.
Environmental issues: Plant and animal species threatened and endangered due to hunting, overfishing, overgrazing by wild and introduced animals, and invasive alien plants

Hawai'i is not a state of mind, but a state of grace.

Paul Theroux

Economy

Tourism and federal defense spending continue to drive the state's economy. Efforts to diversify in the areas of science and technology, film and television production, sports, ocean research and development, health and education, tourism, agriculture, and floral and specialty food products are ongoing.

GSP: $40.1 billion
Per capita income: $30,000
Inflation: 1%
Unemployment: 4.3%
Work force: 595,450
Debt: $7.3 billion
Major industries: Tourism, Federal government (defense and other agencies)
Agricultural products: Sugar, pineapple, papayas, guavas, flower and nursery products, asparagus, alfalfa hay, macadamia nuts, coffee, milk, cattle, eggs, shellfish, algae

Exports: $616 million
Major export products: Aircraft and parts, naphthas, medical equipment and supplies, fruit, steel scrap, electronic components, unleaded gasoline, artwork, cocoa, coffee, flowers, macadamia nuts
Imports: $2.6 billion
Major import products: Crude oil, electronic and digital equipment, coal, passenger motor vehicles

In what other land save this one is the commonest form of greeting not "Good day," or How d'ye do," but "Love?" That greeting is "Aloha"–love, I love, my love to you . . .It is a positive affirmation of the warmth of one's own heart, giving.

Jack London

Political Climate

Debate has waxed and waned for more than a century over how and when to return to native Hawaiians more than 1 million acres of land and other assets seized when American business interests overthrew the island monarchy in 1893. Certain native factions still advocate a return to independent nationhood. Sovereignty gained new momentum in the 1990s with the passage of a federal law, formally apologizing for the overthrow and urging reconciliation. Momentum has since fizzled. Hawaii's current governor has renewed efforts to have Congress recognize Hawaiians as an indigenous people, much like native americans and Alaskans. The governor also has pledged to support continued funding of health care, language, and other cultural programs, and to achieve state and federal obligations to distribute homestead lands to qualified Hawaiians.

Did You Know?

• Hawai'i is home to the world's most active volcano: Kīlauea, on the Big Island.

• 'Iolani Palace had electricity and telephones installed several years before the White House and is the only palace on U.S. soil.

• Hawai'i has about 12% of all endangered plants and animals in the U.S.; 75% of the country's extinct plants and birds were Hawaiian.

• The Royal Hawaiian Band is the only intact organization from the time of Hawaiian monarchy that is fully functional and still preserves Hawai'i's musical history.

VOCABULARY

Although an understanding of Hawaiian is by no means required on a trip to the Aloha State, a *malihini,* or newcomer, will find plenty of opportunities to pick up a few of the local words and phrases. Traditional names and expressions are widely used in the Islands, thanks in part to legislation enacted in the early '90s to encourage the use of the Hawaiian language. You're likely to read or hear at least a few words each day of your stay. Such exposure enriches a trip to Hawai'i.

With a basic understanding and some uninhibited practice, anyone can have enough command of the local tongue to ask for directions and to order from a restaurant menu. One visitor announced she would not leave until she could pronounce the name of the state fish, the *humuhumunukunukuāpua'a.* Luckily, she had scheduled a nine-day stay.

Simplifying the learning process is the fact that the Hawaiian language contains only eight consonants—H, K, L, M, N, P, W, and the silent *'okina,* or glottal stop, written '—plus one or more of the five vowels. All syllables, and therefore all words, end in a vowel. Each vowel, with the exception of a few diphthongized double vowels such as *au* (pronounced "ow") or *ai* (pronounced "eye"), is pronounced separately. Thus *'Iolani* is four syllables (ee-oh-la-nee), not three (yo-la-nee). Although some Hawaiian words have only vowels, most also contain some consonants, but consonants are never doubled.

Pronunciation is simple. Pronounce *A* "ah" as father; *E* "ay" as in weigh; *I* "ee" as in marine; *O* "oh" as in no; *U* "oo" as in true.

Consonants mirror their English equivalents, with the exception of W. When the letter begins any syllable other than the first one in a word, it is usually pronounced as a V. *'Awa,* the Polynesian drink, is pronounced "ava," *'ewa* is pronounced "eva."

Nearly all long Hawaiian words are combinations of shorter words; they are not difficult to pronounce if you segment them into shorter words. *Kalaniana'ole,* the highway running east from Honolulu, is easily understood as *Kalani ana 'ole.* Apply the standard pronunciation rules—the stress falls on the next-to-last syllable of most two- or three-syllable Hawaiian words—and Kalaniana'ole Highway is as easy to say as Main Street.

Now about that fish. Try *humu-humu nuku-nuku āpu a'a.*

The other unusual element in Hawaiian language is the *kahakō,* or macron, written as a short line (ˉ) placed over a vowel. Like the accent (´) in Spanish, the kahakō puts emphasis on a syllable that would normally not be stressed. The most familiar example is probably *Waikīkī.* With no macrons, the stress would fall on the middle syllable; with only one macron, on the last syllable, the stress would fall on the first and last syllables. Some words become plural with the addition of a macron, often on a syllable that would have been stressed anyway. No Hawaiian word becomes plural with the addition of an S, since that letter does not exist in the *'ōlelo Hawai'i* (which is Hawaiian for "Hawaiian language").

What follows is a glossary of some of the most commonly used Hawaiian words. Don't be afraid to give them a try. Hawaiian residents appreciate visitors who at least try to pick up the local language.

'a'ā: rough, crumbling lava, contrasting with *pāhoehoe,* which is smooth.
'ae: yes.
aikane: friend.
āina: land.
akamai: smart, clever, possessing savoir faire.
akua: god.
ala: a road, path, or trail.
ali'i: a Hawaiian chief, a member of the chiefly class.

aloha: love, affection, kindness; also a salutation meaning both greetings and farewell.

'ānuenue: rainbow.

'a'ole: no.

'apōpō: tomorrow.

'auwai: a ditch.

auwē: alas, woe is me!

'ehu: a red-haired Hawaiian.

'ewa: in the direction of 'Ewa plantation, west of Honolulu.

hala: the pandanus tree, whose leaves (*lau hala*) are used to make baskets and plaited mats.

hālau: school.

hale: a house.

hale pule: church, house of worship.

ha mea iki or **ha mea 'ole:** you're welcome.

hana: to work.

haole: ghost. Since the first foreigners were Caucasian, *haole* now means a Caucasian person.

hapa: a part, sometimes a half; often used as a short form of *hapa haole,* to mean a person who is part-Caucasian; thus, the name of a popular local band, whose members represent a variety of ethnicities.

hau'oli: to rejoice. *Hau'oli Makahiki Hou* means Happy New Year. *Hau'oli lā hānau* means Happy Birthday.

heiau: an outdoor stone platform; an ancient Hawaiian place of worship.

holo: to run.

holoholo: to go for a walk, ride, or sail.

holokū: a long Hawaiian dress, somewhat fitted, with a yoke and a train. Influenced by European fashion, it was worn at court, and at least one local translates the word as "expensive mu'umu'u."

holomū: a post–World War II cross between a *holokū* and a mu'umu'u, less fitted than the former but less voluminous than the latter, and having no train.

honi: to kiss; a kiss. A phrase that some tourists may find useful, quoted from a popular hula, is *Honi Ka'ua Wikiwiki:* Kiss me quick!

honu: turtle.

ho'omalimali: flattery, a deceptive "line," bunk, baloney, hooey.

huhū: angry.

hui: a group, club, or assembly. A church may refer to its congregation as a *hui* and a social club may be called a *hui.*

hukilau: a seine; a communal fishing party in which everyone helps to drive the fish into a huge net, pull it in, and divide the catch.

hula: the dance of Hawai'i.

iki: little.

ipo: sweetheart.

ka: the. This is the definite article for most singular words; for plural nouns, the definite article is usually *nā.* Since there is no *S* in Hawaiian, the article may be your only clue that a noun is plural.

kahuna: a priest, doctor, or other trained person of old Hawai'i, endowed with special professional skills that often included the gift of prophecy or other supernatural powers; the plural form is *kāhuna.*

kai: the sea, saltwater.

kalo: the taro plant from whose root poi is made.

kama'āina: literally, a child of the soil; it refers to people who were born in the Islands or have lived there for a long time.

kanaka: originally a man or humanity in general, it is now used to denote a male Hawaiian or part-Hawaiian, but is occasionally taken as a slur when used by non-Hawaiians. *Kanaka maoli,* originally a full-blooded Hawaiian person, is used by some native Hawaiian rights activists to embrace part-Hawaiians as well.

kāne: a man, a husband. If you see this word on a door, it's the men's room. If you see *kane* on a door, it's probably a misspelling; that is the Hawaiian name for the skin fungus tinea.

kapa: also called by its Tahitian name, *tapa,* a cloth made of beaten bark and usually dyed and stamped with a repeat design.

kapakahi: crooked, cockeyed, uneven. You've got your hat on *kapakahi.*

kapu: keep out, prohibited. This is the Hawaiian version of the more widely known Tongan word *tabu* (taboo).

kapuna: grandparent; elder.

kēia lā: today.

keiki: a child; *keikikāne* is a boy, *keikiwahine* a girl.

kona: the leeward side of the Islands, the direction (south) from which the *kona* wind and *kona* rain come.

kula: upland.

kuleana: a homestead or small plot of ground on which a family has been installed for some generations without necessarily owning it. By extension, *kuleana* is used to denote any area or department in which one has a special interest or prerogative. You'll hear it used this way: If you want to hire a surfboard, see Moki; that's his *kuleana*. And conversely: I can't help you with that; that's not my *kuleana*.

lā: sun.

lamalama: to fish with a torch.

lānai: a porch, a balcony, an outdoor living room. Almost every house in Hawai'i has one. Don't confuse this two-syllable word with the three-syllable name of the island, Lāna'i.

lani: heaven, the sky.

lau hala: the leaf of the *hala,* or pandanus tree, widely used in Hawaiian handicrafts.

lei: a garland of flowers.

limu: sun.

lolo: stupid.

luna: a plantation overseer or foreman.

mahalo: thank you.

makai: toward the ocean.

malihini: a newcomer to the Islands.

mana: the spiritual power that the Hawaiian believed inhabited all things and creatures.

manō: shark.

manuwahi: free, gratis.

mauka: toward the mountains.

mauna: mountain.

mele: a Hawaiian song or chant, often of epic proportions.

Mele Kalikimaka: Merry Christmas (a transliteration from the English phrase).

Menehune: a Hawaiian pixie. The *Menehune* were a legendary race of little people who accomplished prodigious work, such as building fishponds and temples in the course of a single night.

moana: the ocean.

mu'umu'u: the voluminous dress in which the missionaries enveloped Hawaiian women. Now made in bright printed cottons and silks, it is an indispensable garment in a Hawaiian woman's wardrobe. Culturally sensitive locals have embraced the Hawaiian spelling but often shorten the spoken word to "mu'u." Most English dictionaries include the spelling "muumuu," and that version is a part of many apparel companies' names.

nani: beautiful.

nui: big.

ohana: family.

'ono: delicious.

pāhoehoe: smooth, unbroken, satiny lava.

Pākē: Chinese. This *Pākē* carver makes beautiful things.

palapala: document, printed matter.

pali: a cliff, precipice.

pānini: prickly pear cactus.

paniolo: a Hawaiian cowboy, a rough transliteration of *español,* the language of the Islands' earliest cowboys.

pau: finished, done.

pilikia: trouble. The Hawaiian word is much more widely used here than its English equivalent.

puka: a hole.

pupule: crazy, like the celebrated Princess Pupule. This word has replaced its English equivalent in local usage.

pu'u: volcanic cinder cone.

waha: mouth.

wahine: a female, a woman, a wife, and a sign on the ladies' room door; the plural form is *wāhine.*

wai: freshwater, as opposed to saltwater, which is *kai.*

wailele: waterfall.

wikiwiki: to hurry, hurry up (since this is a reduplication of *wiki,* quick, neither W is pronounced as a V).

Note: Pidgin is the unofficial language of Hawai'i. It is a Creole language, with its own grammar, evolved from the mixture of English, Hawaiian, Japanese, Portuguese, and other languages spoken in 19th-century Hawai'i, and it is heard everywhere: on ranches, in warehouses, on beaches, and in the hallowed halls (and occasionally in the classrooms) of the University of Hawai'i.

MENU GUIDE

Much of the Hawaiian language encountered during a stay in the Islands will appear on restaurant menus and lists of lū'au fare. Here's a quick primer.

'ahi: yellowfin tuna.

aku: skipjack, bonito tuna.

'ama'ama: mullet; it's hard to get but tasty.

bento: a box lunch.

chicken lū'au: a stew made from chicken, taro leaves, and coconut milk.

haupia: a light, gelatin-like dessert made from coconut.

imu: the underground ovens in which pigs are roasted for lū'au.

kālua: to bake underground.

kaukau: food. The word comes from Chinese but is used in the Islands.

kimchee: Korean dish of pickled cabbage made with garlic and hot peppers.

Kona coffee: coffee grown in the Kona district of the Big Island.

laulau: literally, a bundle. *Laulau* are morsels of pork, butterfish, or other ingredients wrapped with young taro shoots in ti leaves for steaming.

liliko'i: passion fruit, a tart, seedy yellow fruit that makes delicious desserts and jellies.

lomilomi: to rub or massage; also a massage. *Lomilomi* salmon is fish that has been rubbed with onions and herbs, commonly served with minced onions and tomatoes.

lū'au: a Hawaiian feast, also the leaf of the taro plant used in preparing such a feast.

lū'au leaves: cooked taro tops with a taste similar to spinach.

mahimahi: mild-flavored dolphinfish, not the marine mammal.

mai tai: potent rum drink with orange and lime juice, from the Tahitian word for "good."

malasada: a Portuguese deep-fried doughnut without a hole, dipped in sugar.

manapua: dough wrapped around diced pork.

manō: shark.

niu: coconut.

'ōkolehao: a liqueur distilled from the ti root.

onaga: pink or red snapper.

ono: a long, slender mackerel-like fish; also called wahoo.

'ono: delicious; also hungry.

'opihi: a tiny shellfish, or mollusk, found on rocks; also called limpets.

pāpio: a young *ulua* or jack fish.

pohā: Cape gooseberry. Tasting a bit like honey, the pohā berry is often used in jams and desserts.

poi: a paste made from pounded taro root, a staple of the Hawaiian diet.

poke: chopped, pickled raw tuna, tossed with herbs and seasonings.

pūpū: Hawaiian hors d'oeuvre.

saimin: long thin noodles and vegetables in broth, often garnished with small pieces of fish cake, scrambled egg, luncheon meat, and green onion.

sashimi: raw fish thinly sliced and usually eaten with soy sauce.

ti leaves: a member of the agave family, used to wrap food while cooking and removed before eating.

uku: deep-sea snapper.

ulua: a member of the jack family that also includes pompano and amberjack. Also called crevalle, jack fish, and jack crevalle.

INDEX

NOTES

NOTES

NOTES

NOTES

NOTES

NOTES

NOTES